Fannie Mae and Freddie Mac

Oonagh McDonald

Fannie Mae and Freddie Mac

Turning the American Dream into a Nightmare

Oonagh McDonald

B L O O M S B U R Y
LONDON · NEW DELHI · NEW YORK · SYDNEY

Bloomsbury Academic

An imprint of Bloomsbury Publishing Plc

50 Bedford Square   1385 Broadway
London   New York
WC1B 3DP   NY 10018
UK   USA

www.bloomsbury.com

First published in hardback, 2012
Paperback edition first published 2013

British Library Cataloguing-in-Publication Data
A catalogue record for this book is available from the British Library.

ISBN: HB: 978-1-7809-3002-2
      PB: 978-1-7809-3523-2
      ePub: 978-1-7809-3004-6
      ePDF: 978-1-7809-3005-3

Library of Congress Cataloging-in-Publication Data
A catalog record for this book is available from the Library of Congress.

Printed and bound in the United States of America

Contents

Acknowledgements

I have benefitted from discussions with Mark Calabria, Director of Financial Regulation, Cato Institute and Ed Pinto, Resident Fellow at the American Enterprise Institute. I would especially like to thank Lord Desai, Professor Robert Hudson, Professor of Finance, Newcastle University Business School and Professor Kevin Keasey, Director of the International Institute of Banking and Financial Services, University of Leeds, all of whom were kind enough to read the manuscript in draft and for their constructive comments and criticisms. I would also like to thank John Fawthrop for the provision of the list of Fannie Mae and Freddie Mac campaign contributions, and Mathew Kamisher-Koch, Cicero Consulting, for assisting with some source material. Any errors and misconceptions are mine.

I would also like to thank all those who contributed to the reception of the hardback edition and in doing so made this new paperback edition possible. Michael Lafferty of the Lafferty Group, the American Enterprise Institute, the US Financial Planning Association, the CSFI (Centre for the Study of Financial Innovation) and the Cambridge International Symposium on Economic Crime ran forums on the book, providing me with the opportunity to set out the arguments before an engaged audience. I would also like to thank all those who took the time to review what some might have seen as a daunting 500 pages, including Lord Lawson, the former Chancellor, for his review in the Financial Times, Gene Epstein of Barron's and Peter Wallison, Fellow in Financial Policy Studies at the American Enterprise Institute, for his review in Forbes. Finally I would like to thank the editors of City AM and Company Lawyer, who gave me the opportunity to explain the main themes of the book.

Oonagh McDonald

List of Abbreviations

ABS:	Asset-backed securities
ACORN:	Association of Community Organizations for Reform Now
AHAR:	Annual Homeless Assessment Report
APR:	Annual percentage rate
ARMs:	Adjustable rate mortgages
BIF:	Bank Insurance Fund
BoA:	Bank of America
CalPERS:	Californian Public Employees Retirement System
CBO:	Congressional Budget Office
CDO:	Collateralized Debt Obligation, an investment-grade security, backed by a pool of bonds, loans, and other assets. CDOs represent different kinds of credit risk, usually described as "tranches" or "slices," each of which has a different materiality or risk associated with it
CFCB:	Consumer Financial Protection Bureau
CLO:	Collateralized Loan Obligation, a special-purpose vehicle with securitization payments in the form of different tranches. CLOs allow banks to reduce their regulatory capital requirements by selling large portions of their loan portfolios to international markets, reducing the risks associated with lending
CRA:	Community Reinvestment Act
DU:	Desktop Underwriter (Fannie Mae's automated underwriting system)
ECOA:	Equal Credit Opportunity Act, 1974
Fannie Mae:	Federal National Mortgage Association
FASB:	Financial Accounting Standards Board
FAS:	Financial Accounting Standard
FCRA:	Federal Credit Reform Act
FDIC:	Federal Deposit Insurance Corporation
FHA:	Federal Housing Administration
FHFA:	Federal Housing Finance Agency
FHFB:	Federal Housing Finance Board
FHLB:	Federal Home Loans Banks System
FHESSA:	Federal Housing Enterprises Safety and Soundness Act, 1992
FICO:	Fair Isaacs Corporation, most widely used credit scoring model in the USA

FFIEC:	Federal Financial Institutions Examinations Council
FIRREA:	Federal Institutions Reform, Recovery and Enforcement Act, 1989
FOIA:	Freedom of Information Act
FRB:	Federal Reserve Board
Freddie Mac:	Federal Home Loan Mortgage Corporation
GAAP:	Generally accepted accounting principles
GAO:	Government Accountability Office
GEMICO:	GE Capital Mortgage Insurance Corporation
Ginnie Mae:	Government National Mortgage Association
GLBA:	Gramm-Leach-Bliley Act, 1999
GMS:	Guaranteed Mortgage Securities
GSE:	Government Sponsored Enterprise
HAMP:	Home Affordable Modification Program
HECM:	Home Equity Conversion Mortgage
HERA:	Housing and Economic Recovery Act, 2008
HMDA:	Home Mortgage Disclosure Act, 1975
HOPA:	Home Owners Protection Act, 1998
HOEPA:	Home Ownership and Equity Protection Act, 1994
HUD:	Housing and Urban Development Department
LIBOR:	London Inter-bank Offer Rate
LMI:	Low-to-Moderate Income
LP:	Loan Prospector (Freddie Mac's automated underwriting system)
LP:	First American Loan Performance
LPS:	Lender processing services
LTV:	Loan-to-Value
MBA:	Mortgage Bankers Association
MBSs:	Mortgage-backed securities
MMI:	Mutual Mortgage Insurance
MSA:	Metropolitan statistical area
NACA:	Neighborhood Assistance Corporation of America
NAR:	National Association of Realtors
NASDQ:	National Association of Securities Dealers Automated Quotations
NCRC:	National Community Reinvestment Coalition
OBRA:	Omnibus Budget Reconciliation Act, 1990
OCC:	Office of the Comptroller of the Currency
OFHEO:	Office of Federal Housing Enterprise Oversight
OIG:	Office of the Inspector General
OMB:	Office of Management and Budget
OTS:	Office of Thrift Supervision
PDAMS:	Purchase discount amortization system

PCS:	Participation certificates in a pool of mortgages
PLSs:	Private label securities
RBS:	Risk-based capital requirement
REMICS:	Real estate mortgage conduit
RHS:	Rural Housing Service
RMBS:	Residential Mortgage Backed Securities
SFAS:	Statement of financial accounting standard
SEC:	Securities and Exchange Commission
SFDPA:	Seller funded down-payment assistance
TBA:	To be announced, this refers to a forward mortgage-backed security, indicating that the investor is acquiring some portion of a pending pool of as yet unspecified mortgages, which will be specified at a given delivery date
VA:	US Department of Veterans Affairs

Introduction

The American mortgage market from 2008 to 2012

The Nightmare lingers on

The full impact of the financial crisis of 2008 still reverberates around the globe. It was triggered by events in the US sub-prime mortgage market of 2007–2008. It quickly spread to other financial markets, sometimes unrelated, but also often connected through the banks' activities in the wholesale market. The purpose of this book is to analyse the causes of the development of a vast subprime market in the United States. The mortgage market has reached the point where almost nine out of ten mortgages are currently insured or guaranteed by the US Government. At the beginning of President Obama's second Administration in January 2013, Fannie Mae and Freddie Mac still linger on as do the effects of the subprime market, which they readily assisted in creating.

Turning the dream into reality

The American dream of home ownership had always been part of aspirations articulated by successive governments in the United States, but it was not until President Bill Clinton took office that any President sought to turn the dream into a reality for millions of families. He introduced the "affordable housing" ideology in his 1995 "National Homeownership Strategy," designed in part to cut federal expenditure on public housing, but also to respond to claims that banks discriminated against minorities. The aim was to increase home ownership by entering into a partnership with all those involved in the process of making mortgages available. President Clinton did not just involve the private sector, but also used existing legislation and the long-established federal agencies to achieve his aims.

Using federal agencies and Government-Sponsored Enterprises

The Federal Housing Administration (FHA), Veterans Administration and the "Government-Sponsored Enterprises (GSEs)," (the Federal Home Loan Banks (FHLBs) System, Fannie Mae and Freddie Mac) were all created as part of the

1930s' "New Deal" to get the mortgage market functioning again after the Great Depression. The agencies had evolved over time, but from the mid-90s onwards were co-opted into increasing home ownership among minorities and low-to-moderate income groups.

The Community Reinvestment Act, 1977

The Community Reinvestment Act (CRA) was originally designed to prevent "red-lining" by banks and other financial institutions. The Act was readily to hand and only required amendments in order to incentivise the lenders to increase their lending to minorities and low-to-moderate income groups; to those, in other words, who could not meet the usual loan-to-value, credit scores or debt-to-income ratios required by the so-called conventional 30-year fixed rate mortgages with some 20% down payments. The move away from that type of mortgage had already begun in the early 1980s: a wide range of mortgages, including adjustable rate mortgages, were no longer banned under state laws.

The carrot for the lenders was the regulatory seal of approval, that is, being rated as "outstanding" in their compliance with the requirements of the CRA, as amended, to lend to less creditworthy families or those without any credit rating at all. Such a rating meant that their plans to merge or acquire other banks would be approved by the regulators. Interstate banking had been illegal until the Riegle-Neal Act, 1994 took effect. Thus, the CRA contributed to the subprime debacle.

Fannie, Freddie and the Housing and Urban Development Department

In this book, attention is inevitably focussed on Fannie and Freddie, but the role of the "other" GSEs should not be neglected: such as the FHLBs system, consisting of the 12 banks which provide stable, on-demand, low-cost funding enabling lenders to make home loans. The FHLBs ran into difficulties as well, through bad management and poor supervision. The government agency, which is also part of the Housing and Urban Development Department, and so subject to political direction, is the FHA, which insures mortgages made by lenders to qualifying borrowers against default. Operating at the lower end of the mortgage market, it insures a disproportionate number of black and Hispanic and low-to-moderate income borrowers, often in inner-city areas. In the context of the affordable housing ideology, the FHA was prepared to insure loans with deposits as low as 3% and to accept seller-funded down payments until a long history of fraudulent activities in the market finally ended the practice. But Fannie and Freddie were the key players.

From the beginning of their existence, Fannie and Freddie only operated in the secondary market. They did not make any home loans themselves but were chartered by Congress to provide a stable source of funding for housing finance throughout the country. They carried out that "mission" by purchasing the home loans from the originators, the lenders and then packaging the loans into mortgage-backed securities (MBSs). The MBSs were then sold to investors, along with a guarantee against losses from defaults on the underlying mortgages, or by held in portfolio, financed by the agency debt which the GSEs issued.

The Secretary for Housing was the "mission regulator" for Fannie Mae and Freddie Mac. This involved setting the housing goals, that is, the proportion of mortgages for low-to-moderate income families they were expected to buy each year, goals established by as a result of complex and bureaucratic formulae, but which increased each year, until the goal for 2008 was 57%. The first set of goals was finalised in 1996 for the years 1996–2000 and the process continued throughout the Bush administration, following his announcement of the "Blueprint for the American dream" in 2002.

Fannie and Freddie became the dominant players in the market both in size and in political power, forming partnerships with banks of all kinds, which were lending to minorities and low-to-moderate income families. The partnership agreements meant that banks could sell the mortgages to Fannie and Freddie, paying the guarantee fees in exchange for removing the default risk from their own books. The GSEs spent millions of dollars on lobbying, using every means possible to attack politicians who sought to limit their power, and rewarding many Congressional members of the banking and financial services committees, which were responsible for the way in which Fannie and Freddie operated, by sponsoring housing projects for affordable housing in their constituencies.

The signals from government were clear enough: lend to minorities and less well-off families, and adjust underwriting standards to increase home ownership among these groups. But Fannie and Freddie had a pivotal role in the mortgage market, and so must bear a major part of the blame. They were out of control. They exploited the weakness of their regulator, and engaged in dubious accounting practices, while amassing fortunes for their top executives. All the time, they proclaimed their commitment to affordable housing and were aided and abetted in all their activities by Presidents and politicians alike.

So lend they did: banks, thrifts and mortgage brokers, safe in the knowledge that they need not retain the risks. Fraud and predatory lending practices were rife, not just on the part of banks, but also brokers, appraisers, loan servicers, builders and borrowers. Mortgages were packaged in ever more exotic financial instruments. The regulators failed to act to prevent predatory lending until it was too late. The Commodities Futures Modernisation Act, signed into law in December 2000 by President Clinton, exempted over-the-counter trading in derivatives, including credit default swaps from regulation.

A few voices in Congress and outside in the community and in the banking sector were raised in protest but they were not heard while more and more people could buy their own homes; the affordable housing ideology blinded the rest. Much was hidden while house prices continued to rise but as they faltered in 2006 and began to fall throughout 2007, as interest rates rose, the extent of the subprime market dawned slowly. Decisive action was too late to prevent the collapse of the mortgage market with its misery for millions both in the United States and elsewhere.

As pivotal players in the market, Fannie and Freddie must take a large slice of the blame. But above all, it was the distortion of the banking sector to achieve political ends which ultimately caused the crisis. Politicians with their unthinking political stances must, perhaps for the first time, take the lion's share of the responsibility. The vast subprime market out of which others created over-complex, opaque financial instruments, selling them with only an eye to profit throughout the world, was the child of the affordable housing ideology.

2008 and its Aftermath

The year 2008 saw the failure of 25 American banks, including Lehman Brothers, the fourth largest US investment bank, the largest bankruptcy filing in American history and Washington Mutual, which was seized by federal regulators, who brokered an emergency sale of almost all of its assets to JP Morgan Chase. Altogether 25 US banks failed that year. That destroyed trust in lending. Banks could not be sure of the value of underlying assets on which the collateralised debt obligations (CDOs) and other financial instruments were based, and which had been sold to banks throughout the world. Banks stopped lending to one another, so governments had to step in to ensure liquidity. Banks began to collapse throughout the industrialized world. Shoring them up added to the debts of already weak economies with overheated housing markets. Triggered by the discovery that Greece's debt stood at 126% on GDP in April 2010, and investors feared that Greece would be unable to meet its debt obligations, the banking crisis turned into a sovereign debt crisis. The eurozone crisis continues.

Fannie and Freddie

They were taken into conservatorship on September 7, 2008. Four years later, they remain in conservatorship. No decision has been taken about their future, nor is one likely in the very near future. Secretary Geithner set out three options for the housing finance market and a limited role for government intervention through the FHA, the Department of Veterans Affairs and the US Department of Agriculture, with Fannie and Freddie being phased out of existence. He also stressed the need for good rented accommodation rather than home ownership. These proposals were ignored. They were followed by Edward DeMarco's strategic plan issued in February 2012, of which the most important is to "build a new infrastructure for the secondary mortgage market," as the United States does not have a private sector infrastructure capable of securitising the $100bn per month of new mortgages being originated. The plan envisaged incorporating Fannie, Freddie and Ginnie Mae while acknowledging that the future may not include the two GSEs. The Strategic Plan met with a lukewarm response when it went out for consultation in October 2012. With the departure of Secretary Geithner and the possible departure of Edward DeMarco, the continuing existence and role of Fannie and Freddie remains uncertain.

Meanwhile, the costs of Fannie and Freddie's bail-out continue to rise and may continue to rise in the future. The Federal Housing Finance Agency, the current regulator of Fannie and Freddie, estimated that the costs of keeping the GSEs afloat had already reached $187.5 bn and estimates that by the end of 2015 the costs (on various models) could rise to $191 to $209 bn. Secretary Geithner announced in August 2012 that all the profits made by Fannie and Freddie would be paid in their entirety to the Treasury, since both began to make a profit in the second quarter in 2012. However, the two GSEs guarantee loans amounting to $2.7 trillion and $1.8 trillion, respectively, which do not figure in budget calculations. In December, Chairman Bernanke announced that the Federal Open Market Committee had decided to continue to purchase agency mortgage-backed securities at the rate of $45 bn per month. The purpose is not to assist in ensuring that they would not be able to rebuild their capital base, but to boost employment through the housing market. Meanwhile, little attention is being paid to the FHA, where its Mutual Mortgage Insurance Fund has been shown to be entirely inadequate for the risks it faces. Another bail-out may be looming on the horizon.

The "affordable housing" ideology lingers on. It distorted the provision of mortgages for two decades in the United States, but the lessons may not have been learnt, given Chairman Bernanke's speech on November 15, 2012, in which he pointed out that "terms and standards for borrowers with lower credit scores and less money available for a down payment" and that the "pendulum may have swung too far." The belief in the affordable housing ideology may even have drifted across the Atlantic, and emerged in the form of the NewBuy scheme, which accepts lower down payments with a shared insurance between builders, lenders and the government. A salutary lesson is to look carefully at the suffering of families either from losing their homes or from the effects of foreclosures on the whole neighbourhood.

Instead, attention was focused on numerous law suits. The Securities and Exchange Commission (SEC) brought a complaint against six former executives of Fannie Mae and Freddie Mac for securities fraud, alleging that they knew and approved of misleading statements, claiming that the companies had minimal holdings of higher risk loans, including subprime loans. The announcement, made on December 16, 2011, provides numerous examples, showing that for both the GSEs, all the information on their strategies contained in internal documents does not correspond with its public filings, including statutory disclosures. These discrepancies were not discovered until 2011, showing how ineffective the Office of Federal Housing Enterprise Oversight (OFHEO), the former regulator of the GSEs was. Other cases are quite different. Those brought by the US Department of Justice against leading banks accused the banks of deliberately selling subprime loans to Fannie and Freddie, who were unaware of the nature of the loans they purchased. The claim that Fannie and Freddie were unaware that they had purchased subprime mortgage loans is truly astonishing, especially in the light of the detailed evidence to the contrary produced by the SEC. It also ignores the close relationship which Fannie and Freddie had with Countrywide, the largest subprime lende in the USA, and their commitments to purchase Countrywide's mortgage loans. In these cases, the banks have all settled out of court, paying out billions of dollars to the Treasury. It is clear that the banks simply want to put the whole sorry affair behind them, thus avoiding huge legal fees and continuing reputational damage.

That Fannie and Freddie should be phased out of existence is clear. As they are now making a profit for the Administration, this may not happen in the near future. The story that should have an ending does not have one.

Timeline

1932 Creation of the Federal Home Loan Bank System under the Federal Home Loan Bank Act to promote the use of long-term, fixed-rate, fully amortizing residential mortgages. The FHLBs provide cash advances to their 8,000-odd members, including community banks, thrifts, credit unions and community development financial institutions, as well as all depositary institutions with more than 10% of their portfolios in mortgage-related assets under the 1989 Financial Institutions Recovery and Reform Act (FIRREA). The FHLB System is also known as the "other" Government Sponsored Enterprise (GSE).

1934 The Federal Housing Administration was created under the National Housing Act and later became part of the Housing and Urban Development, in 1965. Its function is to insure loans made by banks and other private lenders for home builders and home buyers.

1938 Fannie Mae, the Federal National Mortgage Association (FNMA), was created as part of the "New Deal" as a government agency, designed to ensure the supply of funding to banks by buying up existing mortgages for cash to enable banks to provide further loans. It created a liquid secondary mortgage market, primarily by buying loans insured by the Federal Housing Administration.

1968 Fannie Mae was converted into a private shareholder corporation to remove its activities and debt from the federal budget, under legislation signed by President Lyndon B. Johnson. At the same time, Ginnie Mae (the Government National Mortgage Association) was formed as a government agency, supporting FHA-backed mortgages as well as the Veterans Administration and Farmers Home Administration (FmHA) mortgages. Ginnie Mae is the only home-loan agency backed by the full faith and credit of the US Government.

1970 The federal government authorized Fannie Mae to purchase conventional private mortgages (that is, not insured by the FHA, VA or FmHA). At the same time, the Federal Home Loan Mortgage Corporation (FHLMC), Freddie Mac, was created to compete with Fannie Mae and ensure a more competitive and efficient secondary market.

1982 Freddie Mac also became a publicly traded, shareholder-owned corporation. The Alternative Mortgage Transactions Parity Act allowed mortgages other than the conventional 30-year fixed-rate mortgage: adjustable rate mortgages; balloon payment mortgages; and interest only mortgages. At the same time, Fannie Mae was funding one in seven mortgages in the USA.

1984 Fannie Mae issues its first debenture in the overseas Euromarket, marking its entry into foreign capital markets.

1992 President George H. W. Bush signed the Housing and Community Development Act, of which the Federal Housing Enterprises Financial Safety and Soundness Act (FHEFSSA) is Title XIII, the Charter for Fannie and Freddie. It established the Office of Federal Housing Enterprises Oversight (OFHEO) within the Housing and Urban Development Department (HUD). Fannie and Freddie would be required to meet the "affordable housing goals" set by HUD and approved by Congress.

2003 Report of OFHEO's Special Examination of Freddie Mac (accounting irregularities).

2006 Report of OFHEO's Special Examination of Fannie Mae (accounting irregularities).

March 2007 HSBC announces one portfolio of purchased subprime mortgages evidenced delinquency that had been built into the pricing of these products.

June 2007 Bear Stearns pledges a collateralized loan to one of its hedge funds, but not the other.

October 2007 Merrill Lynch, Citi and UBS report significant write-downs.

November 2007 Moody's announces it will re-estimate capital adequacy ratios of US monoline insurers/financial guarantors.

November 2007 Freddie Mac announces 2007 Q3 losses and says it is considering cutting dividends and raising new capital.

December 2007 Bear Stearns announces expected 2007 Q4 write-downs.

January 2008 Announcements of significant Q4 losses by Citi Bank, Merrill Lynch and others.

January 2008 Bank of America confirms purchase of Countrywide.

January 2008 Citi announces plans to raise $14.5bn in new capital.

February 2008 American International Group (AIG) announces that its auditors have found a "material weakness" in its internal controls over the valuation of the AIGFP super senior credit default swap portfolio.

March 2008 JP Morgan Chase & Co announces that in conjunction with the Federal Reserve Bank of New York it will provide secured funding to Bear Stearns for an initial period of up to 28 days. Two days later, it agrees to purchase Bear Stearns, with the Federal Reserve providing $30bn no recourse funding.

March 2008 OFHEO gives both companies permission to add as much as $200bn financing into the mortgage markets by reducing their capital requirements.

April 2008 OFHEO report reveals that Fannie and Freddie accounted for 75% of new mortgages at the end of 2007 as other sources of finance sharply reduce their lending.

June 2008 Lehman Bros confirms a net loss of $2.8bn in Q2.

June 2008 Morgan Stanley reports losses from proprietary trading and bad loans.

July 2008 Closure of mortgage lender, IndyMac.

July 2008 Shares in Fannie Mae and Freddie Mac plummet in the face of speculation that a bail-out of Fannie and Freddie may be required, and that such a bail-out would leave little value available for shareholders.

July 2008 US Treasury announces a rescue plan for Fannie Mae and Freddie Mac.

July 2008 Housing and Economic Recovery Act, signed into law by President Bush on July 30. OFHEO replaced as the regulator for Fannie and Freddie by Federal Housing Finance Agency (FHFA).

September 2008 Fannie and Freddie taken into conservatorship on September 7.

September 2008 Lehman Brothers filed for Ch 11 bankruptcy protection on September 15th.

2008–2009 The years of the financial crisis.

February 2011 Timothy Geithner, Secretary to the Treasury, published his proposals for the future of Fannie Mae and Freddie Mac: Reforming America's Housing Market.

December 2011 The Securities and Exchange Commission charges six former Fannie Mae and Freddie Mac Executives with securities fraud. The case continues.

2008–2012 The Government continues to bail out Fannie Mae and Freddie Mac.

2012 Fannie Mae reported first quarter profits, and Freddie Mac reported second quarter profits for the first time since 2006.

August 17 2012 Secretary Geithner announced a quarterly sweep of every dollar of profit to the Treasury.

October 2012 Edward DeMarco, Acting Director of the Federal Housing Finance Agency, published the Strategic Plan for the Enterprises Conservatorships as a consultative document.

November 15 2012 Chairman Bernanke's speech, Challenges in Housing and Mortgage Markets, in which he suggested that a relaxation of underwriting standards for mortgages would be timely.

2012 The US Department of Justice brought a number of civil fraud cases against leading banks. All of the banks settled out of court, including the Bank of America.

January 2013 The Bank of America finally agreed to settle for no less than $11.6 bn on January 7, 2013.
Timothy Geithner leaves the Treasury on January 21, 2013-01-28.

January 21 2013 President Obama's second term of office begins.

1

The Seeds are Sown

Introduction

It is impossible to understand and appreciate the extent of subprime lending and its contribution to the global financial crisis without an analysis of the origins of such lending and the operations of the US mortgage market, especially from the mid-1990s to the time when the bubble finally burst in 2008. The period was dominated by the "American Dream of Homeownership" to which all actors in the mortgage market subscribed, even if it was only a matter of paying lip-service to the dream. What marked the difference between this era and the preceding ones was that successive Presidents espoused the dream, but did little to make it a reality.

What happened subsequently was that politicians recruited all the federal housing agencies to serve the end of "home ownership for all." This book will explore the ways in which every aspect of the market was subsumed to that purpose; how a combination of the contribution of all those agencies, working together with the banks and other players who grabbed money-making opportunities, created a huge pool of subprime mortgages. It was a heady mix of good intentions, the reasonable aspiration of owning one's own home, negligence, greed, fraud on the part of some lenders, some government agencies, and even borrowers as well, driven by politicians of every hue. These all combined to encourage all the players to take on risks, which they either did not understand, or which they thought they could handle in the good times. The good times did not last.

The Clinton era

The crisis arose out of laudable political aims and aspirations: to extend the American dream of home ownership. "You want to reinforce family values in America, encourage two-parent households, get people to stay home? Make it easy for people to own their own homes and enjoy the rewards of family life and see their work rewarded. This is the big deal. This is about more than money and sticks and boards and windows. This is about the way we live as people and what kind of society we're going to have." These were the widely held ideals expressed by President Clinton when he announced the National

Homeownership Strategy in June 1995, which was the beginning of the affordable homes era. These ideas had not been plucked out of the air: much research lay behind them.[1]

The National Homeownership Strategy brought together fifty-six leading organizations concerned with mortgages, affordable home ownership, community activists, state housing provision, government departments and many others as "Partners in the American Dream," including the American Bankers Association; America's Community Bankers; the Federal National Mortgage Corporation, and the Federal Home Loan Mortgage Corporation (commonly known as Fannie Mae and Freddie Mac respectively); the National Association of Realtors; the National Council of State Housing Agencies; the Neighborhood Reinvestment Corporation; and the US Department of Housing and Urban Affairs.

Amongst the Action Points included in the program under the strategy of reducing down-payment and mortgage costs, especially for low- and moderate-income home buyers, were more flexibility in down-payment requirements to include "public subsidies or unsecured loans;" counseling to accompany mortgage financing with high loan-to-value ratios; and flexible mortgage underwriting criteria. The actions of Fannie Mae and Freddie Mac in introducing affordable loans for home purchase, loans requiring only 3% from the purchaser when an additional 2% is available from other funding sources such as gifts, unsecured loans and government aid, were commended in the National Strategy announced in May 1995.

The aim was quite explicit. "Since 1993," the President said, "nearly 2.8 million households have joined the ranks of America's homeowners, nearly twice as many as in the previous two years. But we have to do a lot better. The goal of this strategy, to boost homeownership to 67.5% by the year 2000, would take us to an all-time high, helping as many as 8 million American families to cross that threshold … and we're going to do it without spending more tax money."[2] The reference to not spending any more tax dollars is significant. President Clinton did make further cuts in the housing budget, especially for public housing: here, changes involved the replacement of high-rise concrete blocks with low-level scattered housing. However, the total stock for public housing fell during that period, as did new units for subsidised rental accommodation,[3] and this must also be considered part of the background against which the political push for affordable housing should be assessed.

Racial discrimination and home ownership

The issue of racial discrimination in housing, and hence the need to increase home ownership in low-income and underserved areas, had already come to the fore when the Federal Reserve Bank of Boston published a study entitled

"Mortgage Lending in Boston: Interpreting HMDA data."[4] Based on the Home Disclosure Act data for 1990, together with their own survey, the authors concluded that the data showed substantially higher denial rates for black and Hispanic applicants. Even high-income ethnic minorities, the authors claimed, were more likely to be turned down than low-income whites. They reached this conclusion after finding that the higher denial rate for minorities is accounted for, in large part, by such applicants having higher loan-to-value ratios and weaker credit histories than whites; they are also more likely to seek to purchase a two- or four-unit property than a single family home. A black or Hispanic applicant in the Boston area is roughly 60% more likely to be denied a mortgage than a similarly situated white applicant. "In short," the paper concludes, "the results indicate that a serious problem exists in the market for mortgage loans, and lenders, community groups and regulators must work together to ensure that the minorities are treated fairly."[5] The authors rightly state that "this pattern has triggered a resurgence of the debate on whether discrimination exists in mortgage lending."

The study did more than trigger a debate; it led to increased community activity and encouraged politicians to use legislation and bank lending to achieve social aims. Groups such as the Association of Community Organizations for Reform Now (ACORN) and many other local groups engaged in direct action, such as arranging sit-ins in bank branches until banks agreed to lend more, entering into partnerships with local groups to lend to low-income areas, or demanding that banks publish more of the information they were already required to provide for the authorities under the Home Mortgage Disclosure Act, 1975.

The article also sparked an intense political debate, conducted in the media, and had a major influence on public policy, largely because it came from an important government agency and, as such, was bound to capture public attention. Its central claim did not go undisputed. It led to an avalanche of academic papers, some arguing that the conclusions were based on incomplete data or; that there were serious errors in the data, which, when removed, also removed the evidence supporting the discrimination hypothesis;[6] that several alternative model specifications perform better than the logit regression models used for the Boston study in terms of various econometric performance measures, and do not support the conclusions;[7] or that the model uncertainty can be eliminated using Bayesian model averaging (the result of the latter indicates that race has little effect on mortgage lending.[8]) Another paper rejected the Boston study's market level model, arguingthat the "standard" Boston model can only be used, at best, on the basis of a bank-specific analysis, based on its own particular lending guidelines.[9]

Many studies followed the Boston one in focusing on denial rates. Others argued that this was entirely the wrong approach: they have "not determined the profitability of loans to different groups ... A valid study of discrimination in lending would calculate default rates, late payments, interest rates and other determinants of the profitability of loans" and that "failure to do so is a serious methodological flaw."[10] Still other analyses indicated that black households have higher default rates, suggesting that differences in defaults or transaction costs may explain the results.[11] The wide range of criticisms of the Boston analysis suggests that it may not have been the most reliable foundation on which to build public policy, but neither politicians nor regulators wished to be perceived as being unconcerned about such widely reported racial discrimination in lending.

Lawrence Lindsay, then a member of the Board of Governors of the Federal Reserve, having been informed of numerous problems in the Boston study said, "The study may be imperfect, but it remains a landmark study that sheds an important light on the issue of potential discrimination in lending."[12] This, despite the fact that the vital element missing in the HMDA data is a lack of information about the credit history of the borrower and the difficulties as time went on in tracking default rates. These are both issues regarding data which will be explored at a later stage.

Changing the underwriting standards

Given that the debate about racial discrimination began at the Federal Reserve Bank of Boston, it is small wonder that it was followed by "Closing the Gap: A Guide to Equal Opportunity Lending" with a foreword by Richard Syron, President and Chief Executive, in which he quoted approvingly Lawrence B. Lindley, a member of the Board of the Federal Reserve System: "The regulatory issues in the 1990s will not be limited to safety and soundness, but will increasingly emphasise fairness: whether or not the banks are fulfiling the needs of their communities." Syron states that the Federal Reserve Bank of Boston have developed a comprehensive program for all lenders who wish to ensure that all their borrowers are treated fairly, and to "expand their markets to reach a more diverse customer base." Lenders should review every aspect of their lending practices, staffing and training to ensure that no part of the process is "unintentionally racially biased," since underwriting guidelines are historically based on "data that primarily reflect nonminority mortgage loan participants."[13] In particular, the lack of a credit history "should not be seen as a negative factor," since certain cultures encourage a "pay-as-you go" approach. Instead a willingness to pay debt promptly should be assessed through a review of utility, telephone and medical bills, and rent payments; and past credit problems should be reviewed for extenuating circumstances.

Similar considerations should apply to employment history, where lenders should focus on the applicant's ability to maintain or increase his or her income level. Interestingly enough, the Guide noted that Fannie Mae and Freddie Mac (of which more later) would accept as valid income sources: overtime and part-time work; second jobs (including seasonal work); retirement and Social Security income; alimony and child support; Veterans administration benefits; welfare payments and unemployment benefits. Together with CRA-lending (see below), these recommendations would inevitably weaken underwriting standards, as thrifts and commercial banks sought to increase lending based on this guidance.

Using the Community Reinvestment Act (CRA)

All of these issues lay behind the development of the National Homeownership Strategy as described in an Urban Policy Brief prepared by the Housing and Urban Development Department in 1995. The Strategy was described as an unprecedented public-private partnership, designed to increase home ownership to a record level over the following six years. Home ownership was described in romantic terms: "The desire for home ownership is deeply rooted in the American psyche. Owning a home embodies the promise of individual autonomy and of material and spiritual well-being ... In addition to its functional importance and economic value, home ownership has traditionally conveyed social status and political standing. It is even thought to promote thrift, stability, neighborliness and other individual and civic virtues." The brief then refers to the bi-partisan support for Federal policies designed to encourage home ownership from Presidents Herbert Hoover to Ronald Reagan.

The problem that President Clinton sought to address was the decline in home ownership rates beginning in the 1980s, falling to 64.1% in 1991. The decline was sharpest amongst those for whom the possibility of buying their own homes has always proved more difficult such as low-income families with children (from 39% to 27%). Rates stagnated at about 43% for blacks, but dropped from 43% to 39% for Hispanics between 1980 and 1991. During the late 1960s and the 1970s, it was argued that banks would not lend to specific neighborhoods regardless of the residents' creditworthiness, and that these areas were red-lined largely because of the residents' race, ethnicity and income. Various Acts had been passed to reduce discrimination in the credit and housing markets, including the Fair Housing Act, 1974, the Equal Credit Opportunity Act, 1974 and the Home Mortgage Disclosure Act, 1975. The Community Reinvestment Act, 1977 (CRA) was also designed to encourage depository institutions to meet the credit needs of the communities in which they operate, including low- and moderate-income neighborhoods "in a manner consistent with safe and sound operations." The CRA applies to all federally insured banks.

To deal with all of these issues, President Clinton's approach to the extension of home ownership, especially in low-income and underserved areas, which would greatly assist with the problem of racial discrimination, was two-pronged: the introduction of the Strategy; and the amendments to the regulations under the Community Reinvestment Act as a further step after the Federal Housing Enterprises Safety and Soundness Act, 1992, which, *inter alia*, requires the existence of the Federal National Mortgage Corporation and the Federal Home Loan Mortgage Corporation (commonly known as Fannie Mae and Freddie Mac respectively.) Fannie Mae and Freddie Mac had to meet annual percent-of-business goals established by the Housing and Urban Development Department (HUD) for three categories: low and moderate income; underserved; and special affordable.[14] Clinton regarded the CRA changes as one of the highlights of his presidency:

> One of the most effective things we did was to reform the regulations governing financial institutions under the 1977 Community Reinvestment Act. The law required federally insured banks to make an extra effort to give loans to low- and modest-income borrowers, but before 1993, it never had much impact. After the changes we made, between 1993 and 2000, banks would offer more than $800 billion in home mortgage, small-business and community development loans to borrowers covered by the law, a staggering figure that amounted to well over 90% of all loans made in the twenty-three years of the Community Reinvestment Act.[15]

When Congress passed the Act in 1977, it was built on the straightforward proposition that deposit-taking banking organisations have a special obligation to serve the credit needs of the neighborhoods in which they maintain branches. At the time of the passing of the Act, banks and thrifts originated the vast majority of home purchase loans. Concerns had been expressed not only about racial discrimination, but also about the deterioration in the condition of many of America's cities, especially in low-income neighborhoods, and many believed that this had been caused by limited credit availability, blaming the mainstream depository institutions for their alleged unwillingness to lend to low-income neighborhoods, despite the presence of creditworthy consumers.

The initial focus on the areas in which the CRA-registered institutions maintained branches made sense because of the restrictions, a ban, in fact, on interstate banking and branching activities which were limited to the geographic scope of mortgage-lending operations. Not only were banks prevented from engaging in interstate banking, but intrastate branching was also severely restricted. Other factors included an underdeveloped mortgage market, the lack of a comprehensive national credit reporting system, expensive credit evaluation methods, and unlawful red-lining.

The 1977 Act required insured depository institutions to serve the "convenience and needs" of the communities in which they are chartered to do business, including meeting their credit needs. The Bank Holding Act, 1958 already required the Federal Reserve Board, when considering proposed acquisitions by banks or bank holding companies, to consider how well they were meeting community needs, a factor which became more important under the Riegle-Neal Act of 1994.

Until the Financial Institutions Reform, Recovery and Enforcement Act (FIRREA) came into force in 1989, CRA examinations led to a confidential report and rating, provided only to the bank or thrift. Under FIRREA, the regulators were obliged to make the ratings public and provide written performance evaluations, using facts and data to justify the agencies' conclusions. These were sometimes used in the ways described below, which were perhaps not envisaged in the Act.

The Act itself directs the federal regulators of federally insured commercial banks to encourage their regulated institutions to meet the credit needs, in particular, of low- and moderate-income neighborhoods in a way consistent with "safe and sound" operations, the latter perhaps being a somewhat neglected aspect of the assessment. It was because of the perceived ineffectiveness of the CRA in meeting these requirements, and its apparent failure to ensure that the credit needs of the minorities were met, that the new regulations of which Clinton was so proud were issued at his request by all four of the then federal banking regulators: the Board of Governors of the Federal Reserve System, the Federal Deposit Insurance Corporation (FDIC), the Office of the Comptroller of the Currency (OCC), and the Office of Thrift Supervision (OTS).

The regulations were issued in 1995 and were designed to ensure that banks met the credit needs of the low- to moderate-income areas; that is, any area in which the bank had a branch or an ATM. This, as we have seen, is partly because banks were confined to a particular state and the areas in which they had permission to open a branch. The income area was also strictly defined in terms of "census tracts." In the 1990s, such tracts consisted of between 2,000 and 8,000 people, designed to be relatively permanent and stable in terms of population characteristics, economic status and living conditions.[16] The income levels in a tract could be determined, and banks were "encouraged" to increase lending to those in low-income areas (below 50% of the area median income) and to those on moderate incomes (between 50% and 80% of the area median income).

Banks were required to define their assessment area and ensure that it was updated annually to include any census tract in which a branch or an ATM had been provided. They were free to define one or more assessment areas, but each assessment area must consist of one or more metropolitan statistical areas and include the geographical areas in which the bank had its main office, branches or deposit-taking ATMs, as well as the surrounding areas in which the bank had originated or purchased a substantial part of its loans, including home mortgages. They had to use the areas as defined by the Office of Management and Budget and the Census in force at the beginning of the calendar year, and had to include the whole geographical area. This was designed to ensure that the bank could not select boundaries which reflected illegal discrimination or arbitrarily excluded low- and moderate-income areas.

The basis of the evaluations varied according to the size of the bank: those with assets of $1,061bn faced a lending test, an investment test and a service test. Lending is assessed on both qualitative and quantitative factors and the outcome accounts for 50% of the bank's overall CRA rating. Investment benefitting low- and moderate-income individuals and neighborhoods or rural areas, and services to the entire community are reviewed, with each accounting for 25% of the rating. In a 2002 amendment, financial institutions with assets between $265m and $1,061bn, "designated intermediate small institutions," are evaluated on their record of lending in low- to moderate-income areas and low-income individuals in the institutions' assessment areas. The assessment includes a community development test but allows banks flexibility in allocating their resources where they will produce the greatest benefit. Those institutions with less than $265m are evaluated primarily on their lending performance in their communities, including low- to moderate-income areas and populations, but are not expected to engage in complex and expensive community projects.

To those outside America, such rules will no doubt appear extraordinarily bureaucratic. However, in the context of local banks confined within a state and often within a limited number of counties, the emphasis on geographical location defined in this way made it possible for regulators and others to check on the loans the banks made in any one year, using the assessment areas as defined by the bank. Banks had to keep full records in machine-readable form as prescribed by the regulatory authorities of all their small business and small farm loans, mortgages and consumer loans. Under HMDA, banks with offices in metropolitan areas had to report annually and publicly, itemising each housing-related loan originated or purchased during the year, including the location of the loan and the borrower income.

In a nod to the changing structure of banks, the 1995 regulations did allow banks and other regulated institutions to include lending by mortgage companies or subsidiaries. These changes gave each institution the discretion to exclude or include the activities of affiliated mortgage companies in the CRA examination for specific assessment areas. This was a recognition on the part of the regulatory authorities that some mortgage company affiliates specialized in serving lower-income markets, whilst others wished to serve a larger market; however, it is possible that at the same time it may have weakened the CRA's inducements to expand lower-income lending by allowing institutions to select the combination of reporting that would produce the most favorable lending record. In addition, the revised lending test, which gives lenders credit for certain mortgage loans regardless of the characteristics of the area in which loans are made, represented a move away from the spatial focus of the CRA, but that was not the immediate effect.

The financial institution then had to pass various tests to achieve the most desirable 'outstanding' rating, if it demonstrated responsiveness to credit needs in its assessment areas. That would be shown if "there is an excellent distribution ... of loans amongst individuals of different income levels; an excellent record of serving the credit needs of highly disadvantaged areas in its assessment areas, including low-income individuals ... and extensive use of innovative or flexible lending practices in a safe and sound manner to address the credit needs of low- or moderate-income individuals."[17] The rule also established a "performance context. An institution's performance under the tests and standards in the rule is judged in the context of information about the institution, its community, its competition and its peers."[18]

To encourage such lending, the regulators continued to use publicity from which, during the long consultation period of some two years altogether, the industry requested a "safe harbor" from the activities of community groups, which they were not granted. More important from the banks' point of view was the requirement to have at least a "satisfactory" rating (or better, an "outstanding" rating) as a result of the CRA examination, if a bank was to apply to its regulatory authority for permission to relocate a home office or to open or relocate a branch, to merge with or acquire another insured depositary institution, to convert an insured bank to a national bank charter, or to assume the assets or liabilities of another regulated financial institution. In addition, the assessment of the bank would be adversely affected if there was evidence of discriminatory or other illegal credit practices; the regulator would also take into account any policies and procedures that the bank had in place to prevent such practices.

A bank then had to make available to the public the CRA assessment together with detailed information, such as the number and location of its branches, services generally offered at the branches, and, for banks other than small banks, the number of loans in each income category and the location of those loans in the bank's assessment area, plus the information required under the Home Mortgage Disclosure Act. Large banks needed an "outstanding" rating to excel against their competitors. The regulatory authorities would also take into consideration the public response, including responses from ACORN, the Neighborhood Assistance Corporation of America (NACA), and other consumer advocacy groups. These developments, for which ACORN in particular had long argued, provided such groups with all kinds of new opportunities. Previously, they had used strong-arm tactics, such as sit-ins in bank branches, disrupting tellers' queues, annual meetings, and targeting executives' homes. The amendments to the CRA meant that they would be able to use public information about a bank's CRA rating to force more lending to minorities and low-income families. Many banks caved in and entered into partnerships, promising to spend millions of dollars over the years to various projects. Meanwhile, the organisations were able to cash in, as they received huge grants for mortgage counseling and financial education. NACA apparently decided with what it claimed was delegated underwriting authority from banks to arrange mortgages for low-income families and expected to close 5,000 mortgages in 2001, earning a $2,000 origination fee on each.[19] ACORN focused on providing counseling and training for would-be borrowers.[20]

It is arguable that the CRA and its 1995 amendments became less relevant as the decade progressed, since banking changed in ways which were not envisaged in the Act. These included developments in banking technology, automated mortgage underwriting, telephone banking and the development of ATMs. Banking organisations operating outside their assessment areas expanded rapidly and comprised the fastest-growing segment of the residential mortgage market during that period. As a result, between 1993 and 2000 the number of home purchase loans made by CRA-regulated institutions *in their assessment areas* fell from 36.1% to 29.5%.

The regulatory structure that was in place when the CRA was enacted, in the late 1970s and subsequently, imposed many restrictions on financial institutions in terms of the types of products and services they could offer, the geographical areas in which they could operate, and the range of interest rates they could offer depositors or charge borrowers. In addition, strict chartering requirements raised the cost of setting up new financial services companies. "Redlining may have become a red herring, drawing attention away from the effectiveness of market forces in breaking down the types of financial barriers prevalent when the CRA was enacted."[21] Lending to low- and moderate-income families in underserved areas was not going to be left to market forces and developments in banking. Instead, new legislation coupled with the CRA would provide more tools for community and housing advocacy groups to ensure and some would say, force, some banks to lend to such families, and others to embrace the opportunity.

The implications of the Riegle-Neal Interstate Banking and Branching Act, 1994

Amongst its other effects, this Act increased the importance and value of the "outstanding" rating for banks. The amendment Act enabled full nationwide banking across America, for the first time and regardless of state law, after it came into full effect on June 1, 1997. It allowed branching through acquisition only, which means that a bank must acquire another bank and merge the two structures in order to operate across state lines, unless there existed a reciprocal agreement between states. The states had the power to allow a bank to open a branch in another state without the necessity of acquiring another bank to allow them to open a branch. The Act also allowed states to "opt out" of interstate banking by passing a law to prohibit it before June, 1997, but Texas and Montana were the only two states to do this. The first stage was agreements between states, but finally by 1997, the Act was signed into a law ratifying agreements between states, the FDIC and the Federal Reserve allowing for "seamless" supervision for state-chartered branches with branches across state lines.

It is in this context that the importance of the CRA amendments to the regulations must be seen, as Chairman Ben Bernanke pointed out in a speech in 2007. The 1994 Act was followed by "a surge in bank merger and acquisition activities ... As public scrutiny of bank merger and acquisition activity escalated, advocacy groups increasingly used the public comment process to protest bank applications on CRA grounds. In instances of highly contested applications, the Federal Reserve Board and other agencies held public meetings to allow the public and applicants to comment on the lending records of the banks in question. In response to these new pressures, banks began to devote more resources to their CRA programmes. Many institutions established separate business units and subsidiary community development corporations to facilitate lending that would be given favorable consideration in CRA examinations."[22] The public, of course, already had access to information about the distribution of loans, since banks were required to publish it. Community action groups often used such publicity to "encourage" banks to lend to such areas: indeed, there are examples of banks funding various housing and other development projects or financing community organisations in order to avert bad publicity. These had become more important factors in the context of the Riegle-Neal Act.

The "surge" in mergers and acquisitions

The "surge" in mergers and acquisitions to which Chairman Bernanke referred changed the whole structure of American banking, both within the USA and globally. At the end of 1996, and before Riegle-Neal came into force, the largest American bank was Chase Manhattan Corp., New York, then ranked seventeenth in the world by assets ($333.8 billion), followed by Citicorp, New York, ranked twenty-sixth, then BankAmerica Corp., San Francisco and J.P. Morgan & Co. Inc., New York. At that time, six of the ten largest banks in the world were Japanese. By the end of 2000, the largest banking group in the world was Citigroup at just under $1 trillion, and another two of the top ten banks in terms of asset size were American banks: J.P. Morgan Chase & Co., New York ($715,348,00) and Bank of America Corp., Charlotte, N.C.; a further nineteen significant acquisitions took place between 1998 and 2001, which involved extending the lines of business, such as acquiring trust services, mortgage banking or servicing, securities brokerages and investment advisory. Some of the acquisitions followed the repeal of Glass-Steagal by the Gramm-Leach-Bliley Act in 1999. Overall, the number of banks fell from 14,451 in

1982 to 8,080 in 2001. The total number of branch offices almost doubled during the same period, from 34,791 to 64,087.

Acquisitions and mergers did take place prior to 1997, when the Act was fully implemented. Based on an approach which aggregates all subsidiaries of the target banking organisation and views them all as one acquisition, dating from the completion of the transaction, a study by the Federal Reserve Bank shows that between 1994 and 2003, 3,517 deals were completed and that the target (acquired organisations) had $3.1 trillion in total assets, $2.1 trillion in total deposits, and 47,283 branch offices. The three largest deals of the entire ten-year period (ranked by asset size of the target) all took place in 1998, the year marked by the greatest volume of merger activity. Three other deals among the fifteen largest also took place in that year. Fifteen banking organisations were the acquirers in the twenty-five largest acquisitions. Four of these, First Union, Fleet and its successor FleetBoston, Nations Bank and Washington Mutual, were each of the acquirers in two of the top twenty-five. Two other banks, Firstar and Chemical (and its successor, Chase Manhattan), were each of the acquirers in the top twenty-five. The targets in many of the biggest deals were banks with large retail operations, allowing an expanded service area and greater penetration of established service areas, as well as a large retail customer base.[23]

Mergers and acquisitions are generally the only way to extend the retail customer base. The market share of the fifty largest bank holding companies actually declined from 71% in 1990 to 68% in 1999, reflecting their relatively low internal growth on a pro forma basis. In contrast, the market share of the top fifty in unadjusted terms increased steadily during the 1990s and underwent an especially significant jump in 1998, after the series of mega-mergers referred to above dramatically increased the size of several of the largest bank holding companies. This showed that the largest bank holding companies increased market share through M&As, and that internal growth was an inconsequential factor. It is possible that, with the aim of reducing excess capacity, the consolidated banks removed overlapping operations and became smaller in the short run; lowering costs and increasing efficiency would then enable them to outgrow competitors and thus increase market share. All of these changes meant that the structure of the banking industry changed dramatically during the 1990s, and would change again with the Gramm-Beach-Bliley Act.[24]

The importance of CRA ratings

The result of the regulations and the surrounding publicity led banks to focus on those activities which counted towards the rating, regardless of their impact on strengthening communities; or, as one commentator put it: "It's the rating, stupid!"[25] When a bank wishes to merge with another bank (or open an additional branch or branches) it must submit an application to its federal regulator. Various factors are taken into account, including the bank's record in serving the convenience or needs of the communities under the CRA. A merger application can be denied or delayed based on poor performance in meeting any of the factors considered in the application process, including CRA ratings. Denials of merger or acquisition applications are rare, but delays may occur while the bank answers various questions about its past CRA performance or makes specific commitments to improve its performance. A conditional approval may also be given for a merger or an acquisition, but a bank is required to take steps to remedy the deficiency and improve its rating. The public and community organizations also participate in the process. That is one reason why banks are concerned with the CRA ratings, since delays in planned mergers and acquisitions are costly and may prevent the bank from developing an effective competition strategy. Perhaps because of these and other strategies, based on the Federal Financial Institutions Examination Council (FFIEC) between January 1997 and November 1999, about 20% of all banks received an "outstanding" CRA rating, 79% received a "satisfactory" rating and 1% were advised of their "need to improve" rating.

As a result, CRA agreements are often negotiated between banks and community groups during the merger application process. Banks issue CRA commitments, promising a specific number of affordable home loans and branches in working-class or minority communities.[26] According to the US Treasury, the CRA-covered lenders increased home mortgage loans to low- and moderate-income borrowers by 39% from 1993 to 1998, more than twice that experienced by middle- and upper-income borrowers during the same period.[27] The report relies on an analysis of HMDA data and does not take into account the purchase of loans.

However, neither Chairman Bernanke nor any other analysts took on board the fact that banks could and did purchase loans in order to manipulate CRA examinations through the buying and selling of loans; and that they were able to do this because the data on loan purchases were not analysed separately from loan originations. In 2004, the regulatory authorities proposed separate tables on originations and purchases of loans, only to abandon this proposal. Originating a loan is a more difficult task in low- to medium-income areas, as it requires advertising, counseling, compliance, and more detailed record-keeping. Purchasing a loan has no, or very little, value to the local community, but is a much less time-consuming process; it is therefore not surprising that it was an option.[28] The loan could be purchased and then sold on as a private label mortgage-backed security (MBS), or sold on again to Fannie Mae and Freddie Mac.

Many analysts took the view that it was indeed the case that throughout the 1990s, there was a substantial increase in lending to lower-income populations and neighborhoods. This was due to a number of factors, such as changes to banking regulations and supervision, increased competition among providers of financial services, favorable economic circumstances and the growing demand for credit, as well as advances in technology allowing for better and cheaper evaluations of borrower creditworthiness. The period from 1991 to 2001 was one in which banks often experienced record profits in a time of unprecedented growth in the economy. This led some to claim that the banks moved into subprime mortgage lending to reap vast profits at the expense of low-income families.

Performance and profitability of CRA-related lending

Increasing suspicions about the possibility of excess profits led Congress to request a report from the Federal Reserve System on the performance and profitability of CRA-related lending. The report was presented to Congress in 2000.[29] The authors noted that "little systemic information is publicly available about the delinquency and default (performance) and profitability of CRA-related lending activities." This is partly because banks identified the origination or purchase of such loans, but did not follow through with the identification up to the point where they were paid off or in default; and also because, although delinquency is more consistently defined and recorded across the industry, default is not. Indeed, there is little agreement on the definition of the latter. The lack of such key agreed definitions is significant and a matter to which it will prove necessary to return.

To deal with these problems, Congress directed the Board to produce a comprehensive study which is focused on (i) delinquency and default rates of loans made in conformity with the CRA, and (ii) the profitability of such lending. This resulted in a special survey conducted by the Board of the largest banking institutions, concentrating on their CRA-related lending, that being considered responsible for the origination of the majority of CRA-related loans. Here the authors of the report had to decide what counted as "CRA-related" loans, so the report itself refers to CRA-related lending as "lending by banking institutions to low-and-moderate income populations, low-and-moderate income areas, small businesses within their CRA assessment area(s) and to lending for the purposes of community development" where the lending is in the first instance referred to home purchases and refinancing.[30] In their Economic Commentary on the report, the authors note that their definitions (which covered only federally regulated banking institutions, of course) excluded about half of all lower-income lending done by banking institutions.[31]

Their further notes in the Economic Commentary are also instructive. They found that the focus on home lending in terms of the "relatively narrow group of loans made under the affordable-home-loans programs" often deviated from the definition of CRA-home loans made by other financial institutions, such as mortgage companies. More important, the frequent inclusion of loans made by banking institutions outside their local communities, and loans made to borrowers with incomes exceeding the lower-income criterion, meant that much of the existing research on performance and profitability is unreliable.[32]

However, throughout the report itself, reference is made to affordable lending programmes, which have four distinct elements: targeted groups; special marketing; the application of non-traditional and more flexible underwriting standards; and the proactive use of risk-mitigation activities. Flexible underwriting generally has the following characteristics: relatively low down-payment requirements; higher acceptable ratios of debt to income; the use of alternative credit history information, such as records of payment for rent and utilities; flexible employment standards; and reduced cash-reserve requirements. Some lenders offer reduced interest rates, waive private mortgage requirements, or reduce or waive costs associated with originating the loan. Many of the larger banks, the report states, "have developed new credit products that feature underwriting guidelines that are generally more flexible than those for other products."[33]

The authors set out the way in which they conducted the research, explaining first the data they expected to find. Their survey was restricted to the largest 500 retail banks, because these account for over 70% of one to four family home lending and community development lending, based on their projected total assets as at December 31, 1999. It consisted of 400 commercial banks and 100 savings institutions, ranging in size from about $870m to $500bn. The focus should be on one to four family home purchases and refinance mortgage lending, because the banks are able to identify these CRA-related loans at the time of origination or purchase, and so might be able to provide information on their performance and profitability over time, and because the purchases in these categories have enough borrower and geographic information to estimate the volume of CRA-related and non-CRA-related lending.

They then explain the further complications in the data, arising from the fact that CRA lending also refers to the distribution of loans across the range of borrowers, as well as to any loan made *within* the banking institution's CRA assessment area to a low- or moderate-income borrower regardless of the neighborhood income *or* in a low- or moderate-income neighborhood regardless of borrower income. Then, of course, information could only be collected about loans held in the bank's portfolio or for those loans that were originated, later sold but still serviced by the originating bank. The fact that a major report encountered such difficulties in compiling necessary information and had to look beyond the HMDA data to other sources such as the Reports on Condition and Income (Bank Call reports for commercial banks and some savings institutions) and the Thrift Financial Reports (for the remaining savings associations) indicates the inadequacy of data collection, which may well be significant in terms of the relationship between CRA-lending and subprime loans.

It is estimated that the 500 banks and savings associations originated over $570bn in home purchase and refinance loans in 1999 alone, of which about 10% was CRA-related. The level of profitability depends on whether it is calculated according to the institution or on a per CRA-related dollar basis. The authors point out that it is important to note that the large banks with assets of $30bn or more were far more likely to assess their CRA-related house purchase and refinance lending as being less profitable than other lending in this product category than medium-sized banks ($5bn to $30bn). Overall the majority of banks held that such lending was profitable or marginally profitable. When reported on a per CRA-related dollar basis, 63% said that loans originated in 1999 were less profitable than other home finance or refinance lending, as compared with 44% on a per institution basis.

When it comes to performance, that is, delinquency and default rates, the authors argue that this is more difficult to estimate, as it is not clear what percentage of loans for each type of institution have been sold on. Where banks were in a position to report, about half of the survey respondents had higher rates for delinquency for CRA-related loans for home purchase than for overall lending; one-third reported that there was no difference; and one-sixth reported higher delinquency rates. The same analysis conducted on a per CRA-dollar basis gave higher credit losses for CRA-related loans than for other loans (46% as compared with 28%). The originating costs of CRA-related loans for home purchase are about the same, but in some cases the servicing costs may be higher. In general, most banks, especially the large ones, reported that pricing is similar for both types of loans or in many cases lower than for CRA-related home purchase and refinance loans. When it comes to calculations on a per-CRA dollar basis, many more report that the originating and servicing costs are higher. In other words, the report concluded that most of the banks surveyed at best did not regard CRA-related lending as particularly profitable.

If it was not particularly profitable, then why did banks engage in it at all? The authors of the report note, in their short article in the Economic Commentary, 2000, that only 1% of the respondents stated they did it in order to obtain a "satisfactory" or "outstanding" response, which is hardly surprising: "A large share said they established their programme to meet the local community's credit needs and to promote its growth and stability."[34] Whilst that was no doubt true, in the political context of the time, and given that merger and acquisition proposals could be delayed if they did not reach the CRA goals, it must be seen as just one of the reasons for the banks to engage in CRA-related loans.

The CRA and the subprime crisis

Since the beginning of the financial crisis, a fierce debate has raged. The issue: did the Community Reinvestment Act and its amendments *cause* the crisis? Proponents of the Act both within Congress and amongst many analysts deny that it had such an impact; others argue that the Act did not increase lending to low- and moderate-income families, or to minorities at all, so that it would not have had any impact on the financial crisis, nor did it increase subprime lending; this view is expressed by Christopher Perry and Sarah Lee on the basis of their regression discontinuity design.[35] Using HMDA loan application data, plus bank data from the FDIC Summary of Deposits database and FRB's commercial bank database, and on the basis of their analysis, they find little evidence that the CRA caused a reduction in loan rejection rates for low-to-moderate neighborhoods or individuals between 1993 and 2003. Rejection rates are lower for banks operating in their CRA assessment areas, and this difference holds both for loans to low- and moderate-income borrowers and for loans to high-income borrowers. This study, however, makes no reference to underwriting standards and the encouragement provided by the CRA to introduce "flexible" lending standards.

Others argue that the CRA did fulfil the aims and objectives which President Clinton desired and of which he was so proud. Those who take this view (some of whom still want the Act to be strengthened) accept that while it did bring about an increase in subprime lending, it was such a small percentage of CRA lending that it could not have and therefore did not cause such effects.

Whether or not the CRA contributed to the increase in low- to moderate-income lending, there was undoubtedly a vast increase between 1993 and 2000, according to a number of studies, especially ones conducted by those supporting the CRA. For example, a study by Harvard's Joint Center for Housing Studies found that home purchase loans to such borrowers and neighborhoods rose by 77% during that period, more than the overall increase in lending for house buying, which was 53%.[36]

Others argued that the growth rates were even more impressive, if broken down into different ethnic groups. Michael Barr calculated that between 1993 and 1999, the number of home purchase loans to Hispanics increased by 121%; to Native Americans, by 118%; to African Americans, by 91.0%; to Asians, by 70.1%; and to whites, by 33.5%. Over that period, the number of home purchase loans extended to applicants with incomes less than 80% of the median increased by 86.2%, a much higher rate of growth than for any other income group.[37]

These calculations were based on HMDA data as reported by the Federal Financial Institutions Council, but, as Barr acknowledges, this may overstate the growth in lending to Hispanics, since their household growth was much higher than white households at the time (36.7% as compared with 6.2%.) Adjusting for differential levels of household formation, the growth for whites was 3.58 times its household growth of 6.2%; for Hispanics, 3.31 times; for blacks 7.34 times its household growth of 12.4%; the figures still show progress for minorities. Various other measures are used, all indicating growth in lending to low- and moderate-income areas: for example, in 1990, there were 19.6 million home owners in such areas, 49.65% of the number of home owners in high-income areas. By 2000, the ratio had improved, so that the number of home owners in low- to moderate-income communities was 55% of the number in high-income areas. The number of the former group grew by 26.6% over the decade, while the number in high-income areas grew by only 14% with a net gain for minority home ownership. These figures are based on Michael Barr's calculations using US Census data from 1990 and 2000, and the evidence is supported by a number of other studies, indicating that the CRA improved access to home mortgage credit for low-income borrowers especially after the regulations were amended in 1995. The share of loans to individuals targeted by CRA and fair lending regulations originated by banks, thrifts, and their affiliates increased during the 1990s; other researchers found evidence consistent "with the view that the CRA has been effective in encouraging bank organizations, especially those involved in consolidation, to serve lower income and minority borrowers and neighborhoods."[38]

By themselves, these growth rates do not show that this was due to the influence of the CRA alone. The method Michael Barr uses is to compare the growth in CRA lending by each CRA-regulated bank or thrift with the growth in its non-CRA lending. What emerges is interesting, and perhaps the most relevant argument: the number of CRA-related loans increased by 39% between 1993 and 1998, while other mortgage loans increased by only 17%. Even excluding affiliates, which are there by the lenders' discretion, they increased their lending to the target groups by 10%, whilst the lending to affluent areas did not increase at all. Over this period, the portfolio share of CRA-covered lender and affiliate mortgage loans going to these low- and moderate-income borrowers and to the relevant areas increased by 3%. There are indications that the growth in CRA lending to these groups continued to increase during the early part of the following decade.

The CRA and community groups

The argument that the impact of CRA-related loans did not spill over from the 1990s into the following decade has to take into account the fact that community groups not only continued to be relevant for low- to moderate-income areas, but pressed for it to be strengthened. Here the annual reports of the National Community Reinvestment Coalition (NCRC), an association of over 600 community-based organizations that promote access to basic banking services, including credit and savings, create and sustain affordable housing, promote job development and ensure vibrant communities for America's working families are relevant. It includes a wide variety of organizations in its membership, ranging from community reinvestment bodies to local and state government agencies, amongst others. In its contribution to a forum on the future of the CRA, John Taylor and Josh Silver, NCRC President and Vice President respectively, point out in *The Community Reinvestment Act: 30 Years of Wealth Building and What We Must Do to Finish the Job* that "the CRA's effectiveness can also be measured by comparing the lending patterns of CRA-covered banks with those of lending institutions not covered by CRA exams. NCRC found that in 2006, depository institutions extended 23.5% of home purchase loans to LMI (low- to moderate-income borrowers), whereas non-CRA covered lenders extended 21.5%."[39] Their comments on the approach to CRA enforcement are also illuminating, and are as follows:

(i) "Though the CRA regulation stipulates that the assessment areas include geographical regions containing bank branches, the regulation also states that the assessment areas include other regions in which the bank has originated or purchased a substantial portion of its loans.[40] Despite this regulatory clause, the federal agencies usually adopt a narrow definition of assessment areas for banks or thrifts that issue most of their loans through non-branch channels. For these banks, it is not unusual to encounter CRA exams that cover only the geographical area of the bank's headquarters."

(ii) In a later paragraph, the authors point out that, "under the CRA banks have the option of including their non-depository affiliates, such as mortgage companies, on CRA exams. Banks are tempted to include affiliates on CRA exams if the affiliates perform admirably, but they will opt against inclusion if the affiliates are engaged in risky lending or discriminatory policies. This is counter to the essential purpose of the CRA, which is to ensure that the institution as a whole is meeting credit needs in a responsible manner."[41]

The NCRC welcomed the CRA Modernization Act, 2007 as a way of ending "this serious gap" in enforcing the CRA, as banks would be obliged to include all their affiliates in CRA exams. The submission argues strongly for this and other improvements in the CRA legislation, including its extension to nonbank financial institutions, including credit unions, securities companies, mortgage companies, insurance firms and investment banks. It is interesting that, in spite of this recognition of the changing structure of the financial services industry, they still make the point that "credit unions and independent mortgage companies do not offer as high a percentage of home loans to LMI borrowers as banks."[42] In addition, safety and soundness examination should be integrated with fair lending reviews and CRA examinations. For these organisations and other witnesses, such as Michael Barr, the Community Reinvestment Act still had an important role to play in ensuring that low-to moderate-income borrowers have access to credit.[43]

Of course, it can be argued that these are interested parties to a greater or lesser extent, but their views are supported by other analyses to which reference has been made, such as the view that of the banks responding to the Federal Reserve's survey, most found that low- to moderate-income lending was at least marginally profitable, if not profitable. Another analysis examines the effects of CRA on lending patterns from different point of view, namely empirically, modeling changes in aggregate lending as a function of local economic characteristics and changes in those characteristics, based on changes in mortgage lending activity over three-year intervals and CRA lending agreements. The results of the analysis are "consistent with the view that institutions increase targeted conventional mortgage lending upon the introduction of the CRA agreement ... that it is new lending ... and is relatively short-lived. The results are broadly consistent with the notion that lenders view CRA agreements as a form of insurance against potentially large and uncertain costs of fair lending violations, poor CRA performance ratings, and adverse publicity from CRA-related protests of mergers and other applications."[44]

This analysis ties in with the behavior one would expect a bank's executives to recommend to the board. The decision may even have been taken in such a context for such lending not to be a short-term activity, when it was open to public view. Analysts have taken note of the regulatory and broad political pressures to increase low- and moderate-income lending, especially for mortgages; it should be noted that CEOs and their boards would undoubtedly take account of pressures exerted by Congressional members as well as the wide range of community organizations, who would ensure that their criticisms of bank lending policies in low- to moderate-income areas were fully covered by the local media.

As critics alleged that the CRA was the cause of the recent mortgage crisis, a useful summary of the view taken by the Federal Reserve and other regulators is found in a speech given by Governor Randall Kroszner, a member of the Board of Governors of the Federal Reserve System.[45] Once again, this both insists that the CRA was effective *and* that it was not a cause of the subprime crisis. The governor refers first of all to the study of 2000, to which reference has already been made, to the effect that during the 1990s the CRA-prompted lending to lower-income individuals and communities was "nearly as profitable and performed similarly to other types of lending done by CRA-covered institutions." Thus, with the backing of the Federal Reserve's research, the CRA "has encouraged banks" to pursue "lending opportunities in all segments of their local communities," which by implication they would not have done without the CRA. If that was not the case, then the CRA would have been completely useless, whereas in fact regulators, politicians and community organizations alike argued that it was effective, with many strongly opposing its abolition. Thus the CRA may well have contributed to the growth in subprime lending in the period 2001 to 2006, although the governor insists that only "6% of the higher-priced loans were extended by CRA-covered lenders to lower-income borrowers or neighborhoods in their CRA assessment areas, the local geographies that are the primary focus for CRA evaluation purposes ... (banks) can also purchase loans from lenders not covered by the CRA, and in this way encourage more of this type of lending ... Specifically, less than 2% of the higher-priced and CRA-credit eligible mortgages sold by independent mortgage companies were purchased by CRA-covered institutions."[46] It should be noted that subprime lending is here identified with 'higher-priced' lending, an inadequate definition, as will be shown in the next chapter.

Since Governor Kroszner refers to the lines of business not "previously tapped by forming partnerships with community organizations and other stakeholders to identify and help meet the credit needs of underserved areas," it is worth exploring what such partnerships could entail. The 2007 Annual Report of the National Community Reinvestment Coalition provides an excellent account of the number and dollar value of such partnerships, based on a careful analysis of all the data provided by its member organizations.

The report covers the period from 1977 to the first part of 2007. Negotiations with lenders by community organizations have led to the former committing $4.56 trillion in reinvestment dollars, of which $4.5 trillion was committed between 1992 and 2007, whereas only $8.8 billion was negotiated between 1977 and 1991. Apart from the increasing sophistication of the much larger numbers of community organizations, the NCRC argues that as banks became regional and national in scope, they recognized the importance of maintaining their local community lending and investing capacity. Not all of the lending went into meeting housing needs, and not all of the monies "committed" may have been actually lent, as some of the agreements cover several years.

The preface to the report notes that banks increasingly entered into unilateral agreements, presumably, and if for no other reason, to avoid public criticism; but it also describes the fluctuation in dollar amounts, which it relates to mergers and acquisitions. Examples are 1998, a year of mega-mergers, including the merger of the Bank of America with Nations Bank as well as Citigroup's merger with Travelers, leading to the Bank of America pledging $350 bn over ten years and to Citigroup pledging $115 bn over ten years as a result. Fewer mega-mergers and less reinvestment were the characteristics of the following years, until 2003 and 2004, when the pledges increased dramatically with the watershed mergers of the Bank of America's acquisition of Fleet, J.P. Morgan Chase acquiring Bank One, and Citizens taking over Charter One. The dollar amounts comprising the 2007 total achieved since 1977 consists of (a) agreements negotiated between community organizations/state and local governments with lenders during the merger application process, and (b) voluntary CRA programs or commitments unilaterally announced by a lender. The largest community development was announced in 2008 at a Federal Reserve Bank Hearing on the proposed merger between the Bank of America and Countrywide Financial Corporation. It was for $1.5 trillion, and the Bank of America would embark on the program once the merger was completed.[47]

The point here is to look at the basis of lending agreements to lower- and moderate-income borrowers for single family units, since the vast amounts listed above were not all directed to housing. The examples selected show that the agreements were spread over the years between 1992 and 2006, and indicates the wide range of arrangements the banks agreed to make:

(i) In its 2006 agreement with the Greenling Institute and California Reinvestment Coalition, Wachovia Bank pledged $10.3bn for both single-family and multi-family loans with higher debt to equity ratios than usual, flexible credit history requirements, low down-payment requirements ($15m commitment to down-payment assistance) and no closing costs. This followed agreements during its planned merger with SouthTrust in 2004 to include a lending goal of $15bn in mortgages to low- to moderate-income borrowers and neighborhoods in seven different states, including Alabama, Florida, Georgia, Mississippi, North and South Carolina, Tennessee, Texas and Virginia. These were designed for lenders with impaired credit with no requirement for private mortgage insurance, up to 100% financing and low or no down-payment requirements.

(ii) Others offered refinancing loans at lower rates: for example, in the 1999 agreement with New Jersey Citizen Action and the Affordable Housing Network of New Jersey, the Bank of New York pledged $10m under a pilot project to offer refinance loans to borrowers with subprime mortgages. Borrowers were not required to have a minimum credit score provided they could demonstrate 18 months of satisfactory mortgage payments.

(iii) As part of its 2003 pledge, CitiMortgage offered a closing cost assistance program for buyers in certain areas. The bank also agreed to allow borrowers with past credit difficulties to obtain a mortgage rate 2% lower than was usual for such borrowers to pay.

(iv) The 1999 agreement between Sovereign Bank, New Jersey Citizen Action and the Affordable Housing Network of New Jersey committed the bank to offer a mortgage product with no private mortgage insurance, housing and debt ratios of 33/40, 1–1.5% below the market interest rate, 95% loan to value and up to 3% of the down-payment in the form of a gift or second mortgage. Over a period of three years, the bank will offer $41m per year of such mortgages.

(v) In their 1998 agreement, New Jersey Citizen Action and the Philadelphia Association of CDCs committed First Union to providing affordable home loans with no private mortgage insurance, down payments from "sweat equity" (i.e. recognition of work done to improve the property), debt to income ratios as high as 33 and 38%, and loans as low as $10,000. Similarly, the Maryland Center for Community Development and First Union agreed that the bank would provide a 100% loan-to-value product with no down-payment or mortgage insurance and $500 of the borrower's own funds at closing, which can be a gift or paid by the seller.

(vi) In its $1.25bn agreement with the Ohio Community Reinvestment Project (OCRP) and the Coalition of Homelessness and Housing in Ohio (COHHIO) signed in 1998, Fifth Third bank agreed to maintain a "Home Sweet Home" mortgage with no private mortgage insurance and 3% down payments.

(vii) In 1998, Household International signed a $3bn agreement with Inner City Press/Community on the Move and the Delaware Community Reinvestment Action Council. Household specializes in offering subprime, high-interest loans to those with blemished credit histories. As part of the agreement, Household committed itself to set up a lower-interest home equity product for those borrowers with "A" or "A-minus" credit histories. This was welcomed as a precedent-setting agreement for minorities, whom, it was claimed, were regarded as subprime borrowers in numbers disproportionate to their population.

(viii) In its $200m CRA agreement with the City of Cleveland, Firstmerit would offer a "First Choice Mortgage" with a 97% loan-to-value ratio, 33/44% housing and debt ratios, no private mortgage insurance and no application or origination fee, starting in the year 2000.

Fewer specific examples are given of other aspects of flexible lending standards, except that the report refers to many CRA agreements which adopt a more flexible approach to credit histories, given that many low-income and minority applicants lack traditional credit histories or have a record of late payments. With regard to employment history, most lenders require borrowers to have between two and five years at the same job to qualify for a loan. This often excludes low-income and minority applicants, who change jobs frequently but may maintain a steady source of income. Many CRA agreements have included provisions to address this problem.

The damage which was done by pushing banks to make such commitments can be seen from the following: Wachovia Bank collapsed in September 2008 and was taken over by Citibank, with losses of $42bn; Sovereign Bank went through a series of mergers and acquisitions until it was taken over by Santander in 2009; First Union was taken over by Wachovia in 2001; Household International was purchased by HSBC in 2003, but in September 2007, HSBC took a write-down of $800m and closed it down.

The report is valuable, in that it gives further insight into what "flexible underwriting standards" were taken to mean. The true impact of the Community Reinvestment Act and hence of its contribution is difficult to assess for a variety of reasons: the inadequacy of the HMDA statistics; the apparent "safety and soundness" of subprime lending during the 1990s and the years immediately following; the extent to which banks and thrifts purchased subprime loans from non-CRA-lenders; and the lack of data linking loan origination with loan performance. Those who argue that the CRA did not cause the crisis point to the lack of an agreed definition of "subprime" loans; instead many euphemisms were used, such as the references to "flexible" underwriting standards. But these standards involved high LTV ratios, high debt-to-income ratios, low credit scores or no credit history at all; in short, the key characteristics of a subprime loan. The Boston Handbook spelt out what the standards were from the start. It was a clear signal to the banks. The CRA provided strong incentives, and even pushed banks into lowering their lending standards. It may not have been *the* cause of the crisis, but it undoubtedly played a part. The inadequacy of the data and the longest period of economic expansion between 1992 and 2000 served to hide the effects of the growth of subprime lending, which began then. The CRA was an important cause of the subprime crisis, but by no means the only one.

2

Two More Tools in the Tool-Kit

To reach the targets for extending home ownership especially to low- and moderate-income families, both Congress and the Administration were aware that two more avenues were open to them. Both were long-established. Both were originally part of the New Deal. One, the Federal Housing Administration, was part of a government department and the other, the Federal Home Loan Bank System, was a government-sponsored enterprise. Two more tools to be used.

The Federal Housing Administration (FHA)

The FHA was originally established in 1934 under the National Housing Act and was incorporated into the Department of Housing and Urban Affairs in 1965. Its function is to insure loans made by banks and other private lenders for house building and home purchase, and has insured over 34 million properties since it came into existence. A New Deal phenomenon which has probably outlived its usefulness, it came into being when a million construction workers were unemployed and most people were unable to obtain a mortgage. Mortgage terms then were limited to 50% of the property's market value, with a repayment schedule of three to five years, ending with a balloon payment.

As an agency within HUD, the FHA oversees two mortgage insurance programmes to insure lenders against loss from loan defaults by borrowers through the Mutual Mortgage Insurance/Cooperative Management Housing Insurance fund account (MMI/CMHI). Another account, the General Insurance/ Special Risk Insurance Fund account (GI/SRI), covers more risky home mortgages, multifamily rental housing and an assortment of special-purpose loans for hospitals and nursing homes. Only the first fund is relevant here, providing insurance for mortgage loans backed by the "full faith and credit of the United States." Since the purchaser pays for the insurance as part of the monthly mortgage payments, and the proceeds are set aside in a separate account, which is used to operate the whole program, the insurance is regarded as self-financing and is designed to protect the lender from the losses incurred if the borrower defaults on the mortgage. The advantage of FHA loans from the borrower's point of view is that the required down payment is the high LTV, and there is greater flexibility in calculating household income and payment ratios.

This is the way in which HUD presents[1] the value of FHA-insured loans to would-be borrowers.

The FHA has traditionally been a major source of funding for first-time, low-income and minority home-buyers, but during the 1990s, substantial program and policy changes enabled it to extend that role. Between 1993 and August, 2000, the share of home purchase loans insured by the FHA and the VA (Veterans Home Loans Program) going to first-time buyers increased from 67% to 81%; that is, 4.2 million first-time buyers, especially minorities, have been assisted to buy their own homes, according to HUD. FHA-insured loans to African-Americans and Hispanics increased from 19.5% in 1993 to 34% by August, 2000. The share for all minorities rose from 22.5% in 1993 to 41.8% in the same period.

By contrast, the conventional conforming market funds low-income and minority borrowers and their neighborhoods at much lower rates than the FHA. Based on HMDA figures for 1999, African-American (minority) borrowers accounted for 14.6% of all FHA loans in metropolitan areas, compared with only 5.4% for the conventional conforming market. More than 40% of FHA loans financed properties in underserved neighborhoods, compared with only 26% of conventional conforming loans.

President Clinton saw the FHA as another way of achieving the aim of increasing home ownership. His 1998 Budget called for helping "hundreds of and thousands of hard-working, middle-class Americans qualify as homeowners by raising home mortgage insurance limits used by the FHA. Despite record national home ownership rates, many Americans, including young, first-time home buyers, city center residents, and racial and ethnic minorities, are shut out of home ownership because they have difficulties in accessing mortgage credit."[2] He asked for a single nationwide figure of $222,150, which would put FHA-insured loans on a par with the conventional loan limits set by Fannie Mae and Freddie Mac. The limit itself was well above the median price for houses in the USA, which ranged from $148,000 in January 1998 to $152,000 in December. This was not agreed; instead the limits for FHA single family loans continued to be set by county in accordance with the National Housing Act. The basic nationwide limits for single family units ranged from $121,296 to $219, 849 for high-cost areas in 2000, and from $160,176 to $290,319 in 2004.

Changes in FHA requirements

This "success story" was achieved by persuading Congress, whose responsibility it is to set the maximum and minimum loan terms as well as loan-to-value, to allow lower down payments. The National Housing Act was amended in 1999 (and extended in 2002) to allow the FHA to use a simplified formula for assessing the down payment for borrowers buying houses with FHA-insured loans.

The formula still seems quite complicated, but in effect it means that the down payment is about 3% of the appraisal price of the property. Borrowers also have to pay closing costs, prepaid fees for insurance and interest, escrow fees and property taxes, but the loan could be structured so that borrowers do not pay more than 3% of the total out-of-pocket funds, including the down payment. After this change, the FHA doubled the percentage of loans it insured with down payments of less than 5%, from 23% in 1998 to 44% in 1999, and increased its share of house purchase loans from 12% to 15%. It was setting lower underwriting standards with greater reliance on minimum down payments and increasing the total debt-income ratio to 41% and beyond on very low down-payment loans, and it had no minimum FICO score. Indeed, the FHA focused only on the borrower's last year to two-year credit history. With loans like this on offer, the FHA's market share rose from 11% to 15% in 1999–2000, but began to fall in 2001 and 2002 as it faced increased competition from the GSEs. By 2004, its share had fallen to about 3%.

HUD also persuaded Congress to increase the dollar loan limits on FHA mortgages in 1998. These had previously been set at 95% of the area median home sale price within a county, and ranged between a statutory minimum of 38% of the conforming loan limit for conventional loans purchased by Freddie Mac and Fannie Mae and a statutory maximum of 75% of the conforming limit, which could change annually with the general level of house prices. At HUD's request in 1998, Congress raised the respective statutory minimum and maximum limits to 48 and 87% of the conforming limit respectively, thus making FHA loans available more widely, especially to those in high-cost areas who could not use conventional mortgage products. By 2000 the loan limits for single units stood at a minimum of $121,296 to a maximum of $219,849.

Seller down-payment program

Underwriting guidelines were also relaxed: gifts could be used to cover the whole down payment in the seller-funded down-payment program; this was introduced in the 1990s and brought to an end in 2008, although loans from a family member will still be considered as cash for this purpose. Congress was also persuaded to authorize a simpler method of calculating the minimum down payment required so that an FHA borrower must put a minimum cash investment of 3% of the purchase price towards the acquisition cost of the home (price plus closing costs), together with whatever additional cash is required to achieve a maximum LTV that varies with loan size and whether the property is located in a state with high closing costs.

The seller down-payment program allowed non-profit consumer advocacy groups to "donate" the 3.5% down payment to low-income buyers seeking an FHA-insured loan.[3] Having introduced the program, the FHA was extremely reluctant to abandon it, despite the concerns expressed by both HUD and the

FHA itself.[4] In her written statement to Congress in June, 2007, for example, Margaret Burns, Director of the FHA's Single Family Program Development, admitted their concerns and refers to the "recently published rule" that the "funds cannot be derived from sellers or any other party that stands to benefit financially from the purchase transaction."[5] Loans that rely on these "gifts" had higher foreclosure rates than other FHA loans, not necessarily because the buyers were riskier, but because seller-funded down payments were offered in weak real estate markets, often accompanied by property overvaluation. These were very popular loans, accounting for about 30% of FHA loans in 2005.[6]

Congressional reluctance to limit the seller down-payment scheme continued even after the Internal Revenue Service (IRS) issued a new ruling in 2006, for which the press release stated that funneling down-payment assistance from sellers to buyers through "self-serving, circular-financing arrangements is inconsistent with operation as a section 501© (3) charitable organization." The so-called "charities" were often set up by the builders, who covered their costs simply by increasing the cost of the home. They "contributed" the funds to the non-profit organization, which passed on the increased costs to the buyer. They were roundly condemned by the Chairman of the IRS as "scams" which "damage the image of honest legitimate charities." This weakness in lending standards cost the FHA some $10bn according to the FHA's independent Actuarial Report, 2009; the report states that "if the FHA had not insured any loans with seller-funded down payment assistance, the net capital ratio today would still be above the statutory required 2%. FHA's estimated economic net worth would be $10.4 billion higher today were it not for those loans."[7] These "gifts" not only benefited the non-profits, but also house builders and many others, since the non-profit was at times a front for them. The program was often fraudulent as well.

Margaret Burns' statement also provided the examples of Ohio and Indiana, where, in 2006, more than 50% of FHA's purchase mortgage business was for borrowers who relied on non-profit seller-funded gifts, these being states in which house values have been stagnant or declining. Borrowers who face any kind of financial hardship and have no or negative equity slip into foreclosure fairly quickly. As a result, the high foreclosure rates in these communities contribute to additional decline in home values and a vicious cycle of property deterioration.

The seller down-payment program was regarded as being an extremely risky one. For example, HUD had proposed a series of reforms, which were incorporated into H.R. 5121, as passed by the House. An administrative provision in the bill the House passed would have amended the National Housing Act, raising the loan limits for low-cost areas from 48% to 65% of the Freddie Mac limit, and would have given the FHA authority to insure 100% mortgages, with HUD determining what, if any, down payment would be required based on the likelihood of borrower default, with the insurance premium being based on the risk the borrower posed to the insurance fund.

Senate declined to include these provisions in its version of H.R. 5576, partly because it did not believe that the proposal included the reforms necessary to allow HUD to compete in the private market without increased financial risk to the FHA insurance fund, and without subjecting the proposal to significant fraud and abuse. Interestingly enough, the Committee was concerned that the proposals would move the FHA closer to becoming lender of last resort. Neither proposal was enacted by the end of the 109th Congress.[8]

Senators may have been fortified in their views by the 2005 Government Accountability Office (GAO) report on the risks involved in the seller down-payment programme.[9] GAO noted that the risks had grown substantially over the previous few years, between 2000 and 2004 increasing from 35% to nearly 50%, with seller non-profit having reached about 30%. Involving a non-profit alters the transaction in a variety of ways:

(i)   When a home buyer receives assistance from a seller-funded non-profit, many require the property sellers to make a payment to the non-profit that equals the amount of assistance the home buyer receives plus a service fee after the closing. This requirement creates an indirect funding stream from property sellers to home buyers that does not exist in other transactions, even those involving some kind of down-payment assistance.

(ii) GAO found from market participants and a HUD contractor study that the property sellers who provided down-payment assistance through non-profits often raised the price of the house so that they recovered the cost of the contributions to the non-profits. This meant larger loans for the purchaser and higher LTV ratios. The differences were significant, about 2% to 3% more than comparable homes without such assistance. The FHA requires lenders to inform appraisers of the presence and source of down-payment assistance, but does not require the lenders to identify whether or not the provider receives funding from the property sellers. Some mortgage lenders regard seller-funded non-profits as an inducement to a sale and so its use should either be restricted or banned. The FHA did not.

(iii) The GAO report notes that examples of seller-funded non-profits that provide the most down-payment assistance to home buyers with FHA-insured mortgages include the Nehemiah Corporation of America, Ameridream, Inc. and The Buyers Fund, but all these require contributions from sellers. Examples of those which do not include, but still provide, the most down-payment assistance to buyers with FHA-insured mortgages include the Clay Foundation, Inc. and Family

Housing Resources Inc. It is the lender's responsibility to ensure that the gift meets FHA requirements.

(iv) The GAO report relies on two studies conducted by the Office of the Inspector General, analysing the default rates of FHA loans with down-payment assistance: one sample included loans provided by Nehemiah, and the other did not. In the first study, the default rate was more than double for the loans with down-payment assistance provided by Nehemiah. In the second study (loans endorsed between 1997 and 2001), Nehemiah-assisted loans defaulted at the rate of 19.42% as compared with a rate of 9.7% for loans without assistance from this non-profit.[10] GAO also refers to another report by the Homeownership Alliance of Nonprofit Downpayment Providers (HAND), whose survey based on endorsed loans from 1997 to 2001, evaluated in May 2003, found that the delinquency rates for loans with assistance from non-profits were about 11% higher than for loans with gifts from relatives.

GAO therefore recommended that the FHA should:

(i) Routinely assess the impact that the widespread use of down-payment assistance has on loan performance; it should also target lenders with a high volume of such loans.

(ii) Identify down-payment sources.

(iii) Include the presence and source of down-payment assistance as a variable in the FHA's TOTAL Mortgage Scorecard during the underwriting process.

(iv) Continue to include the presence and source of down-payment assistance in future loan performance models.

The GAO added that a program assessment, which was included with the 2006 President's Budget, showed that the FHA's Loan Performance Model was neither accurate nor reliable, because it consistently failed to predict the level of claims. This was a significant failure then, and was about to become more serious as the economic value of the fund fell dramatically in 2007. FHA's actuaries have also commented on the impact of down-payment assisted loans in the actuarial study of MMI for the fiscal year, 2005. Their conclusion was that the losses on such loans led to a decrease of almost $2bn in the estimated economic value. The independent actuarial report for 2006 showed that the cumulative insurance claim rates for down-payment assisted loans represent a significantly greater risk to the FHA than "no gift" loans. For each origination year, the claim rates are much higher than the rates associated with no gifts.[11]

It was for this and for the reasons cited above that HUD introduced a rule banning seller-assisted down payment, which came into force on October 31,

2007. All organizations providing down-payment assistance reimbursed by the seller "before, during and after" that sale must cease providing grants for FHA-insured loans by October 30, 2007. The Nehemiah Corporation was allowed an extension until April 1, 2008; Ameridream was also allowed to operate until February 29, 2008.

However, life for HUD was not going to be that easy. Nehemiah and several other organizations filed suit to block HUD's implementation of this new rule, which led to the District Court of Columbia issuing a ruling on November 1, 2007, temporarily preventing HUD from implementing the ban. On March 5, 2008, the Court vacated the rule and remanded it to HUD for further processing in line with the Court's opinion. It was, however, a Pyrrhic victory for Nehemiah and others, since the Housing and Economic Recovery Act, 2008 (enacted July 30) ended seller down-payment assistance. Nehemiah, by then, had invested in a for-profit marketing firm, Invision Marketing and Sales Inc., to help it reach real-estate agents, house builders and other industry professionals on the grounds that a for-profit company would perform better than a non-profit group because marketing representatives would work harder. It expanded nationally and became the largest provider of down-payment assistance.

The non-profits share part of the blame for the long period in which this program was allowed to flourish. At the start of 2008, when the FHA announced that such assistance was no longer allowed, it had been required to re-estimate its insurance fund by $6bn due to the high default rate on such loans. It became clear at the beginning of 2009 that the FHA would have to request its first ever Congressional appropriation, if the program were to continue (given the Court ruling). The FHA announced that it was going to introduce risk-based pricing of mortgage premiums instead of its traditional "one-price fits all" approach. After the public comment period, the risk-based pricing approach took effect in mid-2008. Because some industry organizations did not support risk-based pricing (no doubt due to extensive lobbying), Senate placed a one-year moratorium on pricing its mortgage insurance premiums according to the risks of the borrower, even in the midst of the financial crisis.

The costs of the program continued to rise: the seller-assisted loans have claim rates that are three times those of other FHA single-family loans. In their 2009 report, the actuaries note that the net capital ratio would still have been about the statutory 2% if the FHA had never insured those loans, and its estimated net worth would have been $10.4bn higher in 2009 without them. The actuarial estimate in 2010 is that these loans will have a net cost of $13.6bn. The report adds that of the one million seller-assisted loans insured between 1998 and 2009, about 500,000 are still active, and an additional 145,000 were paid-off but re-entered the MMI as stream-lined refinance loans. Of these, 14,000, nearly one in ten, have already gone to claim. The effect of this program was dire and will continue to be so.

The report sums up the current situation as follows: "The sum of house purchase loans with the Seller assisted programme and refinance loans from that portfolio, account for $157bn of actively insured loan balances today. That represents 17% of all active insurance in the MMI Fund ... [Of those] which are still active, 34% are in serious delinquency. Another 12% of the refinance loans are in serious delinquency. This suggests significant additional claims and losses will occur over the next two years. If one-in-three of these loans results in an insurance claim, with current loss-on-claim rates of 54%, the expected two-year losses could be an additional $7.5bn beyond the $6.1bn already incurred."[12]

Congressional efforts to remove the down-payment requirement

But "Congressional efforts have yet to result in the FHA being permitted to offer better and more flexible financing options," and continued to do so until the seller-assisted program was abolished on October 1, 2008. In fact, the Congressional efforts to which Ms Burn referred sought to deal with the problems of the seller down payment by an even riskier proposal, removing the necessity for a 3% down payment altogether. Brian Montgomery, Assistant Secretary for Housing, stated that the FHA wanted to remove the 3% down payment, and cited in support of his request the fact that 43% of first-time buyers purchased their homes with no down payment in 2006. That was to be balanced by a risk-based pricing approach to premiums charged for MMI insurance. In addition, the FHA wanted to increase the loan limits in high-cost areas.[13] In so doing Brian Montgomery failed to understand the risks involved in such mortgages, despite the warnings received: the GAO had issued a number of reports on the inadequacies of FHA's management and the risks of its portfolio, especially in its 2005 report.

Modernising the FHA proved controversial, and although various measures were introduced in Senate and the House, these stalled until 2008. One was introduced Senator Jim Talent (Missouri): "The Expanding Home Ownership Act" was designed to eliminate the 3% down payment, create a risk-free premium structure, and increase and simplify FHA's loan limits. It was welcomed by Alphonso Jackson, Secretary for Housing, but although it had bi-partisan support, it did not become law; it was re-introduced in 2007, but died again. These and other bills were introduced with a blithe indifference to or perhaps a total lack of understanding of the fact that such proposals simply increased the risks and in the longer run would do nothing for the recipients of the largesse.

A similar bill was introduced Senator Hillary Clinton, "The 21st Century Housing Act" (S. 1373). Its aim was to revise the National Housing Act to allow the FHA to offer zero down-payment loans and to increase multi-family loan limits to expand affordable rental housing production in high-cost areas. The bill also proposed 50-year mortgages to reduce monthly mortgage repayments for low-income families: it was never debated in committee. In July of the same year, Senator Clinton introduced "The Federal Fair Housing Act" (which did not make any progress), designed to increase loan limits in high-cost areas. "Many people in New York cannot afford a home within two hours of where they work. If the FHA limits were higher, they could afford a home and we should make that happen."[14] Her legislative proposals were welcomed by the Chairman of the Mortgage Bankers Association in testimony before the Senate Banking Committee. "As mortgage bankers, we look to programs like the FHA to help us provide even more options to consumers and help bridge the affordability gap faced by many first-time buyers and minority and low-to-moderate income families ... S.3173 will make the changes necessary."

Lender perspectives on the FHA's declining market share

A survey of mortgage bankers published in 2006 shows the extent to which the FHA's approach to lending had been adopted by the market as a whole.[15] The survey was conducted during 2005 against the background of a precipitous drop in FHA's share of single-family lending between 2000 and 2005. Between 2000 and 2004, for example, FHA's share of single-family originations declined from 16% to 5%, whilst its share of total mortgage debt outstanding fell from 20% to 9%. Some of this can be accounted for by changes in the overall market: between 2000 and 2004, conventional prime loans (including private and Agency loans, Fannie Mae and Freddie Mac) as a share of total loans outstanding increased from 69% to 76%, while the subprime share increased from 2% to 11% defined as higher priced loans.

Another change was taking place: the conventional conforming market declined to 35% of total originations, from 62% in 2003, as the Alt-A market share increased to 12.5% in 2005 and the subprime market increased to 20% in 2005.[16] The authors point out that the FHA's market share tends to decline during refinancing waves such as took place in 1992–3 and again in 1998, and has increased during the times when home purchase was to the fore, due to the caps on the size of FHA mortgages and the FHA's traditional appeal to first time-buyers. Contributing to the perceived increase in FHA risk were the rising FHA delinquency and foreclosure rates, when about 12% of the FHA book was delinquent in the third quarter of 2005 and about 2.5% was in foreclosure. In 2005, delinquency rates on FHA mortgages were about 7% higher on all loans, compared with a spread of 4% in 1998, that is, before the rules changed on down payments and the seller down-payment programs. Lenders also reported their dislike of higher delinquency rates, since these almost always meant higher servicing costs and the possibility of being called before the HUD Mortgage Review Board, which oversees compliance with FHA/HUD requirements and has the power to impose sanctions, ranging from reprimands to civil penalties and ultimately to the lender's ability to originate FHA loans.

The lenders were most concerned about the FHA's lack of a zero down-payment product, regarding this as one of the most significant weaknesses in its existing product suite, which was then available in both agency and subprime markets. The loan limits were another, but less important, factor. The best way to improve FHA's market share would be to match the down-payment and equity requirements of other market offerings, including agency (that is, Fannie Mae and Freddie Mac) offerings.

Interestingly enough, the lenders surveyed regarded the appraisal process as another important obstacle to considering FHA loans. The appraisal process is usually based on a market-based approach; that is, an estimation of the value of the property for sale, based on recent sales of similar units ("comparables") in nearby areas. The FHA (until 2005) required a much more comprehensive review, involving a meticulously detailed assessment of the property, and required the seller to remedy various deficiencies, such as foundations and structural conditions, roofing, site hazards and nuisances, wood-destroying insects and so on. None of this would be considered in a conventional report. Real estate agents and lenders breathed a sigh of relief when this requirement was removed in 2005. Appraisers generally only sought to assess the market value, and were thought to have frequently inflated those values during the late 1990s and up to 2007, when house prices began to fall.

Undeterred by such concerns, respondents to the survey declared that they would still consider FHA loans if a zero down-payment product was on offer as well as a stronger refinancing product. The FHA had a cash-out refinancing product, and the loan amount was capped at 85% of the home's appraised value. That was about to change with an FHA Mortgagee Letter of 2005, which stated that the FHA would allow such an offer up to 95% of the appraiser's estimate of value, but as this came after the survey was almost completed, it did not affect the response. In respect of the zero option, respondents considered that recent market innovations had put the FHA at a disadvantage, rendering it less able to compete for more creditworthy business, and regarded this as an explanation for the decline in the performance of FHA loans.

The human cost of increasing home ownership

Successive Secretaries of State for Housing and Urban Development and Commissioners for the Federal Housing Administration presented their reports to Congress each year, emphasizing the increase in home ownership for low-income families and minorities. Their claims were not matched by reality, according to one of the community groups, National People's Action.[17] The NPA pointed out that "HUD claims that foreclosures are lower than ever nationally ... The national default rate on FHA loans made between 1996 and

2000 was 6.4%. However, a closer look reveals the startling reality of families losing their homes and communities plagued with abandoned buildings. This situation is most severe in low-income and minority neighbourhoods." NPA argued that the result was increased crime, drug trafficking, prostitution and disinvestment. The examples given include the low-income neighborhoods of Baltimore, where 21% of FHA loans between 1996 and 2000 went into default, as did over 25% of FHA loans made by Los Angeles's third largest lender, and over 20% of the loans made by Cleveland's top FHA lender in minority neighborhoods, statistics which, it is claimed, applied to many other cities. The FHA continued to do business with the majority of these lenders; in fact, it paid out over $5.6 bn to lenders in insurance claims on foreclosed properties. In addition, NPA argued that HUD-approved lenders, realtors, and appraisers often work together to deceive home-buyers by overvaluing homes, selling shoddy properties to unsuspecting borrowers, or promising repairs or loan deals that never materialized. HUD's response under Secretary Mel Martinez was described as being "lukewarm."

The true costs of FHA's mortgage insurance

According to the federal budget accounting rules as specified in the Federal Credit Reform Act of 1990 (FCRA), the subsidy cost of the FHA's insurance program, Mutual Mortgage Insurance, is negative. Indeed, the program's activities are estimated to produce a net gain to the government, excluding administrative costs. The President's budget for the fiscal year, 2007 estimated a net income of 3 cents for each $100 of guaranteed loans. This is why using the FHA to meet the affordable housing objectives appealed to politicians: increase home ownership for minorities and low-income families at no cost to the taxpayer.

Unfortunately, an analysis provided by the Congressional Budget Office (CBO) in 2006 shows that this is not the case. This is partly because budget accounting understates the subsidy cost of credit programs by excluding the cost of market risk and displaying administrative costs separately. It is also because the FHA's Mutual Mortgage Insurance Program imposes costs on the government and taxpayers of between 2% and 5% of the amount of insured loans. The CBO compared the cost of single-family mortgage insurance with that of private mortgage insurance in a highly competitive market, suggesting that the quoted prices are good approximations of the minimum cost of providing such insurance. It is that comparison which provides the basis for the estimated subsidy of between 2% and 5%.

MMI provides lenders with protection against defaults and increases the availability of funds for the kind of higher-risk borrowers whom the FHA insures. Current law allows an up-front fee of up to 2.25% of the loan and an annual fee of 0.55% of the unpaid balance, but the present premium is 1.5%

with an annual fee of 0.5%, which ceases when the loan is reduced to 78% of the initial amount. In 2005, the FHA insured about $58bn in new loans, down sharply from $147bn in 2003, part of the long-term decline in its share of single-family mortgages since the mid-1980s, when the agency insured 15% of all mortgages. The FHA is also limited in the kind of mortgages it insures: 30-year and 15-year mortgages of a limited size with a 3% down payment.

Private mortgage insurers, on the other hand, have noted especially rapid growth in coverage for mortgages with less than 97% LTV, larger mortgages than the FHA amount, deferred principal payment or interest-only mortgages, and adjustable-rate mortgages in which the borrower has an option only to pay a portion of the amount due each month. Eight insurers were providing mortgage coverage, but perhaps more important, a large number of mortgage lenders compete by not selling mortgage insurance directly but by providing equivalent services through second mortgages or home equity loans. Such mortgages for no more than 80% of the purchase price do not need insurance; the second mortgage borrowers take out will finance the remaining 20%, and that will cover the risk of default.

However, the rules under the FCRA, although they include the cost of expected losses from defaults, do not calculate these in the way in which markets do, that is, including the costs of uncertainty and risk. The budget costs only average losses rather than a range of losses, which does not recognize any compensation due to the taxpayers for taking on those risks. A careful analysis of the costs of FHA mortgage insurance with private insurance and the price actually charged to FHA borrowers indicates a subsidy of about 3.5% of the amount of the insured mortgages. Allowing for the uncertainty of the adjustment to the costs of FHA insurance so that the annual net cost is 36 and 76 basis points less than the cost of private insurance, the subsidy costs become between 2% and 5% of the amount of the insured mortgages. If the FHA insures $60bn in new single-family mortgages per year, with a subsidy rate of 3.5%, then the program costs $2bn annually in the form of bearing risks to maintain its activities.[18] The extent to which the risk applied to the inability to meet the rising costs of foreclosures from the capital would cost the taxpayer more than the subsidy for mortgage insurance. The other cost was the encouragement to extend home ownership by increasingly risky loans, in which the FHA played its part as well.

This was revealed in the 2009 independent actuarial report, which showed (for the first time) the extent of risky lending, as defined by those with low FICO scores of 620 or below.[19] Mortgage lenders generally regard scores of 620 and below as ineligible for prime mortgages; scores of 500 and below as extremely risky and liable to default.[20] The FHA was largely squeezed out of the mortgage lending boom between 2003 and 2007, partly because it could not compete with the 100% LTV others were able to offer. However, in 2009, the FHA guaranteed more than $360bn in single-family mortgages, partly due to an increase in refinance activity as interest rates fell from about 6.5% in 2008 to close to 5% in 2009. That represents a 75% increase over activity in 2008, and more than four times the volume of insurance commitments made in 2007.

Even in those boom years, the FHA managed to provide low-income families with mortgages; for each year between 2005 and 2008, the agency recorded high proportions of fully underwritten loans with credit scores of below 620, ranging from 40.57% in 2005 to 46.90% in 2007, and even 33.56% in 2008 of its 1.1 million single-family loans for that year. As for underwriting standards, FHA Commissioner David Stevens in his written testimony to Congress pointed out that 6.2% of the entire loan portfolio had been issued to home buyers with FICO scores of below 500, that is, some 360,000 loans, which are four times more likely to be seriously delinquent than loans above the guidelines. These loans "currently demonstrate a seriously delinquent rate of 31.1%."[21] In the same testimony, Commissioner Stevens pointed out that the FHA assisted 450,000 families in keeping their homes out of foreclosure, but by the first quarter in 2010, 67% of these modified FHA mortgages were in foreclosure again.

It was HUD's responsibility to oversee the activities of the FHA and its lending practices, the dilatoriness in dealing with the issue can be seen from the failure to respond to the recommendations made by the Government Accountability Office (GAO) in 2005. Their report pointed out that almost half the single-family home-purchase mortgages the FHA had insured in 2004 had down-payment assistance, with about 30% of the non-profits receiving at least part of their funding from the sellers. Sales with such assistance were appraised and sold for about 2–3% more than comparable homes bought and sold without it, and these loans were characterized by higher delinquency rates. The GAO's series of recommendations did not include abolition of the practice, but required much stricter oversight of the program, noting that mortgage-industry participants restricted such assistance. The Secretary of HUD took little action apart from requiring more information from the FHA in its quarterly reports until the scheme was finally closed.

Such delays in essential reforms have to be seen in the political context in which both HUD and the FHA operated. Indeed, in view of all the problems in the down-payment program, it is surprising to see that the FHA resisted development of an outright prohibition on seller-funded gifts, and instead tried to obtain an "alternative FHA financing arrangement for borrowers lacking the funds for a down payment." It is true that any such ban may have been prone to loopholes in the rules, such as the Nehemiah Housing Corporation exploited, but the FHA abandoned the attempt in view of strenuous opposition rather than any drafting problems. The agency wanted to eliminate its own 3% cash down-payment requirement: to "offer cash poor, but creditworthy borrowers a safer, more affordable alternative to seller-funded Gift programs," but "Congressional efforts have yet to result in FHA being permitted to offer better and more flexible financing offers."[22]

The FHA to the rescue?

Momentum for FHA reforms grew as the downturn in the housing market worsened in 2008. By then, the fall in house prices, the continuing rise in foreclosures and the meltdown in the mortgage market meant that politicians turned to the FHA as an instrument to add some stability to the mortgage market. Modernizing the FHA became part of the Housing and Economic Recovery Act of 2008 (HERA), which was enacted on July 30 of that year. Title I of Division B of HERA is in fact the FHA Modernization Act, but it does not follow all of the proposals contained in Congressional debates, such as zero down payments. It increased the down-payment requirements to 3.5%, although family loans may be included, or, if the borrowed amount is secured by a lien, then this must be subordinate to the mortgage, and together they must not exceed 100% of the appraised value of the property. Loan limits were increased in relation either to HUD-approved limits or to the Freddie Mac conforming loan limits. Insurance premiums were increased, but these were linked to whether or not the borrower had received counseling.

The FHA Modernization Act sets out significant changes to the law governing the MMI Fund, including: (i) establishing that HUD has the fiduciary responsibility to ensure that it remains financially sound; (ii) that there is an independent actuarial study of the Fund; (iii) that quarterly reports are provided to Congress on the status of the Fund; (iv) that adjustments are made to the insurance premiums when needed; and (vi) that operational goals are established for the Fund. By 2008, the whole tenor of the legislation had changed, as the enormity of the housing crisis had begun to hit home.[23]

Both the independent auditors' report and the independent actuarial report of November 2010 showed the impact of the FHA's past and continuing policies of providing affordable home ownership options for those who would otherwise be unable to purchase their own homes, either as single- or multiple-family units, as well as the costs. Between 2003 and 2007, FHA-insured loans constituted only about 2–3% of the market, but when private capital withdrew at the end of 2008, would-be purchasers turned to the FHA for the insurance that would enable them to borrow. The FHA then insured 30% of purchases and 20% of refinances. From January 2009 to September 2010 the agency helped nearly 3 million Americans to either purchase a home or to refinance into more stable, affordable mortgages.[24] In the fiscal year, 2009, the FHA re-emerged as the primary source of credit guarantees both for home buyers and for home owners wishing to refinance as interest rates fell from around 6.5% to 5%. In 2009, the FHA guaranteed over $360bn in single-family mortgages, a 75% increase over 2008 and four times the volume of commitments made in 2007. In 2010, the FHA served over 1.1 million home buyers, helping 882,000 first-time buyers, which was only the second time that the FHA had helped so many home buyers, the first time being in 1997, when it insured 740,000 single-family mortgages, of which 76% were first-time buyers. In other words, the FHA appears to be retrieving its position in the market between 1986 and 1990, when it was the largest insurer of single-family mortgages.

The immediate cost was that the secondary reserves fell to 0.53% of the total insurance-in-force, below the 2% level required by legislation, according to the 2009 Independent Actuarial Report. The 2010 report found that the MMI Fund remains actuarially sound, but that there are significant risks to the near-term financial outlook, with the capital ratio standing at 0.50%[25], once again below the mandated level. Shaun Donovan, Secretary for Housing and Urban Development (responsible for oversight of the FHA and MMI) noted in his assessment of the actuarial reports that "this has precipitated significant administrative actions at HUD to both protect the ratio from falling below zero, and to assure that a 2% ratio can again be achieved in a reasonable amount of time."[26] HUD argued that the loan book of 2010 was of a much higher quality than in previous years, with credit scores of 680 or over being 12% higher, a dramatic decrease in the share of loans with scores between 600–639, and a virtual disappearance of loans with credit scores below 600. This once again demonstrates the level of credit scores the FHA had been prepared to accept in the past.

One of the highest costs, and likely to continue as such, turned out to be the seller-funded down-payment assistance loans (SFDPA). These proved a disaster, with insurance payments totaling over $5.5bn having been paid out by 2010 and the 2010 actuarial estimate being $13.6bn. The FHA reported a further loss of $600m on subsequent refinance loans for such mortgages, totalling $6bn. The exposure in 2010 of SFDPA mortgages together with refinancing accounted for $157bn of the actively insured loans in that year. With continuing high unemployment in the USA, it is likely that further losses will occur. The failure to understand the risks of such loans, or the unwillingness on the part of Congress to recognize the risks, cost the taxpayer dear; even when the risks of seller down-payment were presented, politicians produced a flurry of bills with a view to the introduction of 100% loan to value mortgages for those with the kind of poor credit ratings that the FHA was willing to accept. The 2009 actuarial study observed that the net capital ratio would still be above 2% but for the SFDPA loans.

Once again the FHA promised a series of significant administrative actions and changes in lending criteria, both to protect the ratio from falling below zero and to ensure that a 2% ratio could be achieved in a reasonable time period. A Chief Risk Officer was appointed in 2009, the first in the FHA's history, and insurance premiums were increased. David Stevens, FHA Commissioner until later that year, when he became Chairman of the Mortgage Bankers Association, reported to Congress. He set up a Mortgagee Review Board, meeting monthly, and no doubt was shocked to find the extent of violations of the FHA's origination and underwriting requirements, including false certifications and failures to verify the borrower's income and creditworthiness. This led to the suspension of well-known FHA lenders and withdrawal of FHA approval from a further 1,500.[27]

Its new guidelines on LTVs and minimum credit scores took effect in October 2010, raising the minimum credit score for those requiring maximum financing to 580 or higher. Those with a credit score of between 500 and 579 are limited to an LTV of 90%, those with a sub-580 FICO score have to make the 10% down payment on a purchase transaction, and those with a FICO score of 500 and under would be refused an FHA loan. These criteria now apply to all single-family mortgages, except for reverse mortgages (home equity conversion mortgages) and Hope for Homeowners. At present, few banks are willing to lend on such low credit scores, even for FHA loans, but that could change when the economy eventually recovers and FHA lending will once again be risky.

Furthermore, it is unlikely that the proposed administrative changes will have any significant effect, despite HUD's repeated assurances to Congress. In November 2010, the auditors reported on the results of their analysis of the FHA's financial management and information system, noting that it was composed of many aging systems developed over 30 years and integrated with the FHA Subsidiary Ledger introduced in 2002. However, little work was undertaken in the intervening years and bringing the system up-to-date will take several years and hundreds of millions of dollars. It is clear from the auditors' assessment that the system has prevented the FHA from carrying out fraud mitigation and counterparty risk-management initiatives, and from acquiring business intelligence. In particular, the current structure of the actuarial model might lead to understatements of the near-term claim levels, especially given the quantum change in the housing market.[28]

The report of HUD's Office of the Inspector General (OIG) for September 2010 illustrates graphically what this meant in practice in its review of HUD's controls over its automated underwriting process. HUD implemented changes to the FHA's Technology Open to Approved Lenders Scorecard review rules without assessing the risks and documenting changes. "As a result, loans valued at more than $6.1bn were automatically approved for FHA insurance despite having debt ratios that exceeded average thresholds for automated underwriting." The Inspector General then adds, "OIG recommended that HUD conduct a risk analysis to determine the appropriate front-end and back-end ratios for the Scorecard's review rules and institute appropriate changes. OIG determined that the full contents of this report would not be appropriate for public disclosure and released a redacted version to the public."[29] The general observations and assessments are followed by several pages of fraudulent activities on the part of lenders, mortgage brokers and counselors in the Single Family Program, which came to light in part because of Operation Watch Dog.

Can the FHA rescue the mortgage market?

The prospects do not look too hopeful, given so many aspects of extensive and all-pervasive mismanagement, the fact that some programs were open to fraud, which went unchecked, and the poor quality of the loans the FHA continues to insure. Add to that the fact that the the agency failed to introduce new rules, even after repeated warnings, and did not seem to appreciate the risks of the mortgages it would insure when it wanted to include zero down-payment mortgages as the market was clearly deteriorating. None of this inspires confidence.

In its report on the financial condition of the FHA's Mutual Mortgage Insurance Fund, issued shortly before the actuarial report of 2010, the GAO noted that "a weakening in the performance of FHA insured loans has heightened the possibility that the FHA will require additional funds to help cover the cost of insurance issued to date."[30] The GAO report contains a number of proposals for improving the actuarial assessment of the Fund's financial condition, including a wider range of economic forecasts as opposed to a single one, so that the variability in future house prices and interest rates that the Fund may face is taken into account. The failure to do so may well lead to an overstatement of the Fund's economic value. The 2010 report reflects a movement in that direction in that it relies on more than one scenario as produced by Moody's Analytics, but does not provide a stochastic simulation, which may explain why the 2010 projections are cautiously optimistic. The projections for house prices in 2012 (HIS Insight, July 2010 and Moody's Analytics, July 2010) suggested house price increases of 7% in 2012; by the summer of 2011 that seemed unlikely, given the overhang of repossessed houses which the banks have to sell and the uncertainties of the economic situation.

In a statement before the Subcommittee on Housing and Community Opportunity in 2009, Edward Pinto outlined some of the factors leading to the likelihood of a bail-out. These include the fact that the FHA (and the Veterans Administration) now account for over 90% of all the high LTV loans being made. The total high LTV lending in the first six months of 2009 was equal to 23% of all originations by lenders, up from 17% in 2006, which was thought to be the peak of risky lending. The FHA's dollar volume in 2009 was four times its volume in 2006, so that FHA- and VA-insured loans comprised 10% of all outstanding first mortgages by the end of 2009. Millions of new ultra-low down-payment loans are being added to a mortgage market that already has vast numbers of borrowers with low or negative equity.

The loan limit was raised to $729,750, a large increase, and now covers areas such as California, which were badly hit by the crisis. Wells Fargo and Bank of America are the two largest FHA lenders with a combined share of 46%, and their combined share of FHA loans in such fragile markets was 10% in 2009. Finally the FHA has a long history of fraud, and its inability to monitor, control and discipline its lenders is a source of additional risk. The agency added thousands of new lenders to its approved lists between 2007 and 2009, but by the time it is able to track them and assess their quality, it may be too late.[31]

By January 2011 the FHA had insured over 6.8m mortgages with an outstanding balance of $947.8bn (HUD, 2011). The 2009 report estimated that the FHA would not require any government support; that has been criticised on the grounds that it underestimated the number of borrowers who had negative equity and were subject to economic shocks, such as unemployment, especially from "streamline" re-finances. These are a modification of an existing loan into a lower interest rate and extended term: what the actuarial report did was to treat them as though the original loan had been paid off and the refinance was a fresh loan, and this procedure, it has been argued, is subject to significant selection biases in the estimation.[32] The 2010 report corrects for some, but not all, of these criticisms, and concludes that the Fund is still solvent. The income from loans made in 2010, when house prices had stopped falling, the quality of the average FHA borrower was higher and the FHA had raised its premiums.

The future of the MMI is uncertain at best. The FHA's insurance in force has doubled over the past two years and is expected to approach $1.5 trillion over the next five years.[33] At present, the FHA is thought not to require any further government support, but that will depend to a large extent on whether house prices decline again in 2012 and on the economic outlook, neither of which look particularly promising at present. It will also depend on further information about the quality of FHA loans.

The White Paper sees a "reformed and strengthened FHA" having a key role in the future, and so that can be achieved, the Administration "will explore ways to further reduce the risk exposure of FHA ... the FHA will consider other options, such as lowering the maximum LTV more broadly. In considering how to apply such options, the FHA will continue to balance the need to manage prudently the risk to the FHA and the borrower with its efforts to ensure access to affordable loans for lower and middle-income Americans."[34] The temptation is to add: not much change there, then. It is the latter aim which cannot be reconciled just with "managing risk;" the reforms would have to be "root and branch" to deal with all the management issues, and would require resources for new systems and highly qualified staff, which would not be removed when successive Administrations needed to reduce federal expenditure. Continuing the traditional role of the FHA in insuring mortgages should be approached with great caution, bearing in mind that many countries have a mortgage market which functions without a state mortgage insurance agency.

The Federal Home Loan Bank (FHLB) System

Origins of the system

The Federal Home Loan Bank System was created in 1932[35] as a collection of wholesale banks, co-operatively owned by its member commercial banks, thrifts, credit unions and insurance companies, designed to restore liquidity to a housing market which had collapsed following the Great Depression. The "System" is still composed of the original 12 Federal Home Loan Banks (FHLBs), where membership of the FHLB was confined to the relevant financial institutions headquartered in the distinct geographical area that the FHLB was originally assigned to serve. Each FHLB is a separate legal entity with its own management, employees, board of directors and financial statements. The function of each FHLB is still to provide reliable long-term funding to specialized mortgage lenders, known to its members as "advances". Thrifts and certain insurance companies were obliged to be members until the collapse of hundreds of thrifts in the late 1980s led to the introduction of the Financial Institutions Recovery, Reform and Enforcement Act of 1989 (FIRREA). Although that Act brought significant changes to the FHLB, the System retained its privileges.[36] Some of its Charter provisions combined with past government actions have given rise to the perception that its obligations are implicitly guaranteed by the federal government; this allows the FHLBs to finance their activities by issuing debt on more favorable terms than any AAA-rated private corporation. Their "advances" or loans to lenders generally have as their collateral mortgage-backed securities and whole loans, US Treasury and Federal Agency securities. In addition to the explicit collateral and a member's capital subscription, the FHLBs also have priority over the claims of depositors and almost all other creditors (including the Federal Deposit Insurance Corporation, FDIC) in the event of a member's default; this is often described as a "super lien" and explains why the FHLBs argued that they would not suffer loses.

Changes following the 1989 Act

The resolution of the Savings & Loans crisis of the late 1980s brought about enduring changes in the FHLB system. The Act made membership voluntary, open to all depository institutions with more than 10% of their portfolios in residential mortgage-related assets. This allowed many commercial banks and credit unions to join the FHLB System for the first time, resulting in an increase in membership from 3,200 in 1989 to over 8,000 in 2005, and 8,075 by the end of 2007; this despite the decline in the number of thrifts, still legally obliged to be members until 1999. Commercial banks accounted for 70% of all System members by 2005.

The 1989 Act also obliged members to pay 20% of their net earnings to cover a portion of the interest on the Resolution Funding Corporation bonds which were used to finance the clean-up of the thrifts, after the

Savings & Loans crisis. Another 10% was set aside for the "Affordable Housing Program," the largest source of private-sector grants for housing and community development, which is disbursed on the basis of advice provided by a 15-member Affordable Housing Advisory Council for guidance on regional and community development issues.

Emerging concerns about the system and the Gramm-Leach-Bliley Act

However, although FIRREA was credited with strengthening the thrift industry and the System in the early 1990s, concerns emerged later in that decade about its capital structure. In particular, it was noted that, since commercial banks could remove stock from FHLBs with six months' notice, the System's commercial stability could be affected. The Gramm-Leach-Bliley Act (GLBA, 1999) created a more stable and risk-based capital structure for the System. This Act established that FHLB membership was voluntary for thrifts as well, but also that those who decided to become members had to invest more permanent stock in their "FHLBank." FHLBanks can issue Class A stock, which can be redeemed with six months' notice; Class B stock, which can be redeemed with five years' notice; or both. To ensure that capital did not dissipate due to redemption in times of stress, the FHLBank, if following the redemption, would not meet the minimum capital requirements.[37] Following the implementation of the Act, each FHLB had to submit a capital plan to the regulator, the Federal Housing Finance Board (FHFB), for review and approval: all had been approved by 2002, and 11 had implemented their capital plans. The regulator noted that 10 of the 12 capital plans relied entirely on Class B stock and just two included Class A stock. As part of the implementation process, the FHLB required the FHLBs to submit plans for modeling interest rate risks and related procedures for managing those risks.

Lenders see the benefits of the system

FHLB advances are usually regarded as an attractive source of wholesale funds. Advance interest rates are set by the individual FHLBs and reflect a mark-up to the cost of Federal Agency debt funding secured by the Office of Finance. Then the "advances" are structured in a variety of ways to suit each member's funding strategy. To qualify for these advances, a member pledges high-quality collateral in the form of mortgages, government securities or loans on small businesses, agriculture or community development; they must also buy additional stock, usually between 2% and 6% of the advance, in accordance with the FHLB's capital plan. Once the FHLBank approves its member's loan requests, it advances those funds to the member. Advances increased rapidly in the late 1990s and the early 2000s following the entry of commercial banks;

from the end of 2005 to mid-2007 the level of outstanding FHLB advances was within the range of $620bn to $640bn, but suddenly increased by 25% to $824bn in August and September and ended the year at $875bn, equalling 6.2% of US GDP. This was due to the development of liquidity pressures during the third quarter of 2007, so that FHLB appeared to be an attractive source of funding in terms of pricing and investors turned to the security of federal guarantees (explicit or implicit).

The increase in the proportion of residential mortgages on the FHLB System's combined balance sheet began with the introduction of the Chicago FHLB's Mortgage Partnership Finance Program in 1997. They continued to purchase fixed-rate mortgages on single-family properties under various programs in which, generally speaking, the seller guarantees most of the credit risk, whilst the interest rate risk is handled by the FHLBs together with mortgage-backed securities. The interest rate risk from these assets requires careful management because changes in interest rates affect borrower prepayment behavior with consequent effects on the life of the mortgage assets. This led to the FHLBs having to manage an increasing amount of interest rate risk, including embedded call options linked with mortgage prepayment.

The composition of FHLB membership changed as the banking system in America changed, and developed throughout the 1990s and from 2000 onwards. The top depository institutions were also the largest users of FHLB advances, even though they had access to various wholesale borrowing mechanisms, as well as having national or regional branch networks. Many of these institutions maintained charters in more than one FHLB area, thus having many channels into the System. These trends have both heightened the competitive pressures within the co-operative and led to the growth in size, complexity and risk in this institution.

Exposure to risk has also increased in that the FHLBanks are jointly and severally liable for their combined obligations, so that if any individual FHLBank was not able to pay a creditor, the other 11 would be required to step in and cover that debt. Joint and several liability for payment of consolidated obligations was taken to give investors confidence that System debt will be paid. In addition, the FHLB System also provides letters of credit for bond issuances guaranteed by members and mortgage programs, thus passing through their triple-A rating to member institutions, while pledging to be a credit backstop. The mortgage programs provide competitive alternatives to the secondary market by taking the interest rate risk of mortgage loans, while members retain the credit risk and customer relationship.

A chance to play the system

However, the structure of banking has changed so much that it appears that large banks, and especially holding companies with mortgage subsidiaries which are members of more than one FHLB district, could play the system. The GAO identified about a hundred such companies in their 2003 report, and noted significant differences in advance-term pricing among the 12 FHLBanks. It also pointed out that the opportunity existed for holding companies to obtain advances from the FHLBank which offered the most favorable terms, and reported that it had been informed by some FHLB officials that holding companies tried to play one bank off against another by creating competition within the System over advance-term pricing. "However, we also found that the FHFB had not identified any material safety and soundness issues related to FHLBanks' advance-term pricing:" identifying and dealing with such issues as they may give rise to unsafe and unsound practices was the responsibility of the FHFB.[38]

The FHLB System developed new programs, such as the direct purchase of mortgages from member institutions, which led to increased interest rate and credit risk, where the former is the potential for loss due to fluctuations in interest rates, while credit risk is the potential for loss from a borrower or counterparty failure to perform on an obligation. By holding mortgages on their books, they increase both types of risks.

The program began with the Chicago FHLB in 1997, not without controversy. It was a pilot program at first, in which the member institutions originated loans that would close in the name of the FHLB, which would then hold them in portfolio. The pilot was obviously successful, since it was supported by all but one of the FHLBs, FHLB San Francisco, where it was subject to a number of threatened but unsuccessful lawsuits.[39] The mortgage purchase program (MMP) was inaugurated and rapidly got underway: total FHLB System whole mortgage assets nearly tripled, from $16bn at the end of 2000 to $47bn by September 30, 2002.[40] As it turned out, the FHLBs found it difficult to manage the risks involved and at first were not in a position to supervise them effectively.

The FHLB System has weak constraints against over-lending, and indeed against extending its purchases of mortgages. Its purpose is to ensure that its members are in a position to make loans, and the FHLBs are lending to their owners, the member banks. The FHLBs do not monitor the loans or the lenders, since that is the role of their borrowers' primary regulators, but they were regulated by the FHFB until October 2008, when the Federal Housing Finance Authority (FHFA) became their regulator.

The regulatory structure

The Board of the FHFB consisted of five directors, four of whom were appointed by the President and confirmed by the Senate; the fifth director was the Secretary for Housing and Urban Development, with the directors serving staggered seven-year terms. No more than three members could be members of the same political party. The criteria for appointment included extensive experience in housing finance or training in that area, together with a commitment to providing specialized housing credit. Another requirement was that at least one appointed director must be from an organization with more than a two-year history of representing consumers or consumer interests in banking services, credit needs, housing or consumer protection.

The FHFB was also responsible for appointing public interest directors to the boards of the 12 banks, a duty which it considered increasingly difficult owing to the conflicts of interest involved: as the then chairman of the Federal Housing Finance Board put it, "the regulator should not appoint the regulated."[41] The FHFB appointed at least six directors to serve on the boards of the FHLBanks, each of whose boards consist of at least 14 members. A minimum of two of the public interest directors are designated as community interest directors, due to their strong ties with the local community. Members of each of the 12 FHLBanks elect the remaining directors. The selection of independent directors of the FHLBanks, stated Chairman Ronald Rosenfeld, would be subject to a new process "by which we can assess the individual needs of each Bank and select public interest directors, who not only have the desire to serve for relatively low compensation and potentially increased liability, but who also possess the requisite qualifications, knowledge and skills necessary to satisfy the needs of the Bank's board."[42]

This was not the only problem encountered in the appointment of public interest or "outside" directors. The GAO's Review of FHFB Operations[43] showed that 50 of the 75 public interest directors appointed for the first time from January 1, 1998 through to May 8, 2002 made one or more political contributions in the eight-year period prior to their initial appointments. They then analysed the available data to cover the tenures of the three FHFB chairmen in office when the FHFB made public interest director appointments during 1998 to 2002: namely Bruce Morrison, 1995–2000; William Apgar, July to December 2000; and John T. Korsmo, December 2001 to the present. During that period just over half the directors had made between one and ten separate donations, and 22% had done so 11 or more times. The amount given varied from a median of $3,250 for the five appointments made during Apgar's tenure, and $8,364 as the median during Korsmo's tenure until he resigned from the chairmanship following the revelation that he had not told the truth about support given to a fundraiser for a Republican congressional candidate. None of the directors who were appointed gave contributions exclusively to the party of the chair of the FHFB, apart from the brief tenure of Apgar, when the three appointed gave exclusively to the party of the chair.

Problems also arose with the FHFB Board itself, partly due to the fact that the legal framework of the agency gives the chair more power to make key administrative decisions, such as the power to appoint and remove officials and to reorganize the agency without recourse to the board. These powers, in the view of the GAO, have "contributed to the sometimes bitter conflicts that have periodically characterized relations amongst board members over the past eight years."[44] However, when the issue was discussed with the members of the board at the time, it was agreed by the majority of the then board members that the delegation of certain powers to the Chairman is the most efficient way of managing the agency's operation, and that board members can state their views under the delegation with two or more members calling for a vote on the actions taken.

From the accounts summarized in the GAO report, it seems the problems with the management of the board had much to do with its political composition, and the fact that the members of the board were political appointees. The FHFB was finally abolished on July 30, 2008 and the FHLB System is currently regulated by the Federal Housing Finance Agency. The FHFA has appointed a board of directors consisting of the presidents of each of the 12 banks and five independent directors, who now have to meet certain strict criteria as well as the minimum requirements for independence. The directors were selected from a slate of at least five candidates, each of whom was identified in consultation with the FHLBanks.[45]

Problems at Seattle and Chicago

These disputes may also have hindered the effectiveness of the FHFB as a regulator. The GAO reports that it first identified weaknesses in the examination program as far back as 1998, but it was not until August 2002 that the FHFB announced plans that would significantly improve the program by more than doubling the number of examiners and revising the examination program. By 2003, it was too early to assess its effectiveness. In 2004, the agency became aware of risk-management deficiencies in both the Seattle FHLB, one of the smallest, and Chicago, the third largest, especially in their mortgage purchase programs, and sought to rectify these deficiencies by entering into written agreements with both banks. Chicago had led the way in the introduction of the mortgage purchase program.

The written agreement with Seattle dealt with its shortcomings in corporate governance, risk management, capital management and financial performance. For several years, the Bank had been seeking growth and profitability by purchasing a portfolio of mortgage loans, agency debt securities, and mortgage-backed securities to supplement earnings for its advance business, without paying due attention to risk management. In 2002, it had decided to change its portfolio structure by substituting mortgage assets for advances by raising interest rates on the latter.

Washington Mutual, the largest borrower from Seattle, decided to move its advance borrowings to other FHLBs in which its affiliates had members. The low-interest-rate environment of 2003 and the mortgage refinance wave, together with poor quality hedging, resulted in a marked decline in Seattle's market value. Seattle then reduced its mortgage purchases but sought to boost returns by investing some $8bn in callable FHLB System debt obligations funded largely with shorter-term, non-callable instruments, and then was caught by the flattening of the yield curve in 2004, resulting in additional market losses of some $260m.

This transaction apparently took place without the full knowledge of the board and senior management, and was perhaps the reason (rather than the efficiency of the examinations[45]) why the banks' regulators stepped in, leading to the written agreement in 2004. As a result of the independent reviews of the board's oversight and risk-management processes, which the regulator had ordered them to carry out, Seattle had developed an acceptable three-year business and capital management plan in 2005. By 2007, the bank seemed to have recovered, with advances at record levels and a $70.7m profit for the year. That may have been due to general market conditions, because it seems that the basic problems had not been solved: as the financial crisis developed, by July 2009 Seattle had accumulated $247m in net losses, mainly due to its investments in mortgage-backed securities issued by Washington Mutual, the Bank of America and others, in which it had invested some $5.6bn. The Bank's financial condition was weakening; its governance was unsatisfactory and its credit risk high and increasing, according to the FHFA.[46]

The path of the Chicago FHLB was a troubled one, even after its agreement with the FHFB as announced in 2006 in its bulletin, "The Chicago Balance Sheet." Following the identification of serious risk-management deficiencies, it was required to submit a three-year business plan. Rectifying the deficiencies included a restatement of its financial results for 2003 and placed limits on its mortgage purchase program until its risk-management practices improved.

The Bulletin for 2005 stated that the Bank would reduce its voluntary stock owned by members from 58% in December 2004 to 43% by the end of 2007, and would delay implementation of the new capital structure until December 2006 (or until a time mutually agreed with the FHFB). The Bank also planned to find other methods of capitalizing and funding its mortgage finance partnership program and reduce its quarterly dividends below 5.5% on an annualized basis.[47] However, by late 2005 it had halted the redemption program and in the following year, in June, the Finance Board allowed the Chicago FHLB to issue $1bn of ten-year subordinated debt (for which the Bank is the sole obligator) and to use that to purchase excess shares. The FHFB treated excess stock as equity for the purpose of assessing compliance with the minimum capital requirements. The implications of this are difficult to determine. Flannery and Scott Frame point out that "one interpretation of this transaction is that it allowed the Chicago FHLB to increase its risk by substituting debt for equity. However, FHLB excess stock itself has debt-like features, and the lack of market pricing for these claims limits their value as market discipline tools."[48]

By 2007, this approach became unsustainable as the Finance Board announced a "cease and desist" order affecting the redemption and repurchase of capital stock and stated that any increases in dividends by any of the FHLBs required its approval. In October the Chicago Bank announced in its "Balance Sheet" that the Board had decided on a voluntary basis not to declare a dividend in "recognition of projected earning pressure in the fourth quarter and in 2008." In August, it announced that it was discussing a possible merger with the Dallas FHLB, an unprecedented move. The merger talks were abandoned in April 2008, when the Chicago Bank announced the resignation of its President and CEO, Mike Thomas, and a return to a more traditional FHLB business model and capital structure. Regrets for past business were perhaps reflected in its decision in 2010 to file complaints against several defendants, such as Wells Fargo and Citigroup, with regard to the private label MBSs sold to them between 2005 and 2007, on the grounds that the quality of the loans was inconsistent with the description in the pre-purchase documents prepared by the underwriters and the issuers, leading the FHLB to believe that they were purchasing higher-quality instruments than turned out to be the case.

By November 2008, the FHLB of Atlanta reported its first quarterly loss ($47.1m qter 3) in two years to the SEC, a decline of $179m from the same period in 2007. This was unusual, as the Atlanta FHLB with $213bn in assets was one of the financially strongest in the System. This was especially true when the Chicago FHLB reported large losses in recent years and almost merged with the Dallas FHLB. Atlanta's loss was primarily attributed to a $170m reserve against credit losses from the Lehman Brothers Special Financing Ch 11 bankruptcy filing on October 3, 2008 and an $87m impairment charge for certain mortgage-backed securities. The MBS investments created the largest problems for the Bank, as during the first nine months of 2008, the securities that were downgraded or put on the watch list by the ratings agencies for a potential credit reduction increased from $637m on January 1 to $2.2bn on October 29 in the same year. The Bank recorded net total assets of $213.7bn that year, due to the fact that advances increased by $21.4bn (some 15%) during this period, and also due to the sale of federal funds and held-to-maturity securities.[49] It is interesting to note that the demand for loans continued to increase in 2008, but the lenders may have used the funds for other purposes besides mortgage lending.

Another risky federal agency

In an interesting paper produced in 2005, the authors put the question: "Should the FDIC worry about the impact of the Federal Home Loan Bank Advances on the Bank Insurance Fund?" The question turned out to be much more prescient than they may have thought at the time.[50] The first point in their argument is that the FHLBanks do not face any credit risk because of their GSE status and monopoly position; they also require collateralization far in advance of that required by other insured creditors. Finally, they have access to confidential commercial bank examination reports, so they are aware of the deterioration in a member's loan portfolio before other creditors, although the events outlined below suggest that they did not make proper use of such information. If a member bank did fail and the collateral prove insufficient, then the FHLB, as noted earlier, can assert its legal lien priority on other assets before all unsecured creditors. "Because of this protection, no FHLBank has ever lost a penny on an advance. So banks can take the risks with advances, keep the upside, and shift the downside to the FDIC."[51]

The authors sought to model the impact on the FDIC, but concluded that "our estimation of resolution costs suggest that FDIC exposure from advances ranges from modest to large depending on the assumptions. But those figures may still understate potential losses ... and [in 2005] US banks held record levels of capital ... High levels reduce expected Bank Insurance Fund (BIF) losses by deterring risk-taking and absorbing losses from any level of risk-taking. Reversion of capital ratios to historical norms would increase both default probability and loss-given default."[52]

They note that the current pricing structure for BIF (the Bank Insurance Fund as part of the FDIC) does not differentiate between different advance levels, but with similar supervisory ratings and capital protection pays the same premiums, and suggest that the FDIC should charge for increases in expected losses arising from advances. That suggestion, which may have required legislative changes, is perhaps one which Sheila Bair, Chairman of the Federal Deposit Insurance Corporation, came to regret in 2008, when she realized that the FHLBank funding provides an easier escape than insured deposits, as the latter are expensive to obtain and the supply is relatively inelastic (which partly explains the attractiveness of such funding). In an interview in the November issue of *Bloomberg Markets Magazine*, she said "we really get a double whammy," adding that the FDIC has "a beef with excessive reliance on FHLB advances." Earlier that year, Bair had stated that the FDIC was developing a plan to raise insurance premiums for the coming wave of bank failures.

The extent of the use of the "advances" can be seen from the cases of Countrywide and Indymac Bank Corps. The latter had increased its advances by 500% between the end of 2004 and early 2008, and had outstanding loans of $10bn, about one-third of its liabilities, when it collapsed on July 11, 2008. That bank failure cost FDIC $9bn to sort out. Similarly, Countrywide's CEO agreed to borrow $51bn from FHLB Atlanta, but even this did not save it, as the Bank of America acquired Countrywide to rescue it from failure in June 2008.

The role of the FHLBanks was upheld by the then Treasury Secretary as a means of ensuring liquidity for their members, the lenders, in his announcement at a press conference on September 7, 2008. But he was careful to point out what had gone wrong. "Prior to the crisis, the FHLBs suffered from inadequate regulatory oversight, and were allowed to build up large investment portfolios that subjected them to excess risk, while providing concentrated funding to banks engaging in unsound business practices. Today, eight of the twelve banks are under regulatory orders with respect to their capital or have voluntarily suspended dividends or the repurchase of excess stock."[53]

The US Treasury extended a secured credit facility to the FHLBs, allowing them to borrow until the end of 2009. But as James Lockhart, then Director of the Federal Housing Finance Agency, which had become their regulator at the end of July that year, pointed out, they were "very unlikely" to need to use the program, as they had larger capital reserves than Fannie Mae and Freddie Mac and all but one of the regional lenders are profitable. The System is the largest US borrower after the federal government, with $1.34 trillion of assets on June 30, 2008, mostly eligible collateral for the lending program, and $1.25 trillion of debt, according to the Finance Office, which manages their collective debt sales.[54] The US Treasury terminated its short-term credit facility, which had been created under the Housing and Economic Recovery Act, 2008 but had never in fact been used.

FHA and FHLB contributions to the total subprime and Alt-A exposure

By June 2008, about 83% of FHA loans consisted of high LTV loans (over 90%) and about 70% had a FICO score of 660 or less. Given these percentages, it is highly likely that at least 90% of FHA-insured loans have one of these two characteristics. Similar data is not available for VA and rural housing loan programs, but it is reasonable to assume that at least 60% of these loans have one or more of the two characteristics. FHA loans have an average loan balance of $103,300, which would give a total loan balance of $394bn, and for the VA, the average may be $150,000, which gives a loan balance of $143bn. This gives a total of $537bn (including VA and rural loans).[55]

As regards the FHLB, at the end of 2008, the various FHLBs were reported as holding $76bn in private MBSs.[56] Moody's commented that, based on market prices in the third quarter of 2008, the banks' total private label MBS portfolio was valued at $62.7bn, thus representing a $13.5bn write-down, which was felt to be unlikely, but it did mean that under the worst-case scenario only four of the 12 FHLBs would remain above the capital minimum. Taking the year end value of the private MBSs, it would be reasonable to assume that 66% of the total or $50bn would be backed by Alt-A (with little or no borrower or income asset documentation) and sub-prime loans. This in turn is based on an average loan amount of $160,000 (blended average used for Fannie and Freddie's holdings of private MBSs and Alt-A private MBS results in 0.13 loans). What this means is that there are more sources of risk in the mortgage finance system than successive governments have been prepared to admit, even today.[57] The FHLB has been weakened by these purchases and also by the continuing fall-out from its inability to manage interest rate risk from their mortgage purchase programs with FHLB members. It has managed to remain solvent, but leaning on the FHLB may turn out to be leaning on a broken reed.

3

The Role of the Housing and Urban Development Department (HUD)

Introduction

This chapter will set out the role of the Housing and Urban Development Department (HUD). It is worth noting that this was a large and rambling government department, which was never well managed and was notoriously involved in corruption in the various housing programs it managed, involving public funds. The Office of the Inspector General provided a large number of reports over the years, detailing HUD fraud and incompetence; such reports will not be described here, as it is HUD's responsibilities for home ownership in general and for the FHA in particular, which illuminate the affordable housing program.

Established as a Cabinet Department by President Lyndon Johnson in 1965, HUD rapidly acquired a wide range of responsibilities for many and varied housing programs, including public housing, voucher assistance for rented accommodation, housing for the elderly, those with disabilities, persons with AIDs, community development block grants, neighborhood stabilization programs (for those hard-hit by foreclosures and delinquencies) and housing for the homeless, to name but a few. Given the number and complexity of these housing programs, it is perhaps small wonder that HUD was subject to frequent criticisms by the GAO and by its own Inspector General on the grounds of lack of proper management and oversight of its many responsibilities and the failures of its accounting systems.

In addition to the above responsibilities, HUD encompassed other important appointments, including the Federal Housing Commissioner, heading up the Federal Housing Administration; and the Director, Office of the Federal Housing Enterprise Oversight (OFHEO), set up under the Housing and Community Development Act, 1992 to ensure that the Federal National Mortgage Association (Fannie Mae) and the Federal Home Loan Mortgage Corporation (Freddie Mac) are adequately capitalized and operating in a safe and sound manner. Other positions include the President of the Government National Mortgage Association (Ginnie Mae), which provides a secondary market for FHA loans, and the Office of the Inspector General, responsible for conducting and supervising audits and carrying out investigations.

The role of HUD during the Clinton administration

Preparing the ground

It was to HUD that President Clinton turned to implement his program to extend home ownership to low- and moderate-income families. He appointed as Secretary, Henry Cisneros, four times Mayor of Clinton's home town of San Antonio, Texas and only the second Hispanic to hold that office. Cisneros had already decided not to seek a further term and became one of Clinton's advisers for his successful Presidential campaign. A strong supporter of the Hispanic community with a commitment to advancing its share of economic life, Cisneros set about the work enthusiastically.

His first challenge once appointed was to fend off the movement in Capital Hill to abolish HUD altogether, following the 1994 Congressional election, when the Republicans won a majority in the House. His prepared reports in defense emphasized the losses that many American families would face if HUD was abolished, and HUD's local offices argued that the elimination of the department would vastly expand America's underclass, leaving many families, including those with children, homeless.

The focus of HUD's work shifted to expanding home ownership, partly through necessity as a result of changes introduced by the Budget. HUD and the FHA were agencies of the federal government and were funded through the Budget. But "in 1990, as part of a new, multi-year Budget agreement, the Congress and the President adopted new procedures for deficit control. These procedures, embodied in the Budget Enforcement Act of 1990, established statutory limits on discretionary spending and a deficit-neutral pay-as-you-go requirement for new mandatory spending and tax legislation."[1] This coupled with the Federal Credit Reform Act, 1990, and the Omnibus Budget Reconciliation Act, 1990, restricted spending on the FHA, for if the expected premiums were not enough to cover losses, these would have to be regarded as a Budget item, and the latter Act required the FHA to establish a reserve fund and set its premiums at a sufficient level to ensure actuarial soundness.

These restrictions did not, however, prevent President Clinton from cutting the mortgage insurance rates three times between 1993 and 1997. This reduced the mortgage insurance premium from 2% to 1.75%, with the cuts taken together, along with savings passed on to home buyers because the increased efficiency of the FHA would save them $1,200 on the closing costs of the average FHA mortgage of $85,000.[2] The reduction announced on June 12, 1997 accounted for $200 of that saving. This was another attempt to reduce the barriers to home ownership, namely the high closing costs. To qualify for that reduction, prospective first-time home buyers had to successfully complete the 16-hour Homebuyer Education and Learning Program; FHA statistics showed that those who completed this course were better prepared for home ownership and were less likely to default.[3] But this also turned out to be a mistake, as the fund ran into difficulties and the premiums had to be raised again in the years to come. In line with the Budget restrictions, it was supposed to be funded by cost-saving management improvements at the FHA. All of this meant that the possibility of providing affordable housing through government funding was no longer open to HUD. Other ways would have to be found for the realization of the American dream. Under President Clinton's direction, Secretary Cisneros began to work out an alternative.

The partnership program

During 1994, Secretary Henry Cisneros conducted meetings with the leaders of major national organizations from within the housing industry with a view to establishing a national home ownership partnership. All agreed to set up working groups to develop various themes, including the availability of financing and opening markets and targeting underserved populations. The entire strategy consisted of 100 actions to be carried out through a national partnership and a series of State and local partnerships, designed to generate up to 8 million additional home owners by the end of 2000.

The key actions in this document to which so many organizations agreed are as follows:

Action 34. Reduce Down-Payment and Mortgage Costs.

Strategy: The Partnership should support initiatives to reduce down-payment requirements, to encourage savings for down payments by first-time home buyers, and to reform the basic contract between borrowers and lenders to reduce interest costs.

In addition, the amount of money necessary for down payment continues to vary greatly from lender to lender based on many factors, including lender criteria, secondary market investor requirements and mortgage insurer guidelines ... Some lenders are not flexible about other forms of down-payment assistance, such as public subsidies or unsecured loans ... Nevertheless great strides have been made by the *lending community* in recent years to reduce down-payment requirements, particularly for low- and moderate-income home buyers. This trend is encouraging and should be continued with support from the Partnership.

The partnership agreement then notes that the monthly costs associated with owning a home also remain an obstacle for many potential home buyers, of which the interest rate charged is the most important. Interest rates are primarily a function of external economic factors, but they are also affected by the "likelihood of mortgage prepayment by the home buyer, loan assumability by future home buyers, mortgage insurance and loan risk."

Action 35: Home Mortgage Loan-to-Value Flexibility.

Lending institutions, secondary market investors, mortgage insurers and other members of the partnership should work collaboratively to reduce home buyer down-payment requirements ... In 1989 only 7% of home mortgages were made with less than 10% down payment. By August 1994, low down-payment mortgage loans had increased to 29%.

The Strategy then suggests that as "members of the Partnership explore creative means of providing low down-payment financing for potential home buyers, a concerted effort should be made to share success stories and to learn what set of factors generated high loan volume and solid payment histories."[4]

In essence, then, the plan advocated "financing strategies, fueled by creativity and resources of the public and private sectors, to help home buyers that lack cash to buy a home or income to make the payments." The result, not surprisingly, was to increase the risks caused by such innovative and flexible features as low down payments and high LTV ratios. This was identified in an analysis provided in the Federal Reserve Bulletin, 1996, which shows conclusively the risk involved in such lending, especially when low credit scores are taken into account.[5]

Handling the risks of affordable housing

As a matter of interest, the authors of the analysis refer to the roundtable discussions held with lenders in preparing the Federal Reserve's 1993 "Report to Congress on Community Development Lending by Depository Institutions." The participants generally took the view that the costs of originating and servicing loans made under the affordable home loan programs were greater than those incurred on other housing loans, but that the delinquency and default experience up to that time had not been worse. Statistical analyses undertaken for that report did not find any special relationship between bank profitability and the level of lower-income mortgage-lending activity. The lenders thought that the increased risks of more flexible underwriting could be mitigated in various ways: for some, by drawing on their knowledge of local market conditions and familiarity with borrowers and affordable lending. Lenders of that kind would soon be much smaller players in mortgage provision, when the 1994 Act allowing for inter-state mergers and acquisitions took effect. They also thought that home-buyer education programmes and credit counseling services would screen out higher-risk applicants and prepare home buyers for the responsibilities of home ownership. The authors note that "until recently, most of the available information on the performance of affordable lending programs has been anecdotal."[6]

It is this lack of hard data, together with little or no statistical analysis in the first half of the 1990s, which no doubt encouraged the politicians to press for affordable lending, especially against a background in which many believed that home ownership was not open to minorities because of discrimination. They were determined to end that discrimination and open up home ownership to low- and median-income families. In this context it was easier to focus on extending home ownership than to consider the risks which might be associated with affordable lending.

Targets, not risks, were the order of the day

Targets, not risks, dominated housing policy; this was clear from HUD's succession of press releases. Even before the National Homeownership Strategy was fully underway, HUD announced the "sharpest rise in the home ownership rates in at least 30 years, with over 1.4 million new homeowners added in 1995."[7] The figure rose to 65.1% in the last quarter of 1995, up from 64.2% at the end of 1994, and included increases in the home ownership rate for minorities and for households under the age of 35. This was ascribed to the Clinton Administration's economic policies, lower interest rates and the public-private partnership with the housing industry. The second press release of that year (August 1996) put home ownership at 65.4%, praising lender efforts to assist working families. Secretary Cisneros noted that the market share of first-time buyers rose from about 40% of all home sales in the 1980s to 47% in 1994–1996, as "lenders are discovering that not only does affordable lending make sense, it makes dollars and cents." The Assistant Vice President of Flagstar Bank said that they could help people purchase a home for as little as 3% down, with the remaining 2% and other costs coming from grants, gifts and even lender-financing.

More targets

Andrew Cuomo was appointed HUD Secretary in January 1997 after Henry Cisneros's resignation. A few months later, he announced initiatives to boost home ownership and create 2 million new urban home owners by the year 2000, calling on the National Partners in Homeownership, a coalition of 63 national groups representing the housing industry, lenders, non-profit groups and all sectors of government to work together to achieve the new goals. Other initiatives included Ginnie Mae stimulation of $1bn in annual mortgage loans to help 15,000 families in inner cities to buy homes each year, and a further $10m to create new Home Ownership Zones to revitalize inner-city areas. The following year, Cuomo announced that three lenders had agreed to make $1.39bn available in home mortgages and to spend $6m on a range of programs to increase home ownership by low- and moderate-income families.[8]

By January 2000, the rate for 1999 had risen to a high of 66.8% for the year as a whole, a higher percentage than at any time in American history, according to Secretary Cuomo. A total of 70.1m families owned their own homes in 1999, but with rates for the minorities still far behind that of the white population: blacks at 46.7%, Hispanics at 45.5%, and others (Asian Americans, Native Americans and Pacific Islanders) at 54%. President Clinton had more than succeeded in achieving his objective of 8.7 million more home owners in 1999 than when he took office in 1993, and indeed by the third quarter of 2000, the rate was 67.7%.[9]

HUD during the Bush administration

In the second year of his Presidency, George Bush turned to social issues, of which home ownership was one of the priorities. "An ownership society is a compassionate society," he told the White House Conference on Increasing Minority Ownership in October 2002, having previously made speeches on the need to extend home ownership especially for minorities on a number of occasions throughout that year.[10] His concerns were the familiar ones: the ownership gap between whites and the minorities, with less than 50% of blacks and 50% of Hispanics owning their own homes, compared with over 70% of whites; closing that gap would not only bring stability to communities, it would also reinvigorate the economy. Even with the surge in home ownership during the 1990s, that gap narrowed by only 1.5%.

A Blueprint for the American Dream

In October 2002, the President and Secretary Mel Martinez launched the "Blueprint for the American Dream." The new goal in the Blueprint was to increase home ownership for minorities by 5.5 million families before the end of the decade. This time, the goal was to be achieved by bringing together 22 public and private partners, including the Mortgage Bankers Association, Mortgage Brokers, Real Estate Brokers, the National Association of Home Builders, the National Association of Hispanic Real Estate Brokers, the National Association of Realtors, the National Credit Union Administrators, Fannie Mae and Freddie Mac, HUD, the US Treasury and others.

The Blueprint Partners identified four key areas on which they would focus in order to increase home ownership:

- Home ownership education and counseling;
- Increasing the supply of affordable homes;
- Providing down payments;
- Improving mortgage lending by increasing funds for affordable loans and redoubling efforts to root-out illegal discrimination.

The context of these proposals differed from that of the 1995 National Partnership. The economy was faltering after the impact of the terrorist attack of 9/11, so part of the emphasis was on the economic benefits that increased home ownership would bring. To accompany the Blueprint, HUD prepared a report on the "Economic Benefits of Minority Homeownership." It demonstrated that in 2001, the combined housing industry together with the sale of associated consumer goods and home improvement totaled $1.45 trillion or 14% of GDP. Achieving the goal of increased minority home ownership would add a further $256 billion over the decade.

Federal help with the costs of home ownership

Once again the down payment was seen as a serious stumbling-block, so President Bush proposed an expansion of the American Dream Down Payment program by increasing this to $200m per year, which at an average cost of $5,000 per household would assist 40,000 low-income families with the down payment and closing costs. This required an Act, which was eventually agreed in December 2003. Other sources of assistance would include FHA and VA mortgages, alliances between national non-profit organizations and community groups, employers, local agencies, individual development accounts and innovative mortgage products with very low or zero down payments.

Earlier that year, two other initiatives had taken place. In January, the FHA home mortgage limits had been increased to $144, 336 in low-cost areas and up to $261,609 in high-cost areas for single-family homes, with similar increases for multi-unit dwellings. HUD announced that this would make FHA loans available for many who had previously been excluded because the limits were too low, and anticipated that it would endorse $120bn for single-family mortgages for 1.2m in 2002. A $1,000 cash-back move-in incentive was introduced in July to help with moving costs and repairs, provided the buyer lived in the property for 12 months.[11]

In the years following the introduction of the Blueprint, fewer announcements were made regarding the increases in minority home ownership. The first came as part of the announcement of Secretary Martinez's resignation as he decided to pursue an open Senate seat in Florida in September 2003. During that year, minority home ownership increased by 1 million, but President Bush had to wait until December to sign the American Dream Down Payment Act. Alphonso Jackson, the Deputy Secretary, was appointed as Secretary.

Alphonso Jackson takes over at a difficult time

Jackson chose to focus on the increase in sales of existing single-family homes. In July 2004 he announced that these had reached 2.1% in June, to an annual rate of 6.95%, an increase of 17.4% from June 2003, adding that "these numbers show that housing still leads the way in our rapidly recovering economy." On July 29, he announced that there were 73.4m home owners, more than at any time in history at 69.2%, with minority home ownership at 51.0%, a net increase of 1.6m since 2002.

In March 2005, sales of new single-family homes rose 9.4% compared with January and 5.2% compared with February 2004. The annual sales rate of 1.226 min February marked the fourth-highest monthly sales rate in the 42-year history of the series. March also recorded a net increase of 2.2m minority home owners, 40% of the goal. For the first time, HUD was able to announce that the 2006 Budget would contain $200m to fully fund the American Dream Down Payment initiative, which, since it had been signed into law, had helped 3,500 families to purchase their first home. By June 2006, this figure had reached 2.5m, but the overall home ownership rate had dropped slightly to 68.5%. On May 8, 2007, Secretary Jackson announced $1.8bn for affordable housing and first-time home-ownership programs.[12]

In his prepared remarks for a somewhat ill-timed conference on "Making Home Ownership a Reality," the Deputy Secretary for Housing, Roy Benardi, referred to the fact that the figure for minority home ownership had reached 3.5m in 2006, but had to focus on the need to educate home owners and modernize the FHA.[13] This was three days before President Bush's Rose Garden address, in which he announced plans for the FHA to help an estimated 240,000 families avoid foreclosure by enhancing its refinancing program through FHASecure plan, to allow families with strong credit histories who had been making timely mortgage payments before their loans reset, but were then in default, to qualify for refinancing. The Administration also required Congress to pass the FHA Modernization Act to enable the FHA to maintain liquidity in the mortgage market, but for that, they would have to wait. The time for enthusiastic announcements about increases in home ownership was over. The surging market had begun to falter and the size of the potential problem was, belatedly, beginning to emerge.

HUD's shortcomings in its oversight role

Numerous press releases give glowing reports of HUD's achievements in encouraging the growth of home ownership, and in the rescue of those with delinquent mortgages and those facing foreclosure. The department was responsible for oversight of the FHA and for Fannie Mae and Freddie Mac, a matter for subsequent chapters. What the press releases fail to mention is that HUD had frequently shown itself unequal to the many tasks with which it was entrusted. Not all of those are relevant to the issues of this book, as they include oversight of the public housing programs, rental assistance and the many other *ad hoc* initiatives to assist those with limited access to housing, such as the elderly or disabled, and the replacement of slum properties. The Office of the Inspector General regularly uncovered mismanagement, mis-spending and fraud at every level within HUD, and even found favoritism or cronyism in contract selection at various levels in the organization, even the highest.

HUD was the only Cabinet Department that was ever identified as a "high-risk agency" by the General Accountability Office in 1994, a designation which was only removed in 2001, but was retained in two areas (the rental assistance programs and the FHA Single Family Mortgage Insurance Programs) as late as 2007.[14] It is the latter area which is the main concern here; HUD was responsible for the oversight of every aspect of the mortgages which the FHA insured.

In order to carry out its mission of expanding home ownership, FHA assumes 100% of the risk for the mortgages it insures, especially as it is more likely than private lenders to insure loans for low-income and minority borrowers (according to the GAO in its July 2001 report). The FHA therefore relies on private lenders to determine a borrower's creditworthiness, and to make and fund loans. It uses private appraisers to assess the value of every property it insures, and relies on contractors to help assess lenders' compliance with its requirements, monitor the performance of appraisers, and manage and sell the properties it acquires through foreclosure. The GAO points out that without "careful oversight of these lenders, appraisers and contractors, the FHA is vulnerable to mismanagement and fraud."[15] But in 1997, as part of its 2020 Management Reform Plan, HUD devolved its Single Family Mortgage Insurance Program, including oversight, to four centers. In January 2001, the GAO reported that this was a high-risk area for HUD, and in the intervening months carried out a thorough assessment, including the centers' monitoring of contractors.

Staff at the centers were supposed to be deployed in sufficient numbers, but were not; they were also supposed to be trained in the new oversight responsibilities, but funds were cut. The result was that the staff were unable and ill-equipped to handle the increased workload, and so expanded their reliance on contractors, contrary to the 2020 Plan, which stated that contractors would only be used to manage and sell the properties acquired through foreclosure. In fact, contractors currently carry out much of the mortgage insurance endorsement activities, including the underwriting quality of the loans insured by the FHA, with staff in the centers being responsible for monitoring contractors. The centers grant FHA-approved lenders direct endorsement authority, which means that they can underwrite loans and determine their eligibility for FHA mortgage insurance without prior approval from HUD. They also oversee contractors who review loan case files by way of a desk audit of the underwriting quality, and endorse or reject loans for FHA mortgages on the basis of these reviews. In addition they are also supposed to conduct on-site evaluations of lenders' operations (lender reviews) as well as the contractors who are managing and selling properties acquired as a result of foreclosures.

The GAO concluded that lack of proper oversight was still a major problem, ranging from a failure to review high-risk lenders due to staff inexperience (no background in lender monitoring or credit issues), and rarely conducted on-site reviews of properties assessed by contracted appraisers, because of lack of staff and travel resources; centers did not track the percentage of each contractor's work that had received reviews, nor evaluate their performance.[16] The GAO spelt out what this meant in terms of the size of the potential risks involved. "In the fiscal year 1999, the centers and the contractors endorsed about 1.3m mortgages, totaling $123.1bn, then a record in dollar terms." The percentage of FHA-insured loans for first-time buyers increased from 70.3% in 1996 to 80.7% in 1999, and for minorities, from 31% in 1996 to 37% in 1999. The processing-time for insurance approvals fell from several weeks to a few days, partly through technology, direct endorsement by lenders and contracting-out. The problems persisted so that in 2005, for example, the Inspector General's semi-annual report to Congress acknowledged that through "their comprehensive audits of poorly performing lenders and effective investigations" they were showing "significant results," as OIG's recommendations have sought monetary recoveries through loan indemnifications exceeding $133 m, and loss reimbursements of more than £10 m.

But between 2007 and 2009, the familiar problems with HUD's oversight persisted, despite the efforts made by the deputy CFO, James Martin (it was not until 2009 that Robert Ryan was appointed as FHA's Chief Risk Officer). The actions taken in 2007 involved improving the procedures for monitoring the performance of 11,000 private lenders and other underwriters, appraisers and services, responsible for processing and servicing FHA-insured mortgages. The FHA would now seek to administer cost-effective contract services for the management and disposition of HUD-held properties acquired through defaults on FHA mortgages. These processes would be accompanied by sound actuarial reviews and credit subsidy cost models.

The corrective actions undertaken included Neighborhood Watch, Credit Watch and Appraiser Watch programs to weed out poor performers, whose actions would increase the risk of mortgage claims. Two further steps involved developing automated algorithms for targeting highest-risk performers for on-site monitoring, and improving the predictive nature and accuracy of FHA's actuarial and credit subsidy models. The effectiveness of these changes was the subject of constant scrutiny following the introduction of FHA Secure and the plans for the FHA to provide refinancing loans to help families at risk of foreclosure, introduced in 2007. The program was expanded in May 2008 to provide lenders with the added flexibility to refinance and insure more mortgages, including those for borrowers who were late on a few payments and/or received a voluntary mortgage principal write-down from their lenders;

however this was terminated shortly afterwards, since "maintaining the program past the original termination date would have a negative financial impact on the fund."

As we have seen, this led to a rapid increase in the number of single-family mortgages insured by the FHA, to more than $180bn at the end of 2008, up from $59bn in 2007, after the Housing and Economic Recovery Act (HERA) was passed in the summer of 2008. This created a new Hope for Homeowners program to enable FHA to refinance the mortgages of at-risk borrowers, authorizing the FHA to guarantee $300bn in new loans to help protect an estimated 400,000 borrowers from foreclosure. The figure then available for the first quarter of 2009 showed that the FHA total endorsements had increased from 21% to 70% of the market, which included both home sales and refinances. In early 2009, it was thought that Congress would introduce additional legislation to increase participation. HERA also authorized changes to the FHA's Home Equity Conversion Mortgage (HECM) to enable more seniors to tap into their home's equity and obtain higher payouts.

The Inspector General attacks the FHA's continuing failings

In his presentation to the Appropriations Subcommittee on Transportation, Housing and Urban Development, the Inspector General was at pains to stress the increased likelihood of fraud.[17] He noted that despite the introduction of management improvement schemes and the various proposals for improving FHA's oversight of all the processes involved in insuring loans, such as those made by James Martin (see above), few of the problems identified since the 1990s had been addressed; and that, too often, OIG recommendations had not been carried out. In the April IOG Report, he pointed out some of the major concerns, once more, including inadequate quality controls; reliance on manual processes; over-dependence on the honesty of program participants to provide accurate and truthful information; and the urgent need to upgrade data systems (the subject of audit work and investigations transmitted to HUD over the years) by deciding on what data should be collected and why.[18]

The April IOG Report was followed by an even more devastating report presented to the Committee on Financial Services, Subcommittee on Oversight and Investigations US House of Representatives in June 2009. This document is worthy of careful analysis, as it reveals the extent to which the FHA was exposed to fraud; the failure to act on its many recommendations, not just for a year or two but for a decade or more. Above all, it was and is impossible to make any statements about the nature and quality of the loans insured by the FHA, not just during the surge in such applications from mortgage lenders which began in late 2007, but in previous years of high demand for FHA insurance during the late 1990s. For the year in question, the FHA Budget for single- and multi-family properties was $45bn plus mortgage insurance premiums, and its predominance in the mortgage market in 2009 was unparalleled. The program FHA Secure was introduced to refinance existing subprime mortgages and, since it was expanded in May 2008, was terminated in 2009 as the new programs under HERA and HECM came into play.

The first concern expressed by the Inspector was that the weaknesses in FHA's systems and the increases in demand for the FHA program would have collateral effects on the integrity of Ginnie Mae's (Government National Mortgage Association) mortgage-backed securities (MBSs), including the potential for fraud in that program. HUD should also take into account the downstream risks of Ginnie Mae's eventual securitization of HECM Single-Family Loans, since these are the only MBSs to carry the full faith and credit guarantee of the USA. Ginnie Mae had also seen an increase in its market share during 2007 and 2008, with $150bn in outstanding mortgage-backed securities without the resources to keep pace with the increase. Its struggle to keep up with the FHA was also noted by the industry at the time, as it could also reduce liquidity in the market at a critical time. OIG was concerned because an audit of the Ginnie Mae program revealed that it did not take any steps to check that MBS pools were in fact insured with the FHA within a reasonable period after the pool issuance. The full extent of the problems is best illustrated by the case recorded in the report.

"Two former corporate officers of a Michigan financial company were convicted of defrauding Ginnie Mae by retaining the funds obtained from terminated and/or paid-off loans. The defendants failed to disclose to Ginnie Mae that the loans were terminated, while one of the defendants utilized the funds from paid-off loans to invest in the stock market and make fraudulent monthly payments to Ginnie Mae on the loans that were paid-off to conceal the fraud. *The fraud began during July, 1998 and continued until October, 2007, resulting in a loss of approximately $20,000,000*".[19] HERA now includes a stiff penalty provision, specifically for fraud against the FHA. This is clearly important, but only if the systems allow for its detection.

The heightened risks to the FHA included its approval of a large number of new lenders, up from 997 at the end of 2007 to 3,300 by the end of 2008, with a further 11,600 lender approvals in the first half of 2009. It was not just a matter of fraudulent or unscrupulous lenders turning to the FHA, but also the fact that the agency had started to serve several new metropolitan areas with which it had had little contact in the past and with the maximum loan limit having been raised to $729,750. The FHA, due to the loan limit increases, $729,750, was able to serve new metropolitan areas with which it has had little interaction. With entry into these new markets came new players and unknown hazards, which would potentially lead to much greater losses being sustained by the FHA on defaulted loans; such loans may then become more attractive to fraudulent lenders, as they would get large payouts from the FHA's insurance scheme.

The report highlights cases of fraud and abuse arising from the lender approval process, but this is clearly not the only problem; the FHA has no means of identifying the key individuals involved in the transaction, such as the originating loan officer, who is responsible for initiating the loan where due diligence should be done (i.e. credit scores, appraisals, etc.). FHA systems should also be able to capture information on the real-estate agent for both the seller and the buyer. These and other changes in the system have long been proposed but never introduced, since the FHA cannot use any of its revenues to invest in new technology. This means that not only can it not keep pace with the industry in the development of technology, but that the agency has been reduced to relying on random, manual processes by contractors to select for review about 2% of lender endorsements, a further reduction of 3%.

Two other significant areas of concern were identified. First the appraiser roster (a separate function), which the FHA was supposed to monitor, ensuring quality control was clearly not fit for purpose. OIG's review found that the roster contained listings of 3,480 appraisers with expired licenses and 199 appraisers that had been state sanctioned. Inflated appraisals were common, which would obviously increase the costs of the loans and insurance costs with foreclosures. The second matter included a rule change, which had been introduced by the FHA in 2005 and announced through a Mortgagee Letter, altering the requirements for late endorsements for single-family insurance, where the endorsement was considered late if it is received by the FHA more than 60 days after the mortgage loan settlement or funds disbursement. This letter removed the prior six-month good payment history requirement for these loans, and added a 15-day grace period before the current month's payment was considered late.

The FHA did not carry out a risk analysis at the time, but the OIG did, and found that their review of loans from seven prior late endorsement audits (including Wells Fargo, National City Mortgage, Cendant and others) revealed a three-and-a half times higher risk of claims when loans had unacceptable payment histories within the previous six months. That was in 2006. Since then, the default rate has increased significantly for such loans. What was even more extraordinary was that the FHA continued to dispute the audit and did not publish a reversal of the rule, leaving the matter unresolved until 2009, when the whole matter was reported to Congress. All of this was despite the fact that HUD's own Handbook stated that, "Past credit performance serves as the most useful guide in determining a borrower's attitude toward credit obligations and predicting a borrower's future actions."[20]

A year later, in May 2010, Kenneth Donohue Inspector General again appeared before the same Senate subcommittee, and was able to acknowledge the considerable assistance given to him by the then Commissioner, David Stevens, "who has tried to do more in this last year than I saw in all the previous years combined."[21] A few months later, Stevens departed to become Chairman of the Mortgage Bankers Association. Despite such efforts, Donohue's report showed that little had changed, apart from the OIG and FHA's decision to investigate 15 mortgage companies with significant claim rates. The result, as announced later that year, was that a further $11m was lost due to non-complying loans. Fraudulent activities noted in his report included those of Lend America, which in 2008 alone made $1.5bn in loans, and Taylor Bean Whittaker Mortgage Corporation and Colonial Bank with the result that the latter was taken over by the FDIC and sold to BB&T Bank, and the former was subject to seizure but at the time was servicing federally insured and guaranteed loans with a remaining principal balance of about $26bn.

Once again, the point is not just the extent of the frauds, although they ran into billions of dollars. The real cause for concern was the ever-increasing size of the Single-Family FHA-insured loan portfolio, up to $800bn in March 2010; by June 2010 it had reached $865bn. The FHA insured 6.5m mortgages, of which 3.5m were put in place during 2008 to 2009. Its total endorsements increased to 74% of the insured mortgage market, which includes both home sales and refinances. Although fraud attracts attention because of the shock value of the bare-faced behavior of some of its perpetrators, the report is rightly focused on the FHA's inability to assess the quality of the loans or the behavior of the lenders. The latest FHA report showed that net losses on claims were averaging 60%, which was 13% higher than predicted.

The report noted that the same problems arise with Ginnie Mae, which should also improve its approval process and recertification of issuers. The Taylor, Bean and Whitaker Mortgage Corporation (TBW) case exposed weaknesses not only in the FHA program, but also in Ginnie Mae's program. Following the conviction of TBW, and the failure of the company to make the required pass-through payment of principal and interest to MBS investors, Ginnie Mae is required to assume responsibility for it. Ginnie therefore defaults the issuers and assumes control of the issuer's MBS pools. Their securities are the only ones to carry the full faith and credit guaranty of the US Government. In the case of the Colonial Bank, the FDIC temporarily froze the Ginnie Mae custodial accounts at the bank and as a result, Ginnie Mae was forced to make a $1bn pass-through payment of principal and interest to investors. Such issues could arise again for Ginnie Mae, as the number of banks on the FDIC's watch list continues to grow.

In his March statement to Congress, Commissioner Stevens explained the further actions that the FHA was taking to shore up its Capital Reserve Account, including the withdrawal of approval from 354 lenders; increases in premiums and the two-tier FICO requirement. These changes did not prevent the continuing rise in delinquent FHA loans throughout 2010, a figure which has been increasing over the past four years. It reached 619,712 in February 2011, for which the seriously delinquent mortgages are likely to end in default, foreclosure or short sales as only 1% become paying loans, leaving the FHA exposed to $1 trillion in FHA-insured mortgages.

Conclusion

This brief survey of HUD and its failure to oversee the federal affordable housing programs, taken together with the weakness of OFHEO, strongly suggest that it is simply not possible for the federal government to manage to provide affordable housing by these means. It never had the resources to do so, and successive Administrations were unwilling to provide them. Without proper oversight, millions, not to say billions of dollars were wasted on trying to provide affordable housing to those who did not have the income or assets to pay for them. The many-faceted nature of HUD requires careful examination of its role in ensuring that the FHA and Fannie and Freddie carry out their role of providing affordable housing with the interests of the minorities and low- to moderate-income families alone in mind.

4

Mortgage Data

The collection of mortgage data is clearly basic to an understanding of developments in the mortgage market, both for market participants, analysts, economists and regulators, and for home owners and those aspiring to home ownership. A comprehensive and reliable set of data, regularly updated and analysed for emerging trends, is vital for government, policy makers and politicians so that the implications of such trends are properly understood and evaluated, thus giving rise to appropriate policy responses. One of the many problems between 1995 and 2008 is that no one had access to consistent, reliable and adequate data so that the developments taking place in the mortgage markets could be charted. This was one of the reasons why the extent of the growth in both number and quality of subprime mortgages was not observed until the rate of delinquencies and foreclosures began to reach alarming proportions. The purpose of this chapter is to look at the available data and to explain why it was so inadequate.

Sources of mortgage data

The Home Mortgage Disclosure Act, 1975 and the American Housing Survey

Information under this Act and data from the bi-annual American Housing Survey, conducted by HUD and the US Bureau of the Census, is available to the public free of charge. The latter survey is occasionally used to supplement HMDA data but it is not generally used for regulatory purposes. It does provide a picture of changes in patterns of home ownership over the years, as it covers the same 60,000 housing units, including the demographics of the occupants, details of the amount of the mortgage and the interest rate charged, the value of the property, and taxes and other housing costs. However, the HMDA data is the most widely used.

First American Loan Performance (LP)

This is the most important proprietary source of information, with a data base of over 100 million active and paid-off loans tracked for delinquency, prepayment and foreclosure. LP provides loan-level details of non-agency, publicly traded mortgage and asset-backed securities, including all mortgages purchased by Fannie Mae and Freddie Mac, as well as non-agency securitized loans. It also owns the country's largest servicing performance data repository. One of LP's main attractions is its compilation of the largest credit and prepayment performance data base of subprime loans, but it has less coverage of the subprime market.

Lender Processing Services (LPS)

Lender Processing Services (formerly known as McDash) includes 18 large mortgage servicers, 9 out of the top 10, but does not include portfolio loans. LPS data and analytics grant access to loan-level data on about 40 million active first loans and 9 million second mortgages; more data, it claims, about US mortgages than is provided by any other single company. Its Credit Model exposes subsets of the loan population that have a greater tendency to default by examining interest rate projections, geographical factors and other ways to manage portfolio risk. LPS claims to cover 57% of the market, with larger shares in some areas, whereas LP is thought to cover between 78% and 80%.

The National Delinquency Survey (NDS)

This is published by the Mortgage Bankers Association, and is a long-established source of delinquency and foreclosure rates, based on a sample of about 44 million loans serviced by mortgage companies, commercial banks, thrifts, credit unions and others. The NDS provides quarterly delinquency and foreclosure statistics at the national, regional and state levels. These rates are broken down into loan types (prime, subprime, VA and FHA), fixed and adjustable rate products. At each geographical location, the data is further broken down into total delinquencies, delinquency by past due (30–59 days, 60–89 days, 90 days and over), new foreclosures, foreclosures inventory and seriously delinquent. The total number of loans serviced in each quarter, as compiled in the survey, is also included in the data. As of 2008, there were 55 million loans outstanding.

None of the above sources covers the entire mortgage market. They are all incomplete and are collected on different bases and for different purposes. For this reason, use of the available data is not without its problems. The commercial sources are also expensive and not freely available to researchers and policy makers. Nor do the commercial data providers make information freely available to regulators, perhaps due to perceived conflicts, in that some private subscribers have concluded that matching the data with HMDA data may not be in accordance with their contract terms, and that so doing could possibly provide information which could be used against them in fair lending disputes.

However, more recently, some researchers who have purchased the data have tried to marry up the HMDA with, say, LP data by various complex procedures. One example is the use made by Elizabeth Laderman and Carolina Reid, who sought to draw together the various sources of data in their case to show that the minorities were disproportionately offered and obtained subprime mortgages (defined as higher-priced loans), and that these loans ended in default and foreclosures to a greater extent than for the white population in California. The methodology involved a multi-nominal logit regression to predict the relative probabilities of four categories of mortgages (prime fixed rate; prime adjustable rate mortgages (ARM); subprime fixed rate; and subprime ARM ending in default or foreclosure.)[1] In this paper, they define subprime simply as higher-priced lending, and in passing refer to an important gap in the HMDA statistics: namely, that these do not record loan performance over time.

This is one of several attempts to bring together data from various sources in order to understand both the subprime market and the collapse of the mortgage market in 2008 and 2009. Policy makers and analysts alike sought reliable data sources so that models could be developed to provide a means of understanding the extent of the crisis. It is worth noting that the interest in such research, with a few notable exceptions, began in 2007 and continued throughout 2008 to the present. It is difficult to understand why the HMDA statistics seem to be lacking in such important areas, when these are the statistics on which the various regulators rely, given that a key element of their remit is to ensure the "safety and soundness" of the lenders. The reasons will become clear from a brief history of the Home Mortgage Disclosure Act (HMDA) and its relationship to other legislation.

A brief history of the Home Mortgage Disclosure Act

The HMDA was enacted by Congress in 1975 and is implemented by the Federal Reserve Board's Regulation C. In 1980, amendments to the HMDA required the Federal Financial Institutions Examinations Council (FFIEC) to compile annually aggregate lending data for each Metropolitan Statistical Area (MSA) by Census tract for certain lenders. The FFIEC is a formal inter-agency body empowered to prescribe uniform principles, standards and reports for the federal examinations of financial institutions by the Federal Reserve, the Office of the Comptroller of the Currency, the Office of Thrift Supervision and the Federal Deposit Insurance Corporation. The only way to change the data requirements was through amending the law, which then allowed the FFIEC to issue regulations.

Further amendments enacted by Congress in 1988, 1989, 1991, 1993 and 1994 introduced additional amendments, not all of which were major changes but still required an act of Congress or Congressional approval.

The coverage of HMDA reporting was extended to non-majority-owned savings and loan service corporations, mortgage banking subsidiaries of bank holding companies, and mortgage banking subsidiaries of savings and loan holding companies (1988), followed by mortgage lenders not affiliated with depository institutions or holding companies. In 1991, through the Federal Deposit Insurance Corporation Improvement Act, an exemption was introduced for non-depository mortgage lenders, but this was restricted a year later, in 1992, so that non-depository mortgage lenders with an office in an MSA are included if they meet either an asset-sized test or a lending activity test.

By 1992, lenders in the above categories were required to report on the disposition of applications for mortgages and home improvement loans and to identify the race, sex, and income of loan applicants and borrowers. In addition, they were required to identify the class of purchaser for mortgage purchases sold and were allowed to explain the reasons for their lending decision. Each lender had to submit a loan application register, showing the applications, loans originated and loans purchased, as well as loans originated through a mortgage broker or correspondent. Other changes introduced in 1994 and 1995 concerned making the data available to the public, and making a modified version of the loan register available to the public within 30 days of the lender's regulatory report.

Further significant changes cover raising the exemption limits for reporting requirements for depository institutions from $10m to $28m in assets, effective 1997, and to $29m in 1998 in accordance with changes to Regulation C, which allowed for an annual adjustment to the exemption limit in accordance with the year-to-year changes in the average of the Consumer Price Index for Urban Wage Earners and Clerical Workers. (The asset threshold for non-depository institutions remained at $10m.) The threshold was increased to $30m for 2000, $31m for 2001, and $32m for 2002 and 2003. The basis for the annual adjustment had nothing to do with the risks of lending even for small institutions, which had no doubt complained about the regulatory burden.

In June 2003, the Office of Management and Budget issued a revised list of metropolitan statistical areas and metropolitan divisions, micro-statistical areas and combined statistical areas, based on data from the 2000 Census. The reasons for the changes in suitable ways of classifying centers of population are interesting, but beyond the scope of this book; "Census tracts" are regarded as having less stable boundaries than other units (such as counties), and zip codes were rejected as not having specific boundaries. The changes in the definition reflect population shifts as well as changes in travel-to-work patterns. The new boundaries following changes in the 2000 Census added 242 zip codes to the HMDA coverage area and increased the number of reporting lenders by 9%. All of the Census tract changes made a longitudinal analysis of HMDA data more difficult.

Various changes took place for reporting from 2004 onwards. These included an expansion of the coverage of non-depository lenders by adding a $25m dollar volume test to the existing percentage-based coverage test, based on the above index. The most significant change from the point of view of regulators, Congress, consumer advocacy organizations and analysts was the introduction of data related to loan pricing from January 1, 2004. Lenders were required to report loan originations in which the annual percentage rate (APR) exceeds the yield for comparable Treasury securities by a specified amount or threshold. The thresholds are a spread of 3 percentage points for first lien loans and 5 percentage points for subordinate lien loans. Lenders must also report whether a loan is covered by the Home Ownership and Equity Protection Act (HOEPA), and whether the application or the loan involves a manufactured home. This was an attempt to identify subprime loans, which will be discussed in more detail elsewhere.

Few important changes followed in the years 2004 to 2008, apart from raising the exemption threshold until it reached $39m for data collection in 2009 and the asset threshold for non-depository institutions remained unchanged at $10m (or less when combined with the assets of any parent corporation) or originated 100 or more home purchase loans, including refinancings of home purchase loans) in the preceding year. The only other significant change in 2008 was to require the lender to report the spread between the loan's APR and a survey-based estimate of the APRs currently offered on prime loans of a comparable type if the spread is equal to or greater than 1.5 percentage points for a first lien loan or 3.5 percentage points for a subordinate lien loan.

Most of the bureaucratic paraphernalia accompanying the HMDA data has to do with the main purpose of the data collection, which had nothing to do with identifying loans and lenders at risk of default. This is why HMDA data did not help the analysts and economists who tirelessly examined all the statistics in an effort to find out what was really going on the mortgage market. That is clear from an understanding of the purpose of the Act and the context in which it was introduced.

The purpose of the Home Mortgage Disclosure Act

The collection of data was for an entirely different purpose: to ensure that minorities had equal access to credit. The Act itself was a further attempt to improve the effectiveness of existing legislation which included the Fair Housing Act, 1968 and the Truth in Lending Act of the same year. The former was designed to ensure that access to mortgage loans could not be denied on grounds of religion, sex, race, color, national origins, disability or familial status, nor could loans be offered on different terms on those grounds. The Truth in Lending Act required full disclosure of the terms of credit.

Two further Acts followed: the Equal Credit Opportunity Act, 1974, the purpose of which was to end discrimination on the grounds of sex and marital status; then in 1994, President Clinton signed the Home Ownership and Equity Protection Act, of which Section 32 applies to mortgages. The Law sets out clear requirements for the disclosure of information to a prospective borrower. It also bans various lending practices, such as balloon payments (for loans in which the regular payments do not entirely pay off the principal balance, and a lump sum of more than twice the amount of regular payments is required for loans with less than five-year terms); negative amortization; and most prepayment penalties. Such practices would inevitably be an important concern for regulators.

The regulators also had to spend a considerable amount of time both in ensuring that the Community Reinvestment Act was being implemented, and in rooting out discrimination in lending. The extent to which such efforts were successful continues to be a matter of considerable dispute, and is still under discussion in the process of reforming the entire regulatory framework. The reference to the surrounding laws concerned with eliminating discrimination in lending serves to underline the fact that data collection was undertaken with that aim in mind, a major reason for the highly significant omissions in the HMDA data. It was never intended to enable regulators and others to track developments in the mortgage market and thus aid the "safety and soundness" assessments. It was only designed to stamp-out discrimination in lending. But as time went on, the focus of regulators, analysts, economists and policy makers shifted to the behavior of the mortgage market and away from discrimination in lending. This is clear from the increasing number of articles about the market which struggle to make sense out of the HMDA data.

Gaps in the HMDA data

Borrower's income

First of all, although the data record the borrower's income, they do not provide any further information about the borrower's employment, gaps in employment, sources of income used to obtain the mortgage (which could have covered a wide range, such as alimony payments and social security benefits, as indicated in earlier chapters), or the borrower's credit history or substitutes for credit history, such as regular payment of rent, or utility bills. Nor do they include the FICO score. This means that key issues of credit risk are not included in the data, although the inclusion of credit scores was discussed for at least a decade, so that by 2010, the Federal Reserve was still considering what changes should be made to Regulation C, which determines the content and timing of HMDA data.

Loan-to-value ratios and the price of the loan

Other aspects of the risks involved in lending were not included in the data. These consist of two important elements: loan-to-value ratios, and the performance of the loan. The data on purchased loans, that is, loans purchased by lenders in order to improve their CRA ratings, is virtually non-existent, so that a lender's portfolio could include mortgages the lender has originated for which the reporting had to comply with the existing regulations, and purchased loans, which did not. The lender could then package and sell on a bundle of mortgages which included the loans originated by the lender and the purchased loans for which little information was available, either for the regulators or for the buyers of the MBSs.

High LTVs have long been recognized as a risk factor. "Empirical investigations have found that both equity and adverse changes in borrowers' circumstances are related to mortgage loan performance, as predicted by theory (option-based theories and triggering-event theories, such as unemployment). Studies consistently find that the level of equity (whether proxied by the loan-to-value ratio or by a contemporaneous measure of the ratio) is closely related to both the likelihood of default and the size of the loss in the event of default." So wrote Robert Avery and others in 1996, all from the Federal Reserve Board's Division of Research and Statistics, pointing out a significant risk factor which was clearly forgotten in the years that followed, as it was left out of the HMDA statistics.[2]

Credit scores

As well as high LTVs, the credit scores to which reference has already been made are a significant factor. The borrower's income was recorded, but no further information was required, such as the debt-to-income ratio of the mortgage, employment prospects or the sources of the borrower's income. It appears that no record was made of other debts which the borrower had to service at the time of taking out the mortgage, nor the length of such commitments. As time went on, lenders offered loans without the customary full documentation of the creditworthiness of the borrowers. More than that, loans were issued to borrowers on the basis of their stated income and assets, without documentation, or else on the basis of no income at all. The HMDA statistics do not record such information.

Type of mortgage

The other issue concerns the nature of the mortgage, including such features as the length of the mortgage, and the type of mortgage, such as whether it was a fixed or adjustable rate mortgage, an interest only mortgage, prepayment penalties or a so-called "trigger" mortgage. These features were not required for HMDA returns; eventually the focus was on higher-priced loans, but this was because such loans were thought to be both subprime and discriminatory. Minorities, it was frequently alleged, had to pay more for their mortgages than the white population, and the price of the mortgage was a means of identifying such discrimination. Consumer groups had stressed the need to end "predatory lending", and as a result the price of the loan had to be reported from January 1, 2004 onwards.

Price of the mortgage

Whatever the measure used, the rate spread between US Treasury securities and the interest rate charges on mortgages is both misleading and, further, was introduced at just the wrong time. It reflects an assumption that high interest rates on mortgages represent an increase in the reported higher-priced and therefore subprime loans, whereas the changes from year to year may simply reflect changes in the relationship between short- and long-term interest rates.

An analysis of the rate spreads between five-year and 30-year Treasury securities over the past two decades shows that 2003 and 2004 were unusual: the yield curve was steep during that time because of the low short-term interest rates, and as a result, the gap between the two rates was exceptionally large. For example, in mid-January 2004, the yield on five-year Treasuries was 2.97% and on 30-year securities, 4.87%; but the gap narrowed to a limited extent during the year, so that by early January 2005 the yield on five-year Treasuries rose to 3.71% while on 30-year Treasuries it had fallen to 4.72%. Shorter-term interest rates continued to rise throughout 2005, but the longer-term rates continued to rise as well, so that by the end of 2005 the two rates were much closer.

This explains why the gap between the effective interest rate as measured by the APR on most mortgages and the HMDA threshold for reporting higher-priced loans narrowed between 2004 and 2005. For loans priced in the week beginning January 15, 2004, the average APR on the conventional first lien fixed rate 30-year prime loans as reported by Freddie Mac was 5.72%. That meant that the gap between the APR of the typical prime loan priced during that week and the HMDA reporting threshold was 215 basis points, but by December 15, 2005, this had decreased to 140 basis points. Regardless of the nature of the loans and any other factors, the reported incidence of higher-priced loans would have increased during 2005, but subprime lending may not have increased.[3] That would be the case, if subprime loans are defined entirely in terms of higher-priced loans.

The situation is more complicated for adjustable rate mortgages (ARMs), as Robert Avery points out in the same article. Under the Federal Reserve Board's Regulation Z, when calculating the APR for such loans, lenders assume that the interest rate environment at the time of origination will remain the same for the term of the loan, itself an extraordinary assumption. Because of this "regulatory construct," when the yield curve is positively sloped, the APRs for ARMs tend to be lower than those for fixed rate loans of similar term and credit risk.

The flattening of the yield curve can have two effects: (i) narrowing the gap between the longer-term rates used for the HMDA reporting threshold and the shorter-term rates used for pricing the loans; and (ii) narrowing the APR gap between adjustable and fixed rate loans because, as short-term interest rates increase, it reduces the differences in APR between fixed and adjustable rate mortgages. The result, according to Avery, was an increase in the proportion of adjustable rate loans that exceeded the HMDA price reporting thresholds, because many relatively high-rate ARMs would not have been reported as higher-priced in 2004, since comparatively low APRs were reported that way in 2005.

By comparison with prime 30-year fixed rate loans, the gap narrowed much more, from 404 basis points at the beginning of 2004 to only 75 basis points at the end of 2005. Avery's most illuminating comment on this whole analysis lies in his conclusion that "fully quantifying this effect would be difficult even if the HMDA data distinguished fixed from adjustable rate mortgages."[4] As will be seen later, it was not only the numbers of ARMs, but also the structure of the latter mortgages and the relationship to changes in the interest rates that were significant. The same article points out that the "HMDA data do not include all of the factors considered in evaluating and pricing credit," but the rest of the article makes it clear that the purpose was to examine whether or not higher-priced loans were more likely to be extended to minorities, rather than the risks of lending.

Application of reporting requirements

The Federal Reserve Board apparently interpreted the requirement to issue regulations on data for the loans that financial institutions sold, as implying that the data need not be collected for the loans that an institution purchases. This was based on the wording of FIRREA 12 U.S.C., section 2303 (h), which referred only to the loans sold and not to the loans purchased. So loans purchased through securitization and packaged as MBSs soon "lost" the reported information.

The gaps in HMDA reporting requirements identified here are explained by the original purpose of collecting the data, and by understanding how and why that changed over time. The requirement to report on subprime loans did not exist. Instead, HUD chose to identify subprime lending first by the originator, and later by the price of the loans. The next section deals with the identification of subprime loans, first setting out the historical background.

HMDA and the identification of subprime lenders

The introduction of the APR data was regarded as a step forward, since subprime mortgages were identified as subprime if they were originated by a lender on the Subprime and Manufactured Home Lender list maintained by the Department of Housing and Urban Development (HUD). The list consisted of lenders that specialized in subprime or manufactured home lending; it was designed to accompany HMDA data and was available on an annual basis from 1993 to 2005. HUD removed lenders specializing in manufactured housing in 2004, when a means of identifying loans based on manufactured loans was added to HMDA data. It continues to produce the subprime lender list because of concerns that the higher-priced variable might not be sufficient to identify subprime loans. In its description of its own methodology, HUD states that it continues to produce the list because subprime loans do not necessarily have APRs that are above a comparable Treasury APR. Some lenders whom HUD contacted stated that their APR information was incorrectly reported after HUD asked them why their lending portfolios had significant percentages of high APR loans. Then a number of lenders described themselves as "multi-purpose lenders" and pointed out that their high percentage of loans with spreads of 3% or more were due to their broker channels. "These lenders did not feel that they were necessarily subprime."

In addition, some prime lenders informed HUD that their higher APR loans were not necessarily subprime and could reflect fees and yield spread premiums. For these and other reasons associated with changes in connection with the yield curve, HUD decided to retain its list of subprime lenders. Furthermore, some subprime lenders enter and leave the list, and HUD does not alter the records dating from previous years, so that, for example, if a lender identifies itself as a subprime lender in 2004, that same lender could also have been a subprime lender in some of the preceding years. The list contains a few Alt-A specialists which had similar characteristics to subprime lenders, and were also more likely to have a higher proportion of higher APR loans.

The list itself is based on reviews of each lender's HMDA filings. Lenders that have higher denial rates, higher shares of mortgage refinancing loans and few loan sales to government-sponsored enterprises or more higher-priced loans are deemed to be subprime lenders. HUD then follows this up with the possible subprime lenders to discuss their area of specialization. The list is updated and revised annually based on the feedback from lenders, policy analysts and housing advocacy groups. Not all lenders specialize in prime or subprime loans, so some subprime loans could be classified as prime and vice versa, but as it was not possible to add subprime loans originated by prime lender, it is possible that the HUD measure understates the number of subprime originations.

HUD then provides a further description of its methodology, which is interesting and worth quoting in full: "First subprime lenders typically have lower origination rates than prime lenders. Second home refinance loans generally account for higher shares of subprime lenders' total originations than prime lenders' originations. Third lenders who sell a significant percentage of their portfolios to the GSEs do not typically specialize in subprime lending ... HUD called the lenders identified on the potential list or reviewed their web pages to determine if they specialized in subprime lending. A large number of lenders told us that they offer subprime loans but they do not constitute a large percentage of their overall conventional mortgage originations. Most lenders readily identified themselves as prime or subprime lender specialists. Some lenders identified themselves as all-purpose lenders and broke out their loan portfolios by mortgage product. In a couple of cases, we identified a lender as subprime if their subprime mortgages exceeded 50%."

In the additional information provided, HUD points out that they treated all credit unions as prime lenders. "Second, we treat the loans sold to the GSEs by subprime lenders as prime loans. Similarly, the government-insured loans originated by subprime lender specialists are treated as government-insured loans ... users of the list should be reminded that not all of the loans reported by subprime lender specialists are subprime loans. In fact, a number of subprime lenders also originate prime loans. Similarly, a number of large and predominately prime lenders originate a significant number of subprime loans."[5]

Phases of the HMDA

Once again, it should be stressed that the purpose of HMDA data collection was not to provide detailed statistics about the operation of the mortgage market. In a useful analysis, Joseph Kolar and Jonathon Jerrison describe how its history can be divided into three major phases, reflecting the "changes in perception by the industry's critics in the advocacy community and on Capitol Hill regarding how the industry serves low-income communities and members of minority groups."[6]

Phases one and two

In the first phase of the Act, HMDA focussed on concerns about loans by banks and thrifts, reflecting the perception that they were taking deposits from low-income neighborhoods but not reinvesting that money by lending in the same neighborhoods. This pre-dated the introduction of FIRREA (the Financial Institution, Reform, Recovery and Enforcement Act, 1989) and will not be described here. The second phase came about as a result

FIRREA, which led to greatly extended reporting requirements, including data about most bank and non-bank lenders in urban areas. The data collected had to include information about race, ethnicity and gender, as well as each applicant's income, and both accepted and rejected applications for loans that did not close. In implementing the legislative changes, the Federal Reserve Bank (FRB) decided to require public disclosure of each application and closed loans, with any personal identifying information removed.

This is where the Boston Fed report of 1992 came in: as noted in Chapter 1, the report argued that there was still a disparity between white and majority rejection rates. Despite criticisms of the original study, much ink was spilt in the following years in scrutinizing the HMDA data to prove or disprove discrimination against minorities. Community activists seized on HMDA data of individual financial institutions and used it to try to delay or prevent bank mergers, to attack their reputations, or to get funding commitments from them.

The 1989 extensions to HMDA were very clearly designed to be a means of identifying discrimination against minorities. The 1989 Conference Report on the legislation stated: "The Home Mortgage Disclosure Act, as amended by this Act, requires amongst other things, reporting by mortgage lenders to the appropriate regulatory agencies. A primary purpose of such reporting is to assist regulatory agencies in identifying possible discriminatory lending patterns that warrant closer scrutiny. To accomplish this purpose it is essential that the data submitted to the agencies be in a form that facilitates the task of identifying any discriminatory lending patterns that disadvantage women, minority borrowers or predominantly minority or low- or moderate-income neighborhoods."[7]

The Federal Reserve Bank of Boston's 1992 study, purporting to show racial discrimination in mortgage lending, though deficient in many respects, did make one useful point, namely that it is not possible to rely on HMDA data alone to determine whether or not a lender had discriminated against an applicant for a loan on the basis of race, ethnicity or sex. In the years that followed, government agencies responsible for enforcing fair lending laws did not regard the HMDA data as sufficient, and also did not use the many statistical analyses of HMDA data, even if additional information had been given about the underwriting processes, which is not reported under HMDA data.[8]

Lenders were equally unimpressed by the Boston Fed Study, but considered it prudent and a matter of good public relations to be seen to be more active in preventing discrimination. A series of agreements was reached between HUD and the Mortgage Bankers Association (MBA): in September 1994 they came together and agreed a voluntary Fair Lending "Best Practices" Agreement, the first of its kind between a federal agency and a national lending trade association. In December 1997, the MBA and HUD renewed this partnership, signing the Master II Agreement. The Fair Lending "Best Practices" initiative is also an integral part of the National Homeownership Strategy, which aimed to add up to eight million new homeowners by the year 2000. Since then HUD and the MBA have been engaged in a cooperative effort to assist mortgage lenders and mortgage associations in the negotiation and signing of individual Fair Lending accords. The Agreements offer an opportunity for lenders to incorporate fair housing and equal opportunity principles into their mortgage lending standards, as well as to increase low-income and minority lending: "*Lenders are expanding to new and untapped markets, while minority and low-income applications have risen.*"[9]

Lenders responded in more than one way. They began to change their underwriting standards so that impediments to loan approvals were removed, and created what were often called "new products" (inevitably sub-prime loans) for low-income and credit-impaired borrowers (they could be nothing else, since these two categories were often less likely to be able to meet the conditions necessary for prime loans). The lenders also encouraged the GSEs to make their underwriting standards more "flexible" and to purchase loans which were appropriate to that market. This was necessary as bank regulators began to use HMDA data, especially denial disparity rates, to identify institutions on which they would focus fair lending examination efforts."[10]

Phase three

The next stage was what was dubbed the "Predatory Lending/Price Discrimination Model", which led to the introduction of detailed reporting on pricing and its relationship to the yield on US Treasuries. The model arose from the criticisms by community advocates that lenders were "expressly seeking out minority or low- or moderate-income lenders for non-prime loans at higher rates and more onerous terms than conventional conforming loans." The Federal Reserve Board responded not only to the change in focus, but also sought to improve the general quality, consistency and presentation of HMDA reporting. The Federal Reserve reviewed and revised Regulation C (which sets out the details of the reporting requirements under HMDA), which was its responsibility, but Congress did not act to alter the underlying legislation.

The changes in Regulation C on January 1, 2004 required not only information about pricing, but also whether the loan is a first lien loan and whether it is covered by the Home Ownership and Equity Protection Act (HOEPA). The Board of Governors of the Federal Reserve System hoped that this would reveal whether or not certain lenders are targeting minorities or lower-income borrowers for above-threshold loans. In their comment on the final rule, it was stated that "obtaining loan pricing data is critical to address fair lending concerns related to loan pricing and to better understand the mortgage market, including the subprime market."[11] The main focus is still on lending to minorities and low- to moderate-income borrowers.

However, the authors point out that the data still fail in their purpose. The federal agencies responsible for enforcing the fair lending laws do not use HMDA data, since they do not include the factors actually considered in deciding whether a mortgage should be offered and at what price. The data simply do not cover "the underwriting factors that are most important to the loan decision, including the lender's assessment of the applicant's credit and employment history, the applicant's assets and debt-to-income and loan-to-value ratios."[12] The HMDA data did not serve a useful purpose throughout their history until 2010, despite the numerous analyses and attempts to improve the data carried out by so many scholars over the years as they tried to interpret the ways in which the mortgage market was developing.

Recent developments

The Wall Street Reform and Consumer Protection Act, perhaps better known as the Dodd-Frank Act, was signed into law on July 21, 2010. Amongst its many provisions relating to the nature and quality of mortgages, it significantly amends the requirements for data to be submitted under the HMDA to include borrower age and gender, credit score, points and fees at origination, the difference between APR for loan and benchmark rate for all loans, and loan features such as prepayment penalties (HMDA amendment, Section 1094).

The Federal Reserve held a series of public hearings throughout the autumn of 2010 to consider the proposed amendments to Regulation C, which covers HMDA reporting. One such hearing was held at the Federal Reserve Bank of Chicago under the chairmanship of Elisabeth Duke, a member of the Board of Governors, with representatives of researchers, credit unions, community banks and other banks, amongst others.[13] The rule-making authority for amendments to Regulation C was still with the Federal Reserve until the new Consumer Financial Protection Bureau was established.

Elizabeth Duke restated the purposes of the HMDA data: namely to show whether or not lenders are serving the housing needs of the neighborhoods and communities in which they are located; to help government target public investment to promote private investment where required; and to help identify discriminatory lending practices. Elizabeth Duke stressed that the time had come to reconsider the purposes of data collection in the light of the financial crisis. However, the contributors, for various reasons, nevertheless all recommended additions which would undoubtedly have assisted with the identification of the development of the subprime market and the risks involved. The Act itself requires the introduction of a universal mortgage identifier, which is essential for tracking the performance of a particular mortgage.

Participants in the hearing had a much clearer idea of the data which lenders should be required to report under Regulation C, including information on foreclosures and loans sold back to lenders on recourse, and a means of identifying reverse mortgages. Listed are the key data which all participants argued should be included:

- Cumulative loan-to-value ratio.

- Total debt-to-income ratio. Some recommended recording the back-end ratio, because it includes other types of monthly debt payment obligations in addition to the mortgage and is a better reflection of the borrower's overall debt burden.

- HMDA origination data linked to other types of mortgage data, especially on loan performance, using the universal loan identification number (required under the Dodd-Frank Act). This would enable analysts (and regulators) to track the performance of loans with different underwriting and product characteristics.

- Information concerning the level of documentation used in underwriting a mortgage, especially with regard to the borrower's income.

- Refinance mortgages, indicating whether it is a cash-out refinance versus a term or rate refinance.

- Data on purchasing loans. Loans originated in low- and moderate-income neighborhoods or to low- and moderate-income borrowers can be purchased by banks from other lending institutions in order to obtain credit on the Community Reinvestment Act lending test. Purchasing lenders do not have to report the same data on purchased loans as they do for directly originated loans. "It is therefore impossible to tell if banks are purchasing higher-cost, potentially abusive loans for which they would get CRA credit. Just to give a sense of scale, in 2006, the tail end of the subprime boom, depository institutions or affiliates purchased over 35,000 conventional home purchase or refinance loans in low- and moderate-income Census tracks in the Chicago region. So there were a substantial number of loans for which banks are likely getting CRA credit that we know little about. Purchased loans should be subject to the same recording requirements as directly originated loans."[14]

- Participants said they would value the introduction of appraisal identification numbers as well as unique broker identification numbers from existing and newly created databases.

- They also made a plea for public access to all the data, and for greater ease of accessibility to data on the websites.

According to the Federal Register, the Bureau published for public comment an interim final rule establishing a new Regulation C (Home Mortgage

Disclosure), but it "does not impose any new substantive obligations on persons subject to the existing Regulation C," apart from those set out in Section 1094 of the Dodd-Frank Act. The final version published in January 2013 raised the exemption limit for the application of Regulation C.

However, under Subtitle B of the Act, Minimum Standards for Mortgages, Section 1411, lending standards do appear to have been tightened. These rule changes came in with the establishment of the Consumer Financial Protection Bureau (CFCB), and it is not yet clear how they will affect the reporting requirements when the responsibility for this is transferred to it from the CFBC. Under the provisions for the ability to repay loans, lenders would not be able to make residential mortgage loans unless they make a "good faith determination, based on verified and documented information, that at the time the loan was consummated, the consumer had reasonable ability to pay the loan according to its terms, and all applicable taxes, insurance and assessments. It also provides that nothing in the title should be construed as requiring the depository institution to apply mortgage underwriting standards that do not need minimum underwriting standards required by the appropriate regulator of the depository."

The lender is now required to assess the consumer's ability to repay a residential mortgage loan, based on his or her credit history, current and expected income which s/he is reasonably assured of receiving, current obligations, debt-to-income ratio or residual income after paying non-mortgage debt and mortgage-related obligations, employment status and any other financial resources beyond the equity in the property s/he proposes to buy. The income must be verified by tax returns, payroll receipts or any relevant third-party documents. If the income is properly documented, the lender may also consider seasonality and irregularity of income in the underwriting process. The lender must also consider the consumer's ability to repay using a payment schedule fully amortizing the loan over its term.

The new legislation does exempt certain streamlined loans made, guaranteed or insured by federal departments or agencies from verification requirements as long as certain conditions are met, such as the borrower not being more than 30 days behind on the existing loan; refinancing does not increase the principal balance outstanding on the prior loan except for fees and charges allowed by the department or agency making, guaranteeing or insuring the refinancing. There are also rules regarding such loans, limiting the extent of the fees and points, the interest rate, which must be lower than the interest rate of the original loan, the refinancing, which must be fully amortized in accordance with the department or agency regulations, and ruling out balloon repayments, amongst others.

The criteria for a qualified mortgage are also set out in Section 1412 of the legislation, which allows the lender and any assignee of a residential mortgage loan subject to liability under title to presume that the loan meets the "ability to repay" requirement if it is a "qualified mortgage", that is, if it meets the following conditions:

- If regular repayments do not result in an increase in the principal, and, apart from balloon loans under specified circumstances, does not allow the borrower to defer the principal;

- Except for balloon loans under specified circumstances, does not include a balloon payment that is twice as large as the average of earlier specified payments;

- For which the income and financial resources of the borrower are verified and documented;

- For fixed rate loans, underwriting based on a payment schedule fully amortizing the loan over the loan term and taking into account all applicable taxes, insurance and assessments;

- For adjustable rate loans, underwriting based on the maximum rate permitted under the loan during the first five years, a payment schedule that fully amortizes the loan over the loan term and takes into account all applicable taxes, insurance and assessments;

- Complies with guidelines or regulations established by CFPB relating to ratios of total monthly debt to income or alternative measures of the ability to pay regular expenses after payment of total monthly debt, taking into account the income of the borrower and such other factors CFPB considers relevant and consistent with its purposes;

- For which total points and fees payable in connection with the loan do not exceed 3% of the total loan amount;

- For which the loan term does not exceed 30 years, except as such terms may be extended by CFPB, such as in high-cost areas; and

- In the case of a reverse mortgage, one which meets the standards for a qualified mortgage.

Prepayment penalties are to be phased out for qualified mortgages and are prohibited for all mortgages which are not qualified mortgages. There is an exception for government loans in that HUD, Veterans Administration and the Agriculture and Rural Housing Service, together with the CFPB, prescribe the rules defining the type of loans they insure, guarantee or administer that are qualified mortgages but which may not conform to the rules above.

Apart from the rules governing mortgages, there are new rules governing the activities of appraisers and mortgage brokers, who are now included in the definition of mortgage originators. They must be qualified and licensed, if applicable, in accordance with the relevant state or federal law.

In July 2011, the responsibility for Regulation C was transferred to the newly established Consumer Financial Protection Bureau (CFPB). The new Regulation C substantially duplicates the Federal Reserve's Regulation C and does not impose any important new requirements, but only adds a few technical revisions of no particular significance, in terms of data that would help regulators understand developments in the mortgage market. The Bureau will be financed from the fees received by the Federal Reserve, rather than Congressional appropriations, but already disagreements over the cost may mean that the Bureau receives $80m in set-up funds instead of the $134m in the President's Budget. Professor Elizabeth Warren, who was charged with establishing the CFPB, referred to caps on the dedicated funding that currently governs it, and pointed out that "it would take nearly twenty years to invest as much money in protecting consumers and consumer financial markets as it cost the government to resolve IndyMac, a single institution that failed in the financial crisis of 2008."[15]

Subprime mortgages

As has been established, for much of the period between 1995 and 2008, it was argued that there was no generally accepted definition of "prime" and "subprime" mortgages in the market place, or amongst analysts and perhaps even regulators. Without an agreed definition, it was difficult, if not impossible, to assess the growth and development of the subprime market. It was easy and useful to all the parties involved to base their analyses on the two identifiers the HMDA offered, that is, the number of mortgages offered by the lenders who chose to identify themselves as subprime lenders in the years up to 2004, and then to identify "subprime" mortgages as higher-priced mortgages with all the difficulties of identification that involved.

Another method of identifying subprime lending is to focus on the attributes of the borrower, regardless of the lender involved. In a joint proposal to provide guidance to the financial institutions that engage in subprime lending, the agencies involved in supervising them, that is, the Office of Thrift Supervision*, the Office of the Comptroller of the Currency, the Federal Deposit Insurance Corporation, and the Board of Governors of the Federal Reserve System, decided that "subprime" referred to the credit characteristics of individual borrowers.

> Subprime borrowers typically have weakened credit histories that include payment delinquencies, and possibly more severe problems such as 'charge-offs', judgments, and bankruptcies. They may also display reduced repayment capacity as measured by credit scores, debt-to-income ratios, or other criteria that may

---

*Notes to state that the Office of Thrift Supervision ceased to exist in October, 2011, when it was merged with the Office of the Comptroller of the Currency. (OCC).

encompass borrowers with incomplete credit histories. Such loans have a higher risk of default than loans to prime borrowers. Generally, subprime borrowers will display a range of credit risk characteristics that may include one or more of the following:

- Two or more 30-day delinquencies in the last 12 months, or one or more delinquencies in the last 24 months;

- Judgment, foreclosure, repossession or charge-off in the prior 24 months;

- Bankruptcy in the last 5 years;

- Relatively high default probability as evidenced by, for example, a credit bureau risk score (FICO) of 660 or below (depending on the product/collateral), or other bureau or proprietary scores with an equivalent default probability likelihood; and/or

- Debt service-to-income ratio of 50% or greater, or otherwise limited ability to cover family living expenses after deducting total monthly debt-to-service requirements from monthly income.

The agencies add the caveat that the "list is illustrative, not exhaustive and is not meant to define specific parameters for all subprime borrowers," which is interesting as it does not include any reference to verification of income and employment, including future expectations of employment.[16] By March, 2007, in a Proposed Statement on Subprime Mortgage Lending, also issued by the agencies, they state that the term "subprime" is "defined" in the Expanded Guidance.[17] So by then the agencies regarded subprime lending as being defined by borrower characteristics, perhaps most succinctly defined as a FICO credit score of 660 and below. In its review of non-prime mortgage conditions in the United States, the Federal Reserve Bank of New York stated that "typically a FICO score of 660 or above is required to obtain prime financing."[18]

It is noteworthy, first, that the reference to the FICO score was not recognized in HMDA data and tended to be ignored by analysts; and secondly, that the other aspects of subprime loans were not recognized as being part of the nature of the subprime, or riskier, loan, namely, the combined loan to value of the property at the time of the mortgage origination, and the nature of the loan. Yet in their analysis of credit risk of July 1996, Robert Avery and others recognized the significance not only of FICO scores but also of high LTV ratios, which were much more likely to default, even with conventional mortgages. An analysis of 450,000 loans originated over the period from 1975 to 1983 showed that LTV ratios at origination in the range of 91–95% default more than twice as often as LTVs of 81–90% and more than five times as often as loans with LTVs in the range of 71–80%.[19] A full understanding of the borrower's credit rating, high LTV ratios and the nature of the loan as serious risk factors is shown, belatedly, in the contents of the Dodd-Frank Act.

If the fact that the combination of low FICO scores and high LTVs was known to increase the risks of default and foreclosure for so long, then why did Congress and the regulators allow subprime borrowing to take place for well over a decade? The answer lies partly in the way in which the statistics were collected and analysed, and partly because other definitions of subprime lending were used (such as higher-priced loans). In fact, they concealed the true extent of subprime lending.

The Guidance issued by the regulators in 2001 was designed to expand the previously issued examination guidance for supervising subprime lending in 1999. In the introduction, the agencies stated that they continued "to believe that responsible subprime lending can expand credit access for consumers and offer attractive returns. However, we expect institutions to recognize that elevated levels of credit and other risks arising from these activities require more intensive risk management, and, more often, additional capital."[20]

The benefits of what should have been described as subprime loans were emphasized at every level, both politically and within government agencies. The view that mortgages should be made available to low- to moderate-income families and minorities as part of the overriding commitment to the American dream of home ownership for all pervaded every aspect of government and almost the entire political class. In April 2005, Alan Greenspan, then Chairman of the Federal Reserve System, praised the "improved access to credit ... [which] has had significant benefits ... Home ownership is at a record high and the number of home mortgage loans to low- and moderate-income and minority families has risen rapidly over the past five years."[21] Where the risks were recognized, it was assumed that they could be managed.

Instead, the risks were ignored. The extent of the growth of the subprime market was not observed, because there was no means of observing it. Neither was there a will to see and understand what was happening, because too many legislators, policy makers and regulators either believed or thought it prudent to believe that lending to low- and moderate-income borrowers and minorities was a "good thing," as it extended home-ownership opportunities to those who would not otherwise be able to share in the American dream. Analysts lacked the raw data to be able to describe what was happening, and no amount of applying sophisticated modeling techniques would replace such a lack of data. Articles which began by stating that, based on HMDA data, such and such a conclusion could be reached, should, unfortunately, be disregarded, since it was not possible to arrive at any conclusion even about the extent of racial discrimination based on such information. Even combining it with LP or MBA data did not help, because they were not collected in the same way; nor is it possible to be sure that sets of raw data were about the same sets of mortgages.

The way forward is to review all minimum standards for mortgages (which includes fully documented and verified information that the borrower at that time had a reasonable ability to repay the loans according to its terms), the additional HMDA requirements, and the Dodd-Frank Act's mandatory requirement that a publicly available mortgage data base should be created. The reference in Section 1447 is to a default and disclosure data base, recording the number and percentage of loans that are delinquent by more than 30 days, 90 days, that are real-estate owned, and that are in foreclosure. This and such other information that the Secretary of Housing and the new Consumer Protection Bureau require shall be recorded in the data base.

The Uniform Mortgage Data Program was announced in May 2011, when the FHFA directed the GSEs to develop uniform standards for data reporting on mortgage loans and appraisals, designed to improve the consistency, quality and uniformity of data collected at the front-end of the mortgage process. This should improve the quality of the mortgage purchases and thus reduce the repurchase risk for originators. The FHFA Director argued that developing standard terms, definitions and industry-wide data-reporting protocols will also create new efficiencies for originators and appraisers.[22] It is not clear how this fits in with the revised HMDA data. What is clear, however, is that data collection is primarily of interest and importance to the prudential supervisor, as the huge number of subprime mortgages led to the collapse or forced takeovers of so many banks and thrifts. Further clarity on the function of a publicly accessible data base is required, and once again the proposals on the table are still affected by the "affordable housing" ideology and concerns with lending to minorities and low-income families, rather than on the price that all will have to pay if there is another surge in subprime lending in the future.

5

The "Mission Regulator" for Fannie Mae and Freddie Mac

A brief introduction

The Housing and Urban Development Department (HUD) was established as the "mission regulator" for Fannie Mae and Freddie Mac under the Federal Housing Enterprises Financial Safety and Soundness Act (FHEFSSA), 1992. The Act made HUD responsible for setting the GSEs' affordable housing goals, including monitoring and enforcing them, and with overall oversight authority to ensure that they complied with the public purposes of their charters. This included approving new programs; collecting loan-level data from the GSEs on their mortgage purchase activities; making available to the public a data base of non-proprietary GSE loan-purchase information; reviewing and commenting on the GSEs' underwriting guidelines; and ensuring GSE compliance with fair lending requirements. HUD also had "general regulatory powers" over the GSEs and was required to "make such rules and regulations as shall be necessary and proper to ensure" that the Act's provisions and the GSEs' charters were fulfilled; this included meeting the requirements of the Fair Lending Act (it was HUD's responsibility to review their appraisal and underwriting guidelines to that effect). In addition, the Office of Federal Housing Enterprise Oversight (OFHEO), an independent office of HUD, regulated the GSEs for safety and soundness. OFHEO was responsible for ensuring that the GSEs were adequately capitalized and operated their businesses in a "safe and sound manner." HUD was not confined to oversight of the GSEs, but was responsible for a wide and ever-changing range of public housing programs, and voucher schemes for privately rented housing.

Setting the housing goals

This was HUD's most important activity as far as the GSEs were concerned. The refinements to the Community Reinvestment Act (CRA) were the first step in increasing home purchase for minorities and low- to moderate-income families, as discussed in previous chapters. The second step was to use the GSEs, originally set up after the Great Depression to bring liquidity to the market, which they did by purchasing loans directly from private mortgage originators, such as mortgage bankers and depository institutions, and then either holding these loans in portfolio or selling them in mortgage-backed securities (MBSs), which are then sold into the capital markets to a wide range of investors. When the GSEs bought loans, they assumed the credit risk, and charged guaranty fees by way of compensation for the credit risk they assumed, as they guaranteed timely payment of both the interest and the principal. They guaranteed that the loan would be paid on time, at a time when prepayment risk was thought to be a more serious risk than credit risk; these risks were then taken on by Fannie and Freddie when they purchased the loans. Having passed on the risks by paying the guaranty fee, the lender then had the resources to provide more mortgages. In this way, the liquidity of the mortgage market was assured.

The Act and the Administration then decided what proportion of loans should be made by lenders to minorities and low- to median-income families, by laying down the percentage of loans made to such categories that Fannie and Freddie had to purchase. Since the GSEs had to buy the loans, lenders could afford to lend, supplying millions of loans to minorities and to low- to medium-income borrowers, secure in the knowledge that they had passed on the risks. The politicians, on the other hand, thought that their main concerns were being met: banks were no longer taking monies from low-income and underserved borrowers and transferring them to more affluent neighborhoods; they were lending to the underserved areas and helping many more achieve the American dream.

By 1998, HUD estimated that 11.7m homes were financed by "conventional conforming" mortgages, and that the GSEs provided financing for each of these homes. "Conventional" mortgages exclude loans which are insured by the Federal Housing Administration, the Rural Housing Administration or the Veterans Administration. "Conforming" loans refers not to the structure or characteristics of such loans, but to the level of the unpaid principal balance, which must be no greater than the maximum allowable under the GSEs' charter acts. In 2000, that limit was $252,700 for single-family homes in most parts of the USA, and the limit was raised from time to time as house prices rose. The proportion of mortgages financed by the GSEs continued to grow: they came to dominate the market, but it was a gradual process.

A cautious approach at first

"The housing goals play an important role in encouraging mortgage originators to undertake more affordable lending." So stated HUD in its Issue Brief of January 2001.[1] The department set the transitional goals for 1993–95 before the goals were revised, and the "final rule" GSE housing goals were established for 1996–99. This transition period was important since, according to Senator Alfonse M. D'Amato, "It's critical that these goals are not unrealistic or unfeasible, because defaults are counterproductive for everyone." There were both penalties and incentives. The penalties for failing to reach the stated goals involved explaining to the Secretary of State why they failed, or having to file an "affordable housing plan" setting out how it was planned to meet these goals in the future.

The incentives were bonus points for the purchase of two types of mortgages: small multi-family properties, or single-family rental properties. HUD also established a "temporary adjustment factor" for Freddie Mac, whereby each goal-qualifying unit in a large multi-family property counted as 1.35 units in the numerator and 1 unit in the denominator, in calculating goal performance. This was introduced by Congress because it was thought that Freddie Mac was disadvantaged in the multi-family market in the early 1990s. It appears that this did have an effect on the small multi-family mortgage purchases between 2001 and 2003. It was withdrawn in 2003.

Defining the affordable housing goals

The focus of HUD's activity was the affordable housing goals, which had to be defined according to the categories established by Congress. As with the CRA requirements, it is difficult to explain the nature of the affordable housing goals without providing a brief summary of rules of mind-boggling complexity. The commitment to the goals has to be seen in the context of the National Homeownership Strategy, announced by President Clinton in 1995 and for which Henry Cisneros worked so assiduously during his time as Secretary for Housing from 1993 to 1997.

The legislation itself called for three broad categories, which were defined in HUD's regulations as follows:

- A low- and moderate-income goal, for families with incomes below area median income;
- A special affordable goal, for very low-income families and low-income families in low-income areas;
- An underserved areas goal, originally established by Congress as a central cities goal, with authority for HUD to broaden the definition of underserved areas.

The "special affordable goal" was designed to meet the "unaddressed needs of low-income families in low-income areas, and very low-income families, for suitable housing." This category was defined in the 1992 Act as: "(i) 45% shall be mortgages of low-income families who live in census tracts in which the median income does not exceed 80% of the area median income; and (ii) 55% shall be mortgages of the very low income families." The Act initially required the GSEs to spend "not less than 1% of the dollar amount of the mortgage purchases by the GSEs for the previous year;" this requirement was increased substantially by HUD in later years, and, unsurprisingly, it was a difficult target for them to meet.

It is useful to have some indication of the meaning of the income requirements. Although the definitions themselves are not stated in dollars, but in relative terms, they do give some indication of just how low the incomes on which Congress, government and others expected families to sustain a mortgage. A low income is defined as not more than 80% of the median income in a metropolitan statistical area or county; a very low income is 50% or less of the median income; and an extremely low income is less than 30% of the median income. Given the wide variation in wages and salary levels in the USA, a national average wage is not a helpful concept. Instead, it might be useful to set these percentages again the national "poverty line" for a family of four, which has generally been taken to be about 40–45% of the national median household income since 1993.

The generally accepted definition of "affordable housing" is that it should be less than 30% of a family's annual gross income (including taxes and insurance for home owners, and often utility costs as well); above that level, the family is considered to be "cost-burdened." Given that, it is hard to see how "affordable" for families with very low incomes could be achieved without the mortgages exceeding 30% of a family's annual income in the years between 1996 and 2008, especially when the sharp rise in housing costs relative to income is taken into account.

The housing goals HUD set out for the GSEs in that period required them to purchase a certain percentage of loans in each category. The percentages increased over the period, every three to four years. All three of the housing goals are expressed as minimum goal-qualifying percentages of all units purchased by each GSE in a calendar year, with the GSEs calculating their performance, and then submitting their loan-level data to HUD, which then analyses these to determine the "official goal performance." The latter is calculated annually. In 1996, HUD also established dollar-based multi-family subgoals, and then in 2004, home purchase subgoals for GSE acquisitions of home purchase mortgages on owner-occupied single-family homes for each of the categories covered by the overall housing goals. In each case the goals described below refers to the purchases of the mortgages, as Fannie Mae and Freddie Mac operated only in the secondary market, not the primary market.

Setting the affordable housing goals

Goals for 1996–2000

(A) The low- and moderate-income (LM) goal: at least 40% of the dwelling units purchased by each GSE had to be for LM families in 1996, and this rose to 42% for 1997–2000.

(B) The special affordable (SA) goal: at least 12% of the units purchased by each GSE had to be for SA families in 1996, rising to 14% for 1997–2000.

(C) The underserved areas (UA) goal: at least 21% of the units purchased by each GSE had to be for families in UAs in 1996, and the goal rose to 24% for 1997–2000.

(D) The special affordable multi-family (SAMF) subgoal: for each year 1996–2000, Freddie Mac had to purchase at least $0.99 billion in special affordable multi-family housing, and Fannie Mae had to finance at least $1.29bn.[2]

In selecting these goals, Secretary Henry Cisneros, anxious as he was to increase home ownership for blacks and Hispanics, and having identified national housing needs, found that the housing goal regulations were necessary to meet these needs. He decided that many Americans were unable to afford adequate housing due to insufficient incomes, high debt levels and rising home prices. The way forward was to ensure that they had a much larger role in promoting affordable housing. Establishing these specific goals was a departure from the way in which the GSEs had operated up until then. The proposals were published on February 16, 1995 and received 163 responses from the industry, Fannie Mae and Freddie Mac (about 200 pages each, mostly strongly opposed), community organizations, Members of Congress, local and state governments, non-profit organizations, governors and mayors. The final rules took the comments into account, but still established housing goals that were much greater than the transitional rules and "will ensure that the GSEs continue and strengthen their efforts to carry out Congress's intent that the GSEs provide the benefits of a secondary market to families throughout the Nation."[3]

HUD's research, as reported in the Federal Register, concluded that "almost three-fifths of American households qualify as low- and moderate-income under FHEFSSA's definitions. Data from the Census and from the American Housing Surveys demonstrate that housing problems and needs for affordable housing are indeed substantial among low- and moderate-income families. These households, particularly those with very low incomes, are burdened with high rent payments and are likely to continue to face serious housing problems, given the dim prospects for earnings growth in entry-level occupations."[4]

Cisneros apparently interpreted the Act to mean that the GSEs should "lead the industry" by using their dominant position to help ensure additional affordable mortgage originations. They should also provide technical assistance for mortgage originators so that they would also extend mortgages to targeted groups and provide financial standards for the industry. The goals he set were with the safety and soundness of the GSEs in mind, and were in fact conservatively set below HUD's estimates of the targeted mortgage originations already occurring in the primary market.[5] He might have been cautious in terms of numbers, but the context meant that underwriting standards were lowered, especially with regard to down payments and the borrower's credit history, or lack of one. HUD acknowledged that mortgages to be purchased by Fannie and Freddie in "underserved" areas had a higher risk of default, but this did not mean that there was a "safety and soundness impediment" to the policy.[6] Other concerns were the heightened credit risk associated with increased multi-family mortgage purchase volumes, and the feasibility of the goals overall. Taking the likely default implications of the goals into account, HUD concluded that they implied no meaningful increase in risk to the sound financial condition of the GSEs' operations.[7] Fannie Mae and Freddie Mac did respond to the goals, and in the case of Fannie Mae, quite quickly. In a press briefing in 1996, Cisneros responded to a journalist's question, "We're working with Fannie Mae and Freddie Mac-to do things they can do to indicate to the banks that have a lower down payment. Fannie Mae has this 97 and 3 – 3% down payment program that they've innovated over the last year."[8] The significance here is that the Secretary for Housing apparently approved of down payments as low as 3%.

Henry Cisneros was not there to see it through. He resigned after admitting that he had lied to the FBI about money he had paid to a former mistress, following a four-year investigation which cost over $9m. He agreed to a $10,000 fine and a $25 court assessment, following which he was free to pursue other careers, including elected office.

In 2000, Cisneros formed a housing development partnership with KB Homes, and became a director along with James Johnson, former CEO of Fannie Mae, which bought many of the mortgages used for developing these homes. It was "a cozy network ... Fannie's biggest mortgage client was Countrywide;"[9] in 2001, Cisneros joined the board of Countrywide, supporting its $1 trillion dollar commitment, the We House America Challenge, announced in February 2005. He resigned from the board on October 18, 2007, saying he needed to spend more time as Chairman of CityView to "put the company in the best position to adjust to the demands of the period ahead." He also stated that Countrywide was a "well-managed company" and that he had "enormous confidence" in its leadership, including its Chief Executive, Angelo Mozilo.[10]

On October 26, 2007, Countywide reported a $1bn loss for the third quarter, much larger than Wall Street expected, but predicted that it would soon return to profitability.[11] It did not.

Andrew Cuomo becomes Secretary for Housing

Following Henry Cisneros's resignation, Andrew Cuomo, who had been Assistant Secretary for Housing since 1993, was appointed as Secretary for Housing in 1997 and remained in that position until 2001.[12] Cuomo was an energetic Secretary, who realised the value of the position in advancing his political career. His administration issued 302 press releases in 2000, almost one a day, and spent almost $1m on brochures dealing with HUD's work, which inevitably highlighted his position, strategies and achievements. When he entered the gubernatorial race for New York, not surprisingly he made 25 official visits to the state, 21 more than to any other.

In January 2001, Cuomo issued a press release entitled, "Success of HUD Management Reforms Confirmed by GAO. Department Removed from High Risk List." It included carefully selected excerpts from the GAO report and cited both the increase in its Budget year on year and the fact that "over the past four years, the staff at HUD have worked tirelessly to ensure that our programs serve the nation's most vulnerable people more efficiently and effectively … We've transformed a monolithic government agency into a model of government reinvention." This was a rosy picture of HUD's achievements, as the GAO report makes clear; in fact, only one program, the Community Planning and Development program, had been removed from the "high risk" category. Whilst recognizing that progress has been made in other areas, such as the re-organization of the department, and some improvements have resulted from the implementation of the 2020 Management Reform Plan, significant weaknesses remain, especially with internal controls, information and financial management systems, organizational deficiencies and staffing problems, particularly in the FHA single-family programs.[13] Even with these efforts, HUD remained a badly managed department, subject to waste, fraud, abuse and mismanagement.

During Cuomo's time, further steps were taken that increased the risks of delinquencies and foreclosures, both in the FHA program, with the introduction of seller down-payment assistance programs as a result of pressures from Nehemiah, and despite the increased risks identified in the OIG audit report.[14] Cuomo did not take any action regarding these risks. The limits for FHA-insured loans were also raised, with the purpose of "creating more homeowners, more home construction, more jobs and more economic growth."[15]

The goals for Fannie and Freddie were raised substantially. Franklin Raines warned that Secretary Cuomo was moving into risky territory, but added,

"We have not been a major presence in the subprime market, but you can bet that under these goals, we will be." He saw that this gave him the cover for moving further into a market in which he was already a player. Secretary Cuomo apparently recognized that the GSE presence in the subprime market could be of significant benefit to lower-income families, minorities and families living in underserved areas. Some see raising the housing goals for low- to moderate-income families as a prime mover in the subprime lending crisis; it may not be quite that, but it undoubtedly played a part as did the failure to impose any new reporting requirements on the GSEs. The goals were agreed but the requirement to provide loan level data was not.

Goals for 2001–2004

The LM (low- to moderate-income) goal was raised to 50%.

The SA (special assistance) goal was increased to 20%, and the dollar-based special affordable multi-family subgoals were also increased for both GSEs.

The US (underserved areas) goal was increased to 31%.

The bonus point and the temporary adjustment system were also introduced for the years 2001–2003.

HUD's failure to require data for its oversight responsibilities

It was HUD's responsibility to monitor the loans the GSEs purchased, not only to ensure that they met their goals, but also to understand the quality of the loans they purchased with a view, for example, ensuring that the GSEs did not receive credit for predatory loans. Under the Federal Housing Enterprises Financial Safety and Soundness Act (FHEFSSA), Congress had indicated that the GSEs' mortgage purchases should be recorded in the GSE public use data base, designed to supplement HMDA data. Such a data base is available, but the data recorded there are carefully structured to exclude information which was considered to be proprietary from other loan level data but without geographical indicators. HUD published this data from 1996 onwards. The purpose of the data base was to enable the public, including mortgage lenders, planners, researchers, housing industry groups, HUD and other government agencies, to examine the GSEs' mortgage activities and the flow of mortgage credit and capital into the nation's communities. The changes HUD proposed would have made publicly available the same data at loan level as primary lenders report under HMDA requirements.

The responses HUD received were almost equally divided between those who approved and those who opposed on privacy grounds. It is, however, the GSEs' responses that are the most noteworthy. Both were strongly opposed to increased disclosure, citing "competitive issues" resulting from the release of what each GSE considered to be proprietary, confidential business information. Fannie Mae and Freddie Mac expressed general concern that recording certain loan level data as non-proprietary at either the Census tract level or national file level would reveal information about lender relationships, pricing arrangements, and management of credit and interest rate risks. Fannie Mae also took issue with HUD's efforts to conform data available in the GSE public-use data base to HMDA data for research purposes, contending that "both data bases are fundamentally different and cannot be reconciled."[16] Some of the GSEs' reasons ought to have given cause for concern, but instead HUD announced that based on the comments received, it was not making a determination based on this matter as part of this rule-making. A decision on which matters were proprietary and which were not would be given in a separate order.

However, HUD also noted that the changes included in the final rule involved changes in data-reporting requirements. Some of these changes were significant, such as the identification of units with estimated affordability data mortgage loans receiving bonus points, the temporary adjustment factor and high cost mortgage loans. HUD noted that the Treasury recommended the Federal Reserve should require the collection of such data, including borrower debt-to-income ratio for HOEPA (Home Ownership and Protection Act) loans under HMDA. That happened eventually, but not until 2005. At this point, however, HUD merely noted that if such recommendations were implemented, they might affect the data reporting required under this rule. In March, HUD admitted that the new purchasing pressures on the GSEs might "warrant increased monitoring and additional reporting." But after all the responses had been received, especially those from the GSEs, the introduction of new reporting requirements was postponed. They did not form part of the Final Rule.

HUD also proposed that high-cost mortgages should be disallowed for credit as far as the GSEs were concerned. The definition of "high cost" was also considered, as to whether it should be defined using the HOEPA or an alternative definition. The former defined high cost as having an APR of 10% above the yield on Treasury securities of comparable maturity as well as prepayment penalties, balloon payments, negative amortization and failure to consider the borrower's ability to repay.[17]

The two GSEs announced corporate policies during the consultation period for the Final Rule on their goals for 2001–2003. Fannie Mae announced that it would not purchase high-cost loans as defined under HOEPA, loans with points and fees charged to the borrower at above 5%, except where this would result in an unprofitable origination. In addition, it would not purchase or securitize any mortgage for which a prepaid single premium credit life insurance policy was sold to the borrower, and would not generally allow prepayment penalties if there was some benefit to the borrower (such as a rate or fee reduction) or if the borrower was offered an alternative, amongst other conditions. Fannie Mae also announced that it would not purchase loans from lenders who steered borrowers towards higher-cost loans if they would have qualified for lower-cost products. Freddie Mac made similar but fewer commitments: it decided that it would not purchase HOEPA loans or mortgages with single premium credit life insurance. Despite the GSEs' apparent commitment to distance themselves from predatory lending, HUD noted that their policies lacked important details and were subject to changes in corporate direction. HUD considered that regulations may be required.

The first issue that HUD considered was whether to allow credit to the GSEs for purchases of high-cost mortgages. They and a number of respondents expressing similar views argued that they should be able to purchase legitimate subprime loans; that is, ones without the predatory features, such as prepayment penalties. It is interesting to note Fannie Mae's arguments, especially in view of all that happened in subsequent years. The GSEs argued that they were using their respective automated underwriting systems "to allow them to offer products targeted toward borrowers with impaired credit, and that they were able to move into the legitimate subprime market in a responsible and prudent manner, bringing liquidity, standardization, and efficiency to that market." Not allowing credit for high-cost mortgages would provide a disincentive for them to reach out to those borrowers, and would do nothing to combat predatory lending practices. It would simply drive predatory lending into "secondary market sources who are less responsible than Fannie Mae on this issue." At any rate, tracking high-cost mortgages would be very difficult, if not impossible, "owing to the lack of reliable mortgage data on loan costs."

HUD's response was to determine that the GSEs should not receive any credit for purchasing high-cost loans with unacceptable features, resulting from unacceptable practices. Their statutory responsibility was to lead the industry in making mortgage credit available to low- and moderate-income families, and therefore they should seek to make the lowest-cost credit available, while ensuring that they do not purchase loans that actually harm borrowers and support unfair lending practices. But HUD also quotes their own report, "While the secondary market could be viewed as part of the problem of abusive practices in the subprime mortgage market, it may also represent a large part of the solution to the problem. If the secondary market refuses to purchase loans that carry abusive terms, or loans originated by lenders engaging in abusive practices, the primary market might react to the resulting loss of liquidity by ceasing to make these loans."[18] The restrictions applied both to mortgages purchased through the GSEs' "flow" business as well as to mortgages purchased or guaranteed through structured transactions.

Then the rest of HUD's determinations with regard to these mortgages are illuminating:

> Since these restrictions and provisions are consistent with the GSEs' own measures, the Department does not believe that any of these restrictions will provide a disincentive for the GSEs to provide financing for borrowers with slightly impaired credit through innovative products that can bring competition and efficiencies to the legitimate subprime market.

> While the GSEs themselves will presumably be obtaining certain additional data and information to carry out their previously announced purchase restrictions and to monitor lending practices, HUD is not establishing any requirements for additional data to carry out these provisions under this rule. Subsequently HUD plans to request only such original data as is necessary. In this regard, HUD will consult with the GSEs, as practicable, to develop reasonable data reporting requirements that will not present an undue additional burden.[19]

In this regard, Secretary Cuomo was particularly concerned to ensure that the GSEs were indeed playing their part in ensuring that mortgages were offered to very low-income families, for whom he increased the goal, and to minorities. William Apgar was quoted in the *Washington Post* at the time: "We believe that there are a lot of loans to black Americans that could be safely purchased by Fannie Mae and Freddie Mac if these companies were more flexible."

HUD's lack of oversight and lack of resources

The GSEs had already made it clear that the data available to identify even high-cost loans was not available. In this and previous responses to the GSEs and other respondents, HUD in turn made it entirely clear that, even if at any time it intended to monitor the GSEs' activities in the secondary market, it did not have the resources to do so. In fact, it was quite clear that HUD did not intend to monitor the GSEs as required; and, indeed, that neither HUD nor the GSEs, on their own admission, had the resources or tools to do so.

The GAO published a report in 1998 on HUD's ability to regulate the GSEs.[20] The report first of all referred to the budgetary constraints and the lack of properly qualified staff (often far too few in number) to carry out that task. Apart from the fact that HUD's research resources were insufficient to enable HUD to set the appropriate goals, or to understand the effect of the goals on promoting home ownership and housing opportunities, the most important issues concerned the shortcomings of the data and HUD's failure to address them.

These included the lack of inspections to assess the accuracy of Enterprise-Supplied Goal Compliance Data. This is especially important, since the data the GSEs collect and report to HUD regarding their mortgage purchases come from many sources, are often complex, and can be subject to errors. The data are supplied by the original lenders to borrowers: the lenders in turn give the data to the GSEs when they sell the loans to them, and the GSEs collect the data and report them to HUD. The GSEs were only able to conduct limited tests to check the data, but at that stage, HUD had not established a program to carry out independent checks, nor was OFHEO's verification of the GSEs' data systems and controls linked to that of HUD.

The GAO notes that HUD took the view that the much-vaunted automated underwriting systems introduced by Fannie Mae and Freddie Mac merited further oversight. In 1996, HUD conducted a review and concluded that, although the systems may require a further assessment in terms of fair lending concerns, they were not new mortgage programs; the department concluded that they were alternative business programs and, as such, did not have to be submitted to HUD for approval.

The report was issued in 1998, but, given the nature of HUD's responses with reference to its proposed new rules in 2000, it is highly unlikely that any further work was carried out to ensure the accuracy of the data or the GSEs' use of the automated underwriting system, apart from the Fair Lending issues. The automated underwriting systems, developed in the 1990s, and in which the GSEs were market leaders in their development and implementation, were also adaptable systems. In 2000, Fannie Mae and Freddie Mac decided to increase their efficiency in the purchase of Alt-As (with little or no borrower income and asset documentation) and A-minus (loans made to borrowers who cannot qualify for prime mortgages because of blemished credit, but whose credit is higher than is typically found for a subprime loan) by altering their automated underwriting systems. Fannie Mae implemented the Expanded Credit Approval System, and Freddie Mac the Loan Prospectus System, to accommodate risk-based pricing.

That nothing had changed was confirmed by Allen Fishbein, a general counsel of the Neigborhood Revitalization Project, in an article entitled "Going Subprime."[21] Fishbein was a senior adviser for Government Sponsored Enterprises Oversight at HUD from 1999 to 2000, where he helped supervise the establishment of new affordable housing goals for Fannie Mae and Freddie Mac. "HUD needs to enhance its ability to monitor the increases in GSE subprime loan purchases. While HUD currently collects loan level data about GSE loan level purchases, this reporting at present does not provide the detail about pricing and loan terms needed to permit effective monitoring activity. Are the GSEs in compliance with their own standards and HUD rules regarding the purchase of loans with predatory features? Are subprime borrowers benefiting from a larger GSE role? These are questions the agency should have the necessary information to answer ... It is ironic that with all the talk in Washington about investor need for transparency about the capital market activities of the GSEs, the discussion does not extend to finding ways to improve the monitoring of their loan purchase activity."[22]

Fishbein also describes the reasons for the GSEs to expand into the subprime market. Their traditional market of conventional prime mortgages had matured and they were looking for new ways to sustain the previous decade's economic success and investor expectations. It was a relatively untapped (for them) but a growing market. It is small wonder, then, that the CEO of Fannie Mae at that time, Franklin Raines, welcomed the goals and the possibility of being recognised as a major player in the subprime market.

In 2000, when introducing the goals for 2001–2004, HUD concluded that the GSEs were in a strong position to handle the increased "affordable lending" goals. "A wide variety of quantitative and qualitative indicators indicate that the GSEs have the financial strength to improve their affordable lending performance. For example, their combined net income has risen steadily over the last decade, from $677m in 1987 to $6.1bn in 1999, an average growth rate of 20% per year. This financial strength provides the GSEs with the resources to lead the industry in supporting mortgage lending for properties located in geographically targeted areas."[23]

There were no further assessments of HUD's oversight of the GSEs or of its inability to carry out this task throughout the whole of the following decade. Fannie Mae and Freddie Mac continued to purchase loans and keep a large and growing proportion in their portfolios, but there was no way of knowing what they had purchased.

No changes for the GSEs with a new Secretary for Housing

With the change in the Administration in 2001, President George Bush appointed as Housing Secretary Mel Martiniz, who had spent two years as head of Orlando's housing authority in the 1980s and two further years as Orange County's Chief Executive before taking up the HUD position. The American Dream Down Payment Initiative was introduced in December 2003, which provided up to $200m annually to help low-income, first-time buyers with down-payment and closing costs. HUD finalized a rule to protect home buyers from predatory lending practices; in this case from fraudulent appraisers, by making lenders accountable for the appraisals performed by the appraisers they hire. This applied particularly to appraisals of properties to be used as security for the FHA-insured mortgages. He is also thought to have quietly opposed the proposal for a National Affordable Housing Trust Fund financed by the federal mortgage insurance surpluses. Martinez announced his candidacy for the Senate for his home state of Florida in December 2003, and resigned from his Cabinet post.

Alphonso Jackson becomes Secretary for Housing

Jackson had already been appointed Deputy Secretary for HUD in 1991 and was acting Secretary for Housing when nominated by President Bush in January 2004, following Mel Matinez's resignation. He had been Chief Executive of the housing authority of Dallas and later President of the Texas General Services Commission. In response to OFHEO's Special Examination, Jackson announced a review of Fannie and Freddie's investments in June 2006, when speaking to a Congressional caucus, but the outcome of the review was never published. In so far as any action was taken to reduce the portfolios, that was in the hands of OFHEO.[24] He can however take credit for some advances with the management of HUD, since in January 2007 the GAO took HUD off the "high risk" list; this was the first time since 1994 that none of the HUD programs was on that list. Jackson stated, "HUD serves the nation best when all its programs are working effectively and efficiently."[25]

However, as with previous Secretaries for Housing, Jackson failed to understand the risks involved in extending affordable housing loans, and the risks accumulating in the programs for which HUD had the oversight. The GAO warned about the risks involved in zero down payments: its report of July 2007 pointed out that if the risk-based pricing proposal had been in force in 2005, then 20% of borrowers would not have qualified for FHA insurance. Without any program changes, the FHA estimated then that the fund would require an appropriation of approximately $143m in 2008. The GAO added that "the proposal to lower down payments is of particular concern given the greater default risk of these loans … One of the ways in which FHA plans to mitigate new or increased risks is through stricter underwriting standards, but it does not plan to pilot any zero-down payment product. Other mortgage institutions use pilots to manage the risks associated with changing or expanding product lines."[26] The increase in the housing goals for the GSEs, which was resisted at first, turned out to be another huge error in the context of the changing mortgage market and the GSEs' purchases of subprime loans. By mid-2007, HUD's attention was inevitably focused on preventing foreclosures.

Secretary Jackson faced calls for his resignation in 2008, arising from allegations that he improperly directed his staff to steer federal housing contracts to political allies. Senate Banking Committee Chairman Christopher Dodd stated in a letter to President Bush on March 21, 2008 that Jackson was "unfit" to run the agency during a national housing crisis, and added in a further statement that he hoped for a "change in policy that brings real solutions to the housing crisis that has triggered this economic recession." Jackson had favored an industry-led program that would encourage lenders to voluntarily refinance troubled loans rather than using federal funds to deal with the crisis.[27] He resigned on March 31, 2008. Two years later, it was announced that the Justice Department had ended its investigations without charges. HUD's Inspector General had previously concluded that Jackson had not exercized any improper influence over contracts.[28]

Goals for 2005–2008

The new rule was finally published in November, 2004 to take effect on January 1, 2005. It differed from previous rules in that it proposed increasing the goals for each year between 2005 and 2008:

Low to Moderate Incomes (LMs) 52% in 2005; 53% in 2006; 55% in 2007; and 57% in 2008.

Special Affordable Goals (SAs) 22% in 2005; 23% in 2006; 25% in 2007; and 27% in 2008.

Underserved areas (US) 37% in 2005; 38% in 2006; 38% in 2007; and 39% in 2008.

In addition, the GSEs minimum special affordable multi-family subgoals were increased to $5.49bn per year for 2005–2008 for Fannie Mae, and to $3.92bn per year for 2005–2008 for Freddie Mac. The Final Rule (which takes up about 50 pages in the Federal Register) contained some interesting additional requirements. These included further regulations preventing the GSEs from double counting mortgage purchases; that is, counting ones in the current year that it had already counted in the previous year. It also prevents the GSEs from counting mortgage purchases where the seller has an option to dissolve the transaction so that credit can only be received when the seller's option is limited by a one-year lockout period.

The other two requirements provide an insight into the way in which the GSEs may have conducted the business of buying mortgages, based on the fact that the new rules are designed to prevent certain transactions. These include measures for dealing with missing borrower income data, and also to ensure the "integrity of data, information and reports provided to HUD by the GSEs, including a requirement that the GSEs submit a certification with certain reports provided to HUD and providing mechanisms for addressing material errors, omissions and discrepancies in current and prior year data submissions."[29] The fact that such rules had to be put in place does tend to undermine the credibility of GSE reporting.

HUD pushed for these more ambitious goals, despite the fact that many doubted such goals could be achieved in a high-refinance period in which higher-income home owners would represent a larger share of the market. HUD's original proposals for 2006 through to 2008 were (apart from one case) reduced by 1% for the years 2006–2008. However, the Housing Secretary, Alphonso Jackson, stated: "These new affordable housing goals will help the GSEs achieve the standard that Congress intended, leading the mortgage finance industry in helping low- and moderate-income families afford decent housing. These new goals will push the GSEs to genuinely lead the market."[30]

HUD's aims and the GSEs

What was the nature of the progress which Secretary Jackson and other Secretaries of State before him wished to achieve? That was set out in an early Issues Brief, provided by HUD, which points out that "given the dominant role of the GSEs in the mortgage market, the housing goals play an important role in encouraging mortgage originators to undertake more affordable lending." The brief reaches the conclusion that "lower-income and minority families have made major gains in access to the mortgage markets in the 1990s. A variety of reasons have accounted for these gains, including improved housing affordability, enhanced enforcement of the Community Reinvestment Act, *more flexible mortgage underwriting*, and stepped-up enforcement of the Fair Housing Act. But most industry observers believe that one factor behind these gains has been the improved performance of Fannie Mae and Freddie Mac under HUD's affordable lending goals. HUD's recent increases in the goals for 2001–2003 will encourage the GSEs to further step up their support for affordable lending."[31]

When HUD again increased the affordable housing goals for Fannie Mae and Freddie Mac in 2004, it responded extensively to the results of the consultation preceding the introduction of the rules. These had to be approved by Congress before their introduction in November of that year. In its response to comments on the consequences of the goals for the subprime market, HUD replied that: "The GSEs' presence in the subprime market benefits many low- to moderate-income families, whose risk profiles differ markedly form borrowers who qualify for prime mortgage products. Millions of Americans with less than perfect credit or who cannot meet some of the tougher underwriting requirements of the prime market for reasons such as inadequate income documentation, limited down-payment or cash reserves, or the desire to take out more cash in a refinancing than conventional loans allow, rely on subprime lenders for access to mortgage financing. If the GSEs reach deeper into the subprime market, more borrowers will benefit from the advantages that greater stability and standardization create."

Later in the same document, HUD stated that, "While the GSEs can choose any strategy for leading the market, the leadership role can likely be accomplished by building on the many initiatives and programs that the enterprises have already started, including:

(i)   Their outreach to underserved markets and their partnership efforts that encourage mainstream lenders to move into these markets.

(ii) Their incorporation of greater flexibility into their purchase and underwriting guidelines.

(iii) Their development of new products for borrowers with little cash for the down payment and for borrowers with credit blemishes or non-traditional credit histories.

(iv) Their use of automated underwriting technology to qualify creditworthy borrowers that would not have been deemed creditworthy under traditional underwriting rules.

In the past, HUD added that the GSEs have always lagged behind the primary market in financing mortgages for low- to moderate-income borrowers, but "over the past three years, Fannie Mae has closed its historical gap in the market and now leads the primary market in funding mortgages for low- to moderate-income borrowers."[32]

But HUD ignored the risks

Ignored the results of its own analyses

HUD commissioned research in 2005 on "Recent House Price Trends and Home Ownership Affordability," which examined amongst other issues, the impact of various factors on the demand for housing, and concluded that one of the significant factors was indeed the role of HUD. It stated that "more liberal financing has contributed to the increase in demand for housing. During the 1990s, lenders have been encouraged by HUD and banking regulators to increase lending to low-income and minority households. The Community Reinvestment Act, Home Mortgage Disclosure Act, the GSEs and fair lending laws have strongly encouraged mortgage brokers and lenders to market to low-income borrowers and minority borrowers. Sometimes these borrowers are higher risk, with blemished credit histories and high debt or simply not enough savings for a down payment. Lenders have responded with low down-payment loan products and automated underwriting, which has allowed them to more carefully determine the risk of the loan. Other factors that have facilitated liberal financing include low and falling interest rates, low default rates, rising house prices, competition from subprime lenders and strong investor demand for mortgage-backed securities. The net effect has been a booming mortgage market that has generated strong demand for housing, which in turn, has boosted house prices."[33]

It is therefore quite clear that HUD did foster the growth of subprime and other forms of high-risk lending from the early 1990s onwards. HUD could only extend lending to low- and moderate-income groups by lowering underwriting standards. That has been seen in the preceding chapters through the FHA, the GSEs and every other aspect of the mortgage market over which HUD had influence. Successive Secretaries for Housing pursued the same policies, which is hardly surprising since these were set out by President Clinton and then by President Bush throughout most of his term. Republicans in the Senate began to be concerned about the GSEs in 2004, and before the end of his Presidency, the Bush Administration had to put the GSEs into conservatorship, when the housing market collapsed in 2008.

HUD was committed to the "affordable housing" ideology

HUD believed it had achieved the change in mortgage lending it had been seeking by 2004, when in the Federal Register, it stated that "over the past ten years, there has been a 'revolution in affordable lending' that has extended home ownership opportunities to historically underserved households. Fannie Mae and Freddie Mac have been a substantial part in this 'revolution in affordable lending'. During the mid-to-late 1990s, they added flexibility to their underwriting guidelines, introduced new low down-payment products, and worked to expand the use of automated underwriting in evaluating the credit worthiness of loan applicants. HMDA data suggest that the industry and the GSE initiatives are increasing the flow of credit to underserved borrowers. Between 1993 and 2003, conventional loans (not insured by the FHA or guaranteed by the VA) increased at a much faster rate than loans to upper income and nonminority families."[34] That, however, did not stop HUD from pushing for yet more loans to these groups.

HUD's determination to push for the GSEs to attain the higher goals set for them is shown in the discussion regarding subgoals and other matters in the Federal Register. For example, with reference to the Special Affordable Housing Goal Multi-Family Subgoals expressed in terms of minimum dollar volumes, HUD wished to retain these goals, but the GSEs were not anxious to do so, this despite the fact that the GSEs had exceeded these targets every year, reaching $12.2bn in 2003 for Fannie Mae (twice its minimum subgoal in every year since 1997); Freddie Mac's performance outstripped Fannie Mae's, reaching $21.5bn in the same year. Only one multi-family lender demurred, expressing his concern that increasing this goal would "push the GSEs to extend credit to unqualified borrowers with poor quality properties that should not be eligible for long-term, low-cost financing."[35] His was a lone voice amongst advocacy groups, all of whom wanted to see increases in multi-family lending.

HUD did not insist on accurate data for Low-Doc or No-Doc loans

The issue of data raised its head again. By this time, HUD was aware of the increase in mortgages termed "Low-Doc" or "No Doc". First of all, an accurate measurement of GSE performance depends on the completeness of data on property location and borrower income. HUD notes that missing or incomplete geographical information constituted 1%, but missing borrower-income data has been "of the order of several percent each year." Low-Doc and No-Doc loans do not require the borrower to provide income information, but the borrower may sometimes provide information on assets because the "assets are easier to document," or the mortgages may be originated entirely on the basis of a credit report, property appraisal, and cash for the down payment, although these may be larger than usual and subject to higher interest rates. HUD had consulted market participants and advocacy groups about the missing data problem and whether or not such mortgages should be accepted for the GSEs' goals.

As a result of the consultation exercise (in which the GSEs participated extensively), HUD came to the following conclusion: that some level of estimation for affordability data is reasonable and consistent with the statutory intent that the GSEs serve the affordable housing needs of families *even if the actual data are not available.*

Other responses indicated that Low-Doc or No-Doc loans might indicate predatory lending, but HUD replied it did not find that "these loans are essentially predatory in nature." Given that the GSEs had publicly announced that they would not finance any loans with predatory features, HUD would rely on its expectation that the GSEs would "continue to vigorously enforce these policies." The department's existing rules contained strong safeguards against abusive lending by excluding loans with excessive fees and prepayment penalties from counting towards affordable housing goals, and would continue to monitor the GSEs' performance where different types of loans with other features such as prepayment penalties after three years were purchased, noting that such features were not taken into account when the regulations were adopted in 2000.[36]

With regard to the Low-Doc and No-Doc loans, HUD decided to allow the GSEs to use an HUD-approved affordability estimation methodology for all single-family owner-occupied units with missing borrower income data up to a specified maximum. This allowed for the distribution of borrower incomes within Census tracts in determining how to treat loans with missing income data, according to a complex formula set out in the Federal Register. The purpose of these complex changes is to enable HUD to determine the number of goal-qualifying loan purchases.[37]

HUD backed down, when it should have insisted on being able to *count* the number of loans the GSEs purchased

The other issues raised in the process of consultation in 2004, as opposed to 2000, show both the changing nature of the business and the increasing difficulties HUD faced even in the most basic aspect of its oversight work; that is, identifying and counting the number of eligible purchases the GSEs were making in order to determine whether or not they had reached the goals set for them. In that regard, it is interesting to note that the GSEs made extensive contributions, designed, it seems, to ensure that they had as much leeway as possible.

The nature of the mortgage purchases by the GSEs had began to change to such an extent that HUD had decided to consult widely on whether seasoned mortgages (those which had been in force for more than a year) should count towards the targets, and whether their counting rules were sufficiently specific to determine which seasoned mortgages or large-scale transactions were equivalent to mortgage purposes.

In late 2003, both GSEs had undertaken large-scale transactions of seasoned loans. One such transaction with Washington Mutual contained an option for dissolution in the following year. HUD again received a variety of responses, with one policy group suggesting that definitions were changed in order to exclude loans with recourse clauses because they did not alleviate risk from the market.

One trade association supported counting bulk purchases that occurred towards the end of the year, stressing the efficiencies of such purchases; for example, the market for multi-family units is large and fragmented, and seasoned portfolio transactions are an efficient way for the GSEs to acquire smaller loans in the under-50 unit segment of the market. For Fannie Mae, every mortgage purchase contributes to its housing mission, so the qualification of mortgages purchased should not change. Large-scale purchases lower transaction costs for the buyers and sellers; bulk purchases serve the purposes of lenders without a direct relationship with Fannie Mae. The GSE added that two-thirds of its bulk purchases between 2001 and 2003 were for new loans, not seasoned loans (that is, those which had been in existence for over a year). The latter loans were an important component of the liquidity of current mortgages. "Knowing that there is a ready market allows financial institutions to hold some of their assets in the form of mortgages, and affords them the opportunity to sell these mortgages later to manage liquidity, improve profitability, strengthen their capital position and manage certain risks."

The GSEs and Fannie Mae in particular also referred to dissolution options, stating that lenders sometimes request the option to dissolve securities swapped with the GSEs. The reason for such options is that they give lenders greater control over their balance sheets, capital position, and other financial concerns. Such options are also requested because they obtain more favorable rates and can make more loans.[38] HUD regarded the the fact that the seller can exercize his option to reverse or wind down a transaction and take back mortgages within a specified time means the transaction appears temporary in nature, although the liquidity that results from the buy-back appears the same. Even if the short-term liquidity is valuable to mortgage sellers, especially for balance sheet management, it does not contribute to longer-term liquidity; the sellers do not need it, especially if alternative solutions are backed by seasoned loans. HUD therefore imposed a one-year lock-out on dissolution securities, taking the view that this would prevent potential misuse and still allow sellers of mortgages to manage their portfolios in the short and long term. HUD decided to monitor the one-year lock-out to observe whether it was still accomplishing its intended purpose. No other restrictions were placed on mortgage purchases.

HUD did not insist on proper verification procedures for GSE loan purchases.

HUD then turned to the issues of verification and enforcement to ensure GSE data integrity. To this end, the department proposed an independent verification authority to attest to the "accuracy, completeness of data, information and reports submitted by the GSEs in addition to the Department's existing authority to conduct on-site verifications and performance reviews." As a result, the GSEs would be required to provide a certification, confirming Annual Housing Activity Reports (AHAR), data submissions and information are "current, complete, and do not contain any untrue statement of a material fact," signed and attested by the GSE Certifying Official. HUD noted that in requiring this information it was "fully aware that the GSEs collect millions of data elements from hundreds of sources and that the GSEs must depend on these sources to provide accurate data. In requiring a certification, HUD intends that the GSEs will use and rely on their internal controls and other due diligence processes and procedures for collecting, verifying the accuracy of, and reporting the data received from sellers."[39]

HUD already conducted computerized consistency checks on the loan-level data provided by the GSEs in their annual returns, tested the data by applying their counting rules to the GSEs' data to ensure that they are consistent with their own, and also reconciled the GSEs' total business volume as in the shareholder reports with the adjusted mortgage purchases provided for HUD. In the light of all of these comments, HUD withdrew the requirement for independent verification and instead simply required the senior officer responsible for submitting the Annual Mortgage Report and other reports to certify that: "To the best of my knowledge and belief, the information provided herein is true, correct and complete." Even then, its evaluation was deferred until the fourth quarter in 2005, but leaving it open as to when further verification regulations might be required if introduced. HUD intended this to apply to the entire AHAR submission, including the narrative text, data tables, and computerized loan level data; and all of this was to be subject to appropriate internal review procedures by the GSEs. Any errors, omissions or discrepancies must be material and must be ones that indicate to HUD, as a result of HUD's review of the reports, a serious problem in the GSEs' internal procedures.

HUD therefore decided to refer to this rule as Procedures for Prior Year Reporting Errors, under which there is a possibility that HUD may discover, during a performance review, that a serious overstatement of credit towards one or more housing goals occurred in the prior year under review. The GSEs firmly resisted the notion that HUD could deduct the previous year's overstatement of housing goal credit (due to errors, omissions or discrepancies in that year) from the current year's housing goal credit. HUD accepted their objections and altered the rule so that discrepancies such as overstatements (that is, the overstated units enabling the GSE to meet a housing goal that it otherwise could not have met) could be rectified up to 24 months after the close of a calendar year's performance. For example, if overstatements were discovered for 2005 and 2006 and the GSE was notified in 2007, then the GSE could be required to make up the overstatements in 2008.

HUD also responded to further issues raised: goal levels and the effects on the FHA, the subprime market and mortgage default rates. In the light of subsequent events and the policies adopted by Fannie Mae in particular at the time, HUD's responses were complacent, to say the least.

HUD overrode risk warnings in favor of affordable housing goals

With regard to the FHA, a number of respondents to the consultation (including the GSEs) took the view that the unrealistically high goals would affect the future solvency of the FHA. One trade association asserted that "excessive goals will push the GSEs to expand into the least risky part of the FHA market and put into question the FHA's long-term viability."[40] HUD then reports that Fannie Mae and Freddie Mac agreed that they would be compelled to "more aggressively compete with the FHA in procuring top quality borrowers." This actually became Fannie Mae's chosen strategy, as opposed to a strategy that was forced upon it, but all of these concerns were dismissed by HUD.

HUD responded by stating that it was not the FHA's mission to compete with the private sector and then to agree that automated underwriting had blurred the underwriting distinctions between prime conventional and FHA loans. For example, an application with high payment-to-income ratios would be processed using an automated underwriting system which scores the application based on a totality of risk factors. The result was that what once may have been an unacceptable payment-to-income ratio for a prime conventional loan may now be acceptable if the application contains offsetting low risks in other key areas such as borrower cash reserves, loan-to-value ratio or credit score.

With regard to subprime loans, both GSEs stated that they would need to increase their purchase of subprime loans in order to meet the higher goals. Freddie Mac, in particular, argued that in order to meet these goals, it might not have the option in the future of turning away subprime loans with less desirable terms than the subprime business it currently purchases. Once again, HUD stressed the GSEs' approach to predatory lending; their prudence in focusing on the higher levels of the subprime market (A-minus and Alt-A segments, the latter group being those who cannot document all the underwriting information). "The GSEs' subprime products are integrated into their automotive underwriting system and are approved based on mortgage scoring models, which has proved to be an effective tool in limiting risk layering. The GSEs charge lenders higher fees for guaranteeing these loans. As a result, these higher risk loans are priced above those offered to prime borrowers but below what subprime lenders would otherwise charge for these loans."

HUD again praised the GSEs' presence in the subprime market. The content of these remarks is worth noting: "Millions of Americans with less than perfect credit or who cannot meet some of the tougher underwriting requirements of the prime market such as inadequate income documentation, limited down-payment or cash reserves, or the desire to take out more cash than conventional loans allow, rely on subprime lenders for access to mortgage financing. If the GSEs reach deeper into the subprime market, more borrowers will benefit from the advantages that greater stability and standardization create."[41]

Respondents recognized that the higher goals would lead to more expanded affordable housing products as well as higher foreclosures, and were extremely concerned about the impact of a higher level of foreclosure on underserved areas, especially inner-city areas. HUD was warned that affordable loans introduced into the market in favorable economic circumstances can experience higher increasing defaults and foreclosures during periods of higher interest rates, higher unemployment and/or lower house price appreciation rates. One respondent estimated that 15% or more of borrowers in some affordable housing products could experience default in an economic downturn.

Once again, all the warnings were dismissed by HUD, which insisted that an active GSE effort in these neighborhoods would encourage traditional, mainstream lenders to increase their lending activities in these underserved areas. This would result in additional funding opportunities for lower-income and minority borrowers, who would otherwise take out high-cost loans. "As a result the Department believes that GSE participation is a net benefit to lower-income households."[42] Despite such reassurances, the serious anxieties of many within the industry remained, and HUD received more than one explicit warning.

The dangers inherent in the 2004 decision to raise the targets to such an extent did not go unnoticed at the time. The National Association of Realtors in their letter to the Federal Housing Finance Agency (the successor body to the OHEO) in April 2010 referred to their previous comments on HUD's 2004 proposals. Their letter of July 2004 had warned HUD that "the Proposed Rule assumes a GSE market share and future economic conditions that are too optimistic. In particular, we were worried that the goals would 'distort mortgage markets' and pointed out that 'goals set too high can be just as damaging as goals that are set too low'." HUD did not heed NAR's warnings.

HUD's litany of oversight failures contributed to the subprime mortgage crisis

In their 2010 letter, NAR pointed out that the post-2005 HUD goals forcing the GSEs to take undue risks to meet their targets appear to have been a factor behind the market dislocations that have led, and are still leading, to millions of foreclosures. Of course, there were many other factors, including the GSEs' overreaching for market share, accepting weak "Alt-A" underwriting, and purchasing tranches of poor-quality private label securities, as well as weak underwriting by too many subprime lenders, inappropriate commercial lending by FDIC-insured institutions that made possible the operations of abusive subprime lenders, and a flood of excess capital worldwide. NAR reviewed abuses in the subprime lending market starting at the end of 2004, and in May 2005 issued its policy calling for underwriting that is consistent with sustainable home ownership. Regulators have "subsequently taken action consistent with many of these regulations."[43]

The lengthy discussions, which lay behind the introduction of the housing goals especially in 2000 and 2004, have been included here, because at every turn they show the weaknesses and indecisiveness of HUD as a mission regulator. HUD's oversight of Fannie Mae and Freddie Mac consisted in ensuring that they were enhancing the availability of mortgage credit by creating and maintaining a secondary market for residential mortgages. HUD is, as set out above, charged with establishing the goals and monitoring the compliance of Fannie Mae and Freddie Mac's financing of housing for low- and moderate-income families, housing in central cities and other "underserved areas". The department failed in every aspect of its mission, including the failure to see the increased risks for borrowers in the categories which the GSEs were supposed to serve of taking on subprime loans, which in fact turned out to be new forms of predatory lending. Even when such issues were raised by respondents to the proposed goal changes, they were either assured that the existing rules on predatory lending were sufficient, or that the GSEs own voluntary restrictions on predatory lending would provide sufficient safeguards, or that the matter required further investigation. For example, in 2000, HUD emphasized that the GSEs "have a public responsibility to help eliminate predatory mortgage practices which are inimical to the home financing and homeownership objectives that the GSEs were established to serve."[44] The rule confirmed the corporate policies adopted by Fannie Mae and Freddie Mac, that they would not purchase predatory mortgages, by disallowing them from receiving goals credit for predatory loan purchases. HUD should have continued to challenge the GSEs by encouraging them to act more aggressively in ending predatory practices in the subprime market; but it did not, and instead took a complacent view of the subprime market and of the risks involved.

A careful reading of all the submissions from Fannie Mae and Freddie Mac shows that they successfully fought off any attempt to monitor their activities more closely. That was especially true of the seller dissolution options on units acquired in transactions with the lenders; that is, where the seller of the mortgages to the GSEs has an option to dissolve or otherwise cancel a mortgage purchase arrangement or a loan sale. The mortgages are then returned to the mortgage lender or seller. The lock-out proposal was a useful solution, but the problem remained as to whether or not HUD would be able to identify such sales, especially where bulk purchases were concerned shortly before the end of the financial year.

This brief history of the role of HUD between 1995 and 2008 shows that the department did not have the resources, even if it had the will, to oversee the GSEs and the FHA. It did not have the will, because the four Secretaries of Housing were committed to the affordable housing ideology, as were the Administrations of which they were part. They pushed ahead with the affordable housing goals and entirely failed to understand, or, if they understood, chose to ignore, the risks involved, until it was too late.

6

The GSEs and the Developing Crisis

A little history

Fannie Mae and Freddie Mac sound like someone's aunt and uncle, just up from the country. They are in fact the two most important Government Sponsored Enterprises (GSEs), charged with creating liquidity in the secondary mortgage market. It is hard to understand what role they have in a mature banking system, and why so many Americans think that if they did not exist, it would be necessary to invent them. A little history is necessary to explain why they came into being; more analysis is necessary to explain why they continue to operate in spite of growing unease about the risks they have posed, not just to the mortgage market but to the economy as a whole.

There are five GSEs, comprising Fannie, Freddie, the Federal Home Loan Bank (FHLB) System, the Farm Credit System (FCS) and the Federal Agricultural Mortgage Corporation (Farmer Mac).[1] All had their roots in the Great Depression, as part of Roosevelt's New Deal; they were designed to handle the lack of liquidity in the housing market, and to quell the rising wave of defaults. The National Housing Act was passed in 1934 to seek to strengthen the market, followed by the creation of the Federal National Mortgage Association (Fannie Mae) in 1938, with the aim of combating the unwillingness or inability of lenders to ensure a reliable supply of mortgage credit throughout the country. Fannie Mae's original purpose was to purchase, hold or sell Federal Housing Association (FHA)-insured mortgage loans, originated by private lenders, followed by Veterans Administration (VA) loans after World War II.

The first changes occurred with the 1954 Charter Act, which set out the basic framework under which Fannie Mae operated until 2008, but did not remove it from direct federal control at that stage. The Act also removed government backing for what Fannie Mae borrowed on the market to fund its secondary market operations. It also laid down the means by which its secondary market operations would be transferred to the private sector; proceeds from the gradual sale of common stock were to be used to retire Treasury-owned preferred stock in Fannie Mae. That process was completed in September 1968 so that Fannie Mae could be transformed into a Government Sponsored Enterprise (or private corporation). The Charter Act also divided Fannie Mae into two parts: Ginnie Mae as above, responsible for the then existing special assistance programs; and Fannie Mae, the transformation of which was completed in 1968. The same Act allowed the issuance of mortgage-backed securities, and provided for HUD's continuing oversight of Fannie Mae's activities to ensure that it fulfilled its public purposes. Ginnie Mae purchases packages of qualifying FHA, VA, RHS (Rural Housing Service) and PIH (Public and Indian Housing) loans, converts them into mortgage-backed securities, and guarantees the timely payment of principal and interest to the lenders. It was the first to introduce MBSs in 1970, and states on its website that it "converts individual mortgages into safe, liquid securities for investors around the world," thus helping to channel global capital into American housing markets, making more mortgages available. These are the only MBSs which are truly guaranteed by the "full faith and credit guaranty of the United States Government." A rider has been added to the effect that "this means that even in difficult times an investment in Ginnie Mae MBSs is one of the safest an investor can make." Ginnie is also closer to the federal government in that the president is appointed by the President and answers to the Secretary of Housing.

The Emergency Home Finance Act 1970 created Freddie Mac and authorized it to create a secondary market for conventional mortgages. Until the Financial Institutions Reform and Enforcement Act of 1989 (FIRREA), Freddie Mac was owned by the Federal Home Loan Bank (FHLB) System; when the Savings & Loans crisis of the late 1980s precipitated the restructuring of the savings industry, Congress transformed it into another independent GSE with an 18-member board and established HUD as its regulator. Both GSEs were then authorized to provide a secondary market for conventional mortgages in addition to government-insured and guaranteed loans.

The key legislation covering the housing GSEs for the years 1992 until 2008 (when it was replaced by the Housing and Economic Recovery Act) was the Federal Housing Enterprise Financial Safety and Soundness Act (FHEFSSA). This created the Office of Federal Housing Enterprise Oversight (OFHEO) as the new regulatory office within HUD, whose main responsibility was to "ensure that Fannie Mae and Freddie Mac are adequately capitalized and operating safely." Under the Act, OFHEO was subject to the Congressional appropriations process but was financed by semi-annual assessments on the GSEs, subject to Congressional approval. HUD has the statutory authority to ensure that the GSEs fulfil their mission of promoting housing and home-ownership opportunities for all. Congress had not been convinced that HUD's regulatory framework sufficiently benefited low- to moderate-income families and those who live in underserved areas, hence the 1992 Act required HUD to develop, implement and enforce a comprehensive housing mission framework and set goals for the GSEs, a process that involved HUD in long and complex discussions with the industry, the GSEs and community advocates, amongst others.

The GSEs' roots lay, not only in the Great Depression and its aftermath, but also in a fragmented banking system with quite different mortgage rates operating throughout the country. Relatively small banks arranged mortgages, which they then held on their books until maturity. As well as being highly fragmented, the banking system remained relatively static between the 1930s and the 1970s, with restrictions on setting up branches that were so severe that most states at the time either limited branching, or prohibited it altogether. By the early 1970s, only 12 states allowed unrestricted state-wide banking, but between 1970 and 1994, 38 states had deregulated their banking restrictions. Until the 1980s, cross-state ownership of banks was effectively prohibited by the application of the Douglas Amendment to the 1956 Bank Holding Company (BHC) Act. This prevented a BCH from acquiring banks outside the state where it was headquartered unless the target bank's state allowed such an acquisition (which they all refused). This was by and large the situation until the early 1990s and the Riegle-Neal Interstate Banking and Branching Efficiency Act, 1994, which led to the wave of mergers and acquisitions already described, transforming the banking industry in the USA and inevitably leading many to doubt the continuing value of the GSEs.

The structure of the GSEs

The peculiar structure of the GSEs as "hybrid institutions" led to them once being described as "serving two masters, but out of control."[2] The reasons for that lie partly in the complex legal structure, making it difficult to amend their Charters or to take legal action against them; to regulate them, control or limit their activities. They are shareholder owned, profit-seeking corporations, created by Congress to help address America's housing needs. The advantage for a hard-pressed government is that they remove housing expenditure from its public-spending balance sheet, providing off-budget, market-based funding, which allows them to continue to grow without going back to Congress. Favored constituencies then receive a benefit for which Congressmen and Senators could claim credit.

The GSEs were owned by their private shareholders and were answerable to their board of directors. Although the government appointed five of the 18 board members, these were not distinguished from the other members by an obligation to represent personal views or those of the Administration. According to their Charters, the GSEs had to serve the public purposes set out in FHEFSSA, under HUD's supervision.

The advantages of GSE status

GSE status carries with it significant advantages, which Fannie Mae and Freddie Mac have exploited to their benefit over the years. Although many observed and deplored their misuse over the years, those very same advantages made it difficult, if not virtually impossible, to implement the changes they saw were necessary.

As private firms, the GSEs were not covered by the laws applying to government agencies, and their directors, officers and employees did not become federal employees as a result of joining them, so were free from all the constraints on resources, staffing, procurement and procedures applying to federal agencies, even when carrying out public purposes. Because of their special status, the GSEs were free from state laws, and did not have to register or obtain a license in whichever state they chose to conduct business.

Congress was able to provide the housing GSEs with an appropriate and reasonably well-defined public purpose when they were established in 1968 and 1970, in terms of the provision of government-backed credit in view of the imperfections and limitations of the housing credit market at that time. The problem, for the Administration and for various Congressmen and Senators in the following years, lay in seeking to amend the statutory purposes in the light of market developments. Three difficulties lay in the way of redefining or limiting the public purposes for the GSEs in the light of market developments:

(i) The problems in obtaining sufficient support in Congress or the Senate or for the Administration to find the political will to make the necessary changes.

(ii) The lack of understanding amongst politicians and their advisors of the consequences of making specific changes to the GSEs' enabling legislation.

(iii) The tendency of Congress to introduce so-called "technical amendments" put forward by the GSEs but without a full debate on the implications of the proposals, and how these might impact on the existing limits imposed on the way in which the housing GSEs fulfil their public purposes, as well as the means by which they do.[3]

The GSEs have two further advantages in both expanding their activities and in overcoming any challenges to their right to do so. Fannie Mae's Charter Act authorizes the company to "do all things as are necessary or incidental to the proper management of its affairs and the proper conduct of its business."[4] Its complex legal framework means that the GSE can always resist a challenge in the courts, responding by claiming that its actions reduced the cost of its public purposes or enabled it to provide the services more efficiently.

The Charter does give HUD considerable authority to direct the activities of the GSEs, including the approval of new programs, when it states: "Except for the authority of the Director of the Office of Federal Housing Oversight ... and all other matters relating to the safety and soundness of the enterprises, the

Secretary of Housing and Urban Development shall have general regulatory power over each enterprise and shall make such rules and regulations as will be necessary and proper to assure that this part and the purposes of the Federal National Mortgage Association Charter Act and the Federal Home Loan Mortgage Corporation Charter Act are accomplished."[5] HUD's lack of will, resources and leadership over the years meant that it could not exercise proper control over them.

HUD's failed attempts to curtail Fannie and Freddie

In March 2000, William Apgar, Assistant Secretary for Housing, announced a wide-ranging review of the GSEs' activities. "HUD's new program review and approval responsibility is an integral part of the Department's regulatory framework. Considerable resources are being made available ... to ensure that new activities are identified, analysed, and, if appropriate reviewed as new programs. HUD monitors the GSEs' business activities on an on-going basis and recently requested information on a number of their initiatives, including their mortgage insurance initiatives and their various internet activities and partnerships." He added, "neither GSE takes the view that these activities constitute 'new programs' as defined in current law, and they did not submit them to HUD for approval prior to introducing them to the market ... HUD staff are reviewing the material [which the GSEs finally submitted] to make these determinations."[6]

Apgar announced that HUD had begun its first review of the GSEs' automated underwriting systems and appraisal guidelines, since these had become the standards which lenders used to decide whether or not the GSEs would buy the borrower's mortgage, allowing him/her to receive the most favorable interest rates. In 1999, HUD had requested extensive information about how the systems were developed and how they worked, including how the "scorecards" function in deciding which loans would be accepted. The GSEs provided huge amounts of information and data, which they claimed was highly confidential or proprietary business information. However, the aim was to see whether the systems helped all would-be borrowers, especially minorities, to obtain mortgages on favorable terms; the focus was on "fair lending" and not on the way in which the systems operated. The review itself took over two years to complete.

The decision to conduct such a review caused great excitement in the market. The Mortgage Bankers Association supported HUD's action, claiming that Freddie Mac's "HomeSteps Program is not in their charter, not in their mission," and adding that the "GSEs should introduce new products and services only when they directly relate to their core functions of providing liquidity and stability in the secondary mortgage market." America's Community Bankers wanted HUD to "use its statutory authority to disallow new or modified programs that are inconsistent with the statutory mission of Fannie and Freddie."[7] Of course, many lenders, appraisers and others wanted to clip Fannie and Freddie's wings. Appraisers had already seen incursions into their territory as the automated underwriting systems began to include external-only property inspection reports as part of the decision-making process of loan purchase.

The GSEs eventually provided information, often unsatisfactory in HUD's view, arguing that much of the information regarding the automated underwriting systems was proprietary, or else they delayed providing it. HUD threatened to use the various enforcement powers at its disposal, if information was not received by the end of January 2000. These included terminating or suspending the Statement of Understanding between HUD and Fannie implementing Fannie's automated underwriting system for FHA loans; on-site verification of the accuracy and completeness of the information already provided by Fannie; cease and desist proceedings; or civil penalties ranging from $5,000 per day to $1m per day for serious violations. In the event, nothing much happened apart from a long-delayed Fair Lending Review, and the excitement died away.

HUD had the power, not only to set goals, but also to monitor and limit the GSEs' new programs. When it came to it, the department did not act. It had neither the resources nor the will to use its powers under the Charter, knowing that the GSEs would simply use the argument that the new programs helped them cut the cost of mortgages for borrowers. HUD knew just how much political clout the GSEs possessed.

Charter Benefits

1. The Law treats the GSEs as "instrumentalities" of the federal government, rather than as fully private entities. Their Charters mean that they are exempt from all state and local income taxes.

2. They are also exempt from the Securities and Exchange Commission's registration requirements and fees, and may use the Federal Reserve as their fiscal agent.

3. The US Treasury is authorized to lend $2.25bn to both Fannie Mae and Freddie Mac, and $4bn to the FHLBs.

4. GSE debt is eligible for use as collateral for public deposits, for unlimited investment by federally chartered banks and thrifts, and for purchase by the Federal Reserve in open-market operations. GSE securities are explicitly government securities under the Securities Exchange Act, 1934 and are exempt from the provisions of many state investor protection laws. These advantages have not been granted to any other shareholder-owned companies.

5. The much-debated "implicit" government guarantee is one which the government explicitly denies, as stated in a typical disclosure from a Fannie Mae prospectus: "The Certificates, together with the interest thereon, are not guaranteed by the United States. The obligations of Fannie Mae are obligations solely of the corporation and do not constitute an obligation of the United States or any agency or any instrumentality thereof other than the Corporation." This was essential to comply with the Charter of each GSE. The Fannie Mae Charter includes the following provision:

"The Corporation shall insert in appropriate language in all of its obligations ... clearly indicating that such obligations, together with the interest thereon, are not guaranteed by the United States and do not constitute a debt or obligation of the United States or any agency or instrumentality thereof other than the corporation."[8]

However, investors looked at the special treatment of GSE securities in their federal charters and concluded that the government would have to back them in the event of any serious problems.[9] In a way, the statement seemed to hint at an implicit government guarantee, since it merely ruled out an explicit one, and such statements are not required in a prospectus issued by any private company. So, despite such explicit statements, Fannie Mae and Freddie Mac would by a nod and a wink imply that the government would not let them down. Anthony Marra, then deputy general counsel to Fannie Mae, argued in his submission to the Office of the Comptroller of the Currency that "Fannie Mae standard domestic obligations, like Treasuries, typically receive no rating on an issue-by-issue basis, because investors and rating agencies view the implied government backing of Fannie Mae as sufficient indication of the investment quality of Fannie Mae obligations."[10]

But the debt issued and the MBSs guaranteed by the housing GSEs are more valuable to investors because of the perception of the government guarantee and other advantages from the federal government. This is the main way in which the federal government conveys a subsidy to the GSEs. Alan Greenspan noted in a letter to Congressman Richard Baker that "the GSE subsidy is unusual in that its size is determined by market perceptions, not by legislation ... The extent to which the subsidy is exploited is determined by the extent to which the GSEs choose to issue mortgage-backed securities, not by legislation."[11] That implicit guarantee is communicated to investors in the capital markets through all the provisions set out above, including the appointment of some directors by the President of the United States. In addition, although federally chartered and federally insured banks face a limit on the amounts that they can invest in other types of securities, that limit does not apply to GSE securities. "Taken together, those statutory privileges have been sufficient to overcome an explicit denial of federal backing that the GSEs include in their prospectuses."[12]

In May 2001, the Congressional Budget Office (CBO) noted that GSE securities were rated as "agency securities" and priced below US Treasuries and above AAA corporate obligations, thus reducing the borrowing costs for the GSEs, partly by promoting institutional acceptance. Then it was possible for the CBO to say that decisions by portfolio managers to invest in GSE securities did not have to be justified in terms of credit risk. The characteristics of acceptability and liquidity contributed to the relatively high price investors were willing to pay for GSE securities.[13] In the event, although investors were wrong about credit risk, the markets were right about the implicit guarantees. Fannie Mae, especially, and Freddie Mac were simply "too big to fail," and the government took them into conservatorship in September 2008.

Implications of the GSEs' benefits

Costs and competition

These were spelt out in a paper by Barbara Miles, Specialist in Financial Institutions, Congressional Research Services, sparked off by Freddie Mac's attempt to enter the mortgage insurance market via a "technical change" to its federal Charter.[14] She noted that the GSE privileges can act as a barrier to entry by competitors and can result in a monopoly. Their exemptions and privileges were only granted to the GSEs to correct certain perceived market failures; once those have been corrected, the privileges then act to hold down the costs of operation for the GSEs, and can act as a barrier to entry by non-favored would-be competitors.

"The GSEs can reap greater-than-competitive profits, even while undercutting pricing of potential competitors. They need only price their products a little below what fully private companies would have to charge." They only have to increase the business volume or risk in order to increase the subsidies; this obviously provides an incentive to dominate the markets in which they are supposed to operate and also to expand into related markets to the disadvantage of the efficient competitors without GSE charters.

The insurance market which Freddie Mac wished to enter already had a number of insurers and reinsurers, who strongly objected to the proposed competition from Freddie Mac. Freddie could undermine their business, since their costs were inevitably higher, given their lack of special privileges. Miles's report is interesting in that she was one of the first to recognize the potential for market domination by Fannie Mae and Freddie Mac, later described as a duopoly.

The size and composition of the subsidy

In 2001, the CBO pointed out that the same combination of federal regulatory provisions and implied guarantees enhances the credit standing, market acceptance and liquidity of MBSs guaranteed by Fannie Mae and Freddie Mac.

(i)   The risk-based capital requirements for banks are lower for GSE-guaranteed MBSs than for private label MBSs. They offer a credit guarantee, which the market recognizes as being more valuable than a similar guarantee offered by a private company, reducing the rate of return that investors require on GSE-guaranteed MBSs below the rates required on private label MBSs. The mortgage pooler pays higher prices for mortgages and passes along the lower interest rates to borrowers and to charge higher guarantee fees than private guarantors. Fannie Mae and Freddie Mac undoubtedly made use of the latter benefit, but it is doubtful that borrowers benefited much from the possibility of lower interest rates.

(ii) The direct benefits of regulatory and tax exemptions, including the lower cost of obtaining credit ratings for debt and MBS issues, are easy to calculate. These had a combined value of $1.2bn in 2000.

(iii) The value of the subsidy to General Obligation Debt Securities is more difficult to calculate and requires comparing the rates paid by the GSEs with the rates paid by comparable financial institutions with a credit rating in the range of AA to A. The entire analysis is not an easy one, partly because the rate reduction on GSE securities may vary with the maturity of the credit issued, and the default risk being lower over a short horizon than over a longer time period. A further problem is that it is difficult to determine the proportion of short-term debt, held by Fannie and Freddie, because of their extensive use of derivative securities such as swaps, which effectively transform short-term borrowing into long-term borrowing and vice versa. To calculate the effective quantity of the GSEs' short-term debt, their positions in derivative securities must also be analysed.

But as the CBO notes, not only is that information not publicly available, but it would be difficult to analyse even if it were. Fannie Mae and Freddie Mac reported that the percentage of debt which was effectively short-term after "synthetic extensions" at year-end 1999 was effectively 13% and 7% respectively. Those amounts contrast with the figures for nominal short-term debt of 41% and 49% reported on their respective balance sheets, especially when percentages of effective short-term debt in earlier years are higher, between 20% and 30%. The CBO decided to take the proportion at 20%, and to evaluate the total subsidy using a method designed to capture the total subsidy in a given year, the "capitalised subsidy."

On this basis, the total value of the federal subsidies for GSE debts from 1995 to 2000 for all three housing GSEs increased from $3.7bn in 1995 to $10.2bn in 1999, and dropped slightly in 2000 to $8.8bn in total. Throughout the period, Fannie Mae generally benefited most from the subsidy, except in 1997, when the

FHLB subsidy stood at $2bn compared with $1.8bn for Fannie Mae, and again in 1999 when the FHLB issuance of debt benefited to the extent of $4.5bn.

The subsidies to mortgage-backed securities are more difficult to calculate, but are deduced from the two components of the total subsidy. The first is that the advantage passed through to conforming mortgage borrowers was approximately 25 basis points. The second is the amount retained by the GSEs because of the higher guarantee fees they can charge as a result of their special status, which is approximately 20 basis points, and that they retain 5 basis points. As a result the total subsidy to Fannie Mae and Freddie Mac rose from $2.5bn in 1995 to $3.6bn in 2000, a fall from $4.2bn in 1999 as a result of slowing economic growth. Putting all the calculations together, the subsidy to all three GSEs rose from $6.8bn in 1995 to $15.6bn in 1999, before falling back to $13.6bn in 2000.[15]

The CBO Director had sent Fannie Mae and Freddie Mac a copy of the report in advance, for their comments on a confidential basis. The GSEs immediately and publicly attacked the study, as being "quite divorced from market reality," saying it "should be completely disqualified from serious consideration" and was "fatally flawed."[16] The Director accused Fannie and Freddie of leaking the report, which of course they denied, but even so they aroused the ire of Congressman Richard Baker, Chairman of the Capital Markets subcommittee of the House Financial Services Committee. "Once more, I find myself forced into the unfortunate position of having to respond to what can only be adequately described as an orchestrated and audacious attack by Fannie Mae and Freddie Mac upon a respected federal government institution and its highest-ranking official ... In return for Mr Crippen's courtesy [the Director of CBO], Fannie and Freddie have instead embarked on a full-scale assault, in public ... [which] began before even members of Congress for whom the report was produced had a chance to view it ... on top of these pre-emptive strikes ... Fannie and Freddie have gone so far as to accuse the Congressional Budget Office of using 'inappropriate methodology, inaccurate assumptions and faulty analysis'."[17]

The subsidies continued to increase over time, rising to $23bn in 2003, an increase of nearly 69% over the $13.6bn in 2000. That jump in the value of the subsidy was brought about by the GSEs' rapid expansion in 2001. These estimates are based on the assumption that any increase in the GSEs' outstanding debt and mortgage backed securities are sustained only until the acquired mortgages mature. Under the alternative assumption that the GSEs' issued debt and MBSs are reissued when they mature, the federal subsidy for 2003 would be over $46bn.[18] Some of these estimates on the part of CBO have been challenged, but even Fannie Mae, after initial objections, did not pursue the matter further. Fannie may have realized that their initial reaction was a blunder, and that perhaps the better approach would have been to argue that the subsidy was passed on to borrowers in the form of lower mortgage rates, saving them billions of dollars. In that approach, they were more likely to keep the support of Congressman Kanjorski, a key Democrat member of the House Financial Services Committee, whose response was that the "numbers themselves were not as significant as to see whether the subsidy is valuable and whether it's going to the consumer."[19] That is, of course, the argument which Fannie and Freddie would pursue, regardless of the fact that most of the subsidy went to their shareholders and had little effect on the cost of mortgages.

Risks posed by Fannie Mae and Freddie Mac

Recognizing systemic risk

As the decade progressed, the focus shifted away from the extent of federal subsidies to awareness of the dominance of the GSEs and the increasing necessity to manage their risks. Once again, Barbara Miles was one of the first to recognize the risks involved in the implied government guarantee for the GSEs.[20] This was as a result of noting the then size of the outstanding debt of the three housing GSEs, which totalled $1.7 trillion, compared with publicly held, marketable Treasury debt which was $2.7 trillion at the end of the first quarter of 2000. At the then rate of growth, GSE debt could surpass Treasury debt by 2003. Adding in Fannie Mae and Freddie Mac's outstanding guarantees of MBSs, which stood at $1.21 trillion, their debts were almost equivalent to that of the US Treasury, raising concerns about the risks posed for the economy and the US government.

In the case of the GSEs, the normal business risks, such as interest rate risk, credit risk, business risks, management and operational risks were increased due to the lack of market discipline and the belief that GSE debt was virtually equivalent to Treasury. The GSEs at this stage were often the largest re-purchasers of their own MBSs. When mortgages were securitized and sold, the GSE retained the credit risk on the loans, but sold the interest rate risk to investors. MBSs are less profitable than portfolio holdings as a result; re-purchase restores profit along with the risk. Fannie Mae and Freddie Mac were the largest holders and purchasers of their own MBSs, holding nearly 30% of their own issuances and sometimes re-purchasing a volume equal to or greater than their issuances. This, of course, increased shareholder value but did little to assist the mortgage markets.

Miles also stressed the increase in systemic risk arising from the fact that the GSE Charter allows depository institutions to hold their debt and MBSs without limit, instead of the normal restriction to no more of 15% of capital in loans to a single borrower. In 1999, banks held over $210bn in GSE debt, which was then about one-third of bank capital, and over $355bn in MBSs. To this is added systematic risk, due to the legal restrictions on their diversification. They can only depend on one section of the economy, the housing market, and could diversify away from this without a change in mission. The GSEs positioned themselves in the market by regular issuances of debt in a way that creates an alternative to the Treasury yield curve. "But a major economic drawback to using GSE securities ... is that for the benchmark to function properly, it should reflect only the risks inherent in the economy overall ... but the GSE securities include ... (only) housing sector risks."[21]

Repeated warnings on the systemic risk of the size of the GSEs' portfolios

Such warnings were not heeded by Congress, which refused to take steps to reduce the size of the GSEs' portfolios, and certainly not by Fannie or Freddie. By 2002, their outstanding securities reached $4 trillion, more than the then entire US public debt, as well as their MBSs, which by then accounted for almost 57% of residential mortgage debt. As the portfolios continued to grow, the new Director of the CBO, Douglas Holtz-Eakin, issued another warning.[22] Once again, the risks to the tax payer were spelt out, described in this statement as interest rate, prepayment and operational risks. The housing GSEs offered public assurances that their assumed risks, especially for credit or default losses, were low in relation to their private capital, especially for credit or default losses. Fannie, one analyst suggested, is "essentially the world's largest hedge fund (albeit an extraordinarily safe one) that profits from the difference between its incredibly low borrowing costs (a by-product of its bonds being implicitly backed by government) and the much higher yield of its $860bn mortgage portfolio." As long as Fannie's borrowing costs remained low and the mortgage-backed securities market stayed open, Fannie's earnings would continue to grow. This puts it all in a nutshell: the interest rate risk to which they were exposed, and the reason for the portfolio; for the yields.[23]

The GSEs refused to recognize their exposure to interest rate risk, since an increase in interest rates would reduce the value of both fixed-rate assets and fixed-rate liabilities, but the value of the assets would be reduced further if the assets have a longer maturity than the liabilities. A rise in interest rates could eliminate their equity capital. The value of a portfolio of fixed-rate mortgages declines when borrowers exercise their right to re-finance and prepay their mortgages in response to a decline in market rates. The prepayment risk and the interest rate risk meant that the GSEs were vulnerable whichever way interest rates went. In order to limit these risks to the tax payer, the statement proposed tougher regulation, and notes that Congress could assist the regulators by increasing the minimum capital standards, or limiting the growth or profitability of the GSEs' portfolio investments, or requiring the SEC registration of GSE securities, as some members of Congress proposed. Congress did not act on any of these proposals in 2003. Fannie Mae and Freddie Mac opposed any attempt to bring about changes.

In 2005, the CBO Director once again appeared before the Committee on Banking, Housing and Urban Affairs, US Senate.[24] The GSEs' two lines of business continued to grow: outstanding MBSs grew from about $600bn in 1990 to $2.3 trillion in 2004, whilst total debt, including the obligation of the FHLBs, increased from less than $300bn to $2.5 trillion over the same period. The risks were the same as those set out in the 2003 statement, the difference being that Fannie Mae and Freddie Mac offset much of the risk in their investment portfolios by issuing callable long-term debt (which matches the cash flows on mortgage debt), interest rate swaps (matching maturities on assets and debts), and other hedging strategies. Not all of the interest rate risk is covered, since it would be too expensive, and the two GSEs determine the level of risk they retain. Credit risk, though present, was not an immediate concern, masked as it was by low interest rates at that time. The statement set out a similar range of proposals for reducing the risks to the tax payer, the difference this time being that legislation was being considered in the Senate.

The GSEs fight against any attempt to reduce the size of their portfolios

The notion of the GSEs posing "systemic risk" of this kind was firmly rejected by Richard Syron, then Chairman and CEO of Freddie Mac, who saw the argument as merely an excuse to "cut the GSEs down to size," more because of their arrogance than because of any risk they posed to the nation's housing system. He argued that if the GSEs were forced to reduce their holdings of mortgage backed securities, these would simply be "shifted to someone else's balance sheet", that is, to one of the largest banks, since 40% of all US banks' mortgage-backed bonds were held by three institutions. This would mean that the systemic risk had only been moved, and not reduced. Outstanding mortgage debt had grown by 80% since 2000: the retained mortgage portfolios of Fannie Mae and Freddie Mac had increased by 75% since then, and the portfolios of the five largest banks and thrifts grown by 132%.[25]

Of course, Syron did not mention the fact that the GSEs' debts alone included the "implicit government guarantee" and benefited from lower capital requirements than the major US banks to which he referred. Finally, the rate at which the GSEs would be required to sell off their MBSs would or could be staggered, and, at that stage, there was certainly no reason to think that US banks would be the only possible purchasers. Taken together as at the end of 2003, the 9,182 commercial banks and thrifts held $3.1 trillion in residential mortgage debt (including whole loans, lines of credit and MBSs) or about 40.8% of the then $7.6 trillion market. The two GSEs' investment portfolios alone accounted for 20.6%. The remaining one-third of residential mortgage debt was held by other US and foreign investors such as mutual funds, pension funds and insurance companies. The other banks and thrifts also have a larger capital cushion than Fannie Mae and Freddie Mac were required to retain.

Syron's remarks were hardly objective, since the GSEs charged fees for the purchase of mortgages, an important source of their income; he seemed to envisage either a straightforward sale or a cap in order to handle the interest rate risk of the portfolios of mortgages they held. Other methods of constraining GSE risk-taking which may also lead to smaller portfolios included increasing capital requirements or imposing use fees on debt issuance. Each of these has different consequences.

The portfolios continued to grow and the warnings were more insistent

In April, 2005, Chairman Greenspan appeared before the Senate Banking Committee, urging Congress to place limits on the GSEs' portfolio of assets. "Almost all the concerns associated with systemic risk flow from the size of the balance sheets of the GSEs, not from their purchase of loans from home-mortgage originators and the subsequent securitization of these mortgages. We have been unable to find any purpose for the huge balance sheet of the GSEs, other than profit creation through the exploitation of the market-granted subsidy ... We at the Federal Reserve remain concerned about the growth and magnitude of the mortgage portfolios of the GSEs, which concentrate interest rate risk and prepayment risk at these two institutions and makes our financial system dependent on their ability to manage these risks."[26]

Greenspan pointed out that the GSEs' annual return on equity often exceeded 25%, far in excess of the industry average of 15% among other large private competitors: "... Virtually none of the GSEs' excess return reflects higher yields on assets; it is almost wholly attributable to subsidized borrowings." The response to Greenspan's testimony was muted, with most preferring to leave the matter to a new, stronger regulator with the ability to determine the proper level of holdings if a risk was posed to safety and soundness. The Senate Committee obviously did not understand the risks, and no action was taken: nor was this the only occasion on which Chairman Greenspan warned of the risks. Unfortunately his words fell on deaf ears as far as Congress was concerned, or perhaps just on incomprehension.[27]

In response to questions at the hearing, Greenspan said, "we do perceive that if the expansion should continue along the lines it's been growing ... and we see no reason that it is going to stop ... something will go wrong ... and since we are sufficiently on the safe side of the systemic risk horizon ... we have time now to make the adjustments in a manner which does not disrupt the economy or the financial system."

By November, 2005, Freddie Mac's retained portfolio grew at an annualized rate of 25.8%, to $692.8bn. After an 11% decline in October, Freddie Mac increased its purchases to $32.8bn, bringing its annualized rate of growth to 6.7%. By the end of November, Freddie Mac's total portfolio size and market capitalization reached $692.7bn and Fannie Mae reported a retained portfolio of $715.5bn. This growth continued in the year in which the CBO advised reducing the portfolio limits and some members of Senate and Congress had set regulatory reform bills in train, and indeed during the time when the accounting scandals at both Fannie Mae and Freddie Mac had been brought to light.

But the size of their outstanding debts remained at almost $1.5 trillion, which was borrowed to buy and carry portfolios of mortgages and mortgage backed securities, exposing them to the prepayment and interest rate risks which the CBO analysed. The risk was hedged in derivative transactions with notional values in trillions of dollars. A study by the Federal Reserve Bank of Atlanta, published in April 2006, argued that the highly leveraged ($1.4 trillion) investment portfolios continued to pose a systemic risk and potential future social costs, in terms of a GSE failure having the potential to "have an adverse effect on the real economy."[28] The authors argued that there were various policy options to be considered: strict portfolio dollar caps; limiting portfolio activity to that required to support the GSEs securitization business and affordable housing missions; or increasing capital requirements or user fees on debt issuance. Each has different implications for GSE risk-taking incentives, portfolio composition and optimal size; for example, charging debt issuance user fees would simply strengthen investors' perception of an implied government guarantee of GSE debt obligations.

"Congress should not set specific limits but should set broad policy goals for regulatory agencies and then direct the agencies to set the specific details of regulatory standards, because the agencies are better versed in the minutiae of specific issues ... Congress could impose a maximum limit on the holding period for mortgage investments that provides more than sufficient time to securitize the assets but is short enough to clearly limit the size of the retained portfolio." On the other hand, if limits mean "putting a cap on the overall size of the retained portfolio it may be best not to leave this to regulatory discretion ... (This) would create an incentive for the politically powerful GSEs to continuously lobby the regulator and influential members of Congressional oversight committees to bring pressure to weaken portfolio constraints." Instead, Congress should "spell out the principles of portfolio limits and require the regulator to promulgate specific regulations."[29] In the light of these discussions, the comment of Douglas Duvall, spokesman for Freddie Mac, is interesting. "We continue to believe that our portfolio is central to our mission and it helps us provide a balance between fulfilling our affordable-housing mission and attracting international investments to America's doorstep."[30]

Meanwhile, the GSEs' resistance to any attempt to curb their portfolios was further undermined by an analysis produced by economists of the Federal

Reserve Board, which showed that they had only helped to reduce US mortgage interest rates by 2 basis points between April 1997 and September 2005, well below their previous estimates of 15 to 18 basis points. The economists concluded that "both portfolio purchases and MBS issuance have negligible effects on mortgage rate spreads" and that "purchases are not any more effective than securitization at reducing mortgage interest rate spreads."[31] In their introduction, they point out that "earnings from mortgages held in portfolio clearly benefit GSE shareholders ... In particular, unusually heavy and sustained portfolio holdings might bid up the price of new mortgages, allowing originators to profit more or giving originators greater scope to lower mortgage interest rates paid by new borrowers."[32] It is possible to deduce from their research that the real purpose of the large portfolios was to increase the GSEs shareholders' profitability (given that the influence on mortgage rates was negligible), and hence the "public benefit" was not obvious.

The battle over the portfolio limits continued throughout 2006 with Treasury Secretary John Snow's statement that "We need to find a way to give the [GSE] regulators authority to ultimately make a decision on the size of the portfolios."[33] The Undersecretary of Treasury for Domestic Finance, Randal Quarles, emphasized their concerns: "It is now widely recognized that the GSEs have relied upon their funding advantage to expend the size of their retained portfolios far beyond the levels necessary to achieve their mission. The concentration of risk inherent in these portfolios, along with the GSEs' thin capital structure, is an important policy concern and a high priority for the Treasury, and we are continuing to urge Congress to take action soon to address these issues."[34]

Fannie and Freddie "voluntarily" agree to limit their portfolios after the accounting scandals

Meanwhile, Fannie Mae had signed a consent agreement with OFHEO agreeing to cap its retained mortgage-related portfolio to the December 31, 2005 level of $727bn, and OFHEO's Acting Director finally reached an agreement with Freddie Mac on August 1, 2006 to limit its portfolio growth to no more than 2% annually of mission-related assets above the June 30, 2006 limit of $710.3bn. The growth should be limited to "purchases of multi-family whole loans, private-label asset-backed securities, commercial mortgage-backed securities and other assets that are intended to help [Freddie Mac] to meet its affordable housing goals or subgoals." In his statement, Director James B. Lockhart III said, "I concur with the decision by Freddie Mac to limit the mortgage portfolio growth as recommended by OFHEO. Freddie Mac has a need to address the size and scope of its portfolio, particularly in the light of current operational problems surrounding accounting and internal controls ... As the Enterprise works to meet its statutory mission, this limit on portfolio growth provides a public assurance that the Enterprise is committed to fixing its internal controls, reducing operational risks, and improving its accounting, and thereby emerging as a stronger firm." In June 2006, the US Treasury and HUD announced separate inquiries that could lead to restrictions on Fannie Mae and Freddie Mac's ability to finance their mortgage-related portfolios.

The Treasury Undersecretary Randal K. Quarles announced at a Women in Housing Finance luncheon that "the time is right for Treasury to review its debt approval process to ensure we continue to act as appropriate custodians of the power that Congress gave us when the Charters of Fannie Mae and Freddie Mac were created ... I have asked the Treasury staff to undertake such a review to ensure that the process by which we exercise this responsibility is appropriate in the light of all circumstances." Those circumstances included the accounting scandals and the continued weaknesses in the GSEs' accounting systems, risk management practices, and internal controls: "The Administration's reform proposals are intended to ensure greater regulatory oversight, appropriate capital requirements, and alleviate systemic risk, and we continue to urge Congress to take action soon to address these issues. We strongly support GSE reform legislation that addresses each of these points, and in particular provides direction to limit the size of the GSEs' investment portfolios."[35] In effect, this meant that the Administration was supporting Senator Shelby's bill.

HUD announces its own review

On the same day, Secretary Jackson announced that HUD would conduct a review of Fannie Mae and Freddie Mac's investments and holdings, including certain equity and debt investments, with a focus on transactions classified on their financial statements as "other assets/other liabilities." "HUD's primary concern is whether the GSEs' investment activities are consistent with their Charter authorities and their public purposes, and whether each is using the profits it derives as a government-sponsored enterprise for the purposes intended." He also made it clear that he wished to work with Congress in establishing a strong new regulator, but until the legislation was passed, he intended to use the authority under the FHEFSSA to increase the transparency of the GSEs. The statement was immediately welcomed by the American Bankers Association in their press release the following day: "The GSEs' business activities should remain focused on their mission of helping low- and moderate-income individuals afford homeownership in America. The announced action by HUD is an important step in clarifying permissible GSE activities ... it is an important step towards much-needed transparency to ensure that the GSEs are using their benefits only for legitimate secondary mortgage market purposes."

The review would examine the reasons for concerns about the size of the portfolios, in the light of the management deficiencies which the accounting scandals had uncovered. The implicit guarantee effectively lowers funding costs for the GSEs below those of other private companies in a similar financial situation. It also allows for high leverage on the part of the GSEs. Less capital is required to assure investors of safety for any given level of assets. Short-term bonds and loans have lower interest rates than long-term ones, so the GSEs use portfolio management techniques to allow them to borrow using short-term bonds to finance long-term mortgages. The key issue is then the extent to which Fannie and Freddie are able to manage interest rate risk, in particular. As the GSEs move mortgages into their portfolio investments, they increase both the expected returns and risks to shareholders, but only the risks increase for taxpayers. The issue of the risks involved continued to be under discussion. It was not only a question of interest rate risk, but also the GSEs' abilities to manage portfolios or credit risks (often considered to be negligible by many analysts, because they considered the mortgage purchases to consist of prime mortgages).

The Administration again seeks to limit the portfolios

Further attempts were made by the Administration during the summer and autumn to improve the chances of legislation in Senate and Congress. On June 26, 2006 another Treasury Secretary, Assistant Emil Henry, in a speech to the Housing Financial Services Roundtable warned that "unless the portfolios are hedged properly, in a period of significant interest-rate movement, there is a risk to the GSEs that their assets and liabilities will … become broadly mismatched, which can lead to insolvency." He put the case even more strongly than most, concluding, "Ignoring all the rhetoric and spin, the simple truth is that there is no need for our financial markets to be exposed to this risk. Passionate statements made by the GSEs to the contrary, the GSEs' investment portfolios are not necessary for them to stay true to their mission … As long as the portfolios of the GSEs are reduced gradually and responsibly, the overall impact to the housing market should be trivial."

And debt issuance

In his testimony before the Congressional Joint Economic Committee, Chairman Ben Bernanke had given his support to the view that the Treasury should consider limiting the debt that Fannie Mae and Freddie Mac can sell if Congress fails to pass the GSE reform legislation. Noting that the Treasury has the power to limit Fannie Mae and Freddie Mac's debt issuance, and perhaps power over the terms and maturities of that debt, the Chairman said, "If we are unable to achieve progress through Congress, I don't think the Treasury should abandon that power. I think the Treasury should consider using it if it believes that the systemic risks being generated by the [GSEs'] portfolios greatly outweigh the benefits that are mandated by the affordable housing mandate." The Treasury, according to some, appears to have that power: "The corporation is authorized to issue, upon the approval of the Secretary of the Treasury, and have outstanding at any one time obligations having such maturities and bearing such rate or rates of interest as may be determined by the corporation with the approval of the Secretary of the Treasury."[36]

After all these statements from the Administration, the Treasury Department announced on November 17, 2006 that it had completed a process by which Fannie Mae and Freddie Mac would submit quarterly debt sales calendars, which would outline the justification for their debt issuance plans and specify the gross and net issuance, before the Treasury would approve the new debt. The process was expected to begin in January 2007, when their plans would be submitted with a senior officer testifying as to their accuracy. When the process was underway early in 2007, the GSEs would submit their sales calendar a month in advance before the beginning of the new quarter so that the Treasury would be able to review the requests and provide the GSEs with their comments so that the GSEs would have sufficient time to make any necessary changes before the beginning of the quarter. The process would also involve annual meetings between GSE managers and Treasury officials to discuss debt issuances. In addition, the GSEs would be required to seek prior Treasury approval for any changes to debt issuances during the quarter. The procedure was designed to add efficiency and transparency to the process, and was not meant to limit Fannie Mae's and Freddie Mac's borrowings or limit their future growth, according to Treasury officials.

Emil W. Henry Jr, Assistant Secretary for Financial Institutions, US Treasury had already expressed the Treasury's concerns about the approval process in a speech to the Real Estate Roundtable in May that year. In his speech, he described the way in which the Treasury's exercise of its authority had changed over time:

In the mid-1990s, Treasury was actively involved in the scheduling of GSE debt issuances, and every GSE debt issuance was submitted to the Treasury for prior approval. This process was cumbersome, caused considerable strain on Treasury's staff resources and provided questionable return for this investment of time and staff. Because of these concerns, Treasury announced a new process that eliminated the need for Treasury to schedule each of the GSEs' securities offerings. This new process was characterized as a voluntary co-operative process that would provide the GSEs with more flexibility to time and size their borrowing transactions. Treasury also made other process changes during this time period. At that time, these changes were viewed as an appropriate response to a process that had become outmoded, especially as the scope of the GSEs' operations was increasing and certain issuances were becoming more routine and regularized.

Since these changes, the debt approval process has continued to evolve. While Treasury continues to exercise this responsibly, the process we use differs for each of the GSEs and has become less standardized. Depending on the particular GSE, we have developed different procedures as to how their debt issuances are approved. The procedure varies from weekly notices to quarterly notices.

Some of these procedures involve notice of expected versus actual debt issuances. The manner in which the Treasury conveys its approval also varies among the GSEs.[37]

In his speech, Assistant Secretary Henry also set out the review of Treasury procedures which was about to begin.

This description of the Treasury's role has been quoted at length, partly because it indicates just when the Treasury's approval process changed (in the mid-1990s, during the Clinton Administration), and because of the cautious, ministerial tone and content. One can almost hear the civil servants advising on its content. It was not until Emil Henry had long left office that he was able to describe what constituted the then procedures: "By the mid-2000s, the GSEs' process of debt approval had devolved to a simple notification of the Treasury, without any formal process of debt approval. The process of debt issuance was so rapid that such notifications came to the Treasury weekly, typically on one piece of paper that simply listed proposed issuances without supporting data (such as income statements or balance sheets) upon which to make informed judgments."[38] Such a cavalier approach to vast amounts of debt is astonishing, bearing in mind that debt issuance by Fannie Mae and Freddie Mac was at times higher than total US government debt and was triple-A rated on the assumption of the "implicit guarantee".

If the new procedures were intended to ensure that Congress and the Senate agreed on the proposed legislation by the end of 2006, as many believed, then it failed. This was in spite of the combined efforts of Barney Frank, the incoming House Financial Services Committee chairman, Michael Oxley, outgoing chairman, and Treasury department officials to reach a compromise on the issue of portfolio limits, partly by obliging the regulator to consider a number of factors including the size and growth of the mortgage markets in order to determine the rate of growth of the portfolios and to issue an order to that effect. But the legislation failed because of the disagreements between Senate and Congress over the conforming loan limits, an affordable housing fund and the appointment of public interest directors at the FLHBs. The failure was aided and assisted by Fannie Mae's expenditure of $10.48m to block the bill, according to the *Washington Post* (14/12/06).

More congressional efforts to regulate the GSEs effectively

Proposed legislation in 2007

The process of legislating for regulatory reform of the GSEs had to begin again in the new session of Congress (110th). Chairman Barney Frank announced that a large measure of agreement had been reached with the Treasury concerning the contents of the Federal Housing Finance Reform

Bill (H.R. 1427) in January, 2007 and predicted that it would be passed by the House of Representatives in time for the Easter recess at the beginning of April. The bill was similar to that passed in the last Congress, except for the improvements worked out with Treasury officials towards the end of 2006. Other issues, which were of concern to the Treasury, remained, such as a provision to raise the affordable loan limits to $625,000, allowing Fannie Mae and Freddie Mac to purchase loans in the high-cost market, a controversial measure. The banking industry strongly opposed this on the groumds that the private sector was already providing sufficient funding for the "jumbo" mortgage market. It was a move which would take them well away from the mission of affordable housing for low- to moderate-income families. The bill also contained provisions for establishing the affordable housing fund, which the Chairman of the Senate Banking Committee rejected.

Discussions continued with the Treasury and between Congress and the Senate throughout February. The original concern with "safety and soundness" and the need to limit the size of the GSEs' portfolios seemed to have been pushed into the background by loan limits and the affordable housing fund. Chairman Bernanke put this concern back on the agenda in February, when he gave his semi-annual monetary policy report before the Senate Banking and House Financial Services Committee. He suggested that controlling the size of the GSEs' portfolios might be to link them with the affordable housing goals: "That would be a direct way to create some limits on the GSEs' rapid expansion, while still having a direct impact on affordable housing ... We need to find some way that we can limit the growth of their portfolios."[39]

A few weeks later, Chairman Bernanke set out the reforms the Federal Reserve wished to see in the legislation under consideration. The Bank was concerned about systemic risk, given its responsibility for financial and economic stability, and once again emphasized the benefit of the implicit guarantee, which allows the GSEs to borrow in the open capital market at interest rates only slightly above that paid by the US Treasury and then to purchase assets, especially MBSs, that pay returns considerably better than the Treasury rate; the GSEs can enjoy profits "of an effectively unlimited scale."[40] Clearly the GSEs had no incentive to reduce their portfolios and, as a shareholder-owned company, had every incentive to maximize profits. The research conducted at the Federal Reserve Board and elsewhere "found that the GSE portfolios appear to have no material effect on the cost or availability of residential mortgages. At the margin, the GSEs finance their purchases of MBSs by issuing equal amounts of debt, and thus the net supply to the market of housing-related debt is unchanged by GSE purchases. Thus, standard economic reasoning does not predict large effects from these purchases on the mortgage market. Indeed contrary to what would be expected if the GSEs lowered the funding costs of mortgages, over the past decade or so the spread between yields on 30-year fixed mortgages and Treasuries of similar duration has tended to rise in periods in which the GSEs have increased the share of single-family residential mortgages held in their portfolios. and to fall when the GSE share has fallen."[41]

Despite such research showing the irrelevance of the GSEs, Bernanke acknowledged the received "wisdom" that the GSEs did have a role in providing liquidity and aiding low- to moderate-income families in order to press for essential reforms. However, the situation was obviously causing concern, as by March 2007 the two housing GSEs had $5.2 trillion of debt and MBS obligations outstanding, exceeding the $4.9 trillion of publicly held debt; they were also among the most active users of derivative instruments. Bernanke also pointed out that given their advantages, it was not possible for other companies to compete with them, so only regulation and not market discipline could hold them in check. In addition, the capital requirements for Fannie Mae and Freddie Mac were lower than those of banks at only 3.5% of assets.

The Federal Reserve first set out the three requirements in 2004 for effective regulation of the GSEs. The requirements remained the same in 2007. They were:

1. The GSE regulator should have the broad authority necessary to set and adjust the GSEs' capital requirements, in line with the risks the GSEs posed.

2. (Perhaps the most prescient.) The GSEs should be subject to a clear and credible receivership process, a process that would establish that both the shareholders and the debt holders of a failed GSE would suffer financial losses, as well as a method for resolving a GSE once it is placed in receivership.

3. The GSEs' portfolios should be anchored firmly to a well-understood public purpose approved by Congress.

In March, the Chairman of the Housing Financial Services Committee Barney Frank introduced the Federal Housing Finance Reform Bill (H.R. 1427). The Treasury reiterated its concerns about increasing the conforming loan level limits in the high-cost markets and the affordable housing fund, but would not oppose the latter, provided the fund would not be controlled by the GSEs themselves, that is, was capped and limited by a sunset provision. The key provisions, as worked out between the Treasury and Congress, included funding the new agency through assessments on the GSEs without regard to the appropriations process; a risk-based capital requirement that is more flexible than the current unworkable statutory scheme which binds the OFHEO. The new regulator would have the authority to raise minimum and critical capital levels; make temporary minimum capital increases for a regulated entity, and establish additional capital and reserve requirements for a particular program or activity.

The new regulator was instructed to establish standards by which the portfolio holdings of the regulated entities or their rate of growth will be deemed to be consistent with their mission and the safety and soundness of their operations. The Treasury had also wanted mandatory receivership, making it obligatory for the regulator to appoint a receiver if:

(a) the assets of the regulated entity are, and during the preceding 30 calendar days have been, less than the obligations of the regulated entity to its creditors and others; or

(b) the regulated entity is not, and during the preceding calendar 30 days has not been, generally paying the debts of the regulated entity ... as such debts become due.

The compromise bill did not quite fulfil the Treasury requirements, as it retains mandatory conservatorship authority in certain circumstances but allowed the new regulator to establish a conservatorship or receivership, at his or her discretion, as appropriate, to reorganize, rehabilitate, or wind up the affairs of a critically undercapitalized entity. However, both the Treasury and the Acting Director of OFHEO were prepared to support the bill, which was also welcomed by Senate Banking Committee Chairman, Christopher Dodd, in a statement issued on March 7, 2007: "In my view, there is broad agreement that we should create a new regulator to oversee Fannie Mae, Freddie Mac, and the Federal Home Loan Banks. The new regulator ... must have certain core powers. These powers include: the ability to set both minimum and risk-based capital levels for the Enterprises; enhanced enforcement and prompt correction powers; the authority to set and enforce prudential management and internal control standards; the ability to put a GSE into receivership; and authority over both safety and soundness and mission."[42] He confirmed that the Senate would begin its consideration in the autumn. A regulatory reform bill was in fact introduced by Senators Hagel, Sununu, Dole and Martinez in April.

The House of Representatives passed the Federal Housing Reform Act (H.R. 1427) in June. Senate did not pass any legislation designed to regulate the GSEs in 2007, so the Treasury and the Federal Reserve did not get the powers they considered necessary; instead, external events dominated the rest of the year in the aftermath of the collapse of two Bear Stearns hedge funds. The first sign of trouble came with Bear Stearns' decision to commit up to $3.2bn to one of two of its hedge funds on June 27, 2007. They had invested heavily in collateralized debt obligations in highly leveraged funds with insufficient insurance in the form of credit swaps, not having seen the extreme deterioration in the subprime market. The decision to inject more capital was in response to Merrill Lynch's seizure of some $800m in collateral from the fund. At first, it looked as though that decision might have stabilized the market, although much greater doubts were expressed regarding the even more highly leveraged fund, High Grade Structured Credit Strategies Enhancement Leverage Fund, which had only been set up in August 2006. On July 17, Bear Stearns was obliged to tell investors that they had lost 90% and 95% of the face value of their investments in the funds: the total losses were in the order of $1.6bn. The focus of attention switched away from regulatory reform to the subprime crisis and protecting or helping subprime borrowers throughout the rest of 2007.

It was not until 2008 that a bill was passed, but it was too late

The lack of proper powers and a new regulator left James Lockhart seeking to manage the OFHEO with "one or two hands tied behind [his] back," as further troubles hit the GSEs in early 2008. Senate inaction continued, partly due to Senator Dodd's absence as he made an unsuccessful bid for selection as the Democrat Party's presidential candidate. That was not the only reason: disagreements remained over the extent of the powers to impose new capital requirements and the Affordable Housing Fund. Both Barney Frank and President Bush called for Senate to pass the necessary legislation for a new powerful regulator, but the moment had passed.

By March, the need for regulatory reform had turned into a wider debate on the subprime mortgage crisis. By July, it became clear that the GSEs were grossly undercapitalized and technically insolvent, and may even require a government bail-out. Their share prices had been falling during the week beginning July 7, but the bail-out itself was, some would claim, caused by remarks made by William Poole during an interview with Bloomberg News on July 10, in which he said that "Congress ought to recognise that these firms are insolvent, that it is allowing them to continue to exist as bastions of privilege, financed by the taxpayer." This was by no means the first time that the former President of the Federal Reserve Bank of St Louis had raised fundamental questions about Fannie Mae and Freddie Mac, with the Bank's most recent article noting that "their capital position is thin relative to the risks they assume."[43] Other analysts pointed out the weakness, if not insolvency, of Fannie Mae and Freddie Mac, thus triggering a sharp fall in the GSEs' share prices (45% and 58% respectively). Emergency action was required. Both Congress and the Senate approved the Housing and Economic Recovery Act and it was signed into law by President Bush on July 29, 2008.

The Act incorporated some of the provisions for regulatory reform of the GSEs which had been debated in Congress and Senate over the years; it took the near collapse of the GSEs and the rapid decline in the housing market for them to act. The Act does not, however, bring about all the reforms for which many proponents of reform have long argued. A new regulator, the Federal Housing Finance Agency, was established, to be independently funded through the assessments of the GSEs and no longer subject to Budget appropriations. The legislation also alters the housing mission to meet new goals established by the regulator for single- and multi-family home purchasers in low- or very low-income areas and other underserved areas. The portfolio holdings of the GSEs would be established by the regulator in terms of safe and sound operations of the GSEs, and the regulator would also impose prompt corrective actions on the part of the GSEs when necessary.

Most important, the legislation gave the Treasury Secretary Henry Paulson the power to provide explicit government backing to Fannie Mae and Freddie Mac through the purchase of their debt and equity securities, if necessary, to stabilize the financial markets, to prevent the disruption of the availability of mortgages in the markets, and to protect the taxpayer. These were the aims of the brief statement Paulson made on July 13, 2008. However, by September 7, 2008 the situation had changed. His September statement included a reference to what some academics, senior federal officials and analysts had long observed; namely, that "their statutory capital requirements are thin and poorly defined as compared with other institutions," and in view of all the circumstances, "conservatorship was the only form in which I would commit taxpayer money to the GSEs." Paulson elaborated the plan: "the primary mission of these enterprises ... will be to proactively work to increase the availability of mortgage finance ... To promote stability in the secondary mortgage market and lower the cost of funding, the GSEs will modestly increase their MBS portfolios through to the end of 2009. Then, to address systemic risk, in 2010, their portfolios will be reduced at the rate of 10% per year, largely through natural run-off, eventually stabilizing at a lower, less risky size." Further actions would be taken by the Treasury to ensure that each company maintained a positive net worth. They were able to continue channeling funds to the mortgage market, but with the consequence that by 2009, they owned or guaranteed all outstanding mortgages in the United States, and they financed three-quarters of all the new mortgages originated that year.

The decision to put Fannie Mae and Freddie Mac into conservatorship did not take place simply because of the state of the Enterprises, the stock market reactions, or the decline in the US housing market. It was also made because the shares of both Fannie Mae and Freddie Mac, both of which at this time guaranteed half of the $12bn US mortgage market, had fallen by more than 72% and 77% between the end of 2007 and August 1, 2008.

Creditors and investors alike reacted both by limiting the credit supply and selling the shares. Foreign investors, primarily the Chinese and Japanese central banks, but also other Asian central banks, who held 35–40% of the debt issued by Fannie Mae and Freddie Mac, began to sell. The market capitalization of Fannie Mae was $7.6bn compared with $38.9bn at the end of 2007, and of Freddie Mac, $3.3bn compared with $22bn at the end of 2007.

It is small wonder that Henry Paulson said these "actions were made necessary by the ambiguities of the GSE Congressional Charters, which have been perceived to indicate government support for agency debt and guaranteed MBSs.

Our nation has heeded these ambiguities for far too long, and as a result GSE debt and MBSs are held by central banks and investors throughout the world, who believe them to be virtually risk-free. Because the US government created these ambiguities, we have a responsibility both to avert and ultimately address the systemic risk now posed by the scale and breadth of the holdings of GSE debt and MBSs."[44] The Bush administration accepted what the Chinese and Japanese governments wanted, by putting them into conservatorship, whilst guaranteeing full payments to bond and security holders. But this meant taking on as Treasury liabilities an amount equal to the sum of the entire federal debt of the United States. China, in fact, held up to one-fifth of its currency reserves in Fannie Mae and Freddie Mac debt, which amounted to $447.5bn as of June 2008. Countries in Asia had stockpiled foreign exchange reserves since the 1997–1998 currency crisis to act as cushion against a run on their exchange rates.[45]

It should come as no surprise that foreign central banks held so much of the GSEs' debt, since from 1997 onwards, both Fannie Mae and Freddie Mac increased their efforts to sell both debt and MBSs to central banks and foreign institutional investors, seeking higher-yielding non-credit-sensitive assets. In 1997, foreign buyers held about 10% of mortgage investments, and Fannie Mae, scanning international markets in order to find investors for its MBSs, was also seeking to find investors for its debt. A year later, Freddie Mac planned to launch a Five Year Bond, comparable with Fannie Mae's "Benchmark Notes" of which $4bn were issued in January 1998, with Freddie Mac following with a $1bn issue of what came to be called its "Reference Notes".

Fannie Mae and Freddie Mac were committed to offering large bullet issues across maturities to improve market liquidity. The FHLBanks, on the other hand, did not commit to a regular issue schedule, instead offering larger issues through the Global Note program but retaining more discretion in the timing and size of their Global Bullet debt. The Office of Finance, their fiscal agent, sought to manage the debt program, using their funds to make "advances" to their members as well as purchasing mortgage-related assets in the secondary market. The market for GSE debt (including the FHLBanks) grew rapidly from the late 1990s to $2.6 trillion in 2003, almost 84% of the Treasury market at that time.

This was not only due to the GSEs' extensive marketing efforts, but also because the housing market continued to expand with an increase in mortgage debt outstanding from $3.9 trillion to $5.6 trillion, a 44% increase. Residential mortgage debt outstanding reached $10.5 trillion in mid-2006. The growth in debt issuance slowed down in 2003 and 2004, owing to the accounting problems at Freddie Mac and then Fannie Mae, although the FHLB System continued to grow despite problems at some of the member banks. However, growth resumed in 2006 and 2007, so that by the end of 2007, non-US investors held $1.47 trillion of $7.397 trillion, of which over 40% was held by foreign central banks. Other large investors were US commercial banks ($929bn), life insurance companies ($388bn), state and local government retirement funds ($317bn), mutual funds ($566bn), asset-backed securities issuers ($378bn) and the GSEs themselves ($710bn). Of these, the US government was more concerned about foreign investors, and the central banks in particular.[46] This was just the systemic risk about which Chairman Bernanke expressed such deep concern, and about which Congress and the Senate refused to take the appropriate action, allowing Fannie Mae and Freddie Mac in particular to persuade them that the risk was non-existent. Indeed, Richard Syron had dismissed it as a "side-show."

At every turn, those who were responsible and in a position to act, failed to take the appropriate actions. Both Alan Greenspan and Ben Bernanke warned the Administration of the risks building up in the GSEs. The Treasury failed to oversee the GSEs' debt issuance program for too long, even though its powers were limited. The GSEs were issuing debt which, despite the disavowals of the government guarantee, was often greater than the government's own, a fact which should have caused disquiet. No doubt for successive Administrations, the fact that such huge amounts of debt were "off-balance sheet" meant that they could pretend it was not there; but then "as everyone should have learnt by now ... keeping liabilities off-balance sheet does not make them any smaller or less real."[47]

7

The Dominance of the GSEs

As has been discussed in previous chapters, there are several reasons for the dominance of the GSEs in the mortgage market, including the advantages of the hybrid structure, the subsidies, and the inability of HUD or Congress to restrain their freedom in building up their portfolios, in spite of the risks to the financial system for which the US is paying bitterly, will be examined. These include the GSEs' use of their automated underwriting system to dominate the market, and the refusal to allow Congress to impede their progress by making higher capital demands or removing any other benefits.

The GSEs' automated underwriting (AU) systems

Fannie and Freddie: First in the market

It may seem odd to describe the introduction of automated underwriting as a reason for the GSEs' domination of the market, but so it was. This was partly because they were early introducers, and used that pole position to hold sway over lenders. James Johnson, then Chairman and CEO of Fannie Mae, invested some $7bn in technology and in underwriting experiments between 1994 and 1997; the automated system was introduced in 1995, and was continually refined and updated thereafter.

The GSEs were able to make use of statistical credit scoring models which had been developed in the 1970s and 1980s, making it possible to price disparate credit risks. Fair Isaac acknowledged that the information they received from credit repositories was deficient in some respects and called for better reporting. Since then their models have been adapted to handle conflicting and duplicate information, and to avoid relying on data they know to be unreliable;[1] despite data inaccuracies and incomplete reporting, credit scores are highly predictive of loan performance. The models were incorporated into the GSEs' automated systems. Then, with the introduction of statistical modeling techniques and automated underwriting, analysts concluded that these new techniques would enable them to be able to assess the risk of lending with far greater accuracy than manual underwriting.

Developing and using the automated underwriting systems

Freddie Mac describes automated underwriting as a technology-based tool that combines historical loan performance, statistical models and mortgage lending factors to determine whether a loan can be sold into the secondary market. Mortgage originators use the system to determine the terms on which the loan could be sold into the secondary market; evaluate the credit, collateral and capacity of borrowers to make their monthly mortgage payments; and identify the appropriate type of loan for the borrower. Freddie's website emphasizes the importance of the three Cs; it also provides specific examples of families who have been helped by automated underwriting, dispelling the myth that low-income families cannot get a conventional loan; that borrowers need almost perfect credit to qualify for a loan; and that a down payment of 20% is required to buy a home. Freddie Mac's system was known as Loan Protector (LP) and Fannie Mae's as Desktop Underwriter (DU).[2]

The system evaluates the likelihood that the borrower will repay the loan, based on data summarizing how borrowers with similar loan, property and credit characteristics have repaid their loans in the past, using statistically based predictive models that correlate the underwriting data to credit performance. These models assign a loan to a risk category based on an estimate of the borrower's likelihood of default. The loan risk categories and the appraisal produced by the AU system form the basis for the lender's underwriting decision. The main three categories are:

- An Accept (LP) or Approve (DU) designation denotes the lowest level of risk and indicates that the GSE in question is willing to purchase the loan with minimal documentation.

- A Refer (LP and DU) designation indicates that the loan application needs to be referred to one of the lender's underwriters for review. Based on additional information, the loan may still be acceptable to the agencies. This category was removed from LP in November 1998.

- A Caution (LP) or Refer with Caution (DU) designation indicates that the application represents substantial risk and extenuating circumstances would have to be present for the loan to be acceptable for the agencies.

- For certain loans, the statistical property appraisal generated by the AU systems can be used in conjunction with an exterior property inspection in lieu of a full appraisal. This streamlined approval process can save from 50–70% of the costs associated with a standard appraisal.

The growth in the use of the GSEs' system was very rapid even in the early years; for example, as at the end of 1997, 51% of all lenders closing loans used it, and amongst lenders originating more than $1bn, 41% used LP and 32% used DU. Quite apart from increasing usage of the system by lenders, it was also expanded by the GSEs, when they released Internet versions of the automated systems in 2001. Freddie Mac estimated that over 10,000 brokers and 300 wholesalers had access to their system alone; by 2003 Freddie Mac was processing 40,000 loan applications a day and expected to reach 10 million by the end of the year. Fannie was much more reticent about the number of loans, but the total value of loans purchased reached over $1.3bn in the same year.[3] Freddie Mac was probably anxious to publicize the number of loans it processed, since it continually competed with Fannie, the much larger Enterprise.

Flexible standards

Right from the start, the underwriting criteria used in the automated system were flexible. In 1999, Franklin Raines announced a pilot project involving 24 banks in 15 markets to encourage banks to extend home mortgages to individuals whose credit was generally not good enough to qualify for conventional loans. This would be rolled-out nationwide in 2000. "Fannie Mae has expanded home ownership for millions of families in the 1990s by reducing down-payment requirements. Yet there remain too many borrowers whose credit is just a notch below what our underwriting has required who have been relegated to paying significantly higher mortgage rates in the so-called subprime market."[4]

Fannie and Freddie certainly offered 100% mortgages (Flex100 Home Purchase Loan, and Flex 97, which required a 3% down payment). Freddie Mac offered similar products, such as Homes Possible 100 and Homes Possible Neighborhood Solutions. My Community Mortgage offered relaxed credit and debt-to-income ratios, provided that the borrower came up with $500 to pay certain costs, e.g. towards the closing costs. In 2000, Franklin Raines urged the housing industry to work together to advocate a Mortgage Consumer Bill of Rights. "The housing industry during the 1990s ... broke down the toughest barriers to equality in home ownership, including income, finance, credit, information and even discrimination." Fannie's strategy is to offer mortgage products that allow lenders to qualify more home buyers for low-cost conventional financing. In 1999, it rolled out its Timely Payments Rewards Mortgage, which allows families with slightly impaired credit to qualify for a mortgage that was about 2% below the subprime rate; after 24 months of consecutive payments on time, the rate drops another 1%.[5] There were frequent announcements on new products throughout the years up to 2008, showing that the underwriting standards were certainly not meeting the usual demands of the three Cs. In June 2006, HUD published its review of underwriting guidelines to identify potential barriers to Hispanic home ownership: often large, poor families, including undocumented illegals, unlikely to be in regular employment. The report is interesting in that, perhaps inadvertently, it shows the weakness of underwriting requirements. The only barriers it could still find were the lack of acceptability of cash income; the requirement that borrowers be legal residents of the USA; and the requirement for homebuyer education and counseling, which might be difficult if there were insufficient Spanish courses available.[6]

Automated underwriting was often praised by those whose major interest in the late 1990s and early 2000s lay in the extension of lending to minorities and low- to moderate-income borrowers. Improved risk assessments, in their view, reduced the variance in the default equation, allowing managers to accept a higher level of risk. Underserved populations, in particular, benefitted from Loan Prospector's increased ability to distinguish between a wide range of credit risks, and "increased accuracy has led to the development of new mortgage products which would have been deemed too risky even just a few years ago. Freddie Mac now uses Loan Prospector to approve higher-risk mortgages, such as zero-money-down loans, Alt A loans, which tend to have non-traditional documentation, and A-minus loans, which pose a significantly higher risk of default. Accurate risk measurement is working in borrowers' favor, not against."[7] It was widely accepted that the flexibility of AU facilitated a growing diversity of mortgage products, those featuring low or no down-payment requirements, higher debt-to-income ratio, reduced cash reserve requirements, flexible employment standards and reduced mortgage insurance. According to Harvard's Joint Center, the development of loan products such as these have enabled the more cash-strapped borrowers at the margin to qualify for mortgage loans."[8]

Given the advantages of such systems, the GSEs used their early entrance to secure certain benefits. Even by 2005, most of the loans purchased by the GSEs used the LP or DU systems, not because other major lenders had not developed their own or were not in a position to do so, but because it was not in anyone's interests to develop another independent system. The GSEs provided various incentives to encourage the use of their systems, such as better guarantee fees (and higher fees for those who did not use DU or LP), and greater legal waivers to prevent possible loan buy-back requirements against the lender. In the last analysis, the GSEs did not approve any other automated underwriting system. Despite claims about reduction in costs, there were costs involved in using the system, such as user training, costs of supporting the interface between a lender's own computer systems and DU and LP, and, for third-party vendors, the fees paid to the GSEs for delivering their products through the systems.

The sale of third-party products through the system was introduced by the GSEs with Fannie Mae's announcement in 2001 that access to its DU system would only be possible through MornetPlus 2000, a proprietary Fannie Mae on-line system that links lenders, realtors and others with providers of services such as appraisals, credit reports and title insurance.

The AU systems are proprietary systems, so that it is not possible to know what the underwriting criteria are; nor is it possible therefore for a lender to know whether or not a loan was going to be accepted (for purchase by the GSEs) until the fee was paid and the loan had been put through the system. The GSEs do not reject all the mortgages which have not been approved by their systems, but they then place more stringent requirements on the lender, who is obliged as a result to carry a greater part of the risk. In certain circumstances, the lender may have to repurchase the loan from the GSEs if the borrower defaults and the loan was not put through their system.

Using automated underwriting as an inducement

However, as Peter Wallison notes, the "strongest inducement to use the GSEs' AU systems is that fact that it is the most effective way of ensuring that a mortgage loan will be purchased by one of the GSEs, thus reducing the lender's cost or risk of carrying the loan ... and, since the GSEs are ... the sole economically feasible purchasers of most of the vast majority of all residential loans made in the United States, lenders that use the GSEs' AU systems gain considerable cost advantages over lenders that do not."[9] By February 1999, the GSEs' combined market share in the use of LP and DU by lenders was 95%. Wallison argued that in comparison with the Court of Appeals decision concerning Microsoft as an attempt to monopolising a trade, so a case could be made that Fannie and Freddie were monopolising the automated underwriting market under anti-trust legislation. Many disagreed with Peter Wallison's analysis, and a case was never brought to the courts.

The GSEs extended and confirmed the use of their automated systems by engaging with various lenders. These partnership deals varied considerably between banks and in the aims and objectives, and were most frequent in the late 1990s and early years of the following decade. A range of examples follows, which, if nothing else, show that Fannie Mae and Freddie Mac searched for every possible opportunity to expand the business.

(1) Fannie Mae teamed up with the Union Bank of California and the Consumer Credit Counseling Service in Santa Clara County and Los Angeles to offer $6.5m in loans to consumers with impaired credit histories, but only to those who had actively participated in the local debt-management and counseling programs and had "graduated" from them within the past year. The funds were issued by Union Bank and underwritten by Fannie Mae. Similar schemes were established in 13 other cities.

(2) In February 1998 both Fannie Mae and Freddie Mac were seeking to make their underwriting systems available directly to consumers. Fannie Mae teamed up with Finet Holdings Corp., a multi-lender website where consumers could send a loan application which was then processed by Fannie Mae's DU, before the consumer selected

a lender from a panel of about 40 lenders chosen by Finet and participating in their program. The lenders paid the cost of running the application through the DU system, and Finet absorbs the cost if the loan is not finalized. The system puts in a merged credit report and a borrower pays a $39 fee online for up to three attempts. Freddie Mac was in the process of a somewhat similar project, using LP and linking borrowers up with its Goldworks subscribers, its lenders' network.

(3) In May 1998, Fannie Mae announced a new low down-payment product called the Flexible 97 Mortgage, offering a conventional fixed-rate 30-year mortgage with a 3% down payment, where the latter could come from a gift, an unsecured loan from the family, a grant from an employer, a non-profit or a government agency. Other features included the ability to pay the future mortgage on the basis of income received but no minimum credit score. The new product was sold through the network of 500 lenders using DU together with two mortgage insurance companies (Mortgage Guaranty Insurance and Commonwealth Mortgage Insurance).

(4) In July 1998, the *Milwaukee Business Journal* reported that lenders were increasing their use of the automated underwriting systems, partly because of efficiency and also because of the fee reductions on offer once they entered into a deal. These included St Francis Capital Core and several other similar banks, as the DU told them whether or not the GSE would buy the loan: as the Journal reported, "this in effect tells the bank whether to approve the loan." The costs were reduced from $60–70 for every loan processed to an undisclosed sum, but less than $60. Another bank, M&I Mortgage Corp., decided to use Freddie Mac's LP system which meshed with their own software.[10]

(5) Freddie Mac announced a partnership with Wendover Financial Services in February 2001, which allowed its licensed real estate brokers to offer customers mortgage applications, customized pricing and loan approvals using LP. At the same time, LoanTrader.com, which was a transactional marketplace for subprime lenders and brokers, was integrated with LP on the Internet, thus enabling automated underwriting decisions for LoanTrader's brokers and lenders. Fannie Mae simultaneously announced a partnership agreement with America's Community Bankers.

(6) Perhaps one of the most important deals Fannie Mae ever made was with Countrywide, given the size and importance of its operations in the mortgage market. Although Countrywide was acquired by the Bank of America in January 2008, at the time this would have appeared to be an excellent partnership, giving access as it did

to Countrywide's mortgages to brokers on Fannie and Freddie's automated systems. Countrywide mortgages became available on Fannie Mae's Desktop Originator on the Web and Freddie Mac's Loan Prospector on the Internet.[11]

This is just a small sample of the various partnerships, relationships and often complex deals that both Fannie Mae and Freddic Mac entered into over the years, especially up to 2003 and 2004, when the accounting problems came to light. The deals helped to ensure that there was little criticism of the GSEs' dominance in the marketplace, but did not succeed in silencing all the critics: for example, John Taylor, President and CEO of the National Community of Reinvestment Coalitions, stated that the GSEs' regulators "should encourage a wide diversity of credit scoring systems, competing with each other in developing sound and flexible underwriting criteria. This will open more doors to home ownership for minorities and low- to moderate-income borrowers. In addition, the regulatory oversight agency should continue conducting fair lending testing of the GSE underwriting systems, as HUD has just started doing."[12]

With a rather different emphasis, the former Treasury Under-Secretary Gary Geinster stated, "To the extent that the GSEs now finance a significant portion of their sector of the mortgage market, the willingness of the GSEs to purchase a mortgage has become a far more significant factor in deciding whether to originate that mortgage. The GSEs automated underwriting systems are increasingly becoming the means by which originators decide to lend. This technology will make the process more efficient. In the long run, however, this trend may result in less diversity in credit decisions and less price competition."[13] Geinster's conjectures were probably correct, but with so many deals and the near-certainty of selling-on the loans to the GSEs, to many, the lack of competition no doubt seemed less important as time went on. The concern which did linger was that the AU systems discriminated against minorities, primarily due to the credit scoring codes, though it appears that other AU systems in use at the time did not lead to quite as high a rejection rate as other automated systems in 1999. These and other complaints led HUD to conduct a fair lending review, which took over two years to complete. In those early days of the use of such systems, and in the context of the prevailing view that it was vital to extend home ownership to minorities, the emphasis was on fair lending rather than the quality of the mortgages.

Automated underwriting fails to measure default risk

This emphasis on fair lending meant that the data issues, which would turn out to be just as significant for minorities with mortgages as for all others, were overlooked. In February 2001, Fannie Mae revealed the contents of the "black box," that is, the range of factors taken into account when giving loan approval. Much as expected, these were borrower characteristics, including, for example, equity, taking appraisal or sales value into account; credit history (FICO scores); debt-to-income ratio; and the borrower's work status (salaried or self-employed). To these factors was added information about the type of loan and the type of property, and information about any previous defaults or foreclosures.

These are all entirely reasonable factors, but what is missing here are any historical data concerning what would happen to mortgages of a particular type in an economic downturn or in a period of falling house prices. Where such data are incorporated into a computerized model, they tend to be of short duration. The model does not take account of any other external risks, such as changes in interest rates, unemployment or lack of stability in employment even where the work status is salaried. Nor is the basis of borrower default predictions explained in this revelation.

All of this depends on the assumption that the full contents of the "black box" have been revealed, and that it is clear what importance was given to each of the factors over time. For example, the acceptability of the source of the down payment changed over time, and automated appraisals of the value of the property were introduced, based on local house-price data, with some kind of external evaluation of the property that allowed what were called "drive by" appraisals rather than a true inspection. Such appraisals may only have verified the existence of the property at the purported address, and perhaps, say, the presence of a roof, but did little to prevent inflated appraisals, which was another contributory factor to the collapse of the mortgage market. The down payment was considered to be merely an impediment to lending, rather than providing some kind of reassurance that the borrower intended to pay the mortgage. Debt-to-income ratio is correctly included, but the means of verifying income cannot be carried out through this kind of system.

Over time (as can be seen from some of the above partnerships and deals), LP and DU allowed for the shift of the underwriting decision from the GSEs to the lenders, and then to the brokers and finally to the borrower. The GSEs would, of course, claim that this was not the case, because use of the system determined the acceptance or rejection of the loan application. But the whole development and use of the AU reduced human input and control and, as time went on, allowed others to "game the system."

The use of DU and LP and the elements in the model apparently led the GSEs and the regulators to believe that loan acceptance depended on the assessments provided by the system, whereas in fact the quality and accuracy of the data submitted was the key. This is not necessarily to imply that the data was submitted fraudulently; only that those using it needed to ensure that all the data given was properly validated or understood instead of being based on a cursory review of documents provided. Under the system, lenders could assess a borrower's creditworthiness based on "a verbal verification of employment" which was "the only required income verification for borrowers with low-risk profiles." Fannie Mae insisted that, "We've researched this very carefully, and we know that people who have certain risk profiles … in a very high percentage of the time, simply do not take on financial obligations that they cannot handle."[14] Reliable third-party data bases should have been used, rather than depending on borrower-supplied data: two years' of tax returns, paychecks and a written verification of earnings from the borrower's employer were the typical requirements. Other problems in the data were set aside, such as proper appraisals (difficult to find, admittedly, in the US in the 1990s and until the rules were changed in 2008). In addition to data issues, the GSEs frequently changed the significance and weight to be attached to the various factors listed above: for example, accepting loan applications with low and borrowed down payments. Fannie and Freddie frequently changed the system as they sought to develop "new" products in their quest for ever-greater market dominance.

"Fannie Mae had constructed a vast network of computer programs and mathematical formulae that analysed millions of daily transactions and ranked borrowers according to their risk. Those computer programs seemingly turned Fannie into a divining rod, capable of separating pools of similar-seeming borrowers into safe and risky bets. The riskier the loan, the more Fannie charged to handle it. In theory, those high fees would offset any losses." DP did not and probably could not achieve that, but it is not possible to tell, as the details of the models were never revealed and the extent to which programs were modified and adapted to meet specific requirements, perhaps of partners such as Countrywide, were never disclosed. One take on the system was provided by Marc Gott, a former director in Fannie's Loan Servicing Department, who said, "We really did not know what we were buying. This system was designed for plain vanilla loans, and we were trying to push chocolate sundaes through the gears."[15]

HUD's demand for full loan level data

Once again, issues regarding data are vitally important. Checking the automated underwriting applications against the original files would clearly be a major undertaking. Even carrying out meaningful spot checks, given the annual volume of applications (running into millions) would be demanding in terms of human and financial resources, even if the GSEs were seriously prepared to provide them. As indicated in Chapter 5, as part of its proposals for new housing goals for Fannie Mae and Freddie Mac HUD included a Notice of Proposed Information Collection for the GSEs, which covered both the Public Use Data Base and Public Information (which was shelved) together with changes in data reporting, designed to assist with the prevention of predatory loans, defined as high-cost loans. The combined report from HUD and the Treasury contained a recommendation that Fannie Mae and Freddie Mac should provide data about the loans accepted through DU and LP: the APR and the cost of credit, together with the borrower's debt-to-income ratio. The recommendation was resisted both by the GSEs and by the industry, on the grounds that the detailed requirements had not been spelt out (apart from the possible rules which would be drawn up by the Federal Reserve and would apply to HMDA data as well). The comment period ended on January 8, 2001 and the joint letter from the trade associations was published on January 5, asking for HUD to withdraw the Notice. The American Bankers Association, America's Community Bankers, the Independent Community Bankers of America and the Mortgage Bankers' Association all wanted HUD to withdraw it, as "interested parties because Fannie Mae and Freddie Mac will look to their customers, primary market lenders, to supply them with additional data necessary to meet their reporting requirements." They added that "Due process and fundamental fairness require that those who will bear the burden be notified specifically of what that burden will be and be given a reasonable opportunity to assess the implications of the proposal and comment on its reasonableness, particularly in the light of the potential burden of dual reporting regimes for a single objective … We [therefore] strongly urge that, at a minimum, the proposal be withdrawn at this time and published in the *Federal Register* with a list of all the date elements to be collected."[16] The then Assistant Secretary, William Apgar, stated that HUD was aware of the extra burdens to be taken into account if new loan data elements were to be included in the reporting requirements, and if they could not be handled by existing systems then HUD would build in a transition period for them. In the event, the whole issue was postponed.

The issue is an interesting one. Reporting requirements do, of course, impose costs on companies and may require transitional periods for systems adjustments. But the resistance on the part of the industry does raise questions about their own control of mortgage credit. In order to assess the credit risks they had taken on in granting mortgages, assuming it was their policy to grant loans where, for example, the borrower's debt-to-income ratio and other features of the loan carried higher risks, then the banks would surely have such data available. There may, of course, be less concern about carrying credit risk, since the agreements to use DU and LP carried with them the near-certainty that the loans would be purchased by Fannie Mae and Freddie Mac. They create mortgage backed securities, the holders of which get the (passed-through) interest and principal payments of the mortgage borrowers, less a "guarantee fee" charged by the GSEs. The guarantees of the GSEs protect the MBS holders against losses due to "credit risk" (the possibility of default). The mortgage originators can sell their swapped MBSs into the secondary market for these securities, or hold them as relatively liquid assets in their portfolios.

Clearly Fannie Mae and Freddie Mac charged different levels of guarantee fees according to the degree of risk involved. To take one such example, Fannie Mae announced new "eligibility standards" for "refinance mortgages" on September 23, 2002, with the aim of aligning their eligibility and pricing policies more closely with the risk profile of the particular mortgage transaction. Their research indicated that "cash-out refinance mortgages default at a higher rate than other refinance transactions, adjusting for other risk factors … We also confirmed that the default rate increases as the new mortgage amount increases beyond the unpaid principal balance of the mortgage that was refinanced."

Fannie Mae distinguished between limited cash-out mortgages and refinance mortgages, and defined the latter as referring to refinance mortgages that involve the refinance of subordinate liens that were not used in whole to purchase the subject property. "Lenders must obtain written confirmation (and maintain such confirmation in the loan file) that all the proceeds of the existing subordinate lien were used to fund part of the purchase price of the subject property, in order to treat the transaction as a "limited cash-out" refinance. Other relevant documents, such as the contract of sale, should be obtained and retained for this purpose. Then the lender was responsible for ensuring that any application for such a loan (after February 1, 2003, and allowing time for systems adjustments) should be entered into the DU as the appropriate refinance type. The guidance also requires lenders to ensure that the valuation appraisals are carefully scrutinized, as these are more likely to be inaccurate in cash-out refinance transactions. Lenders were warned that cash-out refinance loans would be carefully categorized according to the LTV levels; a table of increased loan level charges was also included.

With reference to the alleged difficulties of providing information, it is interesting to note two important points. Fannie Mae and Freddie Mac's systems had become increasingly sophisticated as they introduced new products or accepted the new types of mortgage which the lenders introduced to meet demand, or to meet the requirements for more lending to low- and moderate-income borrowers or those in underserved areas. From the above example, it is quite clear that Fannie and Freddie could (in theory at least) identify the loans they accepted through the automated system, and that they required files to be kept of the relevant information. Since all the parties involved needed to know how many and what types of loans they accepted, agreed or bought in order to assess the credit risk involved, and, in the GSEs' case, with the important element of charging differential fees, then it is difficult to see why providing HUD with the data should present such difficulties. Fannie and Freddie were nonetheless reluctant to provide such information: they did not want the riskiness of the loans they were acquiring to become known. Franklin Raines, in particular, always referred to "meeting our standards," as though these were the highest standards of lending.

"We also set conservative underwriting standards for loans we finance to ensure the homebuyers can afford their houses over the long term. We sought to bring the standards we apply to the prime space to the subprime market with our industry partners primarily to expand our services to underserved families. Unfortunately, Fannie Mae-quality, safe loans in the subprime market did not become the standard, and the lending market moved away from us. Borrowers were offered a range of loans that layered teaser rates, interest-only, negative amortization and payment options and low-documentation requirements on top of floating-rate loans."[17] They set out to offer "high-quality, low-cost, non-predatory loans" to borrowers with blemished history. It is hard to reconcile this statement with the loans which Fannie Mae knowingly bought over the years, and from lenders such as Countrywide.

Fannie Mae, Freddie Mac and Congress

Making sure the 1992 Act did not impose unwelcome restrictions on the GSEs

The Federal Housing Enterprises Financial Safety and Soundness Act, 1992 took shape over three years, during which time the GSEs worked with the Administration to develop the original proposal, and then with Congressional staff to shape the final outcome. That is to say, James Johnson, then Chief Executive of Fannie Mae, used his powerful lobbying position to shape the GSEs as he wished. "Protecting the Charter had become management's pre-eminent concern."[18] The Act, as a result of a series of compromises, mostly to the benefit of Fannie Mae, resulted in the creation of the Office of Federal Housing Enterprise Oversight (OFHEO), as an office within HUD, but a little separate from the department in that the Director was appointed by the President for a five-year term. According to the statute, "The Director is authorized, without the review or approval of the Secretary, to make such determinations, take such actions, and perform such functions as the Director determines are necessary" to set capital standards, issue and enforce regulations, and examine Fannie Mae and Freddie Mac.[19] It was thought that this would sufficiently separate the OFHEO from political influence.

On the other hand, the Secretary for Housing under the legislation retains the right of approval over any OFHEO actions not directly required by the legislation. OFHEO is required under the legislation to submit appropriations requests for Congressional approval, and must clear drafts of proposed regulations through the Office of Management and Budget. OFHEO's function was to ensure the safety and soundness of the GSEs; from the start, Fannie Mae was determined to ensure that it had some protection against regulatory limitations on its activities. The Act therefore included the requirement that OFHEO put all proposed regulations before Congressional oversight committees, and that funding for OFHEO had to go through an annual appropriations review. Some critics recognized at the time that this would give the GSEs "a chance to exercise influence over the regulator by lobbying the Appropriations Committees."[20]

Preserving benefits: Treasury line of credit

This issue arose during a hearing held by Richard Baker, Chairman of the Capital Markets Subcommittee on March 22, 2000.[21] It was the first of a series of bills that he and others introduced for better regulation of the GSEs. Testimony was given by Gary Gensler, Treasury Under Secretary at the time, in the course of which he supported the removal of the Treasury's line of credit from the GSEs. This was first authorized at its current level (it was authorized to purchase up to $2.25bn of Fannie and Freddie's obligations) in 1957. Mr Gensler was at pains to point out that the amount was irrelevant anyway, given the size of the GSEs at the end of 1999: they had grown in size to $1.4 trillion, and either owned or guaranteed about 63% of all outstanding conforming, conventional mortgages, of which the retained portfolio represented 26%. GSE share of the US debt markets was increasing; at $1.4 trillion, it was the same size as the US's entire municipal debt, and over half of the $2.7 trillion privately held marketable Treasury debt. The GSEs also then held $1.2 trillion in GSE MBSs, which Gensler also recommended should be curtailed. As will be seen, it was not possible for the Administration or the Federal Reserve to change any of that without Congressional approval, which is where Fannie and Freddie were able to exercise their powers.

After the hearing, Gensler said in press interviews that debt issued by Fannie and Freddie was not guaranteed by the US government, which was hardly news, although many investors interpreted the line of credit and other ties to the government as an implicit backing by US taxpayers. Gensler's testimony not only upset the markets, but created a veritable storm. It upset the bond markets the following day, but as John Lonski, Chief Economist at Moody's Investor Services, pointed out, "Some credit market participants were lulled into thinking that agency papers and Treasury debt were virtually indistinguishable. We've warned investors about it for a long time. If the market is overreacting, then it may have more to do with its own nervous state than with Mr Gensler's remarks."[22]

The markets calmed down pretty quickly, while volatility remained with Freddie and Fannie, who launched their attacks in the press with CFO Timothy Howard calling Gensler "irresponsible" and "inept." Freddie's spokeswoman Sharon McHale said that he had "showed utter contempt for the nation's housing and mortgage markets," and Fannie's spokesman, David Jeffers, said that the "bond market's reaction raised costs to consumers," adding "frankly we see no reason why Treasury would want to give up a tool that supplies emergency credit at a time of crisis."[23]

Fannie and Freddie both apologized, but then followed this with further attacks. David Jeffers said that "it is unfortunate and regrettable when statements made by the Treasury have such an immediate and profound effect on American consumers ... [those] attempting to purchase homes today will pay about a quarter point more in mortgage rates as a result of the Under Secretary's comments, and that means that they will pay an extra $5,800 over the life of an average Fannie Mae 30-year loan. The rise in mortgage costs caused by the Treasury's remarks means that about 206,000 families will be disqualified for home loans."[24] This again was retracted the next day, but by then the damage had been done.

Through extensive advertising, Fannie was seen as a mortgage provider throughout the country (although, of course, it did not lend anyone any money). As Congress considered one bill after another in the years to come, Fannie and Freddie's tactics were always the same: any change would increase the cost of mortgages. Then they would arrange for various associations, such as the Association of Independent Community Bankers, to write to the Congressional committees and organize constituents to write to their Representatives or Senators with the same message. Their message would also be conveyed to the House Financial Services Committee. The Subcommittee's Ranking Democrat, Paul Kanjorski, hoped the bill (Housing Finance Regulatory Improvement Act, H.R. 3703) was not on a "fast track," but then he thought that they "should not rush into judgment" almost until the end. Congresswoman Maxine Waters was concerned, as ever, that any changes should not hinder the ability of African-American homebuyers to qualify for mortgages. She wanted Freddie Mac and Fannie Mae to expand and provide more mortgages to poor people, which remained her position until the GSEs collapsed. As for removing the Treasury line of credit? Nothing was done until 2008, when Fannie and Freddie needed far more than $2.25bn.

Fending off higher capital requirements

According to the 1992 Act, OFHEO had to develop a risk-based capital stress test to ensure the GSEs held enough capital to cover credit and interest rate risks, plus 30% for management and operational risks. The 1992 Safety and Soundness Act set out a number of factors which OFHEO was expected to take into account; the single assumption was that there would be ten years in which interest rates fell by 6%, while at the same time house prices would fall throughout the country at a rate observed in an area with at least 5% of the population with the highest default rates and credit losses for the GSEs for at least two years. During that time, the test assumed that the GSEs would not conduct any new business for at least two years. It was odd to set out such details in legislation, and even odder to regard its development as essential during a period in which modeling for various risks was being developed.

Work on the test was supposed to be completed by December 1994, but it was not finished until October 1998, when it was sent to the Office of Management and Budget, which did not complete its review until March 1999, when it was sent to Congress for a 15-day review, followed by a four-month period for public comment. OFHEO hoped it would be finalized by the autumn, but that was far too optimistic; the final rule was not published until July 19, 2001 for public comment, and after that, it was published in the Federal Register on September 13, over 100 pages of it including OFHEO's responses to comments.[25]

A brief summary

The housing GSEs are required to hold capital equal to the minimum requirement or the risk-based capital requirement, whichever is the larger. The former is defined as 2.5% of a GSE's assets plus 0.45% of the outstanding MBSs that it guarantees. As at the end of 2002, with the then volume of outstanding MBSs, the minimum capital requirement was about 3% of assets for both Fannie and Freddie.

The risk-based capital requirement (RBC) is defined as the level of capital necessary for a GSE to absorb all losses and survive a ten-year stress period that begins with a sharp upward or downward movement in interest rates and the onset of a sustained decline in house prices. To estimate the GSEs' losses during that period, OFHEO used a computer model, or stress test. OFHEO then had to estimate the effects of upward and downward movements in interest rates to determine which is worse for the GSEs, and to use that shock in the stress test. In addition, house prices are assumed to decline by 11% during the stress period and then to recover to the initial level of the previous five years. Then, OFHEO estimated how those changes in interest rates and increases in credit losses, because of defaults, would affect the GSEs' earnings, in order to calculate the risk-based capital requirement. The amount of capital was then raised by 30% to account for unmeasured management and operations risk. "The test incorporates no new Enterprise business and no asset sales to raise cash. It simply runs off their existing assets, liabilities and off-balance sheet activities under the stress conditions. This no-new-business requirement is explicitly mandated in the 1992 Act."[26]

"No new business" meant that the GSEs could not create or purchase new MBSs, nor actively reset their derivatives portfolios, although it was not entirely clear whether this would hurt the Enterprises or help them survive the test. A dynamic true hedging would help the GSEs, but the wrong strategy might compound losses. If that was the intent in raising the issue, it was scuppered by the Congressional Budget Office and the Government Accountability Office in June 2002, when the latter published its assessment, in its Report to the Congressional Committees entitled "Incorporating New Business is not Advisable", a matter which was still under consideration in 2003. In a letter to the then Chairman of the Senate Committee on Banking, Housing and Urban Affairs, Paul Sarbanes, the Congressional Budget Office summarized the issues raised by the GAO, which it stated might be useful for the Director of OFHEO when considering risk-based capital:

- The current assumption of no new business does not appear to understate the capital required by the GSEs to survive the stress period. Changing the new business assumptions could reduce the ability of the stress test to measure required capital for the GSEs' current stock of business.

- The primary effect of new business on the required level of capital depends on whether the new business is assumed to be voluntary (and thus largely profitable) or compulsory and unprofitable; if the former, it would reduce the capital requirement, and if the latter, it would increase it.

- Assuming that new business would be profitable, following a time lag for the GSEs to adjust to the new level of interest rates and higher credit losses in a stress period, is probably more realistic than assuming that new business would result in continuing losses. The reason is that both the GSEs' management and federal regulators have incentives to ensure the survival of those Enterprises.

Inadequacies of the test

The stress test itself was inadequate in other respects. First of all, under the then Basel I requirements, mortgage loans had a risk weight of 20%, so that the capital requirement for a mortgage loan would be 4%. If Basel II had been applied, then banks would have had to maintain higher levels of capital against mortgage loans than the GSEs, but the Federal Reserve did not approve the final rules implementing the Basel II risk-based requirements until November 2, 2007. Only large, internationally active banks were obliged to apply the rules over the following three years, although other banks could elect to comply with them, leaving smaller banks with a simpler framework.

The stress test was subject to criticism, partly because it assumed uniformly severe economic conditions throughout the USA, whereas economic capital should depend on the degree of geographical diversification of the mortgage portfolio.[27] The GSEs purchased loans from lenders throughout the USA, and the house price collapse occurred first and more extensively in the so-called "sand states" (Arizona, California, Florida and Nevada). It was therefore a limitation of the test that it only envisaged one scenario, whereas stress tests, properly conducted, postulate a range of scenarios, and estimate the capital requirements for each. Because of these and other innovations in handling risk, the test turned out to be less stringent than the minimum standards, and largely irrelevant.

Secondly, the stress test did not distinguish sufficiently between the likelihood of losses from subprime loans and prime loans. According to an OFHEO working paper by Pennington-Cross, an analysis of a synthetic portfolio of Fannie Mae and Freddie Mac mortgages randomly sampled from 30-year fixed rate mortgages and subprime mortgages shows that the expected or mean simulated losses from subprime mortgages are five or six times higher than for prime loans. The paper also argued that the use of simple risk-sharing arrangements could greatly mitigate expected losses and reduce their variation.[28] Such analyses indicate that the single stress test set out, even if applied rigorously throughout, would not have led OFHEO to understand all the risks to which the GSEs were exposed.

Fannie Mae and the stress test

Freddie Mac welcomed the introduction of the stress test and was constructive in its approach. Fannie, on the other hand, was as obstructive as possible. Shortly before the details of the test were sent to OMB, Fannie objected to any OFHEO reference to a specific capital amount or percentage amount of capital, because this would create a false perception of capital inadequacy. Then the GSE claimed that OFHEO had never talked to its own officials in order to understand their business. Although OFHEO could not legally consult Fannie until the proposed rule was issued, the acting Director, Mark Kinsey, stated that his officials had talked to theirs, as well as to mortgage insurers, large banks and thrifts, and other private market institutions about how they handle risk. In fact they had held many meetings with Fannie Mae officials to understand how they measure and model risk.

That move having failed, Fannie Mae then returned to its usual attack: the proposed rule would limit its ability to serve low- and moderate-income borrowers. They did not get very far with that, so the last try was to suggest that the rule might lead to higher guaranty fees for lenders. In 1999 the Executive Summary of the proposed rule pointed out that the ability of Fannie and Freddie to meet the proposed standard while continuing to meet their affordable housing responsibilities was demonstrated by Freddie's risk-based capital surpluses in 1996 and 1997. OFHEO pointed out that Fannie's capital deficits were not caused by the credit risk of affordable loans, but by unhedged rate risk. "The risk-based standard is unlikely to cause any changes in mortgage rates and will not give the Enterprises incentives to raise their credit guarantee fees. Because the rule will help ensure the continued health of Freddie Mac and Fannie Mae, borrowers will, in fact, benefit from the rule."

For once, Raines recognized that he was not going to prevent the introduction of the test, so by April 1999, Fannie was advising equity analysts that even if the OFHEO proposal was carried out, it would not affect their company's performance. Their Chief Finance Officer, Timothy Howard, claimed that Fannie could reallocate its hedging dollars and subordinated debt to meet the requirements: "Even if the regulation does not change at all, Fannie Mae will be able to adapt to it with no measurable impact on earnings per share growth."[29]

By the time the stress test was developed and carried out, Raines was not too concerned about its impact. In fact, he saw that its successful application could be used to his advantage The OFHEO stress test depended on "data that characterize, at a point in time, an Enterprise's assets, liabilities, and off-balance sheet obligations, as well as data on economic conditions, such as interest rates and house prices [from public sources] ... The Enterprises are required to submit data to the OFHEO at least quarterly for all on-and-off balance sheet instruments in a specified format ... This data submission is called the Risk-Based Capital Report and serves as the financial 'starting position' of an Enterprise for the data for which the stress test is run."[30]

The Fannie Mae Papers and the risk-based capital test

The Fannie Mae Papers, produced by housing and other economists, also bolstered Raines' position.[31] One in particular was extremely important, produced by Joseph Stiglitz, Nobel Prize winner, Jonathon Orszag, Managing Director of Compass Lexecon, and Peter Orszag, former Director of the Congressional Budget Office during the Bush Administration and more recently, Director of the Office of Management and Budget in the Obama Administration until 2010. Their much-publicized conclusion (no doubt regretted now) was:

> This paper concludes that the probability of default by the GSEs is extremely small. Given this, the expected monetary costs of exposure to GSE insolvency are relatively small – even given the very large levels of outstanding GSE debt and even assuming that the government would bear the cost of all GSE debt in the case of insolvency. For example, if the probability of the stress test conditions occurring is less than one in 500,000, and if the GSEs hold sufficient capital to withstand the stress test, the implication is that the expected cost to the government of providing an explicit government guarantee on $1 trillion in GSE debt is less than $2m. To be sure, it is difficult to analyse extremely low probability events, such as the one embodied in this stress test (a severe national economic shock that is assumed to last for ten years). Even if the analysis is off by an order of magnitude, however, the expected cost to the government is still very modest.[32]

Deflecting SEC registration

The role of Congressional and Senate Committees has been illustrated in the oversight of the GSEs, HUD and the OFHEO, the necessity of Congressional approval of major rule changes and the long saga of establishing risk-based capital requirements. The bill proposed by Congressman Richard Baker in 2001 would have removed the GSEs' exemption from SEC registration and reporting requirements, and would, amongst other things, have required Fannie and Freddie to publicly disclose at least annually, financial, business and other information that the Fed determines is in the public interest. That bill had been successfully defeated; it never left committee. Then Congressmen Chris Shays and Edward Markey introduced a bill in April 2002 (H.R. 4071) which would repeal Fannie and Freddie's exemption from Securities and Exchange Commission registration requirements, and drew attention to the fact that they were the only two Fortune 500 companies not subject to disclosure and registration rules. Chris Shays issued a press release in support of the bill on March 21, stating that, "This disclosure is paramount to maintaining transparent markets and providing investors with the accurate and timely information they need to make informed financial decisions. The exemption of Fannie Mae and Freddie Mac from federal securities laws flies in the face of good corporate practice. Our legislation simply brings Fannie and Freddie in line with other firms, and gives investors access to vital information ... there is no excuse for private investor-owned corporations to be exempted out of these important investor protection requirements."[33] They may have been emboldened in the forthright nature of this statement by the response of the SEC Chairman, Harvey Pitt, during the hearing on H.R. 3763, the Corporate and Auditing Accountability, Responsibility and Transparency Act:

MR SHAYS: "In 1992, the SEC, the Treasury and the Federal Reserve in a joint report recommended legislation to repeal the GSEs' exemption from the Federal securities law. As you know, Fannie Mae and Freddie Mac are the only two publicly traded firms that aren't. Does the SEC still adhere to the Commission's 1992 report?"

MR PITT: "We have not changed our general position, but we have focused on it again. I will say that in this day and age I believe transparency has to be the order of the day. To the extent that exemptions permit anything less than transparency, which I believe is the case, I believe at least that portion has to be removed. Frankly, I could care less whether the GSEs pay registration fees or things of that nature. But I do believe that disclosure is critical for the GSEs as well as for other public companies." When Mr Shays then asked if he could use the statement that Federal securities regulation is premised on a full and fair disclosure (of accurate, complete and timely disclosure of financial information) of this information, "as a strong support in some cases of such disclosure," the Chairman replied in the affirmative.[34]

Franklin Raines had been present at the hearing, giving testimony on behalf of the Business Forum, an association of CEOs recognized as an "authoritative voice on matters affecting American business corporations and as such has a keen interest in corporate governance." He was quick to note Chairman Pitt's replies and, obviously in response to questions Raines had briefed the media to ask, the SEC quickly issued a "clarification" stating that "neither Chairman Pitt nor the Commission is advocating any change in the legal status of the GSEs." Such a statement was characteristic of Harvey Pitt's approach during his brief period as Chairman.[35]

No doubt fearing that unwelcome requirements would be imposed on them, especially in the post-Enron era, Fannie Mae and Freddie Mac agreed to make certain voluntary disclosures whilst still opposing the bill to make them subject to SEC requirements. This took the form of website disclosure of the purchases and sales by their own senior executives as allowed immediately after the publication of their quarterly earnings. Both GSEs claimed that such information was always made available to investors who contacted the company. These efforts were not enough to stave off further moves to ensure that they conformed to SEC requirements. On May 29, 2002, the Office of Management and Budget issued a "prompt" letter to OFHEO, urging the regulator to strengthen corporate governance at Fannie Mae and Freddie Mac and to require the GSEs to make certain public disclosures.[36] The letter stated: "In September, 2001, OFHEO published a proposed rule to codify the corporate governance requirements for Fannie Mae and Freddie Mac that currently exist in OFHEO's guidance to the Enterprises. We request a further rule-making that would include additional requirements to strengthen the corporate governance of Fannie Mae and Freddie Mac … We [also] request that OFHEO consider a rule-making to require each Enterprise to disclose publicly the information that is required of publicly traded companies by the SEC, including any additional requirements SEC requires in the future. While the Enterprises now voluntarily comply with many of these disclosures, they are not required to do so. Such voluntary compliance might be abandoned at a time when it is most needed." Such moves, the letter added, would advance the goals the President set out in his Ten-Point Plan for Corporate Responsibility and Protecting America's Shareholders.

In his reply of June 28, Armando Falcon stated that OFHEO was considering a rule which would include the following:

1. Periodic reports both quarterly and annually, supplemented by a special report filing for material developments outside the timetable. These filings would be as comprehensive as the current SEC requirements.

2. Registration of Fannie Mae and Freddie Mac's offerings of stock and debt. Here the OFHEO is developing an approach that would facilitate registration in a way which does not impede their ability to meet their financing needs.

3. Supplemental disclosures, additional information above and beyond current SEC requirements, such as interest rate risk, derivatives and mortgage backed securities.

In response to OMB's press release, Fannie Mae and Freddie Mac stated that they wholeheartedly embrace the goals outlined in the President's 10-point plan. Freddie Mac stated that it was already working with OFHEO on its disclosure project; they welcomed the opportunity to continue working with OFHEO and OMB because they were confident that both would recognize that their disclosures already met or exceeded those required by the SEC. Fannie Mae also stated that it already disclosed more information to investors than any other large financial institution.[37]

The outcome was less than the OFHEO's proposals in its letter of June 28. Just two weeks later, the regulator abandoned its plan to issue a rule-making requiring the GSEs to register their debt. On July 12, in a joint press conference with the SEC and OFHEO, Fannie Mae and Freddie Mac announced that they would voluntarily register their common stock with the SEC, but not their debt or MBSs.

In his statement at the press conference, the SEC Chairman said, "Although Fannie Mae and Freddie Mac's decision to subject themselves to the full panoply of the Securities and Exchange Act disclosure is voluntary, it is now irrevocable without SEC approval. This addresses the concern that, however complete their disclosures were, it was a matter of choice, not a requirement of law. Fannie and Freddie will file, for example, complete audited 10-K annual reports, 10-Q quarterly reports, and 8-Ks regarding current events affecting them … And, of course, we will have our full complement of enforcement authority over these periodic disclosures. Similarly, the companies' officers and directors will file reports on their purchase or sale of company stock, and the companies' proxy statements will be subject to SEC staff review, as is true of other public companies."

Chairman Pitt also announced a study of the disclosure requirements applicable to mortgage-backed securities. "The goal is to ensure that the same standards of disclosure apply to all engaged in the distribution of these securities. But this agreement does **not** subject the companies' securities to Securities Act registration requirements applicable to the public offering of new securities." The study would be undertaken by the Treasury, OFHEO and the SEC.

However, it should be noted that Fannie Mae had not issued common stock since the early 1980s, but had made about 1,500 debt issuances and over 40,000 MBS releases annually. Fannie Mae and Freddie Mac were quick to make public announcements to the effect that their exempt security status had not changed, and that there was no effect on the status of Fannie Mae's securities as "government securities." Freddie Mac quoted from the letter it had received from the SEC confirming that "the actions taken have no impact on the status of Freddie Mac's securities as exempt from securities offering registration requirements as well as other aspects of the federal securities laws." As a result, Freddie Mac's access to worldwide capital markets would remain unhindered.[38] It also enabled them to reject the Shays-Markey bill, which would have required them to register their debt and MBSs, on the grounds that this would have caused unnecessary disruption to the market, since the SEC registration process was not designed to handle the unique securities market in which Fannie Mae operates.

The tactic was successful. The bill could now be painted as irrelevant, and indeed, the Treasury Secretary Paul O'Neill both welcomed the self-initiated compliance and stated that the Administration did not intend to support the Shays-Markey bill. This was repeated by Peter Fisher, Undersecretary for

Domestic Finance, on the grounds that the Administration was not prepared to support repeal of their exemptions from the Securities Act, 1933 but believed that they should comply with the same corporate disclosure requirements as all other publicly owned companies under the Securities and Exchange Act of 1934. Fisher reiterated the announcement of a study of the initial offering disclosures for all issuers of mortgage backed securities, to be conducted by the Treasury, the SEC and OFHEO.

"Together we will listen carefully to the securities industry, investors, Fannie Mae and Freddie Mac, Ginnie Mae, private-label issuers and others in the regulatory community to gain a fuller understanding of the market structure, the nature of competition and the risks being priced and transferred. This will serve as background to a fundamental reconsideration of the initial offering disclosures that would best serve all of the participants in mortgage-backed markets."[39] The Task Force reported in January 2003, having concluded that if the GSEs' exemptions were removed, the additional disclosures would be useful to, and not disruptive of, the mortgage-backed securities market. The issue, in other words, had not been settled by the voluntary disclosure announced in July, but came back in 2003, both in the form of a judicious decision to make additional voluntary disclosures on the part of Fannie Mae and Freddie Mac, and in the form of further legislative proposals to be considered.

These attempts to bring Fannie Mae and Freddie Mac under better regulation and to bring about the necessary legislative changes have been covered in some detail, partly because they were significant factors in the subprime mortgage crisis and its part in the financial crisis, but also because it shows how difficult it was for Congress to bring Fannie Mae and Freddie Mac under control, as Congressional oversight responsibilities required. The all-pervasive American dream of home ownership both blurred the vision of politicians and provided the two GSEs with ready weapons to ward off any attempts to limit their powers.

8

The Beginning of the End for Freddie Mac

The end was slow in coming; much slower than it ought to have been. Both the events and the responses to them as set out in this chapter will explain the reasons for that. Moves to improve the regulation of the two GSEs and to remove certain SEC exemptions continued throughout 2003, accompanied by a recognition of the need for full disclosure of the MBSs.

The GSEs' commitment to voluntary disclosure and registration

Mortgage-backed securities

The GSEs were quick to recognize where voluntary commitments were to their advantage. They fended off the removal of their market advantages, and retained their image as virtuously fulfilling their affordable housing mission. OFHEO, the Treasury and the SEC jointly produced a report on "Enhancing Disclosure in the Mortgage-Backed Securities Market."[1] Based on interviews with market participants, lenders and non-GSE-issuers, who all took the view that the market would function more effectively with additional pool level disclosure, the Task Force proposed a number of additional items of information, which should be included in disclosures. These were:

- Loan purpose
- Original loan-to-value ratios
- Standardized credit scores of borrowers
- Service information
- Occupancy status
- Property type

At the time, Fannie Mae and Freddie Mac disclosed information about the underlying mortgages that support mortgage-backed bonds on an aggregate basis for a number of similar issues of securities, rather than for each individual issue. The aggregating of data about such loan characteristics as initial and average time to maturity, interest rates paid by home owners on individual loans, the initial size of the loans, and the geographic locations of mortgaged properties may conceal significant differences in the pool of mortgages backing individual MBS issues. If investors had more specific information about the mortgages behind the pools, they would have a better understanding of the risks they were taking on, and be able to price them more efficiently. The data are important for understanding prepayment risk, which is likely to occur when interest rates fall. Home owners get a better deal in the form of lower interest rates, but the investor then does not receive the expected return on their investment.[2] The Task Force report regarded prepayment risk as the most important, though it also included interest rate and credit risk.

The most common type of MBS is a pass-through security backed by a pool of single-family mortgage loans, created by pooling or packaging mortgages together in a trust or other collective investment vehicle and selling the interests in a trust. In this case, the certificate holders own undivided interests in the pool. All payments on the underlying mortgage loans, including principal, scheduled interest and unscheduled payments, are passed through, on a pro rata basis, to the holders of the pool interest or participation certificates after deducting service fees, Fannie and Freddie guarantee fees and trust expenses. Private label issuers often used REMICs (real estate mortgage investment conduits), where the underlying assets were either other MBSs or whole mortgage loans. The structure allows the issuers to create securities with short, intermediate or long-term maturities. The assets are pooled and the cash flows are distributed to the various REMIC classes according to agreements made in advance. For the GSEs, REMICs are based on the GSEs' own MBSs, for which there are two basic mechanisms: a "cash" program and a "swap" program.

Such disclosures for the GSEs would largely be made after sales, because most securities are initially sold in the To Be Announced (TBA) market before such information is available. In most cases, and especially with a single lender, the mortgage originators pool the loans and then obtain a guarantee from either Freddie Mac or Fannie Mae, which evaluates the loans to ensure that they meet its credit quality standards. In those transactions, the lender swaps a pool of loans for MBSs representing the ownership in the same mortgages. Exchanging pools of mortgages for MBSs is useful to the lenders, because the securities have lower capital requirements and are more liquid. For Fannie Mae and Freddie Mac, agreements were already in place to deliver the MBSs in the market for forward sales (TBAs). In 1998, the Bond Market Association estimated that about 90% of all transactions, measured by dollar volume, were TBAs. Private label MBSs do not trade in the TBA market; because of the varying credit and other risks of private label issues, the market sets prices for those MBSs individually. The prices for TBAs are based on the assumption that the nature of the risks of the GSEs' MBSs is known.

The purpose of the report was to bring Fannie and Freddie's disclosure requirements up to the then level of private label MBS issuances as required by the SEC, where collateral and structural terms sheets together with a prospectus had to be registered with the SEC, unless a specific exemption was sought, subject to Rule 144A (regarding qualified institutional investors). In July 2002, the Treasury, OFHEO and the SEC jointly announced Fannie and Freddie's intention to voluntarily register their common stock under the SEC 1934 Act. This, however, would not apply to disclosure requirements regarding MBSs, which was the point of this report. Therefore the Task Force recommended both enhanced disclosures for private label MBSs, and their application to the GSEs.

In response, on April 1, 2003, Fannie voluntarily began releasing both the weighted average and the quartile loan-to-value ratios, borrowers' credit scores for the loans making up its MBS pools, identifying servicers for the pools, occupancy status of the property, property type (single-family or two-to-four unit dwellings), and the purpose of the mortgage (purchase or refinance). Freddie committed itself to similar disclosures in June 2003. It was not enough to satisfy all market participants, who wanted the points paid by borrowers to be included, together with loan level documentation and borrowers' debt-to-income ratios. Both the Treasury and the SEC wanted such disclosures as well, but, since the basis was voluntary, OFHEO had no means of enforcing them.

Fannie and Freddie saw voluntary disclosure as their solution. They may have overlooked the possibility that, "when voluntary disclosure programs appear to have no harmful effects on secondary market liquidity, on GSE profitability, or on the costs of homeownership, justification for retaining the exemption loses its persuasiveness."[3] Perhaps they thought that once their voluntary disclosures were in place, their extensive lobbying machine would take over.

The voluntary disclosures were never enforced. The examinations of Fannie and Freddie did not cover the mortgages they bought and sold as MBSs. Apart from the unswerving belief in the implicit guarantee of Fannie and Freddie's creditworthiness, the notion that, as the report put it, investors could rely on all their documentation and extensive financial reporting, was shattered by their accounting irregularities. If all this information had been available, and if the risks involved in purchasing the GSEs' MBSs were fully revealed, then the purchasers and packagers of the MBSs, followed by the investors and the CDOs would have known what they were. But Fannie and Freddie consistently represented the mortgages they bought as "conforming" mortgages and as being of good quality.

Voluntary registration under the SEC Act, 1934

However, the decision to register voluntarily under the SEC Act of 1934, rather than the 1933 Act, had certain advantages from the point of view of the GSEs. It enabled them to register one class of securities (common stock) without registering their preferred stock, debt and MBSs. Voluntary regulation also meant that they would not have to face all the SEC's legal requirements. Congressmen Shays and Markey were well aware of the implications and importance of their proposals for legislation, but it often seemed as though some of their colleagues were not; nor were some of the witnesses. They did not win, perhaps partly because of the immediate decision to offer voluntary registration.

The Secondary Mortgage Market Regulation Act, H.R. 2575

Purpose of the bill

On June 25, 2003, Richard Baker introduced another bill to reform and modernize the oversight of Fannie Mae and Freddie Mac, which he introduced by referring to the enhancement of regulatory oversight under the Sarbanes-Oxley Act, following the fall of Arthur Anderson in June 2002. Mr Baker noted that only two Fortune 500 corporations were exempted from the Act, because "they are too well run to worry about. They have set a standard of corporate governance to be emulated by others. And ... we want to make sure we don't throw any out of the opportunity of homeownership."[4] His frank opening statement shows the problems with Fannie and Freddie: they were exempt from relevant regulatory oversight, a remarkably favorable position, and any criticism of them was immediately construed as a denial of the American dream. He also warned that "if the nation's GSEs were to suffer a financial reversal of a similar scale [to Enron], the systemic consequences are difficult to comprehend."[5] He was not the only one to warn of the risks of their failure, but all such warnings went unheeded.[6]

The legislation was designed to fulfil only three goals: an independent regulator; proper funding (which meant that the regulator's budget would not be funded through the appropriations process); and ensuring that the regulator had all the necessary tools, as possessed by any other regulator in the financial market place. Of course, Congress, as Richard Baker reminded them, was "directly responsible for their supervision and regulation." The bill was debated at subsequent meetings of the Committee, notably in September 2003.

Lukewarm support from the Administration

H.R. 2575 did not have the full support of the Administration. The Secretary of the Treasury, John Snow, gave testimony at the September 10 hearing, at which he made it clear that the Administration supported a new Federal agency to oversee the activities not just of Fannie Mae and Freddie Mac, but also of the Federal Home Loan Bank System. Its powers should include the execution of on-site and off-site supervision; the review and rejection of proposals to transfer controlling interests or significant ownership to other parties; the establishment and enforcement of criteria for new lines of business, acquisitions or investments by the GSEs; the ability to supervise consolidated organization; the ability to ensure that the GSEs have adequate measurements, monitoring arrangements and controls over market risk; and the ability to set appropriate capital requirements, together with all the powers and resources required. The duties of the new regulator should reflect the powers it would have. The Administration was prepared to place the new agency within a Cabinet department.

John Snow's testimony was accompanied by that of the Secretary for Housing, Mel Martinez, who stated that the Administration wished to see a new GSE housing authority within HUD to enforce its own housing goals; to introduce civil penalties for its failure to meet housing goals; and explicitly to provide that the GSEs act to increase home ownership. He also referred to expanding HUD's authority to set housing goals and subgoals beyond the current categories. It is at this point that the potential conflict of interests arose, between the persistent and overriding aim of continually increasing home ownership, and the proper regulation of the GSEs.

What crisis?

The response of two members of the House Financial Services Committee was interesting, given that Freddie Mac's accounting difficulties had already come to light, and in the context of the post-Enron era. Barney Frank, who was a member of the Congressional Financial Services Committee since 1981, and who became its Chairman in 2007 until the Democrats lost control of the House in November 2010, was deeply sceptical of the need for reform. This is what he had to say on September 10, 2003:

> I want to begin by saying that I am glad to consider legislation, but I do not consider that we are facing any kind of crisis ... Fannie Mae and Freddie Mac are not in a crisis. We have recently had an accounting problem with Freddie Mac, with people being dismissed ... I do not think at this point that there is a threat to the Treasury. Fannie Mae and Freddie Mac have played a very useful role in helping make housing more affordable both in leveraging the mortgage market ... and they have a mission which this Congress has given them in return for some of the arrangements which enables them to focus on affordable housing and that is what I am concerned about here. I believe that we, as the Federal Government, have probably done too little rather than too much to meet the goals of affordable housing and to set reasonable goals.[7]

Mr Frank had the strong support of Representative Maxine Waters, who stated that she was a member of the Committee, when they enhanced the structure of these GSEs in 1992, to assure the safety and soundness of their housing mission in particular. "However, I have sat through nearly a dozen hearings when we have tried to fix something that wasn't broke. Housing is the economic engine of our economy, and in no community does this engine need to work more than in mine ... We do not have a crisis at Freddie Mac, and in particular at Fannie Mae, under the outstanding leadership of Mr Frank Raines. Everything in the 1992 Act has worked just fine. In fact the GSEs have exceeded their housing goals. What we need to do today is to fix the regulator, and this must be done in a manner so as not to impede their affordable housing mission, a mission that has seen innovation flourish from desktop writing to 100% loans."[8]

The GSEs' "support" for a strong regulator

The last hearing in 2003 took place on September 25, at which Franklin Raines and George D. Gould (Presiding Director, Freddie Mac) gave evidence. Given the questions about the financial status of Freddie Mac, the focus was inevitably on both the evidence and the responses to issues raised by the Committee from Fannie Mae. In his evidence, Raines gave his full support to the existence of a strong, credible and well-funded regulator, and hence to the Department of the Treasury's plan. He was critical of the proposals of H.R. 2575, arguing that it would "harm the functioning of the housing finance system ... It would make unwise changes in our capital standards. It would impose on Fannie Mae an enforcement and prompt correction regime that is far more harsh than the provisions applicable to any other financial institution. It would force disclosures of proprietary information ... we urge the committee to reject H.R. 2575 in its current form ... We believe policy makers will find consensus around the approach outlined by Secretary Snow."[9]

None of the somewhat sweeping assertions made in his testimony were seriously questioned by members of the Committee. One or two issues came to the fore and are valuable in terms of the insight they give into Fannie Mae's practices. Raines strongly opposed prior approval of programs and products, and the reasons for this are clear in his reply to a question from the Chairman (Michael Oxley):

"This committee may be faced with an issue as early as next week in terms of the mark-up and trying to determine how we deal with the program approval, at the same time dealing with the safety and soundness, because ... the Treasury proposal is very heavily tilted towards Treasury ... but the other issue in terms of programs is still kind of out there. From your perspective, and having experience in that area, what would you suggest?" Mr Raines replied, "Our focus in discussions with them (the Treasury) and others has been more on what the decision-making criteria are. And within the context of the Treasury discussions, they have indicated to us that they believe that a prior approval regime isn't necessary at all ... And that has some attractive features obviously from the point of view of innovation. However, we have also been talking to a wide range of our friends in the housing industry who have a very substantial concern that putting together the approval of our new program activities with the safety and soundness regulator might have a detrimental impact on housing. And we share a lot of those concerns ... The most important issue is that there be a standard that encourages innovation and that we not ignore that fact that it has been through innovation that we have been able to serve more and more people. It is not from just doing that same plain vanilla 30-year fixed mortgage that we started doing in 1938. It is by having new programs with low down payments and with the ability to deal with people with impaired credit and other innovations that have really allowed us to expand affordable housing."[10]

Mr Raines was, of course, correct in arguing that it was only through such 'innovations" as disregarding credit history and requiring low down payments that more mortgages could be offered and home ownership extended, especially to those on low or very low incomes. It comes as no surprise that he wanted such approvals (if they were imposed on him) to be quite separate from "safety and soundness" issues when the kind of mortgage products Fannie Mae and Freddie Mac bought, were precisely those which would impact most on the capital required to cover the risks. Their "friends in the housing industry" would naturally be concerned if they would then find it difficult or even impossible to sell their "innovative" loans to the GSEs.

Another bill bites the dust

The bill, however, was too weak to attract the support of the Administration, so that, contrary to Chairman Oxley's hopes, it did not receive a "mark-up" (that is, a reference back to the full Committee for approval, often with amendments and changes to it). The bill simply died in Committee.[11] The debates in the hearings show that H.R. 2575 was weaker than the Administration's proposals, so attention turned to the Senate in early 2004.

Federal Enterprise Regulatory Reform Act, S. 1508

Purpose of the bill

Another bill had been introduced in the Committee on Banking, Housing and Urban Affairs on October 16, 2003 by Senator Hagel, together with Senators Sununu and Dole. This was the Federal Enterprise Regulatory Reform Act, S. 1508. In introducing it, Senator Hagel set out the principles contained in his bill and the Administration's proposals:

> The new regulator at the Treasury Department must have the authority to approve new programs and ensure that Fannie and Freddie continue to focus on their core missions as defined and established by the Congress of the United States.

Second, an effective regulator must have broad authority over capital standards and the ability to adjust them as appropriate to balance risk and ensure safety and soundness.

The Committee held a further four hearings, and called a wide range of witnesses as well as the key players: Secretary John Snow; Secretary for Housing, Mel Martinez; Alan Greenspan;[12] Franklin D. Raines, CEO Fannie Mae; George D. Gould, Presiding Director, Freddie Mac; Norman Rice, President and CEO, Federal Home Loan Bank of Seattle; John Korsmo, Federal Housing Finance Board; Armando Falcon, Jnr, OFHEO; Douglas Holtz-Eakin, Director, Congressional Budget Office: and representatives of the various bankers' organisations and other financial services regulatory bodies, sometimes on more than one occasion. Fannie Mae, in particular, and Freddie Mac held to the positions on proposed legislation that they had spelt out in the Congressional hearings, with the only difference being that questioning was somewhat more rigorous in those of the Senate.

An awkward passage

The bill was reported from the Committee on April 1, 2004, but on March 26, Chairman Shelby of the Senate Banking Committee released a draft bill which was offered as a substitute for S. 1508 during the mark-up. This bill was designed to create a new independent regulator for Fannie, Freddie and the FHLB System, who would be responsible for safety and soundness and the housing mission. The new regulator under the bill would have the power to alter the GSEs' minimum and risk-based capital requirements, and prior approval authority over new lines of business the enterprises wished to undertake. Over 30 amendments were debated during the Committee's deliberations. Shelby's bill contained a proposal to give the director of the regulatory authority power to appoint a receiver for any GSE which failed; this proved to be controversial and Senator Bob Bennett's amendment, which Shelby accepted in exchange for his vote, gave Congress the power of veto. Some members of the Committee regarded the amendment as being designed to confirm the belief in the implicit federal guarantee. The final version was passed by the Senate Committee with several amendments on a 12-9 vote, showing a split along party lines with one Democrat, Senator Zeil Miller, voting with the Republicans.

On the following day, the Secretaries of the Treasury and HUD issued a joint statement of opposition to the revised version of S. 1508. Their statement referred to an amendment adopted in the mark-up, which would allow Congress to overrule the regulator's decision to appoint a receiver. They characterized this amendment as one which would significantly weaken "a core power needed for a strong regulator," which would be likely to "reinforce a false impression" that the GSEs have a government guarantee.

(Under the amendment, Congress would have 45 days after the appointment of a receiver to pass a joint resolution of disapproval.) Not only would it weaken the regulator, but if such circumstances arose, a delay of 45 days would no doubt have disastrous effects.[13]

This in itself made it more difficult to move the bill forward to a full floor vote, especially since, at that time, the Senate had 51 Republicans, 48 Democrats and 1 Independent. After the Committee's decision, Shelby issued a prepared statement in which he said, "I supported the receivership compromise and many other provisions adopted today, in the hopes of putting together a package that might attract support from across the aisle. I will not support such a compromise in the future. I do not believe that the receivership provisions that the committee has adopted today provide a workable solution for resolving a GSE crisis."

Fannie on the attack

Senator Shelby was also aware that the kind of campaign which Fannie Mae, in particular, would continue to wage against any changes in the regulation of the GSEs had already begun the previous day. A widely reported advertisement appeared on TV, featuring a worried-looking Hispanic couple:

MAN: "Uh-oh."

WOMAN: "What?"

MAN: "It looks like Congress is talking about new regulations for Fannie Mae."

WOMAN: "Will that keep us from getting that lower mortgage rate?"

MAN: "Some economists say rates may go up."

WOMAN: "But that could mean we won't be able to afford the new house."

MAN: "I know."

Senator Hagel was shocked. "Here is an organization that was created by the Congress … spending money questioning the Congress's right to take a serious look at oversight," he said during the April 1 hearing. "I find it astounding. Astounding!"[14] Such an advertisement was typical of the tactics which Fannie Mae adopted whenever they thought it necessary. They continually stressed the importance of their role in the housing markets in their public statements, and through the statements that they persuaded various associations to make on their behalf, given that these associations had benefitted from the ever-expanding housing markets and from their relationships with the GSEs, which the latter had carefully cultivated over the years. Later that year, Raines was to find that he had won a battle, but not the war; he had not taken sufficient note of the many voices which had began to criticize Fannie Mae's activities, ranging from those of OFHEO, the Treasury, the Council of Economic Advisers, and the Office of Management and Budget, and still less of the post-Enron context, one in which the Bush Administration did not want to see any further scandals and in which Freddie Mac had already raised anxieties about the extent of accounting malpractices.

Accounting irregularities at Freddie Mac

The accounting scandals of 2001 and 2002 led to the collapse of two of America's largest companies: Enron in December, 2001 and Worldcom in July, 2002. Both Senate and Congress held a large number of hearings regarding the accounting practices that led to their collapse; by July 30, 2002 they had passed the Sarbanes-Oxley Act, designed to enhance corporate governance and strengthen corporate accountability by requiring full transparency. Attention turned to Freddie Mac, partly because the GSE had had the same auditors as Enron, Arthur Andersen, a defunct firm by then, Freddie Mac replaced them with PricewaterhouseCoopers.

Freddie announces the restatement of its earnings

Anxieties were aroused, however, when Freddie Mac announced on January 22, 2003 that it would have to restate its earnings for 2002, 2001 and possibly 2000, because of a change in accounting for certain derivative transactions. Freddie Mac also announced that it would delay its planned issuance of euro-denominated bonds until after it had published its unaudited earning figures for 2002 on January 27, which it expected to be at a record level. The SEC, with its new powers over Fannie Mae and Freddie Mac, would be likely to investigate, and OFHEO was considering restating Freddie's capital adequacy for the third quarter. OFHEO had just declared that both companies met the minimum risk-based capital requirements as of September 30, 2002, with Freddie Mac being better able to withstand severe economic shocks. The initial shock led to a fall in the value of Freddie Mac's shares, dropping $2.30 to close at $61.60 (a 3.5% decline), but Standard & Poor's Ratings Services affirmed all of its ratings in the light of the announcement, stating that the AAA/A-1+ unsecured debt senior ratings on Freddie Mac reflected the "implied government support for the securities of this government-sponsored enterprise (GSE), as elaborated in its charter and governing legislation. The rating agency pointed out that the AA- subordinated debt, preferred stock and risk-to-government ratings are based on an analysis of the company's financial strength and the operating benefits it received as a GSE."

Top management goes

The first announcement was followed on June 9, 2003 by a more significant announcement by the Board of Directors that the President and Chief Operating Officer had been sacked; that the Chairman and CEO had retired; and that the Chief Financial Officer had also resigned (it transpired in a later press release that Brendsel had retired at the request of Freddie Mac). New appointments were announced: Gregory J. Parseghian as Chief Executive Officer and President; Paul Peterson as Chief Operating Officer; Martin Baumann as Chief Financial Officer; and Shaun O'Malley being elected by the Board of Directors as non-executive Chairman of the Board. The same press release stated that David Glenn had been sacked "because of serious questions as to the timeliness and completeness of his co-operation with the Board's Audit Committee counsel, retained in January 2003 to review the facts and circumstances surrounding the principal accounting errors identified in the accounting process." The Dow Jones Newsletter reported that Vaughn Clarke had been asked to resign "due to questions about his honesty to the company's Audit Committee counsel." It also reported that the share price fell with the news, to $50.60, down 15% or $9.20 on the Friday close.[15]

OFHEO stumbles

Unfortunately for OFHEO, it released its annual report to Congress on June 4, the very day that Freddie Mac's alleged employee misconduct came to light. In the course of the report, OFHEO stated that it considered a "re-audit and delay in 2002's statements is prudent and appropriate under the circumstances … In addition, management and its board of directors initiated efforts in 2002 to enhance the expertise and controls in the areas of financial accounting and operational control … We remain satisfied that the Board of Directors and executive management are taking appropriate action."[16] A few days later, OFHEO announced its special examination, which was eventually published in December 2003.

At the same time, Freddie Mac announced that it expected to delay its restated earnings, probably until the third quarter from the previously stated second quarter, but that the likely cumulative effect would be to "materially" increase reported earnings for the earlier periods and "materially" increase the company's capital surplus under OFHEO's minimum capital requirements as at the end of 2002. Freddie also said it expected that there may be significant volatility in quarterly earnings for those periods. Adjustments affecting its income would relate to changes in the timing of income recognition; and, as a result, cumulative increases related to adjustments would have offsetting effects in future periods, which may be accompanied by increased volatility.[17] Freddie Mac released a more detailed statement later the same month, in which they indicated that the restatement would mean the statement of retained earnings as of December 31, 2002 would be in the range of $1.5bn to $4.5bn. In the event, it turned out to be $5.5bn. The increase was due to gains on certain derivatives and mortgage retained earnings marked to fair value during periods in which interest rates were falling.

The new CEO, Gregory Parseghian, announced that "the new management team of Freddie Mac, working closely with our Board of Directors, is determined to set high standards for candor and transparency in our financial reporting. Our investors and the public should expect and demand nothing else ... At the same time we remain focused on our business and our mission."[18] He was also determined to get the message across to the public, so once again the GSE practice of advertising was adopted, this time in major newspapers. The advertisements took the form of an open letter from the new CEO, referring to the "skilled and energetic" new management team, installed by the Board of Directors, which was working with outside auditors to quickly complete the company's restatement of its financial results for 2000–2002.[19]

But by August 21, 2003, OFHEO recommended that Parseghian should be fired, since as the previous Director of the Funding and Investment Division, he had been involved in the accounting problems. He was removed by the Board and replaced in December, 2003 by Richard Syron, former President of the Boston Federal Reserve Bank.[20]

Much more to Freddie's problems than met the eye

The view is sometimes expressed that the accounting irregularities, involving complex rules for accounting for derivatives, rules sometimes regarded as being controversial, in that they involve mark-to-market accounting, were not so serious as to threaten what many saw as the vital role played by Freddie Mac (and Fannie Mae) in enabling those on low-to-moderate incomes, as well as those on very low incomes, to own their own homes.

In fact, the extremely detailed and thorough report produced by OFHEO in December 2003 showed that the "accounting irregularities" were much more than that. Accounting procedures and practices were entirely focused on "earnings management" to such an extent that they were not in any way designed to provide a "true and fair" picture of the company, but instead distorted every aspect of its management. The OFHEO report describes the activities of what was once known as "Steady Freddie," the image which the company promoted of itself in the early 1990s, a company with strong and steady growth in profits. That led to a corporate culture which made its priority one of meeting those obligations. "Freddie Mac cast aside accounting rules, internal controls, disclosure standards, and public trust in the pursuit of steady earnings growth. The conduct and intentions of the Enterprise were hidden and were revealed only by a chain of events that began when Freddie changed auditors in 2002."[21] The executive summary provides key examples of the manipulation of transactions in order to smooth out the volatility of earnings. They were as follows:

- Management executed several interest rate swap transactions that moved $400m in operating earnings from 2001 to later years. These transactions had virtually no other purpose than management of earnings, specifically, making operational results appear to be less volatile than they were.

- Management created an essentially fictional transaction with a securities firm to move approximately $30bn of mortgage assets from a trading account to an available-for-sale account. Other than to reduce potential earnings volatility, the transaction had no other meaningful purpose.

- From 1998–2002, management purposefully kept loan loss reserves at an unusually high level by using aggressive assumptions, even though both actual and foreseeable credit losses were rapidly declining. Both management and the Board of Directors were aware that the Securities and Exchange Commission had criticized that practice as an inappropriate form of earnings management.

These examples show that the whole thrust was to manipulate earnings, and was not due to the difficulties of accounting for derivatives or any difficulties that might have arisen from implementation of the Statement of Financial Accounting Standards 133 (FAS 135). "The management of the Enterprise went to extraordinary lengths to transact around FAS 133 and to push the edge of the GAAP envelope."[22]

Current and former staff members describe what really went on

The interviews with staff and the examination of documents (including emails and tapes) contained in the OFHEO report are illuminating, in that they show the full extent of the deep and persistent faults with the entire conduct of business at Freddie Mac over a decade. The report notes that the use of inappropriate accounting strategies began in 1994, when the Enterprise established a $200m reserve account to cushion itself against the fluctuations caused by the unpredictable amortization of premium resulting from mortgage prepayment speeds. This policy of an FAS 91 reserve was continued until 2002, and then against FAS 133.[23] But senior management and the Board believed that conformity to these standards gave a "distorted impression of the financial performance of Freddie Mac."[24] Worse than that, of course, application of the standards could reduce their earnings.

The first step in the process was to meet the expectations of the Wall Street analysts, which was apparently the main responsibility of Vaughn

Clarke, Freddie Mac's Chief Finance Officer. This was explained in OFHEO's interviews with employees of Freddie Mac, such as the Corporate Controller, Mr E. Sannini:

"There was an objective to try to get as close to the analysts' estimates … forecasts as possible … [this] came in communications to me primarily from Vaughn Clarke," and more particularly in the Deputy Corporate Controller, Lisa Roberts' statements:

> [The issue of meeting analysts' expectations] would be discussed in terms of communicating either Shareholder Relations or Vaughn would inform the group of where the expectation happened to be at that point given the information available to the company. The company would track and monitor where the analysts were expecting the company to come out for a particular quarter, so that knowledge typically was being evaluated and monitored by Shareholder Relations and Vaughn as an individual. So he would come to the table with that … The purpose of providing that information was if the Funding and Investments Division needed to execute a transaction in order to meet that expectation, those types of strategies, alternatives and options were discussed. On the other hand, Vaughn waited to see actually what business activity had been executed for the month and wanted to look at where the results were coming in, and then based on where the results were coming in compared to where he felt the street expectations were, the options and alternatives were discussed.[25]

All of this was being carried out with a serious lack of resources, including the lack of sufficient and skilled staff. Lisa Roberts in her interview stated that "during the past five years (with the exception of 2002), management maintained roughly the same number of resources within the Corporate Accounting Department and the decentralized accounting units. During this time … we increased the complexity of our products and strained our operating systems. In addition to a steady stream of new products and transactions, management was also challenged by a number of major events including the conversion of the general ledger … the implementation of compliant systems (in preparation for Y2K) and the adoption of major accounting principles such as FAS 133 and 140. These challenges redirected key resource and management focus from the baseline operation to the issue at hand and further challenged the remaining resources to maintain the control structure." In 1996, Corporate Accounting still managed the entire portfolio accounting process on Excel spreadsheets, and it was not until 2000 that a more robust Treasury accounting system was introduced.

It was all about earnings management

It is worth noting in further detail the lengths to which the senior management were prepared to go in order to preserve the impression of a steady stream of earnings, especially in 2000. Mr Parseghian (briefly CEO of Freddie Mac in 2003) stated that the management knew the derivatives gain would be substantial, but that the gain would have "detracted from future period earnings;" that is, a transition adjustment from a large derivatives gain in the first quarter of 2001 would be much less desirable than having the same amount of earnings spread out over several quarters. David Glenn's diaries showed that management had been working on such a plan for some time, and that it had been extensively discussed with the Funding and Investments Division. The plan anticipated an exchange of $10bn to $15bn of PCs (participation certificates in a pool of mortgages) with embedded losses in the retained portfolio for a Giant (Coupon Trade-up Giants, or CTUGs). The purpose of this transaction was to move securities with embedded losses from the held-to-maturity category (where losses are unrecognized) into trading (where losses would be immediately recognized in net income and would offset derivative gains) and then into available-for-sale, where securities gains and losses only hit "other comprehensive income," not "net income."

But in November and December 2000, interest rates were falling rapidly, leading to increased market values for PCs in Freddie Mac's portfolio. The losses were now too small, bringing the total amount of PCs to be exchanged up to about $30bn. In addition, the market value of the options-based portfolio was still too high and the management wanted that to be reduced by the losses created by the CTUG transaction. The PCs had been converted into Giants by Freddie Mac when this should have been carried out by the securitization group at the Enterprise instead of by Salomon Smith Barney. An additional problem was that Salomon Smith Barney only held the securities for a few hours before retuning them to Freddie Mac.

When Freddie Mac carried out the transaction in 2001, management did not obtain a legal opinion, because the external counsel considered that "the transaction would fall under the umbrella of the comprehensive legal letter written in connection with the Giant sales in general." This was because "the transaction was considered to be a typical Giant sale from an operational standpoint." It was, however, not only a very large transaction ($30bn), but, as PricewaterhouseCoopers ascertained in 2003, the PCs were not actually sent to Salomon Smith Barney, cash did not move from the firm to the Enterprise and back again, and no fee was paid by Salomon to the Enterprise; instead, Freddie paid Salomon a fee on the transaction.[26]

The ostensible purpose was to stabilize the earnings flow, but that was not the only reason. As OFHEO put it, "the CTUGs are an example of a transaction with little or no economic substance that Freddie Mac manufactured to obtain a particular accounting result."[27] That was not the only problem. Operational risks were created by the transaction, including the fact that CTUGs contributed to the Guaranteed Mortgage Securities (GMS) reconciliation problem in 2001. This was presented to the Audit Committee in December 2001.

The Report then turned to the issue of executive compensation, especially when linked to earnings per share, and concluded that this certainly contributed to the improper accounting and management practices at Freddie Mac. Compensation of executive officers had three key components: a base salary, an annual cash bonus, and a long-term stock incentive (stock options and restricted stock), according to the Charter, which required that a "significant portion of potential compensation" should be based on the performance of the Corporation.[28] About 54% of the total cash pay (salaries, bonuses and other compensation) to executive officers was based on performance. The practice was to set a "target bonus" incentive for each executive, a percentage of the salary at the beginning of each year. The target bonuses were known as the "bonus pool" and then Freddie Mac used a corporate score card to assess how much was in the bonus pool, depending on profitability, core capabilities and strategic positioning, but which ensured that the bonus funding percentage was above plan or on plan. It was always on plan at least, but the way in which the plan and the score card were structured meant that all executive officers had an interest in achieving the bonus plan, since a substantial part of their earnings depended on it. The way in which the whole process was managed, especially to the benefit of David Glenn and Leland Brendsel, is described in detail in the OFHEO report.[29]

The key point, however, is to see just how many transactions Freddie Mac initiated in order to shift and smooth its reported earnings. The report refers to various derivative transactions, including a pair of linked swaps, which were executed in order to move large amounts of operating income into the future.[30] In August 2001, Freddie Mac entered into eight pairs of swaps, each of which had a notional amount of $5bn, resulting in a total notional value of $80bn for the eight pairs. In September, the Enterprise entered into the ninth pair of swaps; this time they were leveraged swaps with a notional value of $5bn, but with the leverage factor of five, they had the same effect as swaps with a notional value of $100bn.

Morgan Stanley also entered into linked swaps with Freddie Mac, but because the terms of the two swaps substantially offset each other, the transactions did not pose any real risk for them. One such conversation is included in the text of the report. A Freddie Mac employee, Mr Powers, called Morgan Stanley to get pricing for one of these swaps and, since it was an unusual request, Brendan Lavelle, who had to approve such transactions, spoke to Mr Powers:

MR LAVELLE (MORGAN STANLEY): "We've been trained whenever people come in and start doing this kind of stuff, we gotta ask why. Like not why but like, everything's ... I don't want to be taken off in handcuffs here for doing something that's not kosher."

MR POWERS (FREDDIE MAC): "How much are you making off this trade? [*Laughs*]"

MR LAVELLE: "I don't know."

MR POWERS: "You haven't even looked at it. [*Laughs*]"

MR LAVELLE: "I'm just … You know what I'm saying … I mean, I don't mind if there's an accounting reason for you to do this and it makes you guys money. That's fine. You know we're OK with it."

MR POWERS: "That's where we are. We have an accounting reason for doing it. And, um, we're basically … we're offsetting some …"

MR LAVELLE: "I mean you could tell me that there's some asset liability reasons for you doing this, and I'm OK with that."

MR POWERS: "Yeah, I think that's as much as I'd … I don't want to tell you …"

MR LAVELLE: "I don't want to be taken into the courtroom, though, Ray, is what I'm saying OK?"

MR POWERS: "Yeah … No, no, no. This is not … This is basically an asset liability, cash flow management issue."

MR LAVELLE: "OK, I'm with you."

MR POWERS: "The thing is … because of the shape of the curve, um, the geography of our carry in terms of the calendar gets screwed up. So all of a sudden, we have an uneven carry picture to manage and we strive for stability."

MR LAVELLE: "What you're trying to do is, yeah, you're evening out the cash flow."

MR POWERS: "Exactly."

MR LAVELLE: "OK. Alright, I'm with you."

MR POWERS: "Otherwise, like we have all of our portfolios, our 30-year portfolios with all the carry in this year."

MR LAVELLE: "If that's what you want to do, I'm, we're OK with that and we're happy to do it with you, so we can do a lot of this if you want."[31]

OFHEO comments that Mr Lavelle seems to propose a business purpose to his customer, and once the customer agrees with that, Mr Lavelle approves the deal. Mr Wong, an operations officer with compliance responsibilities, at Morgan Stanley advised against any further trades of this kind when it came to his attention; Morgan Stanley decided to handle the situation by pricing the transaction unattractively when Mr Powers requested similar trades. It appears that Morgan Stanley was not the only one who was willing to enter into such arrangements. Other examples are given in the report, and the value of such deals in fee income is recorded there. The Salomon Smith Barney deal was approximately $4.7m for receiving Giant securities, holding them for under three hours and then returning them to Freddie Mac, at virtually no risk to themselves, so that Freddie Mac could place them in the 'available for sale' portfolio, which would not be marked to market.

Blaylock and Partners, a small broker-dealer, acted as an intermediary as well for at least ten trades between 2000 and 2001, where the securities went from the Securities Sales & Trading Group (SS&TG) of the Enterprise to the retained portfolio. Charles Foster, then Vice President of the SS&TG, said that the Blaylock trades were "relatively large for an entity of that size in terms of the capitalization of that company." He explained to OFHEO that the trades were done at the request of the Funding and Investment division, because the SS&TG had mortgage securities in their inventory that were either about to pass through a 30-day window (beyond which SS&TG could no longer sell the securities to Funding and Investment), or were already beyond their 30-day window. He recalled a discussion taking place about whether they could take those assets and sell them to a particular counterparty from whom the retained portfolio could later repurchase them. He was also advised by a colleague in Funding and Investment that Blaylock was not highly capitalized and was therefore a credit risk. The result was that approximately $572m in mortgage-backed securities that had been held for longer than 30 days by SS&TG were sold to Funding and Investment, and Blaylock's commission part of those transactions was 0.25%.[32] By October 2004, Richard Syron had announced that the Securities, Sales & Trading Group would be dismantled, accepting the criticisms that the group added to the GSE's risk and profits without making a contribution to further its mission. Freddie Mac would be a less active trader of MBSs. It would purchase MBSs only to retain in its own portfolio and not for trading accounts. It would not deal with the group of relatively small broker-dealers as it had done in the past.

A total failure of governance

The OFHEO report identified the widespread weaknesses in accounting in terms of staffing, skills and resources. The acute shortage of accounting staff, the inadequacies of successive Chief Financial Officers and Controllers, and the outdated or non-existent accounting policies and manuals between 1991 and 2003 are fully documented. John Gibbons, CFO until March 2000, lacked the skills for that position. He was replaced by Mr Vaughn Clarke, "who had even fewer skills, and hoped he would grow into the job." He was appointed as CFO by default, since Freddie Mac, after extensive searches, failed to find anyone else.

Before he left the company, Mr Gibbons told Mr Brendsel that a fully qualified Deputy Controller should be hired, but the Chairman insisted on appointing Mr Brian Green as deputy in August, 2000. He was already in the company, but Mr Gibbons assessed him as a "person who was not a senior executive ... but back to an entry-level type." This led to an excessive reliance on Arthur Andersen even for basic accounting functions and decisions, which meant that the firm was auditing its own work.[33]

As has been pointed out, the problems at Freddie Mac went much deeper than "accounting irregularities" or difficulties in applying complex accounting standards to derivatives, but from the evidence set out in the report, it appears that the GSE did not organize its affairs with due skill, care and diligence, or indeed control them effectively. For example, it did not ensure that there were senior managers and directors who were able to carry out their roles in a proper manner; nor did they set the right "tone at the top", instead involving every aspect of company in the drive for steady mid-teens growth, whatever the circumstances, with a view to the bonuses that executive staff would receive. That this was the case is shown also in the weakness of the internal audit function.

However, internal audit also failed to meet its own principles and purposes, namely, to "add value and improve the operations of an organization by bringing a systematic, disciplined approach to evaluate and improve the effectiveness of risk management, control and the governance process."[34]

OFHEO found significant weaknesses in three areas, including its failure to evaluate the Enterprise's risk exposures, due largely to its failure to take responsibility for the reliability and integrity of financial information. Internal audit failed to ensure that adequate systems and controls were maintained, or to follow up on any actions agreed with the board and senior management. In fact, the internal audit department did nothing beyond reviewing whether or not corrective action had taken place. In response to their reports back to management, management may well have "reset the target completion date based upon priorities or reduced the seriousness of the issue from a major to another because they have partially remediated it and that may have taken it off our screen."[35] OFHEO records that internal audit had identified significant weaknesses in eight areas, dating from 1996: these included multi-family accounting and support; corporate information quality; financial reporting; derivatives and hedging instruments; financial forecasting; SS&TG sales, trading and operations; and corporate management and control systems. Because of endless extensions, none of the target dates were ever met and all of the issues were still outstanding by the time the report was completed in 2003. Alongside internal audit, Freddie Mac had another system, designed to cover every functional area of the organization, called Management Assessment, Risk and Controls (MARC) reports, but this system was very expensive and cumbersome, according to Melvin Kann. The MARC reports did not at any rate comply with IIA risk management or control performance standards.

The Board of Freddie Mac

So far the role of the Board has not been mentioned. According to the Charter, the Board consisted of 18 members, five of whom were Presidential appointees. The latter were appointed for one year and the average period served by the political appointees was 14.6 months between May 1998 and May 2003; since 1990, none of them had ever chaired a permanent Board committee. Clearly in the time spent in the appointment, the initial months would be taken up by understanding the business of a complex company. Of the remainder, three were executive officers and the others were elected by the shareholders, most of whom had been elected in 1990, when the shares of Freddie Mac were first publicly traded. In late 1989 and early 1990, CEO Brendsel recruited the Board within 60 days, "promising prospective board members that Freddie Mac would not make much demand on their time."[36]

The shareholder-elected directors expected to remain on the Board until they reached the mandatory retirement age.[37] In fact there was hardly any turnover. Until May 2001, 11 of the original 13 shareholder-elected directors were still on the Board, ten of the original directors until December 2002, and then nine until from 1990 until Messrs Brendsel and Glenn left abruptly in June 2003. Leland Brendsel served as Chairman and CEO continuously until 2003, and David Glenn was a member until he was appointed as Vice Chairman in 2000.

The issue of corporate governance

OFHEO published its first guidance to the Board in 2000 and strengthened its requirements in 2002. Given the extensive discussion of the late 1990s on improving corporate governance, the guidelines issued in 2000 and again in 2002 do not seem to place sufficient emphasis on the key features of those developments. For example, given the SEC's experience in the late 1990s, with enforcement actions involving financial misstatement or fraud, which involved bringing about 100 cases per year, including 30 cases in just one day in September 1999, OFHEO should have been aware, and its guidance published in 2000 should have reflected that.[38] Following a recommendation by Arthur Levitt, then Chairman of the SEC in 1998, the Blue Ribbon Committee produced its Report and Recommendations on "Improving the effectiveness of the corporate audit committees" in 1999. This was followed by regulations set out by the SEC, New York Stock Exchange and NASDQ in December of that year, as well as the American Institute of Certified Public Accountants. CalPERS had also published a wider ranging series of recommendations on US Corporate Governance principles and guidance in 1998. Its stress was on the independence of directors and the Board's leadership of the company.[39]

Neither Freddie Mae nor Fannie Mac were subject to SEC regulations, but given the context in which such developments were taking place, OFHEO should have demanded more from the Board and more closely examined its financial statements. It refers to "working with the management" to establish the strategy and goals and to "oversee the development of strategies," and to "being provided with accurate information about the operations and financial condition of the Enterprise in a timely fashion."[40] Its 2002 statement was stronger, but already late. OFHEO could, as the regulator, have required Freddie Mac and Fannie Mae to conform to the general principles as set out by the SEC following the Blue Ribbon report.

Given the fact that the majority of directors and the Chairman and the Chief Operating Officer had worked together for so long, the chances of the Board acting independently were remote indeed. Board meetings were rushed, but this was in part because from the start, Leland Brendsel had only allowed for five full Board meetings a year, with one held together with the annual meeting of shareholders, and one held at the end of every quarter, as well as committee meetings. And that was not the only problem. The directors were aware that the executive management tightly controlled the flow on information to the Board, even to the extent that the executives due to give a presentation to the Board were subjected to a "dry run." The Chairman and the Vice Chairman together with the General Counsel reviewed the presentations prepared by senior management, and made" binding decisions" about what information should be included in the presentations and any other information given to the Board. In addition, it was known that reports of internal audit went to the Chairman instead of being reported directly to the Audit Committee, since the General Auditor also went through the "dry run" process.

Even so, by September 2000 the General Auditor was able to convey to the Audit Committee that there were major weaknesses in various aspects of the GSE's financial reporting systems. These included system and data integrity in debt and derivative accounting; staff and skill shortages; account reconciliation issues; outdated accounting policy issues; the lack of sufficient financial reporting standards and performance objectives in the decentralized account units; the lack of an effective process within corporate accounting to react promptly to new transactions; a labor-intesive financial reporting process; and little time allowed in the reporting deadlines for preventative and early detection controls.[41] The then Chairman of the Audit Committee, Mr Palmer, insisted on a report to the full Board, and that progress should be reported on putting these matters right, but a further 18 months passed before the Board finally exercised its authority and agreed that 25% of the bonuses for 2002 would be tied to the successful resolution of these issues.[42]

More Congressional hearings on Freddie Mac

House Subcommittee on Commerce, Trade and Consumer Protection

Further hearings were held by Congressional committees. These included the presentation of the Doty report, commissioned by the Board of Freddie Mac, to the House Subcommittee on Commerce, Trade and Consumer Protection, on September 25, 2003.[43] The report described the way in which Doty stated that the company "transacted around" FAS 133 because the company believed that "it did not reflect the economic fundamentals of the company's business."[44] It also "found weaknesses in the company's internal compliance and governance processes, disclosure practices that fell well below the standards required of a public company, weaknesses in corporate accounting that resulted in excessive reliance on independent auditors."[45] The OFHEO report both echoes and develops some of these criticisms, but it clearly found the Doty report to be inadequate and noted this in the Congressional hearing on January 21, when Mr Falcon, Director of OFHEO, stated that the "law firm's cooperation and disclosures … were inadequate."[46]

A much more robust view of the findings of the Doty report is contained in Professor Baruch Lev's prepared statement to the hearing, concerning what is missing from the report and summing up Freddie Mac's attitude to financial accounting as, "If it complies with GAAP, it's fine." Professor Lev commented that the attitude of the former management of Freddie Mac towards financial reporting seems to be well-represented by Mr Parseghian, briefly Chief Executive of Freddie Mac.

"Parseghian has acknowledged that he was well aware of the use of reserves to meet earnings goals, but he understood that these reserves were being managed consistent with GAAP". Thus according to Parseghian's view, "financial information can be 'managed' by elaborate devices aimed at making investors believe that the company's performance is different from reality … as long as the scheme is within the wide latitude allowed by GAAP … What users of financial reports need is information that *complies with reality*. They need to be assured that the financial reports portray a truthful and unbiased picture of the company's real earnings, assets and liabilities."[47]

That is the purpose of financial reports, but instead Freddie Mac wanted to provide investors with a particular view of its earnings for their own purposes. Professor Lev also rejected the Doty report's claim that the accounting irregularities were merely "blunders."[48] They were designed to "portray a steady growth of earnings; to eliminate reported volatility to meet analysts' forecasts; to hide large gains until 'needed' in the future and so on." They constituted the "climate of manipulation and intrigue which must have permeated Freddie Mac."

Professor Lev was very dismissive of the Doty report, which claimed that Freddie Mac "just" wanted to portray reality. The report concluded that Freddie Mac sought to avoid any disclosure that would require subsequent explanation or lead investors to any conclusion other than the one management believed reflected the economics of the companies' business. Professor Lev found that much of the evidence from witness statements and documents supported the conclusions he had drawn from their report, rather than their conclusions, which he regarded as glossing over their own evidence.

The tone of the subcommittee on Commerce, Trade and Consumer Protection was quite different from that of the House Financial Services Committee, where there were many supporters of Fannie Mae and Freddie Mac. They focussed on cross-examining Professor Lev and to a lesser extent James Doty, about "certain accounting matters,"[49] the implications for Freddie Mac and indeed for GAAP generally. Only one voice expressed the kind of support for Freddie Mac often found amongst members of Congress. Representative Hilda Solis in her written statement said, "We must not allow the reported accounting irregularities at Freddie Mac to obscure the important role the housing GSEs play in making affordable mortgage lending available to communities across the USA." Commitment to the affordable housing ideology led too many to want to ignore failings of the housing GSEs, which they certainly would not have tolerated in any private company.

Regulating the GSEs

Here the issues being discussed were the hearing on the Views of the Department of the Treasury on the regulation of the GSEs on September 10, 2003; and the hearing on H.R. 2575, the Secondary Mortgage Market Enterprises Regulatory Improvement Act and the Administration's proposals for Reform, September 2003. These hearings on reforming the regulation of the GSEs have already been discussed, but it is worth noting that the committee was divided on the significance of Freddie Mac's June announcement of the departure of three of its top executives, and that there would be a further delay of its long-promised restatement of its financial results for three years.

Both the Chairman and other members of the Committee, such as Congressman Christopher Shays, saw the events as requiring a reform of the regulation of the GSEs which others such as Barney Frank and Maxine Waters rejected. On September 10, 2003, Barney Frank stated that "the two government enterprises we are talking about here, Fannie Mae and Freddie Mac, are not in a crisis. We have recently had an accounting problem with Freddie Mac that has led to people being dismissed, as appears to be appropriate. I do not think at this point there is a problem with a threat to the Treasury." Maxine Waters insisted on September 25, 2003, "we do not have a crisis at Freddie Mac ... nothing in the concerns at Freddie Mac had to do with their capital."

At the hearing on the OFHEO report on January 21, 2004, the Committee heard the witness statements of the Director of OFHEO, Armando Falcon and Martin Baumann, the newly appointed Chief Financial Officer of Freddie Mac. Falcon, as OFHEO Director, came in for criticism for only responding after Freddie Mac's announcement of the earnings statement, which only came to light with the change of auditor. This complaint was from the Committee which had over the years refused to increase the annual appropriation for OFHEO's budget. Most members of the Committee were relieved as they concluded that Martin Baumann would be able to bring about the necessary changes. He stated, "We are implementing a corporate-wide remediation program to ensure that the accounting of financial control issues that led to the need for restatement will never happen again ... Freddie Mac has added over 100 professionals in accounting reporting and control areas, including senior officers and senior managers. We have also retained leading experts in the areas of public disclosure and corporate governance to assist the company in designing and implementing processes and practices in these areas."[50]

Freddie Mac struggles to reform itself

Freddie Mac also hired a Chief Compliance Officer, a Chief Enterprise Risk Officer, and was in the process of developing new systems to ensure the quality, integrity, transparency and timeliness of its financial reporting. The GSE's focus at the time was on bringing its financial statements up-to-date and releasing the quarterly and full-year results for 2003 by June 30, 2004; it would only be after these were completed that they would be able to keep their voluntary agreement to conform to SEC registration requirements. The very fact that so much needed to be done and so many qualified staff had to be hired, itself speaks volumes about the deep-seated management failures at the company over many years.

For all their efforts, there were still delays. The 2003 accounts were produced in June, but these included a 52% drop in income for the year, with wide variations in earnings, from a net loss of $288m in the third quarter to earnings of $2.5bn in the second quarter, which the GSE blamed on wide swings in the value of derivative contracts used to hedge its interest rate risks, and on FAS 133. Their earnings were also affected by $2.13bn of losses on securities classified for accounting purposes as available for trading, compared with gains of $291m on such securities a year earlier. It also reported a $208m write-down in the value of securities backed by loans to buyers of mobile homes. Freddie Mac then announced further delays in the reporting of its 2004 results until March 2005; the company could not say when it would be able to make timely financial statements each quarter or fulfil a promise to file financial reports with the SEC.

A major fraud raises the question: Did Freddie really ever know what it was buying and selling?

Further indications of the lack of oversight and control at Freddie Mac emerged with the outcome of the Taylor, Bean & Whitaker Mortgage Corporation in June 2011. The fraud first surfaced in 2000, when Samuel Smith, an executive at Fannie Mae, realized that the company had sold him a mortgage it did not own. Over the following two years, Fannie Mae ascertained that over 200 mortgages obtained from Taylor Bean were bogus, non-performing or lacked critical components such as mortgage insurance. Fannie Mae officials did not, however, report the fraud to law enforcement or indeed to anyone outside the company, but merely cut all ties with Taylor Bean.

A week later, Freddie Mac began to acquire some of Taylor Bean's mortgages and soon became its largest customer and one of its largest revenue producers, accounting for 2% of the single-family home mortgages by volume in 2009. The company's business consisted of originating, selling and servicing residential mortgage loans, which came from a network of small mortgage brokers and banks.

The decision to allow Taylor Bean to continue in business was made by senior officials at Fannie Mae, such as Samuel Smith and Zach Oppenheimer, then Senior Vice President, according to the latter's deposition and a Fannie Mae memorandum, although Fannie Mae officials were not required to appear in court. It seems that Fannie was concerned about the signal this would send to the industry regarding poor loan quality, and that the value of the servicing rights would drop. In April 2002, after Fannie Mae had terminated its relationship with Taylor Bean, the Chief Executive asked Raymond Bowman to call his contact at Freddie Mac, which at that time was buying between 5% and 10% of the loans generated by the company, and in a short time, Freddie Mac had agreed to buy any conventional loans the company originated. Mr Farkas, CEO of Taylor Bean, apparently explained that eight bogus loans sold to Fannie Mae were the result of a clerical error and that the termination was due to a personality clash. Freddie Mac accepted the explanation. The case ended with Mr Farkas receiving a prison sentence of 30 years. The fraud amounted to $3bn.[51]

But during the years 2002 to 2009, despite all the new systems and changes in corporate culture, the fraud remained undetected. That information was obviously not available to members of Congressional and Senate committees at the time, but the Doty report, and still more the OFHEO report, ought to have motivated all the committee members to move ahead with regulatory reform bills. It did not.

9

The Beginning of the End for Fannie Mae

We like to say we are in the American dream business.

This was the way in which Franklin Raines, Chairman and CEO of Fannie Mae, introduced his testimony before the Congressional hearing on the OFHEO report: "Allegations of Accounting and Management Failure at Fannie Mae on October 6, 2004."[1] In this chapter, the events leading up to this unprecedented hearing will be set out, as well as the hearing itself. The latter illuminates the relationship between the GSE and members of the relevant committees of the House of Representatives, and the position of the regulator. It also shows the way in which Fannie Mae conducted its business, and the reasons for growing anxieties about the systemic risks arising from the key position in the market that it occupied.

2004: A year of troubles for Fannie Mae

2004 was to be a year of battles for Fannie Mae, and especially for Franklin Raines. It did not begin well. Plans for the reforming regulation of the GSEs were debated in the House and Senate throughout the year, but the importance of the role of Fannie Mae and Freddie Mac in providing lower-cost mortgages was undermined by a study carried out by a Federal Reserve economist, Wayne Passmore.[2] Chairman Greenspan used the results of the study in his testimony before the Committee on Banking, Housing and Urban Affairs.[3]

The GSE implicit subsidy and the value of government ambiguity

The study carried out by Wayne Passmore once again analysed the implications of the implicit government guarantee, together with the basis for it in the eyes of the market; the context and extent of the government subsidy constituted a fundamental critique of the role of Fannie Mae and Freddie Mac. This perception was reinforced by the size of the GSEs' portfolios; the fact that the government mandates housing goals for them; and the fact that the government provides a line of credit from the Department of the Treasury, fiscal agency services through the Federal Reserve, US agency status for GSE securities, exemptions from securities registration, and bank regulation on securities services. As indicated earlier, all of this gives the GSEs a funding advantage over private financial institutions, an advantage that amounted to some 40 basis points between 1998 and 2003. According to Passmore's estimates, this lowered interest rates on mortgages by some 7 basis points, at an immense cost to the Treasury of between $119bn and $164bn, of which the shareholders retained between $50bn and $97bn. He calculated that between 42% and 81% was due to the implicit government subsidy, and noted that if the GSEs were private financial institutions, then their behavior would change: they would hold fewer of their own mortgage-backed securities, and their capital-to-asset ratio would be more than double. Some of the members of the House and Senate committees understood that, as can be seen from references to the fact that the GSEs were relatively thinly capitalized.[4]

Calculation of the subsidy is difficult and complex, as Chairman Alan Greenspan acknowledged; Passmore's estimate is certainly larger than that provided in 2000 by the Congressional Budget Office of $13.6bn.[5] The differences may be due to methodology, and were certainly disputed by Fannie Mae and Freddie Mac.

The Congressional Budget Office's analysis

Richard Shelby, Chairman of the Senate Committee on Banking, Housing and Urban Affairs, requested the Congressional Budget Office in April 2004 to carry out further work, to see if the CBO's research supported the Federal Reserve's analysis. The CBO estimated that the total budget subsidy for the GSEs rose to $23bn in 2003, an increase of nearly 70% from the estimate of $13.6bn in 2002. This was due to their rapid expansion in 2001.[6]

These estimates are based on the assumption that any increase in the GSEs' outstanding debt and mortgage-backed securities is sustained only until the acquired mortgages mature. On the basis of the assumption that the GSEs issued debt and MBSs are reissued when they mature, the federal subsidy for 2003 would be over $46bn, up from $20bn in 2000. For the CBO, the value of the total subsidy represents the capitalized value of interest savings on newly originated securities in the year. The increase in the estimated subsidy over the past three years was mainly due to the growth in debt and MBSs, as well as to an increase in the value of the state and local tax exemptions, and a decline in discount rates. CBO's base case assumes that mortgages purchased by GSEs and the securities that they issue to finance them have an average life of seven years. That span is longer than the average realized life of mortgages originating in the mid-1990s, when there was a refinancing boom due to the sharp drop in mortgage rates. At that time, Fannie Mae expected the mortgages on its books to run off in three years (the CBO notes that this was information received from a staff member at Fannie Mae in March 2004). It would be interesting to know exactly what assumptions Fannie Mae retained. The GSEs outstanding securities and assets grew year on year over recent years, so it was not unreasonable to assume continued growth.

The CBO compared its results with the Passmore study, and noted that while the gross estimates differ between the two studies, the results are consistent. This is because the Passmore study capitalizes on the benefit to the GSEs on all outstanding debt and the MBSs, whereas the CBO's capitalizes the benefit on the incremental change in the outstanding issues for the current year. That difference, the value of the stock, rather than the change in value, or the flow, is the principal reason why Passmore's estimate of the gross subsidy is so much higher. He also estimates the subsidy pass-through at a much lower, at 7 basis points instead of the 25 basis points used by the CBO. There are two steps in the method he uses; first, he estimated the spread between jumbo and conforming mortgages and found that the difference is between 15 and 18 basis points. The methodology is the same as the CBO's but the time period for Passmore is extended to May 2003. The second point is that factors other than the GSEs' sponsored status, such as the difference in transaction costs, credit risk and prepayment risk determine the size of the subsidy. The CBO concludes that the point is the same: the housing GSEs receive large subsidies and that only a small proportion of the subsidies reach borrowers in the conforming market.[7]

But as the GAO pointed out in February 2004, "without clearly defined measures of GSEs' benefits, it is not possible for Congress, accountability organizations, and the public to determine whether the federal government should be subject to the financial risks associated with the GSEs' activities ... First, isolating the GSEs' effects on mortgages ... is a complex and technical undertaking. Second, the GSEs' financial activities have evolved over the years and have become increasingly sophisticated, which further complicates any analysis of the GSEs' benefits and costs."[8]

In his testimony to the Senate Committee, Chairman Alan Greenspan offered a way forward. "As noted by the General Accounting Office, the task of assessing the costs and benefits associated with the GSEs is difficult. One possible way to advance the technical discussion would be for Congress to request disinterested parties to convene groups of technical experts in an effort to better understand and measure these cost and benefits."[9] Neither Fannie Mae nor Freddie Mac took up the offer. The "subsidies" received by Fannie Mae and Freddie Mac were off-balance sheet as far as the federal budget was concerned. Despite the best efforts of the Federal Reserve, the CBO and Richard

Shelby, neither the Congressional nor the Senate committees were interested in assessing the costs, except to deny that so little was done to lower the costs of mortgages to the low paid and to minorities.

The risks to which Chairman Alan Greenspan referred frequently from 2003 until the end of his tenure, namely, the growth and scale of the GSEs' mortgage portfolios, concentrating interest rate risk and prepayment risk at these two institutions, coupled with the fact that they did not manage that risk by holding greater capital, were simply not recognized by any of those involved. OFHEO considered that its risk-based capital requirement was more than sufficient to guard against potential problems, and too many politicians were primarily concerned about the alleged increase in the cost of mortgages if the GSEs had to hold more capital (especially when they were persuaded to hold that view by Fannie Mae and Freddie Mac). The GSEs themselves "have chosen not to manage that risk by holding greater capital. Instead they have chosen heightened leverage, which raises interest rate risk but enables them to multiply the profitability of subsidized debt in direct proportion to their degree of leverage ... without the expectation of government support in a crisis, such leverage would not be possible without a significantly higher cost of debt."

Chairman Greenspan continues, noting that the management of such risks with very little capital "requires a conceptually sophisticated hedging framework."[10] It is in this context that the OFHEO report discussed later in this chapter has to be seen. Not only did Fannie Mae clearly lack the necessary skills, systems and qualified staff, but the drive behind all the hedging (and other) strategies was to smooth earnings in order to ensure payment of bonuses, not to manage the risks the organization faced. That was a secondary concern.

Setting up the review was not plain sailing for OFHEO

Having announced its proposals for a special review, which would "independently evaluate the accounting policies at Fannie Mae and examine whether their implementation is resulting in a high level of conformance to GAAP," OFHEO issued a request for an accounting firm to assist in planning and completing the work.[11] Deloitte & Touche was appointed in February 2004. Later in the month, Armando Falcon, Director of OFHEO, expressed concerns about the possible destruction of documents, and indeed about access to documents; OFHEO had to resort to issuing subpoenas in order to obtain co-operation with its investigation. Chairman Oxley stated that he was "dismayed to learn" that OFHEO had had to turn to such measures, adding "it is my sense that if OFHEO had the tools possessed by other regulators, this investigation would not have reached the subpoena stage. If we had a

GSE regulator with the power and authority of a world class regulator, it is possible that these problems at Fannie Mae would have been remedied earlier and today's hearing would not be necessary."[12] In the end, OFHEO had to review over 200,000 documents and e-mails as well as hundreds of interviews and depositions of current and former staff of Fannie Mae. One of the many warning signs was that Fannie Mae had to correct an accounting error to the tune of $1.1bn in October 2003.

Fannie Mae's outdated accounting systems

In a letter to Franklin Raines dated February 24, 2004, Armando Falcon stated that Fannie Mae relied on 70 outmoded manual accounting systems, and pointed out the potential problems in the use of so many manual systems ("end user computer systems"), as opposed to fully automated and integrated systems. The former have a significant risk of error and should only be used with "strong controls and as an interim step to full automation. The recent error with Fannie Mae's 3Q03-8-K filing occurred in an end user computing application and highlights a basic flaw of these systems: a lack or failure of change control processes." It was not just one accidental error, as the rest of the letter makes clear; the mistake occurred during the process of marking the SFAS 149 settled commitments designated as available for sale (AFS).

> The error was the result of a computational miscalculation contained in a spreadsheet formula that calculates the gain/loss of the AFS. More specifically, the error resulted when *an employee made an unapproved change to a formula contained within a Microsoft Excel spreadsheet*. The formula error went undetected during the normal management review process ... and was ultimately discovered during the course of the standard review in preparation of the SEC Form 10-Q for the third quarter ... Other flaws found in this specific end user system were lack of technical and user documentation, insufficient testing, and inadequate back-up and recovery techniques.

Director Falcon demanded a remediation plan which would include a schedule for the development and implementation of a fully automated FAS 149 accounting commitment process, and a plan of action to address all financial reporting end user systems. That plan should particularly include (a) an internal assessment of all financial reporting end user computing applications, including the risks and controls surrounding these applications; and (b) a plan and time-table for full automation of the financial reporting end user computing applications and controls. Alternatively, if Fannie Mae believed that any of these systems should not be automated, then an explanation of the special circumstances preventing their full automation should be provided. The plan had to be submitted within 30 days.[13]

A missing balance sheet

In April, Fannie Mae announced its results for the first quarter 2004, but failed to release its balance sheet at the same time, contrary to standard practice, which it was claimed was due to the need to complete a review of the complex figures related to shareholder equity. The GSE announced that the balance sheet would be available on May 10, when it was due to file its IOQ report with the SEC. Franklin Raines stated that the company's financial performance "continued to benefit from the balance and flexibility of our business model. We are well-positioned to continue to support our mission and to capitalize on opportunities for profitable growth in the coming quarters."[14] Its profits fell by 2.1% between March 2003 and March 2004, that is, from $1.94bn to $1.9bn. Losses on derivatives as marked to market reached $959.3m as compared with $624.6m in the previous year. Its profits, derived from its core business, that is, buying home mortgages from lenders and packaging them as securities for sale on Wall Street, rose by 9.2%. Against that background, which lasted from February to July, when Fannie Mae was clearly resisting OFHEO's request for documents, it seems extraordinarily unwise to publish accounts with a missing balance sheet in April of the same year. This did not go unnoticed by the financial press, leading to a scathing *Wall Street Journal* editorial: "There she goes again ... Fannie Mae, the leveraged hedge fund that calls itself a housing finance company."[15]

Losses on derivatives

The publication of their incomplete financial statement followed a series of articles about Fannie Mae's derivative losses, especially in the *Financial Times*. On March 9, Stephen Schurr of the *FT* set out the paper's analysis of Fannie Mae's accounts, which suggested that "it may have incurred losses on its derivatives trading of $24bn between 2000 and the third quarter of 2003. That figure represents nearly all of the $25.1bn used to purchase or settle transactions in that period. Any net losses will eventually have to be recognized on Fannie Mae's balance sheet, depressing future profits."[16] This met with a sharp response from Jayne Shontell, a senior Vice President, in a Fannie Mae press release on March 10, dismissing the claims in no uncertain terms. She stated that "[this] story is based on wholly invented methodology that we told the reporter is wrong. His calculation and methodology are flawed and the subsequent implications are wrong. The methodology he employed incorrectly calculated unrealized losses and as a result he arrived at an erroneous conclusion. This has resulted in a gross misrepresentation. Anyone who is seriously interested in looking at this should wait for our 10-K filing next week."

When the results were released a week later, they revealed for the first time details of the GSE's derivative trading, including losses on positions that could not be recouped. In its SEC filing, Fannie reported losses of $6.86bn as at the end of 2003 from closed hedges. Total losses, including $5.33bn in open hedge positions, were $12.19bn for that period. In his article of March 16, 2004, Stephen Schurr explained that the *Financial Times* estimated Fannie Mae's losses on derivative positions that had been closed but not yet recognized at $24bn. The *FT* also used third-quarter numbers in its assumptions. Fannie Mae's losses in accumulated other comprehensive income, the broad category, which includes realized and unrealized losses, narrowed from $16.1bn to $12.1bn in the fourth quarter. Bloomberg News noted that Fannie Mae's derivatives holdings surged by 59%, to more than $1 trillion by the end of 2003 as the biggest buyer of US mortgages tried to cushion the effect of swings in interest rates on its earnings.[17]

Fannie Mae improperly accounts for its assets

On May 6, 2004, OFHEO announced that it required Fannie Mae to account for manufactured housing and aircraft lease impairments in the periods in which they occured. OFHEO stated that its examination of Fannie Mae had determined that the Enterprise was not applying the appropriate accounting with respect to determining asset impairments and revenue recognition for these securities. "Fannie Mae improperly accounted for these assets in a way that fails to recognize losses," noted Armando Falcon; they were to be restated by May 14.[18] However, the SEC did not require Fannie Mae to restate its earnings, but agreed with OFHEO that its process for determining impairments was "more rigorous and objective" for "determining other-than-temporary impairment, and the SEC encouraged that conclusion." Franklin Raines went on to state that "during the second quarter of 2004, we will implement this new estimation process ... in accordance with the Director's directive."[19]

The results of applying the required method was a reduction in the value of $8bn of securities backed by manufactured housing loans, and $300m of securities backed by aircraft leases. This resulted in a loss of $217m due to an increase in defaults by mobile home owners, and a potential $353m in additional unrealized losses on securities for which OFHEO required a recalculation. Fannie Mae recognized that losses of a further $260m in the second quarter might occur. Franklin Raines insisted that such losses were very small in relation to a trillion-dollar balance sheet.

Fannie Mae's co-operation "has been spotty"

Meanwhile OFHEO's inquiry was continuing, but without much help from Fannie Mae. Chairman Richard Baker took the opportunity to ask the OFHEO

Director about the "forensic audit" of Fannie Mae and "whether the agency is providing access to documents, personnel or other matters as may be deemed appropriate to the accounting firm or to your own inspectors as appropriate, given the circumstance they find themselves in? Are they being co-operative in your view?"

Mr Falcon replied, "I think the cooperation has been spotty, but there are many demands we have placed on them for documents and to employees for scheduled interviews. Given that we find that co-operation has been less than adequate, whether it is deadlines being met or data submissions not being complete, we have taken steps to address these problems and will continue to be as forceful as necessary to make sure we get full co-operation."[20] OFHEO later found that it had no option but to issue subpoenas on August 20, which could be enforced by the Justice Department (it later asked for assistance from the Justice Department in doing so, but neither OFHEO nor Fannie Mae was prepared to comment on the outcome).

At the hearing, Chairman Baker raised a number of other issues, some of which he followed up in a letter to Armando Falcon. He noted the matter of the level of guarantee fees, fees which the Enterprises charge originators when they purchase their loans. The data to which Baker had access indicated that "their credit loss ratios have declined due to improvements in their underwriting and risk management ... while loan loss reserves in the same period of review have declined, principally attributable to reduced losses (from 1995 to 2003). Yet the income flow to the corporation would appear on its surface to have been increased rather dramatically."[21] Later, in response to Chairman Baker's letter, OFHEO stated that Fannie Mae's income from such fees rose in 2003 by a third to a record $2.4bn, or 33% of core earnings totaling $7.5bn.

OFHEO's report of findings to date

Of much greater importance in 2004 was the publication in September of OFHEO's "Report of Findings to Date: Special Examination of Fannie Mae."[22] In its executive summary, OFHEO singled out characteristics of the culture and environment which led to the accounting problems at Fannie Mae, citing a number of characteristics, of which two were key: management's desire to portray Fannie Mae as a consistent generator of stable and growing earnings; and an executive compensation culture which rewarded management for meeting goals tied to earnings-per-share, a metric subject to manipulation since the level of compensation depended on the stability of the earnings stream. However, an examination of the structure of compensation shows that increasing the levels of compensation was the overriding aim, and the presentation of stable earnings was simply a means to that end.

"You must have 6.46 branded in your brain"

For the top five executives, there were four main categories of compensation: (i) salary; (ii) annual bonus; (iii) option/restricted stock grants; and (iv) long-term incentive plan payouts (LTIPs). The last category referred to the number of shares given each year, depending to a substantial extent on the previous year's earnings, with the weight given to earnings determining how many shares to award. Items (ii) to (iv) were a more important part of the total compensation than the actual salary. The arrangements also allowed considerable freedom for executives to sell vested options and shares, which Timothy Howard, the Chief Financial Officer, frequently exercised; in the six-month period before the SEC's announcement that Fannie Mae grossly misstated earnings, he realised about $6m in selling them.

Over 700 employees benefitted from the Annual Incentive Plan, which from 2000 onwards took the form of a special option grant program termed "Earnings per Share Challenge Option Grants." Under the terms of this plan, the options would be vested and would be realized in January 2004, if the reported EPS equalled or exceeded $6.46 by December 31, 2003. Staff were continually exhorted to meet the challenge, which they did: earnings per share reached $7.91 by the end of 2003, and they were able to realize the options. As OFHEO's later report spells out, the commitment by Franklin Raines to the achievement of the EPS targets overrode all other objectives, even to the extent that the December 2001 job descriptions for Mr Raines, Chief Operating Officer Daniel Mudd, CFO Timothy Howard, and Vice Chairman Jamie Gorelick each listed the EPS targets as the primary performance indicator for their positions. They and other senior executives spent a substantial amount of time and effort "managing reported financial performance, at the expense of other goals and objectives associated with safety and soundness and internal control, so that Fannie Mae's reported EPS would hit the announced targets."

That same objective permeated all other levels in the organization; it was the "corporate mantra." Everyone had to play their part in achieving that goal. In 2000 Mr Rajappa, Senior Vice President for Operations Risk and Internal Audit, who became head of the Office of Auditing, made the following speech to the internal auditors: "By now every one of you must have 6.46 branded in your brains. You must be able to say it in your sleep, you must be able to recite it forwards and backwards, you must have a raging fire in your belly that burns away all doubts, you must live, breathe and dream 6.46, you must be obsessed on 6.46 ... After all, thanks to Frank, we have a lot of money riding on it ... We must do this with a fiery determination, not on some days, not on most days but day in and day out, give it your best, not 50%, not 75%, not 100%, but 150%. **Remember, Frank has given us an opportunity to earn not just our salaries, benefits and raises, ESPP, but substantially over and above if we make it 6.46.** So it is our moral obligation to give well above our 100% and, if we do this, we would have made tangible contributions to Frank's goals."[23] This is a quite extraordinary speech for the Head of Internal Audit to make, especially one who had experience in the company actually with internal audit.

In the OFHEO report, the accounting "irregularities" were presented as being part of the aim, or as with the aim, of persuading investors that the GSEs' earnings were steady, predictable and insulated from excessive volatility; and also to ensure specific levels of compensation for executives. They were not designed to hide fundamental problems with the company, such as was the case with Enron and Worldcom. However, the effect of the constant manipulation of earnings and the company's financial position in general may have contributed to just such problems in the longer term, if for no other reason than they absorbed so much of the energy and attention of the senior executives and staff at every level, and may have distorted any proper understanding of the company's true position. Inevitably, as OFHEO pointed out in its executive summary, the manipulation of earnings was serious, since it raised "concerns regarding the validity of previously reported financial results, the adequacy of regulatory capital, the quality of management supervision, and the overall safety and soundness of the Enterprise."[24]

Fannie Mae's failure to conform to accounting standards

The report first of all sets out the events leading up to the development of Fannie Mae's current amortization policies and practices. When Fannie Mae buys mortgages or MBSs, it does not pay the exact amount of the unpaid premium balance outstanding on the loans. If the interest rate (or coupon rate) is below the current market rates, the loan is less valuable and will sell at a discount. To calculate the effective yield on the loan, Fannie Mae must take these premiums and discounts into account. (A loan bought at a premium is less valuable than the coupon rate would imply, and vice versa for loans purchased at a discount.) According to SFA 91, the amount of these premiums and discounts must be amortized, or recognized over the estimated life of the purchased loans or MBSs. The amounts recognized appear on the income statement as an adjustment to current interest income.

In the autumn of 1998, interest rates fell sharply, as central banks sought to manage the effects of the Russian and Hong Kong financial crises and the turbulence in the global financial markets. In such a period of low interest rates, borrowers paid off their mortgages and refinanced them at lower rates. The effect on the unexpected increase in prepayments was an additional expense of $400m, which according to the accounting rule, SFAS 91, should have been recognized and set against the 1998 earnings. However, Fannie Mae chose not to do that and only set $200m against its earnings for that year, deferring the other $200m. Later their auditors, KPMG, identified the $200m deferred expense (the unrecorded amount) as an "audit difference," subsequently agreeing to waive that difference on the grounds that it was immaterial. Partners Ken Russell and Julie Theobold, and senior manager Eric Smith, signed the following statement in waiving the $199m PDA and other audit differences as of December 31, 1998: "I have evaluated the above audit differences individually and in the aggregate, and determined that the waived audit difference would not have material affect on the financial statement as a whole." As it turned out, it *was* material, since not booking that expense increased the EPS by about 12.5 cents, from $3.11 to the $3.23 that was actually reported to the public on January 14, 1999, and in the 1998 Annual Report, including the audited financial statements.[25]

In its Report of Findings to Date, OFHEO refers only to an "audit difference," which is then portrayed as a trivial matter in the course of the December hearing before the House subcommittee on Capital Markets, Insurance and Government Sponsored Enterprises on October 6, 2004. As a consequence, some members of the Subcommittee regarded the failure to record expenses totaling $200m in 1998 as a relatively trivial issue. OFHEO appears to spend too much time on a past event which then seemed trivial; it is not, of course, as OFHEO makes it plain that this was the beginning of a whole series of accounting policies which were designed to fulfil the objectives which Fannie Mae had set itself.

Fannie Mae provided a variety of reasons why the deferral in expenses occurred, such as the fact that it was necessitated by limitations in models and infrastructure, which caused the estimate of expenses to be overstated. However, these did not hold water. For example, in interviews with Mr Howard and Leanne Spencer, Controller, it was indicated that one of the reasons for not recording the additional expenses was that not all REMIC securities (that is, a real estate mortgage investment conduit) are structured into separately traded securities.[26] But then the records show that upon increasing the percentage of REMIC securities which could be modeled, the amount of catch-up expenses actually increased. OFHEO also discovered that, despite insisting that the estimate of loss was overstated, Fannie Mae developed a strategy to record monthly "on-top adjustments" (that is, adjustments made directly to the general ledger during the financial statements close process) to the financial statements to recognize the estimated $200m deferred expense in the subsequent fiscal years, 1999 and 2000.[27]

To see the significance of the catch-up, we need to return to the issue of compensation, which includes the Annual Incentive Plan (AIP) awards, that is bonuses linked to the size of the bonus pool for meeting the annual earnings per share target. For 1998, the size of the annual bonus payout pool was linked to specific EPS targets: $3.13 minimum payout; $3.18 target payout; and $3.23 maximum payout. If Fannie Mae was to pay out the maximum amount in AIP awards in 1998 (about $27.1m), the EPS would have to be $3.23. Bang on target: the 1998 EPS figure turned out to be $3.2309, so this allowed the maximum payout. The annual EPS figure is calculated by dividing the net annual earnings by the average number of shares of common stock outstanding for the year. The 1998 $3.23 EPS was established by dividing the net income available to common shareholders ($3.352bn) by the weighted average number of common shares outstanding (1.037m). If the net income available to common shareholders had been reduced to $125m, the EPS for 1998 would have fallen to $3.11, below the minimum payout level.

Then the "catch-up" of deferred expenses in 1999 began, but with the aim of not exceeding a negative £100m by the end of the year. Fannie Mae had learnt its lesson; it did not want to face any further surprises in sudden interest rate changes which would incur expenses, which it would then have to handle by managing the process of calculating amortization. Part of the $200m that had been deferred was placed into an account described as a "reserve against future interest rate changes."[28]

In its report OFHEO includes various staff memoranda in which they discussed the SFAS 91 accounting standards. They decided not to adopt most of the standards, but only those which allowed them, or could be interpreted as allowing them to: (a) not recognize estimated income or expenses up to certain thresholds, and (b) defer the recognition of income or expenses that exceeded recommended thresholds over a several-year planning horizon.[29] These accounting methods are neither supported by SFAS 91 nor GAAP more broadly, but they were adopted in December 2000 and were still in force at the time of the report. At that time, OFHEO was unable to find any evidence that the policy had been used, although Mr Jonathon Boyles, then Senior Vice President Financial Standards, acknowledged that the methods were not in accordance with GAAP.

OFHEO also noted that the active modeling and management of the catch-up required more robust systems than Fannie Mae had in place. However, Fannie Mae installed a system called BancWare Convergence, "as a tool to facilitate the scenario analysis of our purchase discount/premium and deferred/prepaid fee position ... These upgrades created enhanced cash flows, which improved our catch-up forecasting ability." A specific enhancement was added to BancWare which allowed it to produce modeling reports in dollars, and therefore to bypass PDAMS (purchase discount amortization system), which was used at the time to model catch-up. In his memorandum, Mr Juliane added, "BancWare amortizes premium and discount using an interest proxy method based on a proportionate amount of principal collected. This generates an amortization amount that ensures that the purchase price is maintained throughout the life of the instrument. Consequently, the normal amortization factors BancWare produces assume that you record catch-up in the period when incurred. *However, even though the normal factors assume that you will recognise catch-up in the period incurred, BancWare gives you the flexibility to manipulate factors to produce an array of recognition streams.* With this manipulation you can 'bleed' the catch-up within a specified time period and affect both the subsidiary ledger as well as the general ledger equally. This strengthens the earnings management that is necessary when dealing with a volatile book of business."[30] It is interesting to note that, given OFHEO's later criticism of the number of manual systems and lack of computer systems, one of the earliest robust systems Fannie Mae installed was designed to assist with the preparation of financial reports which suited them and their objectives, rather than providing reliable financial reports for investors.

How Fannie Mae accounted for derivatives

Much of the report is taken up with various difficulties in the way in which Fannie Mae dealt with derivatives accounting. Under SFAS 133, derivatives, including futures, contracts, swaps, and caps, are all financial instruments whose value is linked to changes in a particular economic variable, usually interest rates. Fannie Mae used derivatives to manage interest rate risk. According to the above accounting rule, changes in fair value from the previous accounting period must be reported as current income, unless the derivatives are used for hedging. SFAS 133 allows a company to recognize as earnings both the change in the derivative's value and the offsetting change in the value of the hedged item. If the gains and losses are closely correlated, the net effect on reported earnings will be very small or zero. The report analysed a number of these transactions, and found many practices that did not conform to SFAS 133. It also found that a number of staff involved in the whole process did not understand the accounting practices with which they were dealing, and were even unfamiliar with SFAS 133.

Fannie Mae used a number of shortcuts, which appeared to provide the "perfectly effective" hedge, that is, one which eliminates the risk of an existing position entirely, or which eliminates all market risk from a portfolio. Many would regard "perfect hedges" as being extremely rare, and would refer instead to "effective hedges." OFHEO notes that a great deal of emphasis was placed on treating hedges as "perfectly effective," by which Fannie meant that the hedging relationship was not in any way ineffective, an unlikely occurrence. Fannie Mae, however, did not carry out any assessment or measurement of the effectiveness of the hedging relationship. According to the interview OFHEO conducted with Jonathon Boyles, Senior Vice President of Accounting Standards and Corporate Tax, in August 2004, Mr Boyles stated that he "would guess over 90% of Fannie Mae's hedges are perfectly effective at any point in time."[31] What Fannie Mae did was set aside the very limited circumstances in which SFAS 133 allows for the treatment of hedges to be perfectly effective, with the result that at the end of December 2003, it "had a notional of $1.04 trillion in derivatives of which a notional of only $43m was not in a hedging relationship."[32]

OFHEO identified at this stage in its examination a wide range of examples in which accounting rules had been intentionally misapplied in order to minimize earnings volatility and simplify operations. Fannie Mae failed to carry out a proper assessment of effectiveness, or a measurement of the ineffectiveness with many of its hedges. These calculations together with proper documentation of hedges are essential for hedge fund accounting treatment under SFAS 133. If these derivatives are not to count as hedges then their fair value (or market value) changes should be recorded directly as earnings.

Before 2004, Fannie Mae treated some offsetting derivatives as hedges when they did not qualify as such. In 2001–2002 in particular, the GSE did not properly account for certain purchased interest rate caps, which might have led to significant misstatements of its earnings and Accumulated Other Income Statements (AOCI) during those years. They knew that their accounting treatment did not accord with GAAP.

That was changed in 2004, but without any reference to possible misstatements in the previous years. Fannie Mae disclosed in its first quarter 2004 10-Q that the impact of classifying certain derivatives as non-hedging was approximately $13m on that quarter's pre-tax net income. OFHEO considers that the impact may have been larger. In 2002, Fannie Mae disclosed another change in its methodology in accounting for changes in time and intrinsic value of its purchased interest rate caps. Once again, no reference was made to the implications of such changes on its past financial statements. Again in December 2003, the balance in the AOCI includes $12.2bn in deferred losses relating to cash flow hedges.

OFHEO, with respect to the improper application of hedge fund accounting, correctly comments that this led them to "question the validity of the amounts reflected in AOCI; as well as the amounts reflected as carrying value adjustments, at any point since the adoption of SFAS 133. For hedges which do not qualify for hedge fund accounting, fair value changes should be reflected in earnings in the period in which the value change occurred, and with no offset to AOCI or hedged item carrying value. Additionally, the possible reclassification of these amounts into retained earnings could have a *substantial impact on Fannie Mae's compliance with regulatory capital requirements.*"[33]

There are two further reasons to be concerned. The first is the lack of adequate documentation, which might appear as a regulatory burden, but the rationale is clear enough: without such documentation, it would be impossible to determine the effectiveness of the hedge. For example, SFAS 133 requires that at the beginning of a hedge, the following information should be recorded:

- Management objective and strategy for entering into a hedge
- Identification of the hedging instrument
- The risk being hedged
- How the hedge effectiveness will be assessed

Fannie Mae's system involves entering the hedging instrument with the hedged item in a term sheet, which identifies the hedged item and the linkage between the derivative and the hedged item. Their system also includes the transaction descriptions for the permitted hedging strategies. What is lacking is any reconciliation between the term sheet and ultimate hedge fund linkage in the system. As a result of one of its interviews with a senior financial analyst in the Treasury Middle Office, OFHEO noted that the final decision about the nature of the hedging relationship is made by the Controller's Financial Accounting Group. Clearly this mode of operations with the linkage in what Fannie Mae calls the DEBT system, allows the Financial Accounting Group to change the ultimate treatment of a hedge's designation, and contradicts the regulatory requirements.

In examining the whole process, OFHEO concluded that there were a number of inadequacies in the various systems Fannie Mae employed. These included:

- Ambiguity of the hedging relationship

- Hedged risk not properly defined

- Hedged items not specifically identified in certain fair value hedges

- No term sheet produced for re-linkages

- Designation not contemporaneous

- Unclear definition and probability of hedged transaction in cash flow hedges

- Retroactive linkage of hedging instruments with hedged items

With regard to the latter item, OFHEO includes e-mails which showed that they were given permission by the Controllers to go back and change the linkages to the trader's intent at the time of the buyback.[34] This illustrates the ease with which descriptions could be changed retroactively to achieve a certain accounting result, which is clearly and expressly ruled out under SFAS 133, where paragraph 385 states that the concurrent designation and documentation of a hedge is critical; without it, an entity could retrospectively identify a hedged item, a hedged transaction, or a method of measuring effectiveness to achieve a desired accounting result.

Did the hedge accounting failures matter?

The OFHEO report spells it out: the lack of adequate, contemporaneous hedge designation documentation precludes a company from hedge accounting, which in turn means that the fair value changes for such derivatives should be recorded through the income statement, without receiving any offset, or matching with, the earnings affect of the hedged item. All of this is complex and esoteric stuff. Does it matter beyond that? OFHEO answers: "Given the billions of dollars of mark-to-market value of Fannie Mae's derivatives and the fact that the vast majority of them are currently receiving hedge accounting, the potential impact of these documentation issues on Fannie Mae's reported financial results and regulatory capital appears to be substantial."[35] In other words, Fannie Mae could not be certain of the risks it faced or the capital it had at its disposal at any one time. It also undermines confidence in any other aspect of Fannie Mae's reports of its achievements, including the nature of the loans it purchased, the guaranty fees it charged lenders and, of course, the whole issue of compensation, something Fannie Mae was reluctant, to say the least, to reveal.

The role of senior managers

In the 2004 report, OFHEO concentrates on the responsibilities of senior management and systems and controls, rather than on the role and responsibilities of the Board. That is covered in much more detail in the 2006 report. The issue of systems and controls is tackled in part through accounting policy development and financial reporting responsibilities, which ultimately was the responsibility of the Chairman and Chief Executive, Franklin Raines, Tim Howard, Chief Financial Officer (CFO), and Leanne Spencer, Senior Vice President and Controller. Ms Spencer reported to the CFO; Sam Rajappa, Operations Risk and later Head of Internal Audit, had a dotted line of reporting to the CFO over the previous two years, although he also reports to the Chairman of the Audit Committee. There were two other Senior Vice Presidents: Janet Pennewell, Financial Reporting, and Jonathon Boyles, Financial Standards and Tax, with one vacancy for the SVP of Financial Accounting and Mary Lewers as the Vice President of Financial Accounting.

Jonathon Boyles was responsible for the initial accounting policy development, taking on board the rule changes at the FASB and the SEC, and the impact on business units at Fannie Mae and their views. A draft would then go to the Controller, who would be responsible for reviewing the policies for compliance with GAAP. No formal procedures for the development of accounting policy existed at Fannie Mae, and sometimes the policies which had been developed in such a disorganized fashion were not in accordance with GAAP. What Boyles recognized as "known departures from GAAP" were simply characterized as a "practical application of accounting standards." The CFO claimed in interviews with OFHEO that he was not aware of any departures from GAAP.

Any internal review of proposed accounting policies was conducted by the Controller, Leanne Spencer, whose job it was to decide which policies to approve and implement. Leanne Spencer was not a Certified Public Accountant, but in the event of a difference of opinion between the Controller and the Financial Standards Group, then the CFO is the final arbiter. Nor was the CFO, Tim Howard, a Certified Public Accountant, and his technical background did not include any accounting-related experience. Mr Howard's testimony made it clear that he did not rely on Leanne Spencer for technical expertise, but rather as "an engaged participant" in the process, with Jonathon Boyles being the subject matter expert.[36] However, none of these individuals was regarded as a real expert: the CFO, the Controller, the VP of Financial Accounting and the Head of the Office of Auditing (internal audit) all made it quite clear that they referred to KPMG as the final arbiter of Fannie Mae's compliance with GAAP, which meant that KPMG was effectively auditing itself. The Controller revealed during interviews that she was hardly in a position to do anything else, since when asked about the company's treatment of interest-only and principal-only securities, she admitted that she did not have a detailed understanding. Even the Head of Internal Audit did not consider it his responsibility to ensure compliance with GAAP, but rather "to do audits to ensure that the policies are followed by those they govern in a fashion consistent with our [internal] standards."[37] Neither the Controller nor the Head of Internal Audit were able to or wished to comment on the regulatory accounting standards for which it was the Controller's responsibility to decide which policies to approve and implement. She also ran an under-resourced department and once again admitted that "once we get overloaded, things slip. They don't get done as thoroughly."[38]

OFHEO turned to Tim Howard. As Vice Chairman and CFO, he was able to produce a long list of responsibilities, which included risk management, the retained portfolio, the accounting function, investor relations, Treasury, financial reporting, and evaluating and making compensation recommendations for the Head of the Office of Auditing. As Vice Chairman, he also had a wide range of corporate strategy oversight management responsibilities, and served informally as Fannie Mae's Chief Risk Officer, in flagrant contradiction to the principles set out by the Group of Thirty, of which he was a member: "financial control and risk management must be fully independent of the risk-taking business."[39] Mr Howard also referred to the Steering Committee dealing with the issue of fair value versus historical cost accounting, which Paul Volcker, as Chairman of the Board of Trustees had asked him to join, a group which included Susan Bies from the Federal Reserve.

The report sets out clearly a senior team, many of whom were not qualified for the roles they had; a heavy workload; and a weak review environment, all leading to dependence on a small number of key persons, without a proper segregation of duties or adequate levels of control. But apart from this first report from OFHEO, there were no signs that any one really understood the extent of the disorganization and incompetence (or worse) at the top of such a vast Enterprise.

Testimony of the whistle-blower

Further insights into what this meant for many of those on the inside were provided by Roger Barnes, the whistleblower, who worked at Fannie Mae as Manager of Financial Accounting, Deferred Assets, until his resignation in October 2003. His testimony highlights the extent of false accounting in Fannie Mae, and also indicates that it was deliberate. It was also one of the factors leading to the OFHEO inquiry and obviously indicated the direction in which the inquiry should look. Mr Barnes had begun his employment at Fannie Mae in 1992, in a spirit of idealism; and also to advance, as he says, his own professional career. The testimony itself is a study of growing disillusionment over the years from 1999 onwards.

He was involved in the development of the Amortization Integration Modeling System (AIMS), designed to determine cash flows and income generated by Fannie Mae's deferrals on mortgage and mortgage-backed securities. Mr Juliane led the development of the system, although he was not a certified public accountant. Roger Barnes had doubts about the system from the start, but these were ignored; they were rejected by Ms Pennewell, Ms Lewers and Mr Juliane, as they were working to achieve the objective set by Leanne Spencer and Tim Howard, namely, to reduce earnings volatility. His accounts of specific meetings show the extent of manipulation. One such meeting took place on January 4, 2001, which included Ms Lewers, Richard Stawarz, Director of Financial Reporting and Mr Juliane, with the aim of considering the effects of the Fed's cut in interest rates. The rapid fall in interest rates led senior management to consider adjusting the "on-tops," a term referring to manual journal entries that could be used to adjust arbitrarily Fannie Mae's income as the books were closed each month. Senior management had stated that the "on-tops" could be used to reflect a desired level of income for December 2000. He expressed his concerns about these and other reporting matters to Mr Stawarz, who agreed with him but did nothing about it.

In November 2001, an amortization factor change requested by management resulted in a $100m increase in the company's interest income. "I recognized this increase as concrete evidence that the AIMS system, as developed and used by the company, produced grossly inaccurate and unreliable results when calculating the Fannie Mae's income and expenses."[40]

By September 23, 2002, "it was clear to me that management in the Controller's division had no intention of responding to my disclosures of accounting impropriety. Indeed, the culture in the Controller's division was such that many employees knew or suspected that the company was engaging in improper income management and it became a joke that the Controller's division could produce any income statement the company wanted."[41] Mr Barnes set out all of these practices he had discovered to Mr Raines and Mr Howard, but none was ever investigated; instead, from November onwards, Mr Barnes found that he was excluded from meetings, refused monetary rewards to which he and his staff were entitled, and was not promoted to a position for which he was well qualified.

In April 2003, he again discussed his concerns about Fannie Mae's accounting practices with Mr Stawarz, who advised him not to raise his concerns in a "corporate climate in which employees actually joked about improper incomes management because it was such a regular occurrence," and in which "employee morale suffered because management offered promotions, bonuses and perks only to employees who supported management's improper goals."[42]

After that, Mr Barnes set about researching irregularities as part of his responsibility for 400 ledger accounts, and reviewed the company's amortized transactions, finding "abundant evidence of the same kinds of problematic and unlawful financial practices" that he had identified in his memorandum to Mr Raines and Mr Howard on September 23, 2002. The evidence was presented to the internal auditors and a meeting sought in July with the Head of Internal Audit, Mr Rajappa. The meeting did not take place until August 2003, during which Mr Barnes gave full details of all the errors he had discovered (over 60) and stated that based on his research, he had concluded that Fannie Mae's amortization accounting was not in accordance with GAAP. A copy was given to Ms Spencer, Ms Pennewell, Ms Lewers and Messrs Stawarz and Juliane at a meeting on August 5. He was greeted with anger that he had taken matters to internal audit, and it was claimed that he was "overstating the case." However, the factors generated by AIMS were still used in the amortization processing. After that, a further meeting was held which was not designed to rectify problems, but rather to justify the practices so that Mr Raines could sign off on the financial statements by the August 15 deadline. Franklin Raines did certify the financial statements, which contained all the matters Roger Barnes had questioned. After that, he was excluded from all meetings and even information about OFHEO's investigation, and so felt he had no choice but to leave the company.

Standard & Poor's gives top marks to Fannie Mae's corporate governance

In stark contrast to OFHEO's findings and the testimony of Roger Barnes, Standard & Poor assigned its first Corporate Governance Score to a US company on January 30, 2003, to Fannie Mae. On a scale from 1 to 10, Fannie Mae was given a score of 9. The scores were described on Standard & Poor's website as "independent assessments" resulting from an "interactive process that does not follow a 'check the box' approach." The score is made public at the company's discretion, although according to S&P, a "good majority" of firms do not reveal their scores. Again the website made it clear that, "The resulting report can either be used as a confidential diagnostic by the company or published as a Corporate Governance Score ... funded by the company being analysed and is currently free of charge to investors, insurers and other interested parties." In effect, companies pay a fee to hire S&P, then a score is produced, and the company may decide to disclose this at no extra fee.

The report was based on an examination of Fannie Mae in four key areas: ownership structure and external shareholder influence; investor rights and relations; transparency and disclosure; and board structure and process. It is worth quoting one or two excerpts; although the work was carried out in late 2002 and January 2003, enough had happened in relation to Freddie Mac (see previous chapter) for a somewhat more sceptical approach to have been adopted. With regard to transparency and disclosure, S&P stated that though Fannie Mae's size and the complexity of its particular accounting practices, notably SFAS 133, "make its financial practices subject to a very high level of external scrutiny ... the company's website and the annual report provide a very strong basis of disclosure that meets or in some cases exceeds SEC requirements ... We assess positively Fannie Mae's audit process and how its independence is achieved, but note the high level of non-audit fees paid to the company's auditor."[43] The report notes that KPMG have been the company's auditors since 1968.

The report also notes that although the influence of its regulators and Congress may not materially affect Fannie Mae's corporate governance at present, there is a possibility that this could change in the future. It refers dismissively to Richard Baker, as Chairman of the Capital Markets, Insurance and Government Sponsored Enterprises Subcommittee of the House Financial Services Committee, and his efforts to obtain a Congressional review of Fannie Mae's corporate governance, linking him, for example, to FM Watch, described as a "micro-lobby, backed by some of Fannie Mae's competitors, upset at what they view as unfair government support for the company and for Freddie Mac."[44]

However, the report concludes, "Fannie Mae to this point has been able to use persuasion, its political connections and supportive legal opinion to maintain the status quo that it clearly believes serves the interests of its shareholders ... dealing with external political, regulatory and legislative risk is something the company is quite good at: a skill that has helped the company and its shareholders over the long term."[45] Indeed! The form the application of its political skills took would be revealed to an ever greater extent in the years to come. Even in January 2003, the storm clouds were gathering, and were there to be seen and considered.

A "political lynching" of Franklin Raines?

The Hearing of the Subcommittee on Capital Markets, Insurance and the Government Sponsored Enterprises took place on October 6, 2004. The hearing was dramatic indeed, with one of its members, Rep Lacy Clay, describing it as being "about the political lynching of Franklin Raines ... We are having a trial by OFHEO leaks, trail by newspaper articles, and trial without due process."[46] Others, such as Maxine Waters, echoed the point that the primary motive of the report was political when she said, "I feel like I'm in another round of the battle between FM Watch and the GSEs.[47] FM Watch, financial institutions that decided a long time ago to wage a political war to reduce the GSEs' share of the mortgage market, and of course I must say, Mr Chairman, waged by you."[48] She added, "It is critical that we ensure any action that we may consider not impair the housing mission of the GSEs."

Mr Arthur Davis followed on, saying, "You have imputed various motives to the people running the organization. You then went to the Board and put a 48-hour ultimatum on them without having the specific regulatory authority to put that kind of ultimatum on them. That sounds like some kind of invisible line has been crossed ... as if you have gone from being a dispassionate regulator to someone who is very much involved and has a stake in this controversy ... the political context ... [is] that serious doubts were being raised about the OFHEO."[49]

The focus shifted from claiming that the report was a political attack on Fannie Mae to claims that releasing the report was likely to damage Fannie Mae. Mr Davis asked if it were possible that the "market standing of Fannie Mae could be weakened by your testimony?" He was followed by Rep Joseph Crowley, who said, "I know that Mr Raines has pledged to create 6 million new homeowners, including 1.8 million minority homeowners, by 2014. Do you believe that this goal may be threatened now because of this report?"[50] Mr Falcon gave the obvious answer that the course of action taken by OFHEO was because of the actions of the company, and it is of course those actions which were described in the report.

Mr Kanjorski, a long-standing member of the Committee, who had already lived through the Savings & Loans crisis, adopted a more cautious approach, urging his colleagues on both sides of the aisle to "demonstrate patience and caution." Recognizing the serious nature of the matters raised in the report, he wanted to wait for the process to work itself out, whilst warning against "hyping the initial findings," since they could also raise the price of home ownership.[51]

Apart from Messrs Capuano, Kelly, Toomey, Bachus, Watt and Congresswoman Hart, who all sought to clarify one or other aspect of the report or to emphasize the failings of Fannie Mae, few other issues of substance were raised. These did, however, include the points made by Barney Frank and Maxine Waters. Barney Frank challenged Mr Falcon on the grounds that when he read the Director's testimony, "it seems to me almost boilerplate in his report that he says at the end of every specific, 'and this could raise questions of safety and soundness issues'. It could, but nothing in here seems to me to say that it does ... I think it serves us badly to raise safety and soundness as a kind of general shibboleth."[52]

Later in the hearing, after testimony from Frank Raines and Tim Howard, Barney Frank was again dismissive, both of the report and of the difficulties he alleged in the report's treatment of derivative accounting: "My sense of accounting for derivatives ranges somewhere in between alchemy and astrology. You are accused of being on the alchemy end."[53]

Far from being a challenge to the OFHEO report, this comment indicates the lack of understanding about the whole issue of safety and soundness, which is not just a matter of having sufficient capital, but is also a matter of the reliability of the financial information and the management of risk throughout the whole organization.

With unreliable financial reporting, it is impossible to know what an organization's true assets and liabilities are, and hence to be able to assess the risks to which the organization is exposed. That is why the report, having shown that in respect of key elements of financial reporting, Fannie Mae's figures were unreliable, states that "safety and soundness" were in question. It found an "operating environment that tolerated weak or non-existent internal controls; key person dependencies and poor segregation of duties; ineffective reviews of the Enterprise's office of auditing; and an inordinate concentration of responsibility ... in the Chief Financial Officer."[54] Indeed, any one of these would pose some risk to the safety and soundness of an organization, and the combination could be lethal. It is not clear whether Barney Frank and his colleagues on the Committee understood that; chose not to appear to understand it, preferring to make political points; or could not face up to the fact that Fannie Mae, being in the "American dream business" to which they were all committed, could do anything wrong.

Senior executive compensation at Fannie Mae

As has been discussed, one of the issues raised in the report was that of compensation paid to senior executives. At the beginning of the hearing, Chairman Richard Baker advised the Committee that some 12 months previously, he had corresponded with the Director's office, making enquiries about the levels of compensation for the top 20 executives, information which had not been made public at that time. Within a few days of his enquiries, Fannie Mae had engaged the services of Ken Starr, legal counsel, to warn him and his staff that such information should not be made public and, if it were, civil legal action would follow. He did not reveal the information at the time, because it was not directly relevant to reforming the institutions; nor did he understand why, until he read OFHEO's report.

The extent of systemic risk

A glimpse of the possible extent of systemic risk was revealed by answers to questions posed by Rep Douglas Ose, about the extent to which banks held Fannie Mae's securities and the possible indirect impact. Chairman Baker answered the question in more detail than Armando Falcon did, pointing out that of the 8,400 insured federal depository institutions, more than 3,000 held over 100% (not 50, not 70, but 100%) of their required Tier One capital in GSE securities.[55]

Fannie Mae's defense

Franklin Raines and Tim Howard were also questioned at the same hearing. They spent much of the time denying the contents of the OFHEO report, claiming, for example, "We have looked for the facts. There were no facts in the OFHEO report. None. Other than their calculation that says, 'Oh there seems to be if we subtract one number from another you get this result'."[56] Mr Howard denied that he had the range of roles he had claimed in his interview with OFHEO. Both claimed that they had co-operated all along with the OFHEO, and that the subpoenas had not been necessary. They complained that they had not seen a copy of the report, and that OFHEO had not consulted with them or their very long-standing auditors about the report; also, that it had been presented to Fannie Mae's Board of Directors with 48 hours' notice for reasons that they did not understand. One of the committee members, Congressman Joe Baca, concurred with these complaints, stating, "It seems odd that they did not contact you. Yet … they have gone to the media and they have gone everywhere else."[57] However, under further questioning from Congressman Douglas Ose, Franklin Raines admitted that, prior to the hearing, he and some of his agents, employees or counsel visited members of the committee and discussed the substance of the hearing. In answer to a further question as to whether he, his agents, employees or counsel provided questions to members of the subcommittee for the purpose of having them posed to witnesses during this hearing, Mr Raines admitted that "I believe we talked to members of staff about the questions they might want to pose."[58] That is clear from the hearing, where the lines of attack on the credibility of OFHEO and the manner of its release to the public were obviously planned in advance.

The only issue for which Franklin Raines and Tim Howard were not prepared was the question as to why, if the report consisted of entirely unsubstantiated allegations, the Board had so readily entered into the September 27 agreement, according to which the Board was required to implement correct accounting treatments, hold the 30% capital surplus, recalculate prior period financial statements, using correct accounting, appoint an independent risk officer, and put in place policies to ensure effective adherence to accounting rules and new internal controls. They could not explain in any satisfactory way why that had been agreed.

The final matter of substance raised in the hearing referred to the fact that the issues raised in the report were "brand-new issues" to Fannie Mae, and that they were new to their relationship with OFHEO. In that, Franklin Raines was correct, and the reasons lay with the weakness of the regulator, together with Fannie Mae's resistance to any attempts to strengthen the regulator. The reasons for this will be discussed more fully in the next chapter.

Fannie Mae and the SEC

It was plain from Raines and Howard's statements during the hearing that, knowing the matter was going to be referred to the SEC for a final assessment of the alleged accounting irregularities, they expected to receive favorable treatment from the SEC. Indeed, Fannie Mae requested guidance from the Commission's accounting staff regarding policy matters associated with its compliance with SFAS 91 and SFAS 133. The SEC statement acknowledged that it was unusual for the accounting staff to issue such guidance, whilst there are pending investigations. However, given that Fannie Mae had requested it, "because, in its view, these accounting issues have received extraordinary public attention and resulted in the mortgage and capital markets experiencing uncertainty," the staff agreed to issue guidance, based solely on information provided by Fannie Mae and OFHEO.

Fannie Mae's hopes for SEC support were dashed to the ground by the short and blunt statement issued by Donald T. Nicolaisen, SEC Chief Accountant. "Our review indicates that during the period under our review, from 2001 to mid-2004, Fannie Mae's accounting practices did not comply in material respects with the accounting requirements in Statements Nos 91 and 133." With regard to SFAS 91, he concluded that that Fannie Mae had failed to follow proper accounting procedures in relation to the fees associated with loan origination and purchasing. Fannie appeared to recognize adjustments to the carrying amount of its loans only if it exceeded a "self-defined materiality limit," contrary to the accounting standard.

He added, "Fannie Mae internally developed its own unique methodology to assess whether hedge accounting was appropriate," but its "methodology of assessing, measuring and documenting hedge ineffectiveness was inadequate and was not supported by SFAS 133." Then came the final blows:

Fannie Mae should:

- Restate its financial statements filed with the Commission to eliminate the use of hedge accounting.

- Evaluate the accounting under Statement No 91 and restate its financial statements filed with the Commission if the amounts required for correction are material.

- Re-evaluate the information prepared under generally accepted accounting principles (GAAP) and non-GAAP information that Fannie Mae previously provided to investors, particularly in view of the decision that hedge accounting is not appropriate.[59]

Franklin Raines and Timothy Howard leave Fannie Mae

The SEC met with Franklin Raines, three outside directors of Fannie Mae (Stephen Ashley, Joe Pickett and Thomas Gerrity), OFHEO Director, Armando Falcon, KPMG auditors and criminal prosecutors from the Justice Department at the Commission's HQ on December 15. A week later, the Board of Directors finally gave in to pressure from OFHEO to force both Franklin Raines and Tim Howard from office. According to Fannie Mae's public statement, Franklin Raines accepted early retirement and Tim Howard had resigned. Stephen Ashley then became non-executive Chairman and David Mudd, the Chief Operating Officer, became interim Chief Executive, until March 2005 when his appointment was confirmed. Executive Vice President Robert Levin became interim Chief Finance Officer and the auditors, KPMG, were dismissed.

The departures were accompanied by a flurry of announcements of investigations, including the SEC's inquiry into the reasons for the violations and the conduct of the company's senior executives. The SEC would investigate possible violations of the Sarbanes-Oxley Act, which would cover infringements of the certification requirements (this can lead to criminal as well as civil penalties). OFHEO began investigating bonuses and severance pay for Raines and Howard, especially after Fannie Mae disclosed that the former Chairman and CEO was leaving with a severance package of $24.2m, excluding his $2.4m annual salary for life; another $21m in accelerated stock; potential future stock payments valued at up to $34.6m; and an undisclosed amount in 401(k) benefits. Fannie Mae agreed to maintain a $5m life insurance policy for Raines until he reached the age of 60 and $2.5m insurance cover thereafter, and full medical and dental benefits for life for his wife and dependent children. CFO Timothy Howard did not do quite so well with his minimum severance package, valued at approximately $12m, potential stock payouts valued at up to $6.4m, 401k benefits; Fannie Mae did not include in its severance deal his annual salary of $433,000, and another $15.3m in an accelerated stock payout that he had already earned. His insurance policy would also be maintained at $2m until 2008 and $1m thereafter, with full medical and dental benefits for the rest of his life.

Reactions to the restatement of Fannie Mae's assets

The announcement of the restatement of Fannie Mae's accounts led to calls for fundamental regulatory changes by the Senate Banking Committee Chairman, Richard Shelby. "Now more than ever, it is time to create a regulator with sufficient and flexible authority to take the necessary action to ensure the safe and sound operation of these important housing enterprises."[60] The Chairman of the House Financial Services Committee, Michael G. Oxley, said, "I am deeply disturbed that investors, the markets and Congress were misled by deceptive practices at Fannie Mae. We intend to hold hearings early next year in Chairman Richard Baker's Subcommittee and will continue to work towards sweeping legislative reform."[61]

In his December 16 letter, Chairman Richard Baker, amongst other matters, asked Director Armando Falcon to "recapture all bonus payments from executives that were based upon faulty and deeply flawed earnings statements of the Enterprise ... But for the determined and professional work of OFHEO, investors, the markets and Congress would not have knowledge of the serious problems of Fannie Mae, which jeopardizes the national housing system."[62]

The rating agencies' response was muted, to say the least. Standard & Poor's Governance Services allowed its January 23, 2003 score of 9 to remain, with "negative implications" until discussions with the company had taken place and they had further information about recent events, including the SEC statement, the departures of Franklin Raines and Timothy Howard, and the dismissal of KPMG, the progress of various investigations and the nature of the Board's deliberations, new management and the severance arrangements for departing executives.

On December 23, 2004, Fitch Ratings lowered its credit ratings on Fannie Mae's preferred stock, out of concerns that the company may not be able to pay its dividends in 2005. Fitch also stated that it might reduce that stock from the A+ "materially" if OFHEO forced the company to stop paying dividends, and that it believed further investigations into Fannie may "uncover additional accounting deficiencies."

Moody's Investors Service affirmed Fannie Mae's AAA senior unsecured debt rating and its Prime-1 rating for short-term debt, but said it could cut some of the company's other ratings. The A-Bank Financial Strength Rating remained under review for possible downgrade, reflecting OFHEO's determination that Fannie Mae was significantly under-capitalized, as well as uncertainty about internal control and governance issues. Moody's expected that OFHEO would approve dividend payment and that the non-cumulative dividends would not be interrupted; Fannie Mae's exposure to this risk is inconsistent with the AA rating category for junior securities and A-bank financial rating.

The reaction from the ratings agencies was cautious. The warning from Alan Greenspan was disregarded by most members of the Committee. The treatment meted out to Armando Falcon by many of the Democrat members showed that they were entirely unwilling even to address such basic issues for Fannie Mae and Freddie Mac as upholding proper accounting standards and good governance. Apart from Richard Shelby and Richard Baker, together with some of the members of their respective committees, most simply did not understand the enormity of the risks posed by the Enterprises, risks which would not be addressed by stronger regulation accompanied by a reduction in the size of their portfolios, since these were not the only problems facing Fannie Mae and Freddie Mac. They were large issuers of debt, and they were feeding the market with mortgage-backed securities based to a much larger extent than ever realized on subprime mortgages.

Other warning voices began to be heard. The Organization for Economic Co-operation and Development (OECD), referring to the "rapid growth and systemic importance" of Fannie Mae and Freddie Mac, recommended that their "regulation and supervision" should be "tightened and the Administration has made proposals to this end, including relocating the regulatory authority to the Treasury Department." OECD adds that: "reforms should go beyond that by eliminating their special status ... [which] has led to the market perception of an implicit government guarantee and hence slightly lower borrowing costs, allowing them to expand strongly and go beyond their original mandate of supporting the secondary market for residential mortgages. In any case, the marginal funding advantage is an inefficient way of promoting home ownership ... Altering the GSEs' status, however, may not be sufficient to eliminate their implicit government guarantee. Without reducing the size of the GSEs' portfolios, investors may still perceive them as 'too big to fail'. Limits could be placed on the growth of their mortgage-related asset portfolios, so that mortgage-backed securities traded in public markets, and not GSE debt, became the dominant source of secondary market funding for mortgages."[63]

10

The Years 2005 to 2007

Drinking in the last chance saloon

Introduction

This chapter addresses the story of Congress's failed attempts to restrain the GSEs during the years 2005 to 2007, and its lack of awareness of the storm that was about to break. Even OFHEO's devastating final report of its examination of Fannie Mae's accounting problems did not stir enough of them to action. The case for stronger oversight was crystal clear to the Administration, to all the players in the market place, and to the wider public; it was also obvious to the Chairman of the Senate and House Committees, as both expressed their determination to act, especially in response to the accounting scandals and to revelations about the huge salaries, pensions and compensation that Franklin Raines and Brendsel received on their departure from the GSEs.

Events in 2005

The two Chairmen

At the beginning of the year, it looked as though all was set fair for legislation to restrain the GSEs. The Chairmen of the House and Senate Committees expressed their determination more than once, as part of the reaction to the accounting scandals and revelations about the huge pensions, salaries and compensation that Franklin Raines and Brendsel received on their departure from the GSEs. In two long interviews in late January, Senator Richard Shelby stated that the "climate has improved very much for regulation," but "I don't want a bill that's meaningless. I would not want to be any part of it – the administration won't either. I think the time has come for meaningful reform legislation." He added that he was "sure that there will be opposition to any meaningful legislation to reform the way GSEs work by various people, including some at the GSEs themselves," noting that in 2004, the GSEs "hired everyone in town" and "were obviously against the bill ... They say that they are 'eager for reform' but we are going to test that statement." He added that The White House and the House Financial Services Chairman "will be working with us very strongly to bring about a strong product," and that the GSEs "should be well-capitalized, well-regulated and well-managed."[1]

Richard Baker was reported as saying that he and Michael Oxley intended to set out their proposals for new legislation in February, which would be "the most comprehensive bill we have ever proposed, simply because the environment was so dramatically different from prior sessions when this subject was considered ... Most defenders of Fannie have re-evaluated their positions and are either going to remain quiet or, frankly, are even going to be supportive of some kind of reform."[2] The new regulator would oversee Fannie Mae, Freddie Mac and the FHLBs, replacing OFHEO and the Federal Housing Board.

The Administration again asserted its support for greater regulatory oversight of Fannie Mae and Freddie Mac, when the Treasury Secretary John Snow announced, "We need a strong, credible and well-resourced regulator with a clear mandate and all the powers of other world-class financial regulators," adding that Fannie and Freddie owned or guaranteed almost half the $7.6 trillion mortgage market in the US, making them the second-largest debtor in the country after the federal government. He concluded his speech by saying that "whilst the GSEs have continued to grow in size, complexity and importance, the regulatory structure governing their activities has not. The new regulator should have at heart two guiding principles: promoting a sound and resilient housing finance system, and increasing home ownership for less advantaged Americans."[3] Unfortunately, this indicates a significant failure to recognize that these guiding principles contained an inherent conflict.

Democrats' doubts led by Barney Frank

However, in a press release back in December, 2004, in response to the revelations about Fannie Mae's false accounting, Barney Frank was careful to acknowledge that the SEC's finding that Fannie Mae "used incorrect accounting" was "serious and disturbing." Then he added, "While these improper decisions by Fannie Mae do not threaten the financial soundness of the operation, and *should not be used by anyone in an effort to cut back on Fannie Mae's housing efforts*, they do reveal troubling deficiencies in its corporate governance."[4] This time the response in the Committee from supporters of Fannie Mae and Freddie Mac was muted.

Another bill: The Federal Housing Finance Reform Act H.R. 1461

The Congressional Committee met on April 13 to begin its considerations of yet another bill, or, as Chairman Oxley put it with an air of weariness, "We have been working on this issue for a long time. Since the 106th Congress, this Committee has held 22 meetings and has heard from 101 witnesses on GSE-related matters."[5] The bill, which Richard Baker introduced as the Federal Housing Finance Reform Act, set out to establish a new regulator to replace OFHEO, which, as they had discovered in their hearings, lacked "the critical tools needed to supervise these Enterprises." The bill was also, as Richard Baker was at pains to emphasize, "a collaborative effort, led by the Chairman, in consultation with Secretary Snow, Secretary Jackson, Chairman Greenspan and Director Falcon." Baker also pointed out that any public company which announced that it would have a multi-billion-dollar restatement over multiple years, which could not perform its duty to report its financials in a timely manner to the market, and could not yet give a date by which that financial information would be provided, would not have received the kind of kid-glove treatment which Fannie Mae and Freddie Mac had enjoyed. He concluded that this was because of the market perception of the federal backstop. He might well have added, from his own experience, other reasons, such as the bullying tactics of the GSEs and the millions of dollars spent on lobbying.

Against that backdrop, the bill contained the following proposals:

- Abolish OFHEO and establish an independent agency to oversee the housing GSEs and the Federal Home Loan Banks;

- Enhance the safety and soundness disclosure, and enforcement tools available to the regulator; and

- Increase the budget autonomy of the new regulator by exempting its assessments for the annual appropriations process.

Baker was at pains to point out what the bill did not contain: "It does not, for example, repeal the line of credit; it does not set arbitrary limits on [their] investments portfolio; it does not make immediate or requisite changes to capital. It does create a world class regulator, with the ability to act not only in the interests of tax payers, but in the interests of home ownership. There is the authority to adjust capital, to assess risk, to approve programs and to act in the interest of home ownership."[6]

The bill was met with muted criticism in Committee, with concerns being expressed by Congressman Kanjorski that stronger regulation would become more "bank-like," that an approval process for new products would be "burdensome," and that any "radical proposals" would "fundamentally change the way in which the GSEs operate or undermine their charters," although he did favor strong regulation.[7] Other Congressmen such as Michael Capuano, were anxious about the impact on mortgage rates of tougher regulation. Congressman Clay feared that a substantial reduction in the size of the GSEs' portfolios would result in higher interest rates, although the connection was not entirely clear. Congressman Scott suggested that "if the Treasury Department had full policy control of the GSEs, the markets would perceive that control as the full backing of the GSEs by the government."[8]

Even Barney Frank, a long-time supporter of Fannie Mae, was reluctantly prepared to support the bill in so far as it was a question of enhancing the safety and soundness of the GSEs, but he was lukewarm about it; after the discovery of their highly misleading accounting practices, he had announced in Committee that the "situation is not nearly as critical as people thought. We have found with both Fannie Mae and Freddie Mac inappropriate behavior, bad accounting – I think influenced probably by the compensation schemes of the top officials, and we have been able to step in through the regulator and correct those."[9] The final report by OFHEO on accounting irregularities at Fannie Mae was not completed until 2006. His primary concern was with manufactured housing and affordable housing.

The Administration's position had remained unchanged since 2003, with the key powers being to set both minimum capital standards and risk-based capital standards; the power to assess the entities for independent funding outside the appropriations process; and the ability to place a failed GSE in receivership. The Treasury Secretary had discretion to issue debt in the amount of $2.5bn to Fannie Mae and Freddie, and $4bn to the FHLBs. Treasury Secretary John Snow made it clear that the line of credit was only in the event that a GSE was in significant financial distress and needed the capital to emerge successfully from a receivership process.

The Senate bill: Federal Housing Enterprise Regulatory Reform Act. S. 190

Senators Chuck Hagel, John Sununu and Elisabeth Dole reintroduced their bill on January 26, 2005. Its powers would include approval powers over the new programs and activities proposed by the GSEs, and greater authority to limit exit compensation packages or golden parachutes for executives removed for cause. The bill would also require the GSEs to report mortgage loans that they suspected to be fraudulent, even after the loans have been sold (it also removes the Presidential appointment of directors to the boards of Fannie Mae and Freddie Mac, a right which President Bush did not exercise.) The new regulator would additionally have the power to set limits to the GSEs' secondary market activities, so that they did not participate directly or indirectly in the underwriting of a loan for an organization.

The most important provision of S.190 was to list the types of "permissible assets" that Fannie and Freddie would be allowed to purchase, bearing in mind that the GSEs pay for the mortgage assets by issuing debt securities at rates below what the mortgages and mortgage-backed bonds pay (and also rates that the benefitted from the implicit government guarantee.) The difference between the yield on the mortgage-related assets and the GSEs' cost of funds is profit. It is for this reason that the GSEs had a strong incentive to pursue portfolio growth and also could explain why their chief executives, Richard Syron (Freddie Mac) and Daniel Mudd (Fannie Mae), opposed it. At that time, the two Enterprises had over $1.5 trillion in portfolio assets, leading to the anxieties about concentration risk which are described fully in this chapter.

Section 109 of S.190 as reported limited the GSEs to purchasing mortgages and mortgage-backed securities for the purposes of securitization, and for certain other limited purposes. This would have the effect of radically changing the business model (or actually returning to the model of the early 1990s): the GSEs would no longer be very large investment funds, but would rather be transformed into conduits, buying mortgages from the original lenders, pooling them, packaging them into mortgage-backed securities and selling them to bond investors. This would reduce the risks of the portfolios and also reduce the cost of having to bail out either Freddie or Fannie to avoid the possibility of a systemic catastrophe in the financial markets. The opposition to such a proposal argued that there would then be fewer funds available for low- and moderate-income housing goals. In addition, S. 190 required the Director of the new regulatory authority to conduct a study of guarantee fees and to collect data regarding them. This would be the subject of an annual report to Congress in respect of the amount of such fees, and the way they are set.

Barney Frank's affordable housing fund makes its first appearance

H.R.1461, as reported, covered much the same ground. It required each Enterprise to establish an affordable housing fund to increase home ownership among very and extremely low-income families, to increase investment in housing in low-income and economically distressed areas, and to increase and to preserve the supply of rental and owner-occupied housing for very and extremely low-income families. Each Enterprise shall allocate to the fund 3.5% of its after-tax income during the first year after enactment, and 5% in the following years, unless it was less than adequately capitalized. S.190 did not contain any such provision. Finally, the bills differed in the conforming loan limits, which were not sufficiently high to cover all parts of the country, so H.R.1461 allowed an increase in the conforming loan limit up to a ceiling of 150% of the current limit in metropolitan areas where the median house price exceeds the current limit. S.190 did not contain any such provision.

The Senate Banking Committee met five times during April 2005 to consider the bill, and received testimony from 17 witnesses, including representatives of the industry; Alan Greenspan, Chairman of the Federal Reserve; David Walker, Comptroller General of the USA; Douglas Holtz-Eakin, Director, Congressional Budget Office; and Armando Falcon. The Treasury Secretary, John Snow, and

Secretary for Housing, Alphonso Jackson, gave the same testimony as they had just given to the House Financial Services Committee.

Chairman Greenspan's evidence: Systemic risk and the GSEs

Of all the testimonies, Alan Greenspan's was the most important warning, and one that he had given more than once. He pointed out again that Fannie Mae and Freddie Mac were allowed by law to extend their investments in almost any direction as long as there was some link, however indirect, between these and their mission of supporting conforming mortgage markets. Because they could borrow at a subsidized rate, they were able to pay mortgage originators higher prices for their mortgages than their competitors (this was also facilitated through their guaranties, another area requiring careful oversight.)

Greenspan pointed out that the higher prices paid for mortgages were only one part of the subsidy, the other part being their return on equity, often exceeding 25%, well above the 15% annual returns survivable by other large financial institutions, and almost entirely attributable to their lower borrowing costs. Since the mid-1990s, the rapid growth of the GSEs' portfolios, reaching $1.38 trillion or 23% of the home-mortgage market, was due to no other reason than "profit creation through exploitation of the market-granted subsidy."[10] Hence the growth of their portfolios could only be curtailed by regulatory action, since clearly neither Fannie Mae nor Freddie Mac had any incentive to do so; the size and continued growth of their portfolios "concentrate interest rate risk and prepayment risk in these two institutions and makes our financial system dependent on their ability to manage these risks."[11]

The extent of the interdependence was shown by the fact that over 4,500 banking institutions met all their Tier 1 capital requirements with GSE securities, thereby clearly increasing systemic risk. It was further intensified by the fact that the GSEs' hedging of that risk was concentrated in five or six very large financial institutions. The problem was that few members of the Congressional Financial Services Committee either understood or were ready to listen to Chairman Greenspan's warnings, despite the fact that, as Congressman Royce recognized, it was the "strongest and most stern warning I can recall coming from a Chairman of the Federal Reserve."[12]

Royce was referring to Greenspan's concern that a "stiffening of their regulation might strengthen the market's view of GSEs as extensions of government, and their debt as government debt. The result, short of a very substantial increase in equity capital, would be to expand the size of the implicit subsidy and allow GSEs to play an even larger unconstrained and potentially destabilizing role in the financial markets ... If we fail to strengthen GSE regulation, we increase the possibility of insolvency and crisis ... Almost all the concerns associated with systemic risks flow from the size of the balance sheets of the GSEs, not from their purchase of loans from home-mortgage originators and the subsequent securitization of these mortgages."[13] He was wrong about the latter, as events in 2007 and 2008 would show.

More on systemic risk. Fannie Mae, Freddie Mac and OFHEO

Available to both Committees was a wealth of information about the way in which the GSEs operated, the use to which the implicit subsidies were put, the risks to which they were exposed, and the nature of the growing systemic risk. Interest rate risk for the GSEs is the potential for losses in connection with their portfolios of mortgages and MBSs. They financed these by issuing debt securities with widely varying maturities: for example, if they issued debt securities with a maturity of one year to finance a fixed-rate mortgage of 15 or 30 years, they would face the risk from the rise in market interest rates in the form of higher borrowing costs when they rolled over their maturing short-term debt; but the return on their mortgage portfolio was fixed until the mortgages are paid off. When interest rates fall, more borrowers prepay their mortgages and leave the GSEs with high-cost debt outstanding.

Retained portfolios

In 2004, the GSEs' retained mortgage portfolios were about 40% of their outstanding debt, the remainder of which consisted of the bonds and other securities which they issued, as well as MBSs. In 2004, Fannie's MBSs totalled $1,403 trillion and the remainder of its debt was estimated at $945bn. Freddie Mac's MBSs totalled $852bn and other debt was estimated at $732bn.[14] They issued debt of all maturities, from discount notes with maturities as short as overnight bonds to bonds with maturities as long as 30 years. To manage the interest rate risk and other market risks posed by their rapidly increasing retained mortgage portfolios, they began to issue intermediate and long-term debt securities with embedded call features.[15]

Credit risk

They also faced credit risk due to losses arising from mortgage delinquencies or foreclosures, but up to 2005, such losses were of the order of one to five basis points per year due to rising house prices and low interest rates, a situation which would change if interest rates rose and house prices fell. Although Fannie Mae and Freddie Mac adopted various measures to minimize losses from credit defaults, they continued to retain a substantial amount of credit risk. The extent of operational risk for Fannie Mae was still being uncovered in 2005, but it covered false accounting, fraud, theft, mismanagement and inadequate information and recording systems.

The GSEs issue far more in debt securities than a number of the USA's largest banks combined. The law allows federally insured banks and thrifts to invest in their debt without limitation. It explicitly exempts Fannie Mae's, Freddie Mac's and other GSEs' securities from statutory limitation on commercial banks' investments in the "investment securities" of individual firms, which is generally 10% of the bank's unimpaired capital and surplus. According to the OFHEO report on systemic risk, over 30% of commercial banks with over $1bn in assets held Fannie Mae and Freddie Mac debt equal to more than 10% of their capital, and 10% of such banks held Fannie Mae debt in excess of 50% of their capital. Smaller banks' holdings of GSE securities represented a significantly larger share of their capital; that is, those with less than $1bn in assets.[16] This alone forms part of the interdependency and hence increased systemic risk to which Alan Greenspan referred. The nature of the systemic risks set out in the OFHEO report were clearly summarized and presented in the CBO Director's report.[17]

Interest rate risk

In their management of interest rate risk in particular, Fannie Mae and Freddie Mac numbered amongst the largest end-users of financial derivatives, generally interest rate swaps and swaptions in combination with actual debt instruments, to create long-term debt synthetically and to obtain options to extend or shorten the maturity of their debt. They also used derivative contracts, including futures, options on futures and short sales, to hedge future purchases of mortgages and the issuance of securities against the risk of loss due to adverse interest-rate movements.

In addition, they entered into derivatives contracts (futures, options on futures and short sales) to hedge future purchases of mortgages and the issuances of securities against the risk of loss due to adverse interest-rate movements. They needed debt securities whose principal repayments match the expected repayments of their mortgage asset securities, for which they used interest rate swaps and swaptions, largely to create "synthetic" long-term debt. They bought "put" swaptions to enter into a pay fixed/receive floating swaps, so that they could lengthen their liabilities if interest rates rise and mortgage prepayments slow. According to OHFEO, all of this made it possible for the GSEs to grow their mortgage asset portfolios, hedge their growing interest rate risk and minimize their funding costs.[18]

OFHEO charted the growth in 1993 at $72bn to $1.6 trillion at year-end 2001 for Fannie Mae and Freddie Mac. That was, of course, before the accounting irregularities emerged in 2003 and 2004, so OFHEO's confidence in the figures, the ability of staff in either organisation to use swaps, swaptions and derivatives to hedge against interest rate risk, still less account for them, had been shattered.

The report drew attention to another aspect of systemic risk: namely, that the market for derivatives at that time was highly concentrated among a small number of dealers, primarily brokerage firms and commercial banks, which were counterparties for at least one side of virtually all contracts. The largest dealers included J.P. Morgan Chase, Citigroup (including the large derivatives operation of its broker-dealer subsidiary, Salomon Smith Barney), Deutsche Bank, Goldman Sachs, Lehman Brothers, Merrill Lynch and Morgan Stanley Dean Witter. According to data compiled by the Office of the Comptroller of the Currency, at the end of 2001, seven US banks held nearly 96% of the notional OTC derivatives of the American banking system, and 25 banks held over 99% of the notional OTC derivatives outstanding of all US banks. As far as the Enterprises were concerned, five counterparties accounted for almost 60% of the total notional amount of Fannie Mae's OTC derivatives, and 58% of Freddie Mac's. The Enterprises claimed to have policies in place to limit counterparty credit risk, as all are rated single A or better.

However at the end of 2001, the credit exposure of Fannie Mae's counterparties was about $7bn for Fannie Mae and $2.6bn for Freddie Mac, figures which represent the sum of each Enterprise's exposure to counterparties where the netted value of the contracts favors the company. The issue that emerges from this is not only the interdependency of the various players in the market, but the fact that they were so few in number. Furthermore, in the intervening years since the collection of data for the report, both the debt issued by Fannie Mae and Freddie Mac and the derivative contracts into which they entered continued to increase.

A less obviously important part of Fannie Mae and Freddie Mac's operations is the purchase of mortgages from lenders, which are financed through the issuance of debt securities, or the creation and sale of guaranteed securities backed by pools of loans or by guaranteeing MBSs issued to lenders. Typically, Fannie Mae and Freddie Mac securitize a number of loans from a lender, which retains a portion of the monthly mortgage interest payments as compensation for servicing the loans in the pool. They pool the individual mortgages and then sell to the investors guaranteed claims (MBSs) to the contractual flows from these mortgages. For that service they charge fees, which they expect to cover the cost of defaults on mortgages and earn a return on the investment. Both lines of business have grown significantly: outstanding MBSs grew from about $600bn in 1990 to $2.3 trillion in 2004, while total debt grew from less than $300bn to $2.5 trillion over the same period (including the FHLBs).

Guarantee fees

The issue of the guarantee fees was raised by Mr Bachus in the course of the Congressional hearing on April 13, 2005. The Enterprises charge the guarantee fees on lenders, but this has a direct effect on the costs of the mortgage for borrowers. "I understand that these G-fees are not set on how safe or sound a mortgage is, like an 80% mortgage or 90% mortgage; it is based on volume. And what they do is, they negotiate in private confidential agreements with mortgage originators, and they charge some one fee, they charge others other fees. And I understand that that can vary by as much as 15%. Obviously, the more volumes you do, the lower fee you get ... [it] obviously favors your biggest mortgage companies, and it puts your smaller mortgage companies at a disadvantage ... should not this be made public, where the public can scrutinize it?"[19] Although the Treasury Secretary and the Secretary for Housing agreed, it was plainly a matter that was not going to be taken any further; such agreements and the fees charged were another important source of revenue for the GSEs. What should have caught their attention was the way in which Fannie and Freddie were buying loans, by volume, not by quality.

The bills were delayed until the summer

With bi-partisan support, the House Financial Services Committee passed H.R.1461, the Federal Housing Finance Reform Act, 2005 on a 65-5 vote. Chairman Michael Oxley had engineered the vote by adding the provisions raising the conforming loan limit, introducing the affordable housing fund, and resisting the Administration's call for strict limits on the size of the GSEs' portfolios.

S.190 was "marked up" on July 28, 2005 and passed by a party-line vote of 11–10, but the bill did not reach the floor of the Senate for a vote, despite the fact that the Republicans had a majority in the Senate (55 Republicans, 44 Democrats with 1 Independent aligned with the Democrats). It appears that the reason for this was the nature of the partisan vote: the bill had no Democrat sponsors. Senator Shelby was prepared to work through the summer to get bipartisan support, but he was not prepared to move the Senate bill to the floor, unless he thought that the size of the GSEs' portfolios would be reduced.

Paul Sarbanes had introduced an amendment requiring the GSEs to set aside 5% of their profits into an affordable housing fund in the Committee stage. This was amended again by Senator Jack Reed to prevent its becoming another slush fund for the Enterprises, but the Republicans still voted it down, 11 to 9. Senator Schumer thought the affordable housing fund would not be a difficult issue to resolve, but said that, "The portfolio limits area [is] a very large sticking point for me and I think for just about every one of us [on the Democratic side] ... The bill's portfolio restrictions would result in shifting about $760bn in housing assets from Fannie and Freddie to other private financial institutions. By moving these assets and the risk they encompass out of the GSEs, the bill would simply move them into the portfolios of large institutions that lack Fannie and Freddie's housing focus … and so what we've done is, we haven't reduced the risk, but we've reduced the commitment to housing."[20]

Once again, the domination of the "affordable housing" ideology blinded many politicians to the real risks contained in the size of the GSEs' portfolios, and to the fact that their accumulation of portfolios "is a highly leveraged operation," requiring a "sophisticated hedging of interest rate risk," thus imparting a significant risk to the American financial system." This was the position Chairman Greenspan reiterated more than once, both in his testimony to the House Financial Services Committee and to the Senate Banking Committee. He might have added that, given their demonstrable and abject failure in derivatives accounting and even at the more basic level of record-keeping, there was little reason to believe that the GSEs were able to manage sophisticated hedging of interest rate risk, but the Democrats believed, or chose to believe, that all such arguments and warnings were simply designed to restrict their activities and to remove the GSEs altogether. The affordable housing fund was another canard, which had the effect of holding up or even preventing the passage of bills though the House and Senate.[21]

Further warnings about the risks in the OTC market and the GSEs

Greenspan's warnings were not lightly made, and were repeated on several occasions in 2005. In March, the Federal Reserve published a report evaluating the concerns which had been expressed not only by Federal Reserve officials, but also by foreign authorities and private analysts, about the concentration in the OTC markets for US dollar interest-rate options. There were three major concerns, which the report listed as follows:

- The potential for exit for a leading dealer to result in options market illiquidity and the potential effects of illiquidity on the housing GSEs and other hedgers of mortgages and mortgage-backed securities;

- Market risks to dealers from meeting the demands for options by mortgage hedgers, including whether data indicating the notional value of options sold by dealers significantly exceeds the notional value purchased are accurate and, if so, whether dealers are assuming significant risks; and

- Potential counterparty credit losses to market participants in the event of the failure of a leading dealer or one of the GSEs.

Concentration was relatively high by the end of 2003, when the four largest dealers accounted for 40% of the $37.5 trillion market for US dollar interest rate swaps and forward rate agreements. The report was based on interviews with Fannie Mae, Freddie Mac, several FHLBs, a large mortgage servicer, and seven leading bank and non-bank OTC derivatives dealers. Fannie and Freddie together accounted for more than half of the options demand when measured in terms of the sensitivity of the instruments to changes in interest rate volatility (rather than notional amounts). The supply of interest rate options comprises investors in callable debt issued by the FHLBs (less important than in the past), banks and insurers, non-financial corporations and local governments, investors in structured notes, and hedge funds, which have become an important source of supply and liquidity. OTC derivatives dealers intermediate between options buyers and sellers, but there may well be mismatches between buyers and sellers, leaving them exposed to basis risk.

The GSEs assured Federal Reserve staff that even if a leading dealer left the market, they would be able to use the second tier of dealers, who would step up their activities. Furthermore, if market liquidity were temporarily impaired for some reason, the GSEs did not see themselves as dependent on continuous access to liquidity in the options market, but rather on the liquidity of the swaps market, which is less concentrated and easier to intermediate.

The conclusions of the staff report could be seen as reassuring: concentration was reasonably well-managed. The risk management strategies of Fannie and Freddie (and other mortgage hedgers) rely on continuous liquidity in the swaps markets, where there is less concentration. However, "the GSEs do assume very large net positions in the options and swaps markets. But the potential market impact of dealers' actions to close out and replace those positions following a GSE failure are likely to be substantially offset by the effects of the increases in uncertainty and risk aversion that would be certain to accompany a GSE's failure."[22]

The problem with this report is that it relies too heavily on the GSEs' ability to handle risk, which, given both their abysmal failure to manage accounting for any of the processes involved, as well as the deliberate manipulation uncovered in the first OFHEO report and the lack of skilled staff or proper governance at either institution, should have given cause for doubt. The report ends by recommending that "participants in the interest-rate options markets make more of an effort to think about counterparty risk and market risk in an integrated way when evaluating counterparty credit exposures to large players." Nevertheless, Alan Greenspan referred to the concentration risk for the GSEs in his speech to the Federal Reserve Bank of Chicago,[23] warning again that the sheer size of portfolios exposed them to the risk of market illiquidity, adding that "concerns about potential disruptions to swaps market liquidity will remain valid until the vast leveraged portfolios of mortgaged assets held by Fannie and Freddie are reduced and the associated concentrations of market risk and risk-management responsibilities are correspondingly diminished."[24]

Greenspan pursued the issue of systemic risk, which he had already set out in a testimony to the Congressional Committee in 2004 and 2005, in a speech to a conference at the Federal Reserve Bank of Atlanta,[25] in which he stressed the issue and the difficulty of handling it through the usual means of banking regulation. In the case of the GSEs, he stated once again, these risks can only be handled by reducing the size of their portfolios. The reasons for this were set out in the speech. Regulators could not rely on market discipline to contain systemic risk in the case of the GSEs, owing to the market perception of their special relationship to the government. In addition, given their size in relation to the counterparties to their hedging transactions, the ability of the GSEs to correct any mistakes in their complex hedging strategies "becomes more difficult, especially when vast reversal transactions are required to rebalance portfolio risks."[26] He continued, "a system of diversified and less-leveraged interest rate risk management, away from large, highly leveraged portfolios, would be far more resilient to the inevitable mistakes and shocks of individual risk-mitigating strategies." Greenspan concluded that the "key activity of the GSEs – the provision of liquidity to the *primary mortgage market* – can be accomplished exclusively through the securitization of mortgages: GSEs' portfolios of mortgage-related assets cannot [and do not] serve this function. Such empirical evidence from the history of the GSEs militates against it."[27]

Progress on the House and Senate bills between July and December

The key issue contained in the Senate bill S.190 is the ability to restrict the GSEs' portfolio limits. It directs the new regulatory authority to establish criteria regarding the assets which the Enterprises can hold, and to consider safety and soundness as well as "systemic risk" posed by the size and composition of those investments. In other words, it allows for portfolio limits, which the Congressional bill, H.R.1461, did not. The new regulatory authority should have the powers, in Treasury Secretary John Snow's view, "to allow the GSEs to only hold as much as is necessary to carry out their mission with an appropriate level of safety." Exactly what the principles should be, and whether it should be up to Congress to set out the general framework or for Congress to stipulate, if not the exact ratio, at least the principles that should apply in order to come to conclusions about the portfolio, was left as an open question.

This was the legislative approach which Alan Greenspan recommended to the Senate and Congressional Committees, perhaps in the interests of getting some legislation in place which would include both some limits on portfolio growth, and appropriate receivership arrangements. His view was that the GSEs should "hold only the minimum level of assets needed to accomplish their primary mission mandated by their Charter." In the face of political suspicion, Greenspan may have felt that this was the right approach, but it ran the risk of making the mistakes of the past again: the Charters set out a minimum capital ratio, but one that turned out to be lower than banks were required to provide under Basel I. They also required the regulator, OFHEO, to produce a risk-based capital model, which it then took ten years to develop. But both the House and the Senate were determined to press ahead with their own bills. In the case of the House, this was despite the warnings issued by the Administration and the Federal Reserve.

The result of the legislative process in the Senate and the House was that lawmakers faced a difficult problem in reaching agreement, with two substantially different bills before them. Congressman Richard Baker and Chairman Richard Shelby hoped to reach a consensus, but although Senator Shelby wanted a good bill, he could not accept the affordable housing fund or abandon the question of portfolio limits. The Minority Leader, Senator Harry Reid had made his position clear: he regarded any limitation on the size of the portfolios of the Enterprises as "measures that could cripple the ability to carry out their mission of expanding home ownership ... we cannot pass legislation that could limit Americans from owning homes and potentially harm our economy in the process."[28] Given these opposing views, there was little likelihood that a compromise could be reached, although discussions continued behind the scenes.

The Administration rejects H.R.1461

In September and October, both Chairman Greenspan and the Administration made their positions entirely clear with regard to H.R.1461. In a letter to Senator Robert Bennett,[29] Chairman Greenspan spelt out in more extensive detail, the risks inherent in the strategies for managing the risks involved in the GSEs' portfolios. The interest rate and prepayment risks inherent in mortgages with refinancing options cannot be eliminated, but what can be markedly reduced is the systemic risks involved in such large holdings.

But he added, "Today, the US financial system is highly dependent on the risk-managers at Fannie and Freddie to do everything right, rather than depending on a market-based system supported by the risk assessments and management capabilities of many market participants, who have different views and different strategies for hedging risk." In the case of the Enterprises, there are "no meaningful limits to the expansion of their portfolios," so they must either have the "ability ... to quickly correct the inevitable misjudgments inherent in their complex hedging strategies ... [in a situation which] requires that the ultimate counterparties to the GSEs' transactions provide sufficient liquidity to finance an interest-rate-risk transfer that counters the risk ... or rely on passive hedging." The cost and quantity of derivatives required for the latter approach made this a very expensive way of managing prepayment risks, and again involved "Fannie and Freddie avoiding large errors."

Chairman Greenspan then explained that the reduction in the GSEs' portfolios would have no effect on the availability of home mortgage credit, and that reducing the portfolios would not be difficult, since there were many potential purchasers amongst other financial institutions in the US, including many central banks, which had long purchased agency debt and also hold MBSs in ever-increasing quantities. His final warning at the end of the letter stated, "in the case of GSEs, excessive caution in reducing their portfolios could prove to be destabilizing to our financial system as a whole and in the end could seriously diminish the availability of home mortgage funds;" words which would prove all-too prescient.

The same warning was reiterated in a Statement of Administration Policy, issued on October 26, 2005, which noted that the outstanding debt of the housing GSEs was $2.5 trillion, and that they provided credit guarantees on another $2.4 trillion. By comparison, the privately held debt of the Federal Government was currently $4.1 trillion. Given the size and importance of the GSEs, the Administration noted that Congress must ensure their large mortgage portfolios did not place the US financial system at risk; H.R.1461 "fails to provide critical policy guidance in this area." This statement was issued on the same day that the House was due to vote on the bill on the floor of the House.

The House passes H.R.1461

Despite the Administration's statement, the House of Representatives passed the GSE regulatory reform bill, establishing the Federal Housing Finance Agency, financed through assessments on the GSEs on October 26, 2005 by a bipartisan vote of 331-90. The affordable housing fund was part of the bill, but Democrats and a wide range of 600 faith-based groups opposed a provision which barred organizations involved in voter registration, lobbying activities, and the get-the-vote-out efforts from participating in the fund. They failed to remove these restrictions, but only narrowly. Having failed in this effort, Barney Frank and some other Democrats voted against the final bill. After the vote in the House, Chairman Shelby indicated that there would be no Senate vote on the legislation for GSE regulatory reform in 2005, and that he still wanted to see a reform bill which included the main elements of S.190; they would continue to press for that in 2006.

H.R.1461 was received in the Senate and read twice, and then referred to the Senate Committee on Banking, Housing and Urban Affairs on October 25, 2005. The bill was ordered to be reported favorably, with an amendment in the nature of a substitute, on July 28, 2005. The Administration did not get the bill it wanted and needed; Congress had once again failed to restrain the GSEs. Lawmakers should have paid more attention to OHFEO's report on accounting issues at Fannie Mae, which identified the GSE's failure to follow generally accepted accounting practices, in particular amortization of discounts, premiums and guarantee fees; accounting for financial derivatives contracts and structural problems in accounting operations and review. That report had been released in September 2004, followed by Fannie Mae's announcement in November that it was unable to file a third-quarter earnings statement because its auditor, KPMG, refused to sign off its accounting results. In December, the SEC, after finding serious inadequacies in Fannie's accounting methods, ordered the Enterprise to restate its accounting results from 2001: that had been followed by the departure of Franklin Raines and Timothy Howard. These events ought to have been fresh in the minds of *all* of the members of the House and Senate Committees, and should have required decisive legislative action.

Events in 2006

The Rudman report

The first report had been commissioned by the special Congressional Financial Services Committee, where it was welcomed by Congressman Frank, who commended the Board for its good sense in engaging the former Senator Rudman.[30] He added, "those of us who know him ... have such confidence in his integrity that we benefit from a report that's not being challenged ... I think we should make it very clear ... that we are talking about a betrayal by some of those at Fannie Mae of their high mission ... but this is not something that ought to be used to undo the housing mission."[31] It was more than a few individuals; OFHEO's final report makes it clear that it was a question of the way in which the whole operation was run, and perhaps went even deeper than that. A number of issues were discussed at the hearing, but none of any great moment; the 2,600 pages or so revealed little more than was contained in OFHEO's preliminary audit. It concluded, as OFHEO had done, that "management's accounting practices in virtually all areas that we reviewed were not consistent with GAAP."[32] Perhaps not surprisingly, and in contrast with OFHEO's Special Examination, published some four months later, it concluded: "Overall, we find that Fannie Mae's Board sought in good faith to respond to evolving legal and other standards in the area of corporate governance, that it sought appropriate internal and external support and advice in meeting these standards; and that its aim was to establish governance policies and practices at least in line with those of leading US corporations and peer institutions. The Corporate Governance Benchmarking Project, conducted with the assistance of an outside law firm, reflects the Board's intent that the Board remain up-to-date in the area of governance, consistent with its obligations and responsibilities."[33]

Furthermore, although the report describes all the accounting errors and manipulations in painstaking detail, it does not seek to estimate what Fannie Mae's actual earnings were, nor its true financial condition, and how these differed from its public financial reports. The company ceased to file financial reports from late 2004; it assessed its unrecognized losses as being in the range of $9bn, and later increased that to about $12bn, but there is no indication as to whether or not the estimates still applied, or indeed how Fannie Mae could know, given not only the extent of the accounting errors but also the complete inadequacy of its accounting systems. This led to further questions about the extent to which Fannie's risk management procedures, including especially its hedging activities, were distorted in order to achieve certain earnings goals, thus creating unnecessary exposures in order to reduce the cost associated with its hedging strategies. Fannie Mae and some members of the House Financial Services Committee had hoped that the Rudman report would undermine OFHEO, and that the charges against Fannie Mae would appear much weaker. However, the Rudman report did not quite give Fannie what it wanted, and was overshadowed by that of OFHEO.

OFHEO: Report of the Special Examination of Fannie Mae

The final report was finally published in May 2006, having taken over two years to complete, which was not surprising given the vast number of documents reviewed and the numerous interviews conducted with current and former employees of Fannie Mae, its Board, and KPMG.[34]

The report was precise and to the point, detailing the manifold failings at every level: the GSE's deliberate and improper earnings management, its determination and success in having the "rules written that worked for us," and its arrogance. All of this underlies what Christopher Cox, Chairman of the SEC, had no hesitation in calling the "extensive financial fraud" at Fannie Mae.[35] It is worth setting out just the summary of the report, which is indeed the severest possible indictment of a company, every aspect of which was either fraudulently or incompetently managed but which still managed to present itself to the world as one of the lowest-risk financial institutions and as "best in class" in terms of risk management, financial reporting, internal controls, and corporate governance. This was a "façade" which was unremittingly presented by an army of lobbyists to those who were taken in by or chose to believe it, or who may not have believed it but believed that whatever happened, the government would have to bail them out. The latter proved true in the end. Fannie Mae of course was always ready to use its "housing mission" and its commitment to providing affordable housing for low- and moderate-income families to gild its image. The use of the image also made it much more difficult for the media, politicians and others to criticize the Enterprises.

In their summary, OFHEO states that:

- During the period covered by this report, 1998 to mid-2004, Fannie Mae reported extremely smooth profits growth and hit announced targets for earnings per share precisely in each quarter. Those achievements were illusions deliberately and systematically created by the Enterprise's senior management with the aid of inappropriate accounting and improper earnings management.

- A large number of Fannie Mae's accounting policies and practices did not comply with GAAP. The Enterprise also had serious problems of internal control, financial reporting, and corporate governance. Those errors resulted in Fannie Mae's overstating reported income by some $10.6bn.

- By deliberately and intentionally manipulating accounting to hit earnings targets, senior management maximized the bonuses and other executive compensation they received, at the expense of shareholders. Earnings management made significant contribution to the compensation of Fannie Mae Chairman and CEO Franklin Raines, which totaled over $90m from 1998 through 2003. Of that total, over $52m was directly tied to achieving earnings per share targets.

- Fannie Mae consistently took a significant amount of interest rate risk and, when interest rates fell in 2002, incurred billions of dollars in economic losses. The Enterprise also had large operational and reputational risk exposures.

- Fannie Mae's Board of Directors contributed to those problems by failing to be sufficiently informed and to act independently of its Chairman, Franklin Raines, and other senior executives; by failing to exercise the requisite oversight over the Enterprise's operations; and by failing to discover or ensure the correction of a wide variety of unsafe and unsound practices.

- The Board's failures continued in the wake of revelations of accounting problems and improper earnings management at Freddie Mac and other high-profile firms, the initiation of OFHEO's special examination, and credible allegations of improper earnings management made by an employee of the Enterprise's Office of the Controller.

- Senior management did not make investments in accounting systems, computer systems, other infrastructure, and staffing needed to support a sound internal control system, proper accounting, and GAAP-consistent financial reporting. Those failures came at a time when Fannie Mae faced many operational challenges related to its rapid growth and changing accounting and legal requirements.

These are the main issues set out in the OFHEO report, well attested by all the evidence from the sources outlined above. The arrogance of Fannie Mae was summed up in the words of Mr Daniel Mudd, former Chief Operating Officer (from February 2000), who became Chief Executive of Fannie Mae (in December 2004) after the departure of Mr Raines, in a memo to the latter in November 2004. "The old political reality was that we always won, we took no prisoners, and we faced little organized political opposition … we used to, by virtue of our peculiarity, be able to write, or have written rules that worked for us."[36]

The SEC required Fannie Mae to restate its financial results for 2002 through to mid-2004, and incurred expenses for the restatement process, regulatory examinations, investigations and litigation, which according to Fannie Mae's estimates would exceed $1.3bn in 2003 and 2006 alone. That was in addition to the billions in losses incurred by the company through its corporate failings.

Congressional hearings on the report

There were two hearings on the OFHEO report, one before the Congressional Committee on June 6 and the other before the Senate Banking Committee on June 15. In the Congressional hearing, the report was well-received and the need acknowledged for new legislation to strengthen the hand of the regulator, with a clearer recognition on the part of most members of the Committee of the extent of the risks as evidenced by Congressman Hensarling: "What we have is the second largest borrower in the world, second only to Uncle Sam himself, an institution holding a Federal Charter, an asset portfolio worth over a trillion dollars, and they can't produce a reliable financial statement. That is troubling to say the least."[37]

Congressman Garrett noted the irony of the fact that the hearing was taking place on the same day as Ken Lay received his guilty verdict in the wake of the Enron scandal, yet the Fannie Mae debacle, which the Chairman of the SEC, Christopher Cox, described as "one of the largest restatements in American corporate history" at an "$11bn reduction in previously reported net income"[38] had not resulted in imprisonment for either Franklin Raines or Timothy Howard.

Mr Garrett quoted Armando Falcon's comment that "Fannie Mae is the Enron of government on government steroids" and pointed out that it was due to the government benefits that "their house of cards remains standing." This was in response to Congressman Barney Frank's statement that "what is heartening to me here is that the underlying structure of Fannie Mae and Freddie Mac, the strength of the housing market, the strength of that model, allowed them to withstand being misrun."[39] He failed to understand the value of the implicit government guarantee and the subsidy, or the implications of the OFHEO report, which portrayed an institution which was rotten to the core, or grasp the devastating nature of the comments. The conclusion of the hearing was the need for Senate to act on its bill, since it would only be then that the House and Senate would be able to work together on a conference committee to send the President the GSE bill in this Congress.

The Senate Banking Committee took evidence from Christopher Cox, James Lockhart III, who took over the directorship of OFHEO from Armando Falcon, Daniel Mudd, CEO of Fannie Mae, and Stephen Ashley, the newly appointed Chairman of the Board. Fannie Mae had finally agreed to separate the roles of Chairman and Chief Executive. Apart from his written testimony, Chairman Cox was at pains to stress the enormity of the corporate failings at Fannie Mae, both in terms of the size of the restatement and the fact that the company's internal controls were "wholly inadequate for size, complexity and sophistication of Fannie Mae's business."[40] He explained that, going back to at least 1992, the SEC had continually urged that the GSEs should comply with the disclosure requirements of Federal Securities laws. In July 2002, Fannie Mae entered into a voluntary agreement to comply and register its common stock, and began filing periodic reports with the SEC on March 31, 2003; however, after that date reports became increasingly sporadic and Fannie did not file its annual report for 2004 or 2005, nor did it file its quarterly report (Form 10-Q) for any of the preceding seven quarters. Cox emphasized the point that the $11bn not only falsely enriched its senior managers, but investors (mutual funds, pension funds, local governments and others) paid for $11bn in earnings which were not there. "A company with $47.5bn in market capitalization chartered by Congress, a private company with a public mission, as it calls itself, was for a period of several years raising capital on the basis of financial statements that were the result of fraud ... The harm to investors is both direct and measurable. The stock price of Fannie Mae fell from over $75 to very recently under $49."[41]

Some of the Senators, such as Senator Jack Reed, pressed Mr Lockhart to reassure them that whatever had happened, the company was going in the right direction in terms of risk management, systemic risk, and the retained portfolio. He got short shrift from Mr Lockhart: "They have not handled operational risk yet ... I do not think ... that they actually have a good operational risk capital model ... and they are certainly not complying with Sarbanes-Oxley ... There is no doubt in my mind that these companies are more highly leveraged, potentially, than any other financial institution in this country. They have $1.5 trillion of debt outstanding, and they have used that debt to buy $1.4 trillion of assets. To hedge those assets, they have $1.3 trillion of derivatives, and on top of that, they have $2.6 trillion of guarantees. And that is built on a combined capital of only $75 billion."

Senator Reed then tried to downplay the risk by claiming that their retained portfolio only accounted for 14%, but Lockhart reminded him that the two companies represented 40% of the market, 15% on mortgages owned and 26% on the guarantees, a very large exposure.[42]

The other issues raised concerned the role of Daniel Mudd, appointed as CEO, and corporate governance. It emerged from the Senate Committee hearing that Mudd's earnings over the period in question were $26m, of which $15m was triggered by the accounting irregularities and the total mismanagement of the company. He claimed that, even though he was Chief Operating Officer during that period, his job was focussed on customers and technology systems. That seems to be somewhat of an understatement of the role of COO, who is usually responsible for all the day-to-day operations of the company and reports to the CEO. He added, "I was not responsible for financial accounting. I was not responsible for the mortgage portfolio. I was not responsible for internal audit and I was as shocked as anyone in the company or anyone in Congress or anyone in the market when these issues were uncovered and came to light."[43] He remained as CEO until September 2008.

Senator Hagel questioned Stephen Ashley, the Chairman of the Board. It emerged that he had been a Board member since May 1995, and became Chairman after Franklin Raines' resignation in December 2004, when the decision was taken to separate the roles of chairman and chief executive. He had 40 years of experience in the mortgage business and had served as director or president of a number of businesses.[44] Senator Hagel put it to him that as a member of the Board he had a "fiduciary responsibility," but that according to the reports, "it is pretty clear that you failed ... you did not know anything about what happened, what was developing, the lobbying, the money, the compensation ... was it strange to you at all that was going on, no questions asked?" To which Mr Ashley replied, "I cannot express the deep disappointment and anger that I, as a member of the Board, and I know this is shared by my colleagues on the Board, feel at this moment in time when a company and a management and people that we put our trust in was broken, and not just broken, but shattered ... However, I think it is reasonable for any Board to be able to trust their management."[45] This is an interesting reply, as it refers to trusting the management rather than to any oversight responsibilities. Stephen Ashley remained as Chairman of the Board until September 2008.

Most of the members of the Committee realized the serious nature of the charges against Fannie Mae and the extent of the systemic risks. It has to be said that the Democrat Senators were rather more concerned to play down the extent of the potential damage. A somewhat more extreme version of that position was expressed by Senator Schumer: "I have some real concerns here. Obviously, there have been some misdeeds at Fannie and Freddie. I think a lot of people are being opportunistic, taking those and then throwing out the baby with the bathwater, saying let us dramatically restructure Fannie Mae and Freddie Mac when that is not what is called for as a result of what has happened here. First I want to ask you, Mr Lockhart, the new administration at Fannie and Freddie have taken some real reforms … do you think what they have done is adequate?" To which Mr Lockhart replied that it would take "several years for them to be SEC compliant" and that work on internal controls, risk management, accounting systems and the whole series of actions set out in OFHEO's agreement was taking place slowly.[46]

But still no bill in 2006

Radical action might have been expected after a report of that nature and considering the testimony, but although Chairman Shelby would have preferred another hearing and had hoped to bring the bill forward to a floor vote, no further action was taken on the bill that year. No further hearings on the OFHEO report took place. But as the weeks wore on and the November elections approached, the gap between the two parties on the legislation remained as wide as ever. The nine Democrats on the Senate Banking Committee issued a report, stating that limiting the assets which Fannie Mae and Freddie Mac could hold would limit access to affordable housing, and that "forcing the GSEs both to withdraw from the market and sell off existing bonds would raise the costs of this source of mortgage capital." They reiterated the demand for an "affordable housing fund" financed by a percentage of the GSEs' profits, which was not part of S.190. They concluded that the Committee Bill does not "strengthen the existing affordable housing goals," and "if passed in its current form, could actually weaken affordable housing obligations of the Enterprises by allowing the regulator the authority to 'modify or rescind' existing housing goals."[47]

Senator Bob Bennett pointed out that "if you have a bill reported out of committee on a party line vote in an atmosphere as politically charged as we have with floor time at a great premium going into an election, my guess would be that the leader would say, 'I can't afford floor time to fight over this.' I do not see any indication that there would be an accommodation between the Democratic position and the Republican position on the committee bill."[48]

Michael Oxley, House Financial Services Committee Chairman, wrote to Treasury Secretary, Henry Paulson urging him to redouble his efforts to clear the way for a bill to regulate the GSEs. "Our goal should be to enact robust GSE legislation and send it to President Bush this year," since the "number of legislative working days in the Senate is dwindling quickly." The bill passed in the House in 2005, which would in part establish a new regulator for the GSEs, is the "strongest reform legislation that will ever pass in the House, absent a conference report … As each day passes without news of progress on the other side of the Capitol that will allow the full Senate to act, the likelihood increases that the Congress could close without addressing the serious inadequacies of the current regulatory system and without protecting tax payers, investors and markets."[49]

Voices calling for reform were ignored

These and many other voices called for regulatory reform up to and even after the election in the "lame duck" session. The new Federal Reserve Chairman, Ben Bernanke, in the course of delivering the report on monetary policy to the Senate Banking Committee, was asked by Senator Dole for his views on whether the GSEs' regulator should have the authority to allow the Enterprises to increase their portfolios when there is a downturn in the market. The assumption is that they would thus be able to increase liquidity in the market when there is a downturn.

Chairman Bernanke replied that the Federal Reserve's research indicated that increasing the portfolios had very little effect, and that at any rate liquidity would not be increased by holding MBSs rather than treasuries. However, he continued, "for the purposes of trying to come to an agreement on GSEs' legislation, we could perhaps discuss or consider the possibility that the director might provide some emergency ability to the GSEs to make extra purchases during times in which the director judged the housing market to be in distress for some reason, but then to get rid of that extra portfolio, get rid of the extra MBSs over a period of time when the emergency was eliminated."

In answer to a question from Senator Carper, which was mainly about the affordable housing fund, but also covered the need for regulation before the end of the year, Bernanke stressed the importance of coming to a decision. "The Federal Reserve was drawn to this issue initially because ... we felt that the large portfolios exceeded what was needed for the housing purpose and indeed posed a threat to the stability of the financial system ... The reports we have seen recently on GSE accounting by the OFHEO, which cast into doubt the underlying accounting and internal controls of these agencies, I think just heightens my concern that those large portfolios at some point might create serious problems in the financial markets."[50]

The Administration made its views known once again in pressing for reform, reiterating that the retained portfolios "concentrate rather than distribute the prepayment risk and interest rate risk associated with mortgages and mortgage backed securities held by them, and concentrate them in entities that as a result of the lower levels of capital which they are required to hold are substantially more leveraged than other financial institutions ... hence it is critical that both a strengthened regulator and a mandate to address portfolio size, be included in any final legislation from Congress." This does not mean a "hard" cap expressed in terms of dollars, but the portfolio cap would be a "clear direction" to the new regulator as to the type of assets which could be included in the GSEs' portfolios. The key element for the Administration was not so much the size of the cap but relating this to their mission, which many agreed would result in a substantial reduction in the portfolios. All this would be done through regulation. The legislation would also allow the regulator to increase the cap in times of emergency, temporary disruptions in the mortgage market.

The Treasury Undersecretary for Domestic Finance, Randal Quarles, added an important point. "Secretary Paulson has made it clear to me that he believes that there is systemic risk associated with the GSEs' retained portfolios. While he shares the view that a legislative outcome is preferable, he has instructed us to ensure that the mechanics of our debt approval process are robust enough to give the Treasury the practical options of limiting the GSEs' debt issuance in accordance with our statutory authority should that become necessary. If a legislative solution is not achieved, Treasury will have no choice but to consider additional action."[51]

The first signs of trouble in the mortgage market

In the event, although talks continued up to the eve of the election and even in the lame duck session, a compromise was not reached. The issues which remained unresolved included the creation of an affordable housing fund, changes to the way in which conforming loan limits are set, and the appointment of public interest directors to the FHLBs. Whilst the debates took place about the form legislation should take, members of neither committee had noticed the changes taking place around them. It was left to two subcommittees of the Senate Banking Committee to consider the "Housing Bubble and its Implications for the Economy."[52] They took evidence from the Chief Economists of OFHEO, the Federal Deposit Insurance Corporation, the National Association of Home Builders and the National Association of Realtors. The OFHEO house price index showed that the general level of house prices rose by 56% from the spring of 2001 to the spring of 2006 (inflation-adjusted, a rise of 38%), partly due to lower long-term mortgage interest rates (8% in mid-2000 to less than 6% from early 2003 to mid-2005), building supply constraints, an ageing population and speculation. But pace of increases in house prices had moderated, especially in the most superheated markets. One important indicator was the swelling inventory of unsold houses on the market, up from 3m to 4.5m over 18 months.

The National Association of Realtors reported that existing home sales in July fell by 11.2% from the previous July, and that new home sales were down 22% from 2005. The Association noted that there were wide variations. It is fair to say that neither the witnesses nor the members of the Committee saw any of this as indicating more than a temporary slowdown, or even as Chairman

Bernanke called it, a "substantial correction." Not even UBS's statement that the rate of subprime 60-day delinquencies had already risen from 4.5% to 8% from the previous year, and that such loans were going into foreclosure more quickly than before, made an impact. No doubt with elections looming and the focus on legislation, lawmakers were distracted from such considerations.

The elections were held on November 7, with the Democrats gaining control of the House of Representatives with a majority of 31; each party had 49 seats in the Senate but the two Independents joined the Democrat caucus. Barney Frank became Chairman of the House Financial Services Committee and Senator Christopher Dodd became Chairman of the Senate Banking Committee.

Events in 2007

The whole process of legislation began again in the House under Barney Frank's Chairmanship.

Federal Housing Enteprises Regulatory Reform Act, S.1100

Senators Hagel, John Sununu, Elizabeth Dole and Mel Martinez introduced GSE regulatory reform legislation, S.1100, which was simply a revision of S.190. Their aim was to create an independent regulator to oversee the safety and soundness of the housing GSEs, to focus on the GSEs' combined $1.4 trillion investment portfolio on their housing mission of promoting affordable housing. Amongst the other provisions, the most important was to provide the new regulator with the authority to close down a failing GSE and protect against a taxpayer bailout, but it did not provide for an affordable housing fund. The bill was referred twice in Committee and then referred to the Senate Committee on Banking, Housing and Urban Affairs.

The Committee did not consider any legislation in 2007, although the Chairman stated: "In my view, there is broad agreement that we should create a new regulator to oversee Fannie Mae, Freddie Mac and the FHLBs. This new regulator must have a number of core powers in order to do its job effectively, and to be considered credible in the eyes of the public. These powers include the ability to set both minimum and risk-based capital levels for the Enterprises, enhanced enforcement and prompt corrective action powers, including the authority to set and enforce prudential management and internal control standards; the ability to put a GSE into receivership; and authority over both safety and soundness and mission. The goal in giving the new regulator this broad responsibility is to ensure a more coherent regulatory framework, better enforcement, and a more consistent, deeper and more aggressive effort on affordable housing at all the GSEs. In addition, I believe that the new regulator must be politically independent and funded outside of the appropriations process. It is my hope that this shared consensus can be the basis for moving strong and effective legislation forward."[53] Fine words, expressing a hope which had often been expressed before, to no avail. And again, nothing happened.

Federal Housing Finance Reform Act, H.R.1427

Meanwhile, Chairman Barney Frank introduced H.R.1472 on March 8, 2007. The first hearing was held on March 12 and the second on March 19. In the course of his opening remarks at the second hearing, referring to the debates on the previous bill, he said, "We did disagree that they [the regulators] should be empowered to deal with something called 'systemic risk' over and above safety and soundness. I will continue to be very sceptical that you can have entities that cause risks to the system when they themselves have no problems."[54] The second statement is hard to believe after OFHEO's Special Examination of Fannie Mae. As for the first, unfortunately, he would soon find out what systemic risk meant.

The bill covered much the same ground as the one in the previous session, in that it established the Federal Housing Finance Agency to regulate Fannie Mae, Freddie Mac and the FHLBs and to replace OFHEO. The new independent agency would be headed by a director appointed by the President, confirmed by the Senate for a period of five years, plus three deputy directors. The duties of the director required him to ensure that regulated entities operate in a "safe and sound manner," to maintain adequate capital and internal controls, and contribute to the "liquid, efficient, competitive and resilient national housing finance markets." To achieve these objectives, the regulator would be obliged to issue regulations, setting out the standards for every aspect of the GSEs' operations, such as the independence and adequacy of internal audit systems and the management of interest rate and market risk.

The FHFA would be funded by the annual assessments collected from the GSEs, and would not be subject to the appropriations process, ensuring greater independence. This would allow the regulator to adjust the risk-based capital requirements and provide for minimum capital levels to ensure the safety and soundness of the GSEs. The Director could by order increase the minimum capital levels on a temporary basis, if, for example, an unsafe or unsound condition were to exist. The bill required the Director to conduct a periodic review of the assets and liabilities of each GSE, and, if necessary, to require by order the disposal or acquisition of an asset or a liability. It also allowed for prior approval of new business activities or new programs, and grandfathers any current ones. The Government Accountability Office was required to study the guarantee fees, including the factors determining their amount, and the total revenue from such fees. Each GSE would have to register at least one class of its capital stock with the SEC, and comply with requirements for proxy reporting and transaction disclosure requirements for directors, officers and principal stockholders.

Finally the bill contained Chairman Frank's crowning achievement, the affordable housing fund, funded by the GSEs. This would provide formula grants to increase home ownership for extremely and very low-income families; increase investment in housing in low-income and chronically distressed areas; increase and preserve the supply of rental housing for such groups; increase investment in public infrastructure development related to this housing; and leverage investments from other sources in affordable housing and in public infrastructure development.

This time the Administration did not oppose the bill. The President issued a statement, supporting those elements in the bill which are "essential for proper regulatory oversight of the housing GSEs and for protecting the safety and soundness of the housing finance system and the broader financial system."

The Administration did, however, "oppose provisions that would increase the conforming loan limit, thus diluting the housing GSEs' commitment to low-income buyers," and to the affordable housing fund. It also rejected the Federal Government appointment of directors to the boards of the GSEs, because this would be inconsistent with current corporate governance standards and reinforces the misperception of a government guarantee. The Administration believed that the Board of the FHFA should be composed only of the FHFA Director and the Secretary to the Treasury and the Secretary for Housing. Despite these reservations, the Administration was looking forward to working with Congress on the bill to bring about the much-needed reforms.[55]

The bill was passed in Committee by a vote of 45-19 on March 29. It was the product of careful negotiations between Barney Frank and Treasury officials, and as a result very few changes were made. The Federal Housing Finance Reform Act was passed in the House of Representatives on May 29 by partisan vote of 313 to 104, but, although it was referred to the Senate Banking Committee, it never became law, partly due to deep divisions about how to regulate the Enterprises, and partly because Christopher Dodd had announced his intention to run for President.

By April 2007, attention had shifted away from the GSEs to the subprime mortgage crisis, which began to dominate the headlines. "Who to blame and what to do" became the key issues for both Congress and Senate. Chairman Dodd called for a summit of regulators, lenders and consumer advocates to help identify and reduce the damage from foreclosures rising at an alarming rate, triggered but not caused by the Federal Reserve's string of 17 interest rate rises in the summer of 2005. The next chapter will focus on the causes of the subprime crisis and why no one expected it to happen.

11

The Subprime Market Grew and Grew and No One Knew

Confusion over subprime lending

The language used in describing various kinds of mortgages throughout the period was misleading. Fannie Mae and Freddie Mac were the largest purchasers of "conventional" single-family first mortgages in the secondary mortgage market. The term "conventional" refers to loans that are insured or guaranteed by the federal government. The FHA insures residential mortgages, and the Department of Veterans Affairs (VA) and the Rural Housing Service (RHS) guarantee them. Then conventional single-family loans are often described as being "conforming" or "non-conforming," where the former term means under the loan limits for loans which Fannie and Freddie could buy. Those limits changed from year to year, as house prices rose, but the GSEs were, in theory, not allowed to purchase mortgages above that dollar limit. They did admit to purchasing "jumbo" loans; that is, loans above the "conforming" limit, during the years after the introduction of the National Homeownership Strategy.

Conforming loans

"Conforming" loans were "underwritten according to the standards of Fannie Mae and Freddie Mac", a notion which certainly requires further examination. The term "conforming" implies that the loans conform to certain underwriting standards, but it also has a much narrower meaning, and Fannie Mae played on this ambiguity by constantly referring to the loans Fannie bought as having to "conform" to their standards; it is clear from the comments of regulators and politicians that they usually understood it to refer to the quality of the loan, not its amount. Non-conforming loans would have balances above the dollar limit for that year; these were often called jumbo mortgages and were not underwritten according to the GSEs' underwriting standards.[1] For most people, the loans for single-family homes would be under the limit, which in the late 1990s and in the early part of the following decade looked as though it was more than enough for the purchase of a new single-family home, based on the median price for the whole of the USA. It did not, however, take account of the wide variations in prices in cities such as New York and the District of Columbia, and the "sand" states

(California, Florida, Nevada and Arizona), where house prices soared well above the conforming loan limits. That was especially true between 2004 and 2006, a source of complaint by some members of Congress especially in those years.[2] A jumbo loan will be described as "non-conforming," but that is only in relation to the loan limits and *may* not indicate anything further about the credit quality of the loan. It could be a loan to a borrower with the income and appropriate credit rating, who wishes to purchase a more expensive home than the average-priced home in an expensive urban area, such as Washington DC or New York.[3]

Conforming loans and credit quality

The notion of conforming loans should not therefore be taken to indicate any features of the loan which would enable the assessment of its credit quality. As we saw in Chapter 4, the criteria in use up to 2005 were too limited and did not identify the relevant features of subprime lending, defining them as higher-priced loans and loans from lenders which were on HUD's list of subprime lenders. As John C. Dugan, Comptroller of the Currency, pointed out in his evidence to the Financial Crisis Inquiry Commission in 2010, "OCC analysis has found that national bank subprime origination during the period preceding the financial crisis was small relative to the total subprime market. However, some analyses by others have reached conflicting conclusions, finding significantly higher percentages of overall subprime lending. To some extent the existence of conflicting estimates is not surprising. Developing precise estimates of subprime lending is difficult because comprehensive data for the market *simply do not exist, from either public or private sources.* Statements about subprime activity also suffer from lack of agreement at a more basic level regarding how to define "subprime" or other variants of non-prime loans."[4]

The situation was further complicated by the fact that Fannie Mae classified a loan as subprime if the mortgage loan was originated by a lender specializing in the subprime business, or by subprime divisions of large lenders.[5] This reduced the number of its subprime loans considerably. Similarly, when the Federal Reserve studied the performance of subprime loans, they defined them as subprime if they were reported as high-interest loans under the Home Owners Protection Act (HOPA), which again reduced the number of subprime loans to a very small number. This was important, since when the Federal Reserve studied the performance of CRA loans, they excluded a large number of loans that did not carry interest rates that fell into the HOPA category. The confusion arose, partly for the reasons set out above, but also because many of the participants and reporting agencies used definitions based on the way in which the lender or securities issuer classified the loan, rather than on its objective characteristics.

Subprime loans and lack of data

The acknowledgement of this failure is significant, as it shows quite clearly that the regulators were unaware of the growth of the subprime market. However, they cannot have thought it important to improve data collection by requiring further basic information, such as the credit rating of borrowers, debt-to-income ratios and loan-to-value, for example. Concerns had been expressed about predatory lending, but this was inadequately defined, given regulatory knowledge of the various types of mortgages which were available. It was well known that the size of down payments had been reduced to 5% or 3% or zero in many cases, for example with FHA loans. Some economists applied various modeling techniques to HMDA data in order to identify the proportion of subprime loans, which tended to show that this was quite low and hence unlikely to cause problems; indeed, some argued that subprime loans were just as likely or even less likely to lead to delinquency or foreclosure than prime mortgages, but that was during a period of continually rising house prices and low interest rates. What all failed to take on board was that they simply did not have the raw data. Had HMDA been designed to record the relevant data, from President Clinton's extension of the Community Reinvestment Act, then the risks involved would have become clearer at a much earlier stage. But while the HMDA data were continually examined and analysed, no amount of analysis can bring the raw data into being if they are not there in the first place. No matter how sophisticated and erudite the analyses, how up-to-date the models, the necessary input was simply not available. The trouble was that such work helped to disguise what was really happening in the market.[6]

Belatedly recognizing these issues, the Comptroller in his opening statement pointed out that "poor underwriting practices ... made credit too easy. Among the worst of these practices were the failure to verify borrower representations about income and financial assets; the failure to require meaningful borrower equity in homes in the form of real down payments; the offering of 'payment option' loans where borrowers actually increased the amount of their principal owed with each monthly payment; and the explicit or implicit reliance on future house appreciation as the primary source of loan repayment, either through refinancing or sale.

"In short, at the beginning of the 21st century, the US system for mortgage finance failed fundamentally (yet was so often described as 'world-class' and the 'envy of the world' in the hearings of the House and Senate Committees). The consequences were disastrous not just for the borrowers and financial institutions in the United States, but also for investors all over the world due to the transmission mechanism of securitization ... One [reason why this happened] is that for many years, home ownership has been a policy priority ... we tolerate looser loan underwriting practices ... if they make it easier for people to buy their own homes, sometimes even turning a blind eye to them".[7]

It's too difficult to define subprime loans

In addition to the limitations of the data collected, many commentators and analysts argued that it was difficult to define "subprime" loans, which obviously made it difficult to determine the extent of subprime lending. For many years, researchers and analysts defined risky loans as those loans reported under HMDA that were originated by lenders on the HUD list of subprime lenders, using the assumptions that all loans from these lenders were risky, and no loans from other lenders were risky.[8] This was clearly inadequate, because it helped to obscure the risks that were being taken.

To understand what is meant by subprime mortgages, it is first useful to examine the loans which were being offered, apart the traditional prime mortgage with 80% LTV and a fixed-rate 30-year mortgage. These included adjustable rate mortgages, many of which were short-term hybrids; that is, the interest rate was fixed for the first two or three years and then became an adjustable rate tied to market interest rates. The initial fixed rate of such mortgages is often called a "teaser" rate, because the interest rate on the mortgage is designed to rise by two or more percentage points after the initial period ended. They were sometimes popularly described as 2/28[ths], where the "2" referred to the initial two years of fixed interest rates and the "28" referred to the following 28 years of adjustable interest rates. Other adjustable rate mortgages were floating rate mortgages, where the interest rates varied from the beginning of the loan as market rates changed, and long-term hybrids, where the interest rates were fixed for the first five, seven or ten years before becoming adjustable rates.

Other types of mortgages included "balloon" loans, which could take the form of a short-term mortgage, perhaps 10 years, for which the borrower had to make regular payments and then a final "balloon" payment as one large instalment at the end of the term. They could also be set up as a 30-year fixed-rate mortgage, either as interest only or partially amortizing the mortgage, with an embedded option for a final large instalment. The advantage would be lower rates throughout the life of the mortgage.

At first, Alt-A loans seemed to be quite simple to define as "alternative to agency" and typically loans where the borrower would not provide complete documentation of his or her assets or the amount or source of his or her income. Other characteristics of this classification might include the following: (i) a loan-to-value in excess of 80%, but lacking primary mortgage insurance; (ii) secured by non-owner-occupied property or a debt-to-income ratio above normal limits, or an LTV above permitted thresholds in combination with other factors.[9] Nomura gives examples of Alt-A loans from one lender, whose standard program allows for a maximum LTV of 75% on a $400,000 "stated income" loan to a top-tier borrower. The same lender's Alt-A program allows such a loan to have an LTV as high as 95% but does not allow cash-out refinancing on properties that are second homes or vacation homes. Nomura notes that this approach defines Alt-A loans by what they are not, an approach which, as Nomura states significantly, means that the *"regular programs have expanded the scope of their offerings with the result that many of the loans that would not have qualified several years ago would qualify today."*[10] By the late 1990s, reduced or no documentation loans were lender driven rather than borrower driven, according to Nomura's analysis, with the key issue being whether or not stated income, stated assets and debt-to-income ratios were verified by the lender. Some loans were agreed even though neither assets nor income were verified (apart from a verbal verification of employment), that is, the NINJA loans (no job, no income and no assets). These were probably quite a small proportion of subprime loans, but a proportion which it is difficult to calculate.

Nomura also comments on the "futility" of the effort to define alt-A mortgages on their interest rates relative to contemporaneous conforming loans, since at any time the range of mortgage interest rates on newly originated conforming loans can span several hundred basis points. Some borrowers pay points to get lower interest rates on their loans, and others may accept an above-interest market-rate so that they have "negative points" at the closing of their loans. The same options are available to Alt-A borrowers; hence the interest-rate factor alone is insufficient and may not be relevant. It is all a matter of the terms of the loan. Even in 2003, Nomura noted that "the future of Alt-A is unclear. The GSEs have made major inroads by means of their automated underwriting systems ... [and] already, the GSE 'encroachments' into the Alt-A sector have severely blurred the once sharp line that divided 'conforming' mortgage loans from all others."[11]

All of this shows that the problem of defining subprime lending did not in fact exist: it is a matter of a set of criteria: high loan-to-value, high debt-to-income ratio, and low credit score of the borrower. If the loan fulfils one or more of these criteria, then it is a subprime loan with a higher risk of default. That is clear from the history of the US mortgage market over the years between 1995 until the collapse of the market in 2008.

Subprime mortgages and borrowers

This all became clear in 2008. Writing in that year, Christopher Mayer and Karen Pence, noting the turmoil in the markets, said, "It was not supposed to work out this way. Securitization and other innovations in mortgage markets led to new loan products with the potential to make home ownership easier and more accessible to buyers who could not access credit previously through conventional means. These so-called subprime and near-prime mortgage products allowed buyers with lower credit scores, smaller down payments, and/or little documentation of income to purchase houses. These new products not only allowed new buyers to access credit, but also made it easier for home owners to refinance loans and withdraw cash from houses that had appreciated in value."[12]

This marked a final recognition that subprime mortgages should have been clearly defined in terms of the credit quality of the loan, which would have focused on three features: the loan-to-value; income and debt-to-income ratio; and the credit score of the borrower. The credit status of the borrower may include a range of factors such as recent delinquencies, foreclosures, judgments, bankruptcies and comparably high debt-to-income ratios; a lack of continuity in employment or low incomes, as well as the source of the income, whether from salaries, welfare benefits, child support or alimony; and/or impaired credit or no credit history at all. Credit history and prepayment risk are amongst the factors which should be taken into account in arranging the mortgage and in pricing it.

Of course, much was written and discussed regarding subprime lending almost from the start. An early paper by Robert Avery and others quotes the analysis carried out of loans made under affordable home loan programs, which GE Capital Mortgage Insurance Corporation (GEMICO) had insured. The outcome of GEMICO's analysis was that "delinquency rates on loans extended to borrowers with 'good' credit histories have been lower than the baseline. Conversely, delinquency rates have been particularly high among loans in which the borrowers had marginal credit histories,[13] high ratios of debt payment to income and no cash reserves."[14] Fannie Mae and Freddie Mac announced their intention to move into the subprime market in response to the new housing goals set for them by HUD, to take effect from 2000. At that stage, the GSEs claimed that they only purchased about 14% of the subprime loans originated, but even then "market analysts expect that within the next few years the GSEs could purchase as much as 50% of the overall subprime mortgage volume." Furthermore, it is not always clear what was meant by "subprime." HUD maintained a list of subprime lenders, and classified subprime loans as loans originated by those lenders.

Some subprime lenders stressed that assessing the risks involved is done on an individualized basis, rather than an automated process, but the GSEs stated that they would improve their automated processes on the basis of the subprime loans they purchased and would move into the market in a "slow and prudent manner a reassurance from Fannie Mae accepted with approval in a paper prepared by K. Temkin and others for HUD's policy review. The report recommended the introduction of risk-based pricing, based on the underlying risk of the borrower. Temkin's paper is primarily concerned with the forthcoming role of the GSEs in the subprime market, it is another early indicator of the risks involved in subprime lending, and remarkably prescient about the risks to the GSEs." Although Temkin's paper is primarily concerned with the forthcoming role of the GSEs in the subprime market, it is another early indicator of the risks involved in subprime lending.

Predatory lending and subprime lending

When predatory lending resurfaced as an issue in 2000, the Senate Banking Committee held two hearings in July, 2001. Despite listening with sympathy to witnesses: individuals who had been victimized by predatory lenders, their concerns were that a sharp distinction should be made between predatory lending practices and subprime loans; because "there are people who have credit problems who still need and can justify access to affordable mortgage credit. They may only be able to get mortgage loans in the subprime market, which charges higher interest rates." Others expressed similar concerns, such as Senator Gramm, who was anxious that without a clear definition of predatory lending, the Senate might put in place "policies that destroy a market that is serving an increasing number of people." He explained that his strong feelings were due to his mother's experience: she had three children and no husband but borrowed the money to buy a house at 50% above the market rate, and still paid off the loan. To such Senators and Congressmen, the availability of subprime lending and the importance of home ownership was such a strong and deep emotional issue that they could not see beyond it to the dangers ahead.[15]

Senator Gramm had produced his paper for the Committee on predatory lending practices, based on information received from the regulatory authorities. This concluded that not only was there no definition under federal law of the term "predatory lending," but that the distinction between subprime lending and predatory lending is often blurred; the regulators had no organized system of collecting loan level data on predatory lending.[16] This lay behind his view that the attempt to curb abusive practices could limit access to home ownership through subprime loans. Similar views were shared by the House Financial Services Committee, which conducted a hearing on predatory lending, at which many members of the Committee expressed the need to exercise caution over introducing further restrictions on predatory lending in case it inadvertently limited access to affordable housing.[17] Several bills were introduced in the 109th Congress, but no action was taken on any of the bills, so there were no further attempts to curb predatory lending apart from the Federal Reserve's amendments to Regulation Z to broaden the scope of loans subject to the Home Ownership and Equity Protection Act (HOEPA), which required lenders to document and verify income for loans covered by the Act.[18]

The Federal Reserve and other regulatory agencies did not take further action against predatory lending until 2008, and even then it was limited.[19] The key point here is that for many lawmakers, access to affordable housing was more important than identifying and banning predatory lending. They did not take on board the fact that, even though (in their view) the expansion of subprime lending provides credit access for many people unable to obtain prime loans, it also triggered a rise in exploitative and predatory practices. Hence, even in 2002, HUD noted the extremely high foreclosure rates on subprime loans, suggesting that predatory lending was a serious problem and that many subprime borrowers were entering into mortgages they could not afford. These concerns were identified before the subprime bubble, as were the links between subprime and predatory lending, in that the former all too easily gave rise to the latter.[20]

The GSEs and the subprime market

The belief that loans purchased by the GSEs were not subprime loans arose partly from of the use of the term "conforming," and partly from the way in which the CEOs of both companies referred to their automated underwriting standards as though they had set standards for mortgages to which lenders should aspire. In other words, the impression was somehow conveyed that the GSEs purchased prime loans. That this is not the case can be seen by first examining the Charters under which Fannie Mae and Freddie Mac operated. Section 305 limits the amount of the loan to 80% of the value of the property at the time of purchase, and required that any mortgage with a loan to value of over 80% at origination has private mortgage insurance. This applies to "conventional" mortgages; that is, "a mortgage other than one which has the benefit of any guaranty, insurance or any other obligation by the United States or any of its agencies or instrumentalities."[21] But beyond that, there were no statutory limitations on or means of measuring the credit quality of mortgages which could be purchased. Indeed, Section 1719 of Fannie's Charter stated: "The operations of the corporation ... shall be confined ... to mortgages which are deemed by the corporation to be of such quality, type, and class as to meet, generally, the *purchase standards imposed by private institutional mortgage investors.*"

The Minimum Safety and Soundness Requirements accompanying the Charter took the form of general guidelines, and these seemed to place the onus for assessing underwriting and credit quality on the Enterprise, even when updated in 2005. They stated that "an Enterprise should establish and implement policies and procedures to adequately assess credits before they are assumed and monitor such risks subsequently to ensure that they conform to the Enterprise's credit risk standards on an individual and an aggregate basis."[22]

The guidelines further required the Enterprises to have "prudent underwriting requirements," to consider the borrower's ability to repay, to take account of the implication of a contract with a service provider for their credit risk, and to have procedures in place for identifying and managing declining credit quality. They should also have procedures in place to identify, monitor and evaluate its credit exposures, and to have procedures for handling counterparty risk from engaging in hedging activities and the use of derivative instruments. These comprehensive guidelines should have led to sound risk management procedures. But they required conformity to the Enterprise's credit risk standards, which was obviously the weak link in the chain. In effect, the lawmakers gave Fannie Mae and Freddie Mac a free hand in the purchase of mortgages: a freedom they exercised from the start.

They knew the risks and went ahead anyway

It is clear, both from the programs that the GSEs initiated following the introduction of President Clinton's National Homeownership Strategy in 1995, and from the announcements they made about the changes to their programs (which were designed to promote lending to low- and moderate-income families, and to assist lenders "in their efforts to accurately assess the risks associated with combining various underwriting flexibilities"), that they were always players in the subprime market. They were players in terms of their mortgage purchases, and the "strategic alliance" agreements they made with a relatively small number of lenders.

For Freddie Mac, that began in 1994 with its Affordable Gold Loans program. Fannie Mae had a similar program, the Community Home Buyers Program. These loans were not written according to traditional underwriting standards; for example, for those in which the borrowers were allowed to meet part of the minimum down-payment requirement with funds from a third party, the delinquency rate from 1994 to February 1996 was about four times higher than for the peer group of traditional loans. Other "Affordable Gold Loans" originated in 1994 show a delinquency rate about 50% higher than for the peer group.[23] In other words, right from the start of the Presidential commitment to "affordable homes," it was known that such homes could only be affordable by lowering underwriting standards (flexible underwriting standards), and that the GSEs would purchase such loans. The risks were also recognized from the start, but ignored by many politicians.

According to a report in the *New York Times* in September 1999, Fannie Mae, "under increasing pressure from the Clinton Administration to expand mortgage loans among low and moderate income people" set up a pilot program involving 24 banks in 15 markets to "encourage those banks to extend home mortgages to individuals whose credit is generally not good enough to qualify for conventional loans," which was then designed to become a nationwide program in the following spring. Indeed, such a program would have been required by then, if Fannie Mae was to reach the housing goals set by HUD for 2001 onwards of increasing the purchase of mortgages for low- to moderate-income families to 50% of all mortgages purchased.

Thrift institutions and mortgage companies were "also pressing Fannie Mae to help them make more loans to so-called subprime borrowers." They were pushing at an open door. Franklin Raines said, "Fannie Mae has expanded home ownership for millions of families in the 1990s by reducing the down-payment requirements. Yet there remain too many borrowers whose credit is just a notch below what our underwriting has required who have been relegated to paying significantly higher mortgage rates in the so-called subprime market."[24]

In March 2000, Franklin Raines announced the $2 trillion American Dream Commitment, which would involve new mortgage products, processes and partnerships to close the home-ownership gap between minorities and women-headed households and the majority white population. The emphasis would be on low-cost mortgages on flexible terms. It would enable banks to meet their CRA goals by giving them a suite of mortgage options for low- to moderate-income families.

In particular, the Commitment offered the Timely Payment Rewards mortgages, which were based on "Expanded Approval", an option within the automated underwriting system for those with less-than-perfect credit, past credit problems, or minimal funds for a down payment. A minimum payment of $500 from their own funds was required, or 3% of the loan amount, which could come (as with the FHA) from gifts, grants, or unsecured loans from relatives, employers, public agencies or non-profit organizations. This approval applied to standard fixed-rate loans, such as 30-year, and 5/1 and 7/1 ARMS, but only the former were eligible for a reduction of 1% in the interest rate for timely payments. By March 2001, Fannie Mae reckoned that they had facilitated $190bn for home mortgages.[25] Their Desktop Underwriting had processed over 25 million loan submissions in 2001.[26]

In February 2003, Washington Mutual entered into an agreement with Fannie Mae to boost home lending by $85bn over five years to minorities and to low- and moderate-income families. Washington Mutual would originate the loans and sell them to Fannie Mae, the $85bn being part of the $375bn the thrift pledged to lend in September 2001 over a ten-year period to low- and moderate-income census tracts, the largest commitment of its kind by a financial institution.[27]

With regard to Freddie Mac, it is clear that the decision had been taken right from the start to purchase loans designed to meet the needs of those on low to moderate incomes in the Affordable Gold program. That and other arrangements became more important as HUD's goals became more demanding from 2001 onwards. Other drivers were in place as well: competing with Fannie Mae, the larger and formidable opponent for market share, and restoring confidence after the massive accounting fraud was exposed.

Richard Syron, former President of the Federal Reserve Bank of Boston, was appointed to take over the management of Freddie Mac in 2004. In meeting the HUD goals, however, he was prepared to take risks and rejected internal warnings that the company was financing questionable loans that threatened its financial health. In an interview with the *New York Times*, David Andrukonis, then Chief Risk Officer, stated that he had sent a memo to Richard Syron, warning him that Freddie Mac was financing questionable loans that threatened its financial health. Later in a meeting with Mr Syron, he reiterated his warning, stating that Freddie Mac's underwriting standards "were becoming shoddier and that the company was becoming exposed to losses." However, Mr Syron refused to consider any means of reducing Freddie Mac's risks. Mr Andrukonis also briefed the Risk Oversight Committee of the Board of Directors, but did not share the memo with them. Donald Solberg, Head of Capital Compliance and Oversight at Freddie Mac, advised Mr Syron to maintain a substantial capital cushion, and continued to recommend that until 2007, when he left the company; but again the advice was ignored.[28] In response, Mr Syron and Mr Mudd, Chief Executive of Fannie Mae, both maintained that "one of the reasons why the firms hold so many bad loans is that Congress has leaned on them for years to buy mortgages from low-income borrowers to encourage affordable housing. Freddie Mac warned regulators that affordable housing goals could force the company to buy riskier loans."[29]

They did have a point, in that affordable housing for very low and low-to-moderate income groups would inevitably mean the application of different underwriting criteria, since obviously those whose incomes fell into the categories defined by the CRA and by HUD could not afford to put down 20% of the value of the property and take on a fixed-rate 30-year mortgage. Richard Syron was well aware of that, since it was he who signed off the Boston Handbook in 1992 on lending to low-income families and minorities. He may also have been influenced by his own background as a son of poor Irish immigrants, who were only able to buy their own home by virtue of a VA loan and by sharing it with another family.[30]

Some of their partnership arrangements

The banks from which the Enterprises bought most of their loans were also among the top ten subprime lenders. In 2006, this list consisted of the following:

1 HSBC Finance

2 New Century Financial, CA

3 Countrywide Financial, CA

4 Citimortgage, NY

5 WMC Mortgage, CA

6 Fremont Investment & Loan, CA

7 Ameriquest Mortgage, CA

8 Option One Mortgage, CA

9 Wells Fargo Home Mortgage, IA

10 First Franklin Financial Corp, CA

11 Washington Mutual

This was the list as at 2006,[31] but by April 2007, New Century had filed for bankruptcy. Other lenders selling to the Enterprises included Chase Home Finance and Lehman Brothers.

Contrary to widely held views, Fannie Mae and Freddie Mac were able to purchase such loans, as there was nothing in their Charters to prevent them from doing so. In addition, HUD's mission goals essentially required the GSEs to purchase ever-increasing proportions of lower-quality loans. Many analysts point both to the increase in riskier mortgages between 2004 and 2007 for many lenders, and to the GSEs' increased purchases of such mortgages in that period. This increased the risk in their portfolios, but that risk was ignored by politicians in particular. It was easier to ignore the ever-increasing risks, because aggregate US housing prices increased every month from July 1995 to May 2006.

Even where regulators were aware of the decline in underwriting standards, for example, the Office of the Comptroller of the Currency as a result of its 2005 survey, little action was taken.[32] The OCC discovered the "easing of underwriting standards" in a quarter of the banks surveyed; that is, 28% had eased standards, 10% tightened and 62% made no change, but this was a considerable increase from 2004, when the number easing standards was 13%. "Notably, this is the first time in the survey's 11-year history that examiners reported a net easing of retail underwriting standards, concentrated in home equity products and residential real estate lending ... and affordable housing loans also experiences some easing. According to examiners, banks continue to ease retail standards primarily because of increased competition."[33] The OCC, however, considered that for such banks, appropriate risk management procedures were in place.

The result was that between 2004 and 2007, large national banks continued to make large numbers of low- and no-documentation loans and subprime ARMSs that were solely underwritten to the introductory rate. In 2006, for example, fully 62% of the first lien home purchase mortgages made by National City Bank, NA and its subsidiary, First Franklin Mortgage were higher-priced subprime loans. The bank did not face receivership because a merger with PNC Financial Services Group took place in October, 2008, following further losses of $729 m in the third quarter: PNC announced that it was pleased to have been selected by the Treasury to prevent another collapse, and received federal funds to facilitate the purpose. Other large national banks were also deeply involved in the subprime market, including Citibank, the third-largest bank in the US in 2005; it took over Argent Mortgage, which then became Citi Residential Lending in September, 2007 for subprime lending, but had to dismantle it in May 2008. Wachovia Corporation originated both low- and no-documentation loans through its two mortgage subsidiaries, so that it became the twelfth-largest Alt-A lender in the USA by 2007. Write-offs of these loans increased so much and so quickly that the parent company reported its first quarterly loss for many years, due to rising defaults on option ARMs. When this became public, it led to many customers quietly withdrawing their accounts from the bank after the Lehman Brothers' collapse. Again, to avoid receivership in late September 2008, Wachovia was sold to Wells Fargo.

Washington Mutual, the largest thrift institution with $300bn in assets, was regulated by the Office of Thrift Supervision. On September 25, 2008, it became the largest depositary institution in the US to fail, collapsing in the wake of the Lehman Brothers bankruptcy. It was seized by the government and sold to JP Morgan Chase in 2008. By June 30, 2008, over one-quarter of Washington Mutual's subprime loans which were originated in 2006 and 2007 were at least 30 days overdue. This was not surprising, following the later discoveries about its conduct of business over the preceding years (in spite of the fact that the OTS examiners were stationed permanently on site.) In the mid-2000s, the bank made a conscious decision to focus on high-risk mortgages, which produced higher profits. It increased its securitization of subprime loans sixfold, mainly through Long Beach Mortgage Corporation. Over four years, the bank and Long Beach increased their securitization of subprime mortgages from about $4.5bn in 2003 to $29bn in 2006. From 2000 to 2007, they securitized at least $77bn in subprime loans. Their loan officers were paid according to the volume not the quality of their loans, and were paid more for higher-risk loans. They were also paid more if they got borrowers to pay higher interest rates, even if they were entitled to a lower rate. It was described as the bank that could not say "No," but borrowers certainly paid for it.[34]

Countrywide Home Loans Inc (Countrywide), ranking third in the top 20 subprime lenders in 2006, was one of the closest companies to Fannie Mae. In 2005, one in every four loans purchased by Fannie Mae was from Countrywide and one in every ten by Freddie Mac. This was a mutual interdependence, since almost half of Countrywide's mortgages were sold to Fannie Mae. In addition, Countrywide used Ginnie Mae to guarantee another third of its loans, which meant that about 90% of the loans it originated were bought or guaranteed by the federal government, part of the reason, no doubt, for its spectacular growth. From 2000 onwards, as the mortgage market boomed, no other company pursued growth in home loans more aggressively than Countrywide, which became a $500bn mortgage-producing machine with 62,000 employees, 900 offices and assets of some $200 billion. It had also managed to move from being supervised by the OCC by changing its Charter in March 2007, so that it was subject to less onerous regulation by the Office of Thrift Supervision.

The company almost collapsed in 2008 as it faced an array of law suits. In February 2008, the United States Trustee filed a suit against it concerning a pattern of bad practices in a bankruptcy case, followed by a request for the Bankruptcy Court in Atlanta to sanction the company. This was followed by another suit by the state of Illinois on the grounds that the company had defrauded borrowers by selling them costly and defective loans that quickly went into foreclosure. Ten other states were about to bring similar actions. This led to an $8.4bn loan relief plan for 400,000 borrowers. Countrywide was responsible for about 20% of mortgages granted in the previous few years, so more law suits would follow. A sale to the Bank of America was sought and finally agreed in July 2008.

Fannie Mae and Freddie Mac dominated the secondary market in the number of loans it purchased and either retained in its portfolios, or sold on to investors. They clearly had all kinds of partnerships with the main subprime lenders, but when they dominated the market, what proportion of the market did they purchase, and what was the size of the subprime market by 2008? In answering these questions, the first step is to examine the contributions of the GSEs and other federal agencies to the subprime and Alt-A market.

Federal agency contributions to the subprime and Alt-A market

The brief description above of the kind of strategic alliances into which Fannie Mae and Freddie Mac entered, together with their obligation to meet the "affordable housing" goals, altering their underwriting requirements in order to achieve them and to gain market share, indicates increasing purchases of subprime and Alt-A loans. Fulfilling the affordable housing goals inevitably meant reducing the down-payment requirements, credit scores and debt-to-income ratios. Indeed, when the agencies offered their Expanded Guidance for Subprime Lending Programs in 2001, they both stated that "responsible subprime lending can expand credit access for consumers" and described "subprime" as referring to the credit characteristics of individual borrowers, of which an illustrative but not exhaustive list was given. Such characteristics would properly be summed up in a FICO score of 660 or below.

Hence, assessing the numbers of subprime loans for the federal agencies involves a definition, which encapsulates these features. The definition covers self-denominated subprime by the originator or the securities issuer, or placed in a subprime private MBS or with a rate of interest higher than HOPA, or loans with FICO scores of below 660, a demarcation line first recognized in 1995, as defined in Freddie Mac's industry letter.[35] It can be argued that the GSEs implicitly recognized this when listing the serious delinquency rates by FICO score, where the lowest rate is 11.32% compared with 1.78% for prime loans.[36] Alt-A loans may be self-denominated by the lender or placed in an Alt-A, but with the primary characteristics of low or no-documentation or with an LTV in excess of 80% but without primary mortgage insurance.

Other such loans included adjustable rate mortgages (ARMS) which began with a low rate of interest, which then increased after a certain number of years. These were known as "teaser" rates, as they were used to entice buyers into mortgages that they may not be able to afford. The rates would then be adjusted in accordance rates and margins, which were structured so that the rate was adjusted upwards. Other types of mortgages may have appeared attractive, as the monthly payments would have been affordable, but were subject to negative amortization, as they would not have covered all the interest on the mortgage. There were many variations of loans on offer, such as hybrid mortgages, with fixed rates for a number of years after which interest rates were adjusted each month; no down payment or low downpayments of 5% or less of the value of the property, or loans with flexible underwriting requirements or higher debt-to-income ratios. This range also included high combined LTV, where a combined first and second lien was used to reduce the down payment required. This lending commonly involved an 80% first and a 20% second loan.

On the basis of these definitions, Pinto assesses the federal government and federal agency contributions:

Subprime and Alt-A loans	$ in billions	Number of loans in millions
Fannie Mae	$1,077	7,026
Freddie Mac	$758	4,913
FHA/VA/Rural Housing	$537	4,760
FHLB	$50	0.313
CRA & HUD program	$512	2,240
Total	$4,622	26.7

Mr Pinto justifies these figures as follows:

Step 1 At the end of June 2008, Fannie held $36bn in self-denominated subprime private MBS with an average principal balance per loan of $153,400 for 235,000 loans, plus $30bn in self-denominated Alt-A private MBS with an average principal balance per loan of $171,269 for 0.175m loans.

At the same time, Fannie's single-family mortgage credit book of business holdings of subprime by characteristic loans, self-denominated Alt-A and Alt-A covered a range of high-risk whole loans, which consisted of loans with FICO scores <620, FICO of 620–659, negatively amortizing loans, interest-only loans, loans with an Original LTV>90%, loans with combined LTV>90%, and self-denominated Alt-A.[37]

Step 2 Pinto notes that Fannie and Freddie's disclosures about these seven loan types have evolved over time, and that this has generally resulted in additional information being provided. By Q.2.2009, Fannie listed six of the seven product features in its "Credit Profile by Key Product Features," but also provided additional information about loans where more than one feature was provided.[38] This gave individual dollar amounts for each of the six features (all but Combined LTV>90%), and a subtotal which eliminated any double counting. Although Freddie does not provide so much detail, the information Fannie provides helps to rule out double counting for Freddie as well.

The conclusion of Step 2 is that by the end of June 2008, Fannie's six key product features came to $1,214 trillion gross dollars and 7.944 million gross loans. Pinto then multiplies by 80% to adjust for duplicates, which gives $971 billion and 6.354 million net loans.

Step 3 To this has to be added Fannie's seventh and final key category, Combined LTV>90%. What should also be noted is what Fannie said in its 2007 10-K:

"In recent years there has been an increased percentage of borrowers obtaining second lien financing to purchase a home as a means of avoiding paying primary mortgage insurance. Although only 10% of our conventional single-family mortgage credit book of business had an original average LTV ratio greater than 90% as of December 31, 2007, we estimate that 15% of our conventional single-family mortgage credit book of business had an original combined average LTV ratio greater than 90%. The combined LTV ratio takes into account the combined amount of both the primary and second lien financing of the property. Second lien financing on a property increases the level of credit risk (on the first lien) because it reduced the borrower's equity in the property and may make it more difficult to refinance. Our original combined average LTV ratio data is limited to second lien financing reported to us at the time of origination of the first mortgage loan." It is interesting to note the word "estimate" in this statement; a word which surely should not be there, given the virtues of the DU automated system, which Fannie Mae constantly extolled. That should either have given an accurate figure or rejected such mortgages as being too risky. Reliance on estimates would inevitably have made risk management more unreliable.

To return to Pinto's analysis, based on the above and on subsequent filings, this category provides an estimated $133bn of Fannie's portfolio of loans with a combined LTV>90%.[39] However, since no overlap information has been provided, the overlap has been conservatively estimated at $40bn. The result for Fannie is that the net amount of various categories of subprime loans is $1,011 trillion and the net number of loans is 6.616 million.

He performs a similar analysis for Freddie Mac, with the resulting totals based on the same categories as Fannie Mae. Freddie held $82bn in self-denominated subprime private MBS, with an average principal balance per loan of $153,400 for a total of 0.535 million loans. It held a further $41bn in self-denominated Alt-A private MBS, with an average principal balance per loan of $175, 961 for a total of 0.233 million loans. Its single-family credit guarantee portfolio of business holdings subprime by characteristic loans, self-denominated Alt-A and Alt-A by characteristic loans totaled $752bn on June 30, 2008 with the same seven types of high-risk loans as Fannie Mae. Multiplying $752bn by 80% to allow for duplicates gives a figure of $602bn and 3.939 million net loans, basing the average loan size as $152,814; that is, the same as Fannie's average, as Freddie Mac does not give such a figure.[40]

Freddie's seventh category (Combined LTV>90%) is estimated to be $33bn, based on an initial $110bn, but estimating the overlap at 70% yielding the figure of $33bn on the assumption that these loans have an average balance equal to Fannie's average loan amount of $152,814 for key product features gives a net 0.216 million loans.

Thus for all these categories of loans, the net dollars are $635bn and the net number of loans is 4.155 million.

The other two categories, the Federal Housing Administration (FHA) and Veterans Administration (VA), had 3.492 million and 1.122 million loans outstanding, with average balances of $103,300 and $150,000 respectively. For the FHA, 83% consisted of high original LTV lending and about 70% had a FICO of <660. This results in $537bn in net loan dollars from the FHA and VA plus rural loans with a total of 4.76 million loans.[41]

The contribution of the Federal Home Loan Bank System was much less, but it was reported as holding $76bn in private MBS as at the end of June 2008. It is not clear what the constituent elements of this portfolio were, but Pinto considers it reasonable to assume that 66% of the total, or $50bn, would be backed by Alt-A and subprime loans. If the average loan amount was $160,000 (an average based on Fannie Mae and Freddie Mac's holdings of private MBS and Alt-A private MBS), this gives 0.313 million loans.[42]

The impact of the Community Reinvestment Act must also be taken into account, although many deny that it had any part in the crisis at all, perhaps because its scope was limited, and partly because the lenders were allegedly unregulated mortgage companies. The latter claim is not entirely true, since some of the leading banks, and indeed subprime lenders, were included, such as the Bank of America, JP Morgan Chase, Citibank, Wells Fargo and banks and thrifts with which these banks merged or which they purchased. The incentives built into the CRA requirements have already been described in detail, together with its effects on bank lending.

In 2007, the National Community Reinvestment Coalition (NCRC) published a report, which showed that from 1994 to 2007, CRA commitments came to $4.5 trillion, of which 94% were made by the above banks. The outlier was Countrywide, acclaimed as the first mortgage lender to enter into a voluntary agreement for "Fair Lending Goals" with HUD. It became the third largest lender in 2004, and then either the largest or second largest

Alt-A lender; by 2007 it accounted for 29% and 18% of Fannie and Freddie's acquisitions respectively.[43]

Many of the CRA commitments were fulfilled, largely due to the agreements the banks had made, commitments, totaling $3.5 trillion between 1993 and 2007; but these loans were not tracked in any organized manner. About half of these loans went to Fannie and Freddie to meet their affordable housing requirements; about 10% were insured by the FHA; and about 10% were sold as private mortgage-backed securities. Most of the rest remained on the balance sheets of the four largest banks, where by 2009 and 2010 many showed higher default rates than prime mortgages. The CRA delinquency rates did not show up while interest rates were low and house prices continued to rise. Fannie's delinquency rate on its $900bn high-risk mortgages, 85% of which were affordable housing loans, was 11.36% at September 30, 2009 as compared with the 1.8% delinquency rate on its traditionally underwritten loans. The CRA loans were fixed rate and did not have higher interest rates; as with some of the other subprime loans, they inevitably had other high-risk characteristics such as small down payments and low FICO scores. CRA lending had a slow-burn effect and was indeed a contributory factor, as shown especially by the acquisition of Countrywide.

According to Pinto, by the middle of 2008, there were almost 27 million subprime loans in the financial system, which accounts for almost 50% of all mortgages. Over two-thirds of these were held or guaranteed by federal agencies such as the FHA and the GSEs (12 million) and by US banks (about 2.2 million). That is about half of the outstanding first mortgages, estimated at 55 million, a figure which is derived from the National Delinquency Survey and the Mortgage Bankers Association, Q2, 2008. The NDS survey contains 45.4 million first mortgages, covering about 80-85% of outstanding first lien mortgages.[44] The Federal Reserve reports that the dollar amount of outstanding first lien mortgages at June 30, 2008 was $9.42 trillion. If the calculations regarding the number of subprime mortgages are correct, then they reveal the enormity of the problem which was fostered over the years, particularly since 1995. The very complexity of the calculations and the variety of the data bases, none of which are complete, that have to be taken into account show the difficulty for the Administration, federal agencies and regulators, and the Federal Reserve of getting any sort of handle on the size of the problem. No one was looking at the growth of the subprime market, especially with regard to the involvement of the GSEs, for a number of reasons.

James Lockhart described his "significant supervisory concerns" in his letter to Richard Baker, accompanying OFHEO's annual report to Congress. The work involved was not confined to rectifying the accounting irregularities, but every aspect of the GSEs' conduct of business. The analysis of their 10-Q SEC returns, as set out above, was only possible in the case of Fannie Mae, whose first filing took place on November 9, 2007, and with Freddie Mac, the first quarterly report, 10-Q, was filed on July 18, 2008. OFHEO stated in the 2008 report that the Enterprises filed their first clean (that is, properly audited) annual financial statements in a timely manner for the first time for four years. Even then, the 2008 report to Congress refers to concerns about the effectiveness of the remediation processes for both Fannie Mae and Freddie Mac.

The key point here, however, is that the filings prior to 2007 on the part of Fannie Mae cannot be regarded as being reliable, but that the information provided in Fannie Mae's Q2 10-K filing does occur after much remedial work had been carried out on its accounting procedures and other systems (although much remained to be resolved.) As Pinto points out, more investor information was provided than hitherto. The information gap for four years or more meant that the increase in subprime and Alt-A loans purchased by the Enterprises could not be traced with any degree of certainty. Even so, OFHEO reported that "during the past several years, Fannie Mae relaxed its underwriting standards, but not as much as many market players ... but credit losses resulted from their relaxed underwriting standards ... Management has made significant changes to better manage credit risk, including tightened underwriting standards, increased pricing, improved loss control practices and decreased exposure to distressed servicers." Yet earlier in the report, OFHEO cited credit risk management as an ongoing area of concern, noting that the projects were mostly complete, but scheduled for completion by the end of 2008, and other OFHEO requirements such as tightening underwriting standards would not become effective until March 2008.

The report continues: "Loans booked in the last few years have shown relatively unchanged profile characteristics in terms of FICO, loan-to-value, and level of credit enhancement. However, Fannie Mae increased its exposure to non-traditional mortgages and risk layering."[45] Asset credit quality deterioration in the single-family business accelerated in the second half of 2007, with losses exacerbated by both higher volume and loss severity in defaulted loans, which led to the reserves being increased for guarantee losses to $3.3bn at year-end 2007 with a $2.8bn provision in the fourth quarter of 2007. OFHEO recognized some of the growth of Fannie Mae's purchases of subprime and Alt-A loans, but it was too little and too late, obscured by years of false accounting and total mismanagement of the Enterprises.

It was not, after all, until September 2007, and at the direction of OFHEO, that the Enterprises adopted and implemented the bank interagency guidance on non-traditional mortgages and subprime mortgages. These now apply to all the mortgages that the Enterprises directly hold and guarantee, but also the underlying mortgages in private label securities that they acquire. The unanswered question throughout is this: given the sheer volume in 2007 of loans and MBSs purchased and guaranteed, how was compliance checked; and how was compliance checked in the past, when the 25 million loans in a year were processed through the automated underwriting system (DU), given the inadequacies of Fannie Mae and Freddie Mac's systems and controls? Given OFHEO and HUD's paucity of staff and other resources, no one else was in a position to check on compliance, and indeed, guidance of any kind on subprime lending was not agreed by the federal regulatory agencies until 2004 (and even then, weakly enforced.)

In his testimony before the Senate Banking Committee in February 2008, Lockhart was able to give a more up-to-date picture of the increased risks in an unprecedented market for the GSEs.[46] Their market share rose to record levels in the fourth quarter of 2007 to $5.1 trillion; that is, their debt and guaranteed MBSs, to which should be added the rapidly growing FHLBanks' debt of about $1.2 trillion. So, $6.3 trillion in debt, compared with the public debt of the United States of $5.1 trillion (of which $700bn is owned by the Federal Reserve.) US debt in public hands at the end of 2007 was $4.4 trillion. In the third quarter of 2007, the Mortgage Bankers Association reported that the delinquency rate was 5.6%, the highest since 1986. In the face of such challenging conditions, Lockhart reported, the Enterprises were securitizing loans at $100bn a month, but the risks implicit in such securitization and the extent of them would emerge more clearly later in the year.

The risks were not quantified even in that report to the Senate Committee. Some of the increase in losses Fannie and Freddie began to experience in 2007 was "because they lowered underwriting standards in late 2005, 2006 and the first half of 2007, by buying more non-traditional mortgages to retain market share and compete in the affordable market." The departure from the traditional market was nothing new, as the strategic alliances into which the GSEs entered showed, and their announcements about reducing down-payment requirements as far back as 1999. Lockhart noted that "they also have very large counterparty risks, including seller/services, mortgage insurers, bond insurers and derivative issuers."[47] In 2006, the Enterprises agreed to restrict the growth of their portfolios and to keep the capital levels 30% higher than the minimum required by law; that made it 3.25% of assets rather than 2.5% legal minimum, but this was still low compared with other financial institutions. In addition, given losses in earnings in 2007, they had only 1.2% of equity backing their mortgage exposure.

It is simply not true to say that the entry into the subprime market was a late development. In an early paper, provided for the Office of Housing and Policy Development, the authors point out that the "GSEs are increasing their business, in part, in response to higher affordable housing goals set by HUD in its new rule, established in October, 2000. *In the rule*, HUD indentifies subprime borrowers as a market that can help Fannie Mae and Freddie Mac achieve their goals, and help establish more standardization in the subprime market."[48] Indeed, Title XIII of the Housing and Community Development Act, 1992 called for a study of the "implications of implementing underwriting standards that would (a) establish a down-payment requirement for mortgagors of 5% or less (b) allow the use of cash on hand as a source for down payments and (c) approve borrowers who have a credit history of delinquencies if the borrower can demonstrate a satisfactory credit history for at least the 12-month period ending on the date of application for the mortgage." Such a study was commissioned by HUD; the authors found that both Fannie Mae and Freddie Mac had indeed adopted more flexible guidelines, such as Fannie Mae's introduction of their Flex 97 product, which required a borrower to make only a 3% down payment if the borrower had a strong credit history.[49]

That was from the beginning, but by 2000, they had expanded their purchases to include Alt-A, A-minus and subprime mortgages in addition to private-label mortgage securities. Fannie Mae implemented the Expanded Approval System and Freddie Mac expanded its Loan Prospector system to accommodate risk-based pricing. Subprime and Alt-A mortgages gave the GSEs a real opportunity to expand their businesses.[50] As these markets exploded over the next six years, Fannie Mae and Freddie Mac took full advantage of the opportunities, as the above analysis shows.

Even as late as 2007, Fannie Mae sought to give the impression that its standards, as incorporated in its underwriting programs, were above those of the rest of the market. Daniel Mudd stated that Fannie Mae "has a history of working with lenders to serve families who don't have perfect financial profiles … we see it as part of our mission and our Charter to make *safe mortgages* to such people … We also set conservative underwriting standards for loans we finance to ensure the homebuyers can afford their loans over the long term." He then referred to Tom Lund, then head of the single-family mortgage business, who said in early 2005, "One of the things we don't feel good about right now as we look into the marketplace is more homebuyers being put into programs that have more risk … Does it make sense for borrowers to take on risk that they may not be aware of? Are we setting them up for failure?"[51] Sadly, no one on the House Committee asked what exactly they were doing about purchasing such loans, or whether or how they imposed their "higher" standards on lenders whose mortgages or MBSs they bought. It was yet another part of the image presentation of being "best in class," as the interviews both Daniel Mudd and Tom Lund subsequently gave to the Financial Crisis Inquiry Commission showed that their concerns about subprime and Alt-A loans did not prevent them from buying them, as indeed they had from the start.

In his interview, Mr Lund claimed that in response to the increasing government pressure to meet housing goals (which were increased yet again in 2004), such as lowering the risk level for a borrower through the DU "bump" (lowering the credit risk of a borrower). If the borrower met a housing goal, then the risk level would be 'bumped up' to 2, and the loan would be priced as such by Fannie Mae. This explains why so many loans purchased by Fannie were in fact risky loans, despite Fannie's assurances that loans had to meet 'their standards'. They reduced the equity requirements for home buyers, and bought bulk loans that contained housing goal loans. His concerns were expressed to HUD, but the goals were still increased, and could only be met if borrowers were taking up option ARMS and low- or no-down-payment loans. However, despite an apparent decision not to move further into the subprime market in June 2005, it seems that his anxieties were ignored; the corporate goals he was given at the beginning of 2006 meant that Fannie Mae would become more aggressive in purchasing Alt-A loans, and that continued after August, 2007.[52]

In a similar interview, Mr Mudd made it clear that there were constant changes to the type of products Fannie Mae purchased and guaranteed, and that subprime and Alt-A products were purchased before he joined the company in 2000, at first as a relatively small proportion of their purchases, but as the decade continued, many new products came onto the market. It was a constant process of development beginning in the mid-1990s, in which Fannie Mae would buy some of the new kinds of loans, which gave them access to the data, then buy whole loans and offer the product to some lender customers, developing that line of business over time. He argued that 2005 was not therefore a moment when the company decided to increase purchases of non-traditional mortgages, but that there was a real explosion of Alt-A, subprime, interest-only mortgages and other "affordability" products. The rapid expansion in the market gave them little alternative but to participate by buying these loans in order to fulfil their role of providing liquidity in the market.[53] The tone and content of the information given in the interview is quite different from his testimony to the House Financial Services hearing.

It should be borne in mind that for Fannie Mae, the period in which they embarked on their most aggressive strategies to purchase mortgages and mortgage assets with questionable underwriting standards, that is, between 2003 and 2006, was the one in which they had to restate all their financial reports from 2001 onwards. It was a period at the end of which, the OFHEO report still described the Enterprises as remaining classified with "significant supervisory concerns." Freddie Mac was still not in a position to register with the SEC, but had produced timely financial statements with a clean audit opinion. Fannie Mae had filed clean financial statements for 2007. Having registered with the SEC, it produced its third quarter report (Form 10 Q) in November 2007 and filed its annual report on Form 10K in February, 2008. This is why the Pinto analysis relies on Fannie Mae's June 2008 10 Q report, because of the progress made in its production of financial statements. It should also be borne in mind that during the whole period from 1999 onwards, the problems with both Fannie Mae and Freddie Mac ran much deeper, to the whole way in which the organizations were managed. The overriding principle was to maximize earnings, and any other aspect of the business was subordinated or distorted to achieve that end. An indication of that is the reference made by Mr Lund to altering the credit status of a borrower.

Even by 2007, the GSEs' risk management procedures left much to be desired. It is indeed hard to see why anyone believed the protestations and assurances about the GSEs' standards and the quality of the loans they bought, as right up to conservatorship they were badly managed and had barely got their financial reporting into any kind of order. Conservatorship was soon to follow, with not only the size but also the content of the GSEs' portfolios being key factors. The private label securities and investments in assets collateralized by subprime and Alt-A mortgages probably precipitated their collapse, with private label securities contributing significantly; in many cases their value fell as much as 90% from the time of purchase.

By 2007, it should have been clear that a serious crisis was developing. Chairman Bernanke in his May speech referred to the sharp increase in foreclosure rates in subprime mortgages with adjustable interest rates, which then accounted for two-thirds of the first-lien loans or 9% of all first-lien loans outstanding. This was against a background of house prices decelerating or even falling in some areas, whilst interest rates on loans moved upwards, reaching their highest levels for many years in mid-2006. Once again, the Federal Reserve stated that "the expansion of subprime mortgage lending has made home ownership possible for households who in the past might not have qualified for a mortgage … minority households and households in lower-income Census tracts have recorded some of the largest gains in percentage terms." Relying on HMDA data, the Chairman said, "We believe the effect of the troubles in the subprime sector on the broader housing market will likely be limited."[54] The failure even then to recognize the risks of subprime lending and all the issues raised in this chapter will be pursued in the next.

12

Why Did Fannie Mae and Freddie Mac Get Away with It for So Long?

A weak regulator

Limits of its authority

Quite simply, there were two reasons for this: the "weakness" of the regulator (the Office of Housing and Enterprise Oversight, or OFHEO), and the lobbying conducted by Fannie Mae and Freddie Mac. The first reason makes it look as though OFHEO was simply asleep on the job or in the grip of the Enterprises, but a brief examination of the powers and resources available to the regulator will show that things were not quite that simple. OFHEO was established as part of the Act which gave Fannie and Freddie their Charters in 1992.[1] It was the GSEs' "safety and soundness regulator" and an independent agency within the Department of Housing and Urban Development (HUD) until it was abolished in 2008. HUD was the "mission" regulator of Fannie Mae and Freddie Mac, charged with ensuring that the Enterprises enhanced the availability of mortgage credit by creating and maintaining a secondary market for residential mortgages. HUD was also responsible for setting the housing goals.

OFHEO, as the safety and soundness regulator, was authorized to set risk-based capital standards, conduct examinations, and take enforcement actions if unsafe or unsound financial or management practices were identified. Its Director was nominated by the President, and confirmed by the Senate, for a five-year term. Both HUD and OFHEO were however seen as ineffective regulators. One example, as far as OFHEO is concerned, was the length of time it took to develop and finalize its risk-based capital regulation. That was later dismissed by OFHEO Director James Lockhart as a "stress-test", and both it and the capital surcharge, which OFHEO eventually imposed after the discovery of the "accounting irregularities," was still inadequate, since their regulatory capital was composed of each other's bonds, deferred tax assets and what Henry Paulson later described as "flimsy" capital.[2] When the GSEs were finally taken into conservatorship, they were found to have inflated their capital by using deferred tax assets, that is, credits that companies build up over the years to offset future profits. Fannie argued that its worth was increased by $36bn through such credits, and Freddie claimed $28bn benefit. Such credits have no value until the companies generate a profit, which they had not done over the previous four quarters, and which was unlikely to happen in the near future. Even with a rapid increase in profits, the credits would not have been usable, as the Enterprises had large numbers of affordable housing tax credits, which themselves offset profits.[3]

The weakness overall, as Secretary John Snow observed in his testimony before the House Financial Services Committee, was that "the supervisory system for the housing GSEs neither has the tools, nor the stature, to effectively deal with the current size, complexity and importance of these Enterprises."[4] A number of such failings were revealed when OFHEO published its reports on accounting irregularities. The accounting irregularities and the extensive management and system failures had apparently gone unnoticed for many years. The question remains as to why the regulator was so ill-equipped in every way for effective regulation.

By design

That did not come about by accident. James Johnson took up the reins in 1991 as CEO of Fannie Mae, having been a consultant to the company prior to joining it in the same year. He had been campaign manager for Walter Mondale's failed Presidential bid in 1984, and chairman of the selection committee for the Presidential campaign of John Kerry, which meant that he was well-connected in Washington DC. The GSE had only recently become profitable again, and already had a small but effective lobbying unit. Those who were there at the time recalled that the GSE's Charter was his overriding concern; he aimed to secure the Enterprises' hybrid status and above all to ensure that the controls on their activities were as light as possible. To that end, the legislation would give HUD, and OFHEO in particular, severely limited powers. The most efficient way to do that was to restrict the funds available to OFHEO and to make sure that Fannie Mae and Freddie Mac did not suffer for it. This did not go unnoticed at the time. The debate on a new regulator was brief, but Congressman Jim Leach warned at the time that Congress was "hamstringing" this new regulator at the behest of the companies. He pointed out, presciently, that they were changing "from being agencies of the public at large to money machines for the stockholding few." Barney Frank, on the other hand, argued that the companies served a public purpose, lowering the price of mortgage loans.[5]

The upshot was that OFHEO funded its operations through assessments made on Fannie Mae and Freddie Mac, but could only collect the assessments when approved by the appropriations bill and at a level set by its appropriators (other regulators, such as the banking regulators, are exempt). GAO recognized the severe constraints this placed on OFHEO's ability to carry out its regulatory tasks and to hire additional resources to carry out its oversight. Furthermore, without the timing constraints of the appropriations process, the regulator would be able to respond more quickly to budgetary needs created by any crisis at the GSEs. Predictable income would also assist with hiring and retaining the right quality of staff, and building up experienced teams.

Successive GAO reports covered the failings of OFHEO over the years of its existence. It was not until 2004–2006 that the regulator's oversight improved; but even then, it was the change of auditor which did more than anything to bring Freddie Mac's manifold failings to light. Indeed, OFHEO's 2001 and 2002 examinations of Freddie Mac gave high marks to the GSEs in such relevant areas as corporate governance and internal controls, despite the widespread deficiencies later identified in these areas. It was then that the Director (in 2004) announced their intentions to strengthen the examinations program, create an office of the Chief Accountant, and include corporate accounting (for the first time) into its oversight process.[6]

Hiring the right level of staff with appropriate experience for such an Office was costly, and indeed, additional funds were made available by the Bush Administration for further examination of Fannie Mae's accounting problems. Even as late as 2007, James Lockhart complained about the lack of tools available to a very small agency to do the job, especially as "Fannie Mae and Freddie Mac lost sight of their mission in the early 2000s and used their GSE status to grow out of control."[7] He also pointed out that Congress was considering a budget of $60m for OFHEO, 11% lower than the President's request, leading to cuts in planned supervisory areas.

Limited powers

Apart from insufficient funding, OFHEO simply did not have the powers given to other banking regulators. The minimum capital requirements, and even the so-called risk-based capital requirements, were too restrictive, and other powers were absent, limited or vaguely defined (giving the GSEs scope to mount a legal challenge). OFHEO did not have the authority to remove officers and directors, place an enterprise into receivership, or bring suit on the agency's behalf; ithad to rely on the Attorney General for that. The lack of these potential measures, and perhaps the regulator's own timidity, meant that informal means were used, with OFHEO officials pointing out to the GAO that the Enterprises were keen to resolve issues early and expeditiously.[8] This explains OFHEO's reliance on agreements with Fannie Mae and Freddie Mac, both then and in the years to come. To a weak and underfunded regulator should be added the other concessions afforded to the GSEs, including an exemption from the 1933 and 1934 Securities and Exchange Acts, the ability to borrow more cheaply than their competitors owing to the implicit government guarantee, and the Treasury line of credit. James Johnson had worked assiduously and played the Washington scene to achieve the result he wanted. The money-making machine was underway.

He then laid down the ground rules for running the organization, courting and pleasing the advocacy groups working to expand home ownership among low-income people and minorities. Wall Street appreciated the consistently high returns: "Washington insiders respect him as the most skilled political operator in corporate America, protecting Fannie Mae's franchise with an influential network that extends from the highest reaches of the Clinton Administration to the ranks of conservative Republicans on Capitol Hill."[9] James Johnson, however, would have none of it. "The reason Fannie Mae has broad political support is that we do our job. We effectively promote more homeownership for more people at a lower price."[10] That would be the theme in the years to come. The nature and extent of the political lobbying has to be understood in order to see why a regulator might be intimidated by it. Lobbying for Fannie Mae and Freddie Mac did not just take the form of gentlemanly discussions, issuing reports and engaging in public debate. In fact, there was very little of that, perhaps because the stakes were high: James Johnson himself earned some $28m, including a final bonus of $1.9m, when he left Fannie Mae. Lobbying was just another means of weakening or attempting to control OFHEO, as the regulator revealed.

Lack of market discipline

OFHEO could not look to the markets to assist in the task of regulating Fannie and Freddie; the GSEs had the facility to borrow in the federal agency debt market, and to issue debt obligations and mortgage backed securities with the implicit government guarantee, thus providing them with significant economies of scale. The low capital requirements also worked to their advantage. Banks and thrifts had to hold 4% capital against a residential mortgage, and Fannie and Freddie had to hold much less capital to fund the same mortgage, so clearly, it benefits the bank to sell the mortgage or at least swap it for a GSE-backed MBS. This was the effect of the legal structure and requirements applying to the GSEs. Their expansion came about as a result of the subsidies they received, rather than by them offering clearly more efficient combinations of quality and price; in addition, the implicit government guarantee shielded them from any market discipline. The ever-growing size of the subsidy has been described elsewhere, but as the CBO pointed out in 1996, "one further concern is that Fannie Mae and Freddie Mac rather than public officials substantially control the amount of the subsidy provided to the GSEs."[11] Basically, this meant that Fannie and Freddie were always in a poll position to be ahead of the market: they had the resources for it.

Discrediting OFHEO

As part of its Special Examination, OFHEO reported on four attempts to discredit the organization and its report. Fannie Mae's Government and Industry

Relations Department had close relationships with selected Congressional staff with whom they co-operated. In the spring and again in the autumn of 2004, Fannie Mae's lobbyists, with the knowledge and support of senior management, used their connections to instigate three investigations to undermine OFHEO in general terms. Two of these concerned OFHEO specifically: compensation levels of OFHEO's public and Congressional relations staff, and whether the regulator was in compliance with a provision of the VA-HUD-Independent Agencies Appropriation Act for the Fiscal Year 2004, which required an agency to allocate at least 60% of its budget to examinations and safety and soundness. Fannie Mae staff had helped to formulate the VA-HUD provision, with a lengthy exchange of correspondence to establish the exact percentage. The HUD Inspector General concluded that OFHEO met the 60% level, but that further testing was necessary. The second conclusion was that OFHEO was comparable to other federal financial regulators in its allocation of resources and staffing.[12]

However, a potentially more damaging attempt to discredit the regulator was made in April 2004, when the HUD Inspector General received a Congressional request to conduct a fourth investigation. This time the subject was OFHEO's conduct of its Special Examination of Fannie Mae, in particular that the agency had improperly leaked confidential information obtained during the investigation into the GSE. The attempt was not very intelligently carried out, as it happened; OFHEO found a draft of the Congressional request letter on Fannie Mae's computer system, which was nearly identical to the request letter that was finally sent to the HUD Inspector General. It was dated almost two weeks before the actual request letter was sent.

Duane Duncan, Head of Fannie Mae's Government and Industrial Relations Department, admitted as much under oath in his interview with OFHEO. They also knew about the contents of the OIG report before it was published, and wanted it published even though it was a legally restricted document. A sustained campaign to get it published succeeded, and it was put on a Congressional website for one hour, which was long enough to distribute it to their board of directors, analysts and Congressional staff. Mr Duncan made it quite clear that Franklin Raines, the Executive Vice President for Law and Policy, Thomas Donilon, and the General Counsel, Ann Kappler, were all involved. (The allegations in the fourth OIG report, that OFHEO overstated Fannie Mae's accounting problems were, of course, thoroughly discredited.[13])

The last push was an attempt to use the Appropriations Process to force a change in OFHEO leadership. There were repeated discussions with Fannie Mae's lobbyists to insert into the Independent Agencies' Appropriations Act for the fiscal year, 2005 a provision to withhold $10m until a new director was found.

Despite these may distractions, OFHEO published its Report of the Findings to Date on September 17, 2004, which, of course, brought about the "resignation" of Franklin Raines amongst others. All that scheming did nothing to obscure the report's findings. But that report was published a few weeks after Freddie Mac paid a record $3.8m fine in settlement with the Federal Election Commission and restated lobbying disclosure reports from 2004 to 2005.

At every turn, Fannie Mae and Freddie Mac sought to defeat any restrictions on their Charters or their activities. This was essential for them, as they lived or died by their Charters. "A federal charter means the politics rather than the market determines its major issues ... such as whether the government will charter other firms on the same terms, the financial services that the GSE may provide, how much capital the GSE should hold, the extent that the government will restrain risk-taking by the GSE, and whether it will go out of business if its net worth drops to zero."[14]

The Enterprises employed various approaches to achieve these ends: spending on lobbying; involving Congressmen and Senators in local housing projects; partnership schemes; and donations from their charitable foundations. Partly owing to the millions spent on lobbying and shrewd appointments to the Board and to senior positions, and partly through the use of their "affordable housing mission," which politicians dared not disavow, Fannie, in particular, and Freddie were extremely powerful and well-connected companies in Washington DC. As far as lobbying expenditure was concerned, they spent a combined $174m between 1998 and 2008, positioning them amongst the USA's top twenty spenders, rather less than the American Medical Association and just ahead of General Electric.

"They have always understood the political risk was huge for them, and they put millions of dollars into using contributions, jobs and consulting contracts to stay in the good graces of people in power. They had both parties, and particularly the Democrats, under incredible control," according to Wright Andrews, a "veteran banking lobbyist."[15] Their main aim was to ensure that the government did not change anything about their special status, and that OFHEO continued to lack the resources to carry out effective supervision. In 1999, Franklin Raines stated, "We manage our political risk with the same intensity as we manage our credit and interest risks."[16]

When the GSEs faced all the problems arising from the accounting irregularities, they campaigned even more vociferously against the proposed legislation to impose stronger regulation and controls on their activities. Freddie Mac spent $12.6m on lobbying in 2005, down from $15.44m in 2004 but still enough to place it 11th among corporations which had filed at that time. Fannie Mae's spending rose from $8.78m to $10.1m. Fannie did reduce spending on outside lobbyists by about 24%, but in-house lobbying costs increased by 67%.

In 2005, Freddie Mac secretly paid a Republican consulting firm about $2m to put a stop to Senator Hagel's bill. At the time at which he introduced the bill, most Republicans supported it, but DCI, the consulting firm, undermined his efforts by targeting and convincing various Republican supporters to withdraw support. Senator Hagel and his supporters wrote to the Senate majority leader, Bill First, telling him that "If effective regulatory reform legislation ... is not enacted this year, American taxpayers will continue to be exposed to the enormous risk that Fannie Mae and Freddie Mac pose to the ... financial system and the economy as a whole."[17] Of course the legislation did not pass. And a year later, Freddie Mac was caught again: it had used corporate resources to stage 85 fundraising dinners that raised $1.7m for candidates for federal office. In internal documents, Freddie Mac described the events as an exercise in "political risk management." The fine of $3.8m civil penalty to the Federal Election Commission still stands as the largest in the FEC's 35-year history.[18]

Fannie Mae and Freddie Mac did not use a scatter-gun approach in lobbying expenditure. They have strategically given more contributions to members of the committees which primarily regulate their industry. Fifteen of the 25 lawmakers who have received most from the two companies combined since the 1990 election have either been members of the House Financial Services Committee, the Senate Banking, Housing & Urban Affairs Committee, or the Senate Finance Committee. The others sit on the powerful Appropriations or Ways & Means Committees, are members of the Congressional leadership, or have run for President. A full list of contributions to members' campaigns from Fannie Mae and Freddie Mac directly, and via their Political Action Committees, is given in the Appendix. It should also be noted that expenditure did not only involve campaign contributions, but may be donated to caucuses of members. In 2007, for example, Fannie and Freddie each gave $100, 000 to the Black Causus Foundation, Inc.

Expenditure on lobbying did not end when the companies were running into serious difficulties in 2007, nor in the months up to the takeover in 2008. Fannie Mae managed to spend $3.8bn lobbying the federal government in that year, and Freddie Mac spent $5.78m; in 2007 they spent $2.9m and $4.28 m respectively. One of the first actions Lockhart took when Fannie and Freddie were taken into conservatorship was to end all lobbying activities. "There's no doubt that the legislation was delayed for many years because of the strength of their lobbying power," he said, after issuing the order. At the time, the companies employed 20 in-house lobbyists, who lost their jobs, and 48 outside firms, who looked for their fees elsewhere.[19]

Partnership Offices

It was James Johnson who first established the Partnership Offices in 1994: regional offices, which Fannie Mae regards as catalysts for housing projects in their local communities. He had announced the "Trillion Dollar Commitment" in 1994, enabling it to help 10 million families nationwide, along with the Partnership Office Initiative; the latter was to create partnerships with housing advocacy groups, community development organizations, lenders, house builders, real estate agents, and local government, all designed to work towards expanding affordable home ownership and affordable renting in their areas. The *New York Times* described one such office opening in Phoenix, with four members of Congress from the area (one Democrat and three Republicans) in the front row, whilst the TV cameras were running. One of the Republicans, Representative J. Hayworth, explained his support, despite philosophical differences, saying that "in many cases, like here, there is broad unanimity in wishing to empower people to achieve the American dream."[20] This was just one of the offices. In 1998, for example, another Partnership Office was opened in Oklahoma, with Governor Keating and Senator Nickles present as James Johnson announced that this was another example of the intention to expand affordable home ownership by working with housing partners state-wide to develop a comprehensive investment plan addressing Oklahoma's specific housing needs. Senator Nickles added that they looked forward to having Fannie Mae as their new neighbor, and that Fannie's presence on the ground would help their local mortgage lenders, community groups and housing advocates who are waiting to make the mortgage finance industry more accessible and user-friendly to Oklahoma's families.[21] What should also be noted is that in both cases, help would take the form of "promoting products like mortgages requiring as little as 2% down, and to introduce low down-payment loans to Oklahomans who can afford a monthly down payment but have not accumulated enough savings for a down payment."[22]

Johnson achieved his goal of opening 25 Partnership Offices by 1998, when he retired. He described his achievement and his purpose to the Capital Markets, Securities and Government-Sponsored Enterprises Subcommittee of the US Banking Committee in 1996, in these words: "When we announced our Trillion Dollar Commitment two years ago, we realized that we couldn't do it all from Washington and our five regional offices. One solution was to have people on the ground in 25 communities. In these Partnership Offices, as we call them, small numbers of professionals are in place to custom-tailor our mortgage products to meet the needs of the specific city or state ... So far 20 ... are open and working with local and state governments, local mortgage lenders, and nonprofit and neighborhood groups. Together with three additional cities, they have put together a total of more than $57bn in comprehensive investment plans. As we make and carry out these investment plans around the country, we tell local communities that, above all, we will be accountable to them ... It is one of the most visible and successful of the 11 initiatives that comprise our Trillion Dollar Commitment, and we are extremely gratified by its success to date."[23]

Franklin Raines was quick to realize the value of the Partnership Offices and over the years more than doubled their numbers, to 44 by 2000.

They were used even more extensively for media events, typically announcing a new partnership with a bank or mortgage company or to welcome a family into their new home; for example, with Representatives Luis Gutierrez and Blagojevich and CitiMortgage to announce a new partnership to finance $2.7bn in affordable mortgage lending to Chicago families, and with Representatives Larson and Hartford with Hartford Mayor Peters and GMAC Mortgage to welcome a family into their new home made possible by Fannie's Flex 97 mortgage product through GMAC. A statement of support by Rep. Larson was included in Fannie Mae's press release.[24]

Fannie Mae, of course claimed that these offices were simply created to get away from Washington DC, and that the media events were not directed from Washington. The events were basically product introductions, where a member of Congress asked Fannie Mae to participate in a program; it was all part of the development of relationships in local communities. By 2002, the company had 51 Partnership Offices, which Fannie Mae continued to use for such announcements. For example, Senator Mary Landrieu, Rep. Jefferson and State Treasurer John Kennedy were joined by Fannie Mae to announce a new $1.25bn lending partnership between the Standard Mortgage Corporation and Fannie on July 15, 2002. Rep. Robert Matsui, Fannie, the Sacramento Realist Association and Countrywide Home Loans sponsored a training seminar for brokers and real estate professionals on new mortgage and technology products. The press release issued by Fannie on July 18, 2002 included a statement of support from the Congressmen. *The Wall Street Journal* commented, "Fannie wins the gratitude of politicians by staging local events with them, often to 'announce its plans to buy local mortgages'."[25]

A year later, Fannie had 57 Partnership Offices and held at least another 21 press events with Congressmen and some Senators. The process continued, but in 2004 but it attracted some unwelcome attention. This was partly the result of a teleconference with Duane Duncan, Senior Vice President of Fannie Mae's Government and Industrial Relations team, during which he presented a slide listing 70 members of the House Financial Services Committee and the Senate Banking Committee, and pointed out that the Partnership Offices stayed in close contact with each one. "In every one of these offices, we have evidence of what we have done from the business side." The offices tended to be staffed with former aides from Capitol Hill from the banking, financial services and appropriations committees or others who were likely to be politically useful. Even as far back as 1996, a CBO study noted that "although these offices may conduct some mortgage-related business, their principal purpose is to enhance Fannie Mae's political base." Fannie Mae seemed to confirm this when it opened offices in the districts of the new members of Congressional committees overseeing the GSE; for example, it opened its Charlotte office to cover the state of North Carolina in June 1999, after the newly elected Senator John Edwards joined the Banking Committee.

The partnerships at the offices tended to be, as noted above, with a wide range of interest groups, who could serve as lobbying allies to help fend off any Congressional moves to limit their activities or remove their special privileges or status. It meant that they had an army at their disposal, ready to put Fannie's case to lawmakers, often by arguing that changes would increase the cost of mortgages to the poor and underserved or reduce liquidity in the market. Such "partners" were also arguing Fannie's case in their own interests, or as housing advocacy organizations.

The network of offices also provided a grassroots political organization in key legislative districts. Office directors were expected to maintain a list of contacts for generating calls and letters during political crises, encouraged by regional "franchise preservation" awards to those who had helped Fannie defeat an attack (that is, legislative proposals).

The offices were supposedly designed to help Fannie Mae implement its flagship affordable housing program, the American Communities Fund (ACF), a debt and equity investment fund providing financing for underserved communities, where traditional capital is limited or unavailable. The aim was to fund high-impact investments that serve as catalysts for further revitalization. The Fund started off in 1996 at $100m, by 1999 made almost $300m in investments, and in 2000 Fannie Mae increased its capitalization and committed it to invest $3bn over the next ten years. By 2004, the Fund had invested in some 500 housing deals around the country. Fannie Mae made sure that politicians were aware of the ACF investments made in their districts. But there was more to it than that. A *Wall Street Journal* review of 90 ACF press releases since 1998 found that of those which mentioned an individual member of Congress, the Senator or Congressman was either a member of the Senate Banking Committee or the House Financial Services Committee, or the Appropriations Housing Subcommittee, which funds the federal regulator, whereas only 22% of Congress sits on these bodies. Some did much better than others; for example, Senator Bennett was in the top ten by the number of ACF deals.

The review prodded HUD into action. In July 2004, HUD opened a formal inquiry into the political activities of Fannie Mae's regional offices. The report was completed a year later, but HUD refused to publish it in full; instead, the Department released a statement, saying that Fannie's Congressional Charter allowed it to set up regional offices to promote affordable housing. "However, the Department also concluded from its review that the activities of the Partnership Offices were not confined to affordable housing initiatives. Rather, a central purpose of the Partnership Offices was to engage in activities that were primarily designed to obtain access to or influence members of Congress."[26] However, HUD did release its August 31 letter from Brian Montgomery to Daniel Mudd, stating that the Partnership Offices were really "assigned to the duty of assisting in outreach efforts to members of Congress ... collectively this information indicates that a central purpose of the Partnership Offices is to obtain access to or influence members of Congress." The letter specifically referred to "Rob Bennett, the son of Senator Rob Bennett is the deputy director of Fannie Mae's Partnership Office in the Senator's home state. Jeffrey Bennion, Utah's partnership director, worked for the former Utah Governor, Michael Levitt." This was an example, based on information provided by Fannie Mae, that many offices were located and staffed based on criteria related to Congressional districts represented by various members of Congress, including party affiliation and the committee assignments of the representatives in those districts.[27] The example was apparently greeted with mirth at a closed meeting of Washington lobbyists, when HUD's statement was announced with an addition: HUD was also shocked to discover that gambling went on at Las Vegas.[28]

HUD ordered Fannie Mae to carry out an internal review of the political activities of its regional offices. As a result, Fannie Mae sacked 20 lobbyists and publicists at its Partnership Offices outside Washington and decided to dismantle its grassroots lobbying network. But the offices were only another part of Fannie's array of weapons; it had others in its armory. These included the Fannie Mae Foundation, which was used, sometimes to support other political groups such as the Black Caucus, but also to pump $500m into "highly visible and heavily promoted projects and grants in an effort to sway public opinion and to shape federal regulations." The author of a paper on the need to reform Fannie Mae and Freddie Mac, Ronald Utt, was honest enough to admit to another aspect of the GSE's attempt to control the environment in which it operated, when he pointed out that "even America's college professors became objects of Fannie Mae's affection." This was when it created and financed two academic journals, *Housing Policy Debate* and *Journal of Housing Research*, focusing on a wide range of housing issues. "The exception is that both journals generally avoid discussing the GSEs' role in the mortgage market and whether they make much of a difference. With many professors still confronting a publish-or-perish environment in pursuit of tenure and promotion, common sense argues against irritating a wealthy and influential publisher. As a result, academia has not been a reliable source of dispassionate inquiry into the GSEs' role in the American housing market."[29]

The Fannie Foundation

The Fannie Mae Foundation also donated funds to various housing advocacy and community-based organizations; it is not clear whether or not any money was actually given to the Association of Community Organizations for Reform Now (ACORN), or whether that association with ACORN was only an indirect one through Countrywide, with whom Fannie had a long-standing partnership.

The funding of various community organizations did, however, provide Fannie Mae with yet more voices to be used in opposition to any legislative proposals which threatened its status and which would then be presented as restrictions on GSE lending to low-income families and minorities. The Foundation was closed in February 2007, a "longtime lightning rod for criticism that the company was using tax-exempt contributions to advance corporate interests."[30] Not all of these were directly connected with housing: recipients included Harvard University and Arena Stage, a District theatre where Franklin Raines' wife was Chairman of the Board, and to the John F. Kennedy Center for Performing Arts. Millions of dollars were also spent on advertising to educate home buyers, and the construction of housing in depressed neighborhoods. For example, The Foundation spent $44m on television "outreach" advertising so that consumers could request brochures about obtaining a mortgage in 2001. The Foundation was replaced by charitable giving by the company itself, but some sceptical observers noted that the company would not be under a legal obligation to identify the recipients of the gifts to the public as the Foundation was obliged to do.

Fannie Mae and Freddie Mac used all their allies to intimidate those who tried to restrict their activities. Congressmen and women in particular would suddenly receive floods of emails and telephone calls from anxious voters, saying that the costs of their mortgages would increase or that they would be unable to afford to buy a home. Congressman Shay's experience of a telephone call from Duane Duncan, Fannie's chief lobbyist, when he had only just mentioned ensuring greater disclosure of the state of the GSEs' finances to a couple of staffers the previous evening, was typical. Congressional sources also said that the company tried to get critical Hill staffers sacked, and that after Richard Baker proposed a stronger regulator for the GSEs in 2000 (his first attempt), Fannie Mae hired a phone bank to call constituents on behalf of the Coalition to Preserve Home Ownership, a front for Fannie and Freddie, real estate agents and homebuilders. Some members of the House Subcommittee on the bill were "enraged after they received anonymous boxes filled with thousands of letters from constituents protesting a so-called Congressional proposal to raise mortgage costs."[31]

Other means

Campaign contributions

Harassment was not the only method used. Campaign contributions helped to ensure that many Representatives and Senators remained onside. Other sweeteners were available as well, not directly from Fannie Mae, but from Countrywide, with whom Fannie Mae had a longstanding partnership.

The relationship was such that Angelo Mozilo, Countrywide CEO said, "They have given us a liquid, organized market. If you took them away, it would be a disaster." Angelo Mozilo had driven Countrywide to a dominant position in the mortgage market, beyond the Citigroups and Wells Fargos, but he knew on whom he depended. "If it wasn't for them," he said of Fannie and Freddie, "Wells knows they'd have us."[32] His dependence on Fannie and Freddie led him to ensure their status, as well as giving him the connections and status he craved.

Friends in high places

Until 2004, when President Bush refused to make any more Board appointments, Fannie had another weapon to hand: the five Board appointments in 2002 included Ann McLaughlin Korologos, Labor Secretary under Ronald Reagan; Ken Duberstein, Reagan's Chief of Staff; William Daley, Commerce Secretary in the Clinton Administration and Al Gore's spokesman during the 2000 election controversy; and Jack Quinn, Counsel to Bill Clinton. Freddie Mac's Presidential Board appointments do not seem to have made as much impact, apart from the widely reported appointment of President Clinton's former senior adviser in the White House, Rahm Emanuel, in February 2000. Emanuel had served in that position from 1993 to 1998, but had joined Wasserstein Perella, an investment bank, in 1998, where he stayed until 2002. His stay on the Board of Freddie Mac was short but lucrative, as he received some $320,000 in compensation (including Freddie Mac shares, which he sold). At the time of writing, he is currently Mayor of Chicago. Other Board members included Robert Glauber, Undersecretary of the Treasury under President George W. Bush; and Harold Ickes, Adviser to President Clinton and Senator Hillary Clinton, and member of the Democratic National Committee. Former Board members included Dennis Deconcini, former Board member and US Senator from Arizona; and David J. Gribbin, former Board member, aide to Vice President Dick Cheney, Assistant Secretary of Defense under President George W. Bush.[33] These are just some examples of those appointed to the Board, and whatever relevant skills and experience they may have had, their political connections were clearly vital. They could be relied upon to act when Fannie and Freddie considered that they were threatened. It was because the GSEs were hybrid organizations that the Presidential appointments were made, but that practice was ended by President Bush Jnr. The Boards were abolished when the GSEs were taken into conservatorship.

Apart from Board membership, others were appointed to senior executive positions. Franklin Raines himself was Director of President Clinton's Office of Management and Budget; Jamie Gorelick was Deputy Attorney General in the Clinton Administration, and became Vice Chair of Fannie Mae despite having no background in finance, from 1997 to 2003 (with $26.4m in total compensation); Robert Zoellick served in both the Reagan and the first Bush Administration in various roles, including Deputy Secretary to the Treasury and Deputy Chief of Staff, before becoming Executive Vice President for Public Affairs and Affordable Housing from 1993 to 1997 at Fannie Mae.

Other connections over the years included John Buckley, who worked at Fannie from 1991 to 2001, but took leave of absence to run Bob Dole's campaign for the Presidency. In 2002, for example, the Enterprise's lobbying team included former Congressmen, such as Tom Downey (Democrat) and Ray McGrath (Republican), as well as Steve Elmendorf, Democrat strategist and Donald Pierce, a GOP operative. McCain's economic adviser, Aquiles Suarez was Fannie Mae's Director of Government and Industry Relations. Arne Christensen, a former Newt Gingrich aide, was Senior Vice President for Regulatory Policy; Tom Donilon was Fannie Mae's Executive for Law and Policy as well as being Secretary to the Board of Directors until 2005, and was in the Clinton state department. William Maloni worked for Congressman W. Moorhead and for the Federal Home Loan Bank and the Federal Reserve before joining Fannie Mae.[34]

"Friends of Angelo"

Countrywide's Angelo Mozilo adopted a "softly, softly" approach to obtain influence. A report, entitled *Friends of Angelo's*, sets out the way in which the company sought to buy influence.[35] The company dispensed favours to those whom it believed might be valuable. They would be known as "Friends of Angelo" who had been given loans on favorable terms. These borrowers included legislators, Congressional staffers, lobbyists, opinion leaders, business partners, local politicians, house builders and law enforcement officials. The VIP Loan Program, as it was called, was designed to build its relationship with members of Congress and Congressional staff and also to protect its relationship with Fannie Mae. Senior Countrywide staff and its lobbyists assessed the value of relationships with potentially influential borrowers, the most important of whom were given preferential treatment as part of an expansive effort by Countrywide to "ingratiate Countrywide with people in Washington who may be able to help the company down the road."[36]

The report notes that Countrywide made sure that the "Friends of Angelo" knew they were receiving special pricing and preferential treatment, and that Mozilo had personally priced their loans. They relied on their status as Friends to guarantee such treatment for themselves and others. If they had previously had a loan, then they could expect discounts on subsequent refinancing. A particular loan officer's business card was attached to their loan documents, which clearly indicated that the officer worked in the VIP unit. The loans were classified into seven categories according to the status of the person concerned, and also to ensure that the "origination and routing of VIP loans is handled flawlessly."

The report provides some examples of the individuals with prime responsibility for the oversight of Fannie and Freddie, who received (or were offered) such benefits. They were:

> Senator Kent Conrad, Chairman of the Budget Committee and a member of the Finance Committee, for whom Mozilo instructed the VIP department to take off 1 point.

> Senator Christopher Dodd, Member of the Committee on Banking, Housing and Urban Affairs and Chairman in 2007, who saved about $75,000 by refinancing his home at a reduced rate.

> Senator John Edwards, Member of the Judiciary Committee, who was referred to the "Friends of Angelo's" program when trying to finance the purchase of a $3.8m home in Georgetown.

> Alphonso Jackson, Secretary of Housing and Urban Development, who received two loans through the VIP program and whose daughter was referred to the program by a Countrywide lobbyist in 2003. To make sure she received preferential treatment, when the loan was confirmed in 2004 the loan officer told the Senior Vice President that her father, Alphonso, was expected to be confirmed as Secretary for HUD.

> Clinton Jones III, Senior Counsel of the House Financial Services Subcommittee on Housing and Community Opportunity, was referred for "specialized handling" to the "Friends of Angelo" program by a Countrywide lobbyist, resulting in "0.5 off and no garbage fees."

All of these were confirmed by email correspondence and other documents inspected by Congressional staff, as is clear from the full report and copies of various loan documents. The benefit for Countrywide? The company found that Congress turned to them when the industry-related legislation was being considered to share expertise and to provide insight. Lenz, who was in charge of government relations for the company, said that, "Countrywide had an incredibly good relationship with Congress. It was not unusual for us to get a call, saying, 'A bill's being introduced. It's a little technical, and there are parts we don't understand. Can you educate us on this?"[37]

For the lawmakers concerned, there was surely a reputational risk. Although the existence of "Friends of Angelo" was at least common knowledge, if not public knowledge, through much of the period in question, damaging hints could be dropped, enough to undermine a lawmaker's reputation, such that his contributions on certain topics would not be taken seriously. It also exposed a lawmaker to having to take positions on certain issues that he may not wish to take. In the process of getting a loan, the fact that documentary evidence of an explicit sort would exist (the business card of a specific loan officer, who may leave the company and not feel bound by any rules or loyalty to it) did not seem to weigh on the borrower's mind.

Fannie Mae and Freddie Mac were not the only ones to spend millions of dollars on lobbying. At the end of 2007, the *Wall Street Journal* reported that two of the largest mortgage companies had spent vast amounts of money on political donations, campaign contributions, and lobbying activities between 2002 and 2006. Ameriquest and Countrywide fought hard against anti-predatory legislation in Georgia, New Jersey and other states as well as at the federal level.[38] The largest suppliers of securities to Fannie and Freddie included New Century Financial Co., and Ameriquest, as well as Countrywide, of course. Their lobbying and the expenditure on it were mutually beneficial, so Fannie and Freddie should always be included in any assessment of the impact of lobbying. A recent study, *A Fistful of Dollars*, examined the relationship between lobbying by financial institutions and mortgage lending, and sets out to show that it contributed to the accumulation of risks leading to the financial crisis. The study argues that "lenders which lobbied more intensively on these specific issues have (i) more lax lending standards measured by loan-to-income ratio (ii) greater tendency to securitize (iii) faster growing mortgage loan portfolios. It can now be seen that delinquency rates are higher in areas in which the lobbying banks; mortgage lending grew faster, and during key events of the crisis, these lenders experienced negative abnormal stock returns. These results are consistent with certain lenders having more to gain from lax regulation. Such risk-taking exposed them to worse outcomes during the crisis ... With the caveat that empirical evidence cannot pin down whether lobbying is for signaling information or is motivated by rent-seeking, our analysis suggests that the political influence of the financial industry can be associated with the accumulation of risks."[39] That might be true in general, but it does not fully explain the mortgage market in America between 1995 and 2008.

Fannie Mae and Freddie Mac were not lenders, of course, but buyers of MBSs. The lobbying was mutually beneficial for both the lenders and the buyers. It was clearly rent-seeking behaviour, in that, in effect, *retaining* the kind of legislation which enabled the lenders and Fannie Mae and Freddie Mac wanted for their own purposes required payment. Nor were the lenders, Fannie and Freddie the only rent-seekers involved. The whole context in which the lobbying operated during this period was unusual. It was dominated by the affordable housing ideology, which, *inter alia*, meant that in practice the standards had already been lowered; and it was only at state level (and not with all states) that any serious effort was made to ban predatory lending. Congress had already given the status and benefits to Fannie Mae and Freddie Mac through their Charters, and most lawmakers did not see the need to alter the Charters. They believed or chose to believe that Fannie Mae and Freddie Mac's underwriting practices imposed the highest standards, and the GSEs maintained that myth. The lawmakers did not see, and were helped not to see, that affordable housing for low-income groups inevitably required lower down payments. If anything, the lobbying was designed to signal disinformation, not information. Clearly lobbying by the banks played a significant role in the crisis, but the context in this case was unusual in that it was dominated by the desire of politicians to see home ownership rates increase, and the desire of all the other interested parties to see that happening.

13

The End Cometh

This chapter will trace the changes in market and the events of 2007 and 2008, leading up to conservatorship. In the course of this account, the failure to grasp the dangers of subprime lending on the part of regulators and, above all, politicians will become clear, together with the disastrous effects of the continuing management failures and relentless pursuit of profit above all else on the part of Fannie and Freddie.

The year 2007

The mortgage market began to change in 2006, when house sales peaked in mid-year and began their steep decline thereafter. The price of an average home, which had increased by 124% between 1997 and 2006, began to drop. Interest rates, which had fallen from 6.5% to 1% between 2000 and 2003, began to rise, from 2.6% in December 2004 to 4.16% in December 2005, remaining at about 5% until December 2007, when rates began to fall again.

Other stresses in the mortgage market escalated sharply in the first quarter of 2007. There was a sharp increase in debt servicing and property liability tax for many borrowers, arising mainly from the "ARM reset" issue, leading to an equally sharp jump in mortgage delinquency and foreclosure rates, especially in subprime mortgages. The rise in foreclosures led to increases in the annual flow of housing inventory coming back into the housing market, further depressing prices. Commercial banks, reporting to the Federal Reserve, experienced a reduction in liquidity and funding sources in the mortgage credit supply markets, which had the greatest impact on subprime and Alt-A lenders.

At that time, the ARM reset and related affordability issues were probably the most important sources of stress. The share of ARM mortgages reached about a third of mortgage originations, increasing over the business cycle. These loans had become very popular, when short-term interest rates fell to historically low levels between 2002 and 2004 as the Federal Reserve sought to restart the economy from a long period of sub-potential growth, following the shocks to the financial system after Enron and Worldcom and then 9/11. Lenders also offered "teaser rates" that were below market-indexed rates, enabling more borrowers to enter the market (either subprime borrowers or home owners buying second properties for vacation, retirement or investment; often Alt-A borrowers). The rate reset problem did not only apply to teaser rates, which had expired; market-indexed rates also rose during this period. Some of these loans had caps on the rate increment and might be reset over a relatively short period of time. Property taxes increased too. The sharp rise in delinquency rates, especially in the subprime market at the end of 2006, set off alarm bells in the mortgage credit and equity markets, and led to the tightening of credit by the commercial banks, followed by the disappearance of the subprime lenders from the market. Some took note of these signs, but the majority of regulators and politicians did not (perhaps choosing not to); this failure to understand the significance of these such events explains why the end seemed to come so abruptly for the GSEs.

The number of outstanding mortgages in some sort of foreclosure was 1.2m in 2006, up 83.6% from the previous year. It rose to 2,203,295 in 2007, a 73% increase from the previous year, and again to 3,157,806 in 2008, an increase of 43% over 2007. In other words, about 1 in 54 housing units received some sort of foreclosure notice in 2008.[1] As can be seen from these figures, the decline in mortgage lending and the increases in the housing inventory slowly gathered pace in 2006 and 2007, until the full-blown crisis struck in 2008.

Closure of subprime mortgage companies

Foreclosures were only part of the story. In February 2007, HSBC wrote down its holdings of subprime MBSs by $10.5bn; a further 100 mortgage companies were closed, suspended their operations, or were sold. Lehman Brothers Holdings shut down its subprime mortgage unit, BNC Mortgage, bought in 2004 to expand lending to borrowers with weak credit. It became the first of Wall Street's five largest securities firms to close its subprime business. Until 2006, sales of mortgage companies fetched hundreds of millions of dollars, as illustrated by Merrill Lynch's $1.3bn purchase of First Franklin on December 30, 2006. The industry slump pushed shares of mortgage companies down by 58% from June 2005, with over half of the top twenty subprime lenders, as ranked by Inside Mortgage Finance, trying to sell themselves or leaving the business.[2]

Congress only gradually realized what was happening

The dangers of the subprime market only slowly dawned on Congress and on the Administration during 2007, partly due to the fact that they were unaware of the size of the problem. It was only when the "media frenzy" hit them that Congress began to take action. Even then, the first move was the blame game, with the Chairman of the Senate Banking Committee repeatedly accusing "our nation's regulators" of "being spectators for far too long." He stated that, "By the spring of 2004, the regulators had started to document the fact that lending standards were easing. At the same time, the Fed was encouraging lenders to develop a market alternative, adjustable rate mortgages, just as it was embarking on a long series of hikes in interest rates (17 in all). In my view these actions set the conditions for an almost perfect storm that is sweeping over millions of American homeowners in this country."[3] In an interview after the hearing, Greenspan made it plain that his previous comments referred to a small segment of borrowers, who could indeed save money by using adjustable rate mortgages, rather than the American standard loan of fixed-rate 30-year mortgages.

Congress eventually stopped blaming the Federal Reserve, and both spent the next few months more constructively in examining ways to curb market abuses in the subprime market. This led to the introduction of a further statement issued by the Federal Financial Regulatory Agencies on subprime lending, following the guidance on non-traditional mortgage risks which had been issued the previous year.[4] The 2006 guidelines were insufficient; the 2007 guidelines, which took effect on July 10, were an improvement, but unfortunately far too late.

In September 2007, James Lockhart issued a press release commending Fannie and Freddie for their implementation of the new guidelines: "The application to private-label securities further demonstrates the leadership role of the Enterprises in establishing standards for the secondary mortgage market. The extension of these standards will help to prevent the abuses of the past from recurring ... The Enterprises have also pledged their continued support of subprime borrowers. Freddie Mac said that it will purchase $20bn of subprime loans and Fannie Mae 'tens of billions' of subprime loans over the next several years,"[5] which was an astonishing statement in view of the GSEs' inability to manage risks or hold sufficient capital of suitable quality. However, OFHEO's Director sought to reassure his audience by saying that Fannie Mae and Freddie Mac's programs for subprime borrowers would serve the "cream of the market," relying on the federal regulatory agencies' new guidelines and to considering how to apply these to the GSEs' bond portfolio holdings.[6]

In May, Chairman Bernanke made a speech to which reference has already been made, in which he explained that the serious delinquencies in subprime ARMS were due to a variety of factors, but, most importantly, house prices had began to fall after increasing at an annual rate of 9% between 2000 and 2005. Interest rates on both fixed rate and adjustable rate mortgages also increased, reaching levels unknown for many years in mid-2006; many who had hoped to refinance were unable to do so because they had insufficient equity or may simply have walked away from the property (so-called "no recourse" mortgages were available in many states). The Chairman expected to see further increases in delinquencies and foreclosures in 2007 and 2008 as many adjustable rate loans faced interest-rate resets, but "we do not expect significant spillovers from the subprime market to the rest of the economy or to the financial system."

Given the fundamental factors in place that should support the demand for housing, we believe that the effect of the troubles in the subprime sector on the broader housing market will likely be limited ... The vast majority of mortgages, including even subprime mortgages, continue to perform well. Past gains in house prices have left most homeowners with significant amounts of home equity, and growth in jobs and incomes should help keep the financial obligations of most households manageable.[7]

Congress continues to miss the point

Two Bear Stearns hedge funds filed for Chapter 15 bankruptcy on July 31, as the company effectively wound down the funds and liquidated all of its holdings. These funds were significant since they depended on high leverage to purchase CDOs, consisting of AAA-rated tranches of subprime, mortgage-backed securities, using credit default swaps, as insurance against movements in the credit market. The substantial increases in delinquencies meant that the hedge funds required more capital as the value of the CDOs they owned was falling. They had to sell bonds to raise more cash, but as their predicament became known, competitors moved in to drive down the value of their bonds. It was a real indicator of what was really happening in the subprime market, and what was to come.

Christopher Dodd and Barney Frank continued to blame the Federal Reserve for its inaction, claiming that they and their colleagues had insisted that the Federal Reserve had a clear duty to provide extensive protection to subprime borrowers. Barney Frank warned Governor Kroszner at the hearing on Consumer Protection, "If the Fed doesn't start to use that [HOEPA, the Home Ownership and Equity Protection Act], then we will give it to somebody who will use it ... Use it or lose it."[8]

Bernanke had already responded to the challenge a few days earlier in a speech to the IMF conference. The "patchwork nature of enforcement authority in subprime lending poses a special challenge ... rules issued by the Federal Reserve under HOEPA apply to all lenders but are enforced – depending on the lender – by the Federal Trade Commission, state regulators, or one of five regulators of financial institutions ... We are committed to working closely with other federal and state regulators to ensure that the laws that protect consumers are enforced ... We undertake that effort with the utmost seriousness because our collective success will have significant implications for the financial well-being, access to credit and opportunities for home ownership of many of our fellow citizens."[9] That was a step forward. In July, Congressmen Bachus and Gillmor together with Congresswoman Bryce introduced a bill (H.R.3012) to create a national licensing and registry system for mortgage brokers, which also required very minimal training in loan rules, laws and ethics, a move which was long overdue. A similar bill was introduced in the Senate.

Some of America's major lenders began to make substantial changes in their home loan standards and mortgage offerings, including raising their rates and imposing stricter standards. These included National City Corps, Wachovia and Wells Fargo, partly in response to the federal guidance, but also because investors were unwilling to take on riskier loans. Wachovia stopped offering Alt-A mortgages through brokers, and Wells Fargo ceased to provide 2/28 loans. IndyMac said that the secondary mortgage market had ground to a halt in July and that the bank had "very strong liquidity, a good amount of excess capital ... [but] we cannot continue to fund $80-100bn of loans through a $33bn balance sheet ... unless we know that we can sell a significant portion of these loans into the secondary market."[10]

Red lights continued to flash in the markets: a national survey found that 57% of mortgage broker customers were unable to finance their adjustable rate mortgages in August, because many loan programs were no longer available. The survey also found that a third of home purchase closings were cancelled in August, 64% of subprime closings, and 21% of prime borrower closings.[11] Originators specializing in refinancing or nonconventional lending were "hurting terribly" and no "subprime loans [were] being done and little Alt-A."[12]

A flurry of initiatives

The blame game in Congress came to an end, leading to a flurry of initiatives, such as a hearing on subprime lending before the House Financial Services Committee, the introduction of another bill by Barney Frank, and Senator Schumer's efforts to increase the GSEs' portfolio limits (despite the fact that Fannie Mae's retained mortgage portfolio shrank by an annualized 8% in September, 2007).

Fannie Mae and Freddie Mac lobbied to increase their portfolio caps so that they could help ease the credit crunch. In fact, Freddie Mac sold more mortgages ($19.1bn) in September 2007 than in any other month during the previous four years. Fannie Mae had reduced just its portfolio of mortgage-related investments by $5.1bn, leading James Lockhart to suggest that discussions about increasing the portfolios were "a sort of red herring," as mortgages were always being paid off. They could buy up to $30bn of mortgages per month or up to $180bn over the next few months. But OFHEO would prefer to be able to insist on higher capital reserves and better risk management techniques first.[13]

The Mortgage Reform and Anti-Predatory Lending Act of 2007 (H.R.3915) set national standards for mortgage originators and imposed "assignee liabilities" on securitizers. If lenders did not conform to the standards, they had 90 days in which to bring the mortgage up to standard or had to adopt a policy against purchasing questionable loans. The bill was passed in the House of Representatives on a roll call vote, went to Senate, where it was read twice, and was referred to the Senate Committee on Banking, but it did not become law.

Senator Schumer, Chairman of the US Congress Joint Economic Committee, issued a report on subprime lending. It set out to analyse the effects of the "the current tidal wave of foreclosures," which soon turned into a "tsunami of losses and debt for families and communities." This report concluded that there would be 2 million foreclosures in 2008, in contrast to the GAO's estimate of 1.1 million foreclosures in the following six to seven years.[14] Neither Congress nor the Administration, with such widely varying estimates based on different data, was in a position to grasp the extent of the problem they were facing.

President Bush announced the HOPE plan (Homeowner Protection Effort) at the end of August. As part of HOPE, the Treasury Department and HUD began working on foreclosure prevention initiatives, helping consumers to understand their financing options so that they could stay in their homes.[15] Community organizations, mortgage servicers, the FHA and the GSEs were involved in developing "mortgage products that borrowers can use to refinance existing obligations."[16] Secretary Paulson stressed that without a proper regulatory framework for the GSEs it would be "unreasonable and irresponsible" to expand their businesses. The Administration was clearly considering raising the "conforming" loan limits to allow for jumbo loans and to assist more borrowers who represented a significant credit risk. The GSEs "would have to re-evaluate their own underwriting standards and develop new products that can help reach troubled homebuyers."[17] Chairman Bernanke took up the issue of jumbo mortgages in November, and suggested that liquidity in this market could be improved by allowing Fannie and Freddie to securitize them and then have the federal government act as "guarantor" to these products. He regarded this as being only a very temporary measure, and, in addition, pressed for legislation to modernize the FHA.[18] The Democrats warmly welcomed the proposal, and Senator Schumer immediately offered to draft a bill to that effect, with a second version in October. The aim of the bill would be to make higher-cost loans available for purchase by Fannie and Freddie, bringing liquidity to metropolitan areas where the median price for a single family-home was above the conforming limit of $417,000. It was meant to be a temporary bill, allowing an increase in portfolio caps for that time. It was referred to Committee, but did not become law.[19]

It was just as well that none of Congress's efforts to use Fannie Mae and Freddie Mac to handle the increasing problems of subprime loans came into being. The regulator and the Administration made it quite clear that neither increasing the size of the portfolios nor raising the conforming loan limit would be acceptable. The risks of the former to the financial system have already been spelt out; the cost of higher jumbo rates was not thought to be worthwhile, given the risk to the federal government of the implicit federal guarantee supporting the GSEs. All of these reservations disappeared the following year, as the market continued to deteriorate.

The year 2008

The collapse of Countrywide

The Bank of America rescued the embattled mortgage lender, Countrywide Financial Corporation, with a $4bn all-out stock deal in January. For Angelo Mozilo, it was the destruction of 40 years' work in which he had made Countrywide the largest home-loans lender in America, specializing in subprime loans. It was the business that he and his co-founder, David Loeb, had started in a New York storefront. At its zenith, Countrywide was worth $599bn. By 2007, it had originated $408bn in mortgages and serviced about 9 million loans worth about $1.5 trillion.

During 2007, Countrywide had struggled to deal with rising delinquencies and defaults, especially among subprime mortgages given to customers with poor credit history. It had announced its first quarterly loss in the third quarter, of $1.2bn. As it teetered on the edge of bankruptcy, the Bank of America stepped in, with the aim of extending its operations in the mortgage market. The deal was brokered by the then CEO, Mr Lewis, and it is one which the Bank has regretted ever since; even the current CEO has hinted that the purchase of Countrywide took place "just when you shouldn't have done it." The Bank's real-estate division has lost over $17bn mostly from assets inherited from Countrywide, as well as further costly settlements with investors in Countrywide's mortgage bonds, lawsuits, foreclosure snarl-ups and writing-off the value of its mortgage business.

According to a *Wall Street Journal* article, the previous CEO had had his eye on Countrywide for more than a decade, when the Bank was searching for market share in every part of the US banking industry.[20] He should have kept a closer eye, since Angelo Mozilo made his views about lending standards very clear, especially in his Harvard lecture of 2004. Here he advocated the removal of the down-payment barrier, stating that it "must be eliminated by offering customized programs to those borrowers who cannot meet current down-payment requirements." He then criticized the automated underwriting process, which he claimed "kicked far too many applicants down to the manual underwriting process, thereby implying that these borrowers are not creditworthy," which means back to FICO scores. "The system should say 'No' only to those deemed unwilling to make their mortgage payments."[21]

The no-down-payment policy was hastily abandoned in an e-mail to brokers telling them not to offer such mortgages after March 12, 2007, thereby abandoning one of Mozilo's key commitments.[22] Many borrowers were badly damaged as a result, as all too often the bank had not honored their commitment to house purchase by completing the process so that they could prove ownership. It emerged in February 2008 that Fannie Mae had acquired

$203.3bn in mortgages from sellers and servicers in the fourth quarter, about 30% of their business.

The Economic Stimulus Act

Awareness of the deepening crisis was expressed in the Economic Stimulus Act, which was signed into law by President Bush on February 13, 2008, a package that was expected to cost $152bn in that fiscal year and a further $16bn in 2009, and amounted to 1% of the US economy. The Act was designed to give tax rebates to individuals and to businesses to encourage investment. When signing the bill at the White House ceremony, President Bush announced that "we have come together to put the people's interests first," and that the package was a "booster for the economy."

The bill increased the conforming loan limits for Fannie and Freddie to $729,500 based on median area prices for mortgage originations between July 1, 2007 and December 31, 2008. The FHA conforming loan limit was increased from $367,000 to $729,750 for mortgages for which the agency's credit approval was issued before December 31, 2008. This bill was negotiated with the House, but the Senate sought to introduce another bill with the Democrats there planning a somewhat more expansive stimulus; however, the final bill signed into law was the House bill.

The OFHEO Director said, "We are very disappointed in the proposal to increase the conforming loan limit, as we believe it is a mistake to do so in the absence of comprehensive GSE regulatory reform. To restore confidence in the markets we must ensure that the GSEs' regulator has all the necessary safety and soundness tools."[23] He also made it clear that the 30% capital surcharge at both companies would remain, especially since they were stretched very thin. Lockhart made it clear that he was still hoping Senator Dodd would complete legislation reforming the regulation of the GSEs during 2008. "I'm an advocate of the GSEs. We're going to get the bill done."[24]

When he appeared before the Senate Banking Committee on February 7, Lockhart continued to press for a single regulator with powers of receivership, independent litigation and budget authority, and especially the flexibility to adjust capital requirements, both the statutory minimum and the risk-based capital requirements, which "are not even working at the moment."[25] In his testimony, he pointed out that the GSEs "had been reducing risk in the market by concentrating risk on themselves ... During 2007, the housing GSEs' debt and guaranteed MBS outstanding grew 16% to $6.3 trillion, which is larger than the $5.4 trillion debt of the US with Fannie and Freddie's debt equal to that of the US and the FHLBs' accounting for the rest. House prices are weak, and the Enterprises have provided stability and liquidity to the conforming mortgage market, securitizing about almost $100bn per month in mortgages, which has led to a dramatic reversal in their market share, from 38% to 76%, so they are effectively the mortgage market, and it might be 90% if you added in the FHLBs." He added that the "jumbo loans would present new risks to the already challenged GSEs. Underwriting them successfully will require new models, systems and tough capital allocation decisions."

The advice given by Lockhart was overruled by the Treasury Secretary, Henry Paulson, in his determination to secure a deal with the Democrats on the Economic Stimulus Act, which the Administration urgently required. A second and final hearing on the proposed legislation took place on March 6, in which the Chairman, Christopher Dodd, although in favor of legislating for a more effective regulator of the GSEs, wanted the "GSEs to do more to help subprime borrowers to get out of abusive subprime loans into safer, more affordable and stable markets. As Fannie and Freddie successfully address their accounting and management problems, I think it would be very helpful for them to devote a portion of the surplus capital they have been required to provide for purchase and work-out of these troubled loans."[26] This illustrates the lack of understanding of Lockhart's response to a similar question about the possibility of using the GSEs' surcharge ($17-18bn) into subprime rescues, when he said, "My recommendation is that we need to be very careful when we take this off the added risk these companies have ... I would be much more comfortable taking this [surcharge] off if I had the regulatory power to look at capital. At the moment, I really don't. They were only imposed because of the consent agreement. I think what we need is to give the regulator power to look at minimum capital."[27]

Losses at Fannie and Freddie

Meanwhile attention elsewhere was focussed on the huge losses posted by Fannie Mae and Freddie Mac for the fourth quarter: $3.6bn and $2.5bn respectively. The loss for Fannie Mae was triple the Wall Street analysts' estimates, and over 60% more than their estimates for Freddie Mac. For the 2007 financial year as a whole, Fannie Mae recorded losses of $2.05bn for 2007 (compared with $4.1bn profit for 2006); Freddie Mac reported a $3.1bn loss for 2007 (compared with $2.3bn profit for 2006). In its Investor Summary, Fannie Mae said its 2007 results "accurately reflect the most severe housing dislocation in decades ... Our primary focus is protecting our capital, mitigating losses, and taking steps to emerge from the crisis on a solid footing."

In his statement, Richard Syron said that, "Throughout 2007, Freddie Mac had worked tirelessly to protect distressed homeowners by stabilizing the conforming mortgage market and reducing mortgage foreclosures. In addition to leadership on behalf of homeowners, we are keenly focussed on managing our business through this difficult cycle towards a stronger future. As a clear sign of our progress, we are gratified that today's release marks Freddie Mac's return to timely financial reporting ... We remain extremely cautious as we enter 2008. If the economy weakens substantially from here, a possibility for which we need to be prepared as a company, it will have a further negative effect on homeowners across the country and drive credit costs higher. However, we have taken steps to add capital, tighten our management of credit risk and institute pricing policies that are more consistent with the risks we bear."[28]

The collapse of Bear Stearns

In mid-March, there was another blow to confidence in the market-place: the bail-out of Bear Stearns. The crisis for the company had begun in earlier in the month, when the share price fell by about 20% over the previous ten days. Despite the fact that Bear was paying its counterparties and trades were clearing, customers and counterparties were losing their faith in the bank, and that in itself undermined its ability to continue. After the collapse of its hedge funds in the summer of 2007, the company saw itself as recovering from that episode and strengthening its capital base. Others did not see the recovery and restoration of its capital base, which Bear Stearns claimed was taking place, following the closure of its two hedge funds. Instead, they focussed on the fact that the closures had brought nearly $1.6bn of subprime assets onto Bear's books, contributing to a $1.9bn write-down on mortgage-related assets in November. That prompted a scrutiny of the company's assets.

A major bank refused a short-term loan for $2bn, after which credit gradually dried up completely within a few days, and Bear turned to JP Morgan, probably because the bank was already one of the investment firm's main lenders and hence had an interest in it staying in business. By March 13, liquidity was plummeting, falling to $2bn. To address these needs and to ensure that Bear Stearns would be able to meet its obligations for that day, the Federal Reserve Bank of New York was authorized to make a $12.9bn loan to Bear Stearns through JP Morgan on March 14, but the markets apparently viewed this as a sign of terminal weakness and, after they closed on Friday, Henry Paulson and Timothy Geithner informed Bear that the loan would not be available until after the weekend. A buyer had to be found.[29]

JP Morgan informed the New York Fed and the Treasury that it was interested in a deal if there was financial support from the Fed. This took the form of placing mostly mortgage-related securities, other assets and hedges from Bear's mortgage trading desk to the tune of $28.82bn under the management of the New York Fed, and to which JP Morgan contributed a $1.15bn subordinated loan. On the Sunday, JP Morgan announced a deal to buy Bear Stearns for $2 a share, later increased to $10 to get shareholder approval.

The collapse of the company was less sudden than it appeared; after the closure of its two hedge funds in July 2007, its exposure to the mortgage market was of the order of $56bn, including $13bn in ARMS, which was reduced to $46.1bn in the fourth quarter. It also reduced its unsecured commercial paper when one of the major money-market fund managers dropped it as an approved counterparty, and replaced it with secured repo borrowing, which reached $102bn by the end of 2007. Bear became increasingly reliant on JP Morgan and BNY Mellon: by the end of January 2008, it reported an internal accounting error, which showed the company had less than $5bn in liquidity, which again led to daily reporting to the SEC. By mid-February, lenders and customers were less willing to deal with the company, which then had $36.7bn in mortgages, mortgage-backed securities and asset-backed securities on its balance sheet, of which almost $26bn were subprime, or Alt-A mortgage-backed securities or CDOs. The risks were there, but insufficiently recognized, and the company was too highly leveraged to withstand the market pressures and rumors.

Chairman Bernanke defended the Fed's decision to bail out Bear Stearns to the Senate Committee on Banking, Housing and Urban Affairs, pointing out the complexity and interconnectedness of the financial system. "Bear Stearns participated extensively in a range of critical markets. The sudden failure of Bear Stearns would have led to a chaotic unwinding of positions in those markets and could have severely shaken confidence. The company's failure could also have cast doubt on the financial positions of some of Bear Stearns' thousands of counterparties and perhaps of companies with similar businesses. Given the exceptional pressures on the global economy and financial system, the damage caused by a default by Bear Stearns could have been severe and extremely difficult to contain."[30]

The action taken with regard to Bear Stearns could be seen as in line with the concerted action by the central banks of the G10 countries to increase liquidity in the markets. The Federal Reserve announced that it was making $200bn available to financial institutions to ease the crisis of confidence in the market place. The press release stated that it would increase the amounts the banks could borrow at the Term Auction Facility to $100bn in March (up from $60bn in January and February); thereafter it would make another $100bn available through term repurchase agreements, collateralized by Treasury, agency debt or agency-backed mortgage securities. Again on March 11, the Federal Reserve announced that it would swap $200bn worth of Treasury bills for $200bn of mortgage-backed securities held by major banks which are members of the "prime broker" network on Wall Street. Many in the market took this to mean that the implicit government guarantee for Fannie Mae and Freddie Mac's bonds was being strengthened.[31]

By 2008, the combined GSE market share rose to 72.6% of all mortgage originations, up from 54.5% the previous year. The rapid decline in the value of the mortgage securities which they had bought, especially subprime and Alt-A, combined with mark-to-market accounting rules, forced both Fannie Mae and Freddie Mac to take vast write-offs. The net income losses for the GSEs were $108,826bn by the end of the year.

The focus of Congressional action shifted from regulating the GSEs to bills to prevent foreclosures. Even when faced with the crisis, the bills were passed either by the Senate Banking Committee or the House Financial Services Committee, but not by both. The Congressional Budget Office evaluated the policy options, concluding that "if the objective is to assist homeowners in distress, some of the policies seem likely to succeed at least to some degree. Many policies intended to help homeowners may produce significant benefits for lenders as well. Avoiding some unintended effects will be virtually impossible because it is difficult to distinguish between ... those who were victims of their poor judgment or predatory lenders, those who overstretched their finances for purchasing investment properties, and those who exploited poor underwriting standards."[32]

In conclusion, the CBO noted that most of the proposals under discussion involved modest federal subsidies and would probably affect several hundred thousand homeowners. It was a Presidential election year, and politicians were unlikely to carefully evaluate policy options in the face of the desire to be seen to be Doing Something. The bills kept coming during April and May. The Senate Banking Committee passed a manager's amendment, which encapsulated its housing rescue bill, to the Federal Housing Finance Regulatory Relief Act. Barney Frank foresaw problems over the bill because it diverted money from the affordable housing fund, but before that and other issues could be settled, the Senate Bill stalled in early July. Congress, once again, had f ailed to legislate on its own initiative to deal with the crisis, which was growing steadily worse.

House prices and the mortgage market

House prices peaked in mid-2006. The S&P Case-Schiller national price index for single-family homes was down by 9% in the fourth quarter of 2007 as compared with the third quarter of the same year: a fall of about 12% in real terms. A further fall of 10.7% was recorded for January 2008, according to S&P Schiller index for 20 cities reported monthly. Rapid declines continued throughout 2008, until by the year end house prices had fallen by 20% from the peak.[33] National delinquency and foreclosure rates rose both for prime and subprime loans, especially for adjustable rate loans. For subprime ARMS, 20% were delinquent in the fourth quarter of 2006. The share of subprime ARMS entering foreclosure more than tripled, increasing from an average of 1.5% in 2004 and 2005 but rising to 5.3% in the fourth quarter of 2007, based on the Mortgage Bankers Association's delinquency survey. By the third quarter of 2008, delinquencies reached 6.99% but foreclosures seemed to have levelled off, because of the various moratoria on foreclosures and the mortgage companies holding mortgages for 90 days or more during the modification or work-out process.[34] Such figures did not reveal the full extent of the fragility of home ownership for many people.

In 2006, 17.7 million households (about 15.8%) were spending more than half their income on housing, a huge increase (3.8 million) since 2001. Even 34% of those with incomes one or two times the federal minimum wage, and 15% of those with incomes two to three times the minimum wage, spent more than half of their incomes on housing. These figures were unlikely to have changed for the better by 2008. They show that as the economic situation worsened, many households had very little leeway to help them hold on to their homes. "Sky-rocketing house prices fed many dreams and papered over many ills."[35] The decline in house prices removed the safety valve of selling the property or refinancing. It was also this which led to the general economic decline and recession, rather than the usual sequence of economic decline followed by job losses leading to delinquencies and foreclosures.

Fannie and Freddie providing liquidity to the market

In April 2008, Fannie Mae and Freddie Mac began to purchase "jumbo" loans, (officially) mortgages valued at up to $729,750, in an attempt to stimulate lending in high-cost regions, where the interest rate cuts had failed to increase investors' demand for jumbo loans.[36]

At the same time, OFHEO released its annual report to Congress, in which it reiterated its "significant supervisory concerns." These ranged from the fact that Freddie Mac faced a deterioration in asset quality and a resulting increase in credit risk because of its "strategic decision" to buy and guarantee higher-risk loans over the previous two years. Its accounting problems remained. Fannie Mae's risks included interest rate risks owing to the lack of hedging of its portfolios and related funding. Both Fannie and Freddie pursued policies throughout that inherently exposed the firms to an extreme asset liability mismatch. They held long-term mortgages and MBSs financed by short-term liabilities. Given this strategy, they had to engage extensively in the derivative markets to create synthetically a duration match on the two sides of the balance sheet. These operations exposed the firms to great, but unseen, risks unless their positions were measured at mark-to market value, thus making the extent of the risks more transparent. Counterparty risk for both companies was high, as a significant deterioration in the financial condition of a top counterparty would adversely affect them.[37]

In his Remarks to the Chicago Conference in May, Lockhart outlined the steps he had taken so that Fannie Mae and Freddie Mac would be able to fulfil their mission. "OFHEO recently took several steps that enhanced the ability of Fannie Mae and Freddie Mac to expand their retained portfolios in a prudent manner … in the light of each Enterprise's considerable progress in remediating accounting, control and other management weaknesses. This involved removing the regulatory caps, after they produced timely annual financial statements for the first time for four years for Fannie Mae and six years for Freddie Mac. In response to the market, we lowered their minimum capital requirements from 30% to 20% above the 2.5% statutory minimum, and then with the lifting of the consent order to 15% above the minimum on Fannie Mae's sale of at least $6bn in equity and $5.5bn in equity for Freddie Mac. This allowed the GSEs to add as much as $200bn of MBS to their portfolios. In addition to raising capital through stock options, they have tightened their underwriting standards, increasing the fees they charge for guaranteeing MBS and lowering the prices they pay to purchase whole mortgages."

All this in spite of the fact that "Fannie Mae and Freddie Mac have continued to be a point of vulnerability for the financial system as a whole because they are so highly leveraged relative to their risks. Each Enterprise's core capital ... represents less than 2% of the sum of its mortgage assets and guaranteed MBS ... With that leverage, the Enterprises could pose significant risk to the taxpayers as well as to other financial institutions."[38] The figures involved had grown even further. At the end of March, the two housing GSEs had credit outstanding of $5.3 trillion, including debt of $1.6 trillion and guaranteed MBSs of $3.7 trillion. Little was said about the quality of the capital they held.

Fannie and Freddie could not cope

A few weeks later, Secretary Henry Paulson proposed emergency provisions after concerns that the GSEs were grossly undercapitalized, technically insolvent and may require a government bailout. Turbulence hit their stocks after the publication, ironically enough, of a Lehman Brothers research report, suggesting that proposed accounting rule changes might leave Fannie and Freddie "grossly undercapitalised." Although the report considered that the outcome was unlikely, it speculated that the two Enterprises might need as much as $75bn in new capital between them. This spooked the stock market, sending the shares to 16-year lows. Fannie Mae's shares fell by more than 16% and Freddie's by nearly 18% in value.

Lockhart set out to reassure the markets the following day. On July 8, in an interview with CNBC, he stated that "Both of these companies are adequately capitalized, which is our highest criterion. They have been very active in the mortgage market, and they are continuing to be. And, in fact, Congress has put on them the requirement to do jumbo mortgages and they have been doing those as well." Lockhart also commented that OFHEO was working with the Financial Accounting Standards Board on the revision of FAS 140, since the Board was considering rule changes which would force companies to account for securitized assets such as MBSs on their balance sheets. If that were to happen, then Fannie and Freddie would indeed need a combined $75bn in capital. Since investors had already suffered huge losses, a combined $89bn since August, 2007, the prospect of further losses did indeed shock the markets. Shares rallied to some extent after Lockhart's reassurances, but fell again the following day, as a result of heavy selling and further anxieties. Fannie's shares fell by 13% and Freddie's by nearly 24%.

July 10, 2008

Some attributed further falls to remarks made by William Poole, the former President of the St Louis Federal Reserve, but his comments only confirmed what many in the market had already concluded; namely that under mark-to-market accounting rules, Freddie Mac was technically insolvent. In an interview with Bloomberg, he pointed out that Freddie Mac owed $5.2bn more than its assets were worth in the first quarter, making it insolvent under fair value accounting rules, and the fair value of Fannie Mae's assets fell 66% to $12.2bn and may be negative in the second quarter. Poole had issued many warnings over the years about the GSEs' capital positions as far back as 2003, when he pointed out that they "exposed the US economy to substantial risk, because their capital positions are thin, relative to the risks these firms assume."[39] His remarks were, not surprisingly, followed by another bout of selling; not only of shares, but also of their bonds, in spite of the long-held belief in the government guarantee.

Friday July 11, 2008

Panic sales of shares continued, even although Fannie Mae and Freddie Mac insisted that they were adequately capitalized. Reuters reported late in the afternoon that the Federal Reserve had offered an assurance of access to Fed money if that was required. The Office of Thrift Supervision closed the doors of Indymac in Pasadena at 3 p.m., so that it was taken over by the Federal Deposit Insurance Corporation in what was then one of the most expensive bail-outs at between $4bn and $8bn. The bank specialized in low-doc residential mortgages. No doubt it added another layer of anxiety to the negotiations between the US Treasury Department and the U.S. Federal Reserve which went on over the weekend.

According to the *New York Times*, "government officials said that the Administration had also considered calling for legislation that would offer an explicit guarantee on the $5 trillion of debt owned or guaranteed by the companies. But that is a far less attractive option, they said, *because it would effectively double the size of the public debt* ... Officials have also been concerned that the difficulties of the two companies, if not fixed, could damage economies world-wide. The securities of Fannie and Freddie are held by numerous overseas financial institutions, central banks and investors."[40] These did not only hold MBSs, but also bonds issued by Fannie Mae and Freddie Mac, which often equalled or exceeded US government bonds issued in any one year and over which issuance, the US Treasury exercised very little oversight.

Sunday July 13, 2008

Secretary Paulson announced the GSE initiatives as follows:

- As a liquidity back stop, the plan includes a temporary increase in the line of credit the GSEs have with the Treasury, which will determine the terms and conditions for accessing the line of credit and the amount to be drawn.

- To ensure the GSEs have access to sufficient capital to serve their mission, the plan includes temporary authority for the Treasury to purchase equity in either of the two GSEs if needed.

- The use of either the line of credit or the equity investment would carry terms and conditions necessary to protect the tax payer.

- To protect the financial system from systemic risk going forward, the plan strengthens the GSE regulatory reform legislation currently moving through Congress by giving the Federal Reserve a consultative role in the new GSEs' regulator's process for setting capital requirements and other prudential standards.[41]

Monday July 14, 2008

Freddie Mac conducted an auction of $3bn short-term Freddie Mac debt, which reassured fixed-income investors but not shareholders, who were still unclear about what would happen to them in the event of a government bailout. Fannie's shares fell by 27% and Freddie's by 26%.

July 14 to July 23, 2008

The Administration won some key support for the rescue passage, and stocks in general rose by about 30% on July 17, helped by Wells Fargo's quarterly earnings, which beat analysts' expectations. Freddie Mac filed with the SEC, so that it could register shares in order to raise capital at a later date. It also managed to hold another successful debt sale. The SEC restrictions on short selling took effect. By the July 23, and after further fluctuations in their share prices, Fannie's shares closed at $15 and Freddie's at $10.80, which was the highest price since July 9. This was in response the House's approval of the rescue package bill, which then went to Senate, where it was approved by 72 votes to 13. The bill was signed into law by the President on July 30 as the Housing and Economic Recovery Act.

The Housing and Economic Recovery Act (HERA)

The Act included the proposals set out by Treasury Secretary Henry Paulson; that is, the explicit government backing of Fannie Mae and Freddie Mac through government purchase of the GSEs' debt and equity securities, if that was necessary, in order to stabilize the financial markets, to prevent the disruption of the availability of mortgages in the market place, and to protect taxpayers. The Treasury's increased authority, which was set to expire on December 31, 2009, was limited by the federal debt ceiling (increased from $9.8 trillion to $10.6 trillion in the Act). In exercising this authority, the Treasury Secretary was to take the following considerations into account:

- The need for preferences or priorities regarding payments to the government;

- Limits on maturity or disposition of obligations or securities to be purchased;

- The GSEs' plan for the orderly resumption of private market funding or capital market access;

- The probability of the GSEs fulfilling the terms of any such obligation or security, including repayment;

- The need to maintain each GSE's status as a private company;

- Restrictions on the use of GSE resources, including limitations on the payment of dividends and executive compensation.

Abolishing OFHEO

At long last, but too late for any advantage in terms of the oversight of Fannie Mae and Freddie Mac, the Act abolished OFHEO and created a single housing regulator, the Federal Housing Finance Agency. It had taken eight years and a crisis to reach this point. The legislation included a number of the proposals about which the members of the House and the Senate committees had haggled over for years.

The key features of the legislation are familiar enough. It created a single housing regulator, the Federal Housing Finance Agency (FHFA), independently funded through assessments of the GSEs and no longer subject to the annual appropriations process. Its Director would be appointed by the President and confirmed by the Senate to serve a five-year term; three deputy directors would be appointed by the Director. There would be a five-member Housing Finance Oversight Board, an entirely advisory board consisting of the agency's director, as the board chairman, the Secretaries of the Treasury and HUD, and a further two members appointed by the President and confirmed by the Senate to advise the director on overall strategies and policies. Presidential authority to appoint directors to the boards of Fannie Mae and Freddie Mac was abolished and the number of the GSEs' board members was reduced.

What still remained, however, was the notion that the GSEs had a role in bringing about "affordable housing." The housing missions were altered, and the goals were to be set by the FHFA for single- and multi-family home purchasers in low-income or very low-income areas. These would be defined as 50% of area median income, using three-year averages from HMDA. Both GSEs would be required to serve underserved markets, such as manufactured housing, affordable housing preservation and rural areas. The FHFA may also establish housing goals for the FHLBs, after taking into account the structural and overall mission differences between the FHLBs and the GSEs. The conforming loan limit was raised to the lesser of 125% of an area's median price or $625,000. The loan limit would be allowed to increase in markets where the median house price exceeded the general conforming loan limit, but could not exceed 75% of the area's median home price: the loan limit would be adjusted annually, based on its house price index. Finally, as part of its oversight duties, the FHFA would ensure that the GSEs fostered a healthy national housing finance market that minimized the cost of housing finance.

The legislation was also designed to deal with the issue of the portfolio size of the GSEs, about which lawmakers had been repeatedly warned over the years. The FHFA was now required to measure the portfolio holdings of the GSEs, taking account of the size and growth of the mortgage market; the liquidity needs of Fannie Mae and Freddie Mac, and any other factors the regulator considered appropriate. The regulator could then require the GSEs to dispose of or acquire any asset deemed to be inconsistent with its aims. The FHFA would establish a capital classification system, according to which the GSEs would be rated as (1) adequately capitalized; (2) undercapitalized; or (3) significantly undercapitalized. (2) triggers the development of capital restoration plans by the agency and possible operational restrictions on the GSEs' activities as set out by the FHFA. (3) mandates the election of a new board, selection of executives by the agency, and restrictions on payment of bonuses or salary increases unless approved by the FHFA.

The last condition on which the FHFA could act was if the GSE was critically undercapitalized. Even here, the Congress could not agree on the need for receivership, but instead introduced a compromise. In the FHFA's view, if one or more of the GSEs was judged to be critically undercapitalized, then the FHFA had the power to place it in conservatorship, or receivership with a view to reorganizing, rehabilitating or closing the entity. Finally, a GSE's Charter could be revoked. The Act also contained a temporary provision, requiring the FHFA to consult with the Federal Reserve before issuing any proposed or final regulations, orders or guidelines regarding prudent management, safe and sound operations, capital requirements and portfolio standards at the GSEs.

Senators Richard Shelby and Christopher Dodd issued a joint press release, stating "It is unfortunate that it took the near collapse of Fannie Mae and Freddie Mac to convince a number of colleagues that these entities do indeed pose a systemic risk to the US and global economies. Nevertheless, I am pleased that this legislation now acknowledges and addresses that reality in statute by giving the Federal Reserve a role in advising the new regulator on risks to our financial system. Although the Fed's role is temporary, it now well-established that the systemic risks the GSEs pose are permanent. That debate is now over. The only question now is to whom the Congress assigns that responsibility in eighteen months ..."[42]

The Hope for Homeowners Act

This Act (which is in fact Title IV of HERA) established a new FHA program that would guarantee up to $300bn of loans used for refinancing at-risk mortgages into viable mortgages for a three-year period, ending September 30, 2011. To qualify for participation, all subordinated liens must be extinguished through negotiations with the first lien holder. Borrowers would be required to share the equity and appreciation equally with HUD, until the borrower sold or refinanced the mortgage. Loan servicers were encouraged to participate in the new program through the Act's safe harbor provisions.

The FHA modernization provisions also provided an increase in the loan limits of FHA-insured loans as well as an increase in the loan limits in high-cost real estate markets. The terms of single-family mortgages were extended from 35 years to 40 years. The Act also allowed the FHA to vary the terms of insurance premiums charged to borrowers, based upon their credit risk and a modification of disclosure requirements; and banned sellers or other third parties, other than family members, from providing funds for the purchaser to use as a down payment for an FHA loan. That practice led to fraud and corruption in so many cases, it is surprising it took so long for the lawmakers to ban it.

August 2008

The Administration must have hoped that the bail-out arrangements and the new legislation would calm the markets during August. But once again, the month which politicians and the media regard as the "silly season" turned out to be anything but. All too often, governments find that August is fraught with danger, and so it was for Fannie Mae and Freddie Mac; the measures the Administration had taken had no effect whatsoever on the stock or bond markets: if anything, the anxieties of bond holders were increased. As Professor Lawrence Summers pointed out in an article just after the short-term measures had been introduced: "No one should suppose, however, that the issue is now satisfactorily resolved, even for the short-term. Emergency legislation was necessary because market participants were unwilling to buy Fannie's and Freddie's debt; investors doubted that the GSEs were healthy enough to repay it and did not draw sufficient reassurance from the implicit guarantee of federal support ... A major concern is that receivership would endanger the financial health of the US by taking on the federal government's balance sheet all the liabilities of the GSEs ... Recent statements by the Treasury and the

Federal Reserve Bank have removed any doubt that the US will stand behind the senior debt of the GSEs. Surely everyone will have learned by now that keeping liabilities off balance sheet does not make them smaller or less real."[43]

A week after the July measures, Fannie Mae announced a larger-than-expected loss for the second quarter and slashed its dividend by over 85% in an effort to preserve capital, as the housing market continued to deteriorate. Its losses totalled $2.3bn before preferred dividend statements, bringing the cumulative loss over the previous twelve months to $9.44bn (before preferred dividends). Fannie Mae also announced that it had already reduced its holdings and purchases of Alt-A mortgages by 80% from peak levels, but then far fewer such loans were originated, owing to tighter lending standards. Its core capital, $47bn as of June 30, was $14.3bn above its statutory minimum capital requirement and $9.4bn over its 15% surplus requirement. Fannie Mae also added that it "may from time to time raise capital opportunistically," having raised over $7bn in additional capital in the second quarter, and assured investors that it had not sought access to the Treasury line of credit. The news of Fannie's results came only two days after Freddie Mac's larger-than-expected loss of $821bn.

By August 21 the GSEs' shares dropped in value, as investors feared a government bail-out which would wipe out the shareholders, and then rose as investors made short-term plays with the stocks.[44] Their shares had fallen in value by 72% (Fannie Mae) and 77% (Freddie Mac) between the end of 2007 and August 1, 2008, and were then facing a further hammering in the stock markets. A close watch was also being kept on the companies' ability to access the debt markets, given that they would need to roll over $225bn of debt by the end of September. It was not just the losses that they had incurred or the need to rollover debt, but also the widespread rumors that government officials may have no choice but to effectively nationalize Fannie and Freddie.

The following day, Warren Buffet claimed that Fannie Mae and Freddie Mac were "too big to fail" but that shareholders could lose a lot of money. "The game is over. They were able to borrow without any of the normal restraints. They had a blank cheque from the federal government," and "they do not have any net worth."[45] A few days later, shares of Fannie Mae and Freddie Mac rose again after Freddie completed a $2bn debt sale, although Freddie had to sweeten the terms of the offer in order to create the demand. That led some analysts to take the view that a government bail-out may not be inevitable, but regional banks with significant holdings in Fannie and Freddie's preferred stock "followed the market down." The potential impact of the collapse of Fannie and Freddie on the rest of the market can be seen from JP Morgan's disclosure that it held $1.2bn of Fannie and Freddie preferred shares, which it reckoned had lost $600m since the start of the quarter on July 1.[46]

During August, rumors again abounded that the decision to take the companies into conservatorship was driven, not by the failures of the US mortgage market, but by foreign central banks, sovereign wealth funds and foreign investors throughout the world. They were becoming increasingly reluctant to purchase Fannie and Freddie's debt. The main concern for the Treasury was the $5.2 trillion in Fannie and Freddie's agency debt, of which more than $1.3 trillion was held by foreign investors. At that time, of China's foreign currency reserves, as much as 70% was held in dollar denominated assets. Of that, $376bn was in agency debt, making China the largest holder of their bonds.

September 2008: Announcement on September 7

James Lockhart, Director of the FHFA, announced that a decision had been reached after senior mortgage credit experts from the Federal Reserve and the OCC joined the FHFA teams in countless hours spent reviewing each company's forecasts, stress tests, projections, evaluating the performance of their internal models, discussions with senior management about loss projections, asset valuations and capital adequacy. Not only were their capital reserves too low, but the capital itself was of low quality. Fannie counted $20.6bn in so-called deferred tax credits towards its $47bn of regulatory capital as of June 30, and Freddie applied $18.4bn in deferred tax assets towards its $37.1bn in the second quarter in the second quarter.[47]

This was the "thin" capital held against the $1.46 trillion, or about 47% of the high-risk mortgages purchased by Fannie and Freddie, although it is doubtful that FHFA was aware of the extent of the bad debts that the government was taking on through conservatorship.[48] The companies could not continue to operate safely and soundly and fulfil "their critical public mission" without placing them into conservatorship. The decision was taken after consultation with the Chairman of the Board of Governors of the Federal Reserve System and the Secretary to the Treasury. Conservatorship meant that the FHFA took control of the GSEs, and as such, the powers of the Board of Directors, officers and shareholders were transferred to the FHFA, which in turn meant that both Chief Executives were removed from office. The FHFA's new powers included the power to cancel certain contracts. The purpose of conservatorship was to preserve the GSEs' assets and return them to a sound financial condition that would allow the conservatorship to be ended. This was one of the options, the other being receivership, under the Housing and Economic Recovery Act of 2008, and was one of the outstanding issues which Congress had failed to resolve over the years. Conservatorship may have been the best option, not only for handling Fannie Mae and Freddie Mac's financial problems, but also for speed and ease of acceptance by Congress; the Presidential election was, after all, just over two months' away. It also had the advantage of leaving open any final decision regarding the future of the GSEs.

Between them, the Enterprises had $5.4 trillion of guaranteed mortgage-backed securities (MBS) and debt outstanding, which was equal to the publicly held debt of the United States at that time.[49] Conservatorship meant that the Treasury would buy mortgage-backed securities from the GSEs and raise funds for them. Each GSE gave Treasury $1bn in senior preferred stock and warrants to acquire, at nominal cost, 80% their of the common stock at a nominal price. In return, Treasury announced that it had signed contracts to make short-term collateralized loans to the GSEs with interest rates set at LIBOR (London Inter Bank Offer Rate) plus 50 basis points (0.5%). Treasury also agreed to purchase new GSE MBS on the open market, and to buy senior preferred stock from the GSEs if their liabilities exceeded their assets.

If the GSEs are unable to sell new MBSs, the Treasury has agreed to purchase them using the Federal Reserve Bank as its fiscal agent, the only limit being the debt ceiling. In fact, Treasury announced almost immediately after conservatorship that it had began to purchase MBSs, but did not announce the volume of these purchases, presumably to minimize the risk by acquiring collateral for loans and obtaining first claim on any funds available for dividends. Conservatorship may affect their portfolios, because it gives them access to a new source of funds, the Government-Sponsored Enterprise Facility. This assures Fannie and Freddie access to relatively inexpensive source of funds and a ready market for MBSs if they decide to sell them.

As part of the conservatorship, the FHFA raised portfolio limits to $850bn on a temporary basis; in fact, until December 31, 2009. They would then be gradually reduced by at least 10% annually until each portfolio came to less than $250bn. It *was* an increase, since at the end of August 2008 Fannie Mae reported that its portfolio was $760bn and Freddie Mac, that its portfolio was $761bn. Fannie's portfolio grew at a relatively slow 4.4% annualized rate in August, but Freddie's decreased at an annualized rate of 56.2%. Both GSEs seemed to have been slowing their portfolio growth rates since February 2008, but it had not been a steady decline. Delinquency rates on mortgages had steadily increased between July 2007 and August 2008; if the Enterprises were reducing their portfolio size, it may have been to reduce the need for capital as a cushion against delinquency and losses. Capital requirements have been eliminated and the GSEs can increase their mortgage portfolios by about $90bn very inexpensively.

The temporary increase in portfolio limits would allow the GSEs to provide more liquidity to the mortgage markets during the financial crisis, but the limits would then be reduced to address concerns about systemic risk. This, of course, was the risk which too many members of the House Financial Services Committee and the Senate Banking Committee refused to recognize or address, and about which Alan Greenspan had warned them so often.

Treasury pledged to invest up to $100bn in each GSE, and was committed to invest more if necessary.[50] In July, the Federal Reserve made it possible for Fannie and Freddie to borrow directly from the discount window, a privilege normally available only to primary securities dealers and banks, which are members of the Federal Reserve System. The SEC issued an emergency order restricting short selling of Fannie and Freddie's stock. The July measures had not achieved the objective of calming the markets or of reassuring those overseas investors who held their debt. By contrast, the mortgage bail-out was greeted with relief, especially by non-US investors, who held $1.479 trillion of the debt out of $7, 397 trillion at the end of 2007. Other large investors were US commercial banks ($929bn), life insurance companies ($388bn), state and local government retirement funds ($317bn), mutual funds ($566bn), asset-backed securities issuers ($378bn) and the GSEs themselves ($710bn). Later in 2008, GSE reports indicated that over 40% of certain debt issues were being held by foreign central banks.

The mortgage bail-out was greeted with relief, especially by "nervous foreign finance officials," who had "barraged Treasury Secretary Henry Paulson and Federal Reserve officials to find out what was happening with the mortgage giants." Foreign central banks had been steadily reducing their holdings of debt in the two firms in view of the increasing turmoil. China's four largest commercial banks had pared back their holdings in agency debt, with the Bank of China Ltd, the largest holder of Fannie and Freddie's securities out of the four, stating that it had sold or allowed to mature $4.6bn of the $17.3bn it held since June 30.[51] A spokesman for the Bank of China commented, "We think this is good for Fannie and Freddie because the US government used to be 'invisibly' guaranteeing them, but now it is taking explicit action to [tacitly][52] guarantee them."

After Japan, China was the second-largest holder of US securities in June 2008, but probably became the largest foreign holder in late 2008 or early 2009. Its main holdings were in LT government agency securities (including Fannie Mae and Freddie Mac), estimated at $527bn, with Japan at $270bn out of $1.5 trillion agency debt. The Chinese government was probably pursuing what it considered a relatively low-risk investment strategy, which would explain its heightened anxiety about the special measures for Fannie Mae and Freddie Mac. Its holdings of US agency debt increased between June 2007 and June 2008 by $151bn (all in asset-backed securities), which was larger than any other foreign country over this one-year period. China was by far the largest holder of US agency debt, accounting for 36% of total foreign holdings as of June 2008, up from 29% as of June 2007.

The extent to which China's investments were exposed to US subprime mortgage securities is unclear, although the *South China Morning Post* (September 25, 2008) estimated that Chinese banks held $9.8bn in US subprime at the end of 2007. The Bank of China reportedly had the largest exposure to US subprime mortgage-backed securities among any banks in Asia when the financial crisis began. Despite the September conservatorship, it appears that China sharply reduced its holdings of US agency debt since June 2008. Overall,

China's net purchases of long-term (LT) agency debt fell by $34bn from June 2008 to March 2009.[53]

By purchasing senior preferred stock, the Treasury effectively destroyed the stock value of the common shareholders and the remaining preferred shareholders. Treasury protected all the debt holders, even those holding junior subordinated debt, as the Treasury Senior Preferred Stock Purchase Agreement stated. Given the above figures and the events of August, it is hardly surprising that the Treasury bailed out existing creditors to make explicit the "implicit government guarantee" of Fannie and Freddie, and to make good their "nod and wink" selling practices. As James Lockhart pointed out a year later, the "Senior Preferred Stock Purchase Agreements have given investors confidence that there is an effective guarantee of GSEs obligations, as any negative equity balance at either Enterprise will be offset by the Treasury Department's investment. This support will continue indefinitely into the future subject to the commitment limit of $200bn per Enterprise."[54] Clearly, the Administration needed China, Japan and other foreign investors to continue to buy its debt to finance the deficit, and indeed, to finance the continuing role of Fannie Mae and Freddie Mac in serving the market. Both banks in the US and throughout the world had also invested in the GSEs' bonds as part of meeting their capital requirements.

Conditions leading to the crisis. Why did the market collapse in 2008?

The impact of the collapse of the Bear Stearns hedge funds

In mid-August 2007, the market suddenly denied funding to several financial institutions. This was in fact due to the uncertainties aroused by Bear Stearns' announcement that their two hedge funds, which invested heavily in subprime mortgages, were in difficulties. The securities were estimated to have lost 28% of their value since the beginning of the year. Although Bear only held about $600m in investors' capital, a relatively small amount in terms of the size of the mortgage market, the announcement about the funds created many uncertainties. Hedge funds commonly use leverage to boost returns (borrowed funds or derivatives); as neither the funds nor the derivatives markets were regulated, this led to the belief that many more hedge funds were also in difficulties, and to doubts about which lenders, brokers and derivative dealers might be at risk.

Furthermore, the MBSs held by the funds had been classified as very safe and low-risk by the bond-rating agencies, so the fact that they had lost so much so quickly led to fears about the safety of the ratings of similar bonds.

Suspicions grew that many more financial institutions holding subprime MBSs might be suffering undisclosed losses. This resulted in liquidity drying up for firms and securities with links to subprime mortgages, but it also affected other firms as well, both in the US and elsewhere. The turmoil in the debt markets was quickly reflected in the stock markets, as to investors and creditors, the sequence of events seemed more like contagion. Central banks throughout the world had to act in concert, and the Federal Reserve Bank had to purchase billions of Treasury securities in order to keep the rate at its target and then reduce the discount rate to provide further liquidity.

In mid-September 2007, the Federal Reserve Bank began to cut its main policy interest rate, the federal funds rate, which had stood at 5.25% from June 2006 to mid-August 2007. The first reduction in September was by 50 basis points, instead of the usual 25, and, as the financial strains grew and the economy gradually weakened, the Federal Reserve Bank continued to reduce its Federal Reserve Bank Funds target rate, down to 3% by late January 2008.

Even though the Federal Reserve Bank may have been successful in stemming the worst of the panic, the housing market continued to deteriorate as the rate of default on subprime mortgages rose to 16% and looked set to increase. That was part of a process that had begun in the late spring of 2006, when nationwide, house prices peaked in April and the market downturn started. In October 2006, Moody's chief economist, Mark Zandi, had reached the conclusion that "Nearly 20 of the nation's metro areas will experience a crash in house prices; a double-digit, peak-to-trough decline in house prices. The sharpest declines in house prices are expected [in parts] ... of Florida, metropolitan areas of Arizona and Nevada California, throughout the broad Washington D.C. areas, and in and around Detroit." He expected the declines in various markets to continue into 2008 and 2009, with the odds in favor of national house-price declines in 2007.[55] But it was not until July and then more particularly in the autumn, though into the following year, that the rating agencies began to downgrade their ratings.

A series of downgrades

On July 10, 2007, Moody's downgraded 399 subprime mortgage-backed securities which had been issued in 2006, and put an additional 32 securities on watch. The securities in question, totalling $5.2bn, had all been rated as Baa or lower in 2006. This was attributed to "aggressive underwriting combined with prolonged, slowing home price appreciation," and it was and noted that about 60% of the securities involved were originated by Fremont Investment and Loan, Long Beach Mortgage Company, New Century Mortgage Corporation and WMC Mortgage Corps. A few days later, S&P downgraded 498 similar tranches. Both reduced them by an average of 4 notches per security, where 2 notches would be more usual.

In March 2007, Moody's reported that CDOs with high concentrations of subprime mortgage-backed securities could incur "severe" downgrades. Five days after the report, Yuri Yoshizawa, Group Managing Director of US Derivatives, sent an internal e-mail, explaining to Moody's Chairman McDaniel that one of the managing directors at Credit Suisse First Boston "sees banks like Merrill, Citi and UBS still furiously doing transactions to clear out their warehouses … He believes that they are creating and pricing CDOs in order to remove assets from the warehouses, but they are holding on to the CDOs … in the hopes that they will be able to sell them later." This was noted later in Moody's "Climbing the Wall of Subprime Worry," but they still rated the newly issued CDOs on their existing assumptions. In July, Chairman McDaniel gave a slide presentation to the Board on the 2007 strategy with titles such as "Mortgage Payment Resets are Mounting" and "1–3 m mortgage defaults forecast 2007–2008". Despite all the evidence, Moody's did not make any substantial adjustments to its CDO ratings assumptions until late September, hoping that rating downgrades would be avoided by mortgage adjustments.[56] But as far as Moody's was concerned, it was because it had updated its rating methodology, following the review it had announced early in August. Brian Clarkson, head of the structured finance unit, had replaced Raymond McDaniel as CEO by the time the results of the review were announced in mid-August, as a result of which the analysts saw the severity of the mortgage crisis.[57] Fitch and Standard & Poor's started downgrading MBSs and CDOs as rapidly and extensively as Moody's did from October onwards.

Throughout the autumn, one set of downgrades followed another, often in rapid succession as the rating agencies followed each other's lead. On October 8, Fitch downgraded $18.4bn of MBS, then on October 11 Moody's followed suit with $33.4bn in MBS. Five days later, Standard & Poor's joined in by cutting the ratings on $23.25bn of subprime securities; three days later they downgraded a further $22bn. Then the CDOs came in for downgrades: on October 23, Standard & Poor's announced that it would cut the ratings on $21bn of CDOs. The company also stated that it would continue to monitor its rated CDO transactions and take rating actions when appropriate: "Additionally, Standard & Poor's will continue to review its current criteria assumptions in the light of the recent performance of RMBSs and CDOs."[58]

Moody's made a similar announcement concerning $33.4bn on October 26, and on Oct 29 Fitch stated that it was reviewing ratings on all $300bn of CDOs. Moody's then announced that it would review 500 CDO deals by the following day. By the beginning of November, it was clear that the rapid series of downgrades had led to the crash of the main tracker indices of asset-backed securities. Nor was it just the downgrades, but the extent of them that caused the severity of the shock; for example, Moody's reduced the Aaa rated tranche of a CDO issue called Vertical 07-01, issued by a company called Vertical Capital, by 14 notches to B2 in one decision. The problem for investors was their reliance on the ratings agencies for their investment decisions, given the opacity of CDOs and their generic nature. What is interesting is the fact the there were so many downgrades announced in comparatively small batches, prompting Josh Rosner's comment that "Moody's should have aggregated information about the downgrades. It suggests that they're understaffed and under-automated if they have to do this in such small batches."[59] The number of downgrades continued remorselessly throughout November, and many of them were even more severe, with 500 tranches being downgraded by more than 10 notches. More than 11,000 of the downgrades affected securities which had AAA ratings. Tranches that were rated only by one agency, and those that were rated by S&P in particular, were more likely to be downgraded by the end of January, 2008.[60]

The role of the rating agencies

In 2007 through 2008, the frequency of downgrades of RMBSs and CDOs reached record levels, far outstripping any such rating changes on corporate bonds. Throughout 2006 and the first half of 2007, Moody's had continued to rate large volumes of new CDOs and RMBSs, despite market events suggesting a continued rise in delinquency and foreclosure rates and mass downgrades of CDOs and RMBSs. About mid-2007, when the first downgrades began, the number of new issuances began to decline, but Moody's still gave Aaa ratings to billions of dollars of new CDOs and MBSs, even then. Out of a total of $119bn in RMBSs rated since the downgrades of July 10, 2007, 90% were rated Aaa; and out of a total of $51bn in CDOs, Moody's rated 88% Aaa.[61] By mid-2009, virtually all of these RMBSs originally rated Baa as well as Aaa had been downgraded.

The analysis provided by Benmelech and Dlugosz found that 64% of all structured finance downgrades in 2007 and 2008 were linked to securities that had home equity loans or first mortgages as collateral. CDOs with asset-backed securities (ABS CDOs) accounted for a large share of the downgrades, and some of the most severe. ABS CDOs accounted for 42% of the total write-downs of financial institutions around the world. By October 2008, Citigroup, AIG and Merrill Lynch took write-downs totaling $34.1bn, $33.2bn and $26.1bn respectively, because of ABS CDO exposure.[62]

It is also interesting to see how the rating agencies treated some of the financial institutions which played key roles in the financial crisis, in spite of their own warnings of October 2006 and their own downgrades in July 2007. They did not re-evaluate these companies, which held or insured those securities, until November 2007 at the earliest, apart from Lehman Bros, which two of the agencies had downgraded in June. Not for the first time, the ratings changes proved to be a lagging indicator. In the case of Bear Stearns, the firm had investment-grade ratings just days before JP Morgan acquired it with the help of the US Treasury. The credit ratings of the other major firms at the time of bankruptcy, acquisition or bail-out were as follows:

1. AIG, September 16, 2008. Received an $85bn loan from the Federal Reserve. Moody's A2, S&P A, and Fitch A.

2. Citigroup, November 23, 2008. Received $20bn in equity and guarantees on $300bn of its assets from the US Treasury. Moody's Aa3, S&P AA, and Fitch AA-.

In November 2007, it was announced that Charles Prince, the head of Citigroup, would resign after the bank announced a $5.9bn write-down and a sharp fall in profits. Losses continued throughout 2008, following a Q4 loss of $9.83bn. Chuck Prince had once infamously dismissed fears about an early end to debt frolics in July 2007, when he told the *Financial Times*, "When the music stops [in terms of liquidity], things will get complicated. But as long as the music is playing, you've got to get up and dance. We're still dancing."[63] The complications were left to his successor as CEO, Vikram Pandit.

When Citigroup announced further losses, following the resignation of Chuck Prince in November, Moody's and Fitch lowered their ratings to their third-highest investment grade and S&P warned that it might cut its AA rating. Much of Citigroup's trouble related to $43bn of CDOs linked to lower-quality mortgages, the very ones to which they had awarded high investment grade ratings.

3. Merrill Lynch, September 14, 2008. Struck deal to be acquired by Bank of America. Moody's A2, S&P A, and Fitch A+.

4. Wachovia, March 14, 2008. Offered a $25bn loan for 28 days by the Federal Reserve. Moody's A2, S&P A, and Fitch A+.

5. Citigroup, September 29, 2008. Announced a government-forced sale to Citigroup (later Wells Fargo). Moody's A1, S&P A, and Fitch A+.

6. Bear Stearns, March 16, 2008. Purchased by JP Morgan Chase with the help of a government guarantee on the firm's most toxic securities. Moody's Baa1, S&P BBB, and Fitch BBB.[64]

The downgrading continued with the result that 91% of AAA subprime RMBS securities issued in 2007 and 93% of those issued in 2006 were eventually downgraded to junk status. The numbers for Option Arms were even worse. On January 30, 2008, S&P Rating Services announced that it had either downgraded or placed on serious credit watch 6,389 from US residential mortgage backed securities with first lien subprime mortgage collateral rated between January 2006 and June 2007. At the same time, it placed on credit watch negative 1,953 ratings from 572 global CDOs of asset-backed securities and CDO of CDO transactions.[65] These reflected an issuance amount of $270.1bn or approximately 46.6 % of the par amount of US RMBS backed by the first lien subprime mortgage loans rated by S&P during 2006 and the first half of 2007. For the CDOs this represented $263.9bn or 35.2% of S&P's rated CDO of ABS and CDO of CDO issuance worldwide. S&P stated that these actions "reflected our expectations of further defaults and losses on the underlying mortgage loans and the consequent reduction in credit support from current and projected losses."[66] Indeed, over 18 months, Moody's and S&P downgraded more securities than they had done over their entire 90-year histories.[67]

Criticisms of the rating agencies

In a memorandum to the members of the Permanent Subcommittee on Investigations, Senators Carl Levin and Tom Coburn set out the main problems with the rating agencies, resulting from an inquiry into their activities based on over 100 interviews and depositions, millions of documents, and consultations with a broad range of experts. Their conclusions were that between 2004 and 2007, the agencies had relied on inaccurate rating models, given in to competitive pressures to obtain market share, and failed to re-evaluate existing RMBS or CDO models, even though they knew by 2006 that their models were inaccurate, and revised them.

They then delayed thousands of rating downgrades, allowing those securities to carry inflated ratings that could mislead investors. Between 2004 and 2007, Moody's and S&P knew about the increased credit risks due to mortgage fraud, lax underwriting standards and unsustainable housing price appreciation, but failed to incorporate these adequately into their credit rating models. Not only that, but despite record profits from 2004 to 2007, they failed to assign sufficient resources to rate new profits adequately and test the adequacy of existing ratings.[68]

The SEC report also focussed on the "issuer pays" conflict of interests, clearly manifested in the e-mails which both reports quote and emphasize. Agency personnel are encouraged by clients to provide them with favorable ratings, and "ratings shopping" is an inevitable consequence. The new regulations required agencies to establish and maintain policies and procedures to manage those conflicts, although in the end, they may be irresolvable.[69] Each agency must compete for business, as Moody's Chief Credit Officer told the Subcommittee, "What happened in '04 and '05 with respect to subordinated tranches is that our competition, Fitch and S&P, went nuts, Everything was investment grade."[70]

The Senate Committee report claimed that the endless downgrades from July 2007 through 2008 "helped cause the collapse of the subprime market, triggering sales of assets that had lost investment grade status and damaged holdings of financial firms world wide, contributing to the financial crisis."[71]

However, a better point would be that the subprime market ought not to have been allowed to grow as it did, and that the assets should not have been awarded investment grade status in the first place. The stronger point is the extraordinary incompetence and carelessness, bordering on negligence, with which MBSs and RMBSs were "rated" by the agencies. It is not possible to record all the e-mail traffic here, so only a few examples have been given (showing once again how so many seem to believe that e-mails are a heavily encrypted means of communication, known only to themselves and the person(s) to whom they have been sent!). This selection shows that the shortcomings arose from a variety of sources:

(i) S&P employee 8/17/2004

"We are meeting with your group this week to discuss adjusting criteria for rating CDOs of real estate assets because of the ongoing threat of losing deals ... Lose the CDO and lose the base business – a self-reinforcing loop."

(ii) Moody's BES employee survey 2005

"We are overworked. Too many demands are placed on us for administrative tasks ... and are detracting from primary workflow ... We need better technology to meet the demand of running increasingly sophisticated models."

(iii) Internal S&P emails 3/23/2005

"Version 6 [a new version of the S&P ratings model] could have been released months ago and resources assigned elsewhere if we didn't have to massage the subprime and Alt-A numbers to preserve market share."

(iv) S&P employee 3/21/2006

"The official Moody's line is that there is no 'grandfathering' and that old transactions are reviewed using the new criteria. However, the truth is that we do not have the resources to review thousands of transactions, so we focus on those that we feel are more at risk. Interestingly, Olivier Dufour from Fitch said they 'grandfathered' otherwise it would be unfair."

(v) Moody's employee 5/1/2006

"I am worried that we are not able to give these complicated deals the attention they really deserve and that they [CS] are taking advantage of the 'light' review and a growing sense of 'precedent'."

(vi) Morgan Stanley banker to Moody's employee 8/19/2006

"Since there are no published criteria outlining the change in methodology. how are we supposed to find out about it?"

(vii) S&P employee 12/29/2006

"We ran our staffing model assuming that analysts are working 60 hours a week and we are short of resources ... The analysts on average are working longer than this and we are burning them out."

(viii) S&P employee 1/17/2007

"Can anyone give me a crash course on the 'hidden risks' in CDOs of RMBS?"

(ix) S&P employee 5/08/2007

"No body gives a straight answer about anything round here ... how are we supposed to come out with [new] criteria or a new stress and actually have clear cut parameters on what the hell we are supposed to do?"

(x) S&P 18/07/2005

"I have been a mortgage broker for the past 13 years and I have never seen such a lack of attention to loan risk." (E-mail from Resources Realty re Washington Mutual)

Had the serious faults with the rating agencies been known at an earlier stage, then all the downgrades might not have had such a detrimental effect on the financial institutions. But that is to blame the agencies for the effects of the ever-increasing rates of delinquencies and foreclosures. Highly significant financial institutions announced large write-downs. These included Merrill Lynch, which reported its largest ever quarterly loss in its 93-year history on October 24, 2007, after taking $8.4bn write-downs on subprime mortgages, asset-backed securities, and leveraged loans which led to a third quarter loss of $2.24bn, six times more than it had estimated on October 5. Its stock fell sharply, its credit rating was cut and the perceived risk on the company's bonds rose after the CEO, Stanley O'Neal, said that the company had misjudged the severity of the decline in the debt markets after July.[72] He was later forced to retire. In the same month, UBS downgraded the value of some of its assets by over $3.4bn because of losses linked to the US mortgage crisis, and anticipated a loss for 2007.[73]

The rating agencies' failures were a significant contribution to the crisis

The registration of rating agencies and the insistence on procedures for managing conflicts of interest, the latter being irresolvable, would not deal with the problem. In September 2006, Congress enacted the Credit Rating Agency Reform Act, P.L.109-291, to strengthen SEC oversight of the industry. It took effect in June 2007, when the SEC issued the implementing regulations. The law required the SEC to designate Nationally Recognized Statistical

Rating Organizations (NSROs) and defined that term for the first time. It also prohibited the SEC from regulating the substance, criteria or methodologies used in credit rating models. That would obviously create difficulties, given the extent to which the SEC and other regulators relied on the ratings. However, bearing in mind the evidence of incompetence, negligence and lack of resources, it is clear that the rating agencies do require an independent regulator (perhaps national statistical authorities) to continually check their competence, skills, models and resources, or lack thereof. Inflating ratings due to a lack of competence may well be more important that inflating them because of the fees involved. The big three (Moody's, Fitch, and Standard & Poor's) issue about 98% of the total credit ratings and collect 90% of the total credit rating revenue in the US.

From subprime lending to the financial crisis

The rating agencies were a contributory factor, but their downgrades, belatedly indeed, reflected the quality of the banks' lending practices and their structured financial instruments. Chairman Bernanke identified the basis for the turmoil in the financial markets as increasing anxieties about the credit quality of mortgages, especially subprime mortgages with adjustable interest rates, and spelt out the link between the two elements. "The rising rate of delinquencies of subprime mortgages threatened to impose losses on holders of even [supposedly] highly rated securities, investors were led to *question the reliability of the credit ratings* for a range of financial products, including structured credit products and various special purchase vehicles. As investors lost confidence in their ability to value complex financial products, they became increasingly unwilling to hold such instruments."

Banks came under pressure to take these back onto their balance sheets, which then swelled with nonconforming mortgages, leveraged loans and other credits which brought large losses. Banks responded by protecting their own liquidity, including lending to other banks, so lending became more restrictive and more expensive. That was Chairman Bernanke's analysis at the beginning of 2008, a year which was only going to get worse.[74]

Subprime mortgages. A trigger or a cause?

In September, 2010, in response to the Financial Crisis Inquiry Commission, Chairman Bernanke provided an analysis of the causes of the financial crisis. In it, he described subprime mortgage losses as the "most prominent trigger of the crisis, but by no means the only one. Another, less well-known triggering event was a 'sudden stop' in June 2007 in syndicated lending to large, relatively risky corporate borrowers. Funding for these 'leveraged' loans had migrated in recent years from banks to special purpose vehicles; these vehicles funded themselves by issuing collateralized loan obligations (CLOs), a type of asset-backed security ... As in the case of subprime mortgages, the perceived losses on leveraged loans in the late summer of 2007 were significant, although not large enough by themselves to threaten global financial stability. But they damaged the confidence of short-term investors and, consequently the functioning of the money markets and the broader financial system."

The subprime mortgage market was more than a trigger. It was the root cause of the crisis, with many other factors contributing to the collapse of the mortgage market and its consequences for the global financial system. Unless all of these are understood and acknowledged, then the right policy decisions will not be taken. In the next chapter, the impact of the size of the subprime market and the way in which its effects were transmitted to so many financial markets will be outlined, to clear the way for the political decisions yet to be taken: the future of Fannie Mae and Freddie Mac.

14

Fannie and Freddie:
A story without an ending

Transferring the damage

Fannie Mae and Freddie Mac carried out their mission by purchasing mortgages from lenders. Then they either pooled these loans to create mortgage-backed securities (MBSs), which they guarantee against losses from defaults in the underlying mortgages, selling the MBSs to investors; or they retained them in their portfolios, along with other MBSs that they bought to hold as assets in their portfolios, (both each other's MBSs and those issued by private companies). In 2007, Fannie and Freddie found that they could not sell their mortgage assets, since this would depress the prices of mortgage loans and MBSs still further; nor could they use retained earnings to bolster capital as they had not made a full year's profit since 2006. So, they increased their purchases of mortgage and MBSs as investors came to distrust the market for these securities.

Until 2007, banks and other lenders also sold private label MBSs. From mid-August, there was a broad global reduction in the supply of credit for securities backed by subprime loans. Uncertainty about the decline in the value of subprime collateral especially for private label securities (PLSs) and collateralised debt obligations (CDOs) led to liquidity in these markets virtually disappearing. Far fewer PLSs were issued in the third quarter of 2007, with the fourth quarter being even worse: only $11.9bn subprime PLSs being issued. Investors became less willing to invest in any mortgage-related securities not backed by Fannie, Freddie or Ginnie Mae (always assuming that they understood what they were buying). The result was that the Enterprises' combined share of all MBSs rose to over 75% in the fourth quarter of 2007. Their books of mortgage business rose by 14.3% in 2007 for Fannie and 15.1% for Freddie in 2007 over 2006. Fannie's total book of mortgage business rose to $2.9 trillion and Freddie's to $2.1 trillion.

Residential mortgage-backed securities (RMBSs) and other forms of structured finance related to mortgages had become ever more complex. Issuers bundled up large numbers of home loans into a loan pool, calculated the revenue stream coming into that loan pool from the individual mortgages, and then designed a "waterfall" that assigns the pooled revenues to specific "tranches" set up in a specified order.

The first tranche is at the top of the waterfall and is the first recipient of revenues received from the mortgage pool. The issuer creates a bond linked to the first tranche, which is then rated AAA. The next tranche is the second to receive revenues from the mortgage pool, and is linked to a security that might receive an AAA or lower rating, and so on through the tranches with lower ratings in each case until the equity tranche is reached; this does not have a rating as it must cover the pool's initial losses. Almost every pool has some loans that default, so the equity tranche often offered a high rate of return to compensate for the risks.

CDOs are even more complex, typically including RMBSs from multiple mortgage pools and other types of assets, such as corporate bonds or credit default swaps. These are the "cash" CDOs, to be differentiated from the "synthetic CDOs," which do not contain actual assets but simply reference them. Initially, a CDO is divided into a series of tranches, each of which has a separate rating, with the highest rating reserved for the senior tranche; the middle tranches or the mezzanine tranches usually carry AA or BB rating, and the lowest or junk tranches are called the equity tranches. The senior tranche has the most predictable cash flow and is usually deemed to carry the lowest risk, and the lowest tranches only receive principal and interest payments when all the other tranches have been paid. Senior investors get the benefit of higher pay-outs than they would normally receive from vary safe bonds because they are investing in a pool of loans which includes lower-quality borrowers.

A CDO squared is a CDO that only uses other CDOs as collateral. The CDO cubed is a special purpose vehicle with securitisation payments in the form of tranches. A CDO cubed is backed by CDO squared tranches, allowing the banks to resell the credit risk they had taken once again by repackaging their CDO squared. The complexity of these operations baffled many bankers and others, leading to anxiety as to where the risk really lay. The CDOs cubed were in fact "triple derivatives," sometimes known as "derivatives on steroids."

All of these were typically sold in private placements. The more complex and opaque they became, the more they relied on credit ratings to be marketed and the more investors did, as well.[1] The risks of subprime mortgages were understood, with academic research analysing the risks associated with one or more features, such as high loan-to-value LTVS. But in a rising market, such risks were set aside, since house prices continued to increase. Optimism about how subprime mortgages would perform led to more than 90% of securitised subprime loans being absorbed into securities with AAA ratings.[2]

The vulnerability of leveraged or thinly capitalised investment positions and the illiquidity of many structured credit markets were exposed when trading was disrupted in June 2007. Investors had borrowed heavily or used derivatives to increase returns on capital, and that made investment strategies vulnerable to large market price movements. The main risk-management strategy was to trade rapidly out of a loss-making position, but this, of course failed when the markets became illiquid and no one was quite sure about the quality of the various financial instruments and (indeed the mortgages) they had purchased. In fact, given the size of the subprime mortgage market (about half of the outstanding mortgages in 2008), the contagion would be worse than anyone could have anticipated. Investors began to realise this, when a wave of defaults mostly among subprime borrowers affected some CDO tranches much more than expected. Investors began to question the safety of even the highest tranches in some CDOs, especially the "synthetic" CDOs, which had the highest leverage and the least protection. Mark-to-market requirements made it increasingly difficult to ascribe a value to the CDOs.

Even at that late stage, policy makers seemed unable to relate their demand for lending to low and moderate income borrowers and "flexible" underwriting standards to subprime mortgages.[3] The vast number of subprime mortgages, some 26m, however, were divided into tranches, inevitably adding to the degree of risk involved. About 47% of the mortgages held by Fannie and Freddie were subprime, which makes their conservatorship an expensive affair. The fact that the subprime market was so vast meant that many more of the RMBSs and other financial instruments based on mortgages were "toxic" or contained more toxic elements than had previously been recognised. As that become known or suspected, investors lost confidence and refused to buy or could not sell with the resultant damage. If the risks had then been ascertained to be relatively small, then any market disruption could more easily have been handled and would have been much less damaging than the resultant lack of liquidity.

The ensuing global financial crisis of 2007 to 2009 was caused by the realisation that no one knew how large the losses were or how great the exposure of individual banks actually was, as delinquencies and foreclosures increased rapidly in the United States. Banks throughout the industrialised countries were left with an "overhang" of illiquid assets on their balance sheets. Banks stopped lending to one another, as trust evaporated. Banks realised that they could not be sure of the value of assets held by counterparties. So there were two aspects to the financial crisis: CDS spreads generally rose higher and banks stocks generally fell lower in countries with more exposure to US MBSs and with greater dollar funding needs. "Indirect contagion" may have played a more important role in the global spread of the crisis: a generalised run on global financial institutions, given the opacity of their balance sheets; excessive dependence on short-term funding; the realisation that financial institutions around the globe were pursuing similar flawed business models and global swings in risk-aversion. It was, however, the destruction of trust, which was the ultimate trigger.[4]

The winter of 2008–2009 saw co-ordinated action by the newly formed G20 Group in an attempt to restore liquidity to banks and to prevent the recession from turning into a world slump. At the London summit of the G20 in April 2009, leaders committed themselves to a $5 trillion fiscal expansion and an extra $1.1 trillion of resources for the International Monetary Fund and other global institutions to assist with economic growth.

April 2010 marked the point at which the focus shifted from bailing out banks and ensuring liquidity to sovereign debt. Greece was the trigger. Its debt rose to 126.8% of GDP in 2009, owing to its slow growth, inability to collect taxes, and high expenditure on social welfare programs, which it has been unable or unwilling to cut and which are financed by borrowing. Investors feared that Greece would be unable to meet its debt obligations. Greek bonds were downgraded to junk status in April 2010 and a month later Greece received its first bail-out package from the Eurozone and the IMF. The sovereign debt crisis spread to other member states as investors observed that Ireland, Spain, Italy and Portugal shared similar characteristics, although their debts in no way matched that of Greece. Investors sought higher interest rates on government bonds to compensate for the perceived increased risk. The bailouts of banks added to the sovereign debt problems and also to the unknown risks of the banking sector, which held Greek and other sovereign bonds considered to be at risk of default. The eurozone crisis rumbles on. Major problems remain, made worse by indecisiveness and the inability to agree on solutions or effective bail-out proposals.

Counting the cost of Fannie, Freddie and the FHA

Between November 2008 and December 2012, the Government made net payments to the Government-Sponsored Enterprises (GSEs) of $187.5 bn and is expected to cost between $191bn and $209bn by the end of 2015 according to the Federal Housing Finance Agency FHFA's estimates in October 2012. The Congressional Budget Office takes the view that their conservatorship, which means ownership and control by the Treasury, makes them effectively part of the government and so their costs should be part of the federal budget. The Administration's Office of Management and Budget (OMB) treats them as non-governmental agencies for budgetary purposes. After consultation with the House and Senate Committees on the Budget, the CBO decided that a fair value approach to estimations of the subsidy costs would provide Congress with the most accurate picture.[5]

In August 2009, the CBO estimated that the cost of all of the GSEs' mortgage commitments made in the fiscal year 2009 plus any new commitments made in that year would come to $291bn on a fair value basis. Losses increased to a certain extent because of the continued deterioration of the housing market. Although the subsidy rate declined and has continued to decline, as the housing market recovers, costs will continue to increase. The assets and liabilities on the GSEs' fair value balance sheets provide an indication of how the costs arising from past commitments have changed since then, since on March 31, 2011, the GSEs have reported a fair-value deficit of $187 bn, so the net costs to the Treasury so far amount to $317 bn, representing increasing defaults on distressed mortgages and continued falls in the amounts recoverable following defaults.

The CBO estimates that the new guarantees the GSEs will make over the 2012–2021 period will cost $42 bn (on the basis of the March 2011 baseline projections used for the CBO's analysis of the President's budget). The commitments are extensive. In 2010, as a result of the government's aid and explicit government guarantees, the two GSEs owned or guaranteed about half of all the outstanding mortgages in the United States (including a significant share of subprime mortgages) and they financed 63% of new mortgages originated in that year. Including a further 23% insured by federal agencies such as the Federal Housing Administration (FHA), about 86% of new mortgages in 2010 carried a federal guarantee. [6]

Estimates of the eventual total cost to the federal government of supporting the Fannie and Freddie use different base lines and vary widely. FHFA estimates that the Treasury is likely to purchase $220 bn-$311 bn of senior preferred stock by the end of 2014. The CBO estimates the budget to be more than $300bn.[7]

In addition to direct support, the Treasury and Federal Reserve purchased nearly $1.4 trillion in GSE-issued and guaranteed MBSs. It is also more complicated than that. The GSEs had to pay the Treasury the 10% dividend even when they made losses. They had to borrow from the Treasury to pay the dividend on the preferred stock the government received in exchange for the bailouts. The FHFA estimated that 40–90% of those additional bailout costs would simply be used to pay that dividend, designed to limit losses to taxpayers. The National Association of Realtors lobbied to end the "punitive dividend." "The problem is it's impossible for them to tackle their current problem if they can't rebuild the capital base, and they can't do that paying the dividend level."[8] Then Fannie and Freddie both returned to profit in 2012, due to the continuing improvement in the housing market, which gave them better prices for foreclosures. Fannie Mae's stated profits were $9.7 bn in the first three quarters and Freddie Mac's profits were $6.397 bn reaching $11bn annual net income in 2012 and in 2013, Fannie Mae reported that its net income for the year was $17.2 bn and Freddie Mac's was $11bn.

The companies had to make those dividend payments even in quarters when they have suffered losses, leading to Fannie and Freddie having to pay 10%, which was borrowed from the Treasury. On August 17, 2012, Geithner announced that the 10% dividend would be replaced by a quarterly sweep of every dollar of profit each firm earns going forward to benefit taxpayers, "and support the continued flow of mortgage credit during a responsible transition to a reformed housing finance market."[9] It would end the circular practice of the Treasury advancing funds to the GSEs simply to pay the 10% dividend. In addition, the reduction of the GSEs' investment portfolios must take place at a rate of 15% (as opposed to 10% previously required) and the target of $250 bn must be reached by 2018, 4 years earlier than previously agreed. The changes will prevent Fannie and Freddie from rebuilding their capital base with no opportunity to accumulate retained earnings, no opportunity to function independently of the government and no chance to be released from the conservatorship that now controls their activities.[10] On the other hand, with the GSEs being independently capitalised and making profits, there would be little basis for keeping them locked into conservatorship. They could then be returned to their original status as independent firms with implicit government backing. The GSEs have to produce a plan to the Treasury annually on its actions to reduce taxpayer exposure to mortgage credit risk for both the guarantee book of business and retained investment portfolio. The Secretary to the Treasury, Timothy Geithner, however, left the Administration on January 21, 2013, so another will have to oversee the moves to reform the housing finance market. The August announcement was welcomed by those who wanted to see an orderly winding down of Fannie and Freddie.

Examining the costs of Fannie and Freddie is more complicated than it might at first appear. The first arises because the extent of the loan guarantees extended through Fannie and Freddie and other major federal credit programs are left out of budget calculations, because in the government's view, they are non-governmental agencies. As the CBO regards them as government agencies, they regard the loan guarantees for Fannie and Freddie, which amounted to $3.2 tr and $2 tr, respectively, at the end of 2011, as part of the Budget, together with other major federal credit programs, such as the FHA, Veteran Home Loans and student loans. Taken together, these amount to $7.9 tr outside the budget, then 52% of the USA's GDP. The situation has improved somewhat since then, so that by the end of November 2012, the value of the loan guarantees for Fannie and Freddie fell to $2.7 trillion and $1.8 trillion, respectively, but still do not figure in budget calculations.

In September 2012, Chairman Bernanke announced the purchase of agency MBSs at a rate of $40 bn per month. The purchases are likely to be concentrated in newly issued agency MBSs in the to-be-announced market, because these have greater liquidity and are closely tied to primary mortgage rates. In his press conference of December 12, 2012, Bernanke announced that the Federal Open Market Committee had decided to continue its purchases of agency MBSs at the same pace, and to purchase longer-term Treasury securities, initially at $45bn per month, after its current program to extend the average maturity of its holdings is completed at the end of the year.

For Chairman Bernanke, the purpose of buying Fannie and Freddie's MBSs is not to assist in ensuring that they will not be able to rebuild their capital base. Instead, it is designed to boost employment through the housing market. It is supposed to push mortgage rates down, thus stimulating the market, leading to higher residential investment, rising house prices and stronger consumer confidence and consumption. By increasing MBS prices and lowering yields, it makes them less attractive so that banks will have to look elsewhere for profits. Meanwhile, the Federal Reserve Bank should be aware of another costly problem looming on the horizon, namely, the FHA.

To make matters worse, the FHA's 2011 Actuarial Report estimates that the FHA's Mutual Mortgage Insurance Fund's capital cushion now stands at $2.55 bn, $19 bn below its congressionally mandated level of about $22bn. Its equity cushion on $1.077 trillion of exposure means that the FHA is very highly leveraged, a ratio of 422:1. The report estimates about a 50% chance for home prices to fall further than estimated, exposing the FHA to increased losses, and a negative capital position which could reach $42bn. FHA estimated that it would reach the 2% capital compliance requirement in 2014, but this assumes that the cumulative increase in house prices will be 18% over the years 2012–2015.[11] The latest figures from the S&P/Case Schiller composite index (for September 2011) showed that house prices continued to fall in 20 metropolitan areas. That will mean that more homes will slip into negative equity, according to the 2010 CoreLogic report. The report, which was published in the first quarter of 2010, estimated that 13.5 million were or likely to fall into negative equity (those with less than 5% equity), 28% of all mortgages. That figure decreased slightly to 27.1% by the third quarter of 2011. Very few homes have the conventional 30-year mortgages with 20% down payment, only 12 million of the current 48 million homes. The remaining 75% of mortgaged homes may have an increased risk of falling into negative equity or delinquency, if the mortgages fall into one of the following categories:

- low down payment mortgages
- "exotic" subprime loans
- adjustable-rate mortgages with a reset to higher interest rates after 3 or more years
- two mortgages on the same property-a first mortgage and a "junior lien" such as a second mortgage or a home equity line of credit. Negative equity increases the likelihood of delinquency or foreclosure. The situation has improved somewhat since the publication of that report. The S&P Case Schiller index published in November 2012 showed that house prices rose in the first part of the year and the FHFA index showed a 4.5% increase overall. But to put this in context, house prices are still 30% below the 2006 peak.

The situation with the FHA has continued to deteriorate, as the figures released in the FHA's Actuarial Study in November 2012 for its main single family program[12] show. The capital reserve ratio fell to below zero to a negative 1.44%, that is, by −$13.5 bn, the lower estimate based on Moody's

July forecast projecting 10-year Treasuries in the calendar year Q3:12 to be over 2.2% and rising to 4.59% by 2014.

Loans insured before 2010 continue to be the prime source of stress on the Fund with fully $70bn in future claim payments attributable to the 2007–2009 books of business alone. The so-called "economic value" of the Fund, which means the difference between the expected insurance program revenues and the expected costs associated with defaults on the underlying mortgages is in negative territory.

It represents a shift in the economic value of $23bn in a single year, so the FHA is short of its legal capital requirement of 2% of outstanding mortgages.[13]

The reason for the difference between the estimates of the economic value is in the assumptions made by the independent actuary in his annual report. Basically, it is a bet on the future growth of the FHA's mortgage insurance, and not only for a year ahead. It is an estimate of the net worth of 7 years of mortgage insurance the FHA is expected to write. The true costs of the insurance are being underestimated because the risk and full cost of homeowners becoming unemployed has not been factored in, and the fact that the recent Federal Reserve policy to keep interest rates lower for longer than anticipated by the independent actuary will result in greater losses for the mortgage insurance portfolio. The key point that Congress should take on board is that the "FHA essentially has made an extremely large and highly leveraged bet that it can grow out of insolvency via profitable new insurance business."[14] But over 1 in 6 FHA loans are delinquent by 30 days or more, and most of these loans were originated in 2008, 2009 and 2010. There has been little change in the delinquency rates since 2011: if anything, rates have worsened. In September 2011, the 30-day delinquency rate was 16.78% and in September 2012, it was 17.3%. The serious delinquency rate was 8.77% in September 2011 and 9.62% in September 2012. Despite a slight improvement in the 30-day delinquency rate, which fell to 15.3% in the first three months of 2013, warnings about a bail-out for the FHA should be taken on board by the new Administration.

After conservatorship

The cost to taxpayers of supporting Fannie Mae and Freddie Mac and continuing their operations under conservatorship led to the production of a wide range of proposals for the federal role in the secondary market in the future. Many proposals have been produced with numerous variations on the themes of whether the Federal Government should continue to guarantee payments of certain types of mortgages or MBSs and if so, what the scope, structure and pricing of those guarantees should be. The key proposal, however, was put forward by the Treasury.

The Treasury White Paper

Timothy Geithner, Secretary to the Treasury introduced the White Paper, Reforming America's Housing Finance Market in February 2011. The Administration simply sets out three options and certain criteria. They are as follows:

Option 1 Privatised system of housing finance with government insurance role limited to FHA, USDA and the Department of Veterans Affairs' assistance for narrowly targeted groups of borrowers.

This option would dramatically reduce the government's role in insuring or guaranteeing mortgages, limiting it to the FHA and other programmes targeted to creditworthy lower- or moderate-income borrowers, the vast majority of the mortgage market to the private sector. The ability of the government to step in to ensure access to capital during a crisis would be limited under this option.

Option 2 Privatised system of housing finance with assistance from the FHA, USDA and the Department of Veterans' Affairs for narrowly targeted groups of borrowers and a guarantee mechanism to scale up during a crisis.

As with Option 1, the FHA and other narrowly targeted programmes would provide access to mortgage credit for low-and moderate-income borrowers, but the government's overall role in the housing finance system would be dramatically reduced. But the government would also develop a backstop mechanism to ensure access to credit during a housing crisis. This would mean having a minimum presence in the market during normal times, but the government would be ready to scale up to a larger share of the market as private capital withdraws in times of financial stress.

Option 3 Privatised system of housing finance with FHA, USDA and the Department of Veterans Affairs assistance for low and moderate-income borrowers and catastrophic reinsurance behind significant private capital.

Under this option, the mortgage market outside the FHA and other federal agency guarantee programmes would be driven by private investment decisions, with private capital taking the primary credit risk. To increase liquidity in the mortgage market and access to mortgages for creditworthy Americans as well as to ensure the government's ability to respond to future crises, the government would offer reinsurance for the securities of a targeted range of mortgages. Here Geithner envisages mortgages being insured by a group of private mortgage guarantor companies for which a government reinsurer would provide reinsurance provided certain conditions were met. A special premium would be charged for this to cover future claims and to recoup losses. This one has the advantage of providing the lowest cost access to mortgage credit of all three. None of these options envisage the continued existence of Fannie Mae and Freddie Mac.

The report does, however, contain various proposals designed to reduce the role of Fannie Mae and Freddie Mac in the mortgage system:

- Reduce the GSEs' market share by increasing the guarantee fees charged to lenders who sell mortgages to Fannie Mae and Freddie Mac. In return for this guarantee, Fannie Mae and Freddie Mac guarantee timely mortgage payments to investors that purchase their MBSs. This increase would reduce the profitability from selling mortgages to Fannie Mae and Freddie Mac and could encourage selling mortgages to investment banks and other securitizers;

- Reduce both profitability and risk by increasing capital requirements for Fannie Mae and Freddie Mac. This would require them to purchase credit-loss protection from private insurers;

- Reduce the size of the GSEs by requiring Fannie Mae and Freddie Mac to liquidate their investment portfolios as required under their support contracts with Treasury; and

- Reduce Fannie Mae's and Freddie Mac's share of the secondary mortgage market by lowering the high-cost area conforming loan limits (currently $729,750) to the Housing and Economic Recovery Act, 2008 HERA limits ($625,500). (The Continuing Appropriations Act, 2011 extended the limit until the end of the year).

Since the GSEs are in conservatorship, FHFA could implement all but the last without legislative action. Despite that possibility, Geithner resolutely refused to commit himself or the Administration to any one of them in a House Financial Services Committee hearing. He was equally indecisive about the timing: that should be neither too soon nor too long delayed. Acting too hastily to wind down Fannie Mae and Freddie Mac could destabilize the housing finance market or disrupt the broader recovery. On the other hand, a long-delayed solution would not help. A failure by Congress to approve legislation within the following 2 years would "exacerbate" market uncertainty and leave many of the "flaws in the market" unaddressed. The reason behind Secretary Geithner's stress on the timescale could be that under the present legal framework and conservatorship, only a limited range of options are available, bearing in mind that but for the provisions of HERA, the two GSEs would have been insolvent, owing to the unanticipated but continuing losses from foreclosures. These include the "bad bank" option, which would mean that, given the lack of private investment, the federal government would have to purchase the nonperforming assets. Some would like to see the senior preferred stock dividends reduced, thus saving about $15bn annually but would also reduce the federal government's income by the same amount. This would allow the GSEs to return to shareholder control but at the cost of government support which would then lead to expectations of future government support with the consequent moral hazard, which the GSEs exploited in the past.

If the GSEs were to return to solvency, then the restructuring options would be to

- return Fannie Mae and Freddie Mac to their shareholders with little or no change in their charters;

- eliminate their GSE status and convert them into private corporations;

- eliminate their GSE status and convert Fannie and Freddie into one or more government agencies;

- make supplementary changes to support the secondary mortgage market, such as providing government reinsurance of MBSs, or encouraging the use of covered bonds.

None of these approaches come close to identifying the source of the problems: hence these approaches, involving the retention of the GSEs in some form, even if they were feasible, run the risk of creating similar havoc in the financial system in the future. By intervening once, the federal government has turned the implicit government guarantee into an explicit one, just as investors thought throughout the years and were also encouraged to believe (despite the warnings to the contrary) by the CEOs and senior management of the GSEs. The Enterprises were able to exploit their dominant position in the marketplace through the privileges given to them by their charters. What has not attracted much attention is Secretary Geithner's introduction to the February White Paper. "Our plan champions the belief that Americans should have choices in housing that makes sense for them and their families. This means rental options near good schools and jobs ... and access to credit for those Americans who want to own their own homes ... and a helping hand for lower income Americans, who are burdened by the strain of high housing costs."[15]

In his report to Congress at the same time, Geithner set out his view of the future. "Private markets, subject to strong oversight and standards for consumer and investor protection, will be the primary source of mortgage credit and bear the burden for losses. Banks and other financial institutions will be required to hold more capital to withstand future recessions or significant declines in house prices and adhere to more conservative underwriting standards that require home owners to hold more equity in their homes. Securitisation should continue to play a major role in housing finance subject to greater risk retention, disclosure and other key reforms."[16]

All of the options involve government intervention either in the form of insurance, the use of some of the existing federal agencies or "catastrophic" reinsurance behind significant private capital. There are no clear details of what this would mean in practice and the extent to which government would be exposed to further costs at a time of crisis. The continued use of the FHA is open to the risks of insuring substandard mortgages, as the condition of its Mutual Mortgage Insurance Fund shows. The scandals of the seller down payment fraud should not be forgotten which the FHA knowingly encouraged. The required deposit was only 3% at best. At present, there is a direct endorsement programme in place, which allows lenders to underwrite and close mortgages without prior Housing and Urban Development Department HUD approval or review. Lenders are supposed to comply with all the relevant HUD regulations and to evaluate the borrower's ability to repay the mortgage. However, many examples of fraud or the failure to follow the required underwriting standards have come to light, partly from referrals from HUD to the Office of the Inspector General.[17] Successive federal governments have never provided HUD with adequate resources for the oversight of its own programmes. The reports of the Inspector General, both the brief reports on limited examinations of specific programmes and the overviews reinforce the point time and time again. It seems to be a role that demands the utmost patience, as so many reports result in so little improvement.

A much more radical approach is required, making use of the Geithner report, which does not envisage a future role for Fannie Mae and Freddie Mac. However, Geithner's proposals still lie on the table, and it is entirely unclear whether or not the new Administration will act on them. Given that Fannie and Freddie are now making a profit, which is being paid to the Treasury, (a nice little earner), it is unlikely that any radical change to Fannie and Freddie will take place in the near future.

These proposals were followed a year later by the Federal Housing Agency's strategic plan, which was published in February 2012, setting out three strategic goals of which the first and most important is to "build a new infrastructure for the secondary mortgage market," since the United States does not have a private sector infrastructure capable of securitising the $100bn per month of new mortgages being originated. The aim is to build a new infrastructure for both Fannie Mae and Freddie Mac (and to incorporate Ginnie Mae as well) whilst acknowledging that the future may not include the two GSEs. In the absence of any functioning market on which investors could rely, it was deemed necessary to improve the existing structures or replace the securities platform altogether.

Following the publication of the Strategic Plan in February, the FHFA published a consultation paper in October 2012, setting out the functions to be carried out by the single platform in great detail. Unlike the GSEs' outmoded proprietary infrastructures, the new platform must not be confined to their business models, but must be designed in such a way, that it could be used by any issuer, servicer, agent or any other business which wishes to participate.

It should contain two elements: the usual functions routinely required in the securitisation market, such as issuing securities, providing disclosures, paying investors and disseminating data. The platform would be essential, whether or not policy-makers decided that there should still be a federal guarantor of MBSs. Standardisation across key market functions would add "depth and liquidity to the market."[18]

The platform could provide other important functions as well, such as a master servicing function, including asset and cash management, standardisation interfaces to servicers, guarantors and aggregators, servicing metrics, data validation and reporting or data validation (servicing and issuance) with the securitisation platform storing loan level, pool level and bond level data to improve data integrity and advance transparency and efficiency in the securitisation market. The latter would be facilitated the Uniform Mortgage Data program, a result of Fannie and Freddie working together to produce standard terms, definitions and industry standard data reporting requirements. Together with the Loan Level Disclosure Initiative would produce loan-level investor disclosures both at the point of origination and throughout the life of a security, enabling private investors to efficiently measure and price mortgage credit risk. If all of this had been in place long before 2008, then the quality of the loans incorporated into MBSs would have been transparent and the secondary mortgage market may not have collapsed with such devastating effects on the rest of the world.

However, the strategic plan met with lukewarm support from the industry, to say the least. The FHFA was praised for designing a platform, which could accommodate any conceivable secondary market structure and financing arrangements. A number of problems were identified, including issues around the ownership, governance, management and regulation of the resulting platform and the difficulty of providing enough flexibility to allow for a wide range of credit enhancement structures.

Others insist that the platform should be confined to the GSEs' immediate needs and those of its participating lenders, servicers and investors. Extending the scope to include structured transactions, risk sharing and credit distribution capabilities through a completely different legal framework (based on a model pooling and servicing agreement) are ambitious goals which would take a long time to develop. Furthermore, the largest mortgage lenders have spent extensive resources and time in building their own platforms to meet their own needs and these are increasingly subject to the Security and Exchange Commission (SEC) regulation and the Consumer Financial Protection Bureau rules, designed to achieve the same policy goals. Despite the criticisms of his strategic plan, most agree that his efforts to produce a unified platform or a single national securitisation infrastructure for a post-GSE reform regime are both professional and principled. For his part, however, conservatorship has already continued for too long. The sub-title of his "Strategic Plan for

Enterprise Conservatorships," "The Next Chapter to a Story that Needs an Ending" indicates his views on the indecision of politicians. That may change in President Obama's second Administration, but perhaps without DeMarco's leadership if Washington rumours are to be believed.

The affordable housing ideology lingers on

Whereas home ownership is desirable for many individuals, it is not possible to bring this about for all American families, when individuals and families have low and/or uncertain incomes and are not in a position to make a reasonable down payment and sustain monthly mortgage payments. The attempt to achieve home ownership for such families involved setting "affordable housing" goals and encouraging what were euphemistically called more "flexible" under writing standards. These standards were not set by the banking industry, realtors, mortgage companies, mortgage brokers, appraisers or any other elements of the mortgage finance industry on their own.

Following the Boston Handbook, Clinton's National Partnership Strategy explicitly set out what those lower underwriting standards should be, making it clear that these should be regarded as the appropriate standards by government. Lack of cash for down payments and lack of income, so there should be financing strategies, "fuelled by the creativity of the private and public sectors" to overcome them.

President Bush reintroduced a similar partnership in 2002. "We must begin to close this home ownership gap by dismantling the barriers that prevent minorities from owning a piece of the American dream," setting out to create 5.5 million new minority home owners by the end of the decade. He did at least offer cash. Between 2002 and 2006, the Administration spent $412m on its American Dream Down Payment Initiative to help first-time home buyers with the costs associated with down payments and a further $176m on home ownership counselling to improve financial education and money management (of limited use, since in the last analysis, it cannot create income which is not there).[19]

The Presidents were not the only ones committed to the ideology. It was all-pervasive with one law maker after another stating his public commitment to the belief, and countless others, economists, federal officials, bankers, brokers and realtors at least paying lip service to the ideology. Those wishing to restrain lending practices or to reduce subsidies to Fannie Mae and Freddie Mac were accused of making "affordable housing" more expensive for minorities and low-to-moderate income families and minorities. Many members of the House and Senate did not realise that more flexible underwriting standards inevitably opened the door to predatory and abusive lending practices: they sought to restrict the activities of such lenders, but on the grounds that this made lending more expensive for such groups. Their attempts to curb such lending were relatively ineffective, partly owing to the difficulties of definition and successful court action.

Others adopt the "affordable housing" mantra

Apparently having learnt nothing from the American housing crisis and the extensive damage it inflicted on the rest of the world, Prime Minister Cameron, when he announced a £930m injection into the housing market, said he wanted to make the "dream of home ownership" a reality for more people. "You always remember that moment, if you've done it, when you get that key and you walk into your first flat. It's a magic moment. It's a moment I want everyone in this country to have, not just better off people." His words echo those of President Clinton's announcement of the National Home Ownership Strategy in 1995.

The scheme he announced is indeed limited for now. It covers new build homes for first-time buyers. It is accompanied by an "ambitious scheme" to underwrite mortgages for new homes that would allow banks to cut deposits to 5%, with the government and the builders sharing a proportion of the risk of buyers defaulting on the mortgages, with tax payers having to pick up a maximum of £1 bn in liabilities.[20] Government-backed insurance is a reminder of the activities of the US Federal Housing Administration FHA. Its insurance scheme was supposed to be self-financing, which was not in fact the case, as has been demonstrated in this book, and the FHA itself is teetering on the edge of insolvency. Cutting the required deposits to 5% is an understandable move with such high house prices, for which there are many reasons in the UK. It does carry serious risks.

The NewBuy Guarantee scheme was formally opened in March 2012. "Strong families and stable communities are built from good homes. That's why I want us to build more homes and I want more people to have the chance to own their own home," the Prime Minister stated. The launch went ahead despite reports that some mortgage lenders are wary of participating in the scheme: six mortgage lenders, including Barclays, Nationwide and NatWest, have signed up to take part. They have been persuaded to take part because house builders have agreed to put 3.5% of the purchase price into an indemnity fund for each property sold, while the government will provide a 5.5% guarantee. The Council of Mortgage Lenders (CML) backs the scheme, but has acknowledged concerns about the increased risks of low-deposit mortgages. CML insists that lenders will not be relaxing their affordability criteria. All the mortgages offered are fixed rates for 2 years with the risk of difficulties of remortgaging if property prices fall still further over the next 2 years, when their loan-to-value may have risen above 95%. The other risk is an increase in interest rates, which may make monthly repayments too difficult. By the end of September, it became clear that take-up has been slow, with the largest house builder, Persimmon, having sold only 220 new homes: one reports a weekly total of three or four houses a week and another 70 houses per week. This was followed by the Chancellor's announcement of another risky scheme, called "Help to Buy" in March 2013, due to come into being in January 2014.

Both schemes are limited at present, but political pressures of all kinds will intensify for the schemes to be extended and for the government's insurance to be increased. He would do better to consider the proposals put forward by David Miles, a member of the Monetary Policy Committee, with its examination of various forms of outside equity funding, including shared ownership schemes and equity loans, enabling home owners to decide how much risk they wanted to take on.[21] It is simply not possible, however desirable it may be for everyone to own their own homes. The American experience over the 13 years from 1995 to 2008 amply demonstrated that. For once, the lessons of history should surely be learnt.

A very early warning

The ideology blinded too many to reality. "The ideal of home ownership is so integral a part of the American Dream that its value for individuals, for families, for communities, and for society is scarcely questioned … However, critics of homeownership point out that the economic benefits of homeownership for lower income and minority families should also be balanced against its financial risks. The lower average incomes and educational achievement of these groups make them particularly vulnerable to economic downturns that can result in job loss and, eventually foreclosure." This is the key warning contained in the Urban Policy Brief, which HUD commissioned and which was published in August 1995.[22]

The report also points out that "many external factors can affect whether and at what rate a home's value increases or decreases. Changes in interest rates influence the demand for housing and its attractiveness relative to other investments. Regional economic downturns … can severely depress housing prices. The dynamics of a particular housing market or the fortunes of a particular neighbourhood can also be strong determinants of local home values." It is a pity that President Clinton did not pay close attention to these words in the report, which was prepared for him as part of the National Homeownership Strategy. The dangers of home ownership for those very families and minorities he wished to help are clearly spelt out, as well as the dangers arising from external factors over which families have no control whatsoever and are also ill-equipped to meet, not, for example, having sufficient financial resources to ride out the storm.

Other Presidents before Clinton had supported home ownership as part of the American Dream, but had not sought to use the agencies of the federal government to turn the dream into a reality. President Clinton's plan (and to a lesser extent that of President Bush) was to ensure that all of the federal agencies, working together with all those involved in the financing and construction of housing from every point of view, encouraged or promoted home ownership for low-income families and minorities. Much more than that, he used the federal agencies, and the GSEs in particular, as the levers at his disposal to achieve the target. Five years later, he could boast of a home ownership rate of 67%, and although minorities were still lagging behind, they also made gains. Clinton set the wheels in motion. Bush did little to stop the juggernaut of "affordable," or "subprime lending," which rolled on without any obstacles in its way. But when house prices began to fall and interest rates began to rise, almost half of all outstanding mortgages were revealed as subprime as interest rates rose and house prices began to fall. The juggernaut shuddered to a halt.

The fault did not just lie with the banks, for as Professor Stan Leibowitz succinctly expressed it, "From the current handwringings, you'd think that the banks came up with the idea of looser underwriting standards on their own, with regulators just asleep on the job. In fact, it was the regulators who relaxed these standards-at the behest of community groups and 'progressive political forces'"[23]

Chairman Bernanke, in his description of the causes of the financial crisis, claimed that the "extended use of this model to finance subprime mortgages through securitisation was mismanaged at several points, including the initial underwriting, which deteriorated markedly in part because of incentive schemes that effectively rewarded originators for the quantity rather than the quality of the mortgages extended."[24] This seems to be an extraordinary statement, ignoring as it does, the politicians' insistence on affordable housing at the cost of lowering underwriting standards. That was all undertaken with Federal encouragement and approval. Fannie and Freddie's rush to purchase loans on volume rather than quality was all undertaken to boost their earnings. This is not to suggest that lenders, the originators, were not to blame, but their actions have to be seen in the context of two decades of federal policy.

Professor Lawrence White, in his statement to the House Subcommittee on Capital Markets, Insurance and the GSEs, elaborated on the range of federal responsibilities: "The creation and expansion of Fannie Mae and Freddie Mac did not occur in a vacuum. They were, and continue to be, only one part of a much larger mosaic of governmental policies, at all levels of government, to encourage the construction and consumption of housing ... explicit subsidies for mortgage finance, through the FHA, the Department of Veterans Affairs, Ginnie Mae, as well as through some states' mortgage finance subsidy programmes, implicit subsidies through the GSEs; specialised charters for depositary institutions (thrifts) that are expected to focus on residential mortgage finance..."[25] Not all of these helped to create the huge subprime market, but this does emphasize the extent to which the federal government used so many of these federal agencies as a means of attaining its political aims. When it all went wrong, politicians both in the US and elsewhere sought to deflect attention from their own actions by the ever-popular sport of attacking and blaming the banks. Of course, many of the banks played their part as well, but the prime responsibility is a political one of seeking to increase home ownership at any price.

Has anything been learnt?

On November 15, 2012, in a speech on "Challenges in Housing and Mortgage Markets," Chairman Bernanke remarked that there were improvements in the housing sector, adding much-needed growth and jobs, but the sector still faced significant obstacles. Although house prices had increased nationally, they were nowhere near the peaks in 2006. Residential investment had risen by about 15% and sales of existing and new homes have edged up. Growth was fuelled by record levels of affordability and historically low mortgage rates. But about 20% of mortgage borrowers are underwater and 7% of mortgages are either more than 90 days overdue or are in the process of foreclosure. The national home ownership rate fell to 65% from 69% achieved in 2004. Since the peak of mortgage lending in 2006, the number of mortgages offered to African Americans and Hispanics has fallen by over 65%, whereas lending to non-Hispanic whites has fallen by less than 50%. Most of the hard-won gains in home ownership made by low-income or minority families in the past 15 years or so have been reversed. Among all income groups, between 2007 and 2010, these have fallen most for "households with income of $20,000 or less," which is hardly surprising!

Chairman Bernanke then comments that "lenders began tightening mortgage credit standards in 2007 and have not significantly eased standards since then. Terms and standards have tightened most for borrowers with lower credit scores and less money available for a down payment." He accepts that some tightening of credit standards was an appropriate response to the lax lending conditions in the lead-up to the crisis, but states that "it seems likely at this point that the pendulum has swung too far the other way, and that overly tight lending standards may now be preventing credit worthy borrowers from buying homes, thereby slowing the revival in housing and impeding the economic recovery."[26] A worrying statement from the Chairman, given the history of politically mandated "flexible" underwriting standards over the years leading up to the crisis. Has nothing been learnt? With house prices rising for the first time since quarter 2, 2007 at a rate of 4.34%, and an optimistic outlook for 2013, the past will be too easily forgotten.[27]

The new Consumer Financial Protection Bureau (CFPB) finally published the amendments to Regulation Z (which implements the Truth in Lending Act), which currently prohibits the lender from offering a higher-priced mortgage without regard to the borrower's ability to repay the loan.[28] This complicated regulation (some 150 pages) seeks to prevent the "deterioration of lending standards to the dangerous levels, that contributed to the financial crisis." The regulation introduces the concept of a "qualifying mortgage," which is one in which it can be presumed that the lender made a reasonable determination of the consumer's ability to pay, such as the prospective borrower's current and expected income, employment status and other debts. No particular underwriting model is required. The rule sets the qualified mortgage debt-to-income threshold at 43%, and forbids "no or low documentation loans."

That is an important restriction, but it does not include any consideration and verification of a consumer's credit history, because "the statute is fundamentally about assuring the mortgage credit consumers receive is affordable."[29] This is perhaps the reason why the statute does not require lenders to obtain or consider a consolidated credit score or minimum credit score. A lender "may give various aspects of a consumer's credit history as much or as little weight as is appropriate to reach a reasonable, good faith determination of ability to repay."[30] Add to that the fact that there is no reference to the importance of loan-to-value ratios, the Ability-to-Pay regulation is unlikely to prevent the proliferation of subprime mortgages, as the housing market improves. Yet, just based on a single "qualification," the subprime loan then becomes a prime loan and the non-qualified mortgages become subprime. The regulation also contains a number of references to a "conclusive presumption of complains or a safe harbour" for lenders, rather than for consumers. This is not quite the energetic protection of consumers, which might have been expected. It seems that the inability to identify the features of subprime loans and to recognise their importance persists, leaving open the possibility of further problems in the future.

What happened to those minority and low-income home buyers?

It should be a sobering thought that so many people to whom they sought to extend the "benefits" of home ownership are suffering even more than before. It is true that some brought it on themselves by applying for "liar loans" or buying property carelessly, but many did not. The situation in the housing market is dire with one in seven borrowers delinquent on their mortgages or already in foreclosure and more than one in four mortgages underwater. Various analyses suggest that the number of foreclosures by the time the crisis abates could be anywhere between 8 and 13 million (out of 55 million mortgages outstanding in 2008). Here is one striking and thorough description of what the effects of the fallout from the affordable housing policy are, when market and economic conditions change.

Julia Gordon, in her statement to the House Committee on Oversight and Government Reform, sub-committee on Insurance, Housing and Community Opportunity, describes the effects of foreclosures not just on families losing their homes, but also on whole neighbourhoods which have effectively closed down. States and local authorities have both lost revenue and have had to face additional costs, as the large number of vacant properties attracts crime, arson and squatters. For those who have kept up mortgage payments, the value of their property also falls as the foreclosure signs go up. "Depending on the geography and time period, the estimated impact of each foreclosure ranged from 0.6% to 1.6% in lost value to nearby homes." The losses may be greater, if, with the "no recourse" mortgages, the "owners" trash the property before returning the keys to the lender through the mail. "These losses are on top of the overall loss in property value due to overall house declines."[31]

Those who have owned homes and lost them not only suffer financial losses but also the loss of a roof over their head, and all the money and emotion spent in creating a home. The crisis also affects tenants, who are also affected by foreclosures, since banks now own the housing stock rather than landlords or investors, and, although tenants now have some legal protection, most will ultimately be forced to leave their homes. Some have been kept in their homes through permanent loan modification programmes through the Government Home Affordable Modification Program (HAMP) or proprietary modifications, the numbers in foreclosure continue to overwhelm those borrowers who have been helped. In the end, the federal affordable housing programmes have inflicted more pain and suffering on those it has sought to help than anything else on those it has sought to help.[32]

A plethora of law suits

Attention to Fannie and Freddie's future may be diverted by the law suits against Fannie and Freddie and the banks. The most significant law suits indicate quite different perspectives on the nature and causes of the financial crisis. The size of the subprime market, and Fannie and Freddie's role, both in encouraging its development and in benefitting from it, were confirmed by the SEC's announcement that it had charged six former top executives with securities fraud, alleging that they knew and approved of misleading statements, claiming that the companies had minimal holdings of higher risk loans, including subprime loans.[33]

The details show that Fannie and Freddie made a series of materially false and misleading public disclosures to give the impression that the Enterprises had far less exposure to subprime and Alt-A mortgages than they had between

December 6, 2006 and August 8, 2008. For example, Fannie Mae excluded its Expanded Approval loans, specifically targeted towards borrowers with lower credit histories: for example, Fannie Mae and its senior executives knew and approved the decision to under-report its Alt-A loan exposures, when on March 31, 2007, it declared that its exposure was 11% of its portfolio of single family loans, when it was 18%. Its public disclosures did not include the data on credit risk associated with such loans, when this was reported to and tracked by senior management in terms of acquisition volume, delinquencies and credit losses. In other words, all the information on loans and Fannie's strategy was contained in internal documents, which did not correspond with its public filings.

Freddie Mac led investors to believe that the firm used a broad definition of subprime loans and had disclosed all its single family exposure. By December 2006, the single family business was exposed to approximately $141 bn of loans described internally as "subprime" or "subprime like," accounting for 10% of the portfolio: it grew to about $244 bn or 14% by June 2008. Freddie Mac adjusted its Loan Prospector program in 1997 to allow for subprime loans (described as A-minus loans) on the same terms as an "Accept" loan. Freddie Mac developed Loan Prospector over time, but its strategy was to continue to purchase subprime loans. The meeting notes, warnings from its Enterprise Risk Management Committee and date from its LP Emulator, tracking the risks associated with subprime loans, all show that the senior management knew what was happening at the time. But, during the relevant period (March 23, 2007–August 6, 2008), Freddie Mac provided various estimates of its exposure to subprime loans in its single family guarantee business, ranging from $2bn to $6bn, whereas the real exposure was between $140bn and $244bn of loans (by June 2008), which Freddie internally recognises as "subprime," "otherwise subprime" or "subprime-like." At the same time, Fannie had $641bn in Alt-A loans (23% of the single family loan guarantee portfolio), while investors were told it only had $300bn (11%). Taking these and other details of the complaint into account, their high-risk loans at the time amounted to $2 trillion.[34] This also validates Ed Pinto's estimate that when the full force of the financial crisis hit in 2008, approximately 27m or 49% of the 55 million outstanding single-family first mortgage loans had high-risk characteristics, making them far more likely to default.

That such discrepancies between the internal documents presented to senior executives and public statements, including statutory disclosures, were not discovered until 2011 demonstrate the utter ineffectiveness of the OFHEO and the dilatoriness of Congress in granting neither the resources nor the tools to the former in particular; the effect on the markets of the "affordable housing" ideology, as implemented by the goals set by HUD and successive Secretaries for housing. For example, HUD urged Fannie and Freddie in a 2000 rule-making to "play a significant role in the subprime market," adding that "the line between what is today considered a subprime loan versus a prime loan will likely deteriorate, making expansion by the GSEs look more like an increase in the prime market … This melding of the markets could occur even if many of the underlying characteristics of subprime borrowers and the market's (i.e. non-GSE participants) evaluation of the risks posed by these borrowers remain unchanged … Lending to these credit-impaired borrowers will, in turn, increasingly make good business for the mortgage market."[35]

None of the evidence cited by the SEC and HUD's statement of policy for Fannie and Freddie prevented the US Department of Justice from bringing another civil fraud case concerning mortgage loans sold to Fannie Mae and Freddie Mac on October 24, shortly before the Presidential election on November 6, 2012. Manhattan US Attorney, Preet Bharara, announced that it was suing the Bank of America for a multimillion mortgage fraud against the GSEs. He also stated that it was the sixth time in less than 18 months that his office had been compelled to sue a major US bank for "reckless mortgage practices" in the leadup to the financial crisis. "Countrywide and the Bank of America made disastrously bad loans and stuck the tax payer with the bill … (and) these toxic products were sold to the government sponsored enterprises as good loans." Bharara had also brought mortgage fraud cases against Citibank, Flagstar Bank F.S.B., and Deutsche Bank in February 2012. These three banks settled out of court and paid fines.

The Bank of America (BoA) could have responded by describing the relationship between Countrywide and Fannie from 1999 onwards, but BoA, having spent a year in fractious disputes with Fannie Mae over the extent of the bank's liability for mortgages it sold to them which later incurred losses when the home owners defaulted, agreed to pay $11.6bn to end the dispute over putbacks, the loans that Fannie insists lenders buy back since they were subprime loans. The chief executive, Brian Moynihan stated, "Together, these agreements are a significant step in resolving our remaining legacy mortgage issues, further streamlining and simplifying the company … We sharpen our focus on serving our three customer groups and helping them move the economy forward."

The lawsuit against Wells Fargo also announced in October 2012 that the bank did not underwrite over 100,000 loans to be eligible for FHA insurance. At the time of writing, Wells Fargo planned to vigorously defend itself against this action. No doubt reference will be made to the FHA's continued acceptance of seller-funded down payment mortgages, a scandal which dragged on for many years, and the repeated warnings by the GAO and David Stevens, Commissioner for FHA, about the low credit quality of the loans the FHA insured, as well as HUD's lack of oversight!

It is extraordinary to see Fannie and Freddie presented as innocent dupes, when Fannie Mae had entered into a well-publicised exclusive agreement with Countrywide to purchase billions of dollars at a discounted rate of 13%

for every loan it guaranteed as far back as July 1999. Countrywide was well known as a leading supplier of subprime mortgages; indeed, a study carried out for the Fannie Mae Foundation pointed out that Countrywide "has played a significant role in extending the reach of the secondary mortgage market by working with the GSEs to develop new affordable lending products."[36]

Countrywide and Fannie Mae entered into a further strategic alliance in 2005, so that during each quarter, Countrywide was required to sell at least 70% of all "Expanded Criteria Mortgages" to Fannie Mae. Both companies pledged to continue a "favoured relationship" in which they were "committed to the business success of the other party." By then, one in every four mortgages purchased by Fannie Mae and one in every ten purchased by Freddie Mac was from Countrywide.[37]

Other mortgages were sold to Fannie, Freddie and the FHA by leading subprime lenders, including Wells Fargo, Washington Mutual (now failed), Chase Home Finance, Citimortgage, Lehman Brothers, Morgan Stanley, Goldman Sachs and New Century Financial until March 2007, when Fannie Mae ended the partnership and the bank collapsed shortly afterwards. Contrary to what many believed, there were no legal restrictions on the credit quality of the residential mortgages Fannie and Freddie could buy, despite Franklin Raines' misleading statements about mortgages "conforming to our standards." The only standard set out in their charters was the size of the mortgage loan with an LTV of over 80% when originated, and the requirement for such loans to have private mortgage insurance. Apart from that, the regulations allowed Fannie and Freddie to purchase loans which met the standards set by private mortgage lenders, but also which allowed them to meet the goals set by HUD, thus giving them an entirely free hand. Those underwriting standards were strongly influenced to say the least, by the Administration's insistence that these standards should be "more flexible" so that home ownership would be increased among the minorities and the less well-off.

Fannie Mae and Freddie Mac should be phased out of existence

The federal role in the secondary market was designed to achieve two public purposes: to help to ensure a steady supply of financing for residential mortgages and to provide subsidised assistance for mortgages for housing for low- and moderate-income families. As far as the latter is concerned, the subsidies made very little impact on the cost of loans for the target group. The government achieved the latter policy by using Fannie Mae and Freddie Mac to increase the liquidity of mortgages and MBSs. They were thought to be essential for this purpose. But they are not.

They had such a purpose when banks in the US were restricted to operating in only one state, and then only allowed to open branches with the approval of the regulators. In many states, banks were prohibited from operating more than one branch office. The result was that the banking system of very small banks, even as late as 1994. In June 1994, there were 8,614 FDIC-insured financial institutions with deposits of less than $100m.

The origins of the GSEs are to be found in the restructuring of the banking system after the Great Depression with the establishment of the FHA in 1934, followed by splitting Fannie Mae into two parts in 1968, Ginnie Mae and Fannie Mae, which then became the hybrid organisation it is now, with competition from the then newly established Freddie Mac, created with the same purpose in 1970. Both GSEs were to ensure liquidity in the housing market by purchasing conventional, non-guaranteed loans originated by the savings and loans and other depository institutions through buying the mortgages and repackaging them as bonds. Both grew rapidly during the savings and loans crisis (1979–1981), which was partly due to very small thrifts, inevitably with a small deposit base, lending long and borrowing short. Then, interest rates began to rise and savers turned to the better interest rates offered by money markets. Fannie Mae and Freddie Mac provided the remaining thrifts with liquidity and a means of selling their conventional loans and their adjustable rate mortgages, which were allowed after 1991. Then, the GSEs did have a role in providing liquidity to the market. That role is no longer necessary.

The banking system was transformed in 1994 with the passage of the Riegle-Neal Interstate Banking and Branching Efficiency Act, which allowed banks to operate widespread interstate branching networks, virtually for the first time in American banking. Prior to the Act, there were only 10 commercial banks operating a total of 30 branches across state lines. The Act led to a spate of mergers and acquisitions, creating many more large banks. Such banks do not need Fannie Mae and Freddie Mac to create liquidity. They can build up much larger deposit and savings bases, and sell their own private label securities. Chairman Greenspan spelt out as such in his testimony to the Senate Committee on Banking in 2004:

"The key to developing markets was securitisation, and Fannie and Freddie played a critical role in developing and promoting mortgage securitisation ... Securitisation by Fannie and Freddie allows mortgage originators to separate themselves from almost all aspects of risks associated with mortgage lending ... This development was particularly important before the emergence of truly nationwide banking institutions because it provided a dramatically improved method for diversifying mortgage credit risk.... During the 1980s, the GSEs led the private sector in innovation, and their contribution enhanced the stability of our financial markets. Mortgage securitization continues to perform this crucial function, and *its techniques have now been applied by the private sector in many markets ... Moreover, credit supply is far more stable today than it was because it is now founded on a much broader base of potential sources of funds. The aspiring home owner no longer depends on the willingness of the commercial bank or savings and loan association to hold his or her mortgage.*"(italics mine).[38] Any argument that the GSEs were no longer necessary would simply not have been heard at that time.

Some are beginning to look at the way in which European housing markets operate, to see if anything can be learnt from them. Professor Jaffe argues that the "private market mortgages will be intrinsically safer, with default and foreclosure outcomes that more closely resemble the European markets than the recent U.S. experience." He bases this on the argument that "mortgage default is costly to all parties" and that risk would be priced effectively with the full cost of the risks being met by banks and investors.[39]. This might well be a too optimistic view, unless it is clearly recognised that the proper functioning of the mortgage finance market will depend on good lending and underwriting practices being properly enforced, and the 'no recourse' option for mortgages being removed.[40]

There are, however, two risks which were peculiar to the US mortgage market: the affordable housing ideology and the lowering of underwriting standards which were part of it, and the implicit government guarantee for GSEs MBSs. The removal of these two elements would have the benefit of allowing the mortgage finance market to develop as a private market along European lines. Those looking to the future development of US mortgage finance are increasingly looking to the European markets (as opposed to the repeated refrain over the years that the US mortgage market was "world class" and "the envy of the world."). They note that many other industrialised countries without GSEs have achieved home ownership rates comparable with that of the US or even higher, in fact.

Bernanke points out the difficulties in successful mortgage securitisation. The ultimate investors must be persuaded that the credit quality of the underlying mortgages is high (or even know with a high degree of certainty exactly what the quality of such mortgages is), and that the origination-to-distribution process is managed so that the originators, such a mortgage brokers and bankers, have an incentive to undertake careful underwriting before they will be willing to acquire and trade mortgages.. Because the pools of assets underlying MBSs have highly correlated risks, including interest-rate, prepayment and credit risks, the institutions and other investors that hold these securities must have the capacity to manage their risks carefully. MBSs are complex amalgamations of underlying mortgages, they may also be difficult to price, so that transparency about the underlying assets and the MBSs itself is essential.[41] The chairman is undoubtedly entirely correct, but unfortunately these conditions were not met in the years prior to the crisis. Various aspects of the process were not regulated or inadequately regulated, and that is where full and detailed regulatory preparation will need to be made. The private label MBS market virtually ceased to exist and is unlikely to return in the current circumstances, but presumably will do so in the future.

With fears about the safety of the private label MBS (and the array of complex financial instruments which also helped to bring about the collapse of the market), policy makers have begun to consider the use of covered bonds. These are debt obligations issued by financial institutions and secured by a pool of high-quality mortgages and other assets. These are a major source of mortgage funding in a number of European mortgage markets with about $3 trillion outstanding in 2008. Such instruments are subject to statutory and supervisory regulation, designed to protect the interests of covered bond investors from the risk of insolvency of the issuing bank. The government generally provides strong assurances to investors by having bank supervisors ensure that the cover pool assets backing the bonds are of high quality and that the cover pool is well managed. The market has survived the ongoing crisis well, but investors are aware that these cannot be regarded as risk-free, and both the bank's status and the country of the issuer are more serious considerations than they were in the past.

A look at home ownership rates in 2008 shows that despite all the efforts of the GSEs and the affordable housing programmes, compared with Europe, the US ranked only ninth out of 17 developed countries even when home ownership was at its peak (67.8%).[42] Foreclosure rates are much lower in European countries compared with the higher levels of foreclosures in the US even for the UK, Spain and Ireland. This is why some in the US are looking to Europe as they see a fully privatised market operating successfully without the array of federal agencies and implicit government guarantees.

In doing so, they note that "no recourse" mortgages do not exist. In the US, legal access to recourse varies from one state to another, and even, where it is allowed, it is not often applied, at least until recently. The lack of recourse application arises because a bank must meet quite stringent consumer protection conditions before it can obtain a recourse judgement. Borrowers can always apply for a relatively easy bankruptcy. In Europe, it is possible for a lender to repossess the property, although it is not an option that lenders wish to exercise, except as a last resort. They prefer to renegotiate the terms of the loan, if possible. The "no recourse" approach, as noted, does mean that the borrower simply walks away from the property, often trashing it before s/he goes. From this, it can be seen that many aspects of alternative approaches are being examined in detail and need to be examined in detail, before America takes the plunge into a world without Fannie and Freddie and all the other federal agencies. Policy makers in the US can see that other markets have not only functioned well without Fannie and Freddie, but also most have survived in a somewhat better shape.

Whether law makers will look more closely at the operation of other housing markets is open to doubt. The law suits all give contradictory messages about what really went wrong. All the banks challenged by Preet Bharara have settled out of court. The decision to settle reinforces the view that Wall Street was to blame for the crisis. The SEC Complaint has yet to be decided. Timothy Geithner has left the new Administration, leaving open the possibility of the current Treasury rule, requiring Fannie and Freddie pay their profits to the Treasury being repealed, thus allowing them to rebuild their resources, so that they continue in existence. The current profitability of Fannie and Freddie makes that less likely, since their profits are a welcome addition to the Treasury's funds. Bernanke's suggestion that underwriting rules are too strict, in a speech, which suggests that nothing has been learnt and contains all the "affordable housing" rhetoric, might just be an indication that Congress will postpone action on Fannie and Freddie and maintain the "affordable housing" ideology. If that turns out to be the case, then investors should examine any American MBSs with great care before making any commitment to purchase them.

And the rest of the world?

The future of mortgage finance the United States became a matter of international concern, given the continuing global financial crisis, which clearly started with problems in the US subprime sector, because that sector was much larger than many realised at the time: it was almost half of the outstanding 55 million mortgages in 2008. Subprime loans were part of complex and opaque financial instruments, including MBSs, credit default swaps (CDSs), CDOs and credit derivatives. Risk assessments increasingly lacked clarity, and the incentives for due diligence, never very strong, became weaker. Loan originators concentrated on volume in order to generate fees. Balance sheets had become more opaque. Reliance on wholesale funding increased systemic risk.

That was the background. Then, falling house prices and higher interest rates led to a rising tide of defaults, and the very complex instruments, which had seemed such an innovative way of distributing risk, now undermined price discovery, freezing the market and bringing securitization to a halt. The use of CDOs and special investment vehicles meant that no one knew which banks and other financial institutions held which assets or anything about their quality. As a result, banks were unwilling to lend to one another, thereby causing the credit crunch. That quickly spread to other advanced economies, because MBSs and other instruments were widely held by financial institutions as well as by central banks. Through these direct exposures and associated funding problems, banks throughout Europe were quickly affected, with some significant banks having to be rescued or merged with others.

The sheer size of the US financial market and its central role as an investment destination contributed to the rapid spread of the crisis. At the time, US financial assets constituted about 31% of global financial assets and the US dollar share in reserve currency assets is about 62%. It is not, however, just a question of size, but also of confidence. It is sometimes argued that the direct exposure to US subprime was not so large as to cause the financial crisis, but that is to miss the point. It was both the complexity and opacity of the new structured investment instruments, including the repackaging of US asset-backed securities, which made it difficult to identify counterparties' exposure to the subprime. The shock was further intensified by the fact that foreign banks had substantially increased their cross-border dollar liabilities in recent years, partly to fund their purchases of dollar assets, such as US asset-backed securities. To all of these issues, the facts of instant communication and media speculation should be added as well as the interconnectedness of the banks and other financial institutions, especially between developed countries. All of these factors help to explain how a "domestic housing slump turned into a global financial crisis,"[43] and one which seems never-ending as, it takes yet another twist and turn, with continuing anxieties about the safety and soundness of the banking system and sovereign debt.

All of this seems a far cry from the introduction of the National Home Ownership Strategy in 1995. But that was the first step towards the unchecked and largely unregulated growth of the subprime mortgage market with all the consequences for the rest of the world. Then President Clinton said, "The goal of this strategy, to boost homeownership to 67.5% by the year 2000, would take us to an all-time high, helping as many as 8 million American families to cross that threshold … *and we're going to do it without spending more tax money.*" If the former President were to say that again today, he would be greeted by hollow laughter echoing around the globe.

Notes

Chapter 1 The Seeds Are Sown

1 HUD Urban Policy Brief, Homeownership & Its Benefits, Policy Brief No 2, 1995.
   T. Baum & M. Schwarz, Owner-Renter. Differences in Political and Social Attachment, Nat. Association of Realtors, 1989.
   T. Baum & P. Kingston, Homeownership & Social Attachment, Sociological Perspectives, 27(2), 1984.
   D. Diasquale & E. Glaeser, Incentives and Social Capital: Are Homeowners Better Citizens? Journal of Urban Economics, 1999.
   G. Galster, Homeowner and Neighborhood Investment, Duke University Press, 1987.
   P. Kingston & J. Fries, Having a Stake in the System, Social Science Quarterly 75(3), 1994.
   W. Rohe & M. Stegman, Impact of Homeownership on the Social and Political Involvement of Low Income People, Urban Affairs Quarterly, Sept 1994.
   W. Rohe & L. Stewart, 1996 Homeownership and Neighborhood Stability, Housing Policy Debate.
   W. Rohe, S. Van Zandt & G. McCarthy, Social Benefits of Homeownership, A Critical Assessment of the Research, Joint Center for Housing Studies, Harvard University 2001.
2 Remarks on the National Home Ownership Strategy, June 5, 1995, President William Clinton.
3 Assistance to low-income families in the USA comes in four ways: public housing; federal subsidies to private firms to construct housing for low-income families or individuals; agreements with private landlords to provide subsidized rents for particular units; and a voucher system to pay for rental accommodation. Starting with the Reagan and George Bush I years, new construction in public and subsidized private housing largely stalled, but the Clinton years were a time of even less growth in new commitments for rental assistance than under the previous Republican Administration. For Carter, there were over 300,000 new commitments for subsidized housing, an average of 100,000 p.a. under Reagan and about 75,000 p.a. under George Bush I. But during the period from 1994–1999 only about 30,000 commitments were made, until in 2000–2001 the number jumped to 100,000. For the first time since 1950, the number of public housing units (1.4 million) fell by 10% in view of the increasing emphasis on the voucher system.
4 Working Paper, No 92-7, October, 1992, Alicia Munnell, Lynne E. Browne, James McEneaney & Geoffrey M.B. Tootell.
5 Ibid p. 44.
6 Mortgage lending to Minorities: Where's the Bias? T.E. Day & S.J. Liebowitz, Economic Inquiry, 1998.
7 Stengel, Mitchell & Glennon, Dennis, An Evaluation of the Federal Reserve Bank of Boston's Study of Racial Discrimination in Mortgage Lending, Office of the Comptroller of the Currency, Working Paper, 94-2 April 1994.
8 Discrimination and Mortgage Lending: effects of model uncertainty, C. Goenner, 2007.

9 Evaluating Statistical Models of Mortgage Lending Discrimination: A Bank-Specific Analysis, Mitchell Stengel & Dennis Glennon, Office of the Comptroller of the Currency, May 1995.

10 Professor Gary Becker, The Evidence Against Banks Does Not Prove Bias, Business Week, April 1993.

11 R. Anderson & James Vanderhoff, Mortgage Default Rates and Borrower Race, Journal of Real Estate Research, Vol 18, No 2 1999.

12 Ibid, private correspondence with Professor S.J. Liebowitz, May 1995.

13 Page 9.

14 This Act and the role of Fannie Mae and Freddie Mac will be fully described in subsequent chapters.

15 My Life, Bill Clinton, Arrow Books 2005, pp. 517–518.

16 This "Census tracts" reflects the way in which the Office of Management and Budget and the Census collected statistics and defined income levels.

17 Federal Register, Vol 60 No 86, May 4, 1995, Rules and Regulations 22183–22187, Office of the Comptroller of the Currency.

18 P. 22162, http://www.fdic.gov/news/financial/1995/fil9535

19 The Trillion Dollar Bank Shakedown That Bodes Ill for Cities, H. Hancock, City-Journal, Winter 2000.
     The *Wall Street Journal* reported on Sept 8, 1999, based on a review of documents by a Boston real estate analyst, that Fleet Bank initiated foreclosure proceedings against 4% of loans made for Fleet by NACA in 1994 and 1995, a rate four times the national average.

20 ACORN has become a much larger and more complex organization with several separate nonprofts. These include ACORN Housing Corporation, now operating as Affordable Housing Centers of America (AHCOA). In 2008 and 2009, AHC received $27.6m for counseling services, but the Office of the Inspector General for HUD found that, for example, salary claims were not supported. August 2010.

21 Redlining or Red Herring, J.W. Gunther, K. Klemme & K. Robinson, South West Economy, May/June 1999.

22 "The Community Reinvestment Act: Its Evolution and New Challenges" March 30, 2007. Speech at the Community Affairs Research Conference. Chairman Ben Bernanke.

23 Bank Merger Activity in the United States, 1994–2003, Steven S. Pilloff, Federal Reserve Bank.

24 K.J. Stiroh & J.P. Poole, Explaining the Rising Concentration of Banking Assets in the 1990s, Current Issues in Economics and Finance, Federal Bank of New York, 2000.

25 It's the Rating, Stupid: A Banker's Perspective on the CRA, Mark Willis, Federal Reserve Bank of San Francisco, 2009.

26 National Community Reinvestment Coalition, CRA commitments 7, 2007.

27 The Community Reinvestment Act after Financial Modernization: A Baseline Report, R. Litan & others. US Treasury, 2000.

28 See also John Taylor & Josh Silver, The Community Reinvestment Act at Thirty: Looking back and Looking Forward, New York Law School Review Vol 53, 2008/9 pp 204 ff.

29 The Performance and Profitability of CRA-Related Lending, Report by the Board of Governors of the Federal Reserve System, submitted to Congress pursuant to section 713 of the Gramm-Leach-Bliley Act, 1999, dated July 17, 2000.

30 Ibid, p. 2.

31 The Performance and Profitability of CRA-related Lending, R.B. Avery, R. Bostic & G.B. Canner, Economic Commentary, Federal Reserve Bank of Cleveland, November 2000.

32 Ibid p. 2.

33 Ibid, p. 3.

34 Ibid, p. 4.

35 Christopher Perry & Sarah L. Lee, The Community Reinvestment Act: A Regression Discontinuity Analysis, Harris School Working Paper, series 07.04, 2006.

36 Joint Committee for Housing Studies, Harvard University, The 25th Anniversary of the Community Reinvestment Act: Access to Capital in an Evolving Financial Services System 3, 2002.

37 Michael S. Barr, Credit where it counts: the Community Reinvestment Act and Its Critics, New York University Law Review, Vol 75, 600 2005. The article is based on research Michael Barr directed whilst serving in the Treasury Department, pp 166ff.

38 These are: D.D. Evanoff & L.M. Siegal, CRA and Fair Lending Regulations: Resulting Trends in Mortgage Lending, J. Econ Perspectives, Vol 19 28–38, 1996 & Robert Avery et al, Trends in Home Purchase Lending: Consolidation and the Community Reinvestment Act, Fed Res Bull, 81, 82, 1999; Robert Avery et al Credit Risk, Credit Scoring & the Performance of Home Mortgages, Fed Res Bull, 621, 638–639, 1996.

39 The Community Reinvestment Act: 30 Years of Wealth Building and What we Must Do to Finish the Job," in Revisiting the CRA: Perspectives on the Future of the Community Reinvestment Act, Joint Publication, Federal Reserve Banks of Boston and San Francisco, 2009.

40 See Section 345.41 of the FDIC's CRA regulation.

41 Ibid, p. 151.

42 Ibid, p. 158.

43 Prepared Testimony of Michael S. Barr, before the Committee on Financial Services, US House of Representatives Hearing: Community Reinvestment Act: Thirty Years of Accomplishments, but Challenges Remain, Feb 13 2008.

44 R. Bostic & B.L. Robinson, Real Estate Economics, 31, pp. 23–51, 2003.

45 Speech by Governor Randall Kroszner, The Community Reinvestment Act, December 3, 2008.

46 Ibid, p. 3.

47 Community Development and Investment Goals, Bank of America press release, April 28, 2008.

Chapter 2 Two More Tools in the Tool-Kit

1 From the borrower's point of view, the terms of FHA-insured loans have been changed. In 2011, the agency altered the rules so that borrowers have to pay higher mortgage insurance premiums and seller concessions have been restricted.

2 Testimony of Secretary Andrew Cuomo before the House Appropriations Subcommittee on VA, HUD and Independent Agencies, March 25, 1999.

3 The seller-funded down-payment program has an interesting history. HUD's long-standing policy has been to allow certain third parties (family members and charities) to assist with down payments, but precluded other third parties, such as the home seller from doing so. But these schemes started to surface in the late 1990s. A charity would make a "gift" to the home buyer to provide

the FHA-required 3% down payment with the understanding that the seller would subsequently make an "equal" donation to the charity after the sale was completed. A seller down-payment program was started in California by Nehemiah Progressive Housing Development Corporation. In 1997, Nehemia filed a lawsuit on the basis of differential by HUD loan officers. The law suit settlement allowed Nehemia to continue (1) to provide charitable donations to home buyers, (2) after closing the purchase transaction, to receive donations from the sellers of the properties. HUD's Office of General Counsel found that the scheme did not conflict with the mortgage rule book by then. The FHA published a rule change to ban the practice in 1999 but backed down in the face of a vigorous campaign from down-payment assistance providers. It will be clear that Congress would never have supported any such rule anyway.

4 In fact the down-payment program had been subject to repeated criticism from HUD's Office of the General Counsel in its Memorandum of 1998, the HUD Office of the Inspector General in 2000 and 2002, and the GAO report of 2005.

5 Written statement of Margaret Burns, Director, Office of Single Family Program Development, Office of Housing before the Committee on Financial Services Subcommittee on Housing and Community Opportunity, US House of Representatives, June 22, 2007, p. 1.

6 Government Accountability Office, Mortgage Financing: Additional Action Needed to Manage Risks of FHA-Insured Loans with Down Payment Assistance, GAO-06-24 Nov 9, 2005.

7 Report to Congress on the Financial Status of the MMI Fund, 2009, p. 11.

8 Senate Appropriations Committee, report to accompany H.R. 5576, Transportation, Treasury, Housing and Urban Development Appropriations Act 2007, 109th Congress 2nd session, S. Rept. 109–293 July 26, 2006.

9 GAO Mortgage Finance. Additional Action Needed to Manage Risks of FHA-Insured Loans with Down Payment Assistance, November 2005, GAO-06-24.

10 Office of the Inspector General: Final Report of Nationwide Audit Downpayment Assistance Programs, March 2000.
Final Report, Down Payment Assistance Program operated by Private Nonprofit Entities, Audit Report September 25 2002.

11 Statement of James A. Heist, Assistant Inspector General for the Audit Department of HUD, before the Subcommittee on Housing and Community Opportunity, House Financial Services Committee, June 22, 2007.

12 Financial Status of the FHA Mutual Mortgage Insurance Fund, 2010, p. 24.

13 Statement of Brian Montgomery before the Appropriations Subcommittee on Transportation, Housing and Urban Development, March 15, 2007.

14 Senator Hillary Clinton, Speech on Subprime Lending, NCRC March 15, 2007.

15 Lenders' Perspectives on FHA's declining market share, August 2006, B. Kogler, A. Schnare & T. Willis, Research Institute for Housing America & Mortgage Bankers Association.

16 Alt-A mortgages were typically mortgages provided to borrowers with a good credit record, but without full documentation, particularly regarding the borrower's income. Borrowers were unable or unwilling to provide documentation verifying their income. The loans were often called no-doc or low-doc loans, or stated income loans, and sometimes, pejoratively, "liar loans."

17 FHA: Turning an American Dream into a Neighborhood Nightmare, Washington News and Views, July/August 2002, Inez Killingsworth.

18 Congressional Budget Office, Assessing the Government's Costs for Mortgage Insurance Provided by the Federal Housing Administration, July 2006.

19 FICO scores are used by the major credit rating agencies in the USA (Equifax, Experian and Trans Union, all of which use software developed by Fair Isaac & Co).

20 The range of FICO scores is from 300 to 850, with 60% being 650 or over. FICO assesses the median score as 723.

21 Written testimony of David H. Stevens, FHA Commissioner, "FHA Reforms, Legislative Proposals, and Contributions to the HUD FY 2011 Budget," Hearing before the House Financial Services Subcommittee on Housing and Community Opportunity, March 11, 2010, p. 7.

22 Ibid. Written Statement of Margaret Burns, p. 1.

23 Not for everyone, though. On January 16, 2009, Joe Baca and 9 Democrat Congressmen introduced H.R.600, The FHA Seller Down-Payment Reform Act, allowing sellers to contribute to the borrower's required funds on certain mortgages. Not surprisingly the bill had the support of the Mortgage Brokers Association, the National Association of Realtors, and the National Association of Home Builders. The bill was referred to the Housing Financial Services Committee and did not become law.

24 Written testimony of David Stevens, FHA Commissioner, hearing before Congressional Committee on Financial Services, September 2010.

25 Annual Report to Congress regarding the Financial Status of the FHA Mutual Mortgage Insurance Fund, 2010, p. 1 and 14.

26 Ibid, p. 14.

27 David Stevens, Commissioner, written testimony, hearing before the House of Representatives, September 22, 2010.

28 Audit of the FHA's Financial Statements for Fiscal Years 2009 and 2010. See Appendix A Significant Deficiencies, referring to systems and controls.

29 Office of the Inspector General, Report, Sept 30, 2010, p. 11.

30 Testimony before the Senate Committee on Banking, Housing and Urban Affairs, M. Scire, Director Financial Markets and Community Investment, Mortgage Financing. Financial Condition of FHA's Mortgage Insurance Fund, September 23, 2010, p. 2.

31 Edward Pinto, October 8, 2009.

32 D. Aragon, A. Caplin, S. Chopra, J. Leahy, Y. Lecum, M. Scoffier & J. Tracey, Reassessing FHA Risk, Working Paper, 15802 National Bureau of Economics.

33 Integrated Financial Engineering, Inc. 2010 Actuarial Review of FHA's MMI Fund.

34 US Treasury, White Paper, Timothy Geithner, Reforming the Housing Finance Market, February 2011, p. 19.

35 It is regarded as a government-sponsored enterprise, as it was expressly created by an Act of Congress, The Federal Home Loan Bank Act.

36 These are set out in detail in the Act. The FHLBanks had to meet a leverage requirement and a risk-based capital requirement. The former consists of permanent capital (equal to amounts paid for in Class B stock plus retained earnings) plus Class A stock to be at least 4% of assets. Second Class A stock plus 1.5 times permanent capital must be at least 5% of assets. The risk-based capital standards account for credit risk, for which the regulator specifies capital requirements according to the mix of activities (advances, mortgages, etc.) in which the individual FHLB is engaged. For interest-rate risk, each of the FHLBanks must have an approved interest rate model that provides an estimate of the market value of the FHLB's portfolio during periods of market stress. The capital requirement for operations risk is generally 30% of the total capital charge for credit and interest rate risk.

37 See GAO, "Federal Home Loan Bank System: Key Loan Pricing Terms Can Differ Significantly," GAO-03-973, Sept 8, 2003.
38 Also Federal Home Loan Bank System, An Overview of Changes and Current Issues Affecting the System, Statement of Thomas J. McCool, April 13, 2005, GAO-05-489T, p. 20.
39 See Orla O'Sullivan, Enter the "Third Gorilla GSE." ABA Banking Journal, 1997, Vol 89.
40 Ibid, GAO, p. 1.
41 Testimony of Ronald A. Rosenfeld before the US Senate Committee on Banking, Housing and Urban Affairs, April 21, 2005, p. 6.
42 Ibid, p. 6.
43 GAO-03-364, February 23, 2003, pp 30ff.
44 Ibid, p. 5.
45 Federal Housing Agency Order, Appointment of Directors, Sept 1, 2010.
46 *Seattle Times*, Seattle's Federal Home Loan Bank in Big Money Trouble Again, July 19, 2009.
47 The Chicago Balance Sheet, 2005-1, p. 1 and 3. Interestingly enough, the FHLB did not publish its Chicago Balance Sheet in 2008.
48 Ibid, pp. 49–50.
49 Letter from the President and CEO of FHLBank Atlanta, Nov 17, 2008.
50 Rosalind Bennett, FDIC, Mark Vaughan, Federal Reserve Bank of Richmond, Timothy Yeager, Federal Reserve Bank of Richmond, Working Paper 05-05.
51 Ibid, p. 12.
52 Op.cit, p. 21.
53 Op.cit, p. 9.
54 Bloomberg Sept 7, 2008.
55 Data derived from 2009 Actuarial Review of the Federal Housing Administration Mutual Mortgage Insurance Fund, p. 42 and 44, and the FHA Biweekly report for July 16–31, published by HUD.
56 Reuters, FHLBs may see impairment on $76.2bn MBSs, Jan 8, 2009.
57 These estimates are taken from "Sizing Total Federal Government and Federal Agency Contributions to Subprime and Alt-A Loans in the US First Mortgage Market as of 6.30.08" by Ed Pinto.

Chapter 3 The Role of the Housing and Urban Development Department (HUD)

1 Congressional Budget Office testimony on Budgeting for Emergency Spending, June 23, 1998, p. 5.
2 The mortgage insurance premiums were paid by the borrower with one upfront payment and monthly payments thereafter. The premiums were to protect the lender from defaults on home mortgages. The premiums were paid into the FHA's Mutual Mortgage Insurance fund, which was supposed to be sufficient to meet such losses.
3 President announces cut in Home Mortgage Insurance Premium to reduce Home Ownership Costs for 600,000 families each year. HUD News Release, June 12, 1997.
4 National Home Ownership Strategy 1995, pp. 4–5.
5 Credit Risk, Credit Scoring and the Performance of Home Mortgages, 1996, Robert Avery, R. Bostic, P. Calem & G. Canner.

Ed Pinto in Government Housing Policies in the Lead-up to the Financial Crisis: A Forensic Study, 2010, pp. 82–83 argues that the authors miss the point of a study of the performance of loans. They observe that delinquency rates are low for each loan type and note a 4% rate on government-backed seasoned loans, but do not point out that this rate is 10 times the rate on conventional loans with a FICO score of 660; in 1989, the then median FICO for individuals with mortgages was 730. Of the first-time buyers in 1989 and 1994, 13.3% and 14.5% had a FICO score of 660 and below. The authors also refer to the growth of affordable lending but do not take on board the fact that borrowers with incomes below 80% of the median have a much higher usage of the "innovative" loans or those with flexible underwriting features.

6 Op.cit, Federal Reserve, p. 639.
7 HUD Archives, News Releases, Feb 8, 1996.
8 HUD Archives: News Releases, June 17, 1997 and March 5, 1998.
9 HUD Archives, News Release, January 27, 2000.
10 See also Part of the State of the Union Address, Jan 29, 2002; Remarks at St Paul AME Church in Atlanta, Georgia, June 2002 and Speech at Fort Meade, Maryland, June 2002.
11 HUD Archives News Release, January 2, 2002 and July 30, 2002.
12 HUD Archives News Releases, 2003, 2004, 2005, 2006 and May 8, 2007.
13 Conference in North Carolina, Aug 28, 2006.
14 Presentation by J. Martin, Deputy CFO, "Changing the Face of HUD, Addressing High Risks and Management Challenges," April 17, 2007.
15 GAO Report to Ranking Minority Member, Subcommittee on Housing and Transportation, Committee on Banking, Housing and Urban Affairs, US Senate, Single Family Housing. Better Strategic Human Capital Management Needed at HUD's Homeownership Centres, July 2001, p. 1 GAO-01-590.
16 Op.cit p. 9.
17 April 2, 2009 before the US Senate.
18 Op.cit p. 14.
19 Op.cit p. 5.
20 Op.cit p. 13.
21 Statement of Kenneth M. Donohue, Inspector General, Department of Housing and Urban Development, May 13, 2010.

Chapter 4 Mortgage Data

1 C. Reid & E. Laderman, Untold Costs of Subprime Lending: Examining the Links between Higher-priced Lending, Foreclosures and Race in California, San Francisco Federal Reserve Bank, August 2009.
2 Credit Risk, Credit Scoring and the Performance of Home Mortgages, Federal Reserve Bulletin 82, July 1996, p. 623. The other authors included R. Bostic, P. Calem and G. Canner, all of whom were frequent contributors to research into the developments in the mortgage market for the Federal Reserve throughout the 1990s until the present.
3 See Opportunities and Issues in Using HMDA Data, R. Avery, K. Brevoort & G. Canner, JRER, Vol 29, No 4, 2007, pp. 369–370.
4 Ibid, p. 272.
5 HUD "Subprime and Manufactured Home Lender List" www.huduser.org/portal/datasets/manu/hmtl

6   The Home Mortgage Disclosure Act: Its History, Evolution and Limitations, March 2005, Buckley Kolar LLP.

7   H.R. Conf. report, No 222 at 459, 1989, 101st Session 1989.

8   That did not, however, prevent community housing advocates arguing on the basis of HMDA data that the US mortgage market was riddled with discrimination, even as late as 2006. See evidence presented by the Consumer Mortgage Coalition (including ACORN) to the House Financial Services Commission , subcommittee on Financial Institutions and Consumer Credit, HMDA: Newly Collected Data and What it Means, June 2006.

9   1999, Winning Best Practices, Fair Housing. HUD.

10   Op.cit p. 2.

11   See Board of Governors of the Federal Reserve System, Home Mortgage Disclosure Act: Advance Notice of Proposed Rulemaking, 67 Fed Reg 7228 (Feb 15, 2002).

12   Op.cit p. 20.

13   Public Hearing at the Federal Reserve Bank of Chicago, Sept 16, 2010.

14   Contribution from Geoff Smith, Woodstock Institute, op.cit p. 10.

15   Remarks at the Consumers' Union 75th Anniversary Celebration, Elizabeth Warren, Feb 15, 2011.

16   Subprime Lending. Expanded Guidance for Subprime Lending Programs, January 31, 2001 pp. 2–3.

17   Proposed Statement on Subprime Lending, Footnote 2, p. 6.

18   Technical appendix to the spread sheets, 2008.

19   Op. cit p. 624.

20   Op. cit. p. 1. The additional capital would not be in accordance with the requirements of Basel II. 2001 was too early for final agreement, and at any rate, the USA planned to introduce Basel II in 2008, when a risk-weighted approach to credit risk, for example, would only have applied to the largest banks with assets of $250bn or more.

21   April 8 2005, Speech at the Federal Reserve System's Fourth Annual Community Affairs Research Conference.

22   Statement of Edward D.E. Marco, Acting Director, Federal Housing Finance Agency, Before the House Subcommittee on Capital Markets, Insurance and the GSEs, "Transparency, Transition and Taxpayer Protection: More Steps to End the GSE Bailout," May 25, 2011, p. 4.

Chapter 5   The "Mission Regulator" for Fannie Mae and Freddie Mac

1   HUD's Affordable Lending Goals for Fannie Mae and Freddie Mac, HUD, January 2001.

2   In setting the goals, HUD had to take into account six statutory factors: national housing needs; economic, housing and demographic conditions; performance and effort of Fannie and Freddie towards achieving the goals in previous years; the size of the conventional mortgage market serving the targeted population or areas relative to the size of the overall conventional mortgage market; the ability of the GSEs to lead the industry in making mortgage credit available for the targeted population or areas; and the need to maintain the sound financial condition of the GSEs. HUD did not have the resources available to carry out such complicated analyses. This was outsourced through the Office of Policy Development and Research, which could also draw on outside research.

3   Federal Register, Vol No 60, No 231, Friday December 1, 1995/Rules and Regulations, p. 61848.

4   Op.cit p. 61920.

5   GAO Federal Housing Enterprises: HUD's Mission Oversight Needs to be Strengthened, July 1998, p. 12.

6   Housing-Aid Goals in Underserved Areas Proposed by HUD, *Wall Street Journal*, June 20, 1995.

7   Op.cit p. 61965.

8   Press briefing by Henry Cisneros, Secretary of Housing and Urban Development, June 6, 1996, The Briefing Room.

9   Building Flawed American Dreams, *New York Times*, October 18, 2008.

10 Reuters, Oct 24, 2007.

11 CNN Money, Oct 26, 2007.

12 He then became New York State Attorney General in 2006, following his failed gubernatorial campaign in 2002, and was elected as Governor of New York in November 2010. He became Governor on Jan 1, 2011.

13 GAO Major Management Challenges and Program Risks, Department of Housing and Urban Development, January 2001. See also Statement of Susan Gaffney, Inspector General, Department of Housing and Urban Development before the House of Representatives, Committee on Government Reform, Subcommittee on Government Management and Information Technology, March 22, 2000 in which, inter alia, she referred to an additional 242 adjustments to the financial reports totalling $59 billion for the fiscal year 1999.

14 OIG Audit Report, March 2000 SE 121 0001.

15 Cuomo announces higher FHA mortgage loan limits to help more American families become homeowners, Jan 8, 2000 HUD Press release.

16 Federal Register/Vol 65, No 211, October 31, 2000, Rules and Regulations, p. 05082.

17 This definition covered some of the practices which HUD and the Department of the Treasury issued on June 30, 2000.

18 Joint HUD-Treasury Task Force on Predatory Lending, Curbing Predatory Home Mortgage Lending, June, 2000.

19 Federal Register/Vol.65. No 211, Oct 31, 2000 pp. 65069–65071.

20 GAO Federal Housing Enterprises, HUD's Mission Oversight Needs to be Strengthened, July 1998, GAO/GGD-98-173.

21 Going Subprime, Shelter Force Online, Issue 125, September/October 2002.

22 P. 6.

23 Federal Register op.cit 65168.

24 HUD News Release, Jackson announces review of Fannie and Freddie Investments to ensure Charter Compliance, June 13, 2006.

25 HUD Press Release, GAO recognizes HUD's management reforms, Jan 31, 2007.

26 GAO Federal Housing Administration, Proposed Legislative Changes Would Affect Borrower Benefits and Risks to Insurance Funds, July 18, 2007, p. 2.

27 HUD Secretary Jackson resigns amid Federal Probe, March 31, 2008.

28 *Washington Post*, Probe of former HUD Secretary Alphonso Jackson said to be closed, May 4, 2010. He is Director of the centre for Public Policy and Leadership at Hapton University.

29 News Release. HUD finalizes rule of new housing goals for Fannie Mae and Freddie Mac, Nov 1, 2004, p. 2.

30 Ibid, p. 1.

31 Issues Brief, HUD's Affordable Lending Goals for Fannie Mae and Freddie Mac, January 2001.

32 Federal Register Final Rule, Housing Goals for the GSEs, Determination Regarding the Levels of Housing Goals, November 2004.

33 Prepared for HUD Office of Policy Development and Research, D. Rodda, Abt Associates, J. Goodman, Hartrey Advisers, May 2005, p. 85.

34 Federal Register Vol 69, Nov 2, 2004, Rules and Regulations, p. 6385.

35 Federal Register/Vol 69 No 211, Nov 2, 2004.

36 Ibid, p. 63630.

37 Ibid, pp. 63626–63627.

38 Ibid p. 63628.

39 Op.cit p. 63632.

40 Ibid p. 63598.

41 Ibid p. 63601.

42 Op.cit p. 63601.

43 Letter from V. Cox Golder 2010. President National Association of Realtors to A. Pollard, General l Counsel, Federal Housing Finance Agency, April 12, 2010.

44 Federal Register, Oct 31, 2000, p. 650444.

Chapter 6 The GSEs and the Developing Crisis

1 Two of the five operate in the farm credit market: FCS and Farmer Mac; these are not relevant for this book. Ginnie Mae (Government National Mortgage Association), a US government corporation operating in the US Department of Housing and Urban Development, guarantees investors the timely payment of the principal and interest mainly on mortgage-backed securities from loans issued or guaranteed by the FHA or the Department of Veteran Affairs. Their MBSs were (until 2008) the only ones fully backed by the US government.

2 Title to a collection of papers edited by Peter Wallison, AEI Press, 2001.

3 See Thomas H. Stanton, Government Sponsored Enterprises: Mercantilist Companies in the Modern World, AEI Press, 2002, p. 56.

4 Fannie Mae Charter Act, 12 United States Code sec 1723 (a).

5 Charter Act, United States Code sec 4541.

6 W. Apgar Testimony before the House Committee on Housing, Banking and Financial Services, Capital Markets, Securities and the GSEs, March 22, 2000.

7 The GSE Report, January 14, 2000 pp. 5–8.

8 12 United States Code, sec 1719(b).

9 According to their Charters and subsequent Acts, their debt and mortgage-backed securities were exempt from registration with the Securities and Exchange Commission; they had a line of credit to the Treasury which authorized it to purchase up to $2.25bn of Fannie and Freddie's obligations, and banks were allowed to make unlimited investments in any other debt securities, whereas there are limits on their investments in any other debt securities. Their securities were eligible as collateral for public deposits or for loans from Federal Reserve Banks and FHLBs. Fannie and Freddie's securities were lawful investments for federal fiduciary and public funds, and they were authorized to use the Federal Reserve Banks as their fiscal agents, including issuing and transferring their securities through the book-entry system maintained by the Federal Reserve.

10 Quoted by T. Stanton, Government Sponsored Enterprises: Mercantilist Companies in the Modern World, p. 35.

11 Quoted in the CBO report, p. 2, Letter dated August 25, 2000.

12 CBO Testimony Regulation of the Housing Government-Sponsored Enterprises, Statement of Douglas Holtz-Eakin before the Committee on Banking, Housing and Urban Affairs, Oct 23, 2003, p. 1.

13 Federal Subsidies and the Housing Guarantees, Congressional Budget Office, May 2001, p. 14.

14 Government Sponsored Enterprises: The Issue of Expansion into Mission-Related Business, 1999.

15 CBO, Federal Subsidies and the Housing GSEs, May 2001 and also CBO Testimony before the Subcommittee on Capital Markets, Insurance and the Government Sponsored Enterprises, US House of Representatives, May 23, 2001.

16 Fannie's Senior Vice President for Portfolio Strategy, Peter Niculescu, *Washington Post*, 17 May, 2001 and Freddie's Senior Vice President of Government Relations, Mitch Delk in a letter to Congressman Baker.

17 Press statement by Cong. Richard Baker, May 18, 2001.

18 Updated Estimates of the Subsidies to the Housing GSEs, CBO Office, attachment with letter to Hon. Richard Selby from D. Holtz-Eakin, Director CBO, April 8, 2004.

19 Reuters, May 17, 2001.

20 Statement by Barbara Miles before the Task Force on Housing and Infrastructure Committee on the Budget US House of Representatives, Implications of the Debt Held by the Housing GSEs, July 25, 2000.

21 Op.cit. p. 6.

22 In "Regulation of the Housing Government-Sponsored Enterprises" before the Committee on Banking, Housing and Urban Affairs, US Senate, Oct 23, 2003. p. 2.

23 Jon Birger, *Money Magazine*, CNN Money, Nov 27, 2001.

24 Douglas Holtz-Eakin, "Aligning the Costs and Benefits of the Housing Government-Sponsored Enterprises," April 21, 2005.

25 Prepared Remarks for Richard Syron, Dec 6, 2005, Speech to the Executive Club of Chicago.

26 Testimony of Chairman Alan Greenspan, Regulatory Reforms of the GSEs Before the Committee on Banking, Housing and Urban Affairs, U.S. Senate, April 6 2005 and further comments during the hearing.

27 Testimony, Government Sponsored Enterprises, before the Committee on Banking, Housing and Urban Affairs, Feb 24, 2004 and Remarks by Chairman Alan Greenspan, Government Sponsored Enterprises, Conference on Housing, Mortgage Finance and the Macro-economy, Federal Reserve Bank of Atlanta, May 19, 2005.

28 R. Eisenbeis, W. Scott Frame & L.D. Wall, An Analysis of the Systemic Risks Posed by Fannie Mae and Freddie Mac and An Evaluation of the Policy Options for Reducing Those Risks, Federal Reserve Board of Atlanta working paper, 2006-2. p. 31.

29 Op.cit pp. 40–41.

30 Quoted in Dow Jones Newswires, April 3, 2006.

31 A. Lehnert, W. Passmore & S. Sherlund, GSEs, Mortgage Rates and Secondary Market Activities, Jan 2005, Federal Reserve Board.

32 Op.cit p. 1.

33 Dow International News, 05/18/06.

34 Remarks by Randal Quarles, Under Secretary of Treasury for Domestic Finance, Speech to Money Marketeers at New York University, 5/10/06.

35 Remarks of Randal K. Quarles, Under Secretary for Domestic Finance, US Department of the Treasury before Women in Housing Finance, June 13, 2006, JS-4316.

36 Quoted in the GSE Report, May 6, 2006, p. 4.
37 Remarks of Emil W. Henry Jr, Assistant Secretary for Financial Institutions, US Dept of the Treasury before the Real Estate Roundtable, 15/6/2006.
38 Emil Henry, How to shut down Fannie and Freddie. *Wall Street Journal*, Nov 11, 2010. Quoted by C. Papagianis, before the Subcommittee on Capital Markets and the Government Sponsored Enterprises, Legislative Hearing on immediate steps to protect taxpayers from the ongoing bailout of Fannie Mae and Freddie Mac, March 31, 2011.
39 B. Bernanke, Bloomsberg, reported by James Tyson, 02/15/07.
40 GSE Portfolios, Systemic Risk and Affordable Housing, March 6, 2007, p. 1.
41 Op.cit pp. 1–2. Research sources: The GSEs, Mortgage Rates and Secondary Market Activities, Journal of Real Estate Finance and Economics, A. Lehnert, W. Passmore and S. Sherland, Vol 36, No 3, 2008; The GSEs, Mortgage Rates and Secondary Market Activities, Federal Reserve Bank, W. Passmore & S. Sherland, Jan 2005; Effects of Housing GSEs on Mortgage Rates, W. Passmore, S. Sherland and G. Burgess; The GSEs, Mortgage Rates, and Secondary Market Activities, Sept 2006, Federal Reserve Board.
42 Senate Banking Committee Press Release, 03/07/07.
43 The GSEs: where do we stand? May/June 2007 & GSE Risks, March/April 2005.
44 Treasury press release HP-1129, Sept 7, 2008 and Bloomberg, Sept 7, 2008.
45 Report in China daily, 12/9/2008.
46 CRS Report for Congress, Sept 12, 2008, N. Eric Weiss, p. 5.
47 Lawrence Summers, "The Way Forward to Fannie Mae and Freddie Mac," July 27, 2008.

Chapter 7   The Dominance of the GSEs

1 R. Avery, P. Calem, G. Canner & R. Bostic, An Overview of Consumer Data and Credit Reporting, Federal Reserve Bulletin, 2003.
2 Both Loan Protector and Desktop Underwriter are being replaced by the Uniform Loan Delivery Dataset in 2012.
3 OFHEO's Annual Report to Congress only gave the total dollar value, not the number. OFHEO did not have the total value for Freddie Mac, because it had not submitted accurate financial statements for that year by 2004.
4 *New York Times*, Fannie Mae eases credit to aid mortgage lending, Sept 30, 1999.
5 Speech at National Association of Home Builders, Jan 14, 2000, PR Newswire.
6 Review of Selected Underwriting Guidelines to identify potential barriers to Hispanic Homeownership, prepared for the US Department of Housing and Urban Development, K. Burnett, A. Cortes & C. Herbert, AbT Associates, March 2006.
7 Automated Underwriting and Lending Outcomes: The Effect of Improved Mortgage Risk Assessment on Under-Served Populations, P. Zorn, S. Gates & V. Perry, August 2001, University of California, Berkeley.
8 Joint Center for Housing Studies, State of the Nation's Housing, 1998. The study found that the number of new homeowners grew by 4 million between 1994 and 1997, and the driving force behind the increase was the influx of low-income and minority households into the housing market, p. 13.
9 Applying the *Microsoft* Decision to Fannie Mae and Freddie Mac, July, 2001, AEI Papers and Studies.
10 Milwaukee Business Journal, 7/6/98.
11 National Mortgage News Daily website, 10/10/01.

12 Testimony before Capital Markets Subcommittee, June 15, 2000.

13 Congressional Capital Markets Subcommittee, 22 March, 2001.

14 The Detroit News, 13 Oct, 1997, quoted in Applying the Microsoft Decision to Fannie Mae and Freddie Mac, P. Wallison, July 25, 2001.

15 *New York Times*, October 5, 2008. Article on Daniel Mudd.

16 As reported in The GSE Report, Feb 2, 2001, pp. 22–23.

17 Daniel Mudd, then President and CEO of Fannie Mae, Testimony before the House of Representatives Financial Services Committee, April 17, 2007, p. 1.

18 Examining Fannie Mae, *Washington Post*, May 24, 2006, quoting former Chief Operating Officer of Fannie Mae, Roger Birk.

19 12 US Code 4513.

20 Andrew Taylor, 1992 bill establishing New Overseer for Fannie, Freddie clears, Congressional Weekly Report, October 13, 3138.

21 Testimony of Under Secretary of the Treasury, G. Gensler, before the Capital Markets Subcommittee of the House Financial Services Committee, Hearing on Improving the Regulation of the Housing GSEs, March 22, 2000, p. 3.

22 Quoted in the *Financial Times*, March 24, 2000.

23 *Realty Times*, March 28, 2000 and Dow Jones Newswire, March 22, 2000.

24 Dow Jones Newswire, March 30, 2000.

25 Federal Register, September 13, 2001, pp. 47730–47875.

26 Testimony of the Hon. Armando Falcon Jnr, Director, OFHEO, before the US Subcommittee on Capital Markets, Insurance and GSEs, Aug 1,2001 p. 4. See also the GAO's assessment of the rule, OFHEO's Risk-Based Capital Stress Test: Incorporating New Business is not Advisable," GA0-02-521, June 2002, pp. 6, 10, and 14–15.

27 "Risk-based capital requirements for mortgage loans," P.S. Calem & M. Lacour-Little, Journal of Banking and Finance, 2003, Vol 28(3) pp. 647–672.

28 OFHEO Working Papers 03-1 Subprime and Prime Mortgages: Loss Distributions, A. Pennington-Cross, 2004.

29 National Mortgage News, April 1, 1999.

30 Federal Register, Vol 66, No 178, Sept 13, 2001 p. 47731.

31 The production of such papers, for those regularly writing for the Fannie Mae papers, was often with the research support of the Fannie Mae Foundation.

32 "Implications of the New Fannie Mae and Freddie Mac Risk-based Capital Standard," Fannie Mae Paper, 2002, 1 (2).

33 Statements of Congressman Christopher Shays (in conjunction with Congressman E. Markey on the introduction of H.R.4071, 21/3/2002).

34 Hearing on March 20, 2002, pp. 83–84.

35 He resigned on November 5, 2002 after a turbulent period as Chairman, but provoked in the last instance by the proposed appointment of one William Webster to oversee a panel to review the accounting profession when he had been a director of a company accused of fraud.

36 "Prompt" letters are a device created in 2001 to enable the Office of Management and Budget through the Office of Information and Regulatory Affairs to pro-actively "suggest" issues agencies ought to address. The device has not been used very often, only 12 times since its introduction. Such a letter obviously indicates that the matter is sufficiently important to have attracted the attention of the White House.

37 Dow Jones Newswire, 5/30/02 and Wall Street Journal, 5/29/02.

38 Both Fannie Mae and Freddie Mac had taken care to write to the Office of the General Counsel, Division of Corporate Finance, SEC to have written

confirmation that nothing had changed. The responses from the SEC were dated July 12, 2002. The two GSEs could then be certain that they were on safe ground in issuing the reassurances they did immediately after the joint press conference.

39　Department of the Treasury, Testimony of Peter R. Fisher, Under Secretary for Domestic Finance, before the Subcommittee on Capital Markets, Insurance and Government Sponsored Enterprises, Government Sponsored Enterprises and Financial Disclosure, July 16, 2002.

Chapter 8　The Beginning of the End for Freddie Mac

1　Staff Report of the Task Force: Enhancing Disclosure in the Mortgage-Backed Securities Market, January 2003. The Securities and Exchange Commission, Dept of the Treasury and Office of Federal Housing Enterprise Oversight.

2　The report noted that since Fannie and Freddie guarantee the timely payments of principal and interest on the MBSs, so investors look to their credit quality (not to the US government). The GSEs "provide extensive corporate disclosure and will soon register their common stock under the Exchange Act … Investors in Fannie and Freddie Mac MBSs may look to these disclosures to assess those companies' abilities to fulfil the guarantees of the MBSs. Investors may also look to the information provided by OFHEO about the GSEs' creditworthiness, including results of the examinations and risk-based capital tests,", p. 11.

3　CRS Report for Congress, Fannie Mae, Freddie Mac and SEC Registration and Disclosures, July 11, 2003, Mark Jickling, p. 7.

4　Congressional hearing, Subcommittee on Capital Markets, Insurance and the GSEs, June 25, 2003, p. 1.

5　Ibid.

6　Freddie Mac had just reported that there were failures in their accounting practices.

7　Congressional Financial Services Committee hearing, September 10, 2003, p. 3.

8　Congressional Financial Services Committee hearing, September 25, 2003, p. 9.

9　Congressional Financial Services Committee hearing, Sept 25, p. 31.

10　Op.cit pp. 51–52.

11　The next stage would be for the full Committee to prepare and vote on its final recommendations to the House or Senate. That may be after the Committee has conducted further reviews, held more public hearings, or voted on the Subcommittee's report. Subsequent would be the publication of a Committee report, including items such as the purpose of the bill, its impact on existing laws, budgetary implications, etc. It would then be placed on the legislative calendar of the House or Senate and face another six stages, if it is to have any chance of becoming law, since each stage is a further hurdle.

12　Alan Greenspan's analysis of the risks posed by Fannie Mae and Freddie Mac will be discussed in detail in this and the following chapter.

13　US Department of the Treasury, Office of Public Affairs, Joint Statement of Treasury Secretary John Snow and Housing and Urban Development Secretary Alphonso Jackson, JS-1294, April 2, 2004.

14　As reported by Fortune, Jan 24, 2005, (CNN Money) p. 7.

15　DowJones Newsletter, June 9, 2003.

16　OFHEO Annual Report to Congress, June 2003, p. 38.

17　Freddie Mac's press release, June 9, 2003.

18　Supplementary and detailed statement released by Freddie Mac, June 25, 2003.

19 The GSE report, June 17, 2003 p. 7.

20 CRS Report for Congress, Accounting and Management Problems at Freddie Mac, November 2005, p. 1.

21 Report of the Special Examination of Freddie Mac, OFHEO, December 2003, p. i.

22 These and other examples are given on p. ii of the Executive Summary and OFHEO's conclusion is on p. iii.

23 FAS 133: Accounting for Derivative Instruments and Hedging Activities requires that entities recognize each derivative as an asset or liability on their balance sheets as a fair value or cash flow hedge, or as a derivative with no hedge designation. Different accounting applies to each of these alternatives, with different implications for the equity of shareholders and current earnings. Freddie Mac adopted FAS 133 on January 1, 2001. It was also affected by FAS 140: Accounting for Transfers and Extinguishment of Liabilities, which revises the standards (of FAS 125) for securitization and other transfers of financial assets and collateral and requires certain disclosures, but importantly, provides consistent standards for distinguishing transfers of financial assets that are sales from transfers that are secured borrowings.

24 Op.cit p. 8.

25 Op cit p. 10 and 12.

26 Op.cit pp. 35–36.

27 Op.cit p. 36.

28 Section 303 c of the Federal Home Loan Mortgage Corporation Act, 12 U.S.C. 1452.

29 See especially pp. 63–66.

30 In 2003, OFHEO reported that it was still conducting investigations into the activities of counterparties in improper transactions, which involved some of the members of the Reference Notes Securities Auction Dealer Group, which underwrote the largest debt income issues of Freddie Mac and is a source of substantial underwriting income. The counterparties in the linked swaps also rank highly among the dealers which Freddie Mac used for its usual derivative activities, ibid, p. 74.

31 Audio tape transcript, Ray Powers, Aug 14, 2001. OF 2001659.

32 Op.cit p. 81.

33 Op.cit pp. 88–89.

34 This is one of the principles laid down by the Institute of Internal Auditors, Guidance Overview of the Professional Practices Framework, October 2001. These were the principles to which OFHEO looked in order to assess the internal audit function of Freddie Mac. This was entirely justified, as the Freddie Mac Charter explicitly states that the internal audit function should comply with the standards set out by the standard-setting body, the Institute of Internal Auditors as well as the Senior Vice President-General Auditor.

35 Quoted by OFHEO from an interview with Melvin Kann of the internal audit department, p. 116.

36 Memorandum prepared by Baker Botts re: Mollie Roy Interview, Feb 13, 2003, OF 2000589, op.cit p. 152.

37 Op.cit p. 153.

38 The number of class action suits filed grew steadily following the passage of the Private Securities Litigation Act, 1995. About 60% of these were based on financial reporting misstatements. Source Stanford Securities Class Action Clearinghouse website: http://securities.standford.edu

39 CalPERS is the California Public Employees Retirement System, and with $239.2bn assets under management as at April 30, 2011, the largest pension scheme in America and one of the largest in the world.

40 Op.cit p. 143.
41 Op.cit pp. 159–161.
42 The corporate governance issues described here do not cover other disturbing elements described in an article in the *Washington Post*, August 16, 2004, "Board members, executives and families can still benefit". It covers a range of companies but refers to Fannie Mae, which reported in 2003 that it paid $375,000 to the Duberstein Group, a lobbying and consulting firm led by Fannie Mae Director and former White House Chief of Staff, K. Duberstein and also hired Swyget's son, after Swygert joined the Board.
43 James R. Doty, Partner in charge, Baker Botts, LLP. The references are to his statement to the hearing.
44 Op.cit p. 9.
45 Op.cit p. 8.
46 Hearing before the Subcommittee on Capital Markets, Insurance and the Government Sponsored Enterprises, Jan 21 2004, p. 18.
47 Prepared statement of Baruch Lev, Philip Barnes Professor of Accounting and Finance, Stern School of Business, New York University, p. 17.
48 Op.cit p. 15.
49 Report to the Board of Directors (of Freddie Mac): Internal Investigation of Certain Accounting Matters, July 2003 by Baker Botts L.L.P. with James Doty in the lead.
50 Hearing before the Subcommittee on Capital Markets, Insurance and Government Sponsored Enterprises, p. 28.
51 Bloomberg, June 6, 2011, Fannie Mae Silence on Taylor Bean opened the way to $3bn fraud.

Chapter 9 The Beginning of the End for Fannie Mae

1 Hearing before the Subcommittee on Capital Markets, Insurance and Government Sponsored Enterprises of the Committee on Financial Services, Oct 6, 2004, 108th Congress.
2 Wayne Passmore, The GSE Implicit Subsidy and the Value of Government Ambiguity, 2003-64 Federal Reserve Board, Finance and Economics Discussions Series.
3 Testimony of Chairman Alan Greenspan, Government-Sponsored Enterprises before the Committee on Banking, Housing and Urban Affairs, US Senate, Feb 24, 2004.
4 See Wayne Passmore The GSE Implicit Subsidy and the Value of the Government Ambiguity, 2003-64, Federal Reserve Board, Finance and Economics Discussion Series.
5 Congressional Budget Office, Federal Subsidies and the Housing GSEs, May, 2001.
6 Congressional Budget Office, Updated Estimates of the Subsidies to the Housing GSEs, Director, Douglas Holtz-Eakin, April 8, 2004.
7 Op.cit p. 2.
8 Government Sponsored Enterprises. A Framework for Strengthening GSE Governance and Oversight, David Walker, Comptroller General of the United States, Testimony before the Committee on Banking, Housing and Urban Affairs, US Senate, Feb 10, 2004, p. 9.
9 Testimony of Chairman Alan Greenspan, Government Sponsored Enterprises, before the Committee on Banking, Housing and Urban Affairs, Feb 24, 2002, p. 3.

10 Ibid, pp. 3–4.
11 OFHEO news release, October 9, 2003.
12 The OFHEO Report: Allegations of Accounting and Management Failure at Fannie Mae, op.cit p. 9.
13 OFHEO Letter to Franklin Raines, Feb 24, 2004, pp. 1–2.
14 Business Day, *New York Times*, Fannie Mae's Earnings Drop but its Mortgage Profit Rises, 20 April, 2004.
15 *Wall Street Journal*, April 20, 2004.
16 *Financial Times*, March 9, 2004.
17 Bloomberg, March 16, 2004, James Tyson.
18 OFHEO News Release, May 6, 2004.
19 Quoted by The GSE Report, May 24, 2004.
20 Review of the Office of Federal Housing Oversight and the Federal Housing Finance Board, Joint hearing before the Subcommittee on Oversight and Investigations and the Subcommittee on Capital Markets, Insurance and Government Sponsored Enterprises, July 13, 2004, pp. 34–35.
21 Op.cit p. 17.
22 Office of Compliance Office of Federal Housing Enterprise Oversight, Sept 17, 2004.
23 Address to Audit Group on What We Can Do to Help Achieve $6.46 EPS, Sampah Rajappa, FM SRC OFHEU, Special Examination of Fannie Mae, May 2006, p. 42.
24 Report of Findings to Date Special Examination of Fannie Mae, Sept 17, 2004, p. i.
25 This comes from OFHEO's Report on the Special Examination of Fannie Mae, May 2006, pp. 170–171, which also documents the KPMG work papers and the quoted memorandum, pp. 170–171.
26 A REMIC entitles the investor to a claim on the principal and interest payments on the mortgage underpinning the security. The interest rate paid is usually related to the rates homeowners are paying on their mortgages.
27 OFHEO also discovered that if negative, a deferred expense was calculated as far back as 1995; and that the calculation of a constant effective yield for REMIC securities had not been carried out at all, even though SFAS took effect in 1988.
28 Op.cit p. 13.
29 SFAS 91 Accounting for non-refundable fees and costs associated with originating or acquiring loans, and the initial direct costs of leases, Dec 1986, Financial Accounting Standards Board.
30 Memorandum form Mr Jeff Juliane to Distribution, dated March 12, 1999, OFHEO ibid, pp. 40–41.
31 Op.cit p. 86.
32 Ibid, p. 86.
33 Op.cit p. 93.
34 Op cit. pp. 138 and 144.
35 Op.cit p. 145.
36 Op.cit p. 154.
37 Op.cit OFHEO interview with Sam Rajappa, p. 155.
38 Op.cit p. 165.
39 Enhancing confidence in financial reporting, Group of Thirty, p. 14.
40 Roger Barnes, Written testimony, p. 9.
41 Op.cit p. 11.
42 Op.cit p. 16.

43 Standard & Poor's Corporate Governance Score, Standard & Poor's, January 30, 2003, p. 2.
44 Op.cit, p. 3.
45 Op.cit p. 5.
46 Full hearing p. 11.
47 FM Watch was a group of mortgage insurers and lenders and trade associations, which was opposed to Fannie and Freddie's operations and kept a careful watch on the behaviour of the GSEs. From the point of view of Fannie Mae, they were a group of insurers, high-cost lenders and trade associations representing subprime lenders who wanted to roll back Fannie Mae policies that cut the costs to the consumers.
48 Op.cit p. 19.
49 Op.cit p. 64.
50 Op.cit pp. 65–66.
51 Op.cit pp. 3–4.
52 Op.cit p. 7.
53 Op.cit p. 87.
54 Op.cit p. 23. Armando Falcon's oral testimony to the hearing.
55 Op.cit p. 69.
56 Op.cit Reply of Mr Raines to Mr Scott, p. 90.
57 Op.cit p. 103.
58 Op.cit p. 117.
59 Office of the Chief Accountant Issues Statement on Fannie Mae Accounting, Dec 15, 2004.
60 Press release from the office of Senator Richard Shelby, 12/16/04.
61 Press release form the office of Representative Michael G. Oxley, 12/15/2004.
62 Letter from Rep. Richard H. Baker to the Honorable Armando Falcon, Director of OFHEO, 12/16/2004.
63 OECD Economic Surveys, 2004, United States, p. 17.

Chapter 10 The Years 2005 to 2007:
Drinking in the last chance saloon

1 American Banker, 01/20/2005 and 01/26/2005.
2 Richard Baker, quoted in The Main Wire, 27/01/2005, quoted in The GSE Report, Jan 31, 2005.
3 Bloomberg News, 01/27/05.
4 Press Release from the office of Representative Barney Frank, 12/16/04.
5 Each Congress lasts for two years. The 106th Congress covered the years 1999–2000. Hearing, 109th Congress, April 13, 2005, p. 1.
6 Op.cit p. 6.
7 Op.cit p. 7.
8 Op.cit p. 24.
9 Op.cit p. 4.
10 Statement of Alan Greenspan, Chairman, Board of Governors of the Federal Reserve System before the Committee on Banking, Housing and Urban Affairs, US Senate, April 6, 2005, p. 5.
11 Op.cit p. 7.
12 Op.cit p. 23.

13 Op.cit pp. 2–3.
14 CBO Testimony Douglas Holtz-Eakin, Aligning costs and benefits of the housing GSEs, April 21, 2005, see Table 1, before the Committee on Banking, Housing and Urban Affairs.
15 Systemic Risk: Fannie Mae, Freddie Mac and the Role of OFHEO, 2003, p. 55 (note that all the figures relate to year end 2001).
16 OFHEO's analysis was based on Fannie Mae's analysis and methodology as used in mid-2000 and then updated by OFHEO for the 2003 report; see pp. 75–77 of the report.
17 Statement of Douglas Holtz-Eakin, Aligning the Costs and Benefits of the Housing Government-Sponsored Enterprises, before the Committee on Banking, Housing and Urban Affairs, US Senate, April 21, 2005.
18 Systemic Risk: Fannie Mae, Freddie Mac and the Role of OFHEO, OFHEO, Feb 2003, p. 63.
19 Congressional hearing, April 13, 2005, op.cit pp. 44–46.
20 Concentration and risk in OTC markets for US dollar interest rate options. Staff report for the Federal Reserve, March 2005.
21 Risk Transfer and Financial Stability. Federal Reserve Bank of Chicago's 41st Conference on Banking Structure, May 5, 2005.
22 Op.cit p. 3.
23 Risk Transfer and Financial Stability, Federal Reserve Bank of Chicago's 41st Annual Conference on Bank Structure, May 5, 2005.
24 Op.cit p. 3.
25 Remarks by Chairman Alan Greenspan to a conference on Housing, Mortgage Finance and the Macro-economy, Federal Reserve Bank of Atlanta, May 19, 2005.
26 Op.cit p. 3.
27 Op.cit pp. 4–5.
28 US Fed News, 07/28/05.
29 Dated Sept 2, 2005.
30 A report to the Special Review Committee of the Board of Directors of Fannie Mae, Paul, Weiss, Rifkidn, Wharton & Garrison LLP, and Huron Consulting Group, February 23, 2006.
31 Op.cit p. 2.
32 Op.cit p. 416, Rudman report.
33 Ibid.
34 It was based on the documents it eventually received from Fannie Mae after numerous requests, amounting to some 2.8m pages of hard copy document and 4.1m pages of electronic documents from Fannie Mae and the Special Review Committee, plus over 700,000 work pages and other documents from KPMG, LLP and Ernst & Young. To that total should be added the documents the Counsel to the Special Review Committee received from Fannie Mae, as well as copies of memoranda of 241 interviews it conducted with current and former employees of Fannie Mae and third parties. OFHEO also reviewed the transcripts of 47 interviews of current and former employees conducted by the SEC. OFHEO conducted 26 informal interviews and 55 formal, on-the-record interviews of current and former Fannie Mae employees and board members as well as 7 interviews with current and former KPMG employees assigned to Fannie Mae.
35 Hearing before the Senate Committee on Housing, Banking and Urban Affairs, June 16, 2006, p. 71.
36 Op.cit p. 2.

37 Congressional Committee on Financial Services, Subcommittee on Capital Markets, June 6, 2006, p. 7.
38 Testimony of Christopher Cox, Chairman US Securities and Exchange Commission, "Accounting Irregularities at Fannie Mae," Before the Senate Committee on Banking, Housing and Urban Affairs, June 15, 2006.
39 Op.cit. p. 8 and p. 6.
40 Hearing before the Committee on Banking, Housing and Urban Affairs, June 16, 2006, p. 17.
41 Op.cit p. 19.
42 Op.cit p. 24.
43 Op.cit pp. 43–44.
44 For example, Chairman and CEO of the Ashley Group, since 1997, President of the Genesee Corporation from Dec 2000–May 31, 2004, Chairman and CEO of Sibley Mortgage Corporation & Sibley Real Estate Services, from 1991–96, and various positions in the Manning and Napier Group since 1996, as well as being a former President of the Mortgage Brokers Association. Bloomberg Business Week.
45 Op.cit pp. 47–48.
46 Op.cit p. 30.
47 Dow Jones International News, 07/26/06.
48 Reuters, 07/11/06.
49 Credit Union National Association, News Now Archive, Aug 30, 2006.
50 Senate Banking Committee hearing, Federal Reserve Second Monetary Policy Report to Congress for 2006, July 19, 2008, pp. 30–32.
51 Remarks of Randal K. Quarles, Under Secretary for Domestic Finance, US Department of the Treasury, press release, 7/19/2006 HP-21.
52 Hearing before the Subcommittee on Housing and Transportation and the Subcommittee on Economic Policy, Sept 13, 2006.
53 Senate Banking Committee Press Release, 03/07/2007.
54 Chairman Barney Frank, Congressional Financial Services Hearing, Legislative Proposals on GSE Reform, March 15, 2007, p. 3.
55 George W. Bush, Statement of Administration Policy, H.R. 1427, 2007.

Chapter 11 The Subprime Market Grew and Grew and No One Knew

1 Systemic Risk: Fannie Mae, Freddie Mac and the Role of the OFHEO, Feb 2003, p. 45.
2 Systemic Risk: Fannie and Freddie and the Role of OFHEO, Feb 2003.
3 Conforming loan limits applied throughout the USA apart from specific high-price areas, such as Hawaii, Alaska and the Virgin Islands, set in 1992 with the addition of Guam in 2001.
    Median sales prices of new homes USA (from US census bureau for new homes: 1999 between $153,000 and $172,000: 2003 between $$181,000 and $207,000; and 2006 between $226,700 and $257,000. Conforming loan limits (including both first and second loans) 1999-$240,000: 2003-$322,000 and 2006-$417,000.
4 Statement of John Duggan, Comptroller of the Currency before the Financial Crisis Inquiry Commission, April 8, 2010. Appendix B, p. 1.
5 In November 2008, Fannie acknowledged that it had "other loans with some features that are similar to Alt-A and subprime loans that (it had) not classified as Alt-A or subprime because they do not meet (its) classification criteria." P. 182 of Fannie's Q3: 2008 10-Q.

6　The HMDA data were deficient in many ways, and HUD sought to augment the data by identifying lenders who predominantly originate subprime loans by using a combination of industry trade publications and HMDA analysis. To confirm those lenders thought to be engaging in subprime lending, HUD conducted interviews with lenders and those who confirmed that at least 50% of their conventional originations were subprime loans were included in the list of subprime lenders. This methodology has been used in virtually all studies of subprime lending using HMDA data.

7　Op.cit pp. 1–2.

8　C. Mayer, K.M. Pence & S.M. Sherland, The Rise in Mortgage Defaults, 2008, p. 4.

9　These comments and examples are given in "A Journey to the Alt-A zone" by Nomura, 3 June, 2003. It is especially interesting as it looks at Alt-A mortgages from the point of view of investment in MBSs, and provides an insight into market behavior in 2003, quite early in terms of regulatory and analysts' concerns about subprime lending and foreclosure risks.

10　P. 3., "A Journey to Alt-A," Nomura.

11　Op.cit p. 12.

12　Christopher Mayer & Karen Pence, Subprime Mortgages: What, Where and to Whom?, Federal Reserve Board, 2008–29, p. 1.

13　Subprime Markets, the Role of the GSEs, and Risk-Based Pricing, prepared for HUD by K. Temkin, J. Johnson & D. Levy, March 2002. It is designed as advice to HUD and was based on interviews with subprime lenders amongst others.

14　Credit Risk, Credit Scoring and the Performance of Home Mortgages, Federal Reserve Bulletin, July 1996, Robert Avery, R. Bostic, P. Calem & G. Canner, p. 644. The same paper notes the likely geographic concentration of delinquencies and foreclosures, which is obvious given the impact of the CRA requirements to lend in certain Census tracts defined by low-to-moderate incomes or very low incomes. At that time the research had not been carried out except for a very limited study in Philadelphia, see page 647. For some reason, this seems to have been regarded as a novel consideration by later researchers, no doubt influenced by the concentration of foreclosures, especially in urban areas as 2008 approached.

15　Opening statements of Chairman Sarbanes and Senator Gramm, Senate Committee on Banking, Housing and Urban Affairs, Examination of the Problem, Impact, and Responses of Predatory Mortgage Lending Practices, July 27, 2001, pp. 5–7.

16　Report of the Staff to Chairman Gramm, Committee on Banking, Housing and Urban Affairs, Aug 23, 2000.

17　Joint Hearing Subcommittee on Housing & Community Opportunity and the Subcommittee on Financial Institutions & Consumer Credit of the Committee on Financial Services, Subprime Lending: Defining the Market and Its Customers, March 30, 2004.

18　Federal Reserve Board, press release concerning the final rule to amend its regulations aimed at curbing predatory lending (mandatory on Oct 1, 2002), Dec 14, 2001. It sought to extend the HOEPA requirements more widely by broadening the scope of loans subject to the Act; that is, by lowering the rate-based trigger by 2% for first lien loans and the fee-based trigger to include cost-optional insurance and other provisions at closing. Lenders learnt to evade provisions by slightly lowering the interest rates and fees on subprime loans below the threshold. Enforcement was rather ineffective at any rate.

19　Federal Reserve System, Truth in Lending: Final Rule: official staff commentary, 73 Reg. 44522, 44536, July 30, 2008. Once again, the triggers were first lien loans of 1.5% or more above the average prime offer rate for a comparable transaction, and 3.5% for second lien loans.

20 Subprime Foreclosures: the Smoking Gun of Predatory Lending, HUD, July 2002, H. Bunce, D. Gruenstein, C. Herbert & R. Scheesele.

Preying on the Neighborhood: subprime lending and Chicagoland Foreclosures, National Training & Information Center, September 1999.

21 Federal Home Loan Mortgage Corporation Act, 1992, sec 302, definitions and section 305.

22 12 CFR Appendix A to Part 1720-Policy Guidance: Minimum Safety and Soundness Requirements, Update to December 30, 2005.

23 Credit Risk, Credit Scoring and the Performance of Home Mortgages, op cit, p. 642 ff.

24 *New York Times*, Sept 30, 1999.

25 Business Wire, The $2 trillion American Dream Commitment, March 14, 2001.

26 Fannie Mae, Goldman Sachs &Executive Leadership Council and Foundation, p. 17.

27 The Seattle Post-Intelligence, January 29, 2003.

28 *New York Times*, "At Freddie Mac, chief discarded warning signs," by Charles Duhigg, August 5, 2008.

29 Ibid.

30 Interview with USA Today, August 23, 2004.

31 Source: Origination volumes are from The 2007 Mortgage Market Statistical Annual-Vol 1, p. 209, Inside B&C Lending.

32 Survey of Credit Underwriting Practices, June 2005.

33 The OCC did set out a rule in 2004, prohibiting mortgages to borrowers who could not repay, but it was vague and ineffective. Bank Activities and Operations: Real Estate Lending and Appraisals, 69 Fed. Reg. 1,904, 1,911 (Jan 13, 2004).

34 The Senate Permanent Subcommittee on Investigations, April 2010, Wall Street and the Financial Crisis. Summary of some of the main points from evidence received.

35 Quoted by S&P Structured Finance Ratings, January 1997, p. 14.

36 Fannie Mae 2009 Third Quarter Credit Supplement, p. 5. This is the argument presented by Ed Pinto in Sizing Total Federal Government and Federal Agency Contributions to Subprime and Alt-A Loans in US First Mortgage Market, as at 06/30/2008, p. 3.

37 E. Pinto: Memorandum: Sizing Total Federal Government and Federal Agency Contributions to Subprime and Alt-A loans in US First Mortgage Market as at 30th June 2008. Ed Pinto was formerly Chief Credit Officer at Fannie Mae in the 1980s, and subsequently a consultant to the mortgage-finance industry; he is now a Resident Fellow at the American Enterprise Institute.

These figures are all taken from Fannie Mae 2008, Q.2. 10-Q Investor Summary pages 20 and 30 and p. 5 of the above. With regard to the self-denominated Alt-A and self-denominated Subprime Private MBSs, no average principal balance per loans is provided, Fannie Mae's average loan size for its portfolio of Alt-A loans is provided.

38 Fannie Mae 2009 Second Quarter Credit Supplement, p. 5.

39 Fannie Mae 2008 Q 2 10-Q Investor summary p. 30. This is the result of multiplying the 5% difference noted times Fannie's trillion total single-family portfolio at June 30, 2008. This yields $133bn before addressing overlap.

40 Freddie Mac Second Quarter 2008 Financial Results. Conference Call Slides, p. 36 and p. 26. The latter slide lists five features totaling $588bn, to which sum

a sixth feature was added, FICO 620–659 in the amount of $164bn, bringing the total to $752bn.

41 Pinto bases these results on the MBA's National Delinquency Survey, Q2 2008.

42 Inside Mortgage Finance Data indicates that 66% of MBS private issuances over 2004–2007 were either Alt-A or subprime.

43 Source: Inside Mortgage Finance, quoted by E. Pinto, op,cit p. 12.

44 Between Q1 2008 and Q3 2009, the MBA has reported that it covers between 80 and 85% of outstanding first lien mortgages and the total number of loans reported by the NDS varies by no more than 800,000 over this period, indicating that the variance over this period was about 1 million loans. Pinto argues that using a midpoint of 82.5% coverage and 45. 4 million first mortgage loans covered by the Q2, 2008 survey yields a total of 55m first lien loans.

45 OFHEO Annual Report to Congress, April 2008, pp. 20–21.

46 Reforming the Regulation of the Government Sponsored Enterprises before the Senate Banking, Housing and Urban Affairs Committee, February 7, 2008.

47 Op.cit p. 7.

48 Subprime Markets, the Role of the GSEs and Risk-based Pricing, K. Temkin, J. Johnson & D. Levy, Subprime Markets, the Role of the GSEs, and Risk-Based Pricing, p. vii.

49 B. Ambrose, K. Temkin & T. Thibodeau, 2002, An Analysis of the Effects of the GSE Affordable Goals on Low and Moderate Income Families, Office of Policy Development and Research.

50 T. DiVenti, Fannie Mae and Freddie Mac: Past, Present and Future, Office of Policy Development and Research, 2009.

51 Testimony by Daniel H. Mudd before the US House Committee on Financial Services, April 17, 2007.

52 Memorandum for the record, Group interview with Tom Lund, former EVP of Fannie Mae for single-family business for the Financial Crisis Inquiry Commission, pp. 3–7. The disclaimer on this and the interview summary is that this is a paraphrasing of the interview dialogue, and is not a transcript. I have therefore not quoted from this and the interview with Daniel Mudd, but have summarized what seem to me to be significant parts of it. Both documents are publicly available.

53 Memorandum for the Record of the Interview with Daniel Mudd on March 26, 2010, pp. 2–4.

54 Chairman Ben Bernanke, The Subprime Mortgage Market, May 17, 2007.

Chapter 12 Why Did Fannie Mae and Freddie Mac Get Away with It for So Long?

1 Federal National Mortgage Association Charter Act 12 U.S.C. 1716–1723; Federal Home Loan Mortgage Corporation Act, 12 U.S.C. 1451–1459 Federal Housing Enterprises Financial Safety and Soundness Act, Title XIII of P.L. 92-550 (12 U.S.C. 4501).

2 Memorandum for the Record, Interview with Henry Paulson, April 2, 2010, p. 7.

3 Mortgage Giant overstated its capital base, New York Times, Sept 8, 2008, based on a report prepared by Morgan Stanley and the Treasury.

4 Testimony before the House Financial Services Committee, September 10, 2003, p. 4.

5 Quoted in the *Washington Post*, How Washington Failed to Rein in Fannie and Freddie, Sept 14, 2008.

6 A Framework for Strengthening GSE Governance and Oversight, GAO Report, GAO-04-269T p. 7.

   The GAO published numerous reports critical of the oversight of the GSEs.

   OFHEO Faces Challenges in Implementing a Comprehensive Oversight Programme: GAO Oct 22, 1997.

   OFHEO's Progress in Implementing A Comprehensive Oversight Programme for Fannie Mae and Freddie Mac, July 29, 1998.

   OFHEO's Risk-Based Capital Stress Test Incorporating New Business is Not Advisable, GAO June 2002, GAO-02-521.

   Government-Sponsored Enterprises: A Framework for Strengthening GSE Governance and Oversight, February 2004, GAO-04-269T.

   Housing Government-Sponsored Enterprises: A New Oversight Structure is Needed, April 2005, GAO-05-576T.

7 GSE Reform: A Priority for 2007, NAAHL Legislative Conference, Washington DC, Feb 1, 2007, p. 1.

8 GAO-01-322, Financial Regulators' Enforcement Authorities, January 2001, p. 5.

9 The Velvet Fist of Fannie Mae, *New York Times*, 20 April, 1997.

10 Ibid.

11 Congressional Budget Office, Assessing the Public Costs and Benefits of Fannie Mae and Freddie Mac, May 1996, p. 16.

12 Office of Inspector General, Audit Report 2004-KC-0001 and Audit Report 2005-KC-0001.

13 OFHEO Special Examination of Fannie Mae, 2006, Chapter VIII, Attempts to Interfere with OFHEO's Special Examination.

14 Government Sponsored Enterprises (GSEs): Why is Effective Government Supervision Hard to Achieve?, 37th annual conference on Bank Structure and Competition, Federal Reserve Bank of Chicago, May 10, 2001, p. 6. He also quotes some newspaper headlines illustrating the determination to hold on to the charter:

   "The Money Machine: how Fannie Mae wields power," *Washington Post*, Jan 16, 1995.

   "A Medici with your money: Fannie Mae's Strategic Generosity," Slate, Feb 22, 1997.

   "Firms Report Fannie Mae, Freddie Mac Threats," *Wall Street Journal*, March 8, 2001.

15 Quoted in USA Today, Fannie Mae, Freddie Mac spent millions on lobbying, July 17, 2008.

16 How Washington Failed to Rein in Fannie, Freddie, *Washington Post*, Sept 17, 2008.

17 Freddie Mac paid $2m to thwart regulation, The Boston Globe, October 20, 2008.

18 USA Today, Fannie Mae, Freddie Mac spent millions on lobbying, July 17, 2008.

19 Fannie, Freddie Takeover Ends Lobbying Effort Bigger than GE's, September 9, 2008. Individual companies and organizations have been required to file semi-annual reports to the Secretary of the Senate's Office of Public Records (SOPR), listing the name of each client, the total income received from each of them, and specify the lobbying issues under the Lobbying Disclosure Act, 1995, which chamber of Congress and which executive departments or agencies were contacted. Hence the precise figures for Fannie Mae and Freddie Mac, where it would also figure in their accounts, for whatever that was worth.

20 *New York Times*, April 2, 1997.

21 Allbusiness banking, August 11, 1998.
22 Ibid.
23 April 17, 1996.
24 Fannie Mae press releases, 11 Sept, 2000 and Sept 7, 2000.
25 *Wall Street Journal*, May 7, 2001.
26 Quoted in HUD Review: Fannie Mae Offices Misused, FreeRepublic, Oct 17, 2005.
27 Unfortunately it appears that this press release is no longer on HUD's website, but it is quoted in The GSE Report for Oct 24, 2005, p. 7.
28 Op.cit p. 8.
29 R.D. Utt, Time to Reform Fannie Mae and Freddie Mac, Backgrounder, June 20, 2005, p. 5.
30 *Washington Post*, 23 Feb, 2007.
31 Ibid.
32 Mortgage Makers vs the World, October 16, 2005, *New York Times*.
33 Npr.org July 15, 2008. http://www.npr.org/templates/story/story.php?storyId= 92540620
34 See also Unaffordable Housing and Political Kickbacks, Darrell Issa.
35 Friends of Angelo: Countrywide's Systematic and Successful Effort to Buy Influence and Block Reform, Staff Report, Committee on Oversight and Government Reform, March 19, 2009.
36 Daniel Golden, Angelo Mozilo, Former CEO of Mortgage Lender gave special deals to the Well-Connnected, Including Senators, NBC News, Transcripts, Oct 30, 2008. Quoted in the above report.
37 Op.cit p. 24.
38 Making Friends, Deniz Igan and Prachi Mishra, Finance and Development, June 2011, p. 27.
39 A Fistful of Dollars: Lobbying and the Financial Crisis, D. Igan, P. Mishra and T. Tressel, Research Dept, April 16, 2010, p. 27.

Chapter 13 The End Cometh

1 US Foreclosure Market Reports for 2006, 2007 and 2008, published by Realtytrack. In June 2007, Realtytrack announced that its figures suggested their figures counted only foreclosures, and that future estimates would make it clear that they covered every stage from notice of default to foreclosure, and not all the stages would necessarily lead to foreclosure. In Chairman Bernanke's speech he referred to foreclosure figures based on data from the Mortgage Bankers Association, adjusted to reflect the limited coverage of their sample. Once again the lack of a complete set of data, recording delinquencies and foreclosures, is evident, so that the trends cannot be clearly seen. It is possible that the limited data available led the Chairman to underestimate the effects of subprime lending in May 2007.
2 Bloomberg, Aug 23, 2007, Lehman shuts unit; Toll of Lenders tops 100: Subprime Scorecard.
3 Chairman Christopher Dodd's opening statement, House Financial Services Committee, March 22, 2007, pp. 1–2. In fact, the ban on adjustable rate mortgages was lifted in 1981 (after the Savings & Loans crisis) and Regulation Z was amended to include ARMS disclosure requirements. Christopher Dodd had put his name forward in the race for the Democrat Presidential nomination, but lack of support meant that he withdrew from the contest in the summer.

4 Federal Financial Regulatory Agencies Issue Final Guidance on NonTradtional
   Mortgage Product Risks, September 29, 2006 and their Final Statement on
   Subprime Mortgage Lending June 29, 2006. Interagency Guidance had previously
   been issued on predatory lending on March 1, 1999. This was intended to provide
   the supervisory expectations for examination reviews. The Agencies finally issued
   subprime mortgage lending guidance on June 27, taking effect on July 10, 2007.
   The Guidance still did not provide a definition of subprime lending but provided
   a range of credit characteristics of subprime borrowers as providing illustration.
   Predatory lending would be identified by loan flipping; loans based on the ability
   of the borrower to repay rather than the value of the property and fraudulent
   and/or deceptive practices, and tougher underwriting conditions for hybrid
   ARMS. In May, Chairman Bernanke was able to report that the Federal Reserve
   was conducting a thorough review of all its options under the Truth In Lending
   Act, and held a series of four public hearings on predatory hearings and on the
   effectiveness of the current guidance. His view was that disclosure of the terms
   of the contract was generally sufficient. The aim should be to "curb abuses while
   preserving access to credit."
5 OFHEO James B. Lockhart commends GSEs on Implementation of Subprime
   Mortgage Lending Guidance, September 10, 2007.
6 James B. Lockhart III, speech to the Mortgage Bankers' Association, May 23,
   2007.
7 Chairman Ben Bernanke, May 17, 2007, The Subprime Mortgage Market, p. 3.
8 House Committee on Financial Services, Improving Federal Consumer Protection,
   June 13, 2007.
9 Federal Reserve press release June 5, 2007.
10 IMB Report, August 2, 2007.
11 Survey conducted by Campbell Communications in late August and David Olsen,
   both quoted in Mortgage Brokers Association, November 2007.
12 Ibid.
13 Thompson Financial, Oct 23, 2007 Interview with James Lockhart.
14 Home Mortgage Defaults and Foreclosures, Recent Trends and Associated
   Economic and Market Developments, Briefing to the Committee on Financial
   Services House of Representatives, Oct 10, 2007, GAO Report. These figures are
   based on the National Delinquency Survey produced by the Mortgage Bankers
   Association. The figure of 1.1m loans (about 13% of ARMS) is based on a study
   by C. Cagan in 2007 and is of course limited to one particular subset of subprime
   loans, which is an under-estimate anyway. (C. Cagan Mortgage Payment Reset,
   The Issue and the Impact, First American Corelogic, Inc., March 19, 2007.)
15 The HOPENOW initiative consisted of an alliance of more than 50 mortgage
   servicers, major banks, mortgage companies, the GSEs, mortgage counselors,
   investors and trade organizations. The "aggressive plan" involved direct mail to
   at-risk borrowers, call centers and advertising.
16 Testimony of Treasury Secretary Henry M. Paulson before the Committee on the
   Legislative and Regulatory Options for Minimizing and Mitigating Mortgage
   Foreclosures, Sept 20, 2007.
17 Ibid.
18 Chairman Bernanke: Testimony before the Joint Economic Committee.
19 This is one of several bills which were introduced in the 110th Congress
   (H.R.1427; S.1100 proposed changes in the rules governing the activities of Fannie
   and Freddie; H.R.3777, H.R.3838 and S.1269 and S.2169, focus on allowing the
   GSEs to increase their retained mortgage portfolios as well as S.2036.)

20 The *Wall Street Journal*, BofA Haunted by Countrywide Deal, June 30, 2011.
21 John T. Dunlop Memorial Lecture, Joint Center for Housing Studies at Harvard University, Feb 3, 2004, pp. 10–16.
22 Reuters, March 9, 2007.
23 OFHEO Press Release, 01/24/08.
24 Congressional Quarterly Online, Jan 25, 2008.
25 Senate Banking Committee, Hearing on the Reform of GSE Regulation, Feb 7, 2008.
26 Senate Banking Committee hearing on the Reform of GSE Regulation, Chairman Dodd's Opening Statement, March 6, 2008.
27 Op.cit Senate Hearing Feb 14, 2008.
28 Freddie Mac, Investors Summary, Feb 28, 2008, p. 1.
29 Bear Stearns, JP Morgan and Maiden Lane LLC, Regulatory Reform, Board of the Governors of the Federal Reserve System, last update Feb 10, 2012.
30 Testimony, April 3, 2008.
31 Federal Reserve Press Releases, March 7, 2008 and March 11, 2008.
32 Congressional Budget Office report, Policy Options for Housing and the Financial Markets, p. 2 April, 2008.
33 Other indices include Radar Logic. OFHEO's purchase-only index and S&P Case Schiller indices cover both 20 cities or 10 cities, all of a differing basis.
34 The MBA survey is based on limited data. Press release, December 5, 2008.
35 M. Zandi, Moody's Economy.com.
36 This was part of the stimulus package passed by the House of Representatives allowing the GSEs to buy jumbo loans. Economic Stimulus Act, 2008.
37 OFHEO Annual Report to Congress, 2008, released April 15, 2008.
38 Lessons to be Learned from Mortgage Market Turmoil, 44th Annual Conference on Bank Structure and Competition, Chicago, May 16, 2008, pp. 7–8.
39 W. Poole, Housing in the Macroeconomy, Federal Reserve Bank of St Louis, May/June 2003, p. 2.
40 US Weighs Takeover of Two Mortgage Giants, July 11, 2008.
41 US Department of Treasury Press Release, HP-1079 July 13, 2008.
42 Press Release by Senators Christopher Dodd and Richard Shelby, July 23, 2008.
43 The Way Forward for Fannie and Freddie, Lawrence Summers, July 27, 2008. *Financial Times*.
44 The SEC issued an emergency order restricting short selling in the stock of 19 financial institutions, including Fannie and Freddie. This order expired on July 29, when it was renewed and expired again on August 12 at 11.59 p.m.
45 Interview with the Telegraph, August 22, 2008.
46 CBNC News, August 25, 2008.
47 In a Bloomberg article of September 9, 2008, Fannie and Freddie were described as a "House of Cards."
48 See again, E. Pinto.
49 Statement of FHFA Director James B. Lockhart, FHFA, September 7, 2008.
50 The details of the GSE MBS purchase program and GSE preferred stock were released on September 7, 2008. They are as follows:
    Senior Preferred Stock Purchase Agreement. Treasury will buy preferred stock as needed to ensure that each GSE maintains a positive net worth. The capacity of the agreement is at $100bn for each GSE. In return the government has received warrants to buy up to 79.9% of GSE common stock for $0.00001 per share. (This means that if the GSEs emerge from conservatorship as stock corporations, the government will be the majority owner and will have the option of selling its shares at a profit.)

The GSE MBS purchase program. Treasury will buy newly issued Fannie and Freddie MBSs in the open market as needed to improve the availability and affordability of mortgage credit.

The GSE Credit Facility. The GSEs will have access to short-term loans from the Treasury and will be allowed to post MBSs as collateral.

51 "Mortgage Bailout is Greeted with Relief," September 9, 2008.

52 Quoted by CNNMoney.com September 11, 2008. Money Morning, Foreign Bond Holders – and not the US Mortgage Market – drove the Fannie/Freddie Bailout.

53 US Treasury Department, Foreign Preliminary Holdings of US Securities as of June 30, 2008.

   See also China's Holdings of US Securities: Implications for the US Economy, July 30, 2008, CRS Report for Congress.

54 Statement of James B. Lockhart III, Director FHFA before the Financial Services Subcommittee on Capital Markets, Insurance and the GSEs, June 3, 2009, p. 4.

55 "Housing at the Tipping Point: The Outlook for the US Residential Real Estate Market," Moody's Economy.com (a separate business unit from Moody's Investors Service).

56 Quoted in the "Financial Crisis Inquiry Commission Report" Chapter 11, Te Bust, p. 223.

57 See Sam Jones, "How Moody's Faltered," *Financial Times*, Oct 18, 2007.

58 Standard & Poor's press release, RatingsDirect, Oct 23, 2007.

59 Josh Rosen, Managing Director, Graham Fisher & Co., quoted in Bloomberg, Moody's Cuts Ratings on CDOs Tied to Subprime Bonds, October 26, 2007.

60 The Credit Rating Crisis, E. Benmelech & J. Dlugosz, Harvard University, pp. 162–163.

61 Financial Crisis Inquiry Commission, Credit ratings and the Financial Crisis, Preliminary Staff Report, June 2010, p. 36. The report only refers to Moody's for the sake of simplicity.

62 Op.cit p. 162.

63 *Financial Times*, July 9, 2007.

64 S&P takes action on 6,389 subprime RMBS ratings and 1,953 CDO ratings. Jan 30, 2008, p. 3.

65 S&P Press Release, Jan 30, 2008.

66 S&P Takes Action on 6,389 transactions backed by US first lien subprime mortgage as collateral and rated between January 2006 and June 2007, US Subprime RMBS ratings and 1,953 CDO Ratings, Jan 30, 2008, p. 3.

67 Credit rating agencies use a scale of grades from AAA to C, where the former have historically had a loss rate of less than .05%; for BBB the expected loss rate was about 1 percent. Grades AAA through to BBB were generally called investment grade while those with rating below BBB or Baa3 are called below investment grade or sometimes "junk" investments. Clearly these play a significant role in assessing the safety of investments. In 2006, Congress enacted the Credit Rating Agency Reform Act which took effect in June 2007. The law prohibits the SEC from regulating the substance, criteria or methodologies used in credit rating standards, which as the above sample of e-mail traffic shows should have been one of the major concerns.

68 Wall Street and the Financial Crisis: The Role of the Credit Rating Agencies, p. 11.

69 SEC Summary Report of the Issues identified in the Commission Staff Examination of Select Credit Rating Agencies (which includes Fitch), July, 2008.

70 Op.cit p. 6.

71 Ibid p. 11.

72 Merrill Lynch reports Loss on $8.4bn Write-Down, Bloomberg Oct 24, 2007.

73 Msnbc.com UBS writes off $10bn in subprime losses, Dec 10, 2007.
74 Chairman Ben Bernanke, The Economic Outlook, Testimony Before the Committee on Budget, US House of Representatives, January 17, 2008.

Chapter 14 Fannie and Freddie: A story without an ending

1 The rating agencies perform a critical role in structured finance ... evaluating the credit quality of the transactions ... they are considered credible, because they do not have a financial interest in a security's cost or yield. Ratings are important because investors generally accept ratings by the major public rating agencies in lieu of conducting a due diligence investigation of the underlying assets and the servicer, Comptroller of the Currency Administrator of National Banks, Comptroller's Handbook, 1997.
2 IMF Global Financial Stability Report, 2008.
3 The Commodity Futures Modernisation Act was signed into law by President Clinton, 2000, following the recommendations of the President's Working Group on the Financial Markets, which reported in November 1999. Their recommendations were that derivatives and swaps should be excluded from regulation, with the strong support of Robert Rubin, then Secretary to the Treasury, followed by Lawrence Summers and Alan Greenspan.
4 S. Kamin and Laurie DeMarco: How did a Domestic Housing Slump Turn into a Global Financial Crisis, International Finance Discussion Paper, Federal Reserve Board, January 2010.
5 The CBO points out that another alternative would be to use the Fair Credit Reform Act, 1990, used for federal programmes which provide loans or guarantees. The main difference is the discount rate used to calculate the present value of future costs of guarantees or acquisitions for which the former uses interest rates on Treasury securities. The fair value method is not only more comprehensive, but also recognises the financial risk the government assumes. Under FCRA, the new obligations for Fannie Mae and Freddie Mac and their continuing operations generate budgetary *savings*, under fair-value accounting, they generate *costs*.
6 Congressional Budget Office Statement of D Lewis, The Budgetary Cost of Fannie Mae and Freddie Mac and Options for the Future Federal Role in the Secondary Mortgage Market, before the Committee on Budget, US House of Representatives, June 2, 2011, pp. 3, 7.
7 N Eric Weiss Fannie Mae's and Freddie Mac's Financial Status: Frequently Asked Questions, Congressional Research Service, 27/9/2012.
8 Quoted by CNN Money.com Feb 11, 2011.
9 Treasury Department Press Release, August 17, 2012.
10 Peter Wallison: Did Geithner seal Fannie and Freddie's fate? Orange County Register, August 22, 2012.
11 FHA's 2011 Actuarial Review: A Combination of Rosy Scenarios, Edward Pinto, AEI, Nov 16, 2011.
12 Annual Report to Congress on the Financial Status of the FHA's Mutual Mortgage Insurance Fund for the Fiscal Year 2012.
13 As estimated by FHA Watch in November 2012.
14 FHA, the Next Housing Bailout: Update and Evaluation, Joe Gyourko, Martin Bucksbaum Professor of Real Estate, Finance and Business Economics & Public Policy, The Wharton School, November 2012, p. 2.

15 Op.cit p. 1.

16 Are there government barriers to the housing market recovery? Before the US House of Representatives, Committee on Financial Services, Sub-committee on Insurance, Housing and Community Opportunity, Feb 16, 2011, pp. 6–7.

17 See, for example, OIG's Memorandum 2011-CF-1801 An Underwriting Review of 15FHA Lenders Demonstrated that HUD Missed Critical Opportunities to Recover Losses to the FHA Insurance Fund, March 2, 2011.

18 "Building a Mortgage Infrastructure for the Future." Edward J DeMarco, Speech to SIFMA, Dec 6, 2012, p. 5.

19 President Bush's Administration did at least recognize the dangers posed by Fannie Mae and Freddie Mac, spending most of his Presidency trying to get Congress to restrain their activities through regulation.

20 The Times, Kick-start for housing as Cameron pledges £930m, Tuesday 22 November.

21 Mortgages, housing and monetary policy–what lies ahead? Speech by David Miles.

22 Home Ownership and Its Benefits, August 1995, Urban Policy Brief, No 2.

23 Prof Stan Leibowitz, New York Times, Feb 5, 2008.

24 Chairman Ben Bernanke, Causes of the Recent Financial and Economic Crisis, Before the Financial Crisis Inquiry Commission, Sept 2, 2010, p. 4.

25 "Foreclosures continue: what needs to change in the government response"? Committee on Oversight and Government Reform, US House of Representatives, February 25, 2010.

26 Challenges in Housing and Mortgage Markets, Remarks by Ben S Bernanke, Chairman, Board of Governors of the Federal Reserve System at the Operation HOPE Global Financial Dignity Summit, Atlanta, Georgia, pp. 6–7.

27 FHFA seasonally adjusted house price index for USA.

28 The final rule implements Sections 1411, 1412 and 1414 of the Dodd-Frank Act. Consumer Finance file 201301: Ability-to-repay and Qualified Mortgage Standards. The rule is due to take effect in January 2014.

29 P. 399.

30 Paragraph 43 © (2)(viii) p. 741.

31 P. 5.

32 Are there Government Barriers to the Housing Market Recovery? Before the US House of Representatives, Committee on Financial Services, Sub committee on Insurance, Housing and Community Opportunity, Feb 16, 2011, pp. 6–7.

33 SEC charges former Fannie Mae and Freddie Mac Executives with Securities Fraud, SEC press release, December 16, 2011.

34 An attempt by three former senior executives, including David Mudd, to have the case against them dismissed failed in August, 2012. As of December 31, 2012, the case continues. No final decision has been made.

35 Federal Register Oct 31, 2000, Vol 65, No 211, p. 65106.

36 Case Study: Countrywide Home Loans, Inc. Fannie Mae Foundation, 2000.

37 Mortgage Market Statistical Annual, 2008, Inside Mortgage Finance Publications.

38 Testimony of Chairman Alan Greenspan before the Committee on Banking, Housing and Urban Affairs, February 24, 2004 Government-Sponsored Enterprises.

39 Prof D. M. Jaffe, Bank Regulation and Mortgage Market Reform, Haas School of Business, University of California, March 8, 2011.

40 There are, of course, other aspects of the US mortgage market, which require authorisation and regulation, such as mortgage brokers, appraisers, mortgage companies, to name some of the important players and their practices.
41 Chairman Ben Bernanke, The Future of Mortgage Finance in the US, p. 2.2.
42 These figures are quoted by Prof D Jaffe in "Reforming the U.S. Mortgage Market through Private Market Incentives, November 2010." They are from the European Mortgage Federation Fact Book 2008. Curiously enough, the figure for the UK is incorrect. It should be 68% according to UK government sources.
43 How did a domestic housing slump turn into a global financial crisis, October 7, 2009 Federal Reserve System.

Bibliography

Aaronson, D. A Note on the Benefits of Homeownership, Journal of Urban Economics, 47 (3): 2000, pp 356–369

Abt Associates, Exploratory Study of the Accuracy of HMDA Data, prepared for HUD, April, 1999

ADI Adviser, The Risk of Using the Wrong Risk Metric in HMDA Analyses, June 2005

Adrian, T. & Shin, H.S. The Shadow Banking System, Implications for Financial Regulation, Staff Report, Federal Reserve Bank of New York, July 2009

Alexander, W., Grimshawe, S., McQueen, R. & Slade, B. Some Loans are More Equal than Others: Third-Party Originations and Defaults in the Subprime Mortgage Industry, Real Estate Economics, Vol. 30, No. 4 pp 667–697, 2002

Ambrose, B., Thibodeau, T. & Temkin, K. The Urban Institute, An Analysis of the Effects of the GSE Affordable Goals on Low- and Moderate-Income Families, The Urban Institute, May, 2002

Ambrose, B. & Thibodeau, T. Have the GSE Affordable Housing Goals increased the supply of Mortgage Credit, Regional Science and Urban Economics, 2004, 34 (3) pp 263–273

American Financial Services Association, Prepared Testimony of Mr G. Wallace before US Senate Banking Committee, Predatory Mortgage Lending: The Problem, Impact and Responses, July 27 2001

Apgar, W. and Duda, M. The Twenty-Fifth Anniversary of the Community Reinvestment Act: Past Accomplishments and Future Regulatory Challenges, Federal Reserve Bank of New York, Economic Policy Review (forthcoming)

Ashcraft, A. & Schuermann, T. Understanding the Securitization of Subprime Mortgage Credit, Federal Reserve Bank of New York, Staff report no 318, March 2008

Ashcroft, A., Bech, M. & Scott Frame, W. Federal Home Loan Bank System: Lender of Next-to Last Resort, May 2009

Atlanta Business Chronicle, FHLB of Atlanta Business Chronicle, Nov 24 2008

Avery, R., Bostic, R., Calem, P. & Canner, G. Credit Risk, Credit Scoring and the Performance of Home Mortgages, Federal Reserve Bulletin, July 1996

Avery, R., Brevoort, K. & Canner, G. The 2006 HMDA data, Federal Reserve Bulletin, December 2007

Avery, R., Bostic, R. & Canner, G. The Performance and Profitability of CRA-Related Lending, Federal Bank of Cleveland, Research & Commentary, 2000

Avery, R, Brevoort, K. & Canner, G. Opportunities and Issues in Using the HMDA Data, JRER, Vol 29, No 4 2007

Avery, R., Bhutta, N., Brevoort, K. & Canner, G. The 2009 HMDA Data.

Barnes, Roger. Written Testimony of Roger Barnes, Former Manager of Financial Accounting, Deferred Assets in Fannie Mae's Controller Division, Oct 6 2004

Barr, M. Credit Where it Counts: The Community Reinvestment Act and Its Critics, New York University Law Review, Vol 75, 600

Barr, M. Testimony before the Committee on Financial Services, US House of Representatives: The Community Reinvestment Act: Thirty Years of Accomplishments, But Challenges Remain, February 13, 2008

Barron's Cover, Is Fannie Mae the Next Government Bailout? March 10, 2008

Bebchuk, L. & Fried, J. Executive Compensation at Fannie Mae: A Case Study of Perverse Incentives, NonPerformace Pay and Camouflage, Harvard Law School, Discussion Paper 505, 02/2005

Belsky, E. and Calder, A. Credit Matters: Low Income Asset Building Challenges in a Dual Financial Service System, Joint Center for Housing Studies, February, 2004

Bennett, R.,Vaughan, M. & Yeager, T. Should the FDIC worry about the FHLB? The Impact of FHLB Advances on the Bank Insurance Fund, Federal Reserve Bank of Richmond, WP 05-05

Benmeleh, E. and Dlugosz, J. The Credit Rating Crisis, National Bureau of Economic Research, Working Paper, No 15045, June 2009

Berlin, Mitchell. Bank Credit Standards, Business Review, Federal Reserve Bank of Philadelphia, February, 2009

Bernanke, B. GSE Portfolios, Systemic Risk, and Affordable Housing, March 6, 2007. Before Independent Community Bankers International Conference

Bernanke, B. The Community Reinvestment Act: Its Evolution and New Challenges, March 30 2007

Bernanke, B. The Subprime Mortgage Market, May 17 2007, Speech to Federal Reserve Bank of Chicago's 43rd Annual Conference Bank Structure and Competition

Bernanke, B. Subprime Lending and Mitigating Foreclosures, September 20, 2007

Bernanke, B. The Economic Outlook, Before the Committee on Budget, US House of Representatives, January 17 2008

Bernanke, B. Developments in the Financial Markets, April 3, 2008

Bernanke, B. The Future of Mortgage Finance in the United States, October 31, 2008 to UC Berkeley/UCLA Symposium, The Mortgage Meltdown, the Economy and Public Policy, Berkeley California

Bernanke, B. Causes of the Recent Financial and Economic Crisis, before the Financial Crisis Inquiry Commission, September 2, 2010

Berry, C. & Lee, S. The Community Reinvestment Act: A Regression Discontinuity Analysis, Harris School Working Paper Series 07.04

Bhardwaj, J. & Sengupta. Subprime Mortgage Design, Federal Reserve Bank of St. Louis, October 2008, Revised October 2010

Bhutta, N. GSE Activity and Mortgage Supply in Lower-Income and Minority Neighborhoods: The Effect of Affordable Housing Goals, Journal of Real Estate Finance and Economics, May, 2010

Bhutta, N and Canner, G Staff Analysis of the Relationship between the CRA and the Subprime Crisis, Federal Reserve System, Nov 21 2008

Bies, Susan Schmidt. HMDA, Bank Secrecy and Capital Issues, Member of the Board of Governors of Federal Reserve System, Financial Services Roundtable, March 31, 2005

Bloomberg, Fannie, Freddie Retreat as Mortgage Bonds Mutate, Sept 6 2006

Bloomberg, Moody's Cuts Ratings on CDOs Tied to Subprime Bonds, Oct 26 2007

Bloomberg, US Tosses Lifeline to Lenders Using Home Loan Banks, Oct 30 2007

Bloomberg Businessweek, Bear Stearns Big Bailout, March 14 2008

Bloomberg, Banks' Subprime Losses Top $500bn on Writedowns, Aug 18 2008

Bloomberg, Fannie, Freddie Subprime Spree May Add to Bailout, September 22 2008

Bloomberg Businessweek, A Federal Home Loan Bank System faces risk, Nov 7 2008

Bloomberg, Fannie Mae Silence on Taylor Bean opened way to $3bn Fraud, 30 June 2011

Bostic, R. & Robinson, B. Do CRA Agreements Influence Lending Patterns, July 2002, Journal of Real Estate Economics 31, pp 23–51

Bond, P., Musto, D. & Yilmaz, Bilge. Predatory Mortgage Lending, October, 2008

Bostic, R., Mehran, H., Paulson A. Seidendberg. Regulatory Incentives and Consolidation: the Case of Commercial Bank Mergers and the CRA, Federal Reserve Bank of Chicago, May 21 2002

Brauneis, M. & Stachowicz, S. Subprime Mortgage Lending: New and Evolving Risks, Regulatory Requirements, Bank Accounting and Finance, October–November, 2007

Braunstein, S. The Community Reinvestment Act, before the Committee on Financial Services, US House of Representatives, Feb 13 2008

Bunce, H. & Scheessels. The GSEs' Funding of Affordable Loans, HUD, Office of Policy Development and Research, July 1998

President George Bush, Remarks at St Paul AME Church in Atlanta, June 2002

President George Bush, President Hosts Conference on Minority Home Ownership, Oct 15 2002

President George Bush, Statement of Administration Policy, H.R. 1427, 2007

President George Bush, Just the Facts, The Administration's Unheeded Warnings about the Systemic Risk posed by the GSEs, September 19 2008

Business Insider, FHA Insured Mortgages: A Disaster in the Making, Aug 9 2010

Carr, J. & Lucas-Smith, K. Five Realities about the Current Financial and Economic Crisis, June 3, 2011

Calabria, M. Fannie, Freddie and the Subprime Mortgage Market, Cato Institute, March 7, 2011

Calem, P. & Lacour-Little, M. Risk-based capital requirements for mortgage loans, Journal of Banking and Finance, 2003

Calem, P., Gillen, K. & Wachter, S. The Neighborhood Distribution of Subprime Lending, 2004, Journal of Real Estate Finance and Economics, 2004, Vol 29 Vol 4, pp 393–410

Calomiris, C. The Subprime Turmoil, What's Old, What's New, and What's Next, October 2008

Capozza, D. & Thompson, T. Subprime Transitions: Lingering or Malingering in Default? Journal of Real Estate Finance and Economics, Vol 33 (3), 2006 pp 241–258

Center for Responsible Lending, Subprime Lending: A Net Drain of Homeownership, Issue Paper no 12, March 27 2007

Center for Responsible Lending, Update Projections of Subprime Foreclosures in the United States and their Impact on Home Values and Communities, August 2008

Chinloy, P. & Maconald, N. Subprime Lenders and Mortgage Market Completion, Journal of Real Estate Finance and Economics, Vol 30, (20) 2005, pp 153–165

Chomsisengphet, S. & Pennington-Cross, A. The Evolution of the Subprime Mortgage Market, Federal Bank of St. Louis Review, January/February, 2006

Clinton, Hillary. Speech on Subprime Lending, March15, 2007

Clinton, W. Remarks on the National Homeownership Strategy, June 5 1995

Cisneros, H. Press Briefing by Henry Cisneros, Secretary of Housing and Urban Development, June 6, 1996

CNN Money The Fall of Fannie Mae, January 24 2005

CNN Money, Countrywide: $1.2bn loss now, but profit soon, Oct 26 2007

CNN Money, Countrywide Rescue: $4bn, Jan 11 2008

CNNMoney.com, Fannie, Freddie bailout: $153bn…and counting, Feb 11 2011

Committee on Banking, Housing & Urban Affairs, Report of Staff to Chairman Gramm, Predatory Lending Practices, Staff Analysis of Regulators' Responses, Aug 23 2000

Comptroller of the Currency (Acting) Praises Progress in Community Development Lending, June 1998

Comptroller of the Currency. Comptroller criticizes Subprime lenders who fail to report borrower payment histories, May 5 1999

Comptroller of the Currency before the Committee on Financial Services, House of Representatives, April 1 2004

Comptroller of the Currency, Survey of Credit Underwriting Practices, June 2005

Congressional Budget Office, Assessing the Public Costs and Benefits of Fannie Mae and Freddie Mac, May 1996

Congressional Budget Office, Federal Subsidies and the Housing GSEs, May 2001

Congressional Budget Office, Effects of Repealing Fannie Mae and Freddie Mac's SEC Exemptions, May 2003

Congressional Budget Office, Regulation of the Housing Government Sponsored Enterprises, Statement of Douglas Holtz-Eakin before the Committee on Banking, Housing and Urban Affairs, Oct 23 2003

Congressional Budget Office, Updated Estimates of the Subsidies to the Housing GSEs, April 8 2004

Congressional Budget Office Testimony, Aligning the Costs and Benefits of the Housing Government-Sponsored Enterprises, US Senate, Committee on Banking, Housing and Urban Affairs, Douglas Holtz-Eakin, Director, April 21, 2005

Congressional Budget Office, Measuring the Capital Positions of Fannie Mae and Freddie Mac, June 2006

Congressional Budget Office, Fannie Mae, Freddie Mac, and the Federal Role in the Secondary Mortgage Market, December, 2010

Congressional Budget Office, Testimony, Statement of Deborah Lucas, The Budgetary Cost of Fannie Mae and Freddie Mac and Options for the Future Federal Role in the Secondary Mortgage Market, before the Committee on Budget, US House of Representatives, June 2 2011

Congressional Research Service, The Streamlined FHA Downpayment Program, May 9 2003

Congressional Research Service, Housing Issues in the 108th Congress, Bourdon, E. September 3, 2003

Congressional Research Service, Improving the Effectiveness of GSE Oversight: Legislative Proposals in the 108th Congress, M. Jickling & L. Nott, updated Jan 6 2005

Congressional Research Service, Government Sponsored Enterprises: Regulatory Reform Legislation, updated May 26, 2005

Congressional Research Service, Government-Sponsored Enterprises: Regulatory Reform Legislation, updated October 27 2005, M. Jickling

Congressional Research Service, Accounting and Management Problems at Freddie Mac, M. Jickling, November 15 2005

Congressional Research Service, Limiting Fannie Mae's and Freddie Mac's Portfolio Size, E. Weiss, June 21 2006

Congressional Research Service, Accounting Problems at Fannie Mae, Dec 7 2006, RS21949

Congressional Research Service, Housing Issues in the 110th Congress, March 16 2007, Maggie McCarty et al; Eugene Boyd et al

Congressional Research Service, Subprime Mortgages: Primer on Current Lending and Foreclosure Issues, March 19 2007, E.V. Murphy

Congressional Research Service, Government-Sponsored Enterprises: An Institutional Overview, Kosar, K. April 23, 2007

Congressional Research Service, Securitization and Federal Regulation of Mortgages for Safety and Soundness, Murphy, E. September 17 2007

Congressional Research Service, Financial Crisis? The Liquidity Crunch of August 2007, Getter, D., Jickling, M., Labonte, M. & Murphy, E. Sept 21 2007

Congressional Research Service, Fannie Mae and Freddie Mac: Proposals to regulate their mortgage portfolio size in the 110th Congress, Weiss, N. Nov 5 2007

Congressional Research Service, Financial Institution Insolvency: Federal Authority over Fannie Mae, Freddie Mac and Depository Institutions, D. Carpenter & M. Murphy, September 10, 2008

Congressional Research Service, A Predatory Lending Primer: The Home Ownership and Equity Protection Act (HOEPA), November 26 2008

Congressional Research Service, Fannie Mae's and Freddie Mac's Financial Problems, Weiss, N. September 12 2008

Congressional Research Service, Fannie Mae and Freddie Mac in Conservatorship, M. Jickling, September 15 2008

Congressional Research Service, Fannie Mae and Freddie Mac: Changes to the Regulation of their Mortgage Portfolios, N. Weiss, October 28 2008

Congressional Research Service, Housing Issues in the 110th Congress, updated Nov 4 2008; Perl, L., Foote, B., Jones, K., McCarty,M., Boyd, E., Getter, D. & Gonzales, O.

Congressional Research Service, The FHA Modernization Act of 2008, Foote, B. February, 25 2009

Congressional Research Service, Treatment of Seller Funded Downpayment Assistance in FHA-Insured Home Loans, B.E. Foote, March 11 2009

Congressional Research Service, China's Holdings of US Securities: Implications for the US Economy, Wayne Morrison & Marc Labonte, July 30 2009

Congressional Research Service, The FHA and Risky Lending, D. Getter, April 19 2010

Congressional Research Service, GSEs and the Government's Role in Housing Finance: Issues for the 112th Congress, N. Weiss, March 11 2011

Consumer Bankers Association, Summary of Expanded HMDA Reporting Requirements, Sec 1094 Dodd-Frank Act

Cotterman, R. New Evidence on the Relationship between Race and Mortgage Default: The Importance of Credit History Data, May 23 2002

Courchane, M. & Zorn, P.M. A Changing Credit Environment and Its Impact on Low-income and Minority Borrowers and Communities, August 2010, Joint Center for Housing Studies, Harvard University

Cox, Christopher. Testimony before the Committee on Banking, Housing and Urban Affairs, US Senate, Accounting Irregularities at Fannie Mae, June 15 2006

Cox, Christopher. Testimony Concerning Recent Events in the Credit Markets, before the Senate Committee on Banking, Housing and Urban Affairs, April 3 2008

Cox, Christopher. Oversight of Nationally Recognized Statistical Rating Organizations, Testimony before the US Senate Committee on Banking, Housing and Urban Affairs, April 28 2008

Cox, Christopher. Turmoil in the US Credit Markets: Recent Actions regarding Government Sponsored Entities, Investment Banks and Other Financial Institutions Testimony before the Committee on Banking, Housing and Urban Affairs, US Senate, Sept 23 2008

CSR Press Release, Fannie Mae announces pilot to purchase $2 billion of 'MyCommunityMortgage' Loans; Pilot Lenders to Customize affordable products for Low-to-Moderate Income Borrowers, Oct 29 2000

Danis, M. & Pennington-Cross, A. A Dynamic Look at Subprime Loan Performance, Federal Reserve Bank of St. Louis, May 2005

Day, T. & Liebowitz, S. Mortgage Lending to Minorities: where's the Bias, Economic Inquiry, Jan 1998 pp 1–27

Davies, Howard. The Financial Crisis Who is to Blame? Polity Press, 2010

Deacle, Scott & Scott, J.A. Does Debt Management Policy Matter? The Case of the Federal Home Loan Banks, April, 2008, Fox School of Business, Temple University

Deacle, Scott & Elyasiani, E. The Cost of Debt and Federal Home Loan Bank Funding at US Bank and Thrift Holding Companies, Sept 10 2010

DeMarco, E. Statement of Acting Director, FHFA before the US Senate Committee on Banking, Housing and Urban Affairs, The Future of the Mortgage market and the Housing Enterprises, October 8 2009

Demyanyk, Y. and Hemert, Otto van. Understanding the Subprime Mortgage Crisis, December, 2008

Dell'Ariccia, Igan, D. & Laeven, L. Credit Booms and Lending Standards: Evidence from the Subprime Mortgage Market, IMF Working Paper, April, 2008

DeMong, R. The NonPrime Market in the United States, Statement before the Subcommittee on Financial Institutions and Consumer Credit, and the Subcommittee on Financial Services of the Committee on Financial Services, June 23 2004

DeYoung, R. Safety, Soundness and the Evolution of the US Banking Industry, Federal Bank of Atlanta, Economic Review, first and second quarter, 2007

Diventi, T. Fannie Mae and Freddie Mac: Past, Present and Future, Cityscape, A Journal of Policy Development & Research, Vol 11, No 3, 2009

Doms, M., Furlong, Fred & Krainer, J. Subprime Mortgage Delinquency Rates, Federal Reserve Bank of San Francisco, Working Paper Series, November, 2007

Donilon, T. The First Fannie Mae paper, The Competitive Effects of Fannie Mae, Fannie Mae Foundation, January 2002

Dreier, P. Putting Housing Back on the Political Agenda, Housing Policy in the New Millennium, 2000

Dugan, J. Statement of John C. Dugan, Comptroller of the Currency before the Financial Crisis Inquiry Commission, April 8 2010

Edmiston, K. & Zalneraitis. Rising Foreclosures in the United States: A Perfect Storm, Economic Review, Federal Reserve Bank at Kansas City, Fourth Quarter, 2007

Egan-Jones Ratings Company, for GSE Oversight and the Need for Reform and modernization before the House Subcommittee on Capital Markets, Insurance and Government Sponsored Enterprises, June 25, 2003

Eggers, F. Homeownership: A Housing Success Story, Cityscape, Journal of Policy Development and Research, Vol 5 No 2, 2001

Ellis, L. The Housing Meltdown, Why did it happen in the United States, Bank of International Settlements, Working Paper No 259, September 2008

Elul, R. Securitization and Mortgage Default: Regulation vs Adverse Selection, Federal Reserve Bank of Philadelphia, September 22 2009

Engel, K. & McCoy, P. Turning a Blind Eye: Wall Street Finance of Predatory Lending, Fordham Law Review, March 19 2007

Essene, R. & Apgar, W. The 30th Anniversary of the CRA: Restructuring the CRA to Address the Mortgage Finance Revolution, Federal Reserve Bank of Boston & the Federal Reserve Bank of San Francisco, February 2009

Fannie Mae Flex100 and Flex97 mortgage loans, 1997 and 1999

Fannie Mae, Eligibility Standards for Refinance Mortgages, September 23, 2002

Fannie Mae, Guide to Underwriting with DU, July, 2005

Federal Deposit Insurance Corporation, Supervisory Perspective, FHLBs, June 25 2004

Federal Deposit Insurance Corporation, Breaking New Ground in US Mortgage Lending, 2006

Federal Deposit Insurance Corporation, Supervisory Insights, HMDA Data: Identifying and Analysing Outliers, Dec 7 2007, Winter Vol 4 Issue 2

Federal Housing Finance Agency, Mortgage Market Note 10-2, The Housing Goals of Fannie Mae and Freddie Mac in the context of the Mortgage Market, 1996–2009

Federal Housing Finance Agency, Default Risk Evaluation in the Single Family Mortgage Market, October 2009

Federal Housing Finance Agency, Statement of Acting Director, E.J. DeMarco before the US House of Representatives, Subcommittee on Capital Markets, Insurance and the GSEs, Transparency, Transition and Taxpayer Protection: More Steps to end the GSE Bailout, May 25 2011

Federal Housing Administration, Report to Congress on the Financial Status of the MMI Fund, 2010

Federal Home Loan Bank of Chicago, FHFB accepts Business Plan, 2005-1

Federal Home Loan Bank of Chicago, Board Meeting Up-Date, Oct/Nov 2007

Federal Home Loan Bank, Atlanta, Letter to Members outlining losses, Nov 17 2008

Federal Housing Finance Agency, Statement of Director James B. Lockhart, Sept 7 2008

Federal Housing Finance Board: Performance and Accountability annual reports

Federal Housing Finance Board, Nontraditional and Subprime Residential Mortgage Loans, Advisory Bulletin 2007-AB-01, April 12 2007

Report to Congress, June 13 2011. Fannie Mae and Freddie Mac remain Critical Supervisory Concerns

Federal Reserve System, Concentration and Risk in the OTC Markets for US Dollar Interest Rate Options, prepared by staff of Federal Reserve and the Federal Reserve Bank of New York, May 2005

Federal Reserve Bank, Public Hearings on HMDA, September 2010, Contribution of Governor Elizabeth Duke

Federal Financial Regulatory Agencies, Final Statement on Subprime Mortgage Lending, joint press release, June 29 2007

Federal Financial Institutions Examinations Council, History of HMDA

Federal Reserve Bank of Boston, Underwriting Standards and Practices, 1992

Federal Reserve System, Report by the Board of Governors of the Federal Reserve System, pursuant to section 713 of the Gramm-Leach-Bliley Act, 1999, Report to Congress, The Performance and Profitability of CRA-Related Lending, July 17 2000

Federal Reserve Release, Final Rule to curb predatory lending, Dec 14 2001

Final Guidance on Nontraditional Mortgage Product Risks, Federal Financial Regulatory Agencies, September 29 2006

Financial Crisis Inquiry Commission, Credit Ratings and the Financial Crisis, Preliminary Staff Report, June 10 2010

Financial Crisis Inquiry Commission, The Fall of Bear Stearns, March 2008

Financial Stability Report, Thematic Review on Mortgage Underwriting and Origination Practices, 17 March 2011

Financial Times, Freddie Mac feels subprime flames licking, Nov 24, 2007

Financial Times, Fannie Mae and Freddie Mac, March 28, 2008

Financial Times, BoC cuts Fannie-Freddie Debt, August 29, 2008

Financial Times, Lawmaker accused of conflict of interest, Oct 3, 2008

Financial Times, How Moody's Faltered, Oct 17, 2008

Financial Times, Treasury in grip of Fannie Mae and Freddie Mac: the Sequel, Dec 23, 2009

Financial Times, Nixon Moment for the Ratings Agencies, April 23, 2010

Fishbein, A. Going Subprime, Shelterforce Online, Issue No 125, September/October 2002

Fishbein, A. Testimony before the Committee on Financial Services, Regarding H.R.2575, September 25 2003

Fishbein, A. Fannie and Freddie Under Fire, What's at Stake for Low-Income Housing, Shelterforce Online, Issue No 131, September/October 2003

Fishbein, A. & Essene, R. The Home Mortgage Disclosure Act at Thirty-Five: Past History, Current Issues, August 2010

Fitch Ratings, Structured Finance, The Impact of Poor Underwriting Practices and Fraud in Subprime RMBS Performance, Nov 26 2007

Flannery, M. & Scott Frame, W. The Federal Home Loan Bank System: The "Other" Housing GSE, Federal Reserve Bank of Atlanta

Frank, Barney, Pelosi, N. & other Democrat Congressmen and women: letter to President Bush, requesting his support for the GSEs, June 28 2004

The Free Library, Chairman and CEO Jim Johnson says Fannie Mae's Trillion Dollar commitment already served one million in cities and 500,000 first-time home buyers through $57 billion of investment plans, 17th April 1996

Friends of Angelo's, Countrywide's Systematic and Successful Efforts To Buy Influence and Block Reform, Staff Report, Darrell Issa, Ranking Member, Committee on Oversight and Government Reform, March 19 2009

Freddie Mac Reports on Restatement Progress, June 25 2003

Freddie Mac, Automated Underwriting, 2011

GAO Report, Government Sponsored Enterprises: Advantages and Disadvantages of Creating a Single Housing GSE Regulator, GGD-97-139, July 9 1997

GAO Report, Federal Housing Enterprises, HUD's Mission Oversight Needs to be Strengthened, GAO/GGD 98-173, July 1998

GAO Housing Enterprises, The Roles of Fannie Mae and Freddie Mac in the US Housing Finance System, Statement, Thomas J. McCool, before the House Budget Committee's Task Force on Housing and Infrastructure, July 25 2000

GAO Major Management Challenges and Program Risks, HUD, January 2001, GAO-01-248

GAO Single Family Housing, Better Strategic Human Capital Management Needed at HUD's Homeownership Centers, GAO-01-590, July 2001

GAO OFHEO's Risk-Based Capital Stress Test, Incorporating New Business is Not Advisable, June 2002

GAO Review of FHLB Operations, GAO-03-364, February 28 2003

GAO Consumer Protection, Federal and State Agencies Face Challenges in Combating Predatory Lending, GAO-04-280, January 2004

GAO, A Framework for Strengthening GSE Corporate Governance and Oversight, February 2004, GAO-04-269T

GAO Federal Home Loan Bank System, An Overview of Changes and Current Issues Affecting the System, Statement of Thomas J. McCool, Testimony before the Committee on Banking, Housing and Urban Affairs, US Senate April 13 2005

GAO Housing GSEs: A New Oversight Structure is Needed, Statement by David Walker, Comptroller General, before the Committee on Banking, Housing and Urban Affairs, US Senate, April 21, 2005

GAO Mortgage Financing, Additional Action Needed to Manage Risks of FHA-insured Loans with Down Payment Assistance, November 2005, GAO-06-24

GAO High Risk Series, HUD Single Family Mortgage Insurance and Rental Housing Assistance Programs, High-risk Designation Removed, January 2007

GAO, Home Mortgage Defaults and Foreclosures, October 10, 2007, GAO-08-78R

GAO HUD's Oversight of Housing Agencies should focus more on inappropriate use of Program Funds, June 2009 (public housing)

GAO, Home Mortgage Provisions in a 2007 Reform Bill (H.R. 3915) Would Strengthen Borrower Protection, but Views on Their Long-Term Impact Differ, July 2009, GAO-09-741

GAO Fair Lending Data Limitations and Fragmented US Financial Regulatory Structure Challenge Federal Oversight and Enforcement Efforts, July 2009

GAO Fannie Mae and Freddie Mac, Analysis of Options for Revising the Housing Enterprises' Long-Term Structures, GAO-09-782, September 2009

GAO Analysis of Options for Revising the Housing Enterprises' Long-term Structures, Statement of William Shear, Testimony before the Committee on Banking, Housing and Urban Affairs, US Senate, October 8 2009, GAO-10-144T

GAO Mortgage Financing, Financial Condition of FHA's Mutual Mortgage Insurance Fund, Statement of Mathew Scire, Testimony before the Committee on Banking, Housing and Urban Affairs, September 23, 2010 Garriga, C., Gavin, W. & Schlagenhauf, D. Recent Trends in Homeownership, Federal Bank of St. Louis, September/October 2006

Gates, S. Wharton, Waldron, C. and Zorn, P. (Freddie Mac) Automated Underwriting: Friend or Foe to Low-Mod Households and Neighborhoods, Nov 18–19 Symposium, 2003

Gates, S., Zorn, P. & Perry, V. Automated Underwriting and Lending Outcomes: The Effect of Improved Mortgage Risk Assessment on Underserved Populations, August 2011

Gates, S., Perry, P. & Zorn, P. Automated Underwriting in Mortgage Lending: Good News for the Underserved? Housing Policy Debate, Vol 13, Issue 2, Fannie Mae Foundation 2002

Gensler, Gary, Treasury Under Secretary, House Banking Committee on Capital Markets, Securities and Government Sponsored Enterprises, March 22, 2000

Green, R. & Wachter, S. The Housing Finance Revolution, 31st Economic Symposium: Housing, Housing Finance & Monetary Policy of the Federal Reserve Bank of Kansas, Aug 31, 2007

Godno, James B. House of Cards: What exactly did Mel Martinez accomplish at HUD, NHI, Shelterforce online, May/June 2004

Goldman Sachs, Executive Leadership Council and Foundation, Fannie Mae, 2003

Goldstein, Ira, Bringing Subprime Mortgages to Market and the Effects on Lower-Income Borrowers, Joint Center for Housing Studies, Harvard University, February 2004

Gordon, J. Center for Responsible Lending, Before the US House Financial Services Committee, Subcommittee on Insurance, Housing and Community Opportunity

Gould, George D. Statement of Presiding Director, Freddie Mac, before the Committee on Financial Services of the US House of Representatives, Sept 25 2003

Green, R.K. & Schnare, A. The Rise and Fall of Fannie Mae and Freddie Mac: Lessons Learned and Options for Reform, Nov 19 2009, Empiris LLc

Greenspan, Alan, Irrational Exuberance Speech at the Annual Dinner and Francis Boycr Lecture of the American Enterprise Institute for Public Policy Research, December 5 1996

Greenspan, Alan, Home Mortgage Market, at the Annual Convention of the Independent Community Bankers of America, March 4 2003

Greenspan, Alan, Letter to Senator Robert Bennett, September 2 2005

Greenspan, Alan, Government Sponsored Enterprises, before the Committee on Banking, Housing and Urban Affairs, US Senate, February 24, 2004

Greenspan, Alan, Statement before the Committee on Banking, Housing and Urban Affairs, US Senate, April 6 2005

Greenspan, Alan, Risk Transfer and Financial Stability, Federal Reserve Bank of Chicago's Conference on Bank Structure, May 5, 2005

Greenspan, Alan, Government Sponsored Enterprises, To a Conference on Housing, Mortgage Finance and the Macroeconomy, Federal Reserve Bank of Atlanta, May 19 2005

Greenspan, Alan, Remarks by Chairman Alan Greenspan, Mortgage Banking, to the American Bankers Association Annual Convention, September 26, 2005

Greenspan, Alan, Testimony of Alan Greenspan, Financial Crisis Inquiry Commission, April 7 2010

Greenspan, Alan, The Age of Turbulence, Penguin Books, 2008

Gunther, J., Klemme, K. & Robinson, K. Redlining or Red Herring, Southwest Economy, May/June 1999

Hancock, D., Lehnert, A., Passmore,W. & Sherlund, S. An Analysis of the Potential Competitive Impacts of Basel II Capital Standards on US Mortgage Rates and Mortgage Securitization, Federal Reserve Board, April 2005

Harvard, The State of the Nation's Housing Report, June 23, 2008, The Sharp Housing Downturn continues to pressure the economy

Henry, Emil W., Assistant Secretary for Financial Institutions, US Department of the Treasury before the Real Estate Roundtable, May 15 2006

Henry, Emil, How to Shut Down Fannie and Freddie, Wall Street Journal, November 11, 2010

HMDA data, Frequently asked questions regarding the new HMDA data, April 2006, Federal Financial Institutions Examinations Council website

HUD, A Study of the GSEs' Single-Family Underwriting Guidelines, Temkin, K. Galster, G, Quercia R & O'Leary, S. April 1, 1999

HUD Archives, News Releases, HUD announces Sharpest Rise in Home Ownership Rate in at Least 30 Years; Highest Home Ownership Rate since 1981; Over 1.4 Million New Homeowners Added in 1995

HUD Archives, New Report praises lender efforts to assist working families, August 10, 1996

HUD Archives, Cuomo announces lenders agree to make nearly $1.4 billion in mortgage loans to boost homeownership to low-and-moderate income families and minorities, March 5 1998

HUD Archives, Subprime Lending Report, Unequal Burden: Income and Racial Disparities in Subprime Lending, 1999

HUD Archives, Testimony of William Apgar, Federal Housing Commissioner, March 25 1999 regarding the FHA

HUD Archives, America's Home Ownership Rate Rises to 66.7% including record numbers of black and Hispanic families, April 21 1999

HUD Archives, 1999 Best Practice Success Stories, Mortgage Bankers Association, Fair Lending

HUD Archives, Cuomo announces Higher FHA Home Mortgage Loan Limits to help more American Families Become Homeowners, Jan 6 2000

HUD Archives, HUD reviewing mortgage approval data submitted by Fannie Mae to determine if company provided the required information, Feb 2 2000

HUD Archives, Fannie Mae gives HUD information on 10 million Mortgage Loans for Fair Lending Review, Feb 23 2000

HUD Archives, HUD Reviewing mortgage approval data submitted by Fannie Mae to determine if the company provided the required information, Feb 2 2000

HUD Archives, Statement of William Apgar, Federal Housing Commissioner, before the House Subcommittee on Capital Markets, Securities and Government Sponsored Enterprises, March 22 2000

HUD Archives, HUD releases new study showing explosion of Subprime Home Loans in Black and Low Income Neighborhoods, as Cuomo Raises Concerns of Widespread Consumer Abuses by Predatory Lenders, April 12 2000

HUD Archives, Issues Brief, HUD's Affordable Lending Goals for Fannie Mae and Freddie Mac, January 2001

HUD Archives, Secretary Cuomo's Remarks Predatory Lending Press Conference, New York, October 20 2001

HUD Archives, HUD announces new regulations to provide $2.4 trillion in mortgages for affordable housing for 28.1m families, Oct 31 2000

HUD Archives, President Bush and HUD: Unlocking the American Dream to More People than ever before, January 28 2002

HUD Archives, Barriers to Minority Homeownership, June 2002

HUD Archives, Bush Administration unveils New Homeownership Initiative: $1000 Homebuyer cashback incentive, July 30 2002

HUD Archives, HUD announces New Rule to Protect Home buyers from Predatory Lending Practices, Jan 13 2003

HUD Archives, Martinez endorses American Dream Legislation to increase home ownership among lower income families, April 8 2003

HUD Archives, HUD finalizes rule on New Housing Goals for Fannie Mae and Freddie Mac, Nov 1 2004

HUD Archives, HUD finalizes rule to make more Fannie Mae and Freddie Mac mortgage data available to the public, November 10, 2005

HUD Archives, Review of Selected Underwriting Guidelines to Identify Potential Barriers to Hispanic Homeownership, Office of Policy Development and Research, March 2006

HUD Archives, Jackson announces Review of Fannie and Freddie Investments to ensure Charter Compliance, June 13 2006

HUD Archives, GAO Recognizes HUD's Management Reforms, First time in 13 years no HUD programs on GAO's "High-Risk" List, Jan 31 2007

HUD Archives, HUD Secretary calls for restoring confidence in mortgage lending practices through FHA modernization. Jackson stresses mortgage alternatives and ending predatory lending, April 19 2007

HUD Archives, FHA Modernization, Statement of Brian Montgomery, Assistant Secretary for Housing, Federal Housing Commissioner, Hearing before the Committee on Appropriations, Subcommittee on Transportation, Housing and Urban Developments, March 15 2007

HUD, Statement of L. Carter Cornick, General Deputy, Assistant Secretary, HUD Hearing before the House Committee on Financial Services, Legislative Proposals in GSE Reform

HUD, Subprime and Manufactured Home Lender List, March 16 2007

HUD Archives, HUD Secretary announces $1.8bn for Affordable Housing and First Time Home Ownership programs, May 8 2007

HUD Archives, Promoting and Protecting Home Ownership, Prepared Remarks by Alphonso Jackson, Secretary for Housing, June 4 2007;Prepared Remarks for S. Preston, Secretary for Housing at the National Housing Summit, October 7 2008

HUD Archives, Written Statement of Margaret Burns, Office of Single Family Program Development, Homeowner Downpayment Assistance programs and Related Issues,

June 22 2007 before the House Financial Services Committee, Subcommittee on Housing and Community Opportunity

HUD Archives, Written Statement of Brian Montgomery, Federal Housing Commissioner before the Senate Banking Committee, Oct 23 2008

HUD, Report to Congress on the Root Causes of the Foreclosure Crisis, January 2010

HUD, The Financial Status of the MMI Fund, Independent Actuarial Report, 2010

HUD and the Treasury, Reforming America's Housing Finance Market, A Report to Congress, February 2011

HUD, Briefing by Brian Montgomery, FHA Commissioner, Bush Administration, Plan to help almost a quarter of a million homeowners to avoid foreclosure, Aug 31 2007

HUD, US Housing Market Conditions, Office of Policy Development and Research, November 2007

HUD User, HUD prepares to set new housing goals, Summer, 1998

HUD User, Overview of the GSEs' Housing Goal Performance 2000–2005

HUD User Overview of the GSEs Housing Goal Performance 2000–2007

HUD Using HMDA and Income Leverage to examine Current Mortgage Market Turmoil, US Housing Market Conditions, 2nd qtr, 2008, Office of Policy Development and Research

HUD, Secretary Shaun Donovan, Annual Report on the financial status of the FHA's Mutual Mortgage Insurance Fund, and the Independent Actuarial Report for the FHA, 2009

HUD Audit report, HUD did not have appropriate and effective management control over the automated underwriting process, Sept 15 2010

HUD Office of Audit, An underwriting review of 15 FHA lenders demonstrated that HUD missed critical opportunities to recover losses to the FHA Insurance Fund

HUD, Office of Policy Development and Research, Issue Brief, No V, GSE's Past Performance on the Housing Goals, January 2001

HUD President Clinton announces cut in home mortgage insurance premium to reduce homeownership costs for 600,000 families each year and help boost homeownership rate to record level, June 12 1997

HUD, Secretary Cisneros Calls on Fannie Mae and Freddie Mac to increase financing for Minority Homeowners, before Senate Banking Committee, April 13 1994

HUD Success of HUD Management Reforms confirmed by GAO Department Removed from High Risk List, Jan 17 2001

HUD Secretary Jackson announces $161.5m in down-payment assistance for first-time homebuyers, June 2 2004

HUD Urban Policy Brief, No 2, August 1995

HUD Written Testimony of Shaun Donovan, Secretary of Housing, Before the US Senate Appropriations Committee, Subcommittee on Transportation, Housing and Urban Development, the FHA and the Future of the Housing Market, April 7 2011

Huffington Post, Why Fannie Mae, Freddie Mac continue to cost us taxpayers billions, June 14 2010

Husock, H. The Trillion-Dollar Bank Shakedown that Bodes Ill For Cities, City-Journal, Winter 2000

IMF A Fistful of Dollars, Lobbying and the Financial Crisis, Igan, D., Mishra, P. & Tressel, T., April 16, 2010

IMF Global Financial Stability Report: Market Development and Issues, April, 2007

IMF Lessons and Policy Implications from the Global Financial Crisis, Claessens, S. Dell'Ariccia, Igan D. & Laeven, L. IMF Working Paper, Feb 2010

IMF Outbreak: US Subprime Contagion, R. Dodd & P. Mills, June 2008

IMF Survey: What Next for Fannie and Freddie?, P. Mills, Oct 3, 2008

Inspector General, HUD, Testimony of Susan Gaffney before the Subcommittee on Housing and Transportation, US Senate, Management and Performance Issues facing HUD, March 23,1999

Inspector General, HUD, Susan Gaffney, Before the House of Representatives Committee on Government Reform, Subcommittee of Government Management and Technology, March 22, 2000, regarding the missing $59bn

Inspector General, Semi-annual Report to Congress, Major Challenges Confronting HUD, March 31, 2001

Inspector General, Semi-annual Report to Congress, Major Issues Facing HUD, Oct 2002–March 31, 2003

Inspector General, Final report of the Nationwide Audit, Downpayment assistance programs, March 31, 2000

Inspector General, Statement of James Heist, Assistant Inspector General before the House Financial Services Committee, Subcommittee on Housing and Community Opportunity, June 22, 2007 (FHA and the Nehemiah project)

Inspector General, Statement of Inspector General, HUD, before the Committee on Appropriations, Subcommittee on Transportation, Housing and Urban Development, US Senate, April 2, 2009

Inspector General, Statement of Kenneth Donohue before the Committee on Appropriations, Subcommittee on Transportation, Housing, Urban Development and related agencies, US Senate, April 2009 and June 19 before the House Committee on Financial Services, Subcommittee on Oversight and Development

Inspector General, Written statement of Kenneth Donohue before the Committee on Appropriations, Subcommittee on Transportation, Housing and Urban Development, US Senate, May 13 2010

Inspector General, Preliminary Observations on Funding, Oversight and Investigations and Prosecutions of ACORN or potentially related Organizations, June 2010

Institute of Governmental Affairs, The Role of Government in US Capital Markets, Interagency Guidance on Subprime Lending, March 1, 1999

Issa, D., Ranking Member US House of Representatives, Committee on Oversight and Government Reform, Follow the Money: ACORN, SEIU and their political allies, Staff report, Feb 18 2010

Issa, D. Unaffordable Housing and Political Kickbacks Rocked the American Economy, Harvard Journal of Law and Public Policy, April 1, 2010

Issa, D. The Role of Government Affordable Housing Policy in Creating the Global Financial Crisis of 2008, Staff Report, Committee on Oversight and Government Reform, July 7, 2009

Jackson, Alphonso, Promoting and Protecting Home Ownership, National Press Club Washington, June 4 2007

Jaffee, D.M. The Interest Rate Risk of Fannie Mae and Freddie Mac, Has School of Business, University of California, July 31 2002

Jaffee, D. & Welke, G. The Risk-based Capital Test for Fannie Mae and Freddie Mac, Dec 10, 2003

Jaffee, D.M. On Limiting the Retained Mortgage Portfolios of Fannie Mae and Freddie Mac, June 30 2005

Jaffee, D. Reforming the US Mortgage Market through Private Market Incentives, Nov 15 2010

Jaffee, D.M. The US Subprime Mortgage Crisis: Issues Raised and Lessons Learned, Commission on Growth & Development, Working Paper No 28

Jaffee, D.M. Bank Regulation and Mortgage Market Reform, March 8, 2011, University of California

Kamin, K.B. & DeMarco, L.P. How did a Domestic Housing Slump Turn into a Global Financial Crisis, Federal Reserve Board, January 2010, No 994

Kittle, D. Chairman, Mortgage Bankers Association, Testimony before House Financial Services Committee, Subcommittee on Oversight and Investigations, "Strengthening Oversight and Preventing Fraud in the FHA and other HUD programs," June 18 2009

Kling, Arnold, The Financial Crisis: Moral Failure or Cognitive Failure, Harvard Journal of Law and Public Policy, Vol 33, No 2, pp 507–515

Kogler, B. & Schare, A. Lender Perspectives of FHA's Declining Market Share, Mortgage Bankers Association, August, 2006

Koppell, J.S. Hybrid Organizations and the Alignment of Interests: The Case of Fannie Mae and Freddie Mac, Public Administration Review, July/August, 2001 Vol 61, No 4

Kregel, Jan, Changes in the US Financial System and the Subprime Crisis, The Levy Economics Institute of Bard College, April, 2008

Knowledge@Wharton, Could Tremors in the Subprime Mortgage Market be the First Signs of an Earthquake?, Feb 21 2007

Krosner, R. The Community Reinvestment Act and the Recent Mortgage Crisis, Federal Reserve System, Dec 3 2008

Kyl, J. Problems at Freddie Mac and Fannie Mae, Too Big to Fail? Republican Policy Committee, Sept 9 2003

LaCour-Little, M. The Evolving Role of Technology in Mortgage Finance, Journal of Housing Research, Vol 11, Issue 2, Fannie Mae Foundation

LaCour-Little, M. Economic Factors affecting Home Mortgage Disclosure Reporting, July 28 2007

LaMalfa, T. Testimony before the Financial Services Committee, US House of Representatives, Subcommittee on Housing and Community Opportunity, March 26 1998

Landia, J. & McClure, K. Rethinking Federal Housing Policy, Journal of the American Planning Association, Vol 76, No 3. Summer, 2010

Lanzerotti, L. Homeownership at High Cost: Foreclosure Risk and High Cost Loans in California, Spring 2006

Lea, M. & Sanders, A. Working Paper: The Future of Fannie Mae and Freddie Mac, March 2011

Lev, Baruch, Freddie Mac: Accounting Standards Issued Raised in the Doty Report, September 25, 2003

Lehnert, A., Passmore, W. & Sherland, S. GSEs, Mortgage Rates and Secondary Market Activities, Jan 12 2005, Board of Governors of the Federal Reserve System

Levin, Carl, Senator, Note from the Chairman to Members of the Permanent Subcommittee on Investigations, Wall Street and the Financial Crisis, The Role of Bank Regulators, April 2010

Litan, R., Retsinas, N., Belsky, E. & Haag, S.W. The Community Reinvestment Act after Financial Modernization: A Baseline Report, US Department of the Treasury, 2000

Lockhart, James, B. Statement on OFHEO's Report on the Special Examination of Fannie Mae, House Subcommittee on Capital Markets, Insurance and GSEs, June 6 2006

Lockhart, James B. GSE Reform: A Priority for 2007, Feb 1 2007

Lockhart, James B., Director OFHEO, "Reforming the Regulation of the Government Sponsored Enterprises," before the Senate Banking, Housing and Urban Affairs Committee, Feb 7 2008

Lockhart, James B., Director OFHEO, before the House Committee on Financial Services, Legislative Proposals on GSE Reform, March 15 2007

Lockhart, James B., OFHEO Director Commends GSEs on Implementation of Subprime Mortgage Lending Guidance, September 10 2007

Lockhart, James B. III, Lessons Learned from the Mortgage Market Turmoil, Conference on Bank Structure and Competition, Chicago, May 16 2008

Lockhart, James B. III, Fannie, Freddie Adequately Capitalized, Lockhart, CNBC.com, July 8 2008

Lockhart, James B. III, Director, Federal Housing Finance Agency before the House Committee on Financial Services on the Conservatorship of Fannie Mae and Freddie Mac, September 25 2008

Lockhart, James B. III, Director, Federal Housing Finance Agency, Statement before the Financial Services Subcommittee on Capital Markets, Insurance and Government-Sponsored Enterprises, June 3 2009

Lockhart, James B. III, Testimony before the Financial Crisis Inquiry Commission, April 9, 2010

Lund, T., former EVP of Fannie Mae, Single Family Business, Memorandum for the Record, FCIC, March 4, 2010

Manchester, P. Goal Performance and Characteristics of Mortgages Purchased by Fannie Mae and Freddie Mac, 2001–2005, May 2007, revised, 2008, Office of Policy Development and Research, HUD

Market Watch, Former Fannie executive surprised by extent of crisis, April 9 2010

Martinez, M., Secretary for Housing, Statement before the US House Committee on Financial Services, Sept 10, 2003

Mason, J. & Rosner, J., How Resilient are Mortgage Backed Securities to Collateralized Debt Obligation Market Disruptions, Feb 15 2007

Mattey, J. & Wallace, N. Housing Prices and the (In) stability of Mortgage Prepayment Models, Evidence from California, July 1998, Federal Reserve Bank of San Francisco

Mayer, C. & Pence, K. Subprime Mortgages: What, Where and to Whom?, Divisions of Research & Statistics and Monetary Affairs, 2008-29

Mayer, C., Pence, K. & Sherland, S. The Rise in Mortgage Defaults, Federal Reserve Board, 2008-59

Mayer, C. Housing, Subprime Mortgages and Securitization: How did we go wrong and what can we learn so that this doesn't happen again?, Columbia Business School & NBER, 2010McCoy, Patricia & Elizabeth Renaurt, The Legal Infrastructure of Subprime and Nontraditional Home Mortgages, Joint Center for Housing Studies, February, 2008

Mc Coy, Patricia, Prepared statement, Hearing on "Consumer Protections in Financial Services: Past Problems, Future Solutions," US Senate Committee on Banking, Housing and Consumer Affairs, March 3 2009

McCoy, P., Pavlov, A. & Wachter, S. Systemic Risk through Securitization: The Result of Deregulation and Regulatory Failure, Connecticut Law Review, Vol 41, No 4, May 2009

Media Research Center: Government-Sponsored Enron, Billion Dollar Scandal, Not Ready for Prime Time, March 22 2005

Miles, Barbara, Implications of Debt held by the Housing Related Government Sponsored Enterprises, Statement before the Task Force on Housing and Infrastructure, House Committee on the Budget, July 25 2000

Minton, M. The Community Reinvestment Act's Harmful Legacy, Competitive Enterprise Institute, March 20 2008

Money Morning, Foreign Bondholders – and not the US Mortgage Market – drove the Fannie/Freddie Bailout, Sept 11 2008

Monterrosa, C. Director, Policy and Planning, Los Angelos Housing Department, City of Los Angelos, Regulation C, Implementing HMDA, 1975, before the Federal Reserve Board, Aug 5 2010

Morgan Stanley, Fannie, Freddie and the Road to Redemption, July 6 2005

Mortgage Bankers Association, Statement of Douglas Dugan, Senior Vice President for Research and Business Development, before the Subcommittee on Financial Institutions and Consumer Credit, House Committee on Financial Services, June 13 2006

Mortgage Bankers Association, Testimony of J. Robbins, Chairman, before House Financial Services Subcommittee on Capital Markets, Insurance and Government Sponsored Enterprises, "Legislative Proposals on GSE Reform," March 12 2007

Mortgage Bankers Association, The Future of the FHA and the Government National Mortgage Association, September, 2010

Mozilo, Angelo, Speech, The Home Ownership Gap at Harvard Joint Center for Housing Studies, Feb 4 2003

Mortgage Bankers Association, Delinquencies Increase, Foreclosure starts flat in latest MBA National Delinquency Survey, May 5 2008

Mudd, Daniel, Testimony before the House Committee on Financial Services, March 15 2007

Mudd, Daniel, Interview with Daniel Mudd, former CEO of Fannie Mae, Memorandum for the Record, March 26 2010

Munnell, A., Browne, L., McEnearny & Tootell, G. Mortgage Lending in Boston: Interpreting HMDA data, Working Paper Series, Federal Reserve Bank of Boston, No 92-7, October 1992

Nadar, R. Memorandum, Need for an investigation into misleading statements about the financial health of Fannie Mae and Freddie Mac prior to Conservatorship, April 11, 2011

National Predatory Lending Task Force, Curbing Predatory Home Mortgage Lending: A Joint Report, US Department of Housing and Urban Development and US Department of Treasury, June, 2000

National Public Radio, How Fannie, Freddie became Kings of the Hill, July 15 2008

New York Times, The Velvet Fist of Fannie Mae, April 20 1997

New York Times, Fannie Mae eases credit to aid mortgage lending, Sept 30 1999

New York Times, Fair Game; Home Loans: A Nightmare Grows Darker, April 8 2007

New York Times, Citigroup Chief is set to exit amid losses, Nov 3 2007

New York Times, At Freddie Mac, Chief Discarded Warning Signs, August 5 2008

New York Times, Alphonso Jackson, Sept 13, 2011

New York Times, US Weighs Takeover of Two Mortgage Giants, July 11 2008

New York Times, Interview with Daniel Mudd, Oct 5, 2008

New York Times, Building Flawed American Dreams, Oct 19 2008

Nomura, A. Journey through the Alt-A Zone, June 3 2003

Norberg, John, Financial Fiasco, The Cato Institute, 2009

Norman, A. The CRA and Subprime Lending: Discerning the Difference, Federal Reserve Bank of Dallas, Issue 1, 2009

OECD Economic Surveys, United States, 2004

OFHEO Testimony of Armando Falcon, Director, OFHEO before the US House Subcommittee on Capital Markets, Insurance and Government Sponsored Enterprises, August 1, 2001

OFHEO, Treasury and Securities and Exchange Commission, Special Study, Staff Report on Enhancing Disclosures in Mortgage-Backed Securities, January, 2003

OFHEO, Systemic Risk: Fannie Mae, Freddie Mac and the Role of OFHEO, February, 2003OFHEO Report on the Special Examination of Freddie Mac, December 2003

OFHEO Report on Findings to Date, Special Examination of Fannie Mae, September 17 2004

OFHEO, Statement of Armando Falcon before the Subcommittee on Capital Markets, Insurance and Government Sponsored Enterprises, "Review of OFHEO's Supplemental Agreement with Fannie Mae," April 6 2005

OFHEO Final Report on Special Examination of Fannie Mae, May 2006

OFHEO's Final Report on Fannie Mae, June 6, 2006, Hearing before the Subcommittee on Capital Markets, Insurance and Government Sponsored Enterprises OFHEO Working Paper 07-3, Subordinated Debt Issuance by Fannie Mae and Freddie Mac, V.L. Smith, June 2007

OFHEO's Annual Reports to Congress

Oesterle, Dale Arthur, The Collapse of Fannie Mae and Freddie Mac: Victims or Villains, Entrepreneurial Business Law Journal, Vol. 5.2 pp 744–760

Olsen, M.W. A Look at Fair Lending through the lens of New HMDA data, Member of the Board of Governors of the US Federal Reserve System at the Consumer Bankers Association, Nov 7 2005

Olsen, M. Statement on HMDA before the Subcommittee on Financial Institutions and Consumer Credit of the House Committee on Financial Services, June 13 2006

Park, K. Subprime Lending and the Community Reinvestment Act, Joint Center for Housing Studies, November 2008

Parkinson, P. Deputy Director, Research & Statistics, Federal Reserve System, House Financial Services Committee, Subcommittee on Capital Markets, Insurance and the GSEs, Feb 14 2008

Passmore, W., Sparks, R. & Ingspen, J. GSEs, Mortgage Rates and the Long-run effects of Mortgage Securitization, June 2001

Passmore, Wayne, The GSE Implicit Subsidy and the Value of Government Ambiguity, Federal Reserve Board, 2005-05

Paulson, Henry, Treasury Secretary, before the House Committee on Financial Services on the Legislative and Regulatory Options for Minimizing and Mitigating Mortgage Foreclosures, September 0, 2007

Paulson, Henry, Former Treasury Secretary, Interview, Memorandum for the Record, April 2, 2010

Pennington-Cross, A. & Ho, Giang, The Termination of Subprime Hybrid and Fixed Rate Mortgages, Federal Reserve Bank of St. Louis, Working Paper, July 1996

Pennington-Cross, Subprime and Prime Mortgages: Loss Distributions, OFHEO Working Papers, 03-1

Permanent Subcommittee on Investigations of the Homeland Security and Governmental Affairs, US Senate, Wall Street and the Financial Crisis, The Role of the Credit Rating Agencies, April 23 2010

Perry, V. The Dearth and Life of Subprime Mortgage Data, Jan 8 2008

Pettit, K. & Droesch, A. The Urban Institute, Home Mortgage Disclosure Act Data, 2005, funded by the Fannie Foundation

Pilloff, S. Bank Merger Activity in the US Federal Bank System, Staff Report, May 2004, No 176

Pinto, E. Statement before the Subcommittee on Housing and Community Opportunity of the House Financial Services Committee, October 8 2009

Pinto, E. Government Housing Policy: The Sine Qua Non of the Financial Crisis, The American, July 26 2011

Poole, W. Financial Stability, Federal Reserve Bank of St. Louis Review, Sept/Oct 2002, 84(5) pp 1–7

Poole, William, GSE Risks, Federal Reserve Bank of St. Louis Review, March/April 2005

Poole, William, The GSEs: Where do we Stand? Federal Reserve Bank of Atlanta, January 17 2007

Poole, William, Fannie, Freddie, "Insolvent" after Losses, Bloomberg, July 10 2008

Poole, William, Fannie-Freddie: do US Taxpayers want a repeat performance? Letter to the Financial Times, July 18 2008

Poole, W. Causes and Consequences of the Financial Crisis of 2007–2009, Senior Fellow, Cato Institute, 2009

Poznar, Z., Adrian, T., Ashcroft, A. & Boesky, H. Shadow Banking, Federal Reserve Bank of New York, Staff Reports, No 458, July 2010

PRNewswire, Countrywide Expands Commitment to $1 trillion in Home Loans to Minority and Lower Income Borrowers, Feb 1 2005

Quarles, R., Under Secretary for Domestic Finance, US Department of the Treasury at the Reuters Panel Discussion on Government Sponsored Enterprises, July 19 2006

Raines, Franklin D. calls for Mortgage Consumer Bill of Rights; cites new company initiatives to advance home buyer protections (and highlights Flex 97), Free Library, 2000 Raines, Franklin D., Chairman and CEO, Fannie Mae, Statement before the Senate Committee on Banking, Housing and Urban Affairs, October 16 2003

Raines, Franklin D., Chairman and CEO, Fannie Mae, Statement before the Senate Committee on Banking, Housing and Urban Affairs, February 25 2004

RealtyTimes, Automated Underwriting Decisions Can Be Overruled, 24 July, 2002

Reiss, David, The Federal Government's Implied Guarantee of Fannie Mae and Freddie Mac's Obligations: Uncle Sam Will Pick Up The Tab, July, 2008

Reiss, David, The Role of Fannie Mae/Freddie Mac Duopoly in the American Housing Market, January 2009

Reiss, David, Fannie Mae, Freddie Mac and the Future of Federal Housing Finance Policy; A Study of Regulatory Privilege, Policy Analysis, April 18 2011

Responsible Lending, Neglect and Inaction: Bank Regulators allowed Bad Lending, Why should they remain in charge of Consumer Protection? CRL Policy Brief, November 2009

Reuters, Countrywide says ex-HUD chief Cisneros quits Board, Oct 24 2007

Rodda, D. & Goodman, J. Recent House Price Trends and Homeownership Affordability Trends, for HUD, Office of Policy Development and Research, May 2005

Rohe, W., Van Zandt, S. & McCarthy, G. The Social Benefits and Costs of Homeownership: A Critical Assessment of the Research, Joint Center for Housing Studies, October, 2001

Republican Policy Committee, Problems at Freddie Mac and Fannie Mae: Too Big to Fail, Sept 9 2003

Rosenfeld, R. Testimony of Chairman Federal Housing Finance Board, before the Committee on Banking, Housing and Urban Affairs, April 21 2005

Rudman Report, A Report to the Special Review Committee of the Board of Directors of Fannie Mae, Paul, Weiss, Rifkind, Wharton & Garrison LLP, Feb 23 2006

Salomon Smith Barney, The Evolution of the Mortgage Origination Process, Mortgage Research, January, 1999

Scott Frame, W. Federal Home Loan Bank Mortgage Purposes: Implications for Mortgage Markets, Federal Reserve Bank of Atlanta, Economic Review, 3rd qtr, 2003

Scott Frame, W. & Lawrence White, Regulating Housing GSEs: Thoughts on Institutional Structure and Authorities, Federal Reserve Bank of Atlanta, Second Quarter, 2004

Scott Frame, W. & Tallman, E. Foreign Official Institutions and the Market for US Federal Agency Debt, March 2007

Scott Frame, W. The 2008 Federal Intervention to Stabilize Fannie Mae and Freddie Mac, Working Paper 2009-13, April 2009 Federal Reserve Bank of Atlanta

Scott Frame, W. & White, L. The Federal Loan Bank System: Current Issues in Perspective, V. Ghosal, Editor, Reforming Rules and Regulations, MIT Press, 2010

Seattle Times, Home-Loan Bank steered billions into an unorthodox strategy, May 8 2005

Seattle Times, Seattle's Federal Home Loan Bank in Big Money Trouble Again, July 19 2009

SEC Exchange of Correspondence between Freddie Mac and the Chief Counsel of the SEC, July 12 2002

SEC A Staff Report of the Task Force on Mortgage-Backed Securities Disclosure, January, 2003

SEC Office of Chief Accountant Issues Statement on Fannie Mae Accounting, Dec 15 2004

Sengupta, R. & Emmons, W. What is Subprime Lending? Economic Synopsis, 2007, No 13, Research, St. Louis Federal Reserve

Shadow Financial Regulatory Committee, Strengthening the Capital Structure of Federal Home Loan Banks, May 2006

Shays, C., Congressman, GSE Oversight: The Need for Reform and Modernization, June 23, 2003, Opening Statement, Capital Markets, Insurance and GSE Subcommittee

Scheesele, R. HMDA Coverage of the Mortgage Market, July 1998, HUD, Office of Policy Development & Research

Silver, Joshua, CRA Commitments, September 2007, National Community Reinvestment Coalition

Silver, Joshua & Taylor, John, The Community Reinvestment Act at 30: looking back and looking to the future, New York Law School, Law Review Vol 53 2008/2009

Smith, Brent, The Subprime Market, A Review and Compilation of Research & Commentary, Oct 19 2007

Smith, Brent, C. Mortgage Reform and the Countercyclical Role of the Federal Housing Administration's Mortgage Mutual Insurance Fund, Economic Quarterly, Vol 97, 1st Quarter 2011, pp 95–110

Smith, G., Woodstock Institute, Statement on Subprime Lending and Predatory Lending, before House Financial Services Committee, Subcommittees of Financial Institutions and Consumer Credit and on Housing and Community Opportunity, March 30 2004

Snow, John W., Testimony of Secretary John Snow, before the US Financial Services Committee, Proposals for Housing GSE Reform, April 13, 2005

Snow, J. Testimony of Secretary John Snow before the Committee on Financial Services, September 10 2003

Snow, John W. Testimony before the US Senate Committee on Banking, Housing and Urban Affairs, Proposals for Housing GSE Reform, April 7 2005

Standard & Poor's Corporate Governance Score, Fannie Mae, 30 January 2003

Stanton, T. H. Government Sponsored Enterprises: Why is Effective Government Supervision so hard to achieve?, May 2001

Stanton, T.H. Government-Sponsored Enterprises, Mercantilist Companies in the Modern World, The AEI Press, 2002

Steel, Robert K., Under Secretary for Domestic Finance, Testimony before the House Committee on Financial Services, September 5 2007

Stiglitz, J., Orszag, J. & Orszag, P. Implications of the New Fannie Mae and Freddie Mac Risk-based Capital Standard, Vol 1, Issue 2 March 2002, Fannie Mae Papers

Stiroh, K. & Poole, J. Explaining the Rising Concentration of Banking Assets in the 1990s, Current Issues in Economics and Finance, Vol 6 No 9, August 2000

Stojanovic, D., Vaughan, M. & Yeager, T. Is the FHLB System Funding a Risky Business for the FDIC?, Regional Economist, Federal Reserve Bank at St. Louis, October, 2000

Strahan, P.E. The Real Effects of US Banking Deregulation, Boston School of Management, September 2002

Summers, Lawrence, The Way Forward for Fannie and Freddie, FT July 27, 2008

Syron, Richard, Prepared Statement, Chairman and CEO of Freddie Mac, February 25, 2004

Syron, Richard, Testimony before the House Committee on Financial Services, March 15, 2007, "Legislative Proposals for GSE reform"

Tarr, D. The Political, Regulatory and Market Failures that caused the US Financial Crisis, Policy Research Working Paper, The World Bank, May 2010

Temkin, K., Johnson, J. & Lang, D. Subprime Markets, the Role of the GSEs, and Risk-based Pricing, The Urban Institute, March 2002

Timely Payments Awards with Extended Approval, Fannie Mae, Information sheet: "Helps you buy the home you need … at a competitive interest rate, even if you have less than perfect credit, past credit problems or minimal funds for a down payment or closing costs"

Taylor, J. & Silver, J. The Community Reinvestment Act: 30 years of wealth creation building and what we must do to finish the job, Joint Publication of the Federal Reserve Banks of Boston and San Francisco, February, 2009

Thompson, H. Economic Interdependence and Domestic Politics, Palgrave MacMillan, 2010

Treasury Statement on Fannie Mae and Freddie Mac, September 7 2008

USA Today, CEO throws a rope to mortgage behemoth, August 23 2004

USA Today, Fannie Mae, Freddie Mac spent millions on lobbying, July 17 2008

Utt, R. Time to reform Fannie Mae and Freddie Mac, Backgrounder, The Heritage Foundation, June 20, 2005

Wall Street Journal, Some Appraisers feel Pressure to Inflate Home Values, Feb 10 2004

Wall Street Journal, Mortgage Bailout is Greeted with Relief, Fresh Questions, September 9 2008

Wall Street Journal, How Government Stoked the Mania, October 3, 2008

Wall Street Journal, Whitewashing Fannie Mae, December 11 2008

Wall Street Journal, Loan Losses Spark Concern over FHA, September 4 2009

Wall Street Journal, Acorn and the Housing Bubble, E. Pinto Nov 12 2009

Wall Street Journal, The Price for Fannie and Freddie Keeps Going Up, December 29, 2009

Wall Street Journal, The Next Fannie Mae, Ginnie Mae and FHA are becoming $1 trillion subprime guarantors, 11 August 2009

Wall Street Journal, BofA haunted by Countrywide Deal, June 30 2011

Wallison, Peter, Regulating Fannie Mae and Freddie Mac: Now it Gets Serious, May 2005

Wallison, Peter, The True Origins of this Financial Crisis, American Spectator, February, 2009

Wallison, Peter, On the Future of the Mortgage Market and the Housing Enterprises, October 8, 2009, American Enterprise Institute for Public Policy Research

Wallison, P., Pollock, A. & Pinto, E. Taking the Government out of Housing Finance: principles for reforming the housing finance market, Jan 20 2011

Wallison, P., Dissent from the Majority Report of the Financial Crisis Inquiry Commission, Jan 26 2011

Washingtonian, Fannie Mae before the Meltdown: The View from August 2002, Reprint of Article from 2002 on July 15 2008

Weicher, J. The Affordable Housing Goals, Homeownership and Risk: Some Lessons from Past Efforts to regulate the GSEs, Conference on "The Past, Present and Future of the Government-Sponsored Enterprises," Federal Reserve Bank of St. Louis, Nov 17 2010

The Washington Post, Cisneros Pleads Guilty to Lying to FBI Agents, Sept 8 1999

The Washington Post, High Pay at Fannie Mae for the Well-Connected, December 23, 2004

The Washington Post, Fannie, Freddie will back Regulator but will fight portfolio limits, April 20, 2005

The Washington Post, Examining Fannie Mae, May 24, 2006

The Washington Post, Board Members, Executives and Family Members can still benefit, August 16 2004

The Washington Post Fannie Mae shuts down Foundation, Feb 24 2007

The Washington Post, How HUD policy Fed the Crisis, June 10 2008

The Washington Post, Fannie's Perilous Pursuit of Subprime Loans, August 10 2008

The Washington Post, US seizes control of the Mortgage Giants, Sept 7 2008

The Washington Post, Fannie Mae, Freddie Mac wielded big clout in Washington, Sept 12 2008

Weicher, J. The Affordable Housing Goals, Homeownership and Risk: Some Lessons from Past Efforts to Regulate the GSEs, Nov 17 2010

Whalen, R. The Subprime Crisis-Cause, Effect and Consequence, Networks Financial Institute at Indiana State University March 2008

White, Lawrence, Focussing on Fannie and Freddie: The Dilemmas of Reforming Housing Finance, 9 Jan 2001

White, L. The Community Reinvestment Act: Good Goals, Flawed Concept, A Joint Publication of the Federal Reserve Banks of Boston & St. Louis, February, 2009

White, L.J. Hearing on the Present Condition and Future Status of Fannie Mae and Freddie Mac, before the Subcommittee on Capital Markets, Insurance and Government Sponsored Enterprises, Committee on Financial Services, June 3, 2009

Willis, M. It's the Rating, Stupid: A Banker's Perspective on the CRA, Federal Reserve Banks of Boston and San Francisco, February, 2009

Xudong, A. & Bostic, R., Deng, Y. & Gabriel, S., 2007, GSE Loan Purchases, the FHA, and Housing Outcomes in Targeted, Low-income Neighborhoods, Brookings-Wharton Papers on Urban Affairs

Index

43009957R00240

Made in the USA
San Bernardino, CA
13 December 2016